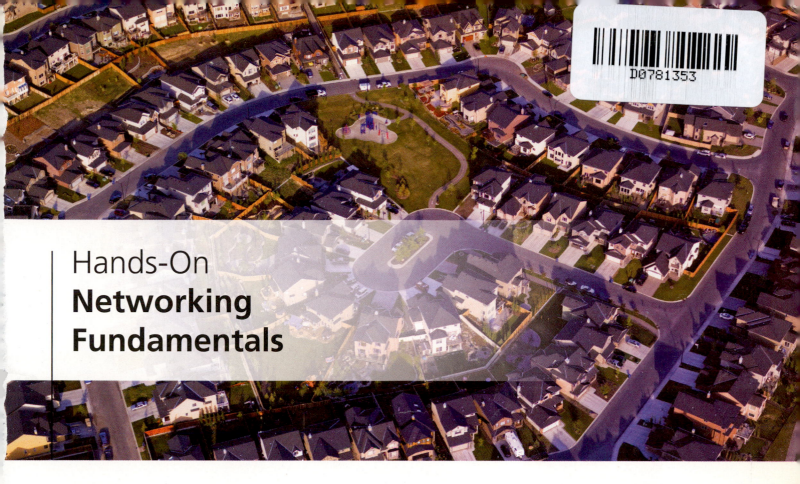

Hands-On
Networking
Fundamentals

Second Edition

Michael Palmer

COURSE TECHNOLOGY
CENGAGE Learning·

Australia • Brazil • Japan • Korea • Mexico • Singapore • Spain • United Kingdom • United States

Hands-On Networking Fundamentals, Second Edition
Michael Palmer

Vice President, Careers and Computing: Dave Garza

Executive Editor: Stephen Helba

Acquisitions Editor: Nick Lombardi

Managing Editor: Marah Bellegarde

Senior Product Manager: Michelle Ruelos Cannistraci

Developmental Editor: Deb Kaufmann

Editorial Assistant: Sarah Pickering

Vice President, Marketing: Jennifer Ann Baker

Marketing Director: Deborah S. Yarnell

Senior Marketing Manager: Mark Linton

Associate Marketing Manager: Erica Glisson

Production Director: Wendy Troeger

Production Manager: Andrew Crouth

Content Project Manager: Brooke Greenhouse

Art Director: GEX

Cover art: © dan_prat/iStockphoto

For product information and technology assistance, contact us at
Cengage Learning Customer & Sales Support, 1-800-354-9706

For permission to use material from this text or product, submit all requests online at **cengage.com/permissions**
Further permissions questions can be emailed to
permissionrequest@cengage.com

Microsoft ® is a registered trademark of the Microsoft Corporation.

Library of Congress Control Number: 2012939052

ISBN-13: 978-1-111-30674-8

ISBN-10: 1-111-30674-5

Course Technology
20 Channel Center Street
Boston, MA 02210
USA

Cengage Learning is a leading provider of customized learning solutions with office locations around the globe, including Singapore, the United Kingdom, Australia, Mexico, Brazil, and Japan. Locate your local office at:
international.cengage.com/region

Cengage Learning products are represented in Canada by Nelson Education, Ltd.

For your lifelong learning solutions, visit **www.cengage.com/coursetechnology**

Purchase any of our products at your local college store or at our preferred online store **www.cengagebrain.com**

Visit our corporate website at **cengage.com.**

Printed in the United States of America
1 2 3 4 5 6 7 16 15 14 13 12

Brief Contents

Contents

CHAPTER 7
Sharing Resources on a Network   **283**

CHAPTER 10
Basic Network Design   **431**

Hands-On Networking Fundamentals, Second Edition opens the world of computer networks to you. Computer networks are a staple in homes, coffee shops, offices, businesses, public places, and organizations. Computer networks involve personal computers, servers, tablet PCs, mobile phones, and other mobile devices. Through sharing information and resources, networks extend the power of computers worldwide. If you are new to networking or just beginning, this book is your chance to learn about networks from the ground up, combining simple and clear explanations of networking concepts and principles with Hands-On Activities to provide a strong foundation in computer networking. Learning about networks enables you to see the larger picture of computing possibilities.

In *Hands-On Networking Fundamentals, Second Edition* you learn what networks are and how they work. You also learn about planning, designing, and installing networks in many different situations. The book introduces you to networking theory and makes the theory come alive through interactive Hands-On Activities. An important element of the hands-on approach is the ability to immediately apply and reinforce what you have learned. Many of the Hands-On Activities use Windows 7, Windows Server 2008/Server 2008 R2, UNIX/Linux, Mac OS X, or any combination of these computer operating systems. You can use just one operating system to practice the concepts, or you can use a combination of operating systems for broader learning. By the time you reach the end of a chapter, what you have learned is real, because you have already practiced it.

Hands-On Networking Fundamentals, Second Edition is written in clear language to enable someone who has never before worked with a network to understand, design, and implement a network. It also provides the essential building blocks for further study toward one of several kinds of network certifications, such as Network+.

Hands-On Networking Fundamentals, Second Edition not only introduces you to networking, but also provides background and experience with the latest networking technologies—wired, wireless, and mobile. You learn to stay current through accessing Web sites for networking standards, technologies, and vendors.

The Intended Audience

Hands-On Networking Fundamentals, Second Edition is written in straightforward language for anyone who is new to networking. No prior networking experience is needed, although some experience in using a computer is helpful. Basic experience with Windows, UNIX, Linux, or Mac OS X operating systems is also helpful. You can use one, a combination, or all of these operating systems for the activities in this book. For the most part, the activities can be performed in a classroom, in a computer lab, or at home.

If you are learning networking for the first time, updating your existing networking knowledge, or interested in further study for a network certification program, *Hands-On Networking Fundamentals, Second Edition* is the book for you.

New in This Edition

Hands-On Networking Fundamentals, Second Edition is fully updated for Windows 7, Windows Server 2008/Server 2008 R2, and UNIX/Linux (with the GNOME 3.x desktop). Also, coverage is added for Mac OS X Snow Leopard and Lion as well as some coverage for the Android (tablet PC and smartphone) and iOS (iPad and iPhone) operating systems. The book discontinues coverage of older operating systems, such as Windows XP and Windows Server 2003. All of the activities and review questions in the book are updated for the new operating systems.

In addition, some of the new topics covered in *Hands-On Networking Fundamentals, Second Edition* include:

- Wireless 802.11n, 802.11ac, 802.11ad, and other wireless networking advancements
- Information about how cellular networks operate
- Advancements in cellular wireless networking and integration with other networks
- 3G and 4G networks and mobile networking devices
- Cloud computing and networks
- Virtual computing and networks
- New network design strategies
- Network and cloud storage
- Far more extensive coverage of IPv6
- Dynamic Host Configuration Protocol version 6
- Simple Network Management Protocol version 3
- 40 and 100 Gigabit Ethernet
- New Digital Subscriber Line and cable TV network capabilities
- New coverage of the tree topology
- Expanded coverage of wireless MANs, including WiMAX and HiperMAN wireless communications
- New coverage of MPLS for WANs
- Advances in shared resource access, including new security options
- New coverage for virtual private networking
- New network security strategies
- Advancements in networking devices and network monitoring
- Server-based network changes related to using Windows Server 2008/Server 2008 R2, UNIX/Linux, and Mac OS X Server

Chapter Descriptions

Consisting of 12 chapters, *Hands-On Networking Fundamentals, Second Edition* is written to provide flexibility for classroom, online, and individual use. The book starts at a beginning level in which you learn about the basics of networking. When you finish the book you should be well grounded in network theory, application, LANs and WANS, mobile networking, wireless networking, network design, security, management, monitoring, and troubleshooting.

- *Chapter 1: Networking: An Overview* describes the purpose of networks and how they benefit homes, businesses, and small to large organizations. The chapter introduces you to basic network concepts and explains network topologies. You also learn beginning network design approaches and apply what you have learned to the design of a local area network.
- *Chapter 2: How LAN and WAN Communications Work* lays the foundation for understanding network communications through the Open Systems Interconnection (OSI) reference model. The model takes the mystery out of how two computers communicate on a network or how a small network connects to a larger network, such as the Internet. In the process of learning the OSI model, you also learn the key network transmission methods, particularly focusing on Ethernet. Toward the end of the chapter you learn wide area network topologies and transmission methods. In addition, you learn about mobile wireless networks that use 3G and 4G communications.

- *Chapter 3: Using Network Communication Protocols* enables you to understand the languages used in network communications through protocols. Some of the protocols you learn include TCP, UDP, IPv4, and IPv6. You additionally learn a suite of practical applications and protocols used with TCP/IP communications. Wide area and telecommunications network protocols used in everyday communications are also presented.

- *Chapter 4: Connecting Through a Cabled Network* teaches you the range of cabled network communications media, particularly focusing on twisted-pair, fiber-optic, and hybrid fiber/coax cable. You learn which cable technologies work best in different network designs and how to upgrade older networks. Popular and new high-speed cable technologies are explained as well as computer interfaces to networks. You learn the specifications for cabled networks to enable you to design, build, and manage your own.

- *Chapter 5: Devices for Connecting Networks* describes an impressive array of network devices from simple repeaters to more complex routers. You learn the specific roles of each network device and different ways to use devices in a network design. At the end of the chapter you learn how to design a router-based network.

- *Chapter 6: Connecting Through a Wireless Network* explains wireless networking technologies. You learn the basic theory of wireless networking and how to apply the theory. The wireless local area network technologies discussed include 802.11, Bluetooth, HiperLAN, and infrared. You also learn wireless communications for metropolitan and wide area networks such as 802.16 (WiMAX), HiperMAN, wireless hotspots, cellular phone/data networking, terrestrial microwave, and satellite microwave technologies. Security is addressed in detail to make wireless networking feasible for many applications. The end of the chapter gives tips for designing home, small office, and much larger wireless networks.

- *Chapter 7: Sharing Resources on a Network* puts the advantages of networking into practice through resource sharing. In this chapter you learn how to create and use peer-to-peer networks in a home, office, or large organization. Particular attention is given to creating user accounts; sharing files, folders, and directories; sharing printers; and Internet connection sharing. In addition, you learn about virtual private networks, cloud computing, and storage area networks. The chapter concludes by showing you how to design a peer-to-peer network.

- *Chapter 8: Using a Server* shows you how to implement a server-based network in different situations. You begin by learning how to install a Windows, UNIX/Linux, or Mac OS X server. In addition, you learn how to employ server virtualization and virtual networking. Next, you learn to set up a server, such as creating user accounts and optimizing a server for specific network uses. After the server is in place, you learn tools for managing servers. At the end of the chapter, you learn to design a server-based network for an office.

- *Chapter 9: Understanding WAN Connection Choices* shows you wide area network technologies used in homes, offices, and large organizations. Wide area networks are key to linking computers, networks, and people over great distances. In this chapter you learn about WANs that have been in use for many years, such as frame relay, and WANs that are much newer, such as DSL, SONET, optical Ethernet, and MPLS. An extensive range of WANs are presented to help you know which WANs work best for specific needs.

- *Chapter 10: Basic Network Design* enables you to put together what you have learned to design networks for a broad range of situations, from small home and office networks to large enterprise networks. You begin by covering network planning issues. Next, you learn to use structured wiring and structured network techniques for successful network designs. You also learn wired and wireless design methods.

- *Chapter 11: Securing Your Network* shows you how to make a network safe. You learn why security is important and how to make security preparations. The anatomy of specific kinds of network attacks is discussed so you will know how to block them. You learn how to secure networks through many approaches, such as updating operating systems, using IPSec, and creating border and firewall security. The end of the chapter focuses on specific security designs.

- *Chapter 12: Maintaining and Troubleshooting Your Network* begins by illustrating many ways to monitor a network. You learn backup strategies to protect valuable network data. The heart of the chapter presents a large array of network problems and how to solve them such as connection problems, cable problems, wireless problems, and printing problems. At the end of the chapter, you learn about developing a solutions strategy for handling any networking problem that comes along.

- *Appendix A: A Short History of Networking* describes how networking technologies have developed since the first WAN was set up in 1965. You trace the development of early networks that led to the Internet, and you learn about the Internet's phenomenal growth period. The history of crucial protocols and networking techniques is presented, and you learn the names of important people and organizations in the development of networks.

- *Appendix B: Network Certifications and Network Equipment Vendors* describes certifications you can pursue as a networking professional. You learn about the certifications and which organizations offer those certifications. Also, there are many network equipment vendors. In this appendix you learn the vendors from "A" to "Z," including the types of products they offer and how to reach the vendors on the Internet.

- *Appendix C: List of Acronyms* enables you to quickly reference a networking term and its acronym or abbreviation. The number of networking terms is impressive and so is the number of terms with acronyms. When you see a networking acronym and are not sure what it means, check this appendix.

- *Appendix D: A Step-by-Step Guide to Using Server Virtualization Software* explains server virtualization options and how to use virtualization to run one or more operating systems on a server, lab PC, or home PC for completing the activities in this book. The virtual software systems discussed are Microsoft Virtual PC, Microsoft Virtual Server, and VMware Player—systems that can be downloaded for free. For each system, you learn how to download it, install it, set up a virtual machine, and configure hardware and networking options.

- *Glossary* includes all of the key terms introduced in the book for fast lookup and review.

Features

To ensure a successful learning experience, this book includes the following features to advance your learning:

- **Chapter Objectives:** Each chapter in this book begins with a detailed list of the concepts to be mastered in that chapter. This list provides you with a quick reference to the contents of the chapter, as well as a useful study aid.

- **Screen Captures, Illustrations, and Tables:** Numerous reproductions of screens and illustrations of concepts aid you in the visualization of theories, concepts, and how to use commands and network administration tools. In addition, many tables provide details and comparisons of both practical and theoretical information and can be used for a quick review of topics.

- **Real-Life Networking Sections:** These short sections present examples from actual networking situations to help your learning come alive. Each Real-Life Networking section shows how what you have learned relates to what users or network professionals have done in real situations.

- **Hands-On Activities:** One of the best ways to reinforce learning about computer networks is to practice configuring specific features or to design a network for a specific purpose. Each chapter in this book contains many Hands-On Activities that give you experience implementing what you have learned.

- **Putting It All Together: Design Sections:** After you learn the network concepts and configuration techniques, a concluding section in each chapter ties together all you have learned into one or more actual design situations. The Putting It All Together sections clearly summarize important design points to help you synthesize and retain them.

- **Case Project:** Located at the end of each chapter is a multipart case project. In this extensive case example, you place yourself in the shoes of a consultant for Network Design Consultants, a fictitious network consulting firm. In your role as a consultant you implement the skills and knowledge gained in the chapter through real-world networking scenarios.

- **End-of-Chapter Study Aids:** The end of each chapter includes the following features to reinforce the material covered in the chapter:

- **Chapter Summary:** A bulleted list gives a brief but complete summary of the chapter.

- **Key Terms:** Each of the key terms introduced in the chapter is defined in this section.

- **Review Questions:** A list of review questions tests your knowledge of the most important concepts covered in the chapter.

Text and Graphic Conventions

Wherever appropriate, additional information and activities have been added to this book to help you better understand what is being discussed in the chapter. Icons throughout the text alert you to additional materials. The icons used in this textbook are as follows:

 The Note icon is used to present additional helpful material related to the subject being described.

 Tips are included from the author's experience to provide extra information about how to configure a network, apply a concept, or solve a problem.

 Cautions are provided to help you anticipate potential problems or mistakes so that you can prevent them from happening.

 Each Hands-On Activity in this book is preceded by the Activity icon and a description of the exercise that follows.

 Case Projects icons mark each case project. Case projects are more involved, scenario-based assignments. In each extensive case example, you are asked to implement what you have learned.

Instructor's Materials

The following supplemental materials are available when this book is used in a classroom setting. All of the supplements available with this book are provided to the instructor on a single Instructor Resources CD (ISBN: 9781111306755) and also available on the textbook's Web site. Please visit *login.cengage.com* and log in to access instructor-specific resources.

Electronic Instructor's Manual. The Instructor's Manual that accompanies this textbook includes:

- Additional instructional material to assist in class preparation, including suggestions for classroom activities, discussion topics, quizzes, and additional exercises.
- Solutions to the Hands-On Activities, including some suggestions for supplementing activities with in-class discussions.
- Solutions to all end-of-chapter materials, including the Review Questions and Case Projects.

ExamView

This textbook is accompanied by ExamView, a powerful testing software package that allows instructors to create and administer printed, computer (LAN-based), and Internet exams. ExamView includes hundreds of questions that correspond to the topics covered in this text, enabling students to generate detailed study guides that include page references for further review. The computer-based and Internet testing components allow students to take exams at their computers and save the instructor time by grading each exam automatically.

PowerPoint Presentations

This book comes with Microsoft PowerPoint slides for each chapter. These are included as a teaching aid for classroom presentation, to make available to students on the network for chapter review, or to be printed for classroom distribution. Instructors, please feel at liberty to add your own slides for additional topics you introduce to the class.

Figure Files

All of the figures and tables in the book are reproduced on the Instructor Resources CD, in bitmap format. Similar to the PowerPoint presentations, these are included as a teaching aid for classroom presentation, to make available to students for review, or to be printed for classroom distribution.

Network Icons

If you are using a drawing package such as Windows Paint that does not have device icons for the network drawings in the activities, you can use the basic icons included on the Instructor Resource CD. The icons are provided in different file formats for versatility.

CourseMate

To access additional materials (including CourseMate), please visit *www.cengagebrain.com*. At the CengageBrain.com home page, search for the ISBN of your title (from the back cover of your book) using the search box at the top of the page. This will take you to the product page for your book, where you will be able to access these resources.

Hands-On Networking Fundamentals, Second Edition, offers CourseMate, a complement to your textbook. Go to *login.cengage.com* to access these resources. CourseMate includes the following:

- An interactive eBook, with highlighting, note taking, and search capabilities
- Interactive learning tools, including quizzes, flash cards, PowerPoint slides, glossary, and more
- Engagement Tracker, a first-of-its-kind tool that monitors student engagement in the course.

CourseMate Printed Access Code with eBook (ISBN: 9781285162072)
CourseMate Instant Access Code with eBook (ISBN: 9781285162089)

System Requirements

This book is written so that you learn a networking concept and then apply that concept using one or more computer operating systems: Windows 7, Windows Server 2008/Server 2008 R2, UNIX/Linux, or Mac OS X Snow Leopard and Lion. You can do well by using only one computer operating system, such as using one that is available on a home or lab computer. If you plan a career supporting a network with multiple operating systems, you can use a combination or all of the operating systems in this book to tailor your learning to your class or learning goals. The book is intended to give you a broad range of knowledge about networking and popular operating systems, while allowing you to practice by using the specific operating system or systems available to you.

Hardware for Windows

- 1 GHz CPU or faster for an x86 computer or 1.4 GHz CPU or faster for an x64 computer
- 1 GB RAM or more (for x86 and x64 computers)
- 50 GB or more disk space (for x86 and x64 computers)
- DVD/CD-ROM drive
- Super VGA or higher resolution monitor
- Mouse or pointing device
- Keyboard
- Network interface card (wired, wireless, or both) connected to the classroom, lab, or school network for on-ground students—or Internet access (plus a network interface card installed) for online students

Hardware for Linux Live Media

- 1 GHz CPU or faster for an x86 computer or 1.4 GHz CPU or faster for an x64 computer
- 1 GB RAM or more (for x86 and x64 computers)
- 50 GB or more disk space (for x86 and x64 computers)
- DVD/CD-ROM drive (Linux Live Media is booted and run from a DVD/CD-ROM drive on a computer with a Windows or Mac OS X operating system and does not require hard disk space because it runs from a combination of the computer's memory and the DVD/CD)
- Super VGA or higher-resolution monitor
- Mouse or pointing device
- Keyboard
- Network interface card (wired, wireless, or both) connected to the classroom, lab, or school network for on-ground students—or Internet access (plus a network interface card installed) for online students

Hardware for Mac OS X

- Macintosh computer with an Intel processor
- 1 GB RAM or more
- 50 GB or more disk space
- DVD/CD-ROM drive
- Mouse or pointing device
- Keyboard
- Network interface card (wired, wireless, or both) connected to the classroom, lab, or school network for on-ground students—or Internet access (plus a network interface card installed) for online students

Software

You can use one or a combination of any of the following operating systems: Windows 7, Windows Server 2008/Server 2008 R2, Fedora Live Media (or any distribution of Linux), and Mac OS X Snow Leopard and Lion.

If you plan to do the UNIX/Linux activities, consider obtaining the free download of Fedora Live Media Linux with the GNOME 3.x desktop. You can run Fedora Live Media from your DVD/CD-ROM drive without the need to install it on your Windows or Mac OS X computer. The GNOME 3.x desktop is designed to resemble the popular Android operating system used by many smartphones and small tablet PCs. You can obtain the free Fedora Live Media download at *fedoraproject.org/get-fedora* along with instructions on how to perform the download and use it from your DVD/CD-ROM drive. Fedora Live Media is a convenient way to learn about Linux.

Virtualization

Windows 7, Windows Server 2008, Windows Server 2008 R2, and Linux, such as Fedora Linux, can be loaded into a virtual server or virtual desktop environment. See Appendix D: A Step-by-Step Guide to Using Server Virtualization Software for tips on how to obtain and use free virtualization software from which to run multiple operating systems on a single computer. If your school or lab has Windows Server 2008/Server 2008 R2, another option is to use the Windows Server Hyper-V virtualization software for running multiple operating systems.

Additional Learning Tools

In addition to the operating systems mentioned, the following elements are helpful for some of the Hands-On Activities:

- A workstation equipped with a Web browser able to access the Internet
- A drawing package, such as Microsoft Paint, SmartDraw (by SmartDraw), Visio (by Microsoft), AutoCAD (by Autodesk), TurboCAD (by IMSI), or DiagramStudio (by Gadwin Systems)
- An Ethernet or wireless network on which to use network troubleshooting software, or access to the Internet
- A TCP/IP network configuration
- A network switch or router and network cable (for a small number of activities)
- Thinnet, twisted-pair, and fiber-optic cable samples or the ability to view these on the Internet
- Cable, connectors, and tools from which to build twisted-pair cable (for one activity)
- Examples of different types of network devices for students to view or the ability to view these via a tour of a business or through the Internet

About the Author

Michael Palmer is an industry consultant, teacher, and author of numerous networking and operating system books, including best-selling books about Windows server systems and UNIX/Linux. He is president of CertQuick, which provides computer and networking consulting services, technical authoring services, and computer science curriculum development for schools. Dr. Palmer has worked for 30 years in higher education and in industry as an instructor, professor, systems and networking specialist, technical manager and department head, and consultant. He holds a doctorate from the University of Colorado.

Acknowledgments

Writing about and sharing ideas in a book is an extraordinarily rewarding opportunity, which is exciting and also represents much hard work on the part of many people. It seems like I can never say enough about how much I appreciate the people with whom I work and the contributions they have made to this book.

I am very grateful to Cengage Learning Acquisitions Editor Nick Lombardi for making this project possible and for his advice on conceptual issues. Senior Product Manager Michelle Ruelos Cannistraci has provided a fine team of people with whom to work and has played a vital role in all phases of this book. Deb Kaufmann, the Development Editor, continues to be simply amazing at providing great ideas, synthesizing reviews, polishing the writing, and giving encouragement. I am truly fortunate to be able to work with such an incredible professional. In addition, I want to thank Brooke Baker, Content Project Manager, for her work in coordinating the book production.

The independent reviewers for this book are Chet Anson, Cloud County Community College; Lisa Bock, Pennsylvania College of Technology; Marc Graustark, ECPI University; Amber Hurst, Wake Technical Community College; Louay Karadsheh, ECPI University; and Dr. Chang-Shyh Peng, California Lutheran University. I am especially grateful to the reviewers for their honest and outstanding advice, which I have worked to implement so that the book more fully meets the needs of you, the reader. Technical Editor Nicole Ashton Spoto has carefully reviewed all technical material in this book for accuracy and completeness. Further, members of Green Pen Quality Assurance have rechecked all technical and writing features of this book.

Dedication

To my parents, Helen and Edward Palmer

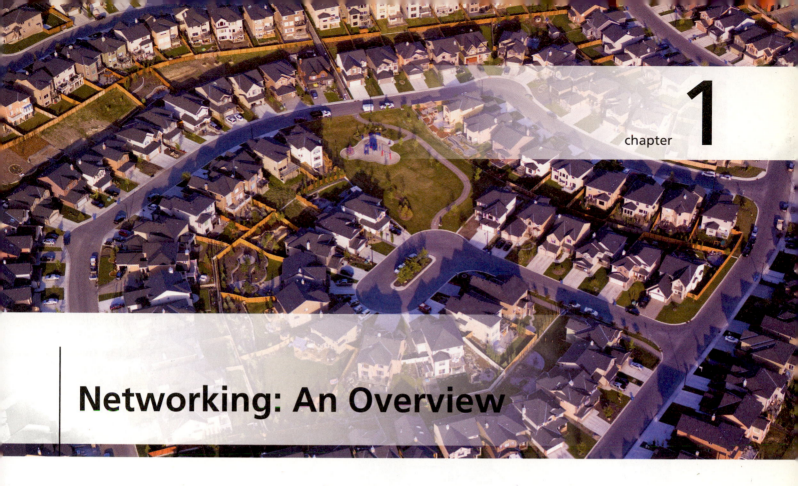

chapter 1

Networking: An Overview

Linking people and ideas through information networks reflects a long-standing human need for communication. In 700 BC, the Greeks used homing pigeons to establish a rudimentary information network. Around a millennium later, in 1819, Hans Oersted proved that a wire carrying an electric current could deflect a magnetized needle, opening the way for wire-based telegraph networks. Today, computer information networks reach millions of people in every corner of the globe.

After reading this chapter and completing the exercises, you will be able to:

- Explain what a network is
- Understand basic networking concepts and terms
- Explain the advantages of using a network in a home
- Discuss the advantages of using a network in an office
- Determine boundaries between networks
- Describe network topologies
- Understand general network design concepts
- Design a simple LAN

Computer networks touch our lives in ways that are sometimes mundane, sometimes dramatic. Every day they enable us to exchange e-mail, learn about the latest news, download software, and participate in electronic commerce. More dramatically, they are used to locate organs for surgery, provide information on road conditions during storms, and immediately transport vital documents.

In this chapter, you explore what networks are and how they can benefit a home or business. You learn some basic networking terms and concepts, and you learn about various network designs, or topologies. At the end of the chapter you apply what you have learned to designing a basic network.

What Is a Network?

The most basic "network" is word-of-mouth communication. Ideas are passed from person to person. It is a practice people learn as soon as they can speak. Another network that people master at an early age is the cell phone or telephone. Each cell phone uses radio waves or microwaves, and the telephone is connected to miles of cable, while both are connected to the world through vast networks of communications equipment. Telephone lines that link homes and cities are easily seen in alleys and along highways, and cellular phones rely on a network of cellular towers.

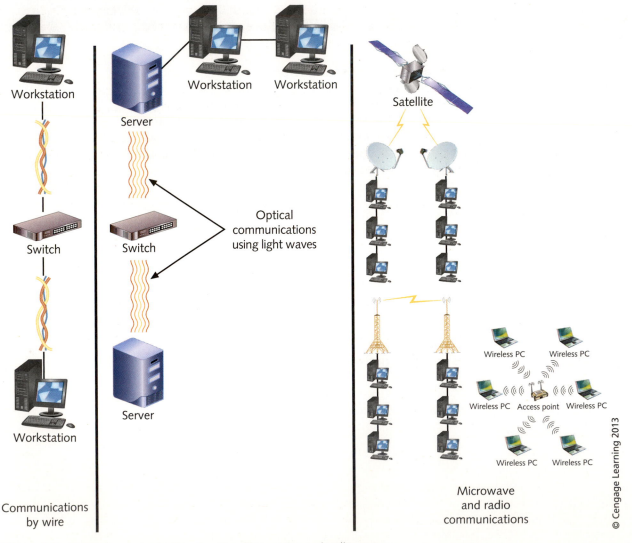

Figure 1-1   Network communications by wire, fiber-optics, and radio waves

© Cengage Learning 2013

Computer networks are simply an expansion of the elements that compose word-of-mouth and cell/telephone communications. Like word-of-mouth communication, a computer network transmits information from one person or group to another. Like the telephone system, computer networks use radio waves and communications cable to carry information from one location to the next, with specialized equipment in between that ensures each message reaches its intended recipient.

A **computer network** is a system of computers, print devices, network devices, and computer software linked by radio waves or communications cable. Most of the first computer networks transmitted data over copper wire, but today networks transmit data, voice, and video communications over wire, fiber-optic media, radio waves, infrared waves, and microwaves, as shown in Figure 1-1. As a technology, computer network communications has advanced at lightning speed, affecting radio, television, and telephone communications along the way.

One of the most important advantages of a computer network is the ability to share information. Sharing documents, data, pictures, printers, and other resources is the hallmark of a computer network. Another advantage of a network is the option to exchange e-mail with someone in the same house, in the same office, or on the other side of the world.

Basic Networking Concepts

A good place to begin learning about networks is through understanding some basic networking concepts. For instance, there are different types of networks. Also, there are different terms that describe the elements of networks. And, there are processes that contribute to general agreement about how networks should work.

Understanding the Types of Networks

Computer networks, typically classified according to their reach and complexity, come in five types: personal area networks, local area networks, metropolitan area networks, campus area networks, and wide area networks, as shown in Figure 1-2. A **personal area network (PAN)**, at one end of the spectrum, is a network that reaches a few meters (such as up to about 10 meters or about 33 feet, but can reach farther). There can be cabled and wireless PAN (WPAN) networks that consist of personal devices, such as mobile computers, smartphones, and handheld devices. PAN Bluetooth is an example of a popular WPAN that uses wireless Bluetooth communications. For instance, a computer with a wireless Bluetooth capability might interconnect to another computer with wireless Bluetooth to share files. You learn more about PAN Bluetooth in Chapter 6, "Connecting Through a Wireless Network." Cabled PAN networks connect to a computer or network using short distance cables typically connected through a **Universal Serial Bus (USB)** port. For example, a mobile tablet computer might connect through a USB connection to a desktop computer to download specific files. Figure 1-3 illustrates a PAN using wireless communications to form a small network between a desktop PC, a smartphone, and a small tablet PC to share picture files.

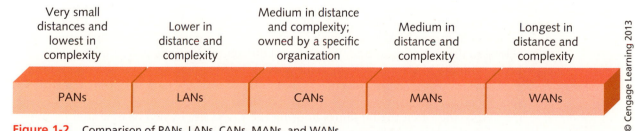

Very small distances and lowest in complexity	Lower in distance and complexity	Medium in distance and complexity; owned by a specific organization	Medium in distance and complexity	Longest in distance and complexity
PANs	LANs	CANs	MANs	WANs

© Cengage Learning 2013

Figure 1-2   Comparison of PANs, LANs, CANs, MANs, and WANs

A **local area network (LAN)** consists of interconnected computers, printers, and other computer equipment that share hardware and software resources in close physical proximity. The service area might be within a house, a small office, a floor in a building, or an entire building. One example of a LAN is a university chemistry department in which the computers in each office and lab are connected by communications cable or wireless devices, as shown in Figure 1-4.

© Cengage Learning 2013

Figure 1-3   A desktop PC, a smartphone, and a tablet PC forming a PAN

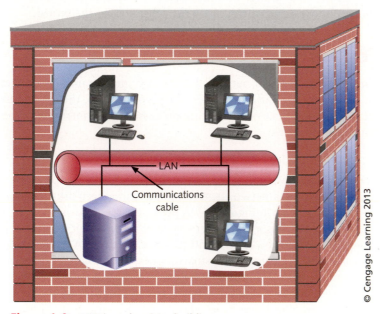

© Cengage Learning 2013

Figure 1-4   LAN in a chemistry building

A **metropolitan area network (MAN)** spans a greater distance than a LAN and usually has more complicated networking equipment for midrange communications. A MAN links multiple LANs within a large city or metropolitan region and typically spans a distance of up to 48 kilometers (about 30 miles). For example, the LAN in the chemistry building described earlier might be linked to a research hospital's LAN and to a pharmaceutical company's LAN several miles apart within the same city to form a MAN, as shown in Figure 1-5. The individual LANs that compose a MAN may belong to the same organization or to several different organizations. The high-speed links between LANs within a MAN are typically made possible by fiber-optic or wireless connections.

The **campus area network (CAN)** is similar to a MAN in that it joins multiple LANs in a specific area, such as in a city or within a defined geographic area. The difference is that all of the LANs and often the buildings housing the LANs are owned or operated by one organization. For example, LANs owned by a large business that is organized into a campus of buildings within a city are united into a CAN. Another example is a college or university that owns buildings and LANs in a specific area and in which the associated LANs are connected into a CAN.

A **wide area network (WAN)** is at the far end of the spectrum because it is a far-reaching system of networks that form a complex whole. One WAN is composed of two or more LANs (or MANs or CANs) that are connected across a distance of more than approximately 48 kilometers or 30 miles. Large WANs may have many constituent LANs and MANs on different continents.

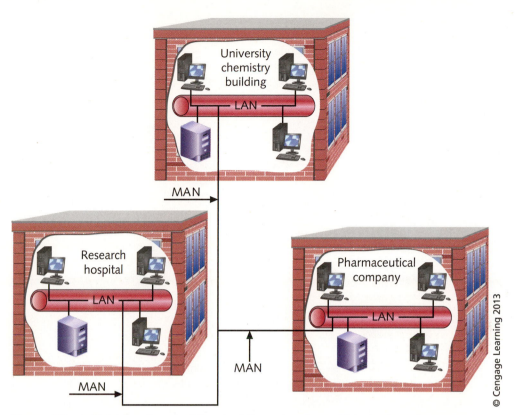

Figure 1-5 MAN joining three buildings in different locations within the same city

 The simplest WAN is a dial-up modem connected to a network provider's services over basic telephone lines. A more complex WAN is a satellite linkup between a LAN in one country and one in another. The most well-known WAN is the **Internet**, which consists of thousands of LANs, CANs, and MANs interconnected by different WAN technologies throughout the world.

In addition to the PAN/LAN/MAN/CAN/WAN classification scheme, another way to classify a network is as an **enterprise network**. This type of network connects many different kinds of users in one organization or throughout several organizations, providing a variety of resources to those users. Note that although a large LAN can be an enterprise network, an enterprise network is more likely to consist of several LANs that compose a MAN, CAN, or WAN.

The key characteristic in an enterprise is the existence of different resources that enable users to fulfill business, research, and educational tasks. For example, a university that brings together academic, accounting, student services, human resources, payroll, and alumni development resources through a vast array of computers and printers on LANs is an enterprise, as shown in Figure 1-6. In Activity 1-1, you learn about the resources that are in your campus' enterprise network.

 Many of the Hands-On Activities in this book use Microsoft Windows 7, Windows Server 2008/Server 2008 R2, Fedora Linux (but you can use most versions of Linux, such as Red Hat Enterprise Linux or SUSE Linux), or Mac OS X Snow Leopard or Lion. The Linux projects typically use the command line from a terminal window, but some activities also illustrate the use of the GNOME 3.x (or higher) desktop. Also, for many projects your computer needs access to a network or to the Internet, such as through a network interface card (card in the computer that connects to a network) connected to a LAN or through a digital or analog modem.

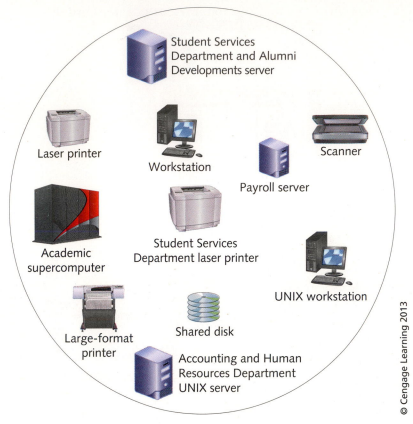

© Cengage Learning 2013

Figure 1-6   Resources in an enterprise network

If you are interested in using Linux with this book, consider download-ing the latest free distribution of Fedora Live Media with the GNOME 3.x desktop. You can run Fedora Live Media from your DVD/CD-ROM drive without the need to install it on your computer. The GNOME 3.x desktop is designed to resemble the popular Android operating system used by many smartphones and small tablet PCs. You can obtain the download at *fedoraproject.org/get-fedora* along with instructions on how to perform the download and use it.

Activity 1-1: Exploring the Composition of an Enterprise Network

Time Required: Time limit set by you or your group
Objective: Explore an enterprise network by locating computers and devices.

Description: In this activity, you learn about the composition of an enterprise network. The activity is intended as a group experience for your class, similar to a scavenger hunt. Consult with your instructor about making arrangements for special access to computer equipment loca-tions on campus and for any assistance offered by your campus' network professionals. If your class cannot gain special access, consider asking the information technology director to arrange a guided tour.

1. Organize into small groups or compete individually to find as many objects as possible attached to your school's network.

2. Set a time limit on the scavenger hunt, such as one hour or by the end of the school day.

3. Each participant should look for the following items and record the location of each item that is found:

- A workstation
- A file or print server
- A network laser printer
- A router, switch, or any combination of network devices
- A connection to a WAN
- A connection between LANs
- A fax machine or fax software
- A large-format printer
- An e-mail server
- A terminator
- Fiber-optic network cable
- Equipment to provide Internet access
- An intranet
- A database server
- A tape drive or array
- A DVD/CD-ROM drive or array
- A wireless network connection
- A modem
- Other devices connected to your network

4. Determine which student or team of students is the first to find the items on the list and check the locations of the items.

If you are using this book as part of an online course or for individual study, consider making arrangements with a local business or organization so you can view the networking devices it uses.

Using Basic Networking Terms

A network is composed of personal computers, servers, mainframes (computers for large processing needs), supercomputers (computers used for highly complex calculations), printers, fax equipment, DVD/CD-ROM arrays, disk arrays, network equipment, and other devices. When directly connected to the network, each of these is a **node** (also called a **station**). Any device connected to a network is a node, such as a personal computer, a server, a tablet computer, network equipment, or a printer. Nodes are physically linked into a network through **communications media** consisting of wire cabling, fiber-optic cable, or radio and infrared waves. The communications media provide a way to transmit a signal containing data or information about network communications. The signal is sent and received by the network nodes.

Three network nodes important to users are workstations, hosts, and servers. A **workstation** is a computer that is home to local applications, such as Microsoft Office, and can run network applications, such as software that accesses data on a server or mainframe computer. The workstation has its own central processing unit (CPU) and operating system. When a workstation accesses software and data through the network on another computer, it is a **client** of that computer. The computer it accesses is a **host**. For example, the client may be a workstation that accesses another computer for a file or a report or to use a software application. The client may use the accessed computer (host) to process data or may process accessed data using its own CPU.

Another meaning of "host" is a computer connected to a network.

The most typical client workstations on a network are personal computers, such as computers that use Intel or AMD microprocessors. Some workstations fulfill roles as both client and host. For example, on a Microsoft network, a Windows 7 workstation may share a folder or an entire disk drive for others to access. In these roles, it acts as a workstation for a user who may be alternating work between a Microsoft Word document and updating payroll information on a server. Functioning as a host, the Windows 7 workstation may be accessed by another workstation to download a spreadsheet to that workstation.

Servers, which are more powerful than workstations, are computers that offer multiuser access. The server acts as a repository for software applications and data files that other network computers can use. A server may allow access for as few as two users or as many as several thousand. A server can host multiple users because it has a network operating system with this capability. For example, a server running the Microsoft Windows Server operating system may host several thousand users at the same time (depending on the server hardware). One user may be accessing a spreadsheet, another may be installing software from the server, a third may be running a database application, while a fourth is running a data report. When you access a Web site, you are accessing a server.

Most networks have a combination of workstation clients and servers. Some networks also have mainframe computers, networked printers, and faxes. Still others may have disk arrays and DVD/CD-ROM arrays available to users. Disk arrays are units containing multiple hard disks that may be used for network access. DVD/CD-ROM arrays offer access to multiple DVDs/CD-ROMs.

Network nodes—workstations, servers, and network devices—are attached to the communications media through a **network interface card (NIC)**. The NIC is a board that is installed in the computer or network device, such as in an empty slot on the main board (or motherboard) inside a workstation. In many computers, the NIC is built into the main board. One end of the NIC is accessible on the outside of the workstation, containing a receptacle or connector for attachment to the communications media (or an antenna for wireless communications, although not all antennas are visible depending on the wireless NIC). Figure 1-7 shows examples of NICs for wireless and cabled network connections.

© Sergei Devyatkin/Shutterstock.com

Figure 1-7   NICs for cabled and wireless connections

When purchasing a computer with a built-in NIC, ensure that you specify the type of NIC that is compatible with the network setup and communications media already in use on your network. Also, some NICs built into the main board are proprietary (with unique or nonstandard capabilities only available from one vendor), so be sure that you receive a DVD/CD-ROM from the manufacturer that contains software for using the NIC (in case you have to reinstall the operating system).

Computers and other network devices communicate with one another through protocols. You might think of a protocol as similar to a language that network devices use for "talking" or exchanging information. The protocol that is the workhorse of network communications is the Internet Protocol (IP). For now, you can think of this protocol as like an envelope with a letter (data) inside and the mailing and return addresses on the outside. IP is explained in Chapter 3 "Using Network Communication Protocols."

Understanding Network Concepts in Historical Context

The history of networking can be fun to read and instructive for several reasons. One reason is that the history can teach you how networking practices and concepts have evolved into what they are today. Another reason for studying networking history is that it provides an understanding of the social, political, and technical factors that have caused networking to develop and flourish. LANs and WANs have roots in early telegraph and telephone systems. Today, networking technology is still closely linked to advances in telecommunications and is driven by the social elements of business, personal communications, and entertainment.

You can learn more about the fascinating evolution of networks by reading Appendix A, "A Short History of Networking." Also, try Activity 1-2 to discover two Web sites that discuss historical events in networking.

Activity 1-2: Learning About the History of Networking

Time Required: 15 minutes

Objective: Use Web resources to learn about historical events in networking.

Description: In this activity, you explore Hobbes' Internet Timeline and the Computer Timeline of History—both Web resources.

1. Open a Web browser, such as Internet Explorer in Windows 7 or Windows Server 2008/Server 2008 R2, Mozilla Firefox in Linux, or Safari in Mac OS X Snow Leopard or Lion. For example, in Windows 7 and Server 2008/Server 2008 R2, click **Start** and click **Internet Explorer** or **Internet Explorer (64-bit)**. In Fedora with the GNOME 3.x desktop, click **Applications** at the top of the desktop, point to **Internet**, and click **Firefox**. In Mac OS X Snow Leopard or Lion, click **Safari** in the Dock.

2. Point your browser to the Hobbes' Internet Timeline 10 (Hobbes' Internet Timeline Copyright © 1993–2012 by Robert H. Zakon) *www.zakon.org/robert/internet/timeline* and press **Enter**.

3. Answer the following questions by researching the timeline:

   a. What group was organized with Steve Crocker as its leader in 1968, and what was the group's purpose?

   b. What was the name of the first full-service bank on the Internet?

   c. In what year were nodes first connected to the early ARPANET network?

   d. What network-related activity did England's Queen Elizabeth II perform in 1976?

   e. In what year did the U.S. White House go online to the Internet for e-mail?

   f. What did the early use of a name server in 1983 mean for network communications?

   g. What protocol was developed in 1973 to facilitate conference calling over a network?

   h. What did NASA test in 2008?

   i. What did Estonia offer in 2007?

4. After you have finished viewing Hobbes' Internet Timeline, access the Computer Timeline of History at *www.computerhistory.org/timeline*.

5. Click '50. What was the name of the National Bureau of Standards computer that was the first computer to use all diode logic?

6. Click '75. What was the name of the first commercial packet-switching network, and how many cities did it connect?

7. Click '90. What important language needed for the World Wide Web was developed, and who developed it?

8. Click '70. What was installed by Citizens and Southern National Bank in this year?

9. Exit your Internet browser.

Using a Network in a Home

Networks are enriching many people's use of computers and digital devices at home. Many homes now are equipped with two or more computers, TVs, radios, other audiovisual entertainment equipment, and various other electrical appliances. A home network can connect computers, entertainment devices, and even appliances. Some prominent uses of home networks include:

- Sharing files and printers
- Accessing the Internet and entertainment resources
- Connecting home resources

These applications for home networks are discussed in the next sections.

Connecting Computers for Sharing Files and Printers

When you have two or more computers in your home, you can share files among the computers. Suppose your daughter is a student who uses a laptop computer to complete a research paper for school, and you are requested to review the paper before she submits it. Your daughter can connect her laptop computer to your home network and share the file containing the paper. You download the file, use change tracking to suggest some changes, and share the file so your daughter can access it and decide which changes to implement.

In another example of file sharing, consider a department head in a company who brings her laptop computer home from work. She prefers to work on her desktop computer while at home, so she connects the laptop to her home network, shares a folder of files from her laptop, and then accesses those files from the desktop computer.

Real-Life Networking

A student who lived in a rural area was working on a 12-page term paper over the span of two weeks. The day before the term paper was due, her father backed up all of the computers on the family's home network, including the file containing her term paper. Later that day a lightning storm caused power line problems and outages that permanently damaged two of the family's computers, including the student's computer. But her important files, such as the term paper, were saved on the computer used for backups, which was undamaged after the storm.

In yet another example, a home network can be used to back up files from one computer to a different computer. If one computer fails, you can still use the backed up files on the other computer. People who have three or four computers at home may even have a server as a central computer from which to share files and to back up the other computers on the network.

Just as you can share files on a network, you can share printers. Three common ways to share printers are:

- Connect a printer to your workstation or server and make it a shared network printer through the computer's operating system, such as through Windows 7. (The limitation is that no one can use the printer if its workstation or server is turned off.)

- Purchase a printer that comes with a built-in NIC so the printer can be attached directly to the network. Many home networks are configured for wireless communications, and printers that wirelessly attach to the network can be purchased (see Figure 1-8).

- Purchase a small network device called a print server that has connections for one or more printers and a NIC. Plug the printer(s) into the print server and connect the print server to the network. Some print server devices can connect more than one printer to the network.

An important advantage to sharing a printer is that you can have only one printer, saving money on printers and headaches from buying multiple types of print cartridges. (You learn more about sharing files and printers in Chapter 7, "Sharing Resources on a Network.")

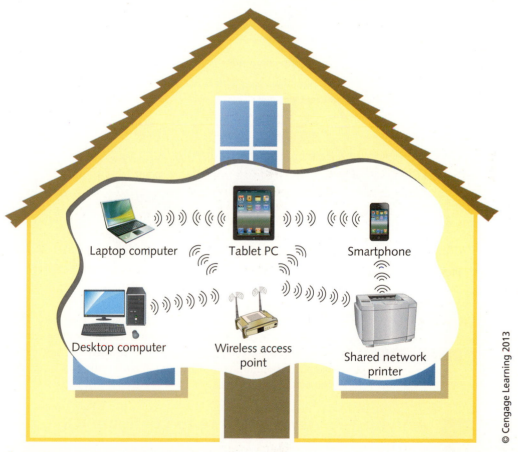

Laptop computer   Tablet PC   Smartphone

Desktop computer   Wireless access point   Shared network printer

© Cengage Learning 2013

Figure 1-8   Sharing a printer on a wireless home network

Using Internet and Entertainment Resources

All of the computers in your home can share the same Internet connection through a network. There are several ways to share an Internet connection, but one of the easiest for home use is to set up **Internet Connection Sharing (ICS)** in Windows 7. All you need to do is have an

Internet connection to a computer running Windows 7, connect that computer to a network, and configure ICS in Windows 7 (see Figure 1-9). The computer configured for ICS acts as a host to the Internet, and other client computers on a network can access the Internet from the host computer. ICS can also be set up in Windows Server 2008 R2. In Activity 1-3 you learn where to set up ICS in Windows 7 and in Windows Server 2008 R2.

Mac OS X Snow Leopard and Lion also offer a means to share an Internet connection through a wireless or cabled connection. You can configure this option from System Preferences as shown in Activity 1-4.

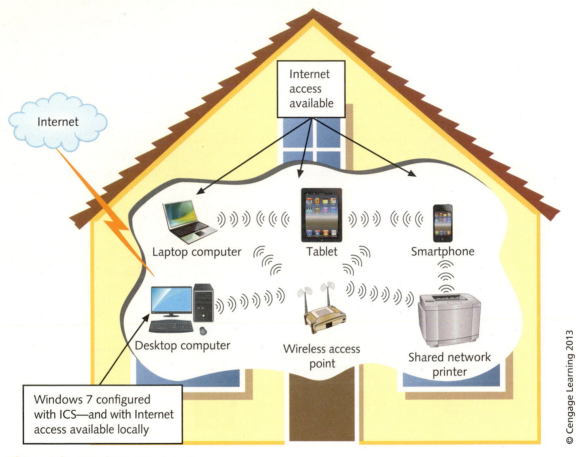

Figure 1-9   Using ICS in Windows 7

© Cengage Learning 2013

In some Windows 7 or Server 2008 R2 projects, you may see the User Account Control (UAC) box, which is used for security to help thwart intruders. The UAC box asks for permission to continue with an action or asks for the administrator password. If you see this box, click **Continue**. Because computer setups may be different, the box is not mentioned in the actual project steps.

Activity 1-3: Viewing Where to Configure ICS

Time Required: 5–10 minutes
Objective: Learn where to configure ICS in Windows 7 or Windows Server 2008/Server 2008 R2.

Description: An easy way to share an Internet connection is through configuring ICS in Windows 7 or Windows Server 2008/Server 2008 R2 (without Active Directory configured). In this activity, you learn where to set up ICS. (Internet access, such as through a dial-up, DSL, or cable modem/adapter, should be configured already. Also, log on using an account with Administrator privileges.)

Security is an important consideration before you share an Internet connection. Make sure that the computer offering the shared connection and the client computers accessing the shared connection all have security features turned on, such as firewalls and virus scanners. Firewalls are introduced in Chapter 5, "Devices for Connecting Networks," and viruses are discussed in Chapter 11, "Securing Your Network."

1. Click **Start** and click **Control Panel**.

2. In Windows 7 and Server 2008 R2 ensure that the **View by** option in the upper right portion of the window is set to **Large icons** or **Small icons**. In Windows Server 2008, select **Classic View**, if it is not already selected.

3. Click (or double-click in Server 2008) **Network and Sharing Center**.

4. In Windows 7 and Server 2008 R2, click **Change adapter settings** in the left pane of the Network and Sharing Center window. Or in Windows Server 2008 click **Manage network connections**.

5. Right-click an active network connection, such as **Wireless Network Connection** or **Local Area Connection** (for a cabled connection). Click **Properties**.

6. Click the **Sharing** tab in the Properties dialog box for the network connection you selected in Step 5.

7. ICS is configured if there is a checkmark in the box for Allow other network users to connect through this computer's Internet connection (see Figure 1-10). Notice there is also an option to Allow other network users to control or disable the shared Internet connection. You might enable this option so that other users who are sharing the connection can manage it, such as other members of your household. Click **Cancel**.

8. Close all open windows.

Figure 1-10 Viewing the ICS configuration in Windows 7

After you have set up ICS, you can enable other computers running Windows 7 to connect to ICS and to your network by using Network and Sharing Center. Open Network and Sharing Center from Control Panel. In Network and Sharing Center, click **Set up a new connection or network**, click **Connect to the Internet**, and follow the steps to set up a connection.

Activity 1-4: Configuring Internet Sharing in Mac OS X Snow Leopard and Lion

Time Required: 10 minutes

Objective: Learn where to configure Internet sharing in Mac OS X Snow Leopard and Lion.

Description: The networking capabilities in Mac OS X Snow Leopard and Lion enable you to share many resources on the computer including files, DVD/CD-ROMs, printers, and an Internet connection. An Internet connection on a Macintosh can be shared with other Macs through a cabled or wireless network connection. In this activity, you learn how to configure Internet sharing from the Mac OS X System Preferences window. When you use a Macintosh, you can configure all types of Mac OS X functions from System Preferences. You need an account that has Administrator privileges to configure System Preferences.

1. Click the **System Preferences** icon in the Dock. (The Dock is similar to the Windows taskbar and is a bar loaded with icons located at the bottom of the Mac OS X desktop.) Another way to open System Preferences is to click the **Apple** icon in the menu bar at the top of the desktop and click **System Preferences** in the Apple menu. Click **Sharing** in the Internet & Wireless section of the System Preferences window.

2. In the Sharing window, click **Internet Sharing** in the left pane that lists services (see Figure 1-11).

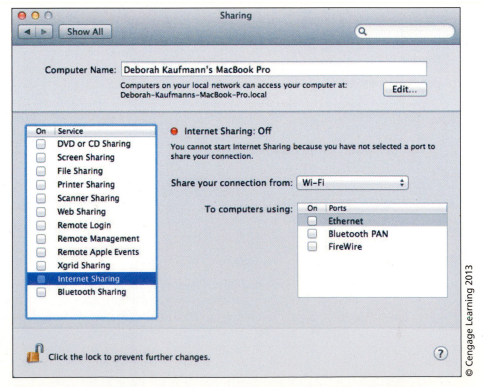

Figure 1-11   Clicking Internet Sharing in the Sharing window in Mac OS X Lion

3. In the right portion of the Sharing window, notice that you can configure the type of connection on your Macintosh, such as AirPort or Wi-Fi for a wireless connection. You can also configure the type of access to be used for the client computers that will share the connection, which you do by configuring the To computers using box for Ethernet (which is a cabled connection), FireWire (which is a wireless connection), or Bluetooth PAN (for a Bluetooth connection in Mac OS X Lion). You must check one or both of these boxes to enable Internet Sharing. For practice, click the box for **Ethernet**.

4. In the Sharing window, click the box for **Internet Sharing**.

5. In the box that asks Are you sure you want to turn on Internet sharing?, click **Cancel** so that you do not start it at this time because this is just practice.

6. Click **System Preferences** in the menu bar at the top of the desktop, and click **Quit System Preferences**.

Having a network at home enables you to enjoy entertainment opportunities through your network. For instance, some digital video devices and TVs come with a NIC. When connected to a network, you can access video files or DVDs loaded on the video device and play them on a network computer. TVs with a NIC can connect to the Internet and play streaming videos and movies. A home media hub enables you to connect a home entertainment center to your network to access photos, music, and video files from a network computer or from an appropriately equipped TV.

Windows Media Center built into Windows 7 enables you to manage and remotely control all types of digital media including DVD movies, photos, music, home videos, games, radio, and live or recorded television. Windows Media Center can also work with cable or satellite TV and a TV tuner for access to regular TV entertainment.

If you have a smartphone or small tablet computer, you already know that you can play streaming video, download music, play movies, and run all kinds of Internet-based applications. These devices have wireless NICs that connect to wireless networks. The iPhone and iPad use **iOS**, which is an operating system tailored for these mobile devices from Apple. Smartphones and tablet computers not produced by Apple typically run the **Android operating system**, which is a product of the **Open Handset Alliance (OHA)**, with Google as a major Android sponsor and promoter. In addition to Google, OHA is composed of organizations such as Motorola, Intel, Dell, T-Mobile, and others. The OHA sponsors standards for mobile devices.

iOS is based on Darwin UNIX, and the Android operating system is based on Linux (which is a UNIX-like operating system). UNIX was the first operating system to support networking, and Linux also supports networking. Consequently, iOS and Android have a solid networking foundation.

Connecting Home Resources

More and more home appliances can be purchased that have communication and control features, which can be used through a network. There are refrigerators that come with digital message boards that connect to a network. These enable you to display messages from the Internet on the refrigerator message board, or to use the message board to send messages to someone's computer or to be picked up on a cell phone via the Internet. Controlling home temperature settings, turning on music, and managing lighting systems are all areas that can take advantage of home networking. Use Activity 1-5 to learn more about appliances compatible with networks.

Activity 1-5: Network-Ready Appliances

Time Required: 10 minutes
Objective: Discover examples of network-compatible home appliances.

Description: More and more companies are offering or developing home appliances that can be managed through a home network. In this activity, you use the Internet to find examples of home appliances that can be managed through a network. You need access to the Internet for this activity.

1. Open a Web browser, such as Internet Explorer in Windows 7 or Windows Server 2008/ Server 2008 R2, Firefox in Linux, or Safari in Mac OS X.

2. Use the search capability in your Web browser or go to *www.google.com* to find three or more examples of home appliances that can be connected to and managed from a home network (or via the Internet). Note the features of these appliances and how they can improve home living. (*Hint*: Try looking for articles about home network appliances at *www.hometoys.com*.)

3. Exit the Web browser when you are finished.

The University of Colorado at Boulder has an experimental project in which a home is not only networked and automated, but the home is designed to adapt to its occupants through determining their lifestyle and preferences. You can learn more about the Adaptive House at *www.cs.colorado.edu/~mozer/nnh/*. Also, of interest to coffee drinkers, there is a networking standard for connecting a coffee brewing device to a network. The standard uses a communications protocol called Hyper Text Coffee Pot Control Protocol (HTCPCP).

Using a Network in an Office

Networks are ideal for most offices because they increase productivity and save money on resources. In the next sections you learn how networks bring these and other advantages to offices.

Using a Network to Save Time and Money

Networks save office workers' precious time and make them more productive. People are able to share information without leaving their offices and can even telecommute to the office via a home network.

Consider an example involving a small tax accounting office. Each of five tax accountants meets with clients and computes a client's taxes on a networked computer. Once the figures are entered, the completed tax documents are sent to a shared network printer. An office associate obtains the documents, checks for printing and data entry errors, compiles the documents, and brings them to the accountant—enabling the accountant to remain in his or her office with the client. After the meeting with the client, a bill is printed, and an office associate checks the billing form and puts it in an envelope to mail to the client.

When people in offices are able to be more productive through networking, the organization saves money. Office workers can spend more time on their work and help generate more income.

Using a Network as a Business Strategy

A well-planned network can be an effective business strategy for any organization, small or large. Consider two small Internet businesses that sell specialty foods, such as chocolates and truffles. When a customer places an order with one company, the order is manually transcribed from a Web-based order form to a piece of paper. An office worker takes that paper to his desk and enters the order into a computer so the customer is billed through the mail. After he has entered several orders, he walks to the processing area and hands the orders to an inventory clerk.

Real-Life Networking

When PCs first came out they offered the promise of helping offices to automate and reduce the use of paper and trips to distribute documents. However, automation never fully took place until those PCs were networked. For example, the process of hiring a new employee in a large organization such as a university often involved manually completing, copying, and distributing job applications and reporting forms. This process was labor intensive in many ways. First, the employee would fill out the application form using a pen, pencil, or typewriter and then send it by mail or hand deliver it to the university's Human Resources Department. Next, Human Resources would make copies of all of the applications for a position and manually pass them out to those doing the hiring and interviewing. After a hiring decision was made, hiring forms were manually completed. These forms were then taken around to each person who needed to sign the forms, such as the department head, dean, vice provost, and human resources director. More forms were manually completed and signed to allocate the budget for the position, complete federal and state forms, and authorize the payroll. The bottom line was that hiring one person required lots of time on the part of those doing the hiring.

Networked servers and workstations have increased productivity in the hiring process through the use of electronic forms that can be distributed over a network. The applicant can complete and automatically send an electronic form, and those doing the hiring can receive and send forms electronically. Budget allocations and federal and state reporting also can be done electronically through networks, and forms can have electronic signatures. These advancements make it easier to hire a new employee and make those doing the hiring much more productive so that they have more time for other work.

The clerk walks to the inventory location, checks the inventory level, notes what is removed, boxes the orders, and prepares them for shipping. In this company most orders take three to five business days before they are shipped.

Consider a second company that is fully networked and automated. When the order comes in over the Web, it is automatically entered into an order-processing server, which generates the bill and sends the information to the processing area for shipment. Inventory is automatically adjusted for each order. The orders processed by this company go out the same day, all made possible by networked systems and automated network-capable software. This company handles more volume and does more business because it is more efficient and customers like receiving their orders sooner.

Connecting Office Resources

Connecting computers, printers, and other resources through a network offers the same advantages as those in a home, but these advantages are multiplied. The effectiveness of printer sharing, for instance, can offer a significant savings. Without a network, an office of 28 people would have 28 computers with one or more printers attached to each one. With a network, the number of printers might be reduced to three or four placed in central locations. The savings in maintenance and printer cartridges can be substantial.

Besides sharing files and printers, an office can also share the following devices that may be connected to a network:

- DVD/CD-ROM arrays
- Network storage through disk arrays

- Centralized tape, disk, or DVD/CD backups of critical files
- Fax machines
- Specialty printers, such as large-format printers
- Network conferencing devices
- Internet connectivity
- Internet telephony

Other resources can be added to the list, but the important concept is that a network can make many resources available to office workers at a reasonable cost. With these capabilities, even a very small business can appear large and effective to a client or customer.

Identifying Boundaries Between Networks

Sometimes the boundaries between networks (LANs, MANs, CANs, and WANs)—or the boundaries between them as a group and enterprise networks—are indistinct, making it difficult to determine where one begins and another ends. However, you can often distinguish one type of network from another by examining these four network properties:

- Communications medium
- Protocol
- Topology
- Network type (private versus public)

Consider the first item in the list. The communications medium is the wire cable, fiber-optic cable, radio/infrared waves, or microwaves used to connect computers and networks to one another. Often a LAN ends where there is a change in the communications medium, such as from wire-based cable to fiber-optic cable. Individual wire-cable LANs are often connected to other LANs over a WAN with fiber-optic cable. Another boundary might be the point at which the communications medium changes from fiber-optic cable to microwaves or radio waves.

The second factor in the list determines LAN and WAN boundaries by the protocol or protocols employed. The protocol specifies how networked data is formatted into discrete units, such as packets or frames (you will learn about packets and frames in the next chapter), how each unit is transmitted, and how it is interpreted at the receiving end.

Note that a single LAN may use one or more protocols, but a change in or an addition to existing protocols can signal the boundary between LANs. For example, a wired network differs from a wireless network in the way data is transmitted.

The third factor that helps to demarcate boundaries is the design layout, called the topology. A network topology has two components: the physical layout of the network cables and devices, and the logical path followed by network packets or frames sent on the cable or by wireless transmissions. In a wired network, the physical layout is the actual path of the cable as it goes through wiring troughs, ceilings, and walls. On a wireless network the path is related to the placement of antennas on network devices and the types of antennas those devices use. The logical path is the direction in which packets or frames flow, which may or may not fully match the physical layout. (You learn more about topologies in the next section.)

Consider an example in which the physical layout matches the logical layout. For example, the physical layout might be in a star shape, with a network device in the center of the star. The logical path of the frames or packets might follow the star pattern, sending the packets and frames to all end points at once. This would be similar to lighting all of the lights in a star ornament at one time.

You can change the preceding example by sending the frames and packets in a logical ring path (even though the cable physically resembles a star). Your frames or packets would go first to one point and then to another. This example is similar to lighting one light in a star ornament, turning that light off and lighting the next light, and so on.

The fourth factor that identifies network boundaries is the network type, as represented by the beginning and end points of private networks and public networks, for example. A **private network** is one owned and maintained by an organization, such as the network inside a bank building or a campus network operated by a college. A **public network** is one that offers services to members of the public, such as network services offered by a telecommunications company or a cable TV company.

As an example of network types, consider a situation in which you work for an accounting firm that has LANs in three branch offices that are connected by the regional telephone system. The boundary between the private LANs and the public WAN is the point at which the LANs connect to the regional telephone network. Another example is a company that enables its employees to use a **virtual private network (VPN)** over the Internet to access confidential data and files so they can telecommute using a computer and modem from home. A VPN is a private network that functions like a tunnel through a larger network—such as the Internet or an enterprise network—and that is restricted to designated member clients. You learn about VPNs in Chapter 7. In Activities 1-6, 1-7, and 1-8, you explore LAN and WAN boundaries.

Understanding the boundaries between networks can be vital in terms of designing security measures, because you may need to place network devices at one or more of these points to lock out intruders or to filter incoming or outgoing information for viruses, for example.

Activity 1-6: Viewing the Connection Point Between a LAN and a WAN

Time Required: 15–30 minutes

Objective: Observe the connection point between a LAN and a WAN.

Description: One way to determine a network boundary is by viewing the location at which a LAN is connected to a WAN, which includes one or more of the boundary elements: a change in communications medium, a change in protocols, a change in topology, and/or a change in network type. In this activity, you view the connection point between a LAN and a WAN.

1. Contact the network administrator at your school or at a business in your community.

2. Ask the administrator if you can view the equipment used to connect the LAN in his organization with a WAN, such as connecting a LAN to a regional telephone company.

3. Ask what type of WAN is connected to the LAN and about the topologies used for the LAN and WAN.

4. Ask what type of equipment is used at the connection point and about the media types used, including types of cable or wireless media.

5. Find out what protocols are used on the LAN and WAN.

6. Find out the speed of the LAN compared to the speed of the WAN.

7. Record your results in your lab journal or in a word-processed document.

As an alternative, your class might arrange to visit the network administrator for a group tour of the LAN/WAN connectivity equipment. You also could invite the network administrator to give a class presentation that describes the LAN/WAN connectivity devices.

Activity 1-7: Viewing Network Links in Windows

Time Required: 5–10 minutes

Objective: View the Windows 7 or Windows Server 2008/Server 2008 R2 LAN and WAN connection options.

Description: Sometimes one network or computer is joined to another through a logical or software link, such as a dial-up connection or through a VPN. Other possibilities include DSL or cable modem connections (you learn about DSL and cable modem connections in Chapter 9, "Understanding WAN Connection Choices"). In this activity, you view the logical links between these types of networks, including dial-up and VPNs, joined through Windows 7 and Server 2008/Server 2008 R2. In both systems you need an account that has Administrator permissions.

1. To view the logical links in Windows 7 or Server 2008 R2, click **Start** and click **Control Panel**. Ensure that **View by** is set to **Large icons** or **Small icons** and click **Network and Sharing Center**. In Windows Server 2008, ensure you are in the **Classic View** and double-click **Network and Sharing Center**.

2. Notice the simple network representation at the top of the Network and Sharing Center window.

3. Click **Set up a new connection or network** in Windows 7/Server 2008 R2 or **Set up a connection or network** in Windows Server 2008 to view the Set Up a Connection or Network window (see Figure 1-12, which is for a Windows 7 computer with a wireless NIC).

4. What types of network connections can be configured on your computer?

5. Click **Connect to a workplace**. Click **Next**.

6. What options do you see?

7. Click **Cancel**.

8. Close the Network and Sharing Center window.

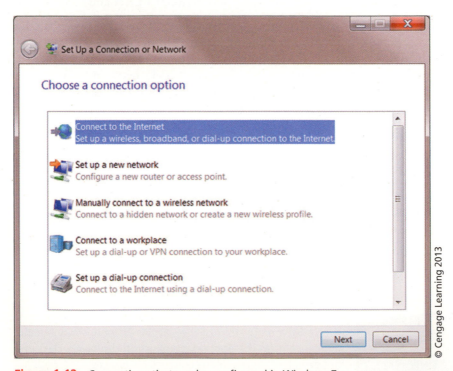

Figure 1-12 Connections that can be configured in Windows 7

Activity 1-8: Determining Network Connectivity in UNIX/Linux

Time Required: 5 minutes

Objective: Viewing LAN and WAN connectivity in UNIX/Linux.

Description: UNIX and Linux systems can have logical LAN and WAN connections. In this activity, you view network connectivity in Fedora Linux (similar steps also work in other versions of Linux and in some versions of UNIX), which is already configured with the X Window GNOME 3.x desktop. In some distributions of Linux, you need to log on using the root account or an account that has superuser (root) permissions. In this activity, you access the root account by using the *su* (switch user) command.

If you are using the Fedora 15 or higher Live Media DVD/CD-ROM, boot your computer from the DVD/CD-ROM and run the operating system from the DVD/CD-ROM. When you turn on the computer, insert the DVD/CD-ROM and use the keyboard key combination specific to your computer for booting from the DVD/CD-ROM drive. The key combination is often displayed when you first turn on the computer, such as pressing F11 or F12 for some computers (consult with your instructor for your particular computer). Allow the automatic boot process to complete so that you are automatically logged in and see the GNOME desktop.

1. In the GNOME 3.x desktop, click **Activities** in the left side of the top panel at the top of the desktop. Click **Applications** on the desktop to view icons of applications that can be opened. Click the **Terminal** icon to open a terminal window. A terminal window enables you to enter Linux commands. (If you are using a distribution of Linux other than Fedora with the GNOME 3.x desktop, follow the appropriate steps in that Linux distribution to open a terminal window or access the command line.)

2. At the command line in the terminal window, type **su root** and press **Enter**. (When you use Fedora 15 Live Media (or higher) you do not need to enter a root password. For other Linux distributions you need to enter the root password at this point. If you do not know the root password, check with your instructor.)

3. Type **ifconfig** and then press **Enter**.

4. Notice the left side of the display. If you see an entry for "wlan0" or "wlan1," the system is configured for wireless access. If you see an entry for "eth0," "eth1," "em0," or "em1," then the system is configured to access an Ethernet network, such as through a NIC connected to a network cable. (Your computer may be configured for one or both of these connections.) You also see "lo" displayed on the left side of the window for a loopback address, which is used for diagnostic testing of network connectivity. Figure 1-13 shows all three connectivity options for "em1," "lo," and "wlan0."

5. Close the terminal window.

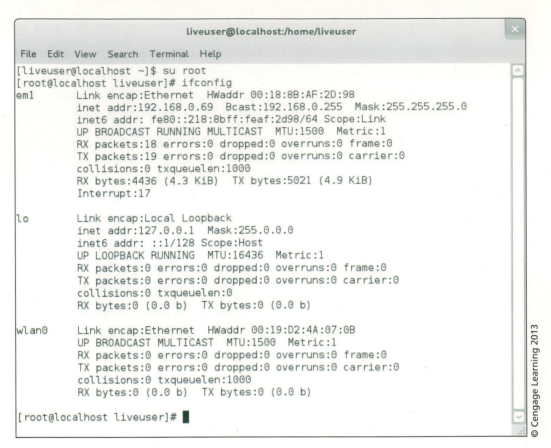

```
                    liveuser@localhost:/home/liveuser                    ✕

File  Edit  View  Search  Terminal  Help

[liveuser@localhost ~]$ su root
[root@localhost liveuser]# ifconfig
em1       Link encap:Ethernet  HWaddr 00:18:8B:AF:2D:98
          inet addr:192.168.0.69  Bcast:192.168.0.255  Mask:255.255.255.0
          inet6 addr: fe80::218:8bff:feaf:2d98/64 Scope:Link
          UP BROADCAST RUNNING MULTICAST  MTU:1500  Metric:1
          RX packets:18 errors:0 dropped:0 overruns:0 frame:0
          TX packets:19 errors:0 dropped:0 overruns:0 carrier:0
          collisions:0 txqueuelen:1000
          RX bytes:4436 (4.3 KiB)  TX bytes:5021 (4.9 KiB)
          Interrupt:17

lo        Link encap:Local Loopback
          inet addr:127.0.0.1  Mask:255.0.0.0
          inet6 addr: ::1/128 Scope:Host
          UP LOOPBACK RUNNING  MTU:16436  Metric:1
          RX packets:0 errors:0 dropped:0 overruns:0 frame:0
          TX packets:0 errors:0 dropped:0 overruns:0 carrier:0
          collisions:0 txqueuelen:0
          RX bytes:0 (0.0 b)  TX bytes:0 (0.0 b)

wlan0     Link encap:Ethernet  HWaddr 00:19:D2:4A:07:0B
          UP BROADCAST MULTICAST  MTU:1500  Metric:1
          RX packets:0 errors:0 dropped:0 overruns:0 frame:0
          TX packets:0 errors:0 dropped:0 overruns:0 carrier:0
          collisions:0 txqueuelen:1000
          RX bytes:0 (0.0 b)  TX bytes:0 (0.0 b)

[root@localhost liveuser]# ▮
```

Figure 1-13   Fedora Linux network configuration

Activity 1-9: Viewing Network Connection Options in Mac OS X Snow Leopard or Lion

Time Required: 5 minutes

Objective: Learn about network connection options in Mac OS X Snow Leopard or Lion.

Description: Mac OS X Snow Leopard and Lion offer Ethernet connectivity for cabled networks and wireless connectivity through wireless cards such as AirPort cards and MacWireless USB network interfaces. Mac OS X also supports FireWire (the IEEE 1394 standard) that enables network and other devices to be connected to a Macintosh computer. In addition, Mac OS X Lion supports Bluetooth PAN, to connect with Bluetooth devices in a PAN. For this activity, you need access to an account that has Administrator privileges.

1. Click the **System Preferences** icon in the Dock, or click the **Apple** icon in the menu bar at the top of the desktop and click **System Preferences**.

2. Click **Network** under Internet & Wireless in the System Preferences window.

3. Notice the network connectivity options listed in the left pane of the Network window, such as Wi-Fi or AirPort. Record the options available on your Macintosh computer.

4. Click **System Preferences** in the menu bar at the top of the desktop and click **Quit System Preferences**.

5. Click **Spotlight** (the magnifying glass) icon in the upper right side of the desktop, type **terminal**, and then click the **Terminal** application. (Alternatively, open Finder (first icon on the Dock), click **Go** in the menu bar, click **Utilities**, scroll down in the Utilities window if necessary, and double-click **Terminal**.) Because Mac OS X Snow Leopard and Lion are built on Darwin UNIX, there is a terminal window available in these operating systems from which to run UNIX/Linux commands.

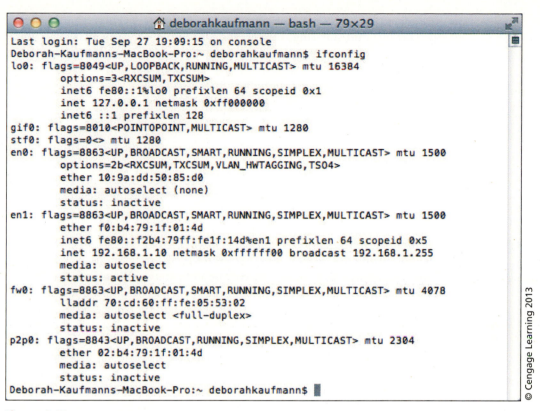

```
 ○ ○ ○            🏠 deborahkaufmann — bash — 79×29

Last login: Tue Sep 27 19:09:15 on console
Deborah-Kaufmanns-MacBook-Pro:~ deborahkaufmann$ ifconfig
lo0: flags=8049<UP,LOOPBACK,RUNNING,MULTICAST> mtu 16384
        options=3<RXCSUM,TXCSUM>
        inet6 fe80::1%lo0 prefixlen 64 scopeid 0x1
        inet 127.0.0.1 netmask 0xff000000
        inet6 ::1 prefixlen 128
gif0: flags=8010<POINTOPOINT,MULTICAST> mtu 1280
stf0: flags=0<> mtu 1280
en0: flags=8863<UP,BROADCAST,SMART,RUNNING,SIMPLEX,MULTICAST> mtu 1500
        options=2b<RXCSUM,TXCSUM,VLAN_HWTAGGING,TSO4>
        ether 10:9a:dd:50:85:d0
        media: autoselect (none)
        status: inactive
en1: flags=8863<UP,BROADCAST,SMART,RUNNING,SIMPLEX,MULTICAST> mtu 1500
        ether f0:b4:79:1f:01:4d
        inet6 fe80::f2b4:79ff:fe1f:14d%en1 prefixlen 64 scopeid 0x5
        inet 192.168.1.10 netmask 0xffffff00 broadcast 192.168.1.255
        media: autoselect
        status: active
fw0: flags=8863<UP,BROADCAST,SMART,RUNNING,SIMPLEX,MULTICAST> mtu 4078
        lladdr 70:cd:60:ff:fe:05:53:02
        media: autoselect <full-duplex>
        status: inactive
p2p0: flags=8843<UP,BROADCAST,RUNNING,SIMPLEX,MULTICAST> mtu 2304
        ether 02:b4:79:1f:01:4d
        media: autoselect
        status: inactive
Deborah-Kaufmanns-MacBook-Pro:~ deborahkaufmann$ ▌
```

© Cengage Learning 2013

Figure 1-14   Using *ifconfig* in Mac OS X

6. At the command line, type **ifconfig** and press **return**.

7. Notice the connection options in the left side of the listing, such as *en1* as shown in Figure 1-14, which in the figure is an active connection for a wireless NIC; (*en* is used to designate cabled or wireless connections in Mac OS X).

8. In the menu bar, click **Terminal** and click **Quit Terminal**.

Network Topologies

Each type of network is constructed of various combinations of cabling, network equipment, servers, workstations, software, and training. You can combine these elements in various ways to create a network to accommodate the needs and resources of a particular organization. Some types of networks have low start-up costs, but are expensive to maintain or upgrade. Others are more expensive to set up, but are easy to maintain and offer simple upgrade paths.

As you learned in the last section, one of the clearest distinctions between types of networks is the network topology, composed of the physical layout of a network, combined with its logical characteristics. On a wired network the physical layout is the pattern in which the cabling is laid in the office, building, or campus. This is often called the **cable plant**. On wireless networks the cable plant is related to the types of antennas, the types of wireless devices, and the direction of wireless transmissions. The logical side of the network is how the signal is transferred from point to point along the cable or through wireless communications.

The network layout may be decentralized, such as with cable running between each station on the network, or the layout may be centralized, with each station physically connected to a central device that dispatches frames and packets from workstation to workstation. A centralized layout is like a star with workstations as its points. Decentralized layouts resemble a team of mountain climbers, with each climber at a different location on the mountain but joined by a long rope. The logical side of a topology consists of the path taken by a frame or packet as it travels through the network.

The main topologies are bus, ring, star, mesh, and tree. There also are hybrid topologies that include star-bus and star-ring. In selecting a topology for your network, you should match the type of network with its intended purpose in an organization. For example, some organizations make more intense use of their network than others. The number and kinds of software applications used by an organization influence the number and frequency of frames and packets to be transmitted—this is known as network traffic. If network users are primarily accessing word-processing software or documents, the network traffic is relatively low, and most of the work is performed at workstations, rather than on the network.

Client/server applications generate a medium to high level of network traffic, depending on the client/server software design. Networks on which there is frequent exchange of database information, such as Microsoft SQL Server or Oracle database files, have medium to high network traffic. Scientific and publications software generate high levels of traffic because they use extremely large data files. Also, graphics-intensive applications, such as streaming multimedia or desktop conferencing, can produce very high levels of network traffic.

The impact of hosts and servers on a network is closely linked to the type of software applications that are used. For example, frequently accessing a database server to generate financial reports and sales figures is likely to generate more network traffic than occasionally accessing a file server containing business correspondence or templates for letters.

You should consider whether other networks will be connected to a network when deciding which topology to use. The network topology for a small business that will never use more than four computers is different from the topology required by an industrial campus that connects via a WAN to other industrial sites. The small business probably does not connect to additional networks, except for perhaps an outside connection to the Internet. The industrial campus can consist of several interconnected networks, perhaps including a network to control machines in the plant, a network for the business systems, a network for the research scientists, and an extended WAN to other locations. Some topologies permit better network interconnectivity than other topologies.

Heavily trafficked networks need high-speed data transmission capabilities. The network speed is important to the productivity of the users. High-speed capability is particularly important when images, graphics, and other large files need to be transported over long distances or onto WANs.

Security, which is the protection of data so that only authorized persons have access, is another issue that influences network design. A secure network uses network devices, passwords, control software, and other techniques to restrict access to information and resources. It also may use data and password encryption, which encodes frames and packets and allows only authorized computers to decode them. High-security networks use fiber-optic cable, which minimizes the risk of data interception by unauthorized users. Another security measure is to place network devices and servers in restricted locations, such as in computer rooms and wiring closets.

Network topology directly affects the network's potential for growth. After you install a network, you will probably need to add more users, perhaps in the same office or in other offices or floors. It is also likely that you will need to connect a LAN to a WAN for long-distance information access.

Bus Topology

The **bus topology** consists of running cable from one PC or server to the next, like links in a chain. Like a chain, a network using a bus topology has a starting point and an ending point, and a **terminator** is connected to each end of the bus cable segment. When you transmit a packet, it is detected by all nodes on the segment and it has a given amount of time to reach its destination, or it is considered late. A bus network segment must be within the **Institute of Electrical and Electronics Engineers (IEEE)** length specifications to ensure that packets arrive in the expected time. The IEEE is an international organization of scientists, engineers, technicians, and educators that plays a leading role in developing standards for network cabling and data transmissions. Figure 1-15 shows a simple bus network design.

You can learn more about the IEEE at its Web site, *www.ieee.org*.

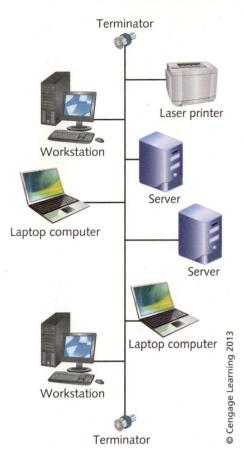

Terminator

Laser printer

Workstation

Server

Laptop computer

Server

Laptop computer

Workstation

Terminator

© Cengage Learning 2013

Figure 1-15   Bus topology

The terminator is critical on bus networks because it signals the physical end to the segment. A terminator is really an electrical resistor that absorbs the signal when it reaches the end of the network. Without a terminator, the segment violates IEEE specifications and signals can be mirrored back or reflected on the same path they just covered. The signal reflection offsets network timing and can interfere with new signals being transmitted on the network, similar to having two conversations happening at once.

 When a terminator is missing or malfunctioning, communications on that segment are unstable and network equipment generally shuts down the segment.

The traditional bus design (as shown in Figure 1-15) works well for small networks and is relatively inexpensive to implement. At start-up, costs can be minimized because on cabled networks it requires less cable than other topologies. It is also easy to add another workstation to extend the bus for a short distance within a room or an office. The disadvantage is that management costs can be high. For example, it is difficult to isolate a single malfunctioning node or cable segment and associated connectors, and one defective node or cable segment and its connectors can take down the entire network (although modern networking equipment makes this less likely). Another disadvantage is that the bus can become very congested with network traffic, requiring the addition of network devices to control the traffic flow.

 The traditional bus topology is used less and less because it can be hard to maintain, and some network and computing vendors no longer support the communication cabling method used in the topology. However, aspects of the bus may be used with other topologies.

Ring Topology

The **ring topology** is a continuous path for data with no logical beginning or ending point, and thus no terminators. Workstations and servers are attached to the cable at points around the ring (see Figure 1-16). When data is transmitted onto the ring, it goes around the ring from node to node reaching its destination and then continuing until it ends at the source node.

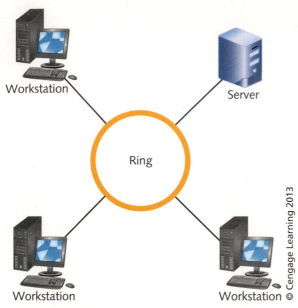

Figure 1-16   Ring topology

When it was first developed, the ring topology permitted data to go in one direction only, circling the ring and ending at the transmitting or source node. Newer high-speed ring technologies employ two loops for redundant data transmission in opposite directions, thus if the loop in one direction is broken, data can still reach its destination by going in the opposite direction on the other loop.

The ring topology is easier to manage than the bus because the equipment used to build the ring makes it easier to locate a defective node, cable, or transmission problem. This topology is well-suited for transmitting signals over long distances on a LAN, and it handles high-volume network traffic better than the bus topology. Overall, the ring topology enables more reliable communications than the traditional bus.

However, the ring topology can be more expensive to implement than the bus. Typically, it requires more cable and network equipment at the start. Also, the ring topology for LAN designs has fallen out of favor, because other topologies and transmission concepts have grown in popularity, such as those that better accommodate wireless networking. Today, it is more common to use the ring topology in some WAN designs as you learn in Chapter 9, "Understanding WAN Connection Choices."

Star Topology

The **star topology** is the oldest communications design method, with roots in telephone switching systems. Although it is the oldest design method, advances in network technology have made the star topology a good option for modern networks. The physical layout of the star topology consists of multiple nodes attached to a central device, such as the workstations and server connected to the switch as shown in Figure 1-17. Typically the central device is a hub, switch, or router that joins single cable segments or individual LANs into one network. Some hubs also are called concentrators or access units. Switches and routers are now typically used instead of traditional hubs because they have built-in intelligence to make network communications go faster. Single communications cable segments radiate from the hub, switch, or router like a star (try Activity 1-10 to create a diagram of a star topology). You learn how hubs, switches, and routers work in Chapter 5, "Devices for Connecting Networks."

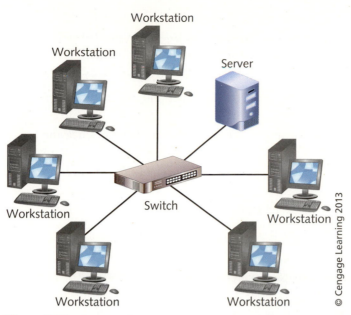

Figure 1-17   Star topology

The start-up costs for the star topology are lower today than those for a traditional bus network. The costs are lower because the prices for network equipment and cable have gone down because so many people use this design. As with the ring topology, the star is easier to manage than the traditional bus network because malfunctioning nodes can be identified quickly. If a node or a cable run is damaged, it can be easily isolated from the network by the network equipment, and service to the other nodes is not affected. The star is easier to expand by connecting additional nodes or networks. It also offers the best options for expansion into high-speed networking. The star is a very popular topology, and thus there is a wider variety of equipment available for this type of network.

A disadvantage is that the central hub, switch, or router is a single point of failure; if it fails, all connected nodes are unable to communicate (unless there is redundancy built into the hub or switch to include backup measures). Another disadvantage is that the star requires more cable than does the bus; however, cabling and connectors for the star topology are less expensive than cabling for the bus.

Activity 1-10: Creating a Network Diagram

Time Required: 15–20 minutes

Objective: Learn how to create a basic network diagram of a star topology.

Description: Learning to diagram a network is particularly valuable for mastering network design now and for troubleshooting later. In this activity you get a first taste of creating a network design by diagramming a star-based network.

1. Start the network drawing software available at your school, such as Visio, AutoCad, or another drawing package. If a network drawing package is not available, use Microsoft Paint in Windows 7. (To open Paint in Windows 7, click **Start**, point to **All Programs**, click **Accessories**, and click **Paint**.)

2. Open to a clear drawing area.

3. Select a switch from a stencil or from the clipart that accompanies the drawing package. If there is no switch included, use the switch.bmp figure file that is available from your instructor.

4. Place or drag the switch to the center of the drawing.

5. Select a PC from a stencil or from the clipart that accompanies the drawing package. If none is included, use the pc.bmp figure file available from your instructor.

6. Place or drag the PC to the upper-left corner above the switch.

7. Copy the PC or repeat Step 5 and place another PC in the upper-right corner above the switch.

8. Add two more PCs, one in the lower-left corner and one in the lower-right corner below the switch.

9. Activate the line draw capability in the drawing package or click the line button, if you are using Microsoft Paint.

10. Create a line between each PC and the switch. The final product should look similar to the drawing in Figure 1-18.

11. Save your work as a file called **starnet**.

12. Print the network drawing.

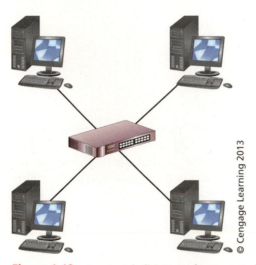

© Cengage Learning 2013

Figure 1-18   A network diagram of a star topology

Star-Bus Hybrid Topology

Modern networks combine the logical communications of a bus with the physical layout of a star, called the **star-bus hybrid topology**. This is also called the **star-wired bus topology**. In this network design, each finger radiating from the star is like a separate logical bus segment, but with only one or two computers attached. The segment is still terminated at both ends, but the advantage is that there are no exposed terminators. On each segment, one end is terminated inside the hub or switch and the other is terminated at the device on the network.

Another advantage of the star-bus network design is that you can connect multiple hubs, switches, or routers to expand the network in many directions, as long as you follow standard network specifications for communications cable distances, the number of hubs or switches, and the number of devices attached. The connection between hubs or switches is a backbone that typically enables high-speed communications between the hubs or switches. A **backbone** is a high-capacity communications medium that joins networks and central network devices on the same floor in a building, on different floors, and across long distances.

Hubs, switches, and routers are available with built-in intelligence to help detect problems. Also, there are expansion opportunities for implementing high-speed networking. Because this is a popular network design, there is a wide range of equipment available for bus networks in the shape of a star.

Star-Ring Hybrid Topology

Today, ring networks are typically designed in the physical layout of a star and called the **star-ring hybrid topology** or the **star-wired ring topology**. There is a hub or access unit that acts as a linking device that replicates transmission of the signal from node to node using the logical communications of a ring. To each computer, the communications appear as though they are in a ring. Because communications are in a ring, there is no need for built-in terminators as used in the star-bus hybrid configuration. (However, star-ring hybrid topology networks are rarely used in LANs, but are used in some WANs.)

Mesh Topology

In the **mesh topology**, every node is connected to every other node on the network. In Figure 1-19 each of the five computers is connected to all other computers for a total of 10 links. This is done so that if a link breaks, every node can still communicate with every other node. This approach gives a network extensive **fault tolerance**, which means there is built-in protection in case there is an equipment or communications failure. The more devices there are in a mesh network, the more alternate communications paths.

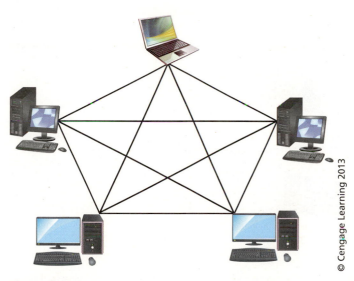

© Cengage Learning 2013

Figure 1-19   Mesh topology

The mesh topology is used less on cabled LANs, because it is expensive to implement, requiring the installation of more cable, multiple hubs or switches, and multiple NICs in each computer. It is, however, often used in MANs and WANs because these can have very large numbers of clients who require reliable communications. The mesh topology is also used on wireless LANs set up so that a node can communicate with any other node in its broadcast range.

Tree Topology

The **tree topology** (also called the expanded star) offers features of the basic bus topology combined with features of the star topology. As the tree analogy suggests, you might think of this topology as consisting of a trunk (or bus) with limbs and branches (star configurations) sprouting out from the trunk. Each limb may contain only one branch or have several clusters of branches growing from an individual limb. Figure 1-20 illustrates a tree topology.

An alternative design for the tree topology is in a hierarchy of nodes, with a main-level node called the root node. Additional nodes may be connected to the root node to compose the second level of the tree. Level three can be built on top of level two, and so on. Figure 1-21 illustrates this design concept, showing three levels.

One advantage of the tree topology is that it is very compatible with segregating network traffic so that network communications in one limb of the tree can be isolated from other limbs. This might be important in the case of a specialized research unit whose computers occupy one limb of the network topology. Communications on that limb can be segregated so that the product plans and other development files for the research unit are accessible only by those involved in the project.

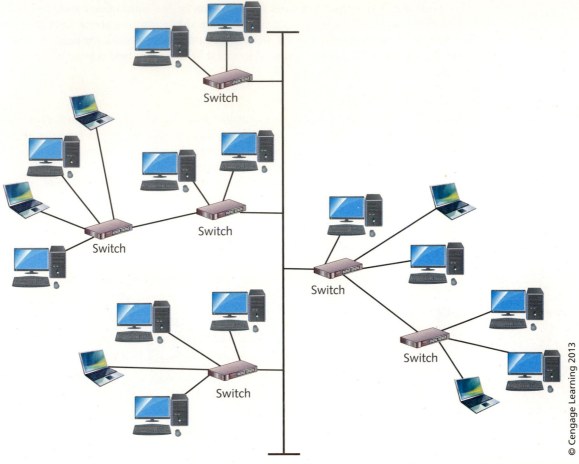

Figure 1-20   Tree topology

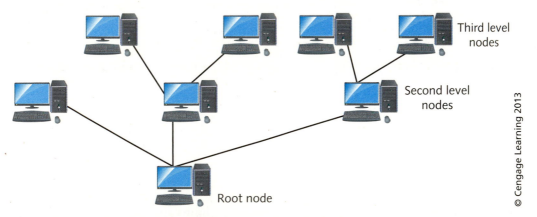

Figure 1-21   Tree topology design with a root node

A disadvantage of the tree topology is that on cabled networks, it may require the use of more cable than other topologies. Another disadvantage is that if communications go down on the main trunk (or backbone) or the root node, then the connected limbs (network segments) can no longer communicate with one another.

Network Design Introduction

Preparing to design networks requires steps that you learn throughout this book. A first step is to understand how networks work in terms of protocols, access methods, and topologies.

For example, the design for a network that uses the Ethernet access method in a bus topology is often different from the design used for a token ring network that uses the ring topology (you learn about access methods including Ethernet and token ring in Chapter 2). In addition, the design for a telecommunications-based WAN is different from the design for a satellite-based WAN.

Another step in the design process is to understand the physical equipment used in networks. The physical equipment includes communications media, such as fiber-optic cable, and network devices, such as routers and switches. A solid design depends on details, such as what communications media are used for a backbone as compared to what media are used to reach desktop computers. Learning the characteristics of different communications media and devices helps you create the most effective network designs.

A third step is to understand basic network design principles. These include how to use structured wiring and structured networking techniques; how to design for multimedia, client/server applications, and cloud applications; and how to take advantage of LAN and WAN device characteristics. For example, in many situations, network performance is enhanced if you place a switch or router at a key junction. In addition, a router can be used to create a firewall for protecting a network or for enabling multimedia communications to be transported quickly.

A fourth step in the design process is to assess the characteristics of your home, office, or organization that affect the design of the network. Your assessment can include answering the following questions:

- What types of computers and operating systems are used, and what are their locations?

- What software applications are used, and what network resources are required to run those applications?

- What work and play patterns are typical in a home, and in what rooms will computers be used, including in a home office?

- What are the business patterns in the organization, and how are those business patterns associated with network use?

- What are the high and low network use periods in the home or organization?

- What features can be designed into a network to make troubleshooting and maintenance easier?

- What type of security is needed for the network?

- What growth is anticipated in home or business use, and in what areas will that growth affect network resources?

Putting It All Together: Designing a Simple LAN

Many small businesses can use a simple LAN design to make business communications easier. For example, consider a small law office that can benefit from having a LAN. The office consists of four attorneys and one secretary. Your research about the law firm's needs reveals that each attorney keeps information about clients strictly on his or her computer, with the exception of sharing case information when they are working with one or more of the other attorneys on a case. When working together, the lead attorney keeps information about that case on her computer and periodically prints a copy to distribute. One problem with this method is that distribution of the information is sometimes forgotten when the lead is busy on another case. When it is time to bill a client, each attorney prints a rough draft of the billable hours and hand carries it to the secretary, who compiles the information and mails the bill. The secretary also keeps the books for the law practice on her computer. Finally, your research shows that each member of the office has his or her own computer and printer. Also, when you research the potential for using a wireless connection in the building, you learn that other offices in the building have decided to use cable connections. Wireless access is intermittent because of the building materials in the walls and because of wireless interference from surrounding electrical devices.

A solid design for this office using what you have learned so far consists of the following:

- A star-bus hybrid topology that is a logical bus network employing the physical layout of a star.
- A switch connecting the computers in the middle of the star layout and connected using network cable (see Figure 1-22).
- The computers are able to share certain information through the network.
- The printers are shared on the network.

The rationale for this design is as follows:

- The star-bus hybrid topology enables the firm to economically connect all of the computers using common network components. The advantage of a star-bus hybrid topology is that it is popular and components are economical, easy to obtain, and relatively easy to support.
- Using cable instead of wireless connectivity due to sources of radio wave interference in the building assures that network communications will be reliable.
- Using a switch to join the links on the network satisfies the need for fast communications between computers.
- The network design enables the law office to share documents through the network using a basic peer-to-peer approach—and without having to configure a server. A **peer-to-peer network** is one of the simplest ways for computers to share information. Through a peer-to-peer network each computer in a small office can share files and printing resources. Modern operating systems, such as Windows 7, UNIX/Linux, and Mac OS X, support peer-to-peer networking. In this way, each computer user controls which files or printers are shared. In the situation described for the law firm, there is no need to have a central server, which would create extra expense and technical support overhead.
- Sharing documents over the network, such as case files and billing information, enables the attorneys and secretary to work more efficiently.
- Creating a network for the law office enables printers to be shared, so that if one or more printers are not working, a different printer can be used.
- The star-bus hybrid design with a switch and peer-to-peer communications keeps the network simple and easy to maintain.
- Using a star-bus hybrid design and switch creates opportunities to easily add Internet communications for all office members.

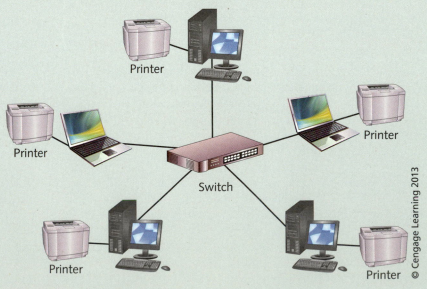

Figure 1-22   Designing a network for a small law office

Chapter Summary

■ A computer network consists of computers, printers, network devices, and software all linked or shared through a system of wired and wireless connections.

■ PANs, LANs, MANs, CANs, and WANs are the five dominant types of computer networks. The main characteristic that differentiates them is their range of operation. Other characteristics include the protocols and topologies used in a network. A PAN is for close-in networked connections, such as a smartphone connecting wirelessly to a nearby computer to download picture files. The term LAN commonly describes smaller discrete networks, and the term WAN is used for the long-distance networks that link LANs. A MAN links LANs within a city or metropolitan region, whereas a WAN can join networks that span long distances. The CAN joins LANs within a specific area, such as on a business campus, and is typically owned by a single business or organization. The relationship between LANs and WANs is analogous to that between a small-office telephone system that is connected to a major telecommunications system. Another way to classify a network is as an enterprise of resources, consisting of computers, servers, mainframes, printers, and other resources brought together in a combination of LANs, MANs, CANs, and WANs.

■ Networks consist of nodes (or stations), such as workstations and servers. The cable or radio waves that link nodes compose the communications media. Nodes are connected to a network through network interface cards (NICs).

■ Networks offer advantages for homes that have two or more computers, such as for sharing files, printers, and an Internet connection.

■ Networks in offices enable businesses and organizations to be more productive and to develop business strategies for optimal effectiveness.

■ Sometimes it is difficult to determine where one network ends and another begins. The ways to determine network boundaries include examining communications media, protocols, topologies, and network types.

■ Networks are designed in terms of topologies. The basic topologies are bus, ring, star, mesh, and tree. Two other topologies are hybrids: star-bus and star-ring.

■ Network design involves many steps. To design networks effectively, you need to thoroughly understand protocols, topologies, network equipment, network design principles, and how to assess the networking needs of an organization. You learn all of these steps and more in the chapters that follow.

Key Terms

Android operating system   An operating system designed for mobile and wireless devices such as smartphones and tablet PCs. Under the hood, Android is based on the Linux operating system.

backbone   A high-capacity communications medium that joins networks on the same floor in a building, on different floors, and across long distances.

bus topology   A network design built by running cable from one PC or file server to the next, like links in a chain.

cable plant   The total amount of communications cable that makes up a network.

campus area network (CAN)   Multiple LANs in a specific area or region, such as in buildings on a college campus, that are managed or owned by one organization.

client   A computer that accesses another computer, such as a workstation that accesses a shared file on another workstation, server, or mainframe. The client may use the accessed computer (host) to process data or may process accessed data using its own CPU.

communications media   The cabling or radio waves used to connect one network computer to another or one network to another and transport data between them.

computer network   A system of computers, print devices, network devices, and computer software linked by communications cabling or radio waves.

enterprise network   A combination of LANs, MANs, CANs, or WANs that provides computer users with an array of computer and network resources to complete different tasks.

fault tolerance   Techniques that employ hardware and software to provide assurance against equipment failures, computer service interruptions, and data loss.

host   (1) A computer (mainframe, server, or workstation) that has an operating system enabling multiple computers to access it at the same time for files, data, and services. Programs and information may be processed at the host, or they may be downloaded to the accessing computer (client) for processing. (2) A computer that is connected to a network.

Institute of Electrical and Electronics Engineers (IEEE)   An international organization of scientists, engineers, technicians, and educators that plays a leading role in developing standards for network cabling and data transmissions.

Internet   A worldwide network of interconnected LANs, MANs, CANs, and WANs that uses the TCP/IP protocol to enable people to share e-mail messages and computer files and to access a vast array of information.

Internet Connection Sharing (ICS)   An option offered on Windows computers that enables one computer connected to the Internet to share its Internet connection with other computers on the same network. This can be a good Internet access solution in a home or small office.

iOS   An operating system developed by Apple for mobile devices such as the iPhone and iPad. Like Apple's Mac OS X for desktop and laptop computers, iOS is based on Darwin UNIX and incorporates concepts from Mac OS X. *See* **Android operating system.**

local area network (LAN)   A series of interconnected computers, printing devices, and other computer equipment that share hardware and software resources. The service area usually is limited to a given office area, floor, or building.

mesh topology   A network design in which every node is connected to every other node, achieving fault tolerance.

metropolitan area network (MAN)   A network that links multiple LANs in a large city or metropolitan region.

network interface card (NIC)   An adapter board or USB device designed to connect a workstation, server, or other network device to a network medium.

node   Any device connected to a network, such as a personal computer, tablet PC, mainframe, server, network equipment, or printer. Also called a station.

Open Handset Alliance (OHA)   An alliance of vendors such as Google, Motorola, Intel, Dell, and T-Mobile that has provided backing for the Android operating system. *See* **Android operating system.**

peer-to-peer network   A network on which any computer can communicate with other networked computers on an equal (peer) basis without going through an intermediary, such as a server. Peer-to-peer networking enables each computer to offer and access shared resources, such as files and printers.

personal area network (PAN)   A network that typically reaches a few meters, such as up to 10 meters (33 feet; although some PANs can reach farther), and consists of personal devices such as mobile computers, smartphones, and handheld devices. A PAN can be cabled or wireless.

private network   A network owned and maintained by an organization, such as a campus network operated by a college.

protocol   Similar to a language, a protocol enables network devices to communicate and exchange information or data. A protocol is an established guideline that specifies how networked data is formatted into a packet or frame, how it is transmitted, and how it is interpreted at the receiving end.

public network   A network that offers services to members of the public, such as network services offered by a telecommunications company or a cable TV company.

ring topology   A network design consisting of a continuous path for data with no logical beginning or ending point, and thus no terminators.

server   A computer that provides extensive multiuser access to network resources, such as shared files, shared disks, and shared printers.

star-bus hybrid topology   Also called the star-wired bus topology, a network design that combines the logical communications of a bus with the physical layout of a star.

star-ring hybrid topology   Also called the star-wired ring topology, a network design in which the logical communications are in a ring, but the physical layout of the network is a star.

star topology   The oldest type of network design, this topology consists of multiple nodes attached to a central hub or switch.

star-wired bus topology   *See* star-bus hybrid topology.

star-wired ring topology   *See* star-ring hybrid topology.

station   *See* node.

terminator   A resistor that is connected to the end of a segment on a bus network, so that data-carrying signals are absorbed at the point where the segment stops. Absorbing the signals ensures that they are not reflected back onto the cable after they reach the end—thus preventing communication errors.

topology   The physical layout of cable and wireless network devices and the logical path followed by network frames or packets sent on the cable or by wireless transmissions.

tree topology   Also called the expanded star, it offers features of the basic bus topology combined with features of the star topology. This topology resembles a tree with a trunk and limbs or represents a root node at the base in a hierarchy of nodes built on levels off of the root node.

Universal Serial Bus (USB)   A serial bus, such as in a computer, designed to support up to 127 discrete devices with data transfer speeds up to 5 Gbits/s (gigabits per second).

virtual private network (VPN)   A private network that functions like a tunnel through a larger network—such as the Internet or an enterprise network—that is restricted to designated member clients only.

wide area network (WAN)   A far-reaching system of networks that usually extends over more than about 48 kilometers (about 30 miles) and often reaches across states and continents.

workstation   A computer that has its own CPU and may be used as a stand-alone computer for word processing, spreadsheet creation, or other software applications. It also may be used to access another computer such as another workstation or server via a network.

Review Questions

1. A computer device manufacturer owns four buildings in downtown Raleigh, North Carolina, and the LANs in each building are connected together for integrated communications and resource sharing. This type of network is an example of which of the following?

   a.   LAN-NET

   b.   TAN

   c.   CAN

   d.   WAN

   e.   none of the above

2. Which of the following are ways to share a printer among computer users? (Choose all that apply.)

   a.   Create a joint area network.

   b.   Connect the printer to a Windows 7 workstation and share it on a network.

   c.   Purchase a printer that has a built-in NIC.

   d.   Use a print server device that connects to a network.

3. A bus topology must have which of the following at each end of the bus? (Choose all that apply.)

    a.   a router junction

    b.   a terminator

    c.   a capacitor

    d.   an amplification connector

4. What advice might a new network designer receive when just starting out? (Choose all that apply.)

    a.   Learn how networks work in terms of protocols, access methods, and topologies.

    b.   Avoid the risks of implementing fault tolerance.

    c.   Start with the safe mesh design in which information is continuously sent around the network ensuring that if a computer misses it the first time there are many other chances to obtain the same information without data loss.

    d.   Understand the physical equipment used in LANs and WANs.

5. Which of the following are reasons why you might have a network in your home of two adults and three teenagers? (Choose all that apply.)

    a.   accessing the Internet

    b.   sharing a printer

    c.   accessing entertainment resources, such as streaming movies

    d.   sharing files between computers

6. In your new building, the contractor is including secure wiring closets, cable, and cable pathways installed in the building as well as backbone cabling into a specialized server room. All of this cabling is part of the _____.

    a.   network data zone

    b.   cable plant

    c.   traffic zone

    d.   throughput byway

7. A large company has many computer resources including computers, servers, mainframes, network devices, computer development labs, computer databases, shared disk arrays, and so on. This is an example of which of the following?

    a.   an enterprise network

    b.   an extended client network

    c.   a radiating network

    d.   network concentration

8. Which of the following are disadvantages of the traditional bus topology? (Choose all that apply.)

    a.   It cannot be connected to the Internet.

    b.   It allows only for a maximum of 16 computers per bus.

    c.   It is subject to network congestion, requiring additional network devices to control traffic flow.

    d.   One defective node or cable segment can take down a network.

9. Assume you are a network consultant for a company that is designing a private WAN to communicate between five locations spread throughout a city. You want to tell the company

president that this WAN will use a design for maximum uptime to all locations. Which of the following designs should you use?

   a.   bus

   b.   star-ring hybrid

   c.   mesh

   d.   traditional ring

10. Assume you have been hired to design a network for a bank. When you determine the factors that affect the network design, you should look at which of the following? (Choose all that apply.)

   a.   software applications to be used

   b.   work patterns in the bank

   c.   the computers and operating systems to be connected to the network

   d.   the security required by the bank and bank regulators

11. Which network topology is no longer used much in modern LANs?

   a.   star

   b.   star-bus hybrid

   c.   ring

   d.   All of the above are commonly used in modern LANs.

12. Which of the following are examples of network nodes? (Choose all that apply.)

   a.   a computer attached to a network

   b.   a DVD/CD-ROM array attached to a server

   c.   a printer attached to a network computer

   d.   a network switch

13. When you design a network that has a bus or star-bus hybrid design, what organization's specifications should you check to make sure you follow the bus segment length requirements?

   a.   Microsoft

   b.   Red Hat

   c.   Institute of Electrical and Electronics Engineers

   d.   National Electrical Contractors Association

14. Your organization has a network that uses the star-bus hybrid topology. A new network associate is in the process of ordering spare network parts and has included 20 terminators in the order. Which of the following is your advice?

   a.   Increase the order, because terminators burn out quickly on busy star-bus networks.

   b.   Be certain to order terminators that contain LEDs to ensure communications can go only one way on the network.

   c.   Order 200 ohm terminators, because the network contains over 50 connections requiring a high overall resistance.

   d.   Omit the portion of the order for terminators, because terminators are built into the devices.

15. High-speed WANs that use the ring topology may use which of the following?

   a.   two loops for redundant data transmission

   b.   ring connectors that work like terminators

   c.   baseband optics

   d.   overflow NICs to regulate the speed of transmission

16. You are researching the possible benefits of a LAN for an advertising firm. Which of the following are benefits that you might include in your report to the firm's partners? (Choose all that apply.)

    a. A LAN would enable the firm to use a DVD/CD-ROM array for sharing commonly accessed DVDs and CDs.

    b. A LAN would eliminate the need for laptop computers (plus laptop computers are not compatible with LAN communications).

    c. Printer expenditures could be reduced.

    d. Centralized backups of client files would be possible.

17. Your company in New York City wants to open a branch office in Richmond, Virginia, and connect the branch office through the Internet. What type of network should be considered for enhanced security?

    a. a closed transmission network

    b. a VPN

    c. a top-down security network

    d. a star-secure network

    e. none of the above

18. Which of the following devices might be used to connect computers in a star topology? (Choose all that apply.)

    a. conjunction box

    b. switch

    c. terminator

    d. router

19. You are setting up a network for your small business of four employees, each of whom has a computer and needs to periodically share files with other employees. Instead of having a server, the files are shared through each computer's operating system. This is an example of a(n) _____ network.

    a. equality

    b. peer-to-peer

    c. jelly-based

    d. open

20. Internet Connection Sharing (ICS) in Windows 7 and Windows Server 2008 R2 can be configured through which of the following?

    a. Network Control icon in the taskbar

    b. Network and Sharing Center

    c. Wide Network Configuration option from the Start button

    d. Office Features menu

Case Projects

You are employed as a network consultant at Network Design Consultants. Your company consists of 15 consultants who assist all types of organizations with issues involving network planning, design, installation, and troubleshooting. The company works on national and international projects, depending on the currently active pool of clients.

Your present assignment is to help a small advertising firm, Harrison and Associates, to consider its options for designing a network. There are eight people in the firm: seven advertising consultants and one office coordinator. Each person has a computer at her or his desk, and every computer has a printer. Harrison and Associates represents a classic small-office situation.

Case Project 1-1: A Preliminary Design Step

As a first step in the design process, what information would you gather about Harrison and Associates?

Case Project 1-2: Creating a Report About Network Topologies

To help prepare the way for the design you plan to suggest, discuss with the firm's management the concept of network topology and the different types of topologies available. Consider making a slide presentation to illustrate what you cover in the discussion.

Case Project 1-3: Recommending a Topology for the Network Design

Prepare a report describing the topology you recommend for Harrison and Associates' network, and include why you recommend it.

Case Project 1-4: Recommending Devices for Network Connectivity

Add to your report in Case Project 1-3 a discussion of the network device or devices you would use for the topology you recommend.

Case Project 1-5: Networking Advantages for the Firm

Finally, add to your report a section that discusses the advantages your proposed network offers to Harrison and Associates.

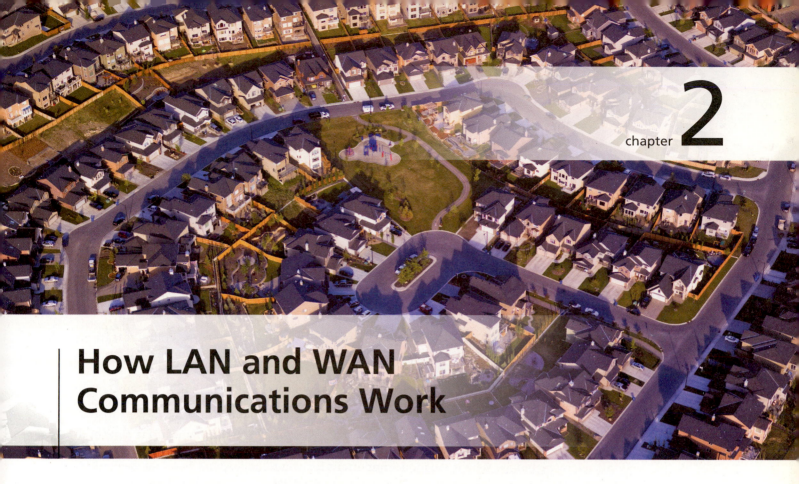

chapter 2

How LAN and WAN Communications Work

If you are interested in learning what makes networks tick, how to make your network work faster, and how to be a better network administrator, start by learning the OSI model. You might think of it as similar to conditioning before starting a race: you'll be better prepared to do your best.

After reading this chapter and completing the exercises, you will be able to:

- Explain the OSI reference model, which sets standards for LAN and WAN communications

- Discuss communication between OSI stacks when two computers are linked through a network

- Apply the OSI model to realistic networking situations

- Describe major LAN transmission methods

- Explain the basic WAN network communications topologies and transmission methods, including telecommunications, cable TV, satellite, and wireless technologies

- Explain the advantages of using Ethernet in network designs

When you connect to a network, how are you able to communicate with all of the other people who are on the same network? When you connect to a WAN from your home or business to send an e-mail, what goes on behind the scenes to enable you to send your transmission across town or to another state? Also, with all of the many LANs and WANs, what enables them to communicate? You learn the answers to these questions in this chapter.

This chapter introduces you to LAN and WAN interconnectivity through the Open Systems Interconnection (OSI) reference model. Without this model, which provides LAN and WAN communication guidelines developed more than 25 years ago, network communications might well be in chaos today. In this chapter, you also learn the key LAN transmission methods that enable users to communicate in an orderly way. Finally, you learn about WAN topologies and transmission methods.

The OSI Reference Model

Networks work because there are standards. Without standards, network communications would be a chaotic accumulation of proprietary devices and protocols established by multiple vendors using different design models. This is how it was in the early computer world—there were no universal standards for devices. For example, a printer from one computer, such as an IBM Displaywriter (an early word processor), could not be used on an early IBM personal computer without physically rewiring the interfaces—the communication port designs were different.

Fortunately, from the early days of networking, LAN and WAN communications have been generally guided by a network communications model called the **Open Systems Interconnection (OSI) reference model**. Why is the model important for you to understand from the beginning? Because if you work with or design networks, then understanding the model enables you to:

- Choose the best equipment for the job at hand
- Create the most effective network designs
- Design networks that will communicate with other networks
- Troubleshoot network problems more effectively

The OSI model is the product of several international standards organizations including the **International Organization for Standardization (ISO)**, the Institute of Electrical and Electronics Engineers (IEEE, see Chapter 1, "Networking: An Overview"), the **American National Standards Institute (ANSI)**, and the **International Telecommunication Union (ITU)**. The ISO is an international nongovernmental organization that establishes communications and networking standards and that is particularly known for its contributions to network protocol standards. ANSI works with U.S. businesses, government agencies, and international groups to achieve agreement on standards for products ranging from bicycle helmets to network equipment. The ITU is a United Nations agency that develops international communications standards; allocates international radio spectrums; and sets standards for modems, e-mail, mobile wireless communications, and digital telephone systems.

To learn more about the ISO, ANSI, and ITU standards organizations, visit their Web sites at *www.iso.org*, *www.ansi.org*, and *www.itu.int*.

Developed in the 1970s, the OSI model applies to LAN and WAN communications and represents an effort to standardize network software and hardware implementation (try Activity 2-1 to learn the ISO's view about the need for standards). Over the years, the OSI model has facilitated the growth in network communications by accomplishing the following:

- Enabling communications between different types of LANs, MANs, CANs, and WANs
- Providing standardization of network equipment so that equipment from one vendor communicates with equipment from another vendor

- Helping customers to retain their investment by enabling older network equipment to communicate with newer equipment, reducing the need for equipment replacement when new devices are installed

- Enabling software and hardware to be developed using common interfaces for communicating within and between networks

- Making possible worldwide network communications, with the Internet as a prime example

Activity 2-1: Learning About the Need for Standards

Time Required: 15 minutes
Objective: Understand why network standards are important.

Description: Standards, such as the OSI model, make universal network communications possible. In this activity, you learn more about the ISO's philosophy concerning why standards are important. You need access to the Internet and to an Internet browser for the activity.

1. Open the Internet browser on your computer, such as Microsoft Internet Explorer, Firefox in Linux, or Safari in Mac OS X.

2. Point the browser to the ISO's home page located at **www.iso.org**.

3. Click the **About ISO** link or tab. Read the information about the ISO and then click **Continue**.

4. Read the Discover ISO section and then click **Why standards matter**.

5. What are the benefits of standardization, as described by the ISO?

6. Click **Who standards benefit**. Record four examples of who benefits from standards.

7. Close your Internet browser when you are finished reading.

Sometimes Internet Web sites and the links on those Web sites change. If you have trouble finding a Web site that is suggested in this book, use a search engine to find a site that may have changed its location. Also, if the Web site's links are changed, search the Web site for the location of the new links or relocated information.

The OSI model predates most of today's network devices, but it has set the stage for cooperative networking and is constantly evolving to accommodate new networking developments. The OSI reference model is not rigorously followed, because new research and technologies sometimes lead in other directions, but it has set a foundation upon which to build (in the following chapters, you learn the extent to which specific protocols and networking devices adhere to the model). It should be emphasized that the OSI model is strictly a theoretical model and not a specific hardware device or a set of software routines. Rather, it is a set of guidelines for vendors to consider and follow when they design communications hardware and software. The guidelines are to protocol and network device development as grammar is to the spoken language. The OSI guidelines specify the following:

- How network devices contact each other, and how devices using different protocols communicate

- How a network device knows when to transmit or not transmit data

- How the physical network devices are arranged and connected

- Methods to ensure that network transmissions are received correctly

- How network devices maintain a consistent rate of data flow

- How electronic data is represented on the network media

The OSI model consists of seven distinct layers stacked on one another: Physical, Data Link, Network, Transport, Session, Presentation, and Application, as shown in Figure 2-1. Each layer handles specific communication tasks and uses specific types of protocols to communicate with the next layer in the stack. Communications between two network devices go up and down the layered stack at each device. For example, when a workstation communicates with a server, communication starts at the workstation's Application layer. It then formats specific information through the lower layers until the data reaches the Physical layer and is transmitted over the network to the server. The server picks up the data at the Physical layer of its stack and sends it up each layer for interpretation until it reaches the Application layer. Each layer is called by its actual name or by its placement in the stack. For example, the bottom layer is called either the Physical layer or Layer 1. (Table 2-1 later in this chapter summarizes features of the OSI layers.)

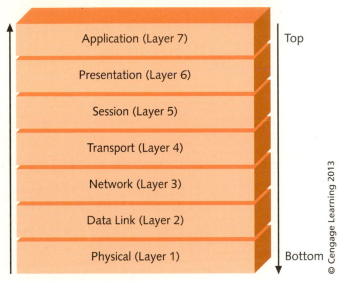

Figure 2-1   The OSI layers

The bottom layers perform functions, such as constructing frames and transmitting packet-containing signals, related to physical communications. The middle layers coordinate network communications between nodes, ensuring that a communication session continues without interruptions or errors, for example. The top layers perform work that directly affects software applications and data presentation, including data formatting, encryption, and data and file transfer management. Taken together, the set of layers is called a stack. In the following sections, you find a detailed description of each of the seven layers.

 Throughout this book you will see references to nodes or stations. These terms are used interchangeably to refer to devices connected to a network, such as computers, printers, and network equipment.

Physical Layer

The lowest layer of the OSI model is the Physical layer (Layer 1), which encompasses the following:

- All data transfer mediums (wire cable, fiber optics, radio waves, and microwaves)
- Network connectors
- The network topology
- Signaling and encoding methods
- Data transmission devices
- Network interfaces
- Detection of signaling errors

The devices used within the Physical layer are responsible for generating, carrying, and detecting voltage in order to transmit and receive signals containing data. Network signals are analog or digital. An **analog** signal can vary continuously, as in a wave pattern with positive and negative voltage levels. An ordinary radio or telephone signal is an example of an analog transmission because it can have an infinite range for sound reproduction. An analog TV or computer monitor can similarly reproduce millions of colors in every range. Analog transmissions are used in WANs that employ analog modems for communications, such as the dial-up modem still in use by some to access the Internet through an Internet service provider (ISP) over a telephone line. Figure 2-2 represents an analog signal.

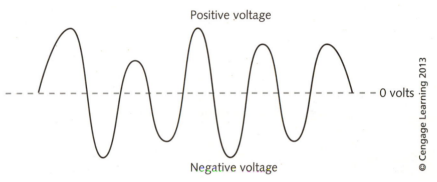

Figure 2-2   An analog signal

A **digital signal (DS)** uses distinct voltage levels to generate binary ones or zeroes and is the most common signaling method used on LANs and high-speed WANs. For example, the presence of voltage, such as +5 volts, can produce a one, and 0 volts can produce a zero (see Figure 2-3). Another way to digitally generate ones and zeros is by using a positive voltage, such as +5 volts, to signify a one and a negative voltage, such as –5 volts, to signify a zero. In fiber-optic transmissions, the presence or absence of light is used to create binary ones and zeroes, as shown in Figure 2-3.

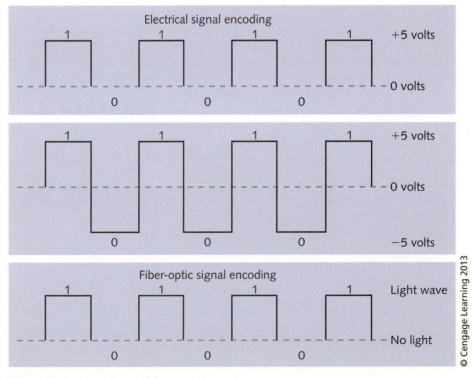

Figure 2-3   Examples of digital signals

Real-Life Networking

To supplement your understanding of the Physical layer, it helps to understand some basic electronics—such as ensuring that your network devices and computers are connected to a true ground (grounded to the Earth) when you plug them into power. This is important for any home, office, or large organization network. At one university, there was a network in a student lab connected to two different main sources of power (on opposite sides of the room), each having a different source of grounding. Because neither was on a true ground, 0 volts on each network was not truly 0 volts, and the base value for 0 volts was different on each network. When a 250-pound network analyst, who was working on the cables from both networks, picked up both cables at the same time, he was thrown to the ground because his body conducted the differences in volts between the wires.

When you encode a signal, you convert it to binary (numeric base 2) format so that it has a particular meaning or value to a computer or network device.

The Physical layer converts bits from the Data Link layer into voltage for transmission. The Physical layer handles the data transmission rate, monitors data error rates, and handles voltage levels for signal transmissions. It is affected by physical network problems, such as a broken communications cable or electrical or magnetic interference. Interference can be caused by nearby electrical motors, high-voltage lines, lighting, and other electrical devices.

Electromagnetic interference (EMI) and **radio frequency interference (RFI)** are two sources of Physical layer interference. EMI is caused by magnetic force fields that are generated by electrical devices such as fans, elevator motors, portable heaters, and air-conditioning units. RFI is caused by electrical devices that emit radio waves at the same frequency used by network signal transmissions. These transmissions include cable TV components, radio and television stations, nearby amateur radio operators, ballast devices in fluorescent lights, inexpensively built computer or TV equipment, and CB radios. Try Activity 2-2 to experiment with the impact of network interference.

Activity 2-2: Testing the Impact of EMI and RFI

Time Required: 20 minutes
Objective: Experience the effects of EMI and RFI in network communications.

Description: This activity examines the impact of EMI and RFI on a network. You need access to a test lab network that has a section of exposed coaxial (legacy cable) or unshielded, twisted-pair cable and an electric drill or a fluorescent light with a ballast.

1. Log onto a workstation on the network and connect to a server or host computer (or if the lab is equipped with Windows 7, access the shared drive of another computer).

2. Turn on the drill or fluorescent light and place it as close as possible to a section of cable that connects to the workstation you are accessing.

3. Download a file from the server, host, or shared drive.

4. Look for problems with the network connection or in downloading the file (if you do not observe problems at your workstation, check other lab workstations for problems).

5. Make sure you log off the workstation and remove the drill or fluorescent light when you are finished.

Another option for this activity is to experiment with a wireless network that operates at 2.4 or 5 GHz. Establish a wireless connection between two computers through an access point (which joins clients on a wireless network) or direct peer-to-peer connection without an access point intermediary. Next, obtain a transmitter (such as a cordless telephone/wireless camera/wireless speaker or old microwave oven or through an amateur radio operator) that can operate at 2.4 or 5 GHz and begin transmitting to see how communications are affected between the computers. Or, to simply read about wireless communications interference, see the National Institute of Standards and Technology publication: *Interference in the 2.4 GHz ISM Band: Challenges and Solutions* by N. Golmie at the Web location: *www.antd.nist.gov/pubs/golmie.pdf*. Also see the publication by Cisco called *20 Myths of Wi-Fi Interference* at *www.cisco.com/en/US/prod/collateral/wireless/ps9391/ps9393/ps9394/prod_white_paper0900aecd807395a9_ns736_Networking_Solutions_White_Paper.html*. You learn more about wireless communications in Chapter 6, "Connecting through a Wireless Network."

Data Link Layer

The task of the Data Link layer (Layer 2) in a LAN is to organize bits so that they are formatted into frames. A **frame** is a discrete unit of data transmitted on a network that contains control and address information corresponding to the OSI Data Link layer, but not routing information (see the next section). Each frame is formatted in a specified way so that data transmissions are synchronized for reliable transmission from node to node. This layer formats the data to be encoded as a frame into an electrical signal, and once it is formatted, the frame is transferred to the Physical layer so that it can be placed onto the communications medium (such as a radio wave or cable) by the transmitting node. The receiving node then picks up the frame via the Physical layer, decodes the electrical signal or radio wave containing bits, organizes the bits into a frame, and checks the frame for errors.

The Data Link layer formats bits into a "data link frame" that contains fields consisting of address and control information, as follows:

- Beginning or start of frame (SOF)
- Address of the device or transmitting node that sent the frame (source address)
- Address of the device or receiving node that picks up the frame after it is transmitted (destination address)
- Administration or communications control information
- Data
- Error-checking information
- Trailer or end of frame (EOF) designator

The communication between two nodes is first established by transmission of a small set of signals used for timing the data stream. After communication is established between the two nodes, their Physical layers are connected via the communications medium (such as radio wave or cable), and their Data Link layers are connected logically through protocols. As soon as the logical link is made, the receiving Data Link layer decodes the signal into individual frames.

The Data Link layer checks incoming signals for duplicate, incorrect, or partially received data. If an error is detected, it requests a retransmission of the data, frame by frame, from the sending node. The Data Link layer handles error detection by using a cyclic redundancy check. A **cyclic redundancy check (CRC)** is an error-detection method that calculates a value for the total size of the information fields (SOF, addressing, control information, data, CRC, and EOF) contained in a frame. The value is inserted near the end of the frame by the Data Link layer on the sending node and checked at the Data Link layer on the receiving node. As the Data Link layer transfers frames up to the next layer, it ensures that frames are sent in the same order as received.

The Data Link layer contains two important sublayers: **logical link control (LLC)** and **media access control (MAC)**. The LLC sublayer is responsible for flow control, error control, synchronizing frames, and generally managing network traffic. LLC also helps to make it possible for multiple protocols to exist on the same network. The MAC sublayer examines the **physical address** or **device address**—sometimes called the **MAC address**—information contained in each frame. For example, the MAC sublayer on a workstation examines each frame received by the workstation and sends the frame to the next higher layer, if the address matches. The frame is discarded if the address is not a match. The MAC sublayer also regulates how multiple devices share communications on the same network.

Network devices have a unique address permanently burned into a chip on the network interfaces of the devices. This address is variously called a device, physical, or MAC address and is coded as a hexadecimal number, such as 0004AC8428DE. (This address could also be represented as 00-04-AC-84-28-DE or as 00:04:AC:84:28:DE in some formats.) The first half of the address is assigned to a specific network vendor, making it possible to tell who manufactured the network device or its interface, and the second half, typically supplied by the vendor, is unique to the interface or the device. Some vendors use a code within the second half to identify the type of device, such as a computer, switch, router, or gateway (you learn about these devices in Chapter 5, "Devices for Connecting Networks"). Also, some devices, such as a server that has two network cards, have multiple interfaces and therefore multiple physical connections to a network. Each network interface in the device still has a unique address, and the device is identified to the network by multiple unique addresses (each address on each network interface).

It is critical that no two network devices or interfaces have the same physical address. Network device manufacturers ensure unique physical addresses by keeping a record of the addresses they use, so that they do not reuse the same address. If two or more devices or interfaces were to have the same address, there would be confusion on the network about how to deliver frames.

When you work on a network, the physical address is a useful troubleshooting aid. For example, you can use it to track excessive activity of a malfunctioning network interface in a computer or device so that you can replace the interface and make the network operate more efficiently. As an alternative, you can track the activities of a network intruder and locate that intruder before there is a serious security problem. In Activity 2-3 you learn how to determine a workstation's physical address.

In some Windows 7 or Server 2008/Server 2008 R2 projects, you may see the User Account Control (UAC) box, which is used for security to help thwart intruders. The UAC box asks for permission to continue with an action or asks for the administrator password. If you see this box, click **Continue**. Because computer setups may be different, the box is not mentioned in the actual project steps.

Activity 2-3: Viewing a NIC's Physical Address

Time Required: 5–10 minutes
Objective: Determine the physical address of the network interface card (NIC) or wireless NIC (WNIC) in a computer.

Description: This activity provides an opportunity to determine the physical address of a NIC or WNIC in a computer. You need access to a computer that is connected to a network and that runs Windows 7, Windows Server 2008/Server 2008 R2, Linux, or Mac OS X Snow Leopard or

Lion. For Linux, you need to use the root account. For Snow Leopard and Lion, you need an account that has Administrator privileges.

To view the network interface's physical address in Windows 7 or Windows Server 2008/Server 2008 R2:

1. Log onto an account.

2. Click the **Start** button and type **cmd** in the Search programs and file box (in Windows 7 and Server 2008 R2) or the Start Search box (in Windows Server 2008). These boxes are below All Programs on the Start menu. Next, click **cmd** in the list of search items.

3. In the Command Prompt window, type **ipconfig /all** at the command line and press **Enter**. Scroll through the window as necessary and look for the physical address of the NIC, such as 0C-60-76-6F-9C-97 (as shown in Figure 2-4 for a wireless NIC in a Windows 7 computer). If there are both wireless and cabled NICs in the computer, look for the physical addresses of each WNIC and NIC.

4. Close the Command Prompt window.

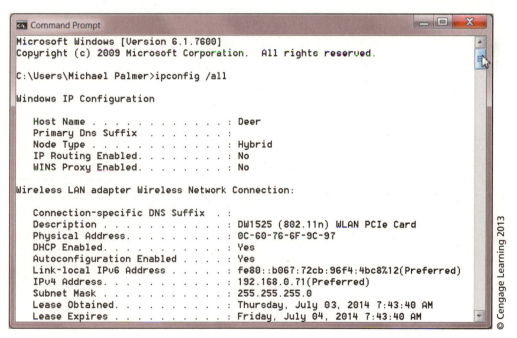

Figure 2-4   *ipconfig* information for Windows 7

To view the network interface's physical address in Linux:

1. Open a terminal window to access the command line. In the GNOME 3.x desktop, click **Activities** in the left side of the top Panel at the top of the desktop. Click **Applications** on the desktop to view icons of applications that can be opened. Click the **Terminal** icon to open a terminal window.

2. Type **su root** and press **Enter**. (When you use Fedora 15 Live Media or higher, you do not need to enter a root password. For other Linux distributions, enter the root password at this point.)

3. Type **ifconfig** *<name of the device>*, as in **ifconfig wlan0** (for a WNIC) or **ifconfig em1** or **ifconfig eth0** (for a cabled NIC), and press **Enter** (see Figure 2-5).

4. What physical address (such as 00:19:D2:4A:07:0B) is displayed in the HWaddr field?

5. If you are using a terminal window, type **exit** and press **Enter** to close the window.

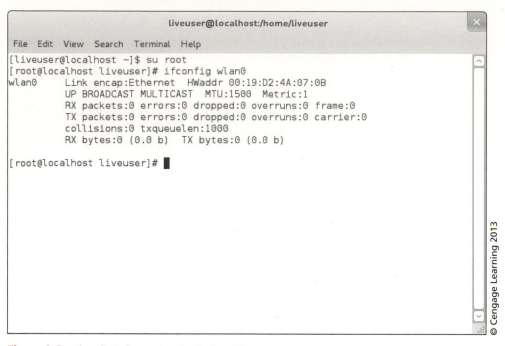

Figure 2-5   *ifconfig* information for Fedora Linux

To view the network interface's physical address in Snow Leopard or Lion:

1. Click the **System Preferences** icon in the Dock, or click the **Apple** icon in the menu bar and click **System Preferences**.

2. In the System Preferences window, click **Network** under Internet & Wireless.

3. In the left pane of the Network window, if necessary click an active network connection (designated by the green dot), such as **AirPort**, **Wi-Fi**, or **Ethernet**.

4. Click the **Advanced** button.

5. Make sure the **Airport**, **Wi-Fi**, or **Ethernet** tab (or other appropriate tab for your connection) is selected.

6. At the bottom of the Network window, notice the Airport, Wi-Fi, or Ethernet ID, which is the physical address of the WNIC or NIC, such as f0:b4:79:1f:01:4d (see Figure 2-6).

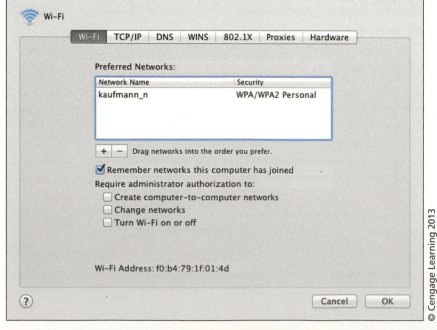

Figure 2-6   Viewing the physical address in Mac OS X Lion

7. Click **Cancel**.

8. Click **System Preferences** in the menu bar at the top of the desktop and click **Quit System Preferences**.

Two types of services are used for communications between the LLC sublayer and the Network layer, which is the next layer up the stack. The Type 1 operation is a **connectionless service**, which does not establish a logical connection between the sending and receiving nodes. In a connectionless service, frames are not checked to ensure that they are received in the same sequence they were sent, there is no acknowledgment that a frame has been received, and there is no error recovery.

The Type 2 operation is a **connection-oriented service** in which a logical connection is established between sending and receiving nodes before full communications begin. Each frame contains a sequence number that is checked by the receiving node to ensure the frames are processed in the same order they are sent. Communications are established such that the sending node does not transmit data faster than the receiving node can handle it. The receiving node provides an acknowledgment to the sending node after the data has been successfully transmitted. If errors are detected, the data is retransmitted.

Network Layer

The third layer up the stack is the Network layer (Layer 3). This layer controls the passage of packets along routes on the network. A **packet** is a discrete unit of data that is formatted as a signal for transmission over a network. In a network transmission, each packet is composed of data bits in fields of information containing transmission control instructions, source and destination information, data, and error-checking information. Packets correspond to the network information sent at the Network layer of the OSI model, which enables the directing of the route (routing) that a packet follows to its destination.

There is some disagreement among networking professionals about strict definitions of the terms "packet" and "frame." Some professionals do not differentiate between the two terms. However, many professionals agree that a frame represents information used in conjunction with Layer 2 of the OSI model and that a packet represents information used in conjunction with Layer 3 of the OSI model.

All networks consist of physical routes (cable and wireless paths) and logical routes (software paths). The Network layer reads packet protocol address information and forwards each packet along the most expedient route, physical and logical, for efficient transmission. This layer also permits packets to be sent from one network to another, through routers (routers are discussed in Chapter 5, "Devices for Connecting Networks").

By controlling the passage of packets, the Network layer acts like a traffic director, routing packets along the most efficient of several different paths. To determine the best path, the Network layer constantly gathers information (metrics) about the location of different networks and nodes, a process called **discovery**.

Not all protocols include information that can be used by the Network layer, which means that these protocols cannot be routed. Two examples of network protocols that cannot be routed are older legacy protocols such as Digital Equipment Corporation's (DEC; now part of HP/Compaq) LAT and Microsoft's NetBEUI. These protocols typically are no longer supported in modern Windows and Linux operating systems or by networks that require routing.

Some destination addresses are assigned to a group. A packet with a group destination address is routed to and acted on by more than one computer or network device.

Real-Life Networking

Knowledge of how the Network layer works arms you with knowledge about how to design and troubleshoot a network to achieve high levels of efficiency. For instance, consider one organization that did not pay attention to a series of routers that were using a router information protocol that was flooding (sending to all nodes but the originator) every area of this large network and causing network slowdowns. When the slowdowns became too unbearable, the organization finally reconfigured the routers to use a more efficient router information protocol. This solution was effective and inexpensive.

The Network layer can route data on different paths by creating virtual (logical) circuits. **Virtual circuits** are logical communication paths set up to send and receive data. The virtual circuits are known only to the Network layer between mutually communicating nodes within that network. Because the Network layer manages data along several virtual circuits, the data can arrive in the wrong sequence. To counteract this possibility, the Network layer checks and, if necessary, corrects the sequence before transporting packets to the next layer. It also addresses frames and resizes them to match the requirements of the receiving network protocol. Then, it ensures that frames are not sent faster than the receiving layer can receive them.

Transport Layer

Like the Data Link and Network layers, the Transport layer (Layer 4) performs functions that ensure that data is sent reliably from the sending node to the destination node. For example, the Transport layer ensures that the data is sent and received in the same order. Also, when a transmission is made, the receiving node may send an acknowledgement, sometimes called an "ack."

When virtual circuits are employed on a network, the Transport layer is responsible for tracking the unique identification value assigned to each circuit. This value is called a **port**, a connection identification, or a **socket**; it is assigned by the Session layer. The Transport layer also establishes the level of packet error checking, with the highest level guaranteeing that packets are sent node to node, without error, and within an acceptable amount of time.

Ports and sockets are very important to understand in relation to computer security and computer forensics, because attackers and malware use these to gain entry into a computer. Good security practice entails closing all unused ports and sockets to thwart attacks. For more information about closing ports, see Chapter 3, "Using Network Communication Protocols" and Chapter 11, "Securing Your Network."

The protocols used to communicate within the Transport layer use several reliability measures. Class 0 is the simplest protocol. It performs no error checking or flow control and relies on the Network layer to perform these functions. Class 1 protocol monitors for packet transmission errors, and if an error is detected, it notifies the sending node's Transport layer to resend the packet. Class 2 protocol monitors for transmission errors and provides flow control between the Transport layer and the Session layer. **Flow control** ensures that one device does not send information faster than can be received by the network or by the receiving device. Class 3 protocol provides the functions of Classes 1 and 2 along with the option to recover lost packets in certain situations. Finally, Class 4 protocol performs the same functions as Class 3, along with more extensive error monitoring and recovery.

Another function of the Transport layer is to break or fragment messages into smaller units when networks use different protocols requiring different packet sizes. Data units that are fragmented into smaller units by the Transport layer on the sending network are reassembled in the right order by the Transport layer at the receiving end for interpretation by the Network layer.

The Transport layer enables you to receive every packet or frame without losing some along the way. Cell phone users know what it is like to miss portions of a conversation because of interference or static. Similarly, you would miss portions of data on a network when the data was sent too fast or too slow. The Transport layer's job is to adjust for these situations so that you don't lose information. Another advantage of the Transport layer is that it can adjust the "window" in which data is sent between acknowledgements, so that more data can be sent in a given time. For example, if your computer is sending one packet and then waiting extra time to receive an ack from the recipient, the Transport layer can adjust the window to send four packets between acks instead of just one packet—making transmission four times faster.

Session Layer

The Session layer (Layer 5) is responsible for establishing and maintaining the communications link between two nodes. It also provides for orderly communication between nodes; for example, it establishes which node transmits first. The Session layer also determines how long a node can transmit and how to recover from transmission errors. If a transmission session is inadvertently broken at a lower layer, the Session layer attempts to reestablish communication.

In some workstation operating systems, you can disconnect the workstation from the network, reconnect it, and continue working without logging on again. You can do this because the Session layer works to reconnect the workstation even after the Physical layer is temporarily disconnected and reconnected.

This layer also links each unique address to a given node, the same way ZIP codes allow mail to be associated with a particular postal region. After the communication session is finished, this layer disconnects nodes.

One example of communications at this layer is when you use a workstation to access a server on the Internet. The workstation and the server each have a unique Internet Protocol version 4 (IPv4), IP version 6 (IPv6), or both addresses. Examples of IPv4 addresses are 122.72.15.122 and 145.19.20.22, which are also called dotted decimal addresses. Here are some examples of IPv6 addresses:

```
1042:0071:28bc00:0001:07ac:0522:210c:425b
0082:05ad:41f8:000a:0010:004d:1800:36bd
```

(IPv6 addresses are in a longer format than IPv4 addresses.) See Chapter 3, "Using Network Communication Protocols," for more in-depth information about IPv4, IPv6, and using IP addressing. The Session layer uses this address information to help establish contact between nodes. After contact is made and the workstation is able to log on, a communication session is established via the Session layer.

The Session layer offers a way to set up communications on a network so that you can increase efficiency twofold. For example, Session layer devices may be set up to send and receive, but not at the same time. At the Session layer, this is called two-way alternate (TWA) mode for dialog control. However, through the Session layer, devices may also be configured to send and receive at the same time, which doubles the speed of communications in a session dialog between two nodes. This is known as two-way simultaneous (TWS) mode.

Real-Life Networking

A network administrator installed an older computer to connect to a newer network switch on a cabled network. When he started the computer, it would not properly communicate on the network. After several delays of checking the wiring, the switch, and the network cable, he discovered the computer's NIC was set for half duplex and the switch connection was set for full duplex. He changed the setting on the NIC to full duplex to solve the problem. Note that many NICs have an automatic negotiation setting so that the NIC can automatically determine the duplex mode. This setting is configured in the driver properties of the NIC and is often set as the default. If a NIC is not communicating on a network, a good troubleshooting tip is to check the properties set for the NIC, such as the duplex setting.

TWA and TWS can be used to enable faster communications between devices on a network. TWA is used in **half-duplex** communications, which means that network interfaces, such as a NIC, can be set up to send and receive on the same medium (such as a cable), but not simultaneously. This means the NIC operates on only one virtual circuit or channel on the medium. At one point in time it may be sending on that channel, and at another point in time it may be receiving. You might think of this as similar to using a walky-talky in which you press a button to talk and then take your finger off the button when you want to listen to the other person.

TWS enables **full-duplex** communications in which the network interface can send and receive at the same time, because there are two channels created over the same medium, one for receiving and one for sending. Beside the TWS capability, full duplex is possible because of buffering at the network interface. Buffering means that the NIC is equipped with memory to temporarily store information that it is not currently processing.

Understanding half- and full-duplex communications is important to you because both represent ways in which networks operate faster and more efficiently. The alternative to these communications is **simplex**, which means that a signal can travel in only one direction on a medium. When you purchase network devices and NICs, ensure that they support both half- and full-duplex communications. Full duplex is most preferred because it enables faster communications than half duplex.

Presentation Layer

This layer manages data formatting, because software applications often use different data-formatting schemes. In a sense, the Presentation layer (Layer 6) is like a syntax checker. It ensures that numbers and text are sent in a form that can be read by the Presentation layer at the receiving node. For example, data sent from an older IBM mainframe or midrange computer may use **Extended Binary Coded Decimal Interchange Code (EBCDIC)** character formatting, which must be translated into **American Standard Code for Information Interchange (ASCII)** character format to be read by a workstation running Windows 7, UNIX/Linux, or Mac OS X. EBCDIC is a character-coding technique used mainly on IBM mainframe computers and consisting of an 8-bit coding method for a 256-character set of letters, numbers, and special characters. ASCII is an 8-bit character coding method consisting of 96 uppercase and lowercase characters and numbers, plus 32 nonprinting characters. **Unicode** is another example of a coding standard that enables consistent coding of characters covering 93 scripts for most languages used throughout the world. Unicode is supported by vendors such as Apple, Microsoft, IBM, Oracle, HP, and many others. Unicode enables data to be translated between different systems and languages (computer and human languages) while retaining the original data integrity. Visit *unicode.org* to learn more about Unicode.

The Presentation layer is also responsible for data encryption. **Encryption** is a process that scrambles the data so that it cannot be read if intercepted by unauthorized users. For example, your computer account password may be encrypted on a LAN or your credit card number may be encrypted through the Secure Sockets Layer (SSL) technique on a WAN. Try Activities 2-4 and 2-5 for more information on Presentation layer security.

 Encryption techniques are key to the success of commerce on the Internet. Without these techniques, few people would be interested in making Internet purchases using credit cards. Clearly, the capabilities of the Presentation layer are very important, especially because awareness of network security has been critical for thwarting attackers.

Another function of the Presentation layer is data compression. When data is formatted, there may be empty space that gets formatted between text and numbers. Data compression removes this space and compacts data so it is much smaller to send. After the data is transmitted, it is decompressed by the Presentation layer at the receiving node.

Activity 2-4: Viewing SSL Setup in Windows

Time Required: 5–10 minutes
Objective: View the SSL configuration for Internet access in Windows 7 and Windows Server 2008/Server 2008 R2.

Description: In this activity, you view the SSL setup (Presentation layer security) for connecting to the Internet in Windows 7 or Windows Server 2008/Server 2008 R2.

1. Click **Start** and click **Control Panel**.

2. In Windows 7 and Windows Server 2008 R2, set **View by** to **Large icons** or **Small icons**. Or in Windows 2008, use the **Classic View**. Click **Network and Sharing Center**.

3. Click (in Windows 7 and Windows Server 2008 R2) or double-click (in Windows Server 2008) **Internet Options**.

4. In the Internet Properties dialog box, click the **Advanced** tab (see Figure 2-7).

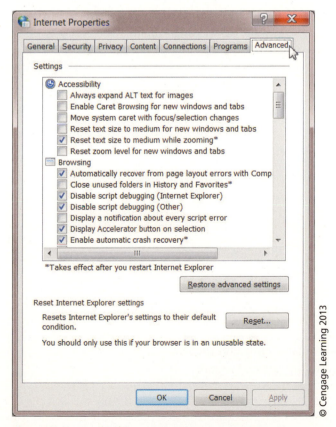

Figure 2-7   Clicking the Advanced tab in Windows 7

5. Scroll to the Security section and notice which, if any, of the SSL security options is checked.

6. Are any other security options checked? Why might these options be checked?

7. Click **Cancel** in the Internet Properties dialog box.

8. Close Control Panel.

Activity 2-5: Viewing SSL Setup in UNIX/Linux

Time Required: 5–10 minutes
Objective: Determine the SSL configuration in the Firefox Web browser in UNIX/Linux.

Description: For this activity you view the SSL setup in the Firefox Web browser that comes with many UNIX and Linux distributions.

1. In Fedora 15 or higher with the GNOME 3.x desktop, click **Activities** and click the **Firefox** icon. In other UNIX or Linux distributions, take the appropriate steps to start Firefox, such as clicking its icon on the desktop.

2. Click the **Edit** menu and then click **Preferences**.

3. Click **Advanced** in the option bar at the top of the Firefox Preferences window (see Figure 2-8).

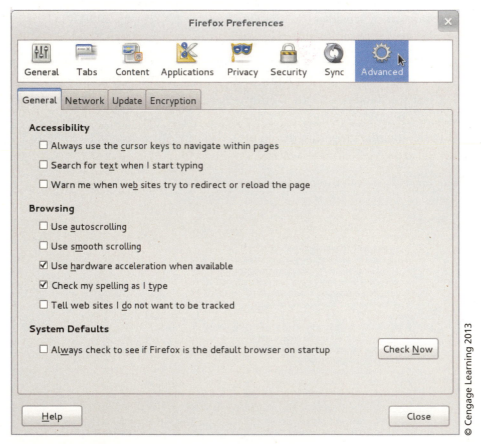

Figure 2-8   Clicking the Advanced option in Firefox Preferences

© Cengage Learning 2013

4. Click the **Encryption** tab.

5. What SSL version is available under Protocols?

6. Close the Preferences window.

7. Close Firefox.

Application Layer

The Application layer (Layer 7) is the highest level of the OSI model. This layer governs the computer user's most direct access to applications and network services. These services include file transfer, file management, remote access to files and printers, message handling for e-mail, and terminal emulation. This is the layer computer programmers use to connect workstations to network services, such as linking an application into electronic mail or database access over the network.

The Microsoft Windows **redirector** works through the Application layer. The redirector is a service that makes one computer visible to another for access through the network. When you share a folder on a Microsoft network, other computers can find your computer and access that folder using the redirector. Activity 2-6 enables you to view the redirector at work in Windows 7 or Windows Server 2008/Server 2008 R2. Also, Activities 2-7 and 2-8 illustrate how the Application layer works in UNIX/Linux and in Mac OS X.

Many of the applications computer users rely on are made possible by the Application layer. Whenever you use an Internet browser, such as Microsoft Internet Explorer or Firefox, or send e-mail, you are working through the Application layer.

Activity 2-6: Viewing Network Objects Using the Windows Redirector

Time Required: 5–10 minutes
Objective: Use the Microsoft Windows redirector.

Description: The Microsoft Windows redirector is one example of the Application layer (Layer 7) at work. In this activity, you view computers, shared folders, and shared printers through a Microsoft-based network, which are made accessible, in part, through the redirector. Your network needs to have at least one workgroup (or homegroup or domain) of computers, shared folders, and shared printers to fully view the work of the redirector. Ask your instructor about which computer or computers to view through the redirector and if you need an account and a password for that computer.

1. Click **Start** and click **Computer**.

2. Click **Network** in the left pane of the Computer window.

3. Notice the computers that are connected to the network.

4. Double-click a computer to see the shared folders or printers that it offers (you may need to enter an account and a password).

5. What objects are shared?

6. Click the **Back** arrow and double-click another computer (if one is available) to see the folders and printers that it offers over the network.

7. Close the Network window.

Activity 2-7: Using the *ping* Utility in UNIX/Linux

Time Required: 5 minutes
Objective: Use the Application layer via the *ping* utility in UNIX/Linux.

Description: Many UNIX/Linux systems automatically configure a "loopback" connection for testing network applications and connections. When you use this connection, you can communicate from your computer over the network and back to your computer. This is another example of using the capabilities of the OSI Application layer. In this activity, you use Linux from your own account. You use the *ping* utility to verify your own network connection. For this activity, log into the root account or stay in your personal account.

1. Open a terminal window to access the command line.

2. Type **ping -c 5 localhost** (or type **ping -c 5 127.0.0.1**, which is the address used for a loopback connection).

3. Notice that you see five transmissions from your computer over its loopback connection (see Figure 2-9). (If the *ping* failed, that means there is a problem with your connection to the network.)

4. Type **exit** and press **Enter** or simply close the terminal window.

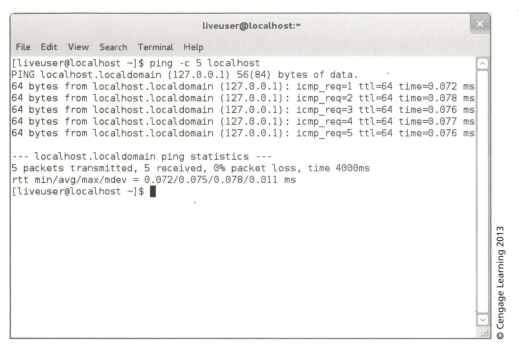

```
                          liveuser@localhost:~                              ×

File  Edit  View  Search  Terminal  Help

[liveuser@localhost ~]$ ping -c 5 localhost
PING localhost.localdomain (127.0.0.1) 56(84) bytes of data.
64 bytes from localhost.localdomain (127.0.0.1): icmp_req=1 ttl=64 time=0.072 ms
64 bytes from localhost.localdomain (127.0.0.1): icmp_req=2 ttl=64 time=0.078 ms
64 bytes from localhost.localdomain (127.0.0.1): icmp_req=3 ttl=64 time=0.076 ms
64 bytes from localhost.localdomain (127.0.0.1): icmp_req=4 ttl=64 time=0.077 ms
64 bytes from localhost.localdomain (127.0.0.1): icmp_req=5 ttl=64 time=0.076 ms

--- localhost.localdomain ping statistics ---
5 packets transmitted, 5 received, 0% packet loss, time 4000ms
rtt min/avg/max/mdev = 0.072/0.075/0.078/0.011 ms
[liveuser@localhost ~]$ 
```

© Cengage Learning 2013

Figure 2-9   Using *ping* in Fedora Linux

Activity 2-8: Using the *ping* Utility in Mac OS X

Time Required: 10 minutes
Objective: Use the Application layer via the *ping* utility in Mac OS X Snow Leopard or Lion.

Description: Mac OS X also uses the loopback connection for testing network applications and connections, and Mac OS X supports the use of *ping* for testing a network connection via the OSI Application layer. In this activity, you use the *ping* utility to verify your own network connection.

1. With Finder open (click an open area on the desktop or click the **Finder** icon in the Dock, if Finder is not open), click the **Go** menu.

2. Click **Utilities**.

3. Double-click **Network Utility**.

4. Click **Ping** in the bar of tab options under the title bar.

5. Enter **127.0.0.1** as the network address to ping.

6. Make sure that **Send only _____ pings** is set to **4**.

7. Click the **Ping** button. You should notice that the address you specified is returned with other information as shown in Figure 2-10. (If the *ping* failed, that means there is a problem with your connection to the network.)

8. Click **Network Utility** in the menu bar and click **Quit Network Utility**.

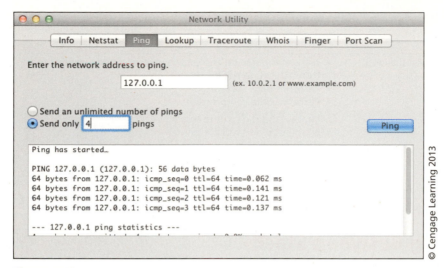

© Cengage Learning 2013

Figure 2-10 Using *ping* in Mac OS X Lion

Table 2-1 summarizes the functions of the seven OSI layers.

Table 2-1 Functions of the seven OSI layers

Layer	Functions
Physical (Layer 1)	• Provides the transfer medium (such as cable) • Translates data into a transmission signal appropriate to the transfer medium • Sends the signal along the transfer medium • Includes the physical layout of the network • Monitors for transmission errors • Determines the voltage levels used for data signal transmissions and used to synchronize transmissions • Determines the signal type, such as digital or analog
Data Link (Layer 2)	• Constructs data frames using the appropriate format for the network • Creates CRC information • Checks for errors using CRC information • Retransmits data if there is an error • Initiates the communications link and makes sure it is not interrupted, thus ensuring node-to-node physical reliability • Examines device addresses • Acknowledges receipt of a frame
Network (Layer 3)	• Determines the network path on which to route packets • Helps reduce network congestion • Establishes virtual circuits • Routes packets to other networks, resequencing packet transmissions when needed • Translates between protocols
Transport (Layer 4)	• Ensures reliability of packet transmissions from node to node • Ensures that data is sent and received in the same order • Provides acknowledgement when a packet is received • Monitors for packet transmission errors and resends bad packets • Breaks large data units into smaller ones and reconstructs them at the receiving end for networks using different protocols
Session (Layer 5)	• Initiates the communications link • Makes sure the communications link is maintained • Determines which node transmits at any point in time, such as which one transmits first • Disconnects when a communication session is over • Translates node addresses

(*continues*)

Table 2-1   Functions of the seven OSI layers (*continued*)

Layer	Functions
Presentation (Layer 6)	• Translates data to a format the receiving node understands, such as from EBCDIC to ASCII • Performs data encryption • Performs data compression
Application (Layer 7)	• Enables sharing remote drives • Enables sharing remote printers • Handles e-mail messages • Provides file transfer services • Provides file management services • Provides terminal emulation services

© Cengage Learning 2013

Communicating Between Stacks

For two computers to communicate within a LAN or across a WAN, they must both be operating under the same communication model, such as the OSI model. The OSI model provides standards for communicating on a LAN, for communicating between LANs, and for internetworking between LANs and WANs and between WANs and WANs.

When information is constructed at the sending node, it starts at the top of the stack with the Application layer. The information is sent next to the Presentation layer and continues down the stack to the Physical layer, where it is sent out to the network as a complete data-carrying signal (see Figure 2-11). You might liken the process to layers in an onion or a message that is sealed in one envelope which is sealed in another, and so on. Each layer contains specific information that

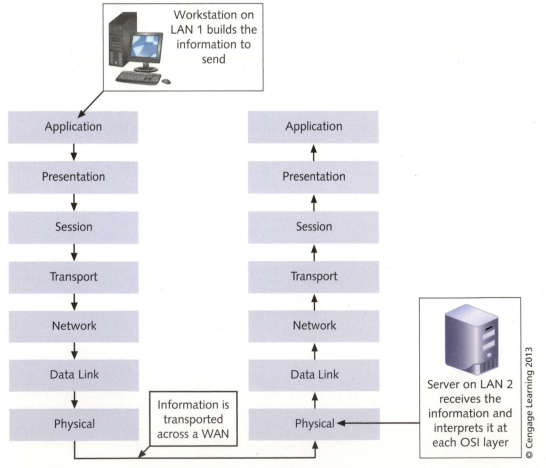

Figure 2-11   Sending information through the OSI reference model

is used between two communicating devices. When the frame or packet is received, the receiving node unwraps each layer, like you might pull off individual layers in an onion. Just as one layer is encapsulated by another in an onion, the same is true in OSI-based communications. In this context, the term **encapsulate** refers to wrapping the information in one layer inside the information within the next layer.

The receiving node receives the information at the Physical layer (at the bottom of the stack) and then sends each discrete information package to be checked as a frame by the Data Link layer, which determines if that frame is addressed to its network interface. The Data Link layer is similar to a postal carrier who checks through all mails to see if any is addressed to your house. Letters with your address are left at the house to be passed along to the right person within the household. Other letters are sent on until their destination is found.

When the Data Link layer finds a frame addressed to that workstation, it sends the frame to the Network layer, which strips out information intended for it and then sends the remaining information up the stack. However, before the frame is transferred from the Data Link layer to the Network layer, the Data Link layer checks the CRC to verify the integrity of the frame.

Each layer in the stack acts as a separate module, performing one primary function, and each has its own format of communication instructions in the form of protocols. The protocols used to communicate between functions within the same layer are called peer protocols (see Figure 2-12). **Peer protocols** enable an OSI layer on a sending node to communicate with the same layer on the receiving node. For example, when the Data Link layer on the sending node packages CRC information, it codes it using a peer protocol that is understood by the Data Link layer on the receiving node.

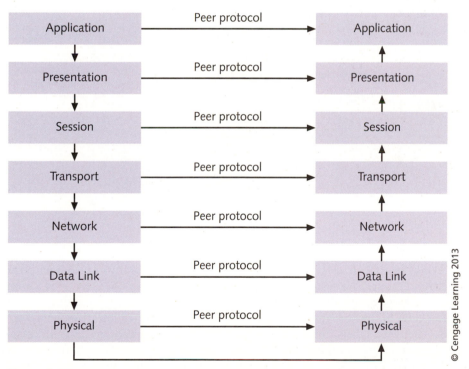

Figure 2-12 Peer protocol communication between the same layers

Information from one layer is transferred to the next by means of commands called **primitives** (see Figure 2-13). The information that is transferred is called a **protocol data unit (PDU)**. As the information goes from one layer to the next (either up or down), new control information is added to the PDU. After the PDU is formed at one layer, it is communicated to the same layer on the companion station by means of peer protocols (see Figure 2-14). At the same time, when the PDU is ready to be passed to the next layer, transfer instructions are added to the PDU by the previous layer.

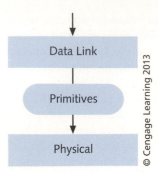

Figure 2-13 Communicating between layers using primitives

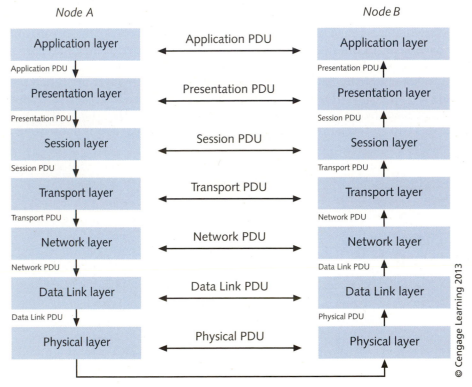

Figure 2-14 Layered communications using PDUs

After the PDU is received by the next layer, the control information and transfer instructions are stripped out. The resulting packet is called the **service data unit (SDU)**. As the SDU travels from one layer to the next, each layer adds its own control information.

At each OSI layer, an SDU is encapsulated with control and transfer information to form a PDU. After the PDU is formed at a particular layer on computer A, for instance, it is then sent to the same layer on computer B. Also, if the layered communications are going down the stack on computer A, for example, then the PDU is sent to the next lower layer in the stack. The control and transfer information is stripped out of the PDU to leave only the SDU. That layer then adds control and transfer information.

Applying the OSI Model

For an example of how layered communication works, think of a workstation accessing a server's shared drive on another network. On the workstation, the redirector at the Application layer locates the shared drive. The Presentation layer ensures that the data format is in ASCII, which is the format used by the workstation and the server. The Session layer establishes the link between the two computers and ensures that the link is not interrupted until the workstation has finished accessing the shared drive's contents. The Transport layer guards against transmission or reception errors, ensuring that the data is interpreted in the order it was sent. The Network layer makes sure packets are sent along the fastest route to minimize delays. The Data Link layer formats frames and ensures they go to the right workstations (via physical addresses). Finally, the Physical layer makes data transmissions possible by converting the information to electrical signals that are placed on the network communications cable or sent over airwaves. As frames and packets are formed, they are adapted for WAN communications between LANs through encapsulation or a process called LAN emulation.

The OSI model is also applied to network hardware and software communications. Network hardware and software that follow accepted standards should function at particular layers of the OSI model to conform to standards. You will find a detailed discussion of network hardware in Chapter 5, but Table 2-2 presents a summary of what network hardware and software match specific OSI layers.

Table 2-2   Network hardware and software associated with the OSI model layers

OSI Layer	Corresponding Network Hardware or Software
Application	Application programming interfaces, Internet browsers, messaging and e-mail software, software to access a computer remotely from another computer, and gateways
Presentation	Data translation software, data encryption software, graphics formatting (.gif and .jpg file formatting), and gateways
Session	Network equipment software drivers, computer name lookup software, half- and full-duplex capabilities, remote procedure call (RPC) capability to run a program on a remote computer, and gateways
Transport	Network equipment software drivers, flow control software and capabilities, Layer 4 switches, and gateways
Network	Gateways, routers, routing protocols, source-route bridges, and Layer 3 switches
Data Link	Network interface cards, intelligent hubs and bridges, Layer 2 switches, and gateways
Physical	Cabling, cable connectors, multiplexers, transmitters, receivers, transceivers, passive and active hubs, repeaters, and gateways

© Cengage Learning 2013

At their core, successful LANs implement the communication guidelines established by the OSI model. An important element in ensuring that a LAN conforms to these guidelines is the method of LAN transmission, presented after the next section. For network professionals, understanding network transmission methods is a direct application of the OSI reference model and is critical to successfully designing a network.

Understanding the Role of Requests for Comments

The implementation of the OSI model and the growth of networking and the Internet have been influenced step by step through the use of **Requests for Comments (RFCs)**. Originated in 1969, an RFC is a document prepared and distributed by any individual or group as a way to further networking, Internet, and computer communications. RFCs help ensure that network standards and conventions are provided so one network can talk to another. Every RFC is assigned a number to distinguish it from other RFCs and to provide a way to track it. Older RFCs are sometimes clarified, built upon, or replaced by newer ones. RFCs build cooperation in a community of equals and play a significant role in advancing network technologies.

When an RFC has wide acceptance in the computer and networking community, it is often adopted as a standard. Today, RFCs are cataloged and managed by the **Internet Engineering Task Force (IETF)**. The IETF is an international group that participates in setting standards for the Internet. Many but not all RFCs are used to set Internet and networking standards, such as for the universal Internet Protocol for transferring information through the Internet. RFCs that are proposed as standards are typically evaluated by a group within the IETF, called the Internet Engineering Steering Group (IESG). Some RFCs are simply used as informational resources; for example, RFC 2555 is used to provide a history of RFCs. Try Activity 2-9 to learn how to view an RFC.

To learn more about RFCs or find a particular RFC, go to *www.rfc-editor* *.org*. For additional information about the IETF, go to *www.ietf.org*.

Activity 2-9: Locating a Particular RFC

Time Required: 5 minutes
Objective: Learn to find an RFC.

Description: In this activity, you find out where to locate information about an RFC.

1. Use a network browser such as Firefox in a UNIX/Linux system, Safari in Mac OS X, or Microsoft Internet Explorer in Windows to access the Internet.

2. Access the **www.rfc-editor.org/rfcsearch.html** Web site.

3. Type **RFC1** in the search box. Make sure that **All** or **RFC** is selected for the category to search and then click the **SEARCH** button.

4. Click **RFC0001** in the list.

5. What is the title of the RFC? Who wrote it, and when was it written? Read the RFC.

6. Click the Back arrow in your browser to return to the RFC Index Search Engine page.

7. Enter **2555** in the search box and click the **SEARCH** button.

8. Click **RFC2555** in the list and read RFC 2555 for a short history of RFCs up to 1999.

9. Click the **Back arrow** in your browser to return to the RFC Index Search Engine page.

10. Enter **5540** in the search box and click the **SEARCH** button. Click **RFC5540** and read the added information for 40 years of RFCs.

11. Close your browser.

LAN Transmission Methods

There are two main LAN transmission or access methods for wire-based networks: Ethernet and token ring. They are defined by the IEEE (see Chapter 1, "Networking: An Overview") through the 802 standards committee and Project 802. Ethernet is defined as a LAN standard in the IEEE 802.3 specifications, and token ring is defined through the IEEE 802.5 specifications. Ethernet is now installed in most places on LANs because it has the broadest options for expansion and high-speed networking. However, it is still valuable to understand token ring communications as an alternative to Ethernet and for token ring's historical significance. A third LAN transmission method, Fiber Distributed Data Interface, is also introduced in this section as a high-speed variation of token ring.

Wireless LAN transmission methods are somewhat different from those used for wired networks, but include one method that is similar to Ethernet. You learn about wireless transmission methods in Chapter 6.

Ethernet

Ethernet transport (the IEEE 802.3 specification) takes advantage of the bus and star topologies. At this writing, Ethernet transmission rates include 10 Mbps, 100 Mbps, 1 Gbps, 10 Gbps, 40 Gbps, and 100 Gbps. Ethernet uses a control method known as **Carrier Sense Multiple Access with Collision Detection (CSMA/CD)**. CSMA/CD is an algorithm (computer logic) that transmits and decodes formatted data frames. Using CSMA/CD, the Ethernet sending node encapsulates the frame to prepare it for transmission. All nodes that wish to transmit a frame on the cable are in contention with one another. No single node has priority over another node. The nodes listen for any packet traffic on the cable. If a packet is detected, the nonsending nodes go into "defer" mode.

Wireless communications use one of two transmission methods, including Carrier Sense Multiple Access with Collision Avoidance (CSMA/CA), which is an Ethernet-related transmission method (see Chapter 6).

The Ethernet protocol permits only one node to transmit at a time. Transmission is accomplished by sending a carrier signal. **Carrier sense** is the process of checking communication media for a specific voltage level indicating the presence of a data-carrying signal. When no signal traffic is detected on the communications medium for a given amount of time, any node is eligible to transmit.

Occasionally, more than one node transmits at the same time, which results in a **collision**. The transmitting node detects a collision by measuring the signal strength. A collision has occurred if the signal is at least twice the normal strength. A transmitting node uses the collision detection software algorithm to recover from packet collisions. This algorithm causes the stations that have transmitted to continue their transmission for a designated time. The continued transmission is a jam signal of all binary ones that enables all listening nodes to determine that a collision has occurred. The software at each node then generates a random number, which is used as the amount of time to wait until transmitting. This ensures that no two nodes attempt to transmit again at the same time.

Frames find their way to a particular destination through physical addressing. Each workstation and server has a unique Layer 2 (MAC) address associated with its NIC, which connects the workstation or server to the network communications cable. That address is burned into a Programmable Read Only Memory (PROM) chip in the NIC.

There are ways to temporarily change or spoof a MAC address through software. Attackers sometimes do this to redirect network traffic so that they can intercept communications from a specific computer or bypass a firewall. This is one reason why using data encryption via the Presentation layer can be important. Refer to Chapter 11 for more information about spoofing and other types of network attacks.

The computer logic that performs these functions is compiled into programs and related files that are called network drivers. Every NIC requires specific network drivers suited for the network access method, data encapsulation format, and addressing method. The driver is installed on the computer.

When data is transmitted in Ethernet communications, it is encapsulated in frames (see Figure 2-15). Each frame is composed of predefined fields:

- *Preamble:* The first field is the preamble, which is 56 bits in length. The preamble synchronizes frame transmission and consists of an alternating pattern of ones and zeros.

- *Start of frame delimiter (SFD or SOF):* The next field is the 8-bit start of frame delimiter. The start of frame delimiter bit pattern is 10101011 and signals that the next portion of the frame contains the beginning of the addressing information.

- *Destination address (DA) and source address (SA):* Following the start of frame delimiter, there are two address fields containing the destination and source addresses. Under IEEE 802.3 guidelines, the address fields can be either 16 or 48 bits (usually set at 48 bits). The source address field contains the address of the sending node, and destination address field holds the address of the receiving node.

- *Length (Len):* Next, the 16-bit length field specifies the length of the data (and pad field, which is the next field in the frame). On a large network that can be divided into multiple virtual LANs (VLANs) for better traffic flow and security, a 32-bit 802.1Q tag can be optionally inserted prior to the Len value in the 802.3 frame to define a VLAN. A **virtual LAN** links together specific switches on a large LAN or on separate LANs so that the switches act as though they compose one logical LAN or VLAN. Switches and VLANs are discussed later in this book.

- *Data and pad:* The data portion of the frame comes after the length field. The length of the encapsulated data must be a multiple of 8 bits (1 byte). A pad field is included if the actual data length is less than 368 bits or is not a multiple of 8 bits. The data field and padding range from 368 to 12,000 bits (or 46 to 1500 bytes).

- *Frame check sequence or frame checksum (FCS):* The end portion of the frame is an FCS or frame checksum field, which is 32 bits long. This field uses a CRC value to enable error detection. The value is calculated from the other fields in the frame at the time of encapsulation. It is recalculated when the destination node receives the frame. If the recalculation does not match the original calculated value, an error condition is generated and the receiving node requests retransmission of that frame. When the recalculation does match the original value, the CRC comparison algorithm yields a result of zero and no retransmission is requested. The CRC algorithm is specified as an IEEE standard.

Preamble 56	S F D 8	Destination address 16 or 48	Source address 16 or 48	Optional 802.1Q tag 32	L e n g t h 16	Data and pad 368–12,000	FCS 32

© Cengage Learning 2013

Figure 2-15   The 802.3 frame format in bits

An important reason for understanding the structure of frames is so you can better understand the portions of a frame that affect network efficiency, troubleshooting, and how attackers break your security. For example, in one type of attack, the attacker alters source and destination addresses so that all of the communication to and from a particular computer first goes through the attacker. In this way the attacker can obtain information, such as passwords or credit card numbers.

Ethernet II is an Ethernet frame-formatting method used on the Internet and other modern networks that varies slightly from the traditional IEEE 802.3 standard (but is now recognized as part of the 802.3 standard and is in RFC 894). Ethernet II makes network transmissions more efficient by having a preamble that is 64 bits long and by combining synchronization information with the start of frame (SOF) delimiter. Destination and source addresses under Ethernet II are strictly 48 bits, as shown in Figure 2-16.

Ethernet II is sometimes called DIX after the three companies that were originally involved in the development of this technology: Digital (Digital Equipment Company, now part of Hewlett–Packard), Intel, and Xerox.

Preamble and SOF	Destination address	Source address	Type	Data	FCS
64	48	48	16	368–12,000	32

Figure 2-16   The Ethernet II (DIX) frame format in bits

Ethernet II uses a 16-bit type field instead of a length field. This field is for upper-level network communications, such as for an 802.1Q tag for VLAN communications. The data field is encapsulated without a pad field and is between 368 and 12,000 bits in length. Minimum and maximum field sizes are used to improve packet collision detection and to ensure that a large packet does not occupy the network for too long. The last field in the Ethernet II frame is the 32-bit FCS field. This field performs a CRC in the same way as the regular 802.3 standard.

 To avoid communication problems, do not use Ethernet II and standard 802.3 frames among the same communicating nodes on the same network.

Both standard 802.3 and Ethernet II can have three optional fields between the length or type field and the data field, as specified by the IEEE 802.2 standard for the Data Link LLC sublayer communications: destination service access point (DSAP), source service access point (SSAP), and control. These fields enable the Data Link layer to manage frames and communicate with higher layers of the OSI model. The DSAP and SSAP are each 8 bits long. Service access points (SAPs) enable the Network layer to determine which network process at the destination node should accept a frame, and they represent communication processes such as OSI, Novell, NetBIOS, TCP/IP, BPDU, IBM network management, XNS, and others (described later in this book). For example, E0 is the hexadecimal value for the Novell SAP and 06 is the hexadecimal code for TCP/IP's SAP. The DSAP specifies the SAP at the receiving node that should accept the frame, and SSAP identifies the SAP on the sending node that issued the frame. The control field identifies the function of the frame, such as whether it holds data or error reporting information. The control field is either 8 or 16 bits long.

 One way that an attacker can strike a network is to change SSAP and DSAP information as a way to interrupt network communications. By using network monitoring devices, a network professional can observe frames to determine if information has been altered.

Another aspect of the IEEE 802.2 standard for LLC is the implementation of the Subnetwork Access Protocol (SNAP), also called Ethernet SNAP. SNAP is used to provide a way to quickly adapt protocols that are not fully compliant with 802.2 standards, such as legacy protocols like AppleTalk and the DEC LAT protocols. When there is no preestablished SAP for such protocols, the DSAP and SSAP fields contain the hexadecimal value, AA, which is the SAP for a SNAP frame. Also, the control field in a SNAP frame is a hexadecimal 03. When a SNAP frame is implemented, a protocol discriminator field is placed just after the control field and before the data field. The vendor of the frame type, such as Apple, is identified in the initial three bytes of the protocol discriminator field, and the type of Ethernet frame is identified in the last two bytes.

Ethernet networks offer a wide variety of equipment options and are widely supported by computer vendors. One reason for the popularity of Ethernet is that it offers many expansion paths to high-speed networking. For example, you can easily upgrade an older 10 Mbps Ethernet network to 100 Mbps Fast Ethernet or 100 Mbps Ethernet to 1 Gbps Ethernet, often using the NICs and cable plant already in place. Also, there are many network testing and management tools available for Ethernet. To learn more about IEEE 802 standards visit *http://grouper .ieee.org/groups/802*. You can purchase information about standards from the IEEE, and you can download for free 802.3 standards that have been approved within the last six months.

Try Activity 2-10 to learn more about Ethernet networks.

Activity 2-10: Examining an Ethernet LAN

Time Required: 15–20 minutes
Objective: View key components on an Ethernet LAN.

Description: In this activity, you visit a LAN in a lab that uses an Ethernet cabled network and observe key elements of the network. Record your observations.

1. Examine the cable used to connect the workstations on the network.

2. Notice how the cable is connected to NICs on the workstations.

3. Ask to see the network equipment, such as hubs, switches, or routers.

4. See if you can determine the topology used by the network, and then ask your instructor what topology is in use.

5. See if you can determine the network transport method, and then ask what is used.

6. Record your observations.

Token Ring

The **token ring** (IEEE 802.5 specification) transmission method was developed by IBM in the 1970s but is no longer popular compared to Ethernet. Even though token ring is not used in modern LANs, it is still valuable to learn token ring basics to help in understanding the ring technologies used in WANs. Token ring works at the OSI Data Link layer (Layer 2).

Data transmission in token ring networks is either 4 or 16 Mbps in older versions and 100 Mbps for fast token ring. The token ring transport method uses a physical star topology along with the logic of a ring topology. Although each node is connected to a central hub, the packet travels from node to node as though there were no starting or ending point. Each node is joined by using a **multistation access unit (MAU)**. The MAU is a specialized hub that ensures the packet is transmitted around the ring of computers. Because the packets travel as though in a ring, there are no terminators at the workstations or in the MAU.

Fast token ring never really caught on. Most vendors that initially offered network devices for this technology eventually withdrew them from the market. Also, a standard for 1 Gbps token ring was formalized in 2001, but no network devices were produced for this standard.

A specialized frame, called the token, is continuously transmitted on the ring to determine when a node can send a packet. In most implementations, there is only one token available on the ring, although the IEEE specifications permit two tokens for networks operating at 16 Mbps or faster. When a node wishes to transmit, it must capture the token. No other node can capture the token and transmit until the active node is finished.

Each token ring network designates one node as the active monitor. Usually this is the first station recognized when the network is brought up. The active monitor is responsible for packet timing on the network and for issuing new token frames if problems occur. Every few seconds, the active monitor broadcasts a MAC sublayer frame to show it is functioning properly. A **broadcast frame** or **broadcast packet** is one that is sent to all points on the network. The other workstation nodes are standby monitors. Periodically, they broadcast frames called "standby monitor present" frames to show they are working normally and are available to replace the active monitor should it malfunction.

If no broadcasts are detected from the active monitor or any one of the standby monitors, the ring goes into a beaconing condition. **Beaconing** starts when a node sends a beacon frame to indicate that it has detected a problem. The ring tries to self-correct the problem, for example, by assigning a new active monitor if the original has gone out of action. After beaconing begins, no data tokens are transmitted until the problem is resolved.

Token ring networks are extremely reliable and were sometimes used in mission-critical situations. One advantage of token ring networks over Ethernet networks is that **broadcast storms** and workstation interference are rare. Broadcast storms sometimes occur on Ethernet networks when a large number of computers or devices attempt to transmit simultaneously or when computers or devices persist in transmitting repeatedly. Network interference also occurs on Ethernet networks when a damaged NIC continues to broadcast transmissions regardless of whether the network is busy. These problems are rare on token ring networks, because only one node is able to transmit at a time. However, with the development of network switches to handle network traffic more efficiently and with ever faster Ethernet speeds, Ethernet came to be preferred over token ring. You learn about switches in Chapter 5, "Devices for Connecting Networks."

Token ring networks were at one time popular in organizations using large and midsized IBM computers and still exists in a few of these older IBM installations.

Fiber Distributed Data Interface

The **Fiber Distributed Data Interface (FDDI)** standard was developed in the mid-1980s to provide higher-speed data communications than that offered by Ethernet (10 Mbps at the time) or token ring (4 or 16 Mbps at the time). However, FDDI faded in use as faster Ethernet alternatives were developed. FDDI is a standard defined by the ANSI X3T9.5 standards committee and provides an access method to enable high-capacity data throughput on busy networks.

At a data throughput rate of 100 Mbps, FDDI was an improvement over 10 Mbps Ethernet and 16 Mbps token ring—but it is rarely used since the development of faster Ethernet technologies. FDDI uses fiber-optic cable as the communications medium. A common application of FDDI has been to provide fast access to network servers (again FDDI has been replaced by faster Ethernet technologies for this purpose).

FDDI is similar to the token ring access method because it uses token passing for network communications. It differs from standard token ring in that it uses a timed token access method. An FDDI token travels along the network ring from node to node. If a node does not need to transmit data, it picks up the token and sends it to the next node. If the node possessing the token does need to transmit, it can send as many frames as desired for a fixed amount of time, called the target token rotation time (TTRT). Because FDDI uses a timed token method, it is possible for several frames from several nodes to be on the network at a given time, providing high-capacity communications.

Two types of packets can be sent by FDDI: synchronous and asynchronous. **Synchronous communication** is used for time-sensitive transmissions requiring continuous transmission, such as voice, video, and multimedia traffic. **Asynchronous communication** is used for normal data traffic, which does not have to be sent in continuous bursts. On a given network, the TTRT equals the total time needed for a node's synchronous transmissions plus the time it takes for the largest frame to travel around the ring.

FDDI employs two rings, so that if one ring malfunctions, data can reach its destination on the other ring. Two classes of nodes connect to FDDI. Class A nodes are attached to both network rings. Class A nodes consist of network equipment, such as hubs. Class A nodes have the ability to reconfigure the ring architecture to use a single ring in the event of a network failure. Class B nodes connect to the FDDI network through Class A devices. Class B nodes are servers or workstations.

WAN Network Communications

WANs, like LANs, are built on topologies and network transmission techniques. Many WANs use variations of the ring or star topologies, but because the major WAN providers keep the specifics of individual topologies confidential to maintain a competitive edge, it is difficult to describe them in detail. WAN network transmission techniques are very complex because new WAN technologies are constantly emerging. In the following sections, general WAN network communications methods are introduced, such as the different switching techniques. Chapter 9, "Understanding WAN Connection Choices," contains a detailed explanation of how switching techniques are implemented in a wide range of WAN transport methods from basic frame relay communications to complex SONET communications.

WAN network services are typically provided by telecommunications companies, cable TV companies, and satellite providers. Currently the providers in the United States with the widest range of services are regional telephone companies—Verizon (formerly Bell Atlantic and GTE), AT&T (which includes the merger of BellSouth, SBC Ameritech, SBC Southwestern Bell, SBC Pacific Bell, and SBC Nevada Bell), CenturyLink (includes the former Qwest)—and long-distance telecommunications companies, such as Verizon (which acquired MCI), AT&T, and Sprint. Regional telephone companies are also called telcos or regional bell operating companies (RBOCs). In Canada, the RBOCs include BellCanada, Manitoba Telecom Services, NorthwesTel, SaskTel, TELUS, Télébec, and BellAliant. Examples of RBOCs in Europe include Deutsche Telekon in Germany and Austria, British Telecom in England, and Swisscom in Switzerland.

Cable television network companies, also called cablecos or multiple system operators (MSOs), are another source of WAN connectivity, such as Comcast and Bresnan/Optimum Communications. Competing with cablecos are satellite Internet companies, such as Hughes Satellite (HughesNet), EarthLink, and WildBlue. Many cell phone companies, such as Verizon and AT&T, also offer wireless Internet access and data communications.

Telecommunications WANs

The telephone companies were the earliest source of WAN connectivity. The most basic WAN communications occur over standard, voice-grade analog telephone lines that compose plain old telephone service (POTS), also called the public switched telephone network (PSTN). There are well over a billion telephone lines all over the world that reach homes, businesses, and educational and government organizations. Communications over POTS include the traditional 56-Kbps access using analog modems and digital-based high-speed access, such as digital subscriber line (DSL) and Integrated Services Digital Network (ISDN), technologies that you learn about in Chapters 5 and 9.

The topology used by RBOCs is often referred to as a "cloud," because the exact path from point to point is difficult to trace and the individual companies closely guard this information. However, there is a known general topology between RBOCs and long-distance carriers. The telecommunications lines supported by an RBOC provide the local access and transport area (LATA) lines. Lines joining RBOCs and long-distance carriers, such as AT&T, are interexchange carrier (IXC) lines. In terms of topology, there is a junction at which LATA lines are connected to IXC lines that is called a point of presence (POP). The POP is highly protected and may even be placed underground for protection from intruders and from adverse weather or disaster conditions. Figure 2-17 represents the general topology linking LATA and IXC lines.

The term "cloud" has more recently been adopted to describe cloud computing, which is based on the same principle as a telecommunications cloud because the point-to-point path of network communications and resources is not apparent to the computer user. You learn more about cloud computing in Chapter 7, "Sharing Resources on a Network."

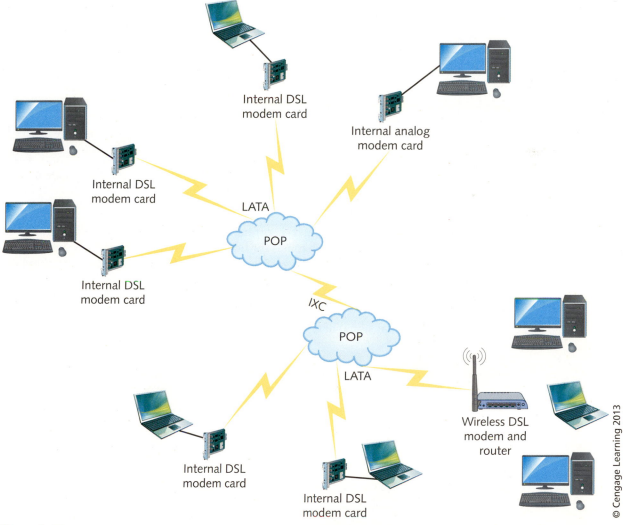

Figure 2-17 POTS topology

Industrial-strength, high-speed data communications through POTS employ dedicated telephone connections, such as T-carrier lines. A **T-carrier** line is a dedicated telephone line that can be used for data communications to connect two different locations for continuous point-to-point communications. For example, some universities use T-carrier lines to connect to one another for Internet communications. Some states use T-carrier lines to connect branch offices and colleges into the government headquarters in the state capitol. These lines offer dependable service over very long distances. T-carriers operate in a logical topology as though no devices are between a LAN at one end and a LAN at the other end, as shown in Figure 2-18.

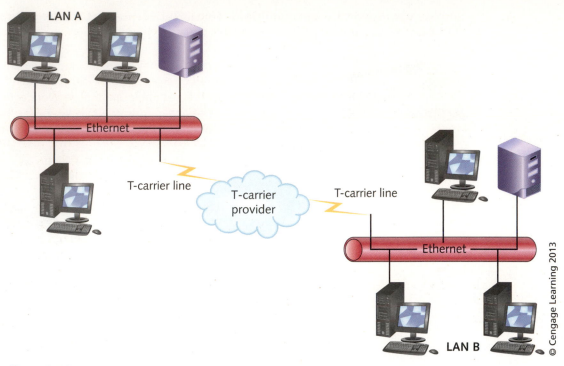

Figure 2-18   Connecting LANs through a T-carrier line

The smallest T-carrier service, T-1, offers 1.544 Mbps data communications that can be switched to create multiple data channels for high-speed communication (as shown in Table 2-3). For example, switching T-1 to the next level of service, called T-2, creates four channels. T-3 has 28 channels, and T4 has 168 channels. Because T-carrier service is expensive, telephone companies offer fractional services that use a portion of the T-1 service and utilize subchannels with 64 Kbps speeds. This is possible because each T-1 service consists of twenty-four 64-Kbps subchannels, called digital signal at level 0 (DS-0) channels.

T-carrier lines are technically called TX/DSx services and correspond to the Physical and Data Link layers of the OSI model. The term "digital signal" refers to electrical transmission characteristics of the Physical layer and the *T* refers to the type of carrier related to the Data Link layer.

Table 2-3   **North American** T-carrier services and data rates

T-carrier	Data Transmission Rate	T-1 Switched Channels	Data Signal Level
Fractional T1	64 Kbps	1 of 24 T-1 subchannels	DS-0
T-1	1.544 Mbps	1	DS-1
T-1C	3.152 Mbps	2	DS-1C
T-2	6.312 Mbps	4	DS-2
T-3	44.736 Mbps	28	DS-3
T-3C	89.472 Mbps	56	DS-3C
T-4	274.176 Mbps	168	DS-4
T-5	400.352 Mbps	336	DS-5

© Cengage Learning 2013

An alternative to T-carrier lines is switched synchronous 56-Kbps communications and switched asynchronous 57.6-Kbps communications. Both provide digital communications through data compression techniques and by using circuit switching (described later in this chapter), methods that combine to yield an actual throughput of up to four times the base rate.

Organizations use switched 56-Kbps communications because the rates are less than those for T-carrier service, and they use them to have a backup line if their main T-carrier service is down.

Cable TV WANs

Cable TV WANs use a distributed architecture that consists of several star-shaped centralized locations. The main focal point in the star is the **headend**, which is the central receiving point for signals from various sources, including satellite, other major cable sources, and local television sources. The headend is a grouping of antennas, cable connections, microwave towers, and satellite dishes, and it distills all incoming signal sources and transfers them to remote distribution centers through trunk lines. In a telecommunications or TV cable system, a **trunk line** is a high-capacity line that goes between two switches (often over several miles) or is generally a main line that has multiple channels.

The distribution centers contain cable transmission equipment that amplifies and transfers cable signals to specific neighborhood distribution points called feeder cables. Individual homes and businesses tap into the feeder cables through smaller drop cables, similar to the small electrical lines that come into homes from the larger lines on telephone poles. The key to providing cable services is to build the right combination of signal amplification and cable lengths to ensure minimal signal loss and distortion at the receiving end. Figure 2-19 illustrates the topology of a cable TV WAN.

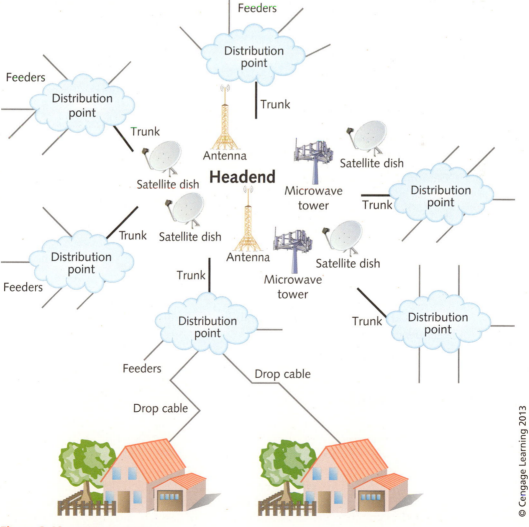

Figure 2-19   Cable TV WAN

© Cengage Learning 2013

Specially designed cable modems are used to convert the cable signal into one that can be used by a computer. The cable modem communicates using upstream and downstream frequencies (channels) that are already allocated by the cable service. The upstream frequency is used to transmit the outgoing signal over a spectrum (contiguous range) of frequencies that are carrying data, sound, and TV signals. The downstream frequency is used to receive signals and is also blended in with other data, sound, and TV downstream signals.

Depending on the modem and the cable provider, upstream and downstream data rates may be the same or they may differ. For example, one vendor's services provide a 10 Mbps maximum upstream rate and a 50 Mbps maximum downstream rate. Another cable provider offers 10 Mbps for both the upstream and downstream rates. However, even though cable modems are built for high speeds and cable providers promote their maximum speeds, at this writing, a single modem user is likely to have realistic access (bandwidth) in the range of 256 Kbps to about 6 Mbps for downloads and 1 to 6 Mbps for uploads. The actual speed is partially dependent on how many of the neighbors are using their cable modems at the same time—because one cable run that connects a group of subscribers to the cable hub can handle a maximum of about 343 Mbps of bandwidth in North America and about 445 Mbps in Europe. Also, a cable service provider may establish a limit on the bandwidth (maximum upload and download speeds) so that the provider can give more users access to the cable network. In addition, new cable TV standards enable bonding communication channels together (so that multiple channels act as one fast channel) to provide even higher speeds for customers. In Activity 2-11 you learn more about cable modems and the cable modem services that are available in your area.

Activity 2-11: Investigating Cable Modem WAN Options

Time Required: 10 minutes
Objective: Discover cable modem WAN options.

Description: In this activity, you learn more about cable modem WAN options for access to the Internet by accessing the *www.cable-modem.net* Web site.

1. Use an Internet browser such as Safari, Firefox, or Internet Explorer to access the Internet.

2. Access the Web site **www.cable-modem.net**.

3. Click the link for **Cable Modems** and read the information about cable modem networks.

4. Click the **Back arrow** or click a link to return to the home page.

5. Click the link for **Service Availability** and follow the instructions to see if there are cable modem services in your area.

6. Close your Web browser when you are finished.

Wireless WANs

Wireless WANs use radio, microwave, and satellite communications. The topology of radio communications requires connecting a LAN to a wireless bridge or switch, for example, which in turn is connected to an antenna. The antenna transmits a radio wave to a distant antenna, which is also connected to a bridge, switch, or router that receives packets and places them on the local LAN. This type of communications is called packet radio and takes place at very high radio frequencies. Figure 2-20 illustrates the topology of a radio wave WAN that joins two LANs.

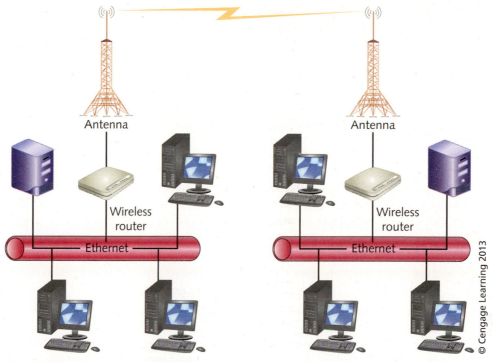

Figure 2-20   Radio wave WAN

Microwave communications operate at a higher frequency than radio wave communications. The topology consists of a microwave dish connected to a LAN, which transmits a signal to a microwave dish at a remote location, which then translates it into network packet communications. In satellite communications, one site uses a satellite dish to transmit the signal to a satellite in space. The signal is retransmitted from the satellite to a dish at a remote location that may be on a continent far from the location that transmitted the signal. Satellite is a more expensive way to build a wireless WAN that connects LANs. Radio waves are the least expensive wireless approach.

Cell phone providers offer three wireless data transmission services that have become popular for Internet access and other data services that can be used alongside traditional voice services: 2G, 3G, and 4G networks. These types of wireless networks are described in the next sections.

2G Wireless Networks   The **2nd generation (2G)** mobile telephone network launched a new era of mobile wireless communications using modern digital signals broadcast from radio transmission antennas instead of analog signals. 2G introduced the use of **codecs**, which are methods of coding and encoding a digital signal to enable loading a specific radio frequency or bandwidth with more individual radio transmissions (calls).

2G has been upgraded to second-and-a-half generation (2.5G) and later to 2.75G capable of up to 236.8 Kbps transmissions on commercial wireless networks.

 The predecessor of 2G, 1st generation wireless (1G) began in 1979 in Japan and spread to Scandinavia in 1981 and then to the United States in 1983. 1G networks used analog instead of digital radio signals and were used for early cell phone communications.

3G Wireless Networks   Cell phone providers and cell phone manufacturers offer **3rd generation (3G)** mobile telecommunications services that enable users to access the Internet and transmit data through a 3G-equipped device, such as a cell phone or small tablet

computer, including the Apple iPad. This capability is enabled through the **International Mobile Telecommunications-2000 (IMT-2000)** standards provided by the ITU. The IMT-2000 standards cover voice, mobile telephone, mobile video, mobile TV, Internet, and mobile data communications through mobile communications devices such as smartphones.

3G communications are capable of up to 5.8 Mbps upstream and 14.4 Mbps downstream for combined voice, data, and Internet services, including multimedia. 3G requires a device—such as a cell phone or smartphone, camera, book reader, tablet, or gaming device—to have a 3G module. There are also USB devices with 3G modules that plug into computers for mobile 3G network access to the Internet.

3G supports digital voice, data applications, streaming music, full motion video, Internet access, voice mail, conference calling, and other wireless communications.

The following 3G communications options have been accepted as following IMT-2000 standards:

- *Code Division Multiple Access 2000 (CDMA 2000):* Broadcasts on up to three combined 1.25 MHz channels (below a total of 5 MHz) for transmission speeds of up to 4.8 Mbps. CDMA 2000 is a product of the Third Generation Partnership Project 2 formed by standards organizations from China, Korea, Japan, and the United States. You can find information about CDMA at the ITU's Web site *www.itu.int*.

- *Digital Enhanced or European Cordless Telecommunications (DECT):* A technology originally developed in Europe by the **European Telecommunications Standards Institute (ETSI)** for cordless telephones and now also used for wireless communications. The DECT 1880 to 1930 MHz broadcast bands (the specific band ranges depend on the country) and 1.9 GHz have been accepted as compatible with the IMT-2000 standards for 3G wireless communications. See *www.dect.org* and *www.dectweb.com/Standards&Regs/StdsOverview.htm* for more information.

- *Enhanced Data Rates for GSM Evolution (EDGE):* Designed to provide higher data rates, EDGE is an enhancement for existing General Packet Radio Service cellular networks operating in the 200 kHz bandwidth using Time Division Multiple Access frame technology (see the section later in this chapter, "WAN Transmission Methods").

- *Universal Mobile Telecommunications System (UMTS):* Uses GSM technologies on the 850, 900, 1700, 1885–2025, and 2110–2200 MHz frequencies to achieve high-speed wireless network communications. Depending on the equipment used, the current user transmission rates are 384 Kbps and 7.2 Mbps and the theoretical transmission capability is up to 45 Mbps. To learn more about UMTS, visit *www.umtsworld.com* and *www.umts-forum.org*.

- *Worldwide Interoperability for Microwave Access (WiMAX):* The IEEE 802.16 standard for wireless MANs, WiMAX operates in the 2–11 GHz and 10–66 GHz frequencies and has a range of about 25–30 square miles (approximately 40–48 square kilometers). Data transfer rates can reach 75 Mbps. You learn more about WiMAX in Chapter 6. Also, visit the Web site *www.wimaxforum.org*.

4G Wireless Networks   **4th generation (4G)** mobile communications use the **International Mobile Telecommunications-Advanced (IMT-Advanced)** standards for mobile communications and follows on from 3G with faster data transfer. The data transfer rate can yield up to 100 Mbps for high-mobility devices, such as those used from a car or bus. For low-mobility or fixed communications situations, such as walking or using a portable device that is not moving, the data transfer rate can go up to 1 Gbps. Besides higher data speeds than 3G, 4G offers:

- Enhanced sound quality
- High-definition streaming video
- Video conferencing
- Better security

Vendors are extending 4G into devices other than just phones, tablet PCs, gaming devices, and video cameras—to also include refrigerators, vending machines, TV phones, and other devices. The technologies employed for 4G (or that are labeled as 4G) include:

- *WiMax:* See the section earlier under "3G Wireless Networks."

- *3rd Generation Partnership Project Long Term Evolution (3GPP LTE):* Also referred to as 3GPP version 8, this standard is offered to advance 3G systems to 4G capabilities. 3GPP LTE is not yet fully consistent with the IMT-Advanced standard. However, at this writing the upcoming 3GPP LTE-Advanced version will fully implement the IMT-Advanced standard. 3GPP LTE is capable of speeds of up 50 Mbps for uploads and 100 Mbps for downloads. 3GPP LTE operates in the 1.4, 3, 5, 10, 15, and 20 MHz frequency ranges and is offered by mainstream providers such as Verizon and AT&T. For more information visit *www.3gpp.org.*

- *Fast Low-Latency Access with Seamless Handoff Orthogonal Frequency Division Multiplexing (Flash-OFDM):* Similar to Frequency Division Multiple Access (see the next section, "WAN Transmission Methods"), Frequency Division Multiplexing is used on logical communications channels, such as for wireless communications, instead of physical communications channels. At this writing, Flash-OFDM operates at 450, 700, and 800 MHz and at 1.9, 2.1, and 2.5 GHz (depending on the country) using layered communications similar to the OSI communications model. The data rates of Flash-OFDM depend on the carrier and frequency, but at this writing the upload rate can be up to 1.8 MBps and up to 5.1 MBps for downloads. (Keep in mind that Bps is bytes per second and bps is bits per second.) This technology is used particularly in Europe.

When you consult with a wireless vendor about data transmission rates, the vendor is likely to quote the ideal rate. Consider asking if there is data on the average transmission rate and the lowest possible rate so that you have a better idea of the realistic estimates for uploads and downloads.

WAN Transmission Methods

WAN transmission methods use different switching techniques. Switching techniques are used to create one or more data paths, called channels, for transmitting data. The channels may be created using one communications cable or using several cables that offer a range of paths along which data can be transmitted. Switching can enable multiple nodes to simultaneously transmit and receive data, or it can enable data to be transmitted over different routes to achieve maximum efficiency in terms of speed and cost. The following is a summary of common switching techniques used in WANs:

- Time Division Multiple Access (TDMA)
- Frequency Division Multiple Access (FDMA)
- Statistical Multiple Access
- Circuit switching
- Message switching
- Packet switching

Time Division Multiple Access (TDMA) divides the channels into distinct time slots. Each time slot is designated for a particular network node, as if it were a dedicated line. The WAN switching device rotates from time slot to time slot for each channel. This is similar to 24-hour television programming, where the 6:00 PM time slot is for the news, 6:30 is for entertainment news, and 7:00 is for a family comedy. TDMA does not guarantee the most efficient use of the network medium, since transmission occurs on only one channel at a time. The timing of node transmission is also important, since a node may transmit at an interval that is out of synchronization with its time slot. (Also, by IEEE specifications, a packet has a designated time by which it must travel the length of the network to avoid a collision with the next packet sent.)

Frequency Division Multiple Access (FDMA) divides the channels into frequencies instead of time slots. Each channel has its own broadcast frequency and bandwidth. The switching device switches from frequency to frequency as it sends data. This is similar to four listeners with headsets sharing a radio modified to have four channels. The first listener might be listening to a classical station, the second to a talk show, the third to a baseball game, and the fourth to the news. Each listener is tuned to a different frequency. The radio sends input to each channel so quickly that none can tell it is quickly switching from channel to channel as it receives the signal on each frequency.

Statistical Multiple Access, or statistical multiplexing, is used by many WAN technologies. This method is more efficient than TDMA or FDMA, because the bandwidth of the communications medium (cable) is dynamically allocated based on the application need. The switching device continuously monitors each channel to determine the communication requirements. For example, at one moment a channel may need to transmit a large graphics file and then be quiet. Algorithms on the switch determine the bandwidth needed to transmit the file. After the file is transmitted, the switch reallocates bandwidth to another channel. This can be compared to the way in which a workstation operating system automatically decides how much memory to give to three applications running at the same time. It might give 40 KB for an active word-processing file, 7 MB for an image from a scanner, and 1.2 MB to print a graphic.

Circuit switching involves creating a dedicated physical circuit between the sending and receiving nodes. This acts as a straight channel on which to send data back and forth without interruption, similar to a telephone call between two parties. The transmission channel remains in service until the two nodes disconnect.

Message switching uses a store-and-forward communication method to transmit data from sending to receiving node. The data is sent from one node to another, each node storing it temporarily until a route toward the data's final destination becomes available. Several nodes along the route store and forward the data until it reaches the destination node. Message switching is used, for example, when you send an e-mail message on an enterprise network with five servers acting as "post offices." The message goes from one post office to the next until it reaches the intended recipient.

Packet switching is a combination of circuit and message switching. It establishes a dedicated circuit between the two transmitting nodes, but the circuit is a logical connection and not a physical one. Although there may be several different physical routes used during the session, each node is aware of only a single, dedicated channel. The advantage of this technique is that the best route can be established for the type and amount of data sent, thus creating an opportunity for high-speed transmissions. Packet switching works like a periscope, which supplies an image that travels from point to point along a nonlinear path. Later in this book, you learn more about how particular WAN technologies use these switching techniques.

Putting It All Together: Designing an Ethernet Network

Ethernet is the most popular transmission method in use on cabled networks and for cabled backbones that join together multiple floors in single buildings and multiple buildings on a CAN (campus area network). Suppose your city's community college has decided to build a new campus because enrollment has increased beyond the capacity of the present campus. Chances are that the network backbone on the original campus already uses Ethernet. Ethernet is still a good choice for the new campus backbone for the following reasons:

- Ethernet is the most popular cabled network transmission method and is a well-tested approach for a backbone on a CAN. The majority of network vendors offer and support a huge array of Ethernet devices. This means the community college does not have to rely on only certain vendors and can take advantage of the best prices.

- The most popular LAN topology, the star-bus hybrid topology, can be used for Ethernet.

- Ethernet's popularity means that there are more network professionals trained in this technology than any other transmission method.

- There are many Ethernet transmission speeds from which to choose, which makes it easier to upgrade a network for more capacity (bandwidth). Ethernet also offers many expansion possibilities so that the network can grow as the student population grows.

- Standards exist for cabled Ethernet and for wireless communications that are fully compatible with Ethernet.

- The vast array of Ethernet vendors and device options makes an Ethernet network relatively easy to expand an Ethernet backbone and cabled Ethernet LANs as more users and buildings are added to the CAN.

- There are many options for connecting an Ethernet network to all types of WAN technologies.

- Many tools are available for monitoring and diagnosing problems with an Ethernet network.

- Many of the network devices used on the original campus can be used on the new campus (depending, of course, on the speed and condition of the devices).

- There are many options for using Internet connectivity on an Ethernet network.

- New standards are constantly evolving to broaden the capabilities of Ethernet.

- Ethernet devices and associated software can be used to help centralize the management of the network for better network function and faster response to problems.

An Ethernet design makes sense for the CAN backbone for areas that require cabled LANs on the new campus. For instance, in student computer labs, the new campus could use wireless access points connected to the Ethernet backbone, so that wireless lab computers can be used and students can use their own wireless laptop and tablet computers at wireless speeds of up to 300 Mbps. Ethernet-compatible wireless communications might also be implemented in the student union, where students go for food and entertainment, and in the campus library. The campus backbone that links the labs and offices to servers can use 10 Gbps or even 100 Gbps speeds. If they start with 10 Gbps for the backbone, they can use cabling to enable them to quickly upgrade to 100 Gbps later by upgrading backbone devices. If more speed is needed for particular labs, such as for graphics, engineering, or computer-aided design software, some labs might use cable connections to individual computers and employ 1 Gbps speeds to the desktop.

Consider another Ethernet design example in which a new three-story psychological counseling office is being built. Ethernet can be used for the backbone between floors and to connect to the Internet; Ethernet can be combined with wireless connectivity to reach users in the offices. There are many equipment options available for Ethernet and wireless communications, making this a sensible design in terms of cost. Also, using Ethernet and wireless services combined makes it likely that network consultants in the community can be found to provide network support. When additional counselors and staff are added, there are many options to match the specific expansion needs.

Chapter Summary

- The seven-layer OSI reference model is the foundation that brings continuity to LAN and WAN communications. Without the OSI model, LAN and WAN interconnectivity might not be feasible today and the Internet might still be a proposition instead of fact.

- Each layer in the OSI model has a vital role in network communications. The bottom layers provide support for physical connectivity, frame formation, encoding, and signal transmission. The middle layers help establish and maintain a communication session between two network nodes and monitor for error conditions. The uppermost layers provide application and software support for encrypting data and assuring the interpretation and presentation of data.

- Information is transported over LANs by using a LAN transmission or access method. Ethernet is the most commonly used cabled LAN transmission method. Token ring was popular in the past, but is virtually nonexistent today. FDDI is a transmission method that was frequently used for high-speed connections to network devices such as servers, but has been supplanted by faster versions of Ethernet.

- WAN network communications architectures are relatively difficult to categorize, because many WAN providers keep specific design techniques confidential. However, the star topology is widely used for WANs as well as LANs. Telecommunications WANs predate LANs in the use of the star topology and continue to apply it today. Cable TV and satellite WAN options are emerging at a fast clip and also employ star-like topologies.

- Wireless WANs have grown exponentially, particularly for mobile telecommunications including voice, video, and data. 2G mobile wireless networks launched the use of digital signals for radio transmissions. 3G and 4G wireless networks have spread to offer faster mobile communications for smartphones, tablets, mobile gaming devices, and even home appliances.

- WAN data transmission methods vary widely, depending on specific technologies, but many employ one or more forms of switching techniques. Switching provides multiple data paths, with the goal of transmitting the maximum amount of data to all designated locations as fast as possible.

Key Terms

2nd generation (2G)   Second generation of mobile telecommunications technology, which is notable because it introduces the use of digital signals instead of analog signals (1G) for mobile radio transmissions and enables the use of codecs for handling many more calls per radio frequency or bandwidth. *See* **codecs**.

3rd generation (3G)   Third generation mobile telecommunications technology for cell phones, tablet computers, and other devices that is based on the IMT-2000 standards for mobile communications. The data transfer rate is up to 5.8 Mbps upstream and 14.4 Mbps downstream.

4th generation (4G)   Fourth generation mobile telecommunications technology that is faster than 3G and is built on the IMT-Advanced standards. Data transfer rates are based on whether a device is used in a low (100 Mbps) or high (1Gbps) mobility situation.

American National Standards Institute (ANSI)   An organization that works to set standards for all types of products, including network equipment.

American Standard Code for Information Interchange (ASCII)   An 8-bit character-coding method consisting of 96 uppercase and lowercase characters and numbers, plus 32 nonprinting characters.

analog   A type of transmission that can vary continuously, as in a wave pattern with positive and negative voltage levels.

asynchronous communication   Communication that occurs in discrete units where the start of a unit is signaled by a start bit at the front and the end of the unit is signaled by a stop bit at the back.

beaconing   An error condition on a token ring network that indicates one or more nodes are not functioning.

broadcast frame   A frame sent to all nodes on a network.

broadcast packet   A packet sent to all nodes on a network.

broadcast storm   Saturation of network bandwidth caused by excessive traffic, as when a large number of computers or devices attempt to transmit simultaneously, or when computers or devices persist in transmitting repeatedly.

cableco   A cable TV company, such as Comcast or Time Warner.

carrier sense   The process of checking a communications medium, such as cable, for a voltage level, signal transition, or light, indicating the presence of a data-carrying signal.

Carrier Sense Multiple Access with Collision Detection (CSMA/CD)   A network transport control method used in Ethernet networks. It regulates transmission by sensing the presence of packet collisions.

circuit switching   A network communications technique that uses a dedicated channel to transmit information between two nodes.

codec   Method of coding and encoding a digital signal to enable loading a specific radio frequency or bandwidth with more individual radio transmissions (calls).

collision   A situation in which two or more packets are detected at the same time on an Ethernet network.

connectionless service   Also known as Type 1 operation, services that occur between the LLC sublayer and the Network layer, but that provide no checks to make sure data accurately reaches the receiving node.

connection-oriented service   Type 2 operation services that occur between the LLC sublayer and the Network layer, providing several ways to ensure data is successfully received by the destination node.

cyclic redundancy check (CRC)   An error detection method that calculates a value for the total size of the information fields contained in a frame. The value is inserted near the end of a frame by the Data Link layer on the sending node and checked by the Data Link layer on the receiving node to determine if a transmission error has occurred.

device address   Also called the physical or MAC address, the hexadecimal number permanently assigned to a network interface and used by the MAC sublayer within the Data Link layer, or Layer 2.

digital signal (DS)   A transmission method that has distinct signal levels to represent binary zeroes or ones, such as +5 volts and 0 volts.

discovery   A process used by routers that involves gathering information about how many nodes are on a network and where they are located.

electromagnetic interference (EMI)   Signal interference caused by magnetic force fields generated by electrical devices such as motors.

encapsulate   In the context of OSI layers, the process of wrapping the information in one layer inside the information within the next layer. In the context of protocols, the process of placing the information formatted for one protocol inside the information formatted for a different protocol, as is done in TCP/IP communications.

encryption   A process that scrambles data so that it cannot be read if intercepted by unauthorized users.

Ethernet   A transport system that uses the CSMA/CD access method for data transmission on a network. Ethernet typically is implemented in a bus or star-bus hybrid topology.

European Telecommunications Standards Institute (ETSI)   Organization that develops "globally applicable" radio and broadcast communications standards and Internet standards under the endorsement of the European Union.

Extended Binary Coded Decimal Interchange Code (EBCDIC)   A character-coding technique used mainly on IBM mainframe computers and consisting of an 8-bit coding method for a 256-character set of letters, numbers, and special characters.

Fiber Distributed Data Interface (FDDI)   A fiber-optic data transport method capable of a 100-Mbps transfer rate using a dual ring topology; largely supplanted today by faster Ethernet methods.

flow control   A process that ensures one device does not send information faster than it can be received by another device.

frame   A unit of data transmitted on a network that contains control and address information corresponding to the OSI Data Link layer, or Layer 2.

Frequency Division Multiple Access (FDMA)   A switching method that creates separate channels on one communication medium by establishing different frequencies for each channel.

full-duplex   The capacity to send and receive signals at the same time on the same medium.

half-duplex   The ability to send or receive signals on a medium, but not at the same time.

headend   On a cable TV WAN, a central receiving point for signals from various sources, including satellite, other major cable sources, and local television sources.

International Mobile Telecommunications-2000 (IMT-2000)   3G standards provided through the ITU that cover voice, mobile telephone, mobile video, mobile TV, Internet, and mobile data communications over mobile communications devices such as smartphones. *See* **3G**.

International Mobile Telecommunications-Advanced (IMT-Advanced)   4G standards provided through the ITU that offer higher data transfer rates, higher quality of services, and better security than IMT-2000. *See* **IMT-2000** and **4G**.

International Organization for Standardization (ISO)   An international body that establishes communications and networking standards and that is particularly known for its contributions to network protocol standards.

International Telecommunication Union (ITU)   A United Nations agency that develops international communications standards; allocates international radio spectrums; and sets standards for modems, e-mail, mobile wireless communications, and digital telephone systems.

Internet Engineering Task Force (IETF)   An arm of the Internet Society (ISOC) that works on Internet-related technical issues. *See* **Request for Comments (RFC)**.

logical link control (LLC)   A Data Link sublayer of the OSI model that initiates the communications link between nodes and ensures the link is not unintentionally broken.

MAC address   *See* **device address**.

media access control (MAC)   A Data Link sublayer that examines addressing information contained in a network frame and controls how devices share communications on the same network.

message switching   A switching method that sends data from point to point, with each intermediate node storing the data, waiting for a free transmission channel, and forwarding the data to the next point until the destination is reached.

multiple system operator (MSO)   A cable TV company that offers WAN or Internet services. *See* **cableco**.

multistation access unit (MAU)   A central hub that links token ring nodes into a topology that physically resembles a star, but in which frames are transmitted in a logical ring pattern.

Open Systems Interconnection (OSI) reference model   Developed by the ISO and ANSI, a model that provides a framework for networked hardware and software communications based on seven layers.

packet   A unit of data formatted for transmission over a network that contains control and other information that corresponds to the OSI Network layer, also called Layer 3.

packet radio   The process of transmitting a data-carrying packet over radio waves through short bursts.

packet switching   A data transmission technique that establishes a logical channel between two transmitting nodes, but uses several different paths of transmission to continually find the best routes to the destination.

peer protocol   Protocol used to enable an OSI layer on a sending node to communicate with the same layer on the receiving node.

physical address   *See* **device address**.

plain old telephone service (POTS)   Regular voice-grade telephone service.

port   *See* **socket**.

primitive   A command used to transfer information from one layer in an OSI stack to another layer, such as from the Physical layer to the Data Link layer.

protocol data unit (PDU)   The information transferred between layers in the same OSI stack.

public switched telephone network (PSTN)   Regular voice-grade telephone service.

radio frequency interference (RFI)   Signal interference caused by electrical devices that emit radio waves at the same frequency used by network signal transmissions.

redirector A service used via the Application layer to recognize and access other computers.

regional bell operating companies (RBOCs) A telecommunications company that provides telephone services to a designated region.

Request for Comments (RFC) A document prepared and distributed by any individual or group as a way to further networking, Internet, and computer communications. RFCs help ensure that network standards and conventions are provided so one network can talk to another. Every RFC is assigned a number to distinguish it from other RFCs and to provide a way to track it. Each RFC is tracked and published by the Internet Engineering Task Force (IETF). *See* **Internet Engineering Task Force (IETF).**

Secure Sockets Layer (SSL) A data encryption technique employed between a server and a client, such as between a client's browser and an Internet server.

service data unit (SDU) A protocol data unit that has been transferred between OSI layers and then stripped of control information and transfer instructions.

simplex The capacity for a signal to travel on a medium in only one direction.

socket A value or means of identifying a service on a network node, such as socket or port 103 for standardized e-mail services in the TCP protocol.

Statistical Multiple Access A switching method that allocates the communications resources according to what is needed for the task, such as providing more bandwidth for a video file and less for a small spreadsheet file.

synchronous communications Communications of continuous bursts of data controlled by a clock signal that starts each burst.

T-carrier A dedicated telephone line that can be used for data communications to connect two different locations for continuous point-to-point communications.

telco A regional telephone company. *See* **RBOC.**

Time Division Multiple Access (TDMA) A switching method that enables multiple devices to communicate over the same communications medium by creating time slots in which each device transmits.

token ring An access method developed by IBM in the 1970s and which is still used on some networks. Variations of the technology are used for WANs. This transport method employs a physical star topology along with the logic of a ring topology. Although each node is connected to a central hub, the frame travels from node to node as though there were no starting or ending point.

trunk line In a cable TV or telecommunications system, a high-capacity communications line that goes between two switches (often over several miles) or it is generally a main line that has multiple channels.

Unicode A character coding standard that enables consistent coding of characters covering 93 scripts for most languages used throughout the world. Unicode enables data to be translated between different systems and languages while retaining the original data integrity.

virtual circuit A logical communications path established by the OSI Network layer for sending and receiving data.

virtual LAN (VLAN) A logical LAN that links together specific switches on a large LAN or on separate LANs so that the switches act as though they compose one unified logical or virtual LAN.

Review Questions

1. You run a machine shop that houses many electrical machines, fans, and an air conditioning unit. All of these devices can contribute to which of the following that must be taken into consideration when designing a LAN? (Choose all that apply.)

   a. electron polarity

   b. electromagnetic interference

   c. radio frequency interference

   d. frame sequencing and timing

2. Which of the following have been facilitated by the OSI model? (Choose all that apply.)

   a.   the development of network hardware that uses common interfaces

   b.   enabling users to retain their investment in network devices by helping to ensure old equipment communicates with new equipment

   c.   protocol stacking so that all network protocols can use 512-bit WEP encryption

   d.   enabling different types of LANs and MANs to communicate

3. A wireless 2G network uses which of the following radio transmitted signals? (Choose all that apply.)

   a.   pause-based

   b.   token-enhanced

   c.   analog

   d.   digital

4. Which of the following fields would you find in a data link frame? (Choose all that apply.)

   a.   address of the transmitting node

   b.   address of the receiving node

   c.   data

   d.   end of frame designator

5. Which of the following is an IEEE standard for Ethernet? (Choose all that apply.)

   a.   802.5

   b.   803.4

   c.   802.3

   d.   800.12ai

6. On your network there is a NIC that is malfunctioning by transmitting many extra frames each time it communicates. Which of the following might help you identify which NIC is having problems so that you can replace it?

   a.   physical address of the NIC

   b.   Ethernet SNAP designator

   c.   IP tag given the NIC

   d.   distance from your computer to the suspect computer as measured in voltage times amperage of the transmitted frames

7. When your computer communicates with a server through the Physical layer (Physical layer to Physical layer), it uses which of the following?

   a.   a code based on Morse code

   b.   peer protocols

   c.   Physical CRC

   d.   module protocol transfer

8. When you configure a computer's operating system to use data encryption for network communications, this occurs at which of the following OSI layers?

   a.   Session

   b.   Physical

   c.   Presentation

   d.   Network

9. When you are purchasing a product through the Internet, which of the following can be used to encrypt your credit card number when you send it to the vendor?

 a. password plus

 b. Ethernet SNAP

 c. 802.08 security

 d. Secure Sockets Layer

10. You have just purchased an Apple iPad tablet so that you can download books, use mapping software, and access your e-mail through the Internet. Which of the following standards makes this possible through a wireless telecommunications network?

 a. IMT-2000

 b. Telnet

 c. TELE400

 d. AppleTalk

11. An Internet browser works at which of the following OSI layers?

 a. Presentation

 b. Application

 c. Network

 d. Transport

12. What types of devices would you expect to see in a headend? (Choose all that apply.)

 a. cable connections

 b. satellite dishes

 c. antennas

 d. trunk lines

13. Which type of switching uses a store-and-forward communication method?

 a. packet

 b. Statistical Multiple Access

 c. message

 d. Frequency Division Multiple Access

14. How is a collision determined on an Ethernet network?

 a. by the size of the frame

 b. when the collision bit is set to 1 in the frame

 c. when a NIC's collision attribute is set to binary 1111

 d. by signal strength

15. A 4G network has which of the following advantages over a 3G network? (Choose all that apply.)

 a. high-definition streaming video

 b. better sound quality

 c. faster possible data transmission rate

 d. improved security

16. You work in a community college system that consists of 15 community colleges throughout the state and a central administration center at one of the colleges. The central administration center processes the payroll and student information and needs to have communications of over 40 Mbps between it and the colleges. Which of the following would best provide this type of communications?

    a. an analog dial-up modem

    b. fractional T-1 communications

    c. T-3 or T-3C communications

    d. a cable modem

17. You are working on security on your company's vice president's computer by closing unused ports for network communications. At what OSI layer are you working while closing the ports?

    a. Physical

    b. Data Link

    c. Transport

    d. Network

18. Enhanced Data Rates for GSM Evolution (EDGE) as used on 3G networks employs which of the following?

    a. Statistical Multiple Access

    b. circuit switching

    c. packet-message switching

    d. Time Division Multiple Access

19. Beaconing occurs on which type of network?

    a. wireless

    b. token ring

    c. Ethernet

    d. 1G

20. You are working on an older network that still uses FDDI on the backbone to connect servers and network devices. What type of cable do you expect to see on the FDDI backbone?

    a. fiber-optic

    b. twisted-pair

    c. copper tubing

    d. TV type case cable

Case Projects

CASE PROJECTS

In the following assignments, you consult for the newsroom of the *Franklin Daily Herald*, a newspaper in a Midwestern U.S. city that is still thriving because of its close ties to the community and first-rate reporting. All of the news reporters have laptop computers, and now their management has funded a project to network the entire newspaper building. Having a network that links all of the departments and enables company-wide exchange of information and Internet access will help position this newspaper to stay competitive with other news sources.

Case Project 2-1: Expanding the Network Backbone

There is already a partial network backbone using Ethernet in the newspaper's building that joins some of the administrative and advertising offices. Prepare a report or slide show that explains why Ethernet is still a good choice for the network backbone.

Case Project 2-2: Creating a Network That Can Communicate with Other Networks

The management wants to know if there are any guarantees that the network you are proposing will communicate with other networks. What is your response?

Case Project 2-3: Questions About the OSI Model

Brett Mason, a new colleague with whom you are working at Network Design Consultants, is unsure about some aspects of the OSI model. He has a list of questions for you and asks that you develop a table that he can use as a reference for the answers. Create a table containing two columns and seven rows. Label the left column "Network Function," and label the right column "OSI Layer." Enter each of the following functions in its own row under the left column, and then specify the OSI layer that performs that function under the right column. Brett's questions about functions are as follows:

- Which layer resizes frames to match the receiving network?
- Which layer performs data compression?
- Which layer ensures data is received in the order it was sent?
- Which layer handles the data-carrying signal?
- Which layer provides file transfer services?
- Which layer enables routing?
- Which layer enables the receiving node to send an acknowledgment?

Case Project 2-4: More Questions About the OSI Reference Model

Brett likes your table and has another question. He would like you to explain MAC addressing.

Case Project 2-5: Implementing T-carrier Communications

After the new network is installed, the newspaper is purchased by a newspaper chain and the coordinators of the purchase transition want to have T-carrier communications with the newsroom network. The *Franklin Daily Herald* management would like you to give them an executive overview explaining T-carrier communications and the possible options.

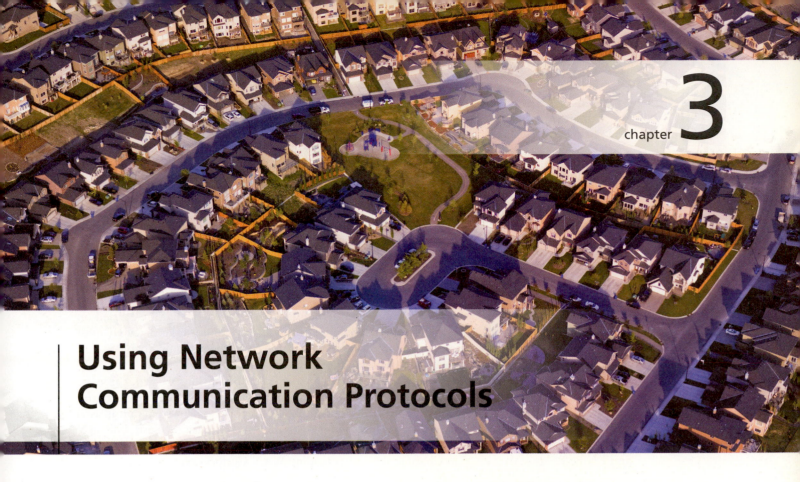

chapter 3

Using Network Communication Protocols

Protocols turn the potential chaos of electronic signals on a network into meaningful patterns of communication, so that when someone sends you an e-mail you can receive and read it.

After reading this chapter and completing the exercises, you will be able to:

- Explain network protocols including TCP, UDP, and IP
- Discuss how IP addressing works
- Understand IPv4 and IPv6
- Explain and use application protocols in the TCP/IP suite
- Explain VoIP
- Compare TCP/IP to the OSI model
- Discuss WAN protocols used for remote communications
- Understand how to design a network to use TCP/IP and application protocols

The early twentieth-century sociologist George Herbert Mead studied the effect of language on human beings and eventually concluded that human understanding flourishes primarily because we have language. Language helps us to find meaning in, and make sense of, our surroundings. Network protocols play a similar role on networks for providing different systems with common contexts for communication.

This chapter explores common protocols used on networks. You learn the advantages and disadvantages of each protocol so that you have a clearer idea of how to employ it. You particularly learn about TCP/IP and how to take advantage of protocols and applications in the TCP/IP suite.

An Overview of Network Protocols

Protocols are like a local language or dialect: on a network, they enable effortless interchange among connected devices. Protocols give meaning to simple electrical signals that are carried on network communications media. Network communications simply cannot take place without protocols. For two computers to fully communicate, they must use the same protocol, just as two human beings communicate best when using the same language.

A LAN can transport several protocols individually or in combinations of two, three, or more protocols. Network devices, such as routers, are often set up to automatically configure themselves by recognizing the different protocols (depending on the operating system that is used with the router). For instance, a router that links two LANs and a WAN must recognize all LAN and WAN protocols in use (see Figure 3-1; TCP, UDP, and IP are discussed later in this chapter, and Frame Relay is discussed in Chapter 9, "Understanding WAN Connection Choices").

Properties of a LAN Protocol

The properties of a LAN protocol include capabilities to do the following:

- Enable reliable network links
- Communicate at relatively high speeds
- Handle source and destination node addressing
- Follow standards, particularly the IEEE 802 standards

Some protocols offer more advantages than others. For example, some protocols enable routing because they have Network layer capabilities, as you learned in Chapter 2, "How LAN and WAN Communications Work." This means that communications using these protocols can be sent along the fastest or most efficient network path. Routable protocols can also be blocked from entering a network as a security measure. Some protocols cannot be routed, which means that they may create unnecessary network traffic. Some protocols that were developed in the early days of networking when network infrastructures were slow are more susceptible to EMI/RFI and are unreliable. Some of these protocols have disadvantages for modern communications. Other protocols have inadequate error checking or were designed for small LANs prior to the implementation of today's enterprise LANs, which require extensive routing.

LAN Protocols and Operating Systems

Protocols that have typically been used on LANs for communications between workstations, servers, and network devices include TCP/IP, IPX/SPX, NetBEUI, and AppleTalk. Of these protocols, TCP/IP is nearly universally used today, in part because of its heritage as the protocol of choice on the Internet. The popularity of TCP/IP has caused IPX/SPX, NetBEUI, and AppleTalk to be replaced or used only on much older networks.

Table 3-1 lists these protocols and the specific network operating systems with which they can operate. In the following sections, you get a short overview of IPX/SPX, NetBEUI, and AppleTalk as legacy protocols. Next, you learn about TCP/IP in much more depth, because it is so universal to networking.

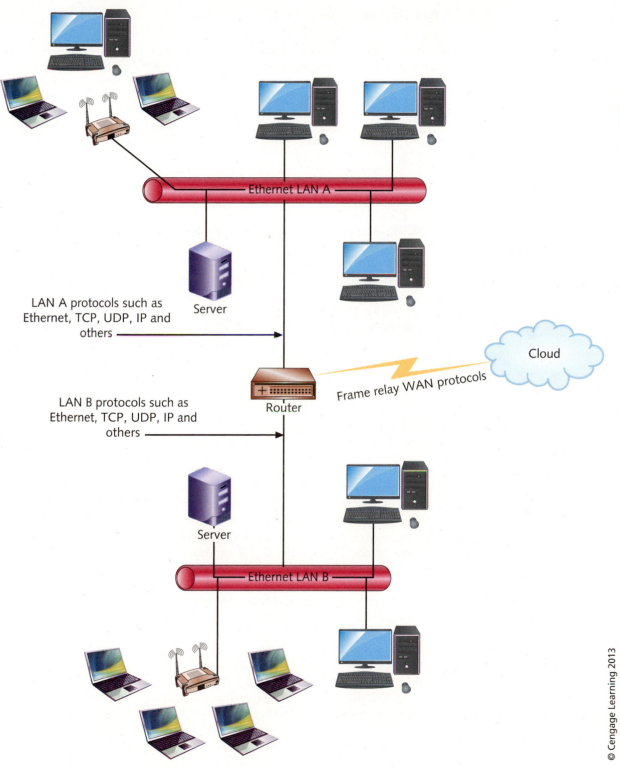

Figure 3-1   Transporting multiple protocols on a network

Table 3-1   LAN protocols and network operating systems

Protocol	Operating System(s)
IPX/SPX	Older Novell NetWare operating systems
NetBEUI	Older Microsoft Windows-based operating systems (support ended with Windows XP and Server 2003)
AppleTalk	Older Apple Macintosh operating systems
TCP/IP	UNIX, Linux, newer Microsoft Windows-based operating systems, modern Apple Macintosh systems, IBM mainframe operating systems

© Cengage Learning 2013

Legacy Protocols

IPX/SPX, NetBEUI, and AppleTalk are older protocols that for the most part have been superseded by TCP/IP. However, you may find these protocols still in use on some older networks, so it is helpful to know a little background about these protocols.

IPX/SPX

The **Internetwork Packet Exchange (IPX)** protocol was developed by Novell for one of the earliest network operating systems with server capabilities, called NetWare. NetWare was originally developed for Ethernet bus, token ring, and ARCnet networks that employed one file server. ARCnet is an early proprietary network alternative that uses specialized packets with tokens and that employs a star-bus hybrid network design. Today, NetWare has been replaced by Novell Open Enterprise Server that can be installed with a NetWare kernel or a SUSE Linux Enterprise Server kernel. A **kernel** is an essential set of programs and computer code built into a computer operating system to control processor, disk, memory, and other functions central to the basic operation of a computer.

Along with IPX, Novell developed a companion protocol called **Sequenced Packet Exchange (SPX)** for use with software applications, such as databases.

IPX/SPX was commonly used on earlier NetWare servers through version 4. When Novell issued NetWare 5, users were encouraged to convert to TCP/IP. Today, TCP/IP is the protocol of preference for Novell Open Enterprise Server installations.

Although it is an early network protocol, one advantage of IPX over some other early protocols is that it can be routed, meaning that it can transport data over multiple networks in an enterprise. A disadvantage is that IPX is a "chatty" protocol, because live stations using IPX frequently broadcast their presence across the network. When there were multiple IPX-configured NetWare servers on early networks and several hundred clients, the IPX "I'm here" broadcasts could amount to significant network traffic.

NetBEUI

Early Windows Server networks used **NetBIOS Extended User Interface (NetBEUI)** as the native protocol. NetBEUI was developed by IBM and Microsoft for LAN Manager and LAN Server before the creation of Windows NT. It was later implemented in the first versions of Windows NT and was also available in Windows 2000. NetBEUI is not supported in Windows XP, Windows Server 2003, or any higher Windows versions and has disappeared from modern networks. NetBEUI proved to have some significant drawbacks because this protocol cannot be routed and can cause unnecessary traffic.

AppleTalk

Apple developed the **AppleTalk** protocol suite to network Macintosh computers running the Mac OS operating system. AppleTalk is a peer-to-peer network protocol, which means it is designed to enable Macintosh workstations to communicate regardless of the presence of a server. AppleTalk Phase I was released in 1983. AppleTalk Phase II came in 1989 and was designed to handle an increased number of networked computers and to be interoperable with large heterogeneous networks that host multiple protocols.

AppleTalk is supported by Mac OS systems up through Mac OS X version 10.5 (Leopard). Starting with Mac OS X version 10.6 (Snow Leopard) AppleTalk is no longer supported.

An advantage of AppleTalk Phase II is that it works well for communications between Macintosh computers, as it is specifically designed for this purpose. Two other advantages are that it is a routable protocol and that it supports multiple logical networks on one physical network through one network interface card (NIC) per computer. As many as 253 nodes can be supported on a single logical network. A disadvantage of using AppleTalk is that it is not as effective as TCP/IP for communicating with non-Macintosh computers and AppleTalk is not used on the Internet.

TCP/IP

TCP/IP is currently the most widely used protocol suite and the protocol of the Internet. Most network server and workstation operating systems support TCP/IP, including UNIX, Linux, all Windows-based systems, Novell Open Enterprise Server, Mac OS X, and IBM's OpenMVS and z/OS (IBM mainframe operating systems). In addition, network device vendors write their operating system software for TCP/IP, including device performance enhancements. TCP/IP was initially used on UNIX systems and then was rapidly adopted on many kinds of networks. Today, TCP/IP enables public and commercial networks to connect to the Internet for access by millions of users. This section outlines the history of TCP/IP, how it works, and the various protocols and applications associated with it.

The History and Role of TCP/IP

In the late 1960s, the Advanced Research Projects Agency (ARPA) was working to make the ARPANET (see Appendix A, "A Short History of Networking") available for universal access. Its goal was to find a common way to enable university, research, and Department of Defense computers to communicate over the ARPANET WAN. One significant impediment to this goal was that computer manufacturers were very proprietary, and information about the internal workings of their systems was closely guarded as trade secrets.

The first attempt to develop a means for different computers to communicate was accomplished through several universities that developed a network protocol, called the Network Control Protocol (NCP), to enable DEC, IBM, and other host computers to exchange information. NCP was a rudimentary protocol that enabled different types of DEC and IBM computers to connect for network communications and to run applications over a network in which the hosts were separated geographically. One application for NCP, for example, was the transfer of files from one computer to another. NCP was a good start, but it was not able to provide wholly reliable communications, and so ARPA launched a project to make improvements. The protocol they developed was actually a combination of two protocols, the **Transmission Control Protocol (TCP)** and the **Internet Protocol (IP)**, which are commonly abbreviated as TCP/IP.

TCP/IP has many advantages that include:

- It is used on most networks and the Internet, which makes it the international language of network communications.

- There is a wide range of network devices designed for use with TCP/IP.

- Most computer operating systems use TCP/IP as their main protocol.

- There are many troubleshooting and network analysis tools available for TCP/IP.

- There is a large body of network professionals who understand TCP/IP.

Protocols and Applications of the TCP/IP Suite

TCP/IP is associated with a suite of protocols and applications that support a vast range of communications capabilities. Table 3-2 provides an overview of the many protocols and applications included in the TCP/IP suite. You learn more about many of these protocols and applications later in this chapter.

Table 3-2 Protocols and applications in the TCP/IP suite

Acronym	Full Name	Description	OSI Layer
ARP	Address Resolution Protocol	Used to enable resolution of IP addresses to MAC addresses	Data Link and Network
DNS	Domain Name System (application)	Used to maintain tables to link IP addresses with computer host names	Application
FTP	File Transfer Protocol	Used to upload and download files	Session, Presentation, and Application
HTTP	Hypertext Transfer Protocol	Used for World Wide Web communications	Application
ICMP	Internet Control Message Protocol	Used for network error reporting particularly through routers	Network
IP	Internet Protocol	Used to handle logical addressing	Network
NFS	Network File System (application)	Used to transfer files over a network (designed for UNIX computers)	Session, Presentation, and Application
OSPF	Open Shortest Path First (protocol)	Used by routers to communicate routing information	Network
PPP	Point-to-Point Protocol	Used as a remote communications protocol in connection with WANs	Network
RIP	Routing Information Protocol	Used to gather routing information to update routing tables	Network
RPC	Remote Procedure Call (application)	Used to enable a remote computer to execute procedures on another computer, such as a server	Session
SLIP	Serial Line Internet Protocol	Used as a remote communications protocol in connection with WANs	Network
SMTP	Simple Mail Transfer Protocol	Used for e-mail	Application
SNMP	Simple Network Management Protocol	Used to monitor network activity	Session, Presentation, and Application
TCP	Transmission Control Protocol	Connection-oriented protocol to ensure the reliability of data transmissions	Transport
Telnet	Telecommunications Network (application)	Used to enable a workstation to emulate a terminal and connect to network servers, Internet servers, mainframes, and routers	Session, Presentation, and Application
UDP	User Datagram Protocol	Connectionless protocol used as an alternative to TCP when reliability is not an issue	Transport

© Cengage Learning 2013

TCP/IP is a layered set of protocols similar to, but not identical to, the OSI protocol layers. TCP/IP consists of nearly 100 standard (nonproprietary) protocols that interconnect computer systems efficiently and reliably. The core component protocols within the TCP/IP suite are:

- Transmission Control Protocol (TCP)
- User Datagram Protocol (UDP)
- Internet Protocol (IP)

Each is discussed in the following sections.

How TCP Works

Transmission Control Protocol (TCP) is a transport protocol (OSI Transport layer or Layer 4) that establishes communication sessions between software application processes initiated by users on a network. TCP provides for reliable end-to-end delivery of data by monitoring the accurate receipt of frames and by controlling data flow. TCP accomplishes this by sequencing and acknowledging frames.

 TCP is initially specified in RFC (Request for Comment) 793.

When two devices communicate, they establish a sequence number for each frame that is transmitted, and the sequence number is placed in the TCP frame header. The sequence number not only shows the frame sequence in a stream of frames, but also indicates the amount of data in the frame. When a frame is received, the receiving node checks the sequence number to make sure it has received the correct frame in the correct order. After the receiving node acquires the frame, it sends an acknowledgement to the sending node. Besides showing successful receipt of the frame, the acknowledgement contains the sequence number of the next frame the receiving node is expecting.

The number of data bytes transmitted in a frame is called the **sliding window** because the number can be increased or decreased from one moment to the next by mutual agreement of the two communicating nodes. The sliding window is dynamically adjusted by the nodes on the basis of two factors: the current network traffic and the amount of buffer space (usually memory) that each node can currently allocate to store frames at a node while the frames are waiting to be processed by that node.

The essential TCP functions are similar to those of the OSI Transport layer:

- Monitor for session requests
- Establish sessions with other TCP nodes
- Transmit and receive data
- Close transmission sessions

The TCP frame contains a header and data payload (see Figure 3-2) and is called the TCP segment.

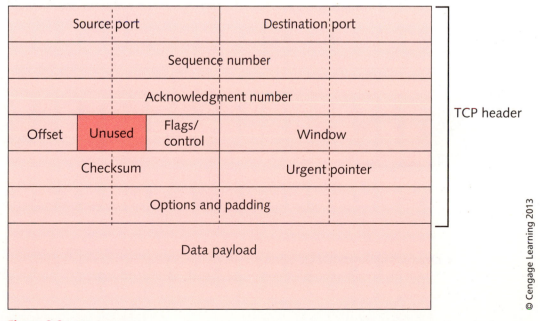

Figure 3-2   TCP frame

© Cengage Learning 2013

The TCP header is a minimum of 20 bytes in length and contains the following fields:

- *Source port*: A **TCP port**, also called a socket or session in other protocols, is similar to a virtual circuit between two communicating processes on two different nodes (as shown in Figure 3-3). The source port is the port on the sending device. TCP ports, also called "well-known ports," are assigned specific tasks for compatibility. For a listing of TCP port assignments, visit *www.iana.org/assignments/port-numbers*. Table 3-3 shows commonly used TCP ports. The implementation of ports in TCP means that more than one process can communicate at a given time during a network session between two connected nodes. For example, one port may communicate about the network status, while another port communicates about e-mail or file transfers.

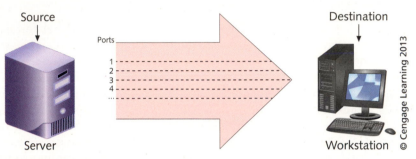

Figure 3-3   TCP source and destination ports

Table 3-3   Sample TCP ports

Port Number	Purpose	Port Number	Purpose
1	Multiplexing	80	HTTP Web browsing
5	RJE applications	93	Device controls
9	Transmission discard	102	Service access point (SAP)
11	Active users	113	Authentication service
20	FTP data	118	SQL database services
21	FTP commands	119	Usenet news transfers
22	Secure Shell (SSH)	139	NetBIOS applications
23	Telnet applications	143	Internet Message Access Protocol (IMAP)
25	SMTP e-mail applications	161	Simple Network Management Protocol
37	Time transactions	443	Transport Layer Security (TLS) or Secure Sockets Layer (SSL)
53	DNS server applications	531	Chat
79	Find active user application	537	Networked Media Streaming Protocol

© Cengage Learning 2013

TCP and UDP ports are often used by computer attackers to break into systems. You can use the knowledge of ports you learn here and in Chapter 11, "Securing Your Network," to foil attackers and protect computers on your network. In Activity 3-1, you learn how to disable a service to essentially close a port for security in Windows 7 and Windows Server 2008/Server 2008 R2. In Activity 3-2 you close a port for security in UNIX/Linux. Also, later in this chapter try Activity 3-10 to learn how to close nonessential ports in Mac OS X.

- *Destination port*: A TCP port on a receiving device (as shown in Figure 3-3) for communication involving an application process, such as a file transfer.

- *Sequence number*: Each frame in a transmission is assigned a 32-bit sequential number, which enables TCP to ensure that all frames are received. The sequence number is also used to identify duplicate frames and to place frames back in the correct order when they arrive through different network routes or channels.

- *Acknowledgment number*: After checking the sequence number, TCP sends back the acknowledgment number, showing that the frame was received. If the acknowledgment number is not sent back, the frame is retransmitted.

- *Offset or header length*: The offset value indicates the length of the header, so that the start of the data portion of the frame can be quickly determined.

- *Flags/control*: Two of the flags in this frame area are used to show the beginning (SYN) and the end (FIN) of the complete data stream. Other flags are for control information, for example, to reset the connection or to show that the urgent pointer field is in effect.

- *Window*: This information works in conjunction with flow control. The window consists of the number of bytes that can be transmitted before the sender receives an acknowledgment of receipt. When the window size is reached, flow control is turned on to stop transmission until acknowledgment is received. For example, if the window size is 64 bytes, then flow control is turned on when 65 bytes have been transmitted without an acknowledgment being returned to the sender. When the network is slow because of heavy traffic, the window size can be increased so that flow control is not turned on needlessly. The window can also be narrowed when the receiving station is slow to respond, for instance, when a workstation is experiencing heavy bus or CPU utilization because of a local application occupying those resources. Sometimes the delay is so long that the allotted window area can no longer hold the entire window size value, resulting in a situation called "long fat network." Although it is typically adjusted automatically by the communicating nodes, the window size can be used by the network administrator for adjusting network performance on slow or fast links to maximize bandwidth. This might be done to minimize retransmissions from misbehaving applications or network congestion, and to correct transmission errors or failures from network-intolerant software applications.

- *Checksum*: The checksum is a 16-bit cyclic redundancy check that is computed by adding the length of all header fields plus the length of the data payload field (the sum of all fields in the TCP segment). The grand total is the CRC checksum, which is placed in the frame by the sending node. The recipient also calculates the checksum and compares its calculation with the value in the checksum field. If they are different, the frame is discarded, and the receiving node requests that the frame be sent again. Added to the front of the checksum value are the source and destination addresses, which are the same as those contained in the IP header of the frame as a check that the frame was sent to the right destination.

- *Urgent pointer*: This header field provides a warning to the receiver that urgent data is coming, and points to the end of the urgent data within the sequence of the transmission of frames. Its purpose is to provide advance information about how much data is still to be received in a connected sequence of one or more frames.

- *Options*: This area in the frame can hold additional information and flags about a transmission.

- *Padding*: The padding area is used when there is too little or no optional data to complete the required header length, which must be divisible by 32.

Note that the actual data carried within the TCP segment is called the data payload, which consists of the raw data transmitted from the sending node to the recipient. In addition, note that TCP and IP ports support full- and half-duplex communications.

Real-Life Networking

A network administrator at a college received a call from a cocky intruder warning that the student registration server would go down in less than half an hour and would be corrupted when brought back up. The network administrator determined that an open TCP port was being used by the intruder and so the administrator shut down the port. Because he understood TCP ports, the administrator was able to immediately stop the attack and keep registration going without a hitch.

TCP acknowledgments can cause significant extra traffic on a network, particularly if the typical sliding window size is relatively small. This is why the User Datagram Protocol is used by some kinds of applications that do not require the level of reliability provided by TCP through sequencing and acknowledgments.

In some Windows 7, Server 2008, or Server 2008 R2 hands-on activities, you may see the User Account Control (UAC) box, which is used for security to help thwart intruders. The UAC box asks for permission to continue with an action or asks for the administrator password. If you see this box, click **Continue**. Because computer setups may be different, the box is not mentioned in the actual activity steps.

Activity 3-1: Closing a TCP Port for Security in Windows 7 and Windows Server 2008/Server 2008 R2

Time Required: Approximately 5 minutes
Objective: Stop the Remote Desktop service in Windows 7 or Windows Server 2008/Server 2008 R2 so that the TCP port for Remote Desktop, which is port 3389, is not available to an attacker.

Description: Windows 7 and Server 2008/Server 2008 R2 offer Remote Assistance so that a person can access and control a remote computer from another location. For example, if you have experienced a computer problem in Windows 7, you can contact a technician who can remotely take over your computer to try and fix the problem. Of course, this also means that a remote attacker can find a way to access your computer (or Windows server) through Remote Assistance. Remote Assistance, depending on the Windows version and how Remote Assistance is employed, uses one or a combination of TCP ports 135 and 3389 and dynamic ports set by the operating system in the range of 49152–65535. Remote Desktop Connection, which is a related remote access service, also uses TCP port 3389. Unless you currently need a technician or computer support person to access your computer remotely or you have a work-related software application that uses Remote Desktop Connection service, then it is a good security measure to close these ports to block possible attacks. You learn how to close access to Remote Assistance and Remote Desktop Connection service in this activity. You need access to an account that has Administrator privileges.

1. Click **Start** and click **Control Panel**.
2. In Windows 7 and Windows Server 2008 R2, set **View by** to **Large icons** or **Small icons**; in Windows Server 2008, use the **Classic View**. Click (in Windows 7/Server 2008 R2) or double-click (in Windows Server 2008) **System**.

3. If necessary, click the **Remote** tab in the System Properties dialog box.

4. In the left side of the System window, click **Remote Settings.**

5. Under the Remote Assistance section, remove the checkmark from the box for **Allow Remote Assistance connections to this computer,** if the box is checked. Note that if your computer or server is not configured for this service, the checkbox will be disabled with no checkmark. Also, under the Remote Desktop section, ensure that the option button is selected for **Don't allow connections to this computer** (see Figure 3-4). Note that for the Home and Home Premium editions of Windows 7, there is no Remote Desktop section with options to select.

6. Click **OK.**

7. Close the System window.

Figure 3-4   Disabling Remote Assistance and Remote Desktop in Windows 7

Activity 3-2: Closing a TCP Port for Security in UNIX/Linux

Time Required: Approximately 5 minutes
Objective: Stop the SSH process in Linux.

Description: Secure Shell (SSH) is a handy tool for accessing one computer from another over a network. Even though it offers some measure of security, when the SSH port is open it is still an invitation to an attacker. SSH is used over TCP port 22. To protect your Linux computer system, plan to ensure that an attacker's access through port 22 is blocked. In this activity, you block access to port 22 using a firewall in Fedora 15 Linux (or higher) with the GNOME 3.x desktop.

1. Log on to your account, such as liveuser.

2. Click **Activities** in the Panel at the top of the desktop.

3. Click **Applications.**

4. Click **Firewall.**

5. Click **Close** if you see an informational note about the Firewall application.

6. Scroll the right pane of the Firewall Configuration window and make a note if any of the services are checked (which means the port is open for use) and note the TCP port used for the service.

7. If there is a check in the box for **SSH**, remove the check (on many Linux systems the box is blank by default; see Figure 3-5).

8. Close the Firewall Configuration window.

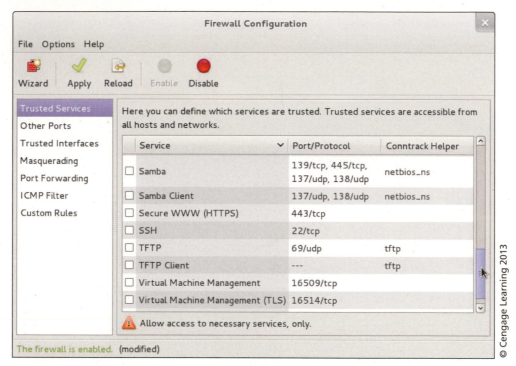

Figure 3-5   Firewall Configuration window in Linux

How the User Datagram Protocol (UDP) Works

When it transmits data, the TCP/IP suite has the option to transmit data in connectionless streams containing virtually no overhead on top of the IP-based datagrams that are sent (as in RFC 1240). The frames are formed, transmitted, and reassembled through a set of algorithms that follow the **User Datagram Protocol (UDP)**, which is used instead of TCP. Like TCP, UDP operates at the Transport layer (Layer 4). Each frame consists of a much simpler header followed by data (see Figure 3-6). UDP is used by network-monitoring applications and by some file transfer applications that do not require the same level of reliability as offered by TCP.

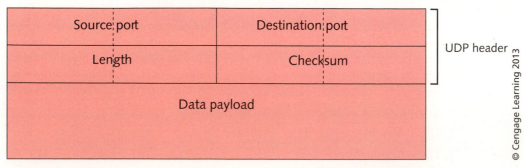

Figure 3-6   UDP frame

The UDP header has the following fields:

- *Source port*: This is a port used for communication about an individual process (at the sender) that is communicating with the same process at the receiver.
- *Destination port*: This is the port at the receiver that is connected to the process with which the sender is communicating. (UDP has nearly the same port assignments as listed in Table 3-3 for TCP.)
- *Length*: The length field contains information about the length of the frame.
- *Checksum*: The checksum is used in the same way as in TCP to compare the received frame with the one that was sent.

UDP does not provide the same level of reliability and error checking as TCP, because it relies only on the checksum to ensure reliability. UDP performs no flow control, sequencing, or acknowledgment. It strictly operates as a connectionless protocol, which enables it to handle and transmit data faster. The advantage of UDP is that it adds little overhead onto IP, and as a way to reduce the network overhead UDP is used with applications that perform transaction processing. Some TCP/IP suite application protocols use UDP as well. For the network administrator, UDP is important in that it carries many of the critical management and network status messages such as RIP, DNS, SNMP, RMON, and BOOTP (discussed later in this chapter).

UDP is used to reduce the overhead of streaming video so there are fewer hesitations. For example, streaming video through Netflix or YouTube uses UDP.

How the Internet Protocol (IP) Works

A LAN may be composed of a series of subnetworks; in contrast a WAN, such as the Internet, may consist of a series of autonomous networks, such as DSL, SONET, frame relay, and MPLS. Internet Protocol (IP) enables a packet to reach different subnetworks on a LAN and different networks on a WAN, as long as those networks use transport options that are compatible with TCP/IP, which include the following:

- Ethernet
- FDDI
- ISDN
- DSL
- Frame relay
- ATM (with conversion)
- MPLS
- SONET

You learn all about these WAN technologies in Chapter 9, "Understanding WAN Connection Choices."

Because IP is employed so universally, it is vital to understand the basic functions of IP and how IP acts as a connectionless protocol.

The Basic Functions of IP

The basic functions of IP are to provide for data transfer, packet addressing, packet routing, fragmentation, and simple detection of packet errors. Successful data transfer and routing to the correct network or subnetwork are made possible by IP addressing conventions. Each network node has a 32-bit address for **IP version 4 (IPv4)** or a 128-bit address for **IP version 6 (IPv6)**. IPv4 is the version of IP most commonly used on networks at this writing, and IPv6 is a newer version that accommodates many more IP addresses and new functions, as you learn in the section, "Using IPv6." When a node's IP address is coupled with the node's 48-bit MAC address, this enables network communications and accurate delivery of a packet.

There is no IPv5. Also, although not designed to be OSI-compliant, IP works at the equivalent of Layer 3, the Network layer, of the OSI reference model, and enables Layer 3 types of routing functionality.

IP as a Connectionless Protocol   IP is a connectionless protocol because its primary mission is to provide network-to-network addressing and routing information and to change the size of packets when the size varies from network to network, such as from Ethernet to FDDI. IP leaves the reliability of communications in the hands of the embedded TCP segment (TCP header and payload data), which is appended after the IP header and which handles flow control, packet sequencing and order verification, and acknowledgment of packet receipt. When the TCP segment is formatted with the additional IP header information, the entire unit is called a datagram or packet, as shown in Figure 3-7.

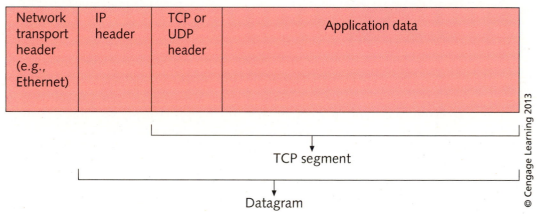

Figure 3-7   TCP/IP packet encapsulation

It is this IP addressing header information that routers check, for example, when determining how to forward an IP packet. The IPv4 packet header consists of the following fields, as shown in Figure 3-8:

- *Version*: This field contains the IP version number, which is 100 (binary 4) for the IPv4 packet header, as shown in Figure 3-8.

- *IP header length (IHL)*: The IP header has a minimum size of 20 bytes, but the size can vary depending on the size of the Options field.

- *Type of service (TOS)*: This field indicates the precedence or priority given to the packet contents. It enables routing protocols, such as Open Shortest Path First (OSPF) and the newer OSPFv2 (for IPv4) and OSPFv3 (for IPv6), to determine the type of path along which to send a packet on the basis of cost (Chapter 5, "Devices for Connecting Networks," discusses routing and OSPF). For example, a regular data packet does not need the same level of throughput as a multimedia packet. TOS recognizes a combination of levels of priority, according to the value and position of the bits within the TOS field: normal, low delay,

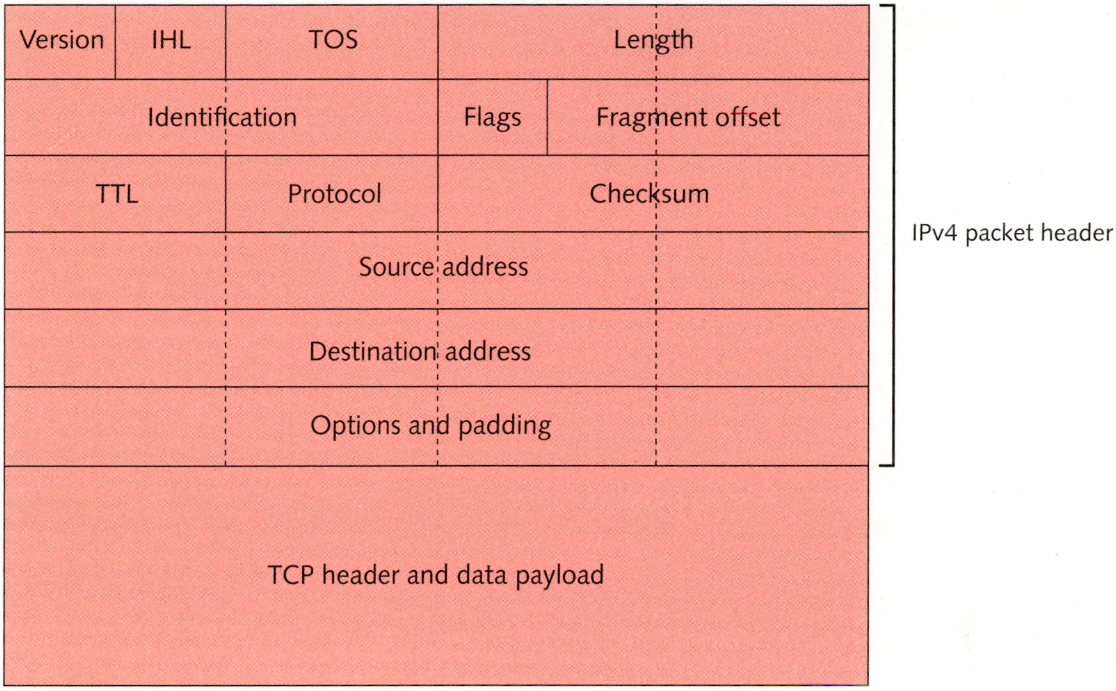

Figure 3-8 IPv4 packet

high throughput, minimum cost, and high reliability. For example, if the normal route is indicated, then a 100 Mbps cable route might be selected, regardless of the number of hops needed to reach the destination. If minimum cost and high throughput are indicated, then a 1000 Mbps cable path with the fewest routers might be used.

- *Length*: The entire IP packet size, which can be up to 65,535 bytes, is provided in this field.

- *Identification*: IP can convert packets from one size to another for dissimilar networks. For example, an Ethernet packet may be 64 to 1526 bytes (counting the preamble) in length, while an FDDI packet can be up to 4472 bytes, and a 16-Mbps token ring packet can be as long as 17,800 bytes. IP is able to transfer packets to different types of networks by fragmenting the packets, perhaps by dividing one FDDI packet into fragments to match the 1526-byte maximum on an Ethernet network. When IP fragments a packet, it assigns a single group number for all of the fragments and places that number in the identification field to ensure that fragments are not reconstructed from the wrong pieces.

- *Flags*: Flags are used with fragmentation to convey information. The information can be that fragmentation is not applicable to the current packet (when it is sent from one Ethernet to another Ethernet network), or it can show when the last fragment in a sequence has been sent (when a packet is fragmented).

- *Fragment offset*: The fragment offset provides information about how to reconnect fragments within a single fragment group.

- *Time to Live (TTL)*: This field contains information that prevents a packet from continuously circulating around a network. The TTL is set as the maximum time (in seconds) to allow a packet to travel. It is checked by each router through which it passes, so that the packet is discarded when TTL equals 0. Each time an IP packet goes through a router, that router reduces the TTL value by a default amount determined by the router or set by a network administrator.

- *Protocol*: This field is used to show which protocol, TCP or UDP, is encapsulated in IP.

Real-Life Networking

When packet size is monitored on a network, improperly sized packets can give you a clue about possible network problems, often related to a sending NIC. For example, an Ethernet packet that is under 64 bytes but that contains all of the normal fields is a called a "runt" and may be the result of a poorly functioning NIC or problems with a NIC driver—or it is a sign there are excessive collisions on a network. An Ethernet packet that is between 1526 to 6000 bytes is known as a "long" packet and may also be caused by a faulty NIC or NIC driver. Long packets are sometimes followed by transmissions of As and 5s that tell other stations that the network is active. This situation, called "jabber," can significantly slow down a network and typically means that the transmitting NIC should be replaced. A packet over 6000 bytes is a "giant" and also may be an indication of a problem at the sending NIC.

- *Checksum*: The checksum is a 16-bit cyclic redundancy check that is the sum of all values contained in every field in the IP header. The IP checksum is calculated in the same way as the TCP checksum, using the Boolean one's complement method; however, the payload data area in the datagram (the TCP segment) is not included in the calculation. The grand total is used to verify that the IP header is received without error. The checksum is examined by each router through which the packet travels, as well as by the receiving node. When the packet is examined by a router, the checksum is updated to reflect changes in values such as TTL.

- *Source address*: This is the network address and the address of the device that sent the packet.

- *Destination address*: This field contains the network address and the address of the receiving device.

- *Options*: There are several options that can be used with IP. For example, the time when the packet is created can be entered, and specialized security can be implemented for military and government implementations.

- *Padding*: Padding fills the options area when there is not enough data to complete the allocated area, because the total size (in bits) of the IP header must be divisible by 32.

The payload data within the IP packet is actually the TCP header and the application data—that is, when connection-oriented services are used. (The IP packet can be the UDP header and application data when connectionless services are used.)

Using IPv4 and IPv4 Addressing

IPv4 addressing is used to identify a specific node and the network on which it resides. For accurate delivery of a packet, it is vital that each IPv4 address be unique. If there are two or more nodes that attempt to access the same network using the same IP addresses, most operating systems display an error message and prevent those nodes from communicating on the network. Understanding IPv4 addressing is important to learning how network communications work.

Basic IPv4 Addressing

The IPv4 address format is called the **dotted decimal notation** address. It is 32 bits long and contains four fields, which are decimal values representing 8-bit binary octets. An IPv4 address in binary octet format looks like this: 10000001.00000101.00001010.01100100. This number converts to 129.5.10.100 in decimal format. Part of the address is the network identifier (network ID), and another part is the host identifier (host ID).

There are five IP address classes, Class A through Class E, and each is used with a different type of network. The address classes reflect the size of the network and whether the packet is unicast or multicast. A **unicast** is a transmission in which one packet is sent from a server to each client that requests a file or an application, as is done with a video presentation, for example. If five clients request the video presentation, the server sends five packets per each transmission to the five clients. In the same example, a **multicast** means that the server is able to treat all five clients as a group and send one packet per transmission that reaches all five clients. Multicasts can be used to significantly reduce network traffic when transmitting multimedia applications. A third type of communication is called a **broadcast**, which sends a communication to all points on a specific network (routers are often configured so that they do not forward broadcasts to other networks).

Many Internet IP addresses for use within classes are assigned by the **Internet Assigned Numbers Authority (IANA)**. Also, blocks of Internet addresses are assigned to other international organizations to dispense on different continents, such as Central and South America, Asia, and Europe. As you can imagine, it is important to have coordination in the assignment of Internet addresses so that duplicate addresses are not used resulting in addressing conflicts. To learn more about IANA addressing assignments, visit *www.iana.org*.

Classes A through C are intended for unicast addressing methods, but each class represents a different network size. Class A is used for the largest networks, composed of up to 16,777,214 nodes. Class A networks are identified by a value between 1 and 126 in the first position of the dotted decimal address. This also means there can be only 126 Class A networks worldwide on the Internet. The network ID is the first 8 bits, and the host ID is the last 24 bits. Table 3-4 lists examples of Class A networks.

Table 3-4   Examples of Class A networks

Network ID	Network ID Owner
3.x.x.x	General Electric (GE)
6.x.x.x	U.S. Army Information Systems
11.x.x.x	U.S. Department of Defense Information Systems
12.x.x.x	AT&T Bell Labs
15.x.x.x	Hewlett–Packard
17.x.x.x	Apple Computer
18.x.x.x	Massachusetts Institute of Technology (MIT)
19.x.x.x	Ford Motor Company
56.x.x.x	U.S. Postal Service

© Cengage Learning 2013

Class B is a unicast addressing format for medium-sized networks composed of up to 65,534 nodes and is identified by the first octet of bits ranging from decimal 128 to 191. The first two octets are the network ID, and the last two are the host ID.

Class C addresses are used for unicast network communications on small networks of 254 nodes or less. The first octet translates to a decimal value in the range of 192 to 223, and the network ID is contained in the first 24 bits, while the host ID is contained in the last 8 bits. Class D addresses do not reflect the network size, but only that the communication is a multicast. The four octets are used to specify the group of nodes designated to receive a multicast, which consists of those nodes that are multicast subscription members. Class D addresses are in the range of 224.0.0.0 to 239.255.255.255. A fifth address type, Class E, is used for experimentation, and addresses range from 240 to 255 in the first octet.

Besides those used for class addressing, there are some special-purpose IP addresses, such as 255.255.255.255, which is a broadcast packet sent to all network locations. Packets that begin with 127 in the first octet are used for network testing. An entire network is referenced by providing only the network ID, with 0s in all other octets, such as 132.155.0.0 for a Class B network or 220.127.110.0 for a Class C network. Table 3-5 summarizes the characteristics of IP address classes.

The address 127.0.0.1 is traditionally called the **loopback address** (for communications that loop back to the computer internally) for IPv4. All other addresses in the 127.0.0.0 to 127.255.255.255 range can be mapped to 127.0.0.1. In IPv6 there is only one loopback address, which is 0:0:0:0:0:0:0:1. When you use tools to look at the IP and MAC addresses of your computer, you may see 127.0.0.1 and 0:0:0:0:0:0:0:1 also listed. Some users worry that the 127.0.0.1 and 0:0:0:0:0:0:0:1 address references for their computers represent an error, but these addresses are assigned intentionally. For more information about this and other IP address designations, including abuses of addresses, visit *www.iana.org/abuse/faq.html*.

Table 3-5   IP address classes

Network Class	Purpose	Beginning Octet	Maximum Addressable Nodes	Number of Octets in Network/Host
A	Large networks	1–126	16,777,214	1/3
B	Medium-sized networks	128–191	65,534	2/2
C	Small networks	192–223	254	3/1
D	Multicast groups	224–239 (224.0.0.0 to 239.255.255.255)	N/A	N/A
E	Experimentation	240–255	N/A	N/A

© Cengage Learning 2013

The Role of the Subnet Mask

TCP/IP addresses require a configured **subnet mask**. A subnet mask is used for two purposes: to show the class of addressing used, and to divide a network into subnetworks to control network traffic. In the first instance, the subnet mask enables an application to determine which part of the address is for the network ID and which is for the host ID. For example, a subnet mask for a Class A network is all binary ones in the first octet and all binary 0s in the remaining octets: 11111111.00000000.00000000.00000000 (255.0.0.0 in decimal). In this instance, the ones represent the network/subnet identification bits and the zeroes represent the host identification bits.

Creating Subnetworks

To divide the network into subnetworks, the subnet mask contains a subnet ID, determined by the network administrator, within the network and host IDs. For example, the entire third octet in a Class B address could be designated to indicate the subnet ID, which would be an octet of 11111111.11111111.11111111.00000000 (255.255.255.0). Another option would be to designate only the first five bits in the third octet as the subnet ID and the last three bits (and last octet as well) for the host ID, which would be 11111111.11111111.11111000.00000000 (255.255.248.0).

Note that using a subnet mask to divide a network into a series of smaller networks enables Layer 3 devices to effectively ignore traditional address class designations, and therefore, it creates more options for segmenting networks through multiple subnets and additional network addresses. This overcomes, or overrides, the four-octet length limitation. A newer way to ignore address class designation is by using **Classless Interdomain Routing (CIDR)** addressing, which puts a slash (/) after the dotted decimal notation.

CIDR provides more IP address options for medium-sized networks, because there is a shortage of Class B and Class C addresses. The shortage is due to the proliferation of networks and the finite number of addresses numerically possible in the basic four-octet address scheme. In CIDR, the fixed network identification designations of 8, 16, and 24 bits for Classes A, B, and C, respectively, are overcome so that unused addresses do not go to waste. This means that if an organization needs 2000 IP addresses on its network, it can use, for example, 11 bits instead of 16 bits for the network ID for a Class B address, thus saving on the number of IP addresses required. Or it could use 11 bits for the network address instead of 8 bits for a Class C address; otherwise several Class C addresses would be needed, which would not be workable.

For instance, consider a Class C network that has only 100 nodes (host identifiers), but is assigned enough addresses for up to 254 nodes. In this case, 154 possible host identifiers go wasted. When using CIDR, the number after the slash is the number of bits in the address that are allocated for the network identifier.

For example, assume a network needs host identifiers for 2048 nodes, which is 2^{11}. To calculate the bits needed for the network identifier, subtract 11 (the bits required for the host identifiers) from 32 (the number of total bits in an IPv4 address). The calculation would be $32 - 11 = 21$, which means that 21 bits are needed for the network identifier and 11 bits for the host identifier—resulting in a subnet mask of 11111111.11111111.11111000.00000000 in binary or 255.255.248.000 in decimal. Also, the IPv4 addresses will end in /21, such as 152.54.28.178/21, which is one address example.

In another example, your network might need enough host identifiers for 16,384 nodes (or 2^{14}). To determine the number of bits needed for the network identifier, you subtract 14 (the bits needed for host identifiers) from 32 (the total number of bits in an IP address): $32 - 14 = 18$. This means that 18 bits are needed for the network identifier and 14 bits are needed for the host identifier (you now have a subnet mask of 11111111.11111111.11000000.00000000, which is 255.255.192.0). An example of an IPv4 address in this second example might be 165.100.18.44/18.

If you use subnet masks to segment network traffic into a series of smaller subnetworks, plan in advance how you will allocate nodes to each segment and how you will assign subnet masks to those segments. Your planning might include network growth projections two to five years away so that you won't have to set up different subnet designations with each future network change. For example, one organization did not plan well and had to change the subnet designations twice; this meant training users to change their own IP addresses, thus creating significant confusion.

There is a handy subnet calculator at *www.subnet-calculator.com* and a CIDR calculator at *www.subnet-calculator.com/cidr.php*. Also, for help with decimal, binary, hexadecimal, and ASCII conversions visit *www .computerhope.com/binhex.htm*.

IPv4 Address Rules

When planning your TCP/IP implementation, you need to consider a few specific addressing rules:

- The network number 127.0.0.0 cannot be assigned to any network. It is used for diagnostic purposes. For example, the address 127.0.0.1 or the loopback address is used for diagnostic testing of the local TCP/IP installation.

- The standard implementation of TCP/IP also reserves a series of addresses known as private addresses. Table 3-6 shows the IP network numbers that have been reserved as private addresses.

Table 3-6   Reserved IP network numbers

Network Number	Subnet Mask	IP Address Range
10.0.0.0	255.0.0.0	10.0.0.1–10.255.255.254
172.16.0.0–172.31.0.0	255.255.0.0	172.16.0.1–172.31.255.254
192.168.0.0	255.255.255.0	192.168.0.1–192.168.255.254

© Cengage Learning 2013

- No one can use these IP addresses on the Internet. They are designed for use on a private network behind a Network Address Translation (NAT) device, such as a firewall or proxy server. If you do have a NAT device, you can use any of these addresses on your own private network.

- You cannot assign a network number to a computer or any other host on the network. For example, your network number might be 198.92.4.0 (subnet mask 255.255.255.0). You cannot assign this number to a computer on the network.

- You also cannot assign the highest number on a network to a computer. In the previous example, you cannot assign 198.92.4.255 to a computer on the network. This address is interpreted as a broadcast message for the subnet, so that all of the computers on the subnet will examine the packet. On the network referred to here, any numbers from 198.92.4.1 to 198.92.1.254 are valid numbers for computers.

In Activity 3-3 you learn where to configure IPv4 communications in Windows 7 and Windows Server 2008/Server 2008 R2. Next, in Activity 3-4 you view IPv4 configuration information in UNIX/Linux. And, in Activity 3-5 you learn where to configure IPv4 and IPv6 in Mac OS X Snow Leopard and Lion.

Activity 3-3: View the IP Address and Subnet Mask Configuration in Windows 7 and Windows Server 2008/ Server 2008 R2

Time Required: Approximately 5 minutes
Objective: View and learn where to configure IPv4 addressing information in Windows 7 and Windows Server 2008/Server 2008 R2.

Description: This activity enables you to view where to set up the IPv4 address and subnet mask in Windows 7 or Windows Server 2008/Server 2008 R2. TCP/IP must be installed before you start. You need an account that has Administrator privileges for this activity.

1. Click **Start** and click **Control Panel**.

2. Set **View by** to **Large icons** or **Small Icons** in Windows 7/Server 2008 R2 or select **Classic View** in Windows Server 2008. Click (in Windows 7/Server 2008 R2) or double-click (in Windows Server 2008) **Network and Sharing Center**.

3. In Windows 7/Server 2008 R2, click **Change adapter settings**. Or in Windows Server 2008, click **Manage Network Connections**.

4. Depending on your type of active network connection (wireless or cabled), right-click **Wireless Network Connection** or **Local Area Connection** in the Network Connections window. Click **Properties**.

5. In the Connection Properties window, double-click **Internet Protocol Version 4 (TCP/IPv4)** in the This connection uses the following items list box. On the General tab, determine which IP addressing option is checked. If Obtain an IP address automatically is checked (see Figure 3-9), this means that your computer obtains its address from a server or device that assigns addresses using the Dynamic Host Configuration Protocol (DHCP, discussed later in this chapter). If Use the following IP address is selected, you can manually specify the IP address and subnet mask. If the IP address is configured manually, determine the IP address and subnet mask for your computer and record your results (see Figure 3-10). (Warning: for this activity only *observe* your address configuration and don't change it as you may create problems with your network connection.)

For a workstation running Windows 7, the automatic configuration selection is often used. For a server running Windows Server 2008 or Server 2008 R2, the IP address is usually manually assigned.

6. Click **Cancel** in the Internet Protocol Version 4 (TCP/IPv4) Properties dialog box.

7. Click **Cancel** in the Connection Properties dialog box.

8. Close the Network Connections window.

9. Close Network and Sharing Center, if it is still open.

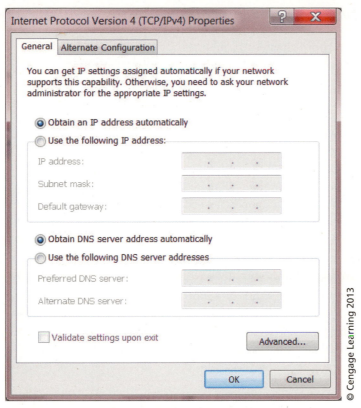

Figure 3-9   IPv4 address configuration in Windows 7 using Obtain an IP address automatically

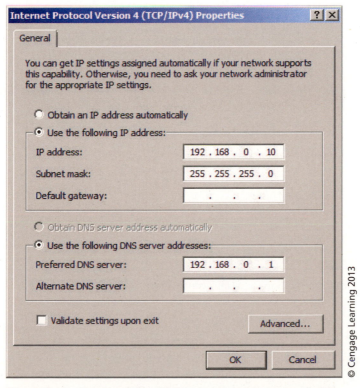

Figure 3-10   IPv4 address configuration in Windows Server 2008 R2 with Use the following IP address

Activity 3-4: View IP Address Information in UNIX/Linux

Time Required: Approximately 10 minutes

Objective: Learn where to view IP configuration information in Linux.

Description: You learned to use the *ifconfig* utility in Activity 1-7 in Chapter 1 to verify a connection to the network. You can also use this utility to determine the IP address and subnet mask assigned to a computer running UNIX or Linux. Further, you can use this utility to manually assign IP address information. In this activity, you use *ifconfig* to determine the IP address of your network connection. You do not need to log into the root account for this activity, but instead can use your own account.

1. Open a terminal window. (In the GNOME 3.x desktop in Fedora Linux 15 and higher, click **Activities** in the left side of the top Panel at the top of the desktop. Click **Applications** on the desktop to view icons of applications that can be opened. Click the **Terminal** icon to open a terminal window.)

2. At the command prompt, type **ifconfig** and press **Enter**. (If *ifconfig* alone does not work, try typing **/sbin/ifconfig** and pressing **Enter**.)

3. In the information for em1, eth0, or wlan0 depending on which is your active connection (em1 or eth0 are for a cabled connection and wlan0 is for a wireless connection), notice the *inetaddr* value, which is the IPv4 address (see Figure 3-11).

4. Next, observe the *Mask* value, which is the subnet mask.

5. Close the terminal window.

```
                              liveuser@localhost:~                              ✕

File  Edit  View  Search  Terminal  Help

[liveuser@localhost ~]$ ifconfig
em1       Link encap:Ethernet  HWaddr 00:18:8B:AF:2D:98
          inet addr:192.168.0.69  Bcast:192.168.0.255  Mask:255.255.255.0
          inet6 addr: fe80::218:8bff:feaf:2d98/64 Scope:Link
          UP BROADCAST RUNNING MULTICAST  MTU:1500  Metric:1
          RX packets:272 errors:0 dropped:0 overruns:0 frame:0
          TX packets:20 errors:0 dropped:0 overruns:0 carrier:0
          collisions:0 txqueuelen:1000
          RX bytes:21120 (20.6 KiB)  TX bytes:4936 (4.8 KiB)
          Interrupt:17

lo        Link encap:Local Loopback
          inet addr:127.0.0.1  Mask:255.0.0.0
          inet6 addr: ::1/128 Scope:Host
          UP LOOPBACK RUNNING  MTU:16436  Metric:1
          RX packets:0 errors:0 dropped:0 overruns:0 frame:0
          TX packets:0 errors:0 dropped:0 overruns:0 carrier:0
          collisions:0 txqueuelen:0
          RX bytes:0 (0.0 b)  TX bytes:0 (0.0 b)

wlan0     Link encap:Ethernet  HWaddr 00:19:D2:4A:07:0B
          UP BROADCAST MULTICAST  MTU:1500  Metric:1
          RX packets:0 errors:0 dropped:0 overruns:0 frame:0
          TX packets:0 errors:0 dropped:0 overruns:0 carrier:0
```

© Cengage Learning 2013

Figure 3-11   IPv4 address information for a Linux connection

You can use the *ifconfig* utility in UNIX/Linux (and in Mac OS X from a terminal window) to configure your NIC or WNIC. For example, if you have one NIC in the computer, you would configure em1 or eth0 as the device. To assign the IPv4 address 172.15.1.19 to em1 or eth0 using the default subnet mask derived from the class of this IPv4 address

(255.255.0.0 for Class B), you would enter *ifconfig em1 172.15.1.19*, for example. If, however, the network is subnetted to make it a Class C network, you could configure the subnet mask for Class C (255.255.255.0) by using the command *ifconfig em1 172.15.1.19 netmask 255.255.255.0*. In Linux, type *man ifconfig* to learn more about using this utility.

Activity 3-5: View the IP Address Configuration in Mac OS X

Time Required: Approximately 10 minutes
Objective: View IP address information in Mac OS X Snow Leopard and Lion.

Description: In Mac OS X Snow Leopard and Lion you can use the Network utility in System Preferences to view the IP address configuration.

1. Click the **System Preferences** icon in the Dock or click the **Apple** icon in the menu bar and click **System Preferences**.

2. In the System Preferences window under Internet & Wireless, click **Network**.

3. In the left pane of the Network window, if necessary click an active network connection (designated by the green dot), such as **AirPort**, **Wi-Fi**, or **Ethernet**.

4. Click the **Advanced** button.

5. Click the **TCP/IP** tab (see Figure 3-12). Record the IPv4 address and subnet mask for the computer. Notice that Mac OS X also can be configured for IPv6, such as to automatically obtain an IPv6 address. (If you change the *Configure IPv6* box to Manually, you can enter a static IPv6 address and prefix length.)

6. Click **Cancel**.

7. Click **System Preferences** in the menu bar and click **Quit System Preferences**.

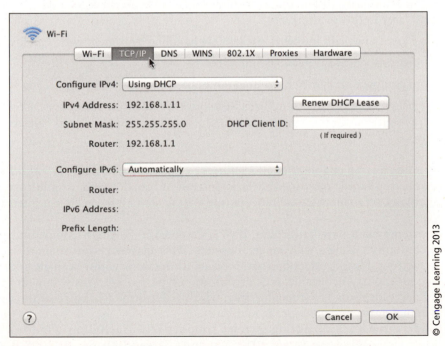

Figure 3-12 Viewing TCP/IP configuration information in Mac OS X Lion

Using IPv6

By the mid-90s, network professionals recognized that IPv4 had some limitations. Chief among the limitations was the 32-bit address, particularly when there were thousands of networks and millions of network users. IPv4 was literally running out of addresses. And in fact, today there is an extreme shortage of IPv4 addresses. IPv4 is also limited because it has no provision for network security or for implementing sophisticated routing options, such as creating subnets based on specific levels of network service and performance. Also, IPv4 does not have many options, other than broadcast and multicast addressing, for handling different kinds of multimedia applications, such as streaming video or video conferencing.

In response to the exploding use of IP, the IP Next Generation (IPng) initiative was started by the Internet Engineering Task Force (IETF). By 1996, IPng resulted in a newly defined standard called IP version 6 (IPv6), defined in RFC 2460. The purpose of IPv6 is to provide a logical growth path from IPv4 so that applications and network devices can handle new demands as they arise.

IPv6 answers a primary concern with IPv4, which is running out of available addresses. IPv6 enables 2^{128} addresses, which is about 3.4×10^{38}—a nearly unimaginable number of addresses (340,282,366,920,938,463,463,374,607,431,768,211,456). This is in contrast to 2^{32} addresses for IPv4, which is about 4,294,967,296 addresses. Currently, IPv4 is used on most networks throughout the world, but the transition to IPv6 is slowly beginning. Some operating system and networking certifications now require knowledge of how to plan for and use IPv6.

Features of IPv6

Among the new features of IPv6 are:

- A 128-bit address capability (16 bytes)

- A single address associated with multiple interfaces

- Address autoconfiguration and CIDR addressing

- A 40-byte header instead of IPv4's 20-byte header

- New IP extension headers that can be implemented for special needs, including more routing and security options

- Use of IP security (IPsec) that is required to enhance network security (you learn about IPsec later in this section)

- The Flow Label field for better packet flow handling by routers using Quality of Service (QoS)

- Simpler automatic address configuration

- More compact and efficient routing tables used by routers through using route aggregation

- Replacement of the use of Address Resolution Protocol by Neighbor Discovery protocol (see the sections in this chapter, "Address Resolution Protocol" and "Neighbor Discovery Protocol")

IPv6 addressing enables one IP identifier to be associated with several different interfaces, so it can better handle multimedia traffic. Instead of broadcasting or multicast grouping, under IPv6, networks transmitting multimedia traffic designate all the recipient interfaces as the same address.

Replacing class-based addresses, IPv6 is designed to be CIDR-compliant, so that addresses can be configured using a wide range of options. This enables better communications for routing and subnetting. Plus, it offers options to create distinctions within a single address for network size, network location, organization, organization type, workgroups within an organization, and so on. IPv6 addressing is autoconfiguring, which reduces the workload of the network administrator in managing and configuring addresses.

Modern network operating systems support IPv6, including Windows 8, Windows 7, Windows Vista, Windows Server 2012, Windows Server 2008/Server 2008 R2, UNIX, Linux, and Apple Mac OS X Leopard, Snow Leopard, and Lion.

 The IPv6 frame structure is not presented here because it is relatively complex and beyond the scope of this book.

IPv6 Addressing

IPv6 uses eight 16-bit fields, each of which can be expressed as a hexadecimal number followed by a colon. The following is an IPv6 address example:

```
1042:0071:0000:0000:07ac:0522:210c:425b
```

One advantage of the IPv6 format is that leading zeros can be removed and contiguous fields containing only zeros can be represented as ::. The example given here can be rewritten as follows:

```
1042:71::7ac:522:210c:425b
```

In another example, the following address:

```
0082:05ad:41f8:0000:0000:0000:0000:36bd
```

can also be represented as:

```
82:5ad:41f8:0:0:0:0:36bd
```

or

```
82:5ad:41f8::36bd
```

The IPv6 addressing rules enable the use of address prefixes. The prefix without a slash shows fixed values in the addressing format, such as fixed values in a range of addresses, and the prefix with a slash shows the network portion of the address or network ID.

The network ID prefix is expressed as the actual prefix numbers followed by a slash and the prefix length. For example, 1042:71::/64 could be the network prefix for the IPv6 address 1042:71::7ac:522:210c:425b. Further, the 1042:71::/64 prefix can represent a subnet on a larger network.

IPv6 Headers

In IPv4 the first portion of the packet or the header that appears prior to the actual data carried in the packet is weighted down by optional information, such as packet fragmenting, authentication, or specialized security information. The IPv4 packet header also contains a checksum. The IPv6 header is streamlined to contain only vital information, such as the packet source and destination addresses. Optional information, such as special security or routing information, is stored in one or more of six types of extension headers, which always are placed after the main header. The use of extension headers enables packets to be processed more efficiently for better network performance. This is because if no optional information is necessary, then the packet is not burdened with reserving empty space for unused information. On the other hand, extension headers enable an IPv6 packet to carry more sophisticated information as needed, such as for security. The packet extension headers are:

- *Hop-by-hop*: Provides better utilization of larger packet sizes, such as jumbograms and multicasts—an IPv6 jumbogram (explained in RFC 2675) can be 4 GB (minus one byte or 4,294,967,295 bytes) whereas the largest data payload in IPv4 (or in IPv6 without this extension header) is 64 KB.

- *Routing*: Used for **source routing**, a routing technique in which the sender of a packet specifies the precise path the packet will take to reach its destination.

- *Fragment*: Houses parameters to enable fragmenting a packet that is too large for the intended path to its destination.

- *Authentication*: Contains information to use in conjunction with IPsec to establish the authenticity of the packet contents.

- *Encapsulating security payload*: Contains information to use in conjunction with IPsec to encrypt data.

- *Destination options*: Used by the receiver of the packet—only two options are defined at this writing, both of which involve padding techniques to accommodate future option storage.

Figure 3-13 illustrates the IPv6 packet and packet header. Compare this figure to Figure 3-8. The important element to remember in the comparison is that using more fields and placing options within the main header, as is done in IPv4, slows network performance. The leaner IPv6 packet header provides a boost to network performance.

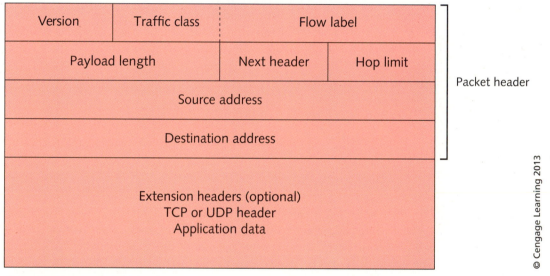

Figure 3-13   IPv6 packet

When using IPv6, the main header must appear in the packet before any extension header. The extension headers are optional and can be used in any combination or not at all. Only one of each type of extension header can be used within a single packet. When one or more extension headers are used, they must follow the order as presented in the previous bulleted list. For example, if the routing header, authentication header, and encapsulating security payload headers are used, the header fields must appear in this order: (1) main IPv6 header, (2) routing extension header, (3) authentication extension header, (4) encapsulating security payload extension header, (5) TCP or UDP header, and (6) application data.

The fields in the IPv6 main header are as follows:

- *Version*: This 4-bit field contains the IP version number, which is IPv6 for the packet header shown in Figure 3-13. For IPv6, the value in the field is 0110 or binary for 6.

- *Traffic class*: This 8-bit field contains two components. The first six bits represent information for Differentiated Services (DiffServ) that is used to classify (prioritize) network traffic and provide information used by Quality of Service to manage traffic. (See the "Quality of Service" section below.) The last two bits are used for Explicit Congestion Notification (ECN), which is used for notification of traffic congestion and alerts both sender and receiver that packets should not be dropped (as long as the network and network nodes support ECN) during traffic congestion.

On networks that do not support ECN, the default is to drop packets as a way to indicate traffic congestion to sending nodes. A network administrator can also monitor network congestion by monitoring dropped packet statistics.

- *Flow label*: This 20-bit field is used for packet flow management for QoS.

- *Payload length*: This 16-bit field provides the payload size plus the size of any extension headers. However, if the field is set to zero, this indicates a jumbogram. A jumbo payload in a jumbogram can be up to nearly 4 GB.

- *Next header*: When extension headers are present, this 8-bit field identifies the first extension header. If no extension headers are used, the next header field denotes the Transport layer protocol (for example, TCP or UDP) in use.

- *Hop limit*: This 8-bit field shows the number of routers through which the packet has passed, which prevents a packet from continuously circulating around a network. The hop limit is set by the sending node and is decremented by 1 each time the packet is forwarded by a router. If a router determines the hop limit field should be decremented to 0, the router discards the packet so that the packet does not continue circulating.

- *Source address*: This 128-bit field is the network address (network ID) plus the address of the device that sent the packet.

- *Destination address*: This 128-bit field contains the network address plus the address of the target device that is to receive the packet.

IP Security

IP security (IPsec) enables IP communications to be secured through authentication certificates and by encrypting data. IPsec is a set of IP-based secure communications and encryption standards created through the IETF (Internet Engineering Task Force). When IPsec communication begins between two computers, the computers first exchange certificates to authenticate the receiver and the sender. Next, data is encrypted at the NIC of the sending computer as it is formatted into an IP packet. IPsec policies can be configured in server operating systems, such as Windows Server 2008/Server 2008 R2.

With IPv4 the use of IPsec is optional, but in IPv6 using IPsec is mandatory. The mandatory use of IPsec is important to assure the security of a network.

Quality of Service and IPv6

As shown in Figure 3-13, the IPv6 header contains the flow label field whereas the IPv4 header (see Figure 3-8) does not. The flow label field enables packet flow management for **Quality of Service (QoS)** at network routers. QoS is a measurement specification of the transmission quality, throughput, and reliability of a network system. For time-sensitive traffic, such as voice and video, QoS refers to providing an assured level of throughput and resources. On network systems equipped for QoS, there are two important advantages:

- Ensuring that network resources are assigned for successful transmission of a specific application

- Ensuring that network resources are not underutilitized

Some device vendors and telecommunications companies offer a guaranteed QoS for their systems.

IPv6 and Routing Tables

As you learn in Chapter 5, "Devices for Connecting Networks," routers maintain information about host addresses and network status in databases called routing tables. Routing table databases contain the addresses of other routers. Routers that are configured for dynamic routing automatically update the routing tables by regularly exchanging address information with other routers. Routers also regularly exchange information about network traffic, the network topology, and the status of the network links. This information is kept in the network status database in each router.

IPv6 enables routers to use global addresses on the Internet, which enhances the use of route aggregation, and makes network communications more efficient by cutting down on the number of routes that need to be advertised by routers. **Route aggregation** is a technique for organizing network routes hierarchically. It also enables routes to be summarized, resulting in smaller router tables and reduced route advertising, both of which mean less network traffic from routers. Consider an Internet Service Provider (ISP) that sets up many subnets containing hosts that use contiguous IPv6 addresses within its larger network. Route aggregation enables the ISP to advertise over the Internet only one route to its main network instead of advertising routes for each subnet.

Types of IPv6 Packets

An IPv6 packet is one of three types: unicast, anycast, or multicast. A unicast packet is identified by its single address for a single interface (NIC) and is transmitted point-to-point. An **anycast** packet contains a destination address that is associated with multiple interfaces, usually on different nodes. The anycast packet goes only to the closest interface and does not attempt to reach the other interfaces with the same address. A multicast packet, like an anycast packet, has a destination address that is associated with multiple interfaces, but unlike the anycast packet, it is directed to each of the interfaces with that address.

Encryption and the IPv6 Packet

Considering today's concern about network attackers, the IP packet payload, or the TCP/UDP header and payload, can be encrypted for security. IPv6 supports encryption techniques that are compatible with **Data Encryption Standard (DES)** security. DES is a network symmetric-key encryption standard developed by the National Institute of Standards and Technology (NIST) and ANSI. The IPv6 encryption capability enables security over the Internet as well as over other types of LANs and WANs.

The downside to using IPv6 encryption is that it can increase the latency of network communications. **Latency** is the time it takes for networked information to travel from the transmitting device to the receiving device.

Activities 3-6 and 3-7 enable you to work with IPv6 in Windows 7/Server 2008/Server 2008 R2 and Linux (you already learned where to configure IPv6 in Mac OS X in Activity 3-5).

Activity 3-6: IPv6 in Windows

Time Required: Approximately 10 minutes
Objective: Learn where to configure IPv6 for use in Windows 7 or Windows Server 2008/Server 2008 R2.

Description: In Activity 3-3 you learned where to configure IPv4 in Windows 7 and Windows Server 2008/Server 2008 R2. In this activity, you learn where to configure IPv6 in these operating systems. You can have both IPv4 and IPv6 configured for use at the same time, in the event you communicate with networks that use IPv6 as well as networks using IPv4.

1. Click **Start** and click **Control Panel**.

2. Set **View by** to **Large icons** or **Small icons** in Windows 7/Server 2008 R2 or select **Classic View** in Windows Server 2008. Click (in Windows 7/Server 2008 R2) or double-click (in Windows Server 2008) **Network and Sharing Center**.

3. In Windows 7/Server 2008 R2, click **Change adapter settings**. In Windows Server 2008, click **Manage Network Connections**.

4. In the Network Connections window, right-click **Wireless Network Connection** or **Local Area Connection**, depending on which connection is active on your computer. Click **Properties**.

5. Double-click **Internet Protocol Version 6 (TCP/IPv6)**. Notice that as is true for an IPv4 configuration, you can also choose to Obtain an IPv6 address automatically or you can manually configure an IPv6 address by selecting Use the following IPv6 address (see Figure 3-14). Also, when an IPv6 address is configured manually you provide the subnet prefix length, which, like the subnet mask used for IPv4, provides information about subnetting. The subnet prefix length is an integer between 1 and 128 and shows the subnet range of IP addresses. For example, if the subnet prefix length is 32, this means that the first 32 bits in the IPv6 address refers to the subnet identification and the last 96 bits refers to the range of host IDs. Using 32 as the subnet prefix example and the subnet identified as 2011:bc7a:xxxx: xxxx:xxxx:xxxx:xxxx:xxxx (where 2011:bc7a is the subnet prefix), the possible addresses are in the range 2011:bc7a:0000:0000:0000:0000:0000:0000 to 2011:bc7a:ffff:ffff:ffff:ffff: ffff:ffff. Besides the subnet prefix, notice also that you can provide the default gateway.

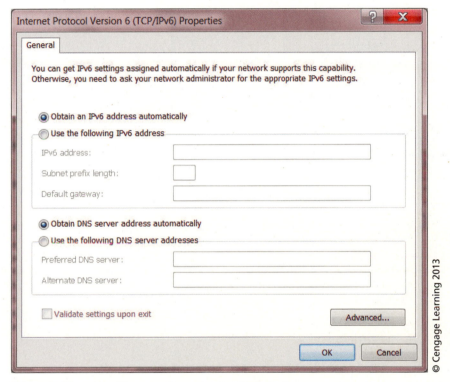

Figure 3-14 IPv6 address configuration in Windows 7

6. Click **Cancel** in the Internet Protocol Version 6 (TCP/IPv6) Properties dialog box.

7. Click **Cancel** in the Connection Properties dialog box.

8. Close the Network Connections window and close Network and Sharing Center, if it is still open.

Activity 3-7: IPv6 in Linux

Time Required: Approximately 10 minutes
Objective: Learn where to configure IPv6 for use in Linux.

Description: Besides the *ifconfig* utility you used in Activity 3-4, Fedora 15 Linux (and higher) and other Linux distributions with the GNOME 3.x desktop offer the Network Connection application for configuring a wired or wireless connection. In this activity you use the Network Connection application to explore configuration options for IPv6.

1. From the desktop, click **Activities** in the top Panel.

2. Click **Applications**.

3. Click **Network Connections** in the display of applications.

4. Click the **Wired** or **Wireless** tab, depending on the type of network you are using.

5. Click your connection as listed under Name and then click the **Edit** button. (If you do not have a working connection, you can instead click the **Add** button and follow the next steps.)

6. Click the **IPv6 Settings** tab.

7. Click the down arrow for the **Method** box. Record the selections that are available.

8. Select **Manual**. Notice that the Addresses area is now activated. Click the **Add** button (see Figure 3-15). You can now choose to assign an IPv6 address, prefix, and gateway address.

9. Click **Cancel** in the Editing dialog box.

10. Click **Close** in the Network Connections window.

Figure 3-15   Configuring IPv6 in the Network Connections application in Linux

TCP/IP Application Protocols

TCP/IP is designed to work with a diverse range of application protocols for e-mail, terminal emulation, file transfers, routing, network management, and other services that collectively are called the TCP/IP suite. The following is a sampling of useful protocols and application services in the TCP/IP suite:

- Telnet
- Secure Shell (SSH)
- File Transfer Protocol (FTP), Trivial File Transfer Protocol (TFTP), and Network File System (NFS)
- Simple Mail Transfer Protocol (SMTP)
- Domain Name System (DNS)
- Dynamic Host Configuration Protocol (DHCP)
- Address Resolution Protocol (ARP)

- Neighbor Discovery (ND) protocol

- Simple Network Management Protocol (SNMP)

- Hypertext Transfer Protocol (HTTP), Secure Hypertext Transfer Protocol (S-HTTP), and Hypertext Transfer Protocol Secure (HTTPS)

- Internet Control Message Protocol (ICMP)

Each of these protocols and applications is discussed in the next sections.

Telnet

Telnet is an application protocol within TCP/IP that provides support for terminal emulation. A terminal is a device that consists of a monitor and keyboard. It is used to communicate with host computers (usually mainframes or servers running terminal services) that run the programs. Programs run on the host because a terminal typically does not have its own processor.

Some examples of legacy terminals include the IBM 3270 terminal or the DEC VT220 terminal. More modern devices that function as terminals are sometimes referred to as thin clients, such as the Wyse C10LE Thin Client or the HP Thin Client t5740e, which primarily consist of a monitor, processor, and RAM with no moving parts.

Terminal emulation involves using software to make a computer, such as a regular PC, behave as though it were a terminal. Today, you can obtain software that emulates IBM 3270 or DEC VT220 terminals and that runs in Windows or Linux.

Telnet enables a user to connect to a host computer so that the host responds as though it were connected to a terminal. For example, Telnet with a 3270 emulator can connect to an IBM mainframe like a terminal. Telnet runs in the TCP/IP layer that is equivalent to the OSI Session layer, but it initiates operation in the Transport layer.

Windows Server 2008 and Server 2008 R2 can be configured as a terminal server (in Server 2008) or a remote desktop services server (in Server 2008 R2) so that programs run on the server, but in this case, Telnet is not used for terminal emulation. Regular terminals can access the terminal server, and PC workstations can be configured with proprietary software to emulate terminals. A terminal server is used, for example, when it is important that software and data files remain in a secure location so that they cannot be downloaded to a PC.

Telnet travels via TCP and has two important features not found in other emulators: it comes with nearly all vendor implementations of TCP/IP, and it is an open standard, meaning that any vendor or developer can easily implement it. Some implementations of Telnet require that the host be configured as a Telnet server. Telnet is supported by a wide range of workstations that run UNIX, Linux, Mac OS X, and any version of Microsoft Windows.

Telnet communications consist of a header and application data that are encapsulated within the TCP data portion of the TCP segment. Also, Telnet uses TCP port 23 at the sender and receiver for dedicated communications.

Telnet includes communications options such as:

- Seven- or eight-bit compatibility

- Use of different terminal modes

- Character echoing at the sending and receiving ends

- Synchronized communications

- Transmission of character streams or single characters

- Flow control

Telnet offers one way for a computer to access another computer over the network or over the Internet. For example, an IBM programmer can use Telnet on a Windows 7 or Linux computer to access a mainframe through the Internet. Some IBM mainframe consultants rely on Telnet so that they do not have to travel to work on a mainframe that may be hundreds or thousands of miles away. Another application is to use a Windows 7 workstation to access files on a UNIX computer or vice versa by using Telnet.

Windows Server 2008/Server 2008 R2 can be configured to operate as a Telnet server, so that information on it can be accessed from any computer using Telnet.

When you use Telnet, ensure that you configure it with a password for better security.

SSH

Secure Shell (SSH) is used on many UNIX/Linux systems, such as Fedora and Red Hat Enterprise Linux, and in Mac OS X to provide authentication security for TCP/IP applications such as Telnet and FTP. If you need to remotely access a computer or upload and download files, use SSH if it is available. You can start this application by entering *ssh* at the UNIX/Linux command line. In Linux and Mac OS X, use the *man ssh* command to learn more about how it is implemented in your particular system.

FTP, TFTP, and NFS

TCP/IP supports three file transfer protocols: **File Transfer Protocol (FTP)**, **Trivial File Transfer Protocol (TFTP)**, and **Network File System (NFS) protocol**. FTP is the most widely used because it is the file transfer option preferred by Internet users. Using FTP, a user in Vermont can log on to a host computer in California and download one or more data files. (The user first must have an authorized user ID and password on the host.) If you are an Internet user, you may have used FTP to download a file such as a NIC driver or an Internet browser upgrade.

FTP is an application that enables the transfer of data from one remote device to another, using TCP. As in Telnet, an FTP header and accompanying data payload are encapsulated within the TCP data payload area. An advantage of FTP over TFTP and NFS is that it uses two TCP ports, 20 and 21. Port 21 is a control port for FTP commands that control how data is sent. For example, the *get* command is used to obtain a file from a host, and the *put* command is used to send a file to a host. FTP supports the transmission of binary or ASCII-formatted files through the commands *binary* and *ascii*. Port 20 is used exclusively for the exchange of data as determined by the FTP commands. Table 3-7 lists sample FTP commands.

Table 3-7   Sample FTP commands

Command	Description
ascii	Transfer files in ASCII format
binary	Transfer files in binary format
bye or *quit*	End the file transfer session and exit the FTP mode
close	End the file transfer session
delete	Remove a file from another computer
dir or *ls*	List the contents of the directory on another computer
get	Obtain a file from another computer
help	Display a description of a particular FTP command
put	Send a file to another computer
pwd	Display the directory on another computer
send	Transmit a file to another computer

FTP supports file transfers for ASCII so that you can transfer plain text files that have no special characters. Binary file transfers are used for files, such as word-processed and spreadsheet files, that have special or control characters.

FTP is designed to transfer entire files only in bulk, which makes it well suited for exchanging even large files over a WAN. It cannot transfer a portion of a file or records within a file. Because they are encapsulated within TCP, FTP data transmissions are reliable and ensured by connection-oriented services, which include sending an acknowledgment when a packet is received. The FTP transmission is composed of a single stream of data concluded by an end-of-file delimiter.

Web browsers, such as Internet Explorer, Safari, and Firefox, provide an easy way to use FTP by connecting to a site and then using the regular browser features, such as drag and drop. In Activity 3-8 you learn how to download a file using FTP in a Web browser.

Activity 3-8: Using FTP via a Web Browser

Time Required: Approximately 10 minutes
Objective: Download a file using FTP in Windows 7 and Internet Explorer, by using Firefox in Linux or by using Safari in Mac OS X.

Description: FTP is easy to use through most Web browsers. In this activity, you learn how to access FTP services through Internet Explorer, Firefox, or Safari.

1. Open the Internet browser on your computer, such as Internet Explorer, Firefox, or Safari, to access the Internet.

2. In the address line, type **ftp://ftp.gnu.org** and press **Enter** (to access the gnu FTP site from which you can download software and utilities for UNIX/Linux systems). In Safari, if you are asked for an account, select to use the **Guest** account and click **Connect**.

3. Notice the folders and files that you can access (see Figure 3-16).

4. Double-click the link for the **gnu** directory or folder.

5. Notice that there are more links containing utilities that can be downloaded and also links pointing to directories that can be opened to more utilities for downloading.

6. Scroll to view more of the gnu directory's contents. You will see many read me files that explain what can be downloaded.

7. If you are using an earlier version of Internet Explorer, click **Page** in the top portion of the Internet Explorer window. If you are using Internet Explorer 9 or later, press **Alt** and click **View** at the top of the window. Click **Open FTP Site in Windows Explorer**. If you see an Internet Security window, click **Allow**. The gnu window that opens contains folders that you can open or drag to a folder on your computer.

8. In your Web browser, double-click a directory and you will see files that can be selected and dragged to a folder on your computer.

9. Close all of your open windows.

If you cannot access FTP using your Web browser and you have a firewall configured, check the firewall settings to enable FTP. If you have trouble accessing an FTP Web site in your version of Firefox, consider installing FireFTP, which is an FTP client for Firefox.

TFTP is a TCP/IP file transfer protocol that is designed for tasks such as the transfer of data to enable a diskless workstation to boot using files transmitted from a server. TFTP is connectionless and is intended for the transfer of small files in situations in which data transmission

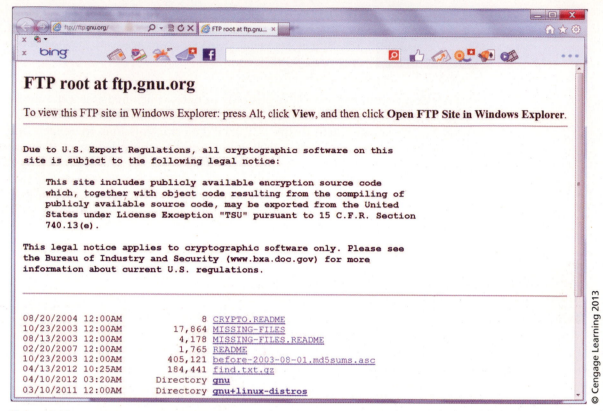

Figure 3-16   Using FTP in Internet Explorer

errors are not critical and there is no need for security. TFTP is connectionless because it runs within UDP (via UDP port 69) instead of within TCP. This means that there are no packet acknowledgments or other connection-oriented services to ensure that a packet successfully arrives at the intended destination.

A popular alternative to FTP is the NFS software originated through Sun Microsystems, which uses a remote procedure call specification via TCP port 111. NFS is installed at the sending and receiving nodes, as is the remote procedure call software, so that one computer's NFS software can run the NFS software on the other computer. NFS, which is frequently used on UNIX/Linux systems, sends data in record streams instead of bulk file streams. Like FTP, NFS is a connection-oriented protocol that runs within TCP. It is particularly suited to computers that perform high-volume transaction processing involving records stored within data files or databases. It is also suitable for situations in which data files are distributed among several servers.

Simple Mail Transfer Protocol (SMTP)

Simple Mail Transfer Protocol (SMTP) is designed for the exchange of e-mail between networked systems, such as between mail servers over a TCP/IP network. UNIX/Linux, Windows-based, Mac OS X, and OpenMVS systems can exchange e-mail over TCP/IP through SMTP. SMTP is also implemented in local e-mail systems so that e-mail can be transported over the Internet.

SMTP provides an alternative to FTP for sending a file from one computer system to another. SMTP does not require use of a logon ID and password for the remote system. All that is needed is an e-mail address on the receiving end.

E-mail messages sent through SMTP have two parts: an address header and the message text. The address header can be very long, because it contains the address of every SMTP node through which it has traveled and a date stamp for every transfer point. If the receiving node is unavailable, SMTP can wait for a period of time and try to send the message again, and then finally bounce the mail back to the sender if the receiving node does not become active within a specified period.

SMTP follows TCP/IP standards, but is not intended to be compliant with the X.400 protocol for e-mail systems. **X.400** refers to a set of standards for global message handling for e-mail. SMTP is sent within TCP, which provides a basic connection-oriented reliability for e-mail. Deployment of SMTP requires an SMTP-compatible e-mail application at the sending and receiving nodes. SMTP applications designate a server as a central mail gateway for connecting workstations and process e-mail distribution through a queue in a file directory or print spooler. The queue serves as a "post office," or domain, for users that connect to that server. Users can log on to the server to obtain their messages, or the server can forward messages to its clients.

Domain Name System (DNS)

Networked computers are often organized into domains. A **domain** is a logical grouping of network resources such as computers, printers, and network devices. A domain is given a name, such as microsoft.com for Microsoft. In addition, computers within a domain are given a unique name, which often parallels the name of a user, such as Sinclair, or is a favorite name, such as antelope or popcorn.

On a TCP/IP network that uses domain naming, each computer is associated with a domain name and an IP address. People who use the network typically use a domain-naming scheme to refer to a specific computer, because a name is easier to remember than an IP address. Note, however, that a TCP/IP network uses an IP address rather than a computer name. Therefore, when a user wants to access a specific computer by name, there must be a way for the network to translate the computer name to an IP address.

The **Domain Name System (DNS)** is a TCP/IP service that converts a computer or domain name to an IP address or that converts an IP address to a computer or domain name. This process is called "resolution." A name is easier for a user to remember than a dotted decimal IP address, but because computers still need the IP address, there must be a way to convert one to the other. DNS uses lookup tables that correlate one value to the other.

Older Windows Server networks may use NetBIOS computer names and applications. For these networks, Windows Internet Naming Service (WINS) is implemented along with a DNS server to resolve IP addresses and NetBIOS computer names.

The computer name is in two parts, similar to the IP network and host IDs. One part is the name of the computer or node, and the other part is the name of the organization, which is the root domain name. The two parts are divided by an "at" (@) character, as in myname@myorganization. The root domain portion of the name is often divided into subparts separated by periods (.) to reflect the name of the organization, the type of organization, and the country in which the organization is located. An example is uwyo.edu for the University of Wyoming (uwyo), which is an educational organization (edu).

The organization part of the name is called a domain name, to show that all individual names associated with that organization are in the same domain of computers. Sometimes large organizations are divided into multiple domains. A large university, for example, might have a student domain (student.uwyo.edu) and a faculty/staff domain (fs.uwyo.edu). Internet host domain names comprise two to three parts: a top-level domain (TLD) (such as country or organization type), an optional subdomain name (such as a university or business name), and a host name (such as the name of a host computer). The **International Corporation for Assigned Names and Numbers (ICANN)** coordinates and registers root domain names and helps to establish policies governing domain registration.

To learn more about ICANN visit *www.icann.org.*

Table 3-8 shows Internet TLD domain naming conventions for many types of organizations, and Table 3-9 shows TLD domain naming conventions for a representative set of countries.

Table 3-8   TLDs for organizations

Type of Organization	Domain Naming Convention
Air transportation	aero
Small to large businesses including partnerships, proprietorships, and corporations	biz
General commercial	com
Business cooperatives (owned by the people who use them)	coop
Educational	edu
Government	gov
Domain name registration organizations	info
International treaty organizations	int
Museums	museum
Domains for individual or personal use	name
Network provider	net
Nonprofit	org
Professionals such as physicians, accountants, and lawyers	pro

© Cengage Learning 2013

Table 3-9   Country names for domains

Country	Domain Naming Convention
Australia	au
Canada	ca
Chile	cl
Finland	fi
France	fr
Hungary	hu
Italy	it
Japan	jp
Jordan	jo
Mozambique	mz
Nigeria	ng
Poland	pl
Qatar	qa
Western Samoa	ws
Sweden	se
United Arab Emirates	ae
United Kingdom	uk
United States	us

© Cengage Learning 2013

The DNS Resolvers and Namespaces   DNS works through a domain name resolver at the client and a domain name server at one or more hosts. DNS servers maintain the **namespace** for an enterprise and provide a way to resolve computer and domain names to IP addresses and IP addresses to computer and domain names. A namespace is a logical area on a network that contains a listing of named objects, such as computers, and that has the ability to perform name resolution.

The Use of Zones   DNS servers maintain tables of information that link computer/domain names and IP addresses. The tables are associated with partitions in a DNS server that are called **zones** and that contain resource records. Each zone houses tables, called the zone file or zone database, of different types of resource records, such as records that link domain servers to the services they provide. Other types of resource records link a computer name to an IP address.

The zone that links computer names to IP addresses is called the **forward lookup zone**; it holds host name records, which are called address records. Each IP-based server and client should have a host record so that it can be found through DNS. For example, if the DNS server name is NetAdmin with the IPv4 address 129.70.10.1, then the forward lookup zone maps NetAdmin to 129.70.10.1. In IPv4, a host record is called a **host address (A) resource record**. An IPv6 record is called an **IPv6 host address (AAAA) resource record**.

When you install a directory service, such as Microsoft Active Directory, you must have at least one DNS server on the network, because the directory service is part of the namespace that is used to coordinate information about objects on a network, such as computers, printers, and shared resources. The directory service relies on interacting with the DNS server to coordinate information about network objects. A directory service is a large container of network data and resources, such as computers, printers, user accounts, and user groups that (1) provides a central listing of resources and ways to quickly find specific resources and (2) provides a way to access and manage network resources.

Another zone, called the **reverse lookup zone**, holds the **pointer (PTR) resource record**, which contains the IP-address-to-host name records. The reverse lookup zone is not used as commonly as the forward lookup zone, but can be important to create for those instances when a network communication requires associating an IP address to a computer name, such as for monitoring a network using IP address information.

Roles of DNS Servers   A DNS server on a network typically plays one of two roles: a primary DNS server or a secondary DNS server. A **primary DNS server** is the DNS server that is the main administrative server for a zone and thus is also called the authoritative server for that zone. For example, when you first create a forward lookup zone on a DNS server for the mybusiness.com domain, you create a **start of authority (SOA) resource record** that identifies that DNS server as authoritative for mybusiness.com. This means that all changes to the zone, such as the creation of host address (A) resource records, must be made on that DNS server.

On medium and large networks, it is common to create one or more backup DNS servers, called **secondary DNS servers**, for each primary DNS server. A secondary DNS server contains a copy of the primary DNS server's zone database, but is not used for administration. It obtains that copy through a zone transfer over the network. A zone transfer involves transmitting the contents of a zone housed on a primary DNS server to a secondary DNS server.

There are three vital services performed by secondary DNS servers. One is to make sure that there is a copy of the primary DNS server's data, in case the primary server fails. Another function is to enable DNS load balancing (via the load sharing resource records) among a primary DNS server and its secondary servers. Load balancing means that if the primary DNS server is busy performing a name resolution, a different request for a name resolution that is received at the same time can be fielded by a secondary DNS server for faster response to users. A third advantage to using secondary DNS servers is that they can be spread to different parts of a network, such as to different sites or geographic locations, so that you can reduce the congestion in one part of the network.

For disaster recovery in medium-sized and large organizations, it is a good idea to create at least one secondary DNS server in a location that is different from the one containing the primary DNS server.

On a larger scale than primary and secondary DNS servers, there are also root servers. **Root servers** are on the Internet and are used to find TLDs, for example, .com or .net. There are 13 root servers throughout the world that act as final authorities for finding a TLD.

DNS Standards   Servers that are authoritative on the network typically support two DNS standards: service resource records and the DNS dynamic update protocol. Outlined in RFC 2052, a **service resource record (SRV RR)** is a type of DNS record that enables DNS to recognize multiple servers and to locate commonly used TCP/IP services that are associated with specific servers. An SRV RR allows a DNS server to generate a list of network servers that provide TCP/IP services. It also gives the protocols supported by those servers and determines a preferred server for a specific service. The SRV record is formatted to include information about the service that is provided by a server, the domain that is serviced by the server, and the protocol used by the server.

The **DNS dynamic update protocol** is outlined in RFC 2136 and enables information in a DNS server to be automatically updated. An example of this is a Windows 7 workstation updating its DHCP-leased IP address. The DNS dynamic update protocol can save network administrators a great deal of time, because they no longer have to manually register each new workstation or to register a workstation each time its IP lease is up and a new IP address is issued.

Dynamic Host Configuration Protocol (DHCP)

The **Dynamic Host Configuration Protocol (DHCP)** is used to enable IP addresses to be assigned automatically by a DHCP server on a network (refer to Activities 3-3 and 3-5). When a new computer is configured to use DHCP and then attached to the network, it contacts the DHCP server. The DHCP server leases an IP address to that new computer via DHCP. The length of a lease is set on the DHCP server by a network administrator. For example, a lease given to a desktop computer might be from several days to several weeks, because the computer is permanently attached to the network. The lease given to a laptop might be several hours to a day because the laptop is frequently moved off of the network or to a different network location. Finally, a server or host computer may be given a lease that does not expire so that its IP address never changes.

To reduce the amount of network administration, choose DNS and DHCP services and servers that are compatible and that support the DNS dynamic update protocol. This helps to ensure that the DHCP server or DHCP clients can automatically update DNS zone information so that the administrator doesn't have to do so.

To accommodate IPv6, DHCPv6 is available for installation on modern server operating systems, such as Windows Server 2008 and Server 2008 R2. Network administrators can combine DHCP (for IPv4) and DHCPv6 to integrate both kinds of communications on a network.

IPv6 uses either stateful or stateless autoconfiguration. **Stateful autoconfiguration** means that a host's IPv6 address is obtained through DHCPv6 and a DHCPv6 server, such as Windows Server 2008 R2 configured in the role of a DHCPv6 server. In **stateless autoconfiguration**, the network host assigns its own IP address without obtaining it from a DHCPv6 server.

Address Resolution Protocol (ARP)

In most instances, the sender needs both the IP and MAC addresses to send a packet to its destination. Multicast transmissions, for example, include both IP and MAC addresses. IP and MAC addresses are never the same and are in different formats, dotted decimal and hexadecimal, respectively.

The **Address Resolution Protocol (ARP)** enables the sending node to obtain the MAC addresses of the intended recipient before packets are sent. When the sending node needs to obtain a MAC address, it sends an ARP broadcast frame containing both its own MAC address and the IP address of the designated receiving node. The receiving node sends back an ARP reply containing its MAC address.

A complementary protocol is **Reverse Address Resolution Protocol (RARP)**, which is used by a network node to determine its own IP address. RARP is used, for example, by diskless workstations that cannot determine their own addresses except by obtaining them through an RARP query to their host server. Also, RARP is used by some applications to determine the IP address of the workstation or server on which they are running.

Neighbor Discovery (ND) Protocol

Neighbor Discovery (ND) protocol uses messages and other means to discover the physical addresses and much more about computers and routers on a network. ND protocol enables a more extensive range of information to be determined beyond the capabilities of ARP. This includes physical addresses, configuration information, and the address prefixes of other hosts. Also, ND protocol can determine the location of nearby routers and whether a computer or router can be currently reached. ND protocol additionally provides information about whether a physical address has been changed, such as when a network interface is replaced. IPv6 replaces the use of ARP with the use of ND protocol for a more effective discovery process.

Simple Network Management Protocol (SNMP)

The **Simple Network Management Protocol (SNMP)** enables network managers to continuously monitor network activity. SNMP was developed in the 1980s to provide the TCP/IP suite with an alternative to the OSI standard for network management, **Common Management Interface Protocol (CMIP)**.

Although it was created for the TCP/IP suite, SNMP nonetheless follows the OSI reference model. Most vendors have chosen to implement SNMP instead of CMIP because TCP/IP is widely used and because SNMP is easier to use. Several hundred networking devices support SNMP, including servers, workstations, NICs/WNICs, routers, repeaters, bridges, switches, and hubs. In contrast, CMIP was used by IBM in some token ring applications, but is not used on modern networks.

Advantages of SNMP
An important advantage of SNMP is that it operates independently on the network, which means that it does not depend on a two-way connection at the protocol level with other network entities. This feature enables SNMP to analyze network activity, such as detecting incomplete packets and monitoring broadcast activity, without depending on possibly faulty information from a failing node. CMIP, on the other hand, connects to network nodes at the protocol level, which means that its analysis of problems depends on the accuracy of a node that may be malfunctioning.

SNMP also has an advantage in that management functions are carried out at a network management station. This is in contrast to CMIP, where management is distributed to the individual network nodes that are also being managed. Another advantage of SNMP is that it has lower memory overhead than CMIP. CMIP needs up to 1.5 MB on each participating node for operation, whereas SNMP needs only a maximum of 64 KB on participating nodes.

Node Types Used with SNMP
SNMP uses two types of nodes, the **network management station (NMS)** and **network agents**. The NMS monitors networked devices that are equipped to communicate via SNMP. The managed devices run agent software that is in contact with the network management station. Most devices connected to modern networks are agents. These include routers, repeaters, hubs, switches, bridges, PCs (via the NIC or WNIC), print servers, access servers, and uninterruptible power sources (UPSs).

You can use the console at the NMS to send commands to network devices and obtain statistics on performance. The NMS can build a map of the entire network. If a new device is added, the NMS can discover it immediately. Software on the NMS has the ability to detect when an agent is down or malfunctioning. That agent may be highlighted in red, an alarm may sound, or both. All NMS software is typically written in GUI format so that it is easy to interpret.

Many NMS software packages have graphical representations of meters that display network utilization, flow of packets, and other network performance information. When there is a malfunction, these graphical representations help to identify which type of agent is affected and the severity of the problem. Some also have application programming interfaces (APIs), which act as doors into the NMS software and enable you to customize programming features by using, for example, Visual Basic.

Each network agent keeps a database of information, including the number of packets sent, the number of packets received, packet errors, the number of connections, and more. An agent's database is called the **Management Information Base (MIB)**. The NMS uses a range of commands to obtain or alter MIB data. The commands are sent through OSI-compliant protocol data units (PDUs) and include message types such as get-request, get-next-request, get-response, set-request, and trap. The retrieved data enables you to determine if a device is down or if a network problem exists. The NMS may even allow you to reboot a device remotely. The messages transmitted between the NMS and the agent are packaged into UDP, with an SNMP header. The SNMP payload contains a **community name**, or "string," which is a password shared by the NMS and the agent.

The MIB stores data on network objects such as workstations, servers, switches, bridges, routers, hubs, and repeaters. The core variables contained in a MIB are listed in Table 3-10. The MIB table was originally defined according to the Management Information Base-I (MIB-I) standard. This standard tracks information about a device, incorporating a range of variables. MIB standards are defined by the IETF.

Table 3-10   MIB variables

MIB Variable	Purpose
Address translation group	Converts network addresses to subnet or physical addresses
Electronic gateway protocol group	Provides information about nodes on the same segment as the network agent
Interfaces group	Tracks the number of NICs and the number of subnets
Internet Control Message Protocol group	Gathers data on the number of messages sent and received through the agent
Internet Protocol group	Tracks the number of input datagrams received and the number rejected
SNMP group	Gathers data about the communications with the MIB
System group	Contains information about the network agent
Transmission Control Protocol group	Provides information about TCP connections on the network, including address and timeout information
User Datagram Protocol group	Contains information about the listening agent that the NMS is currently contacting

© Cengage Learning 2013

A newer and improved standard, MIB-II, provides improved security, support for token ring, support for high-speed interfaces, and support for telecommunications interfaces. MIB-II is supported by many network device vendors. You can read more about MIB-II in RFC 1850 for OSPF; RFC 3418, which is the revised RFC adapted for SNMPv2; and RFC 4750 for compatibility with OSPFv2.

Improvements Found in SNMPv2   The original version of SNMP had some shortcomings that are addressed in a second version, which is called SNMPv2. Perhaps one of the most important of these shortcomings is SNMP's lack of strict security measures. When SNMP is used, the community name is sent by the NMS without encryption, and if captured, this password can be used to gain access to sensitive network management commands. This provides the ability to remotely configure a router or hub and compromises the security on a network.

SNMPv2 provides an encrypted community name, improved error handling, and multiprotocol support. It also adds support for the legacy protocols IPX and AppleTalk. SNMPv2 additionally provides fast data transmission and the ability to retrieve more MIB-II information at one time. RFCs 1909 and 1910 set the foundation for SNMPv2.

Improvements Found in SNMPv3   As set down by RFCs 3410 through 3415, SNMPv3 enhances SNMP-based communications primarily through improving security by encrypting and authenticating SNMPv3 packets. Basically, it has features to make sure that no one has intercepted and changed a packet, that the contents of packets are fully encrypted, and that the source of each packet can be validated.

Monitoring with SNMP, SNMPv2, and SNMPv3

SNMP, SNMPv2, and SNMPv3 can be used to monitor LANs, MANs, CANs, and WANs. There are many network-monitoring tools and network-monitoring software systems that employ SNMP/SNMPv2/SNMPv3. These include NetScout Systems Sniffer software (see *www.netscout.com*) and Microsoft Network Monitor (see *www.microsoft.com*).

"Sniffer" is a general term used to refer to software and hardware that can view network traffic and analyze the characteristics of that traffic, in part by viewing the packet traffic and the contents of packets.

An important SNMP-based tool, used to monitor LANs connected through WANs, is **Remote Network Monitoring (RMON)**, a standard developed in the early 1990s. RMON not only employs SNMP, but also incorporates a special database for remote monitoring, called RMON MIB-II. This database enables remote network nodes to gather network analysis data at virtually any point on a LAN or WAN. The remote nodes are agents or probes. Information gathered by the probes can be sent to a management station that compiles it into a database. RMON MIB-II standards are currently in place for FDDI, Ethernet, and token ring networks.

Activity 3-9 enables you to set up SNMP in Windows 7.

Activity 3-9: Configuring an SNMP Agent

Time Required: Approximately 10 minutes
Objective: Learn to make Windows 7 an SNMP agent.

Description: Windows 7 can be configured to act as an SNMP agent for a network management station. In this activity, you learn how to enable SNMP in Windows 7.

1. Click **Start** and click **Control Panel**.

2. Set **View by** to **Large icons** or **Small icons**.

3. Click **Programs and Features**.

4. In the left pane of the Programs and Features window, click **Turn Windows features on or off**. You may need to wait a few minutes for the features to be displayed.

5. If it is not already selected as signified by a checkmark or blue inside the box, click the box for **Simple Management Network Protocol (SNMP)**, as shown in Figure 3-17.

6. Click **OK** in the Windows Features dialog box. You may have to wait several minutes as Windows makes the change.

7. Close the Programs and Features window.

SNMP is now set up as a service in Windows 7. You can manage the SNMP service and the associated SNMP Trap service by displaying services in the Computer Management tool. Click **Start**, right-click **Computer**, click **Manage**, click **Services and Applications** in the left pane, and double-click **Services** in the middle pane.

HTTP, S-HTTP, and HTTPS

When you exchange information over the World Wide Web you use **Hypertext Transfer Protocol (HTTP)**. HTTP not only enables the establishment of a Web connection, but it also provides for the exchange of resources, for example, displaying a Web page in your browser.

© Cengage Learning 2013

Figure 3-17   Enabling SNMP in Windows 7

The Web page may consist of text, graphics, sounds, and other content. HTTP was introduced in 1990 and has grown in use as the Internet has grown.

When a Web client and a Web server are communicating through HTTP, there are two more secure forms of HTTP available: **Secure Hypertext Transfer Protocol (S-HTTP)** and **Hypertext Transfer Protocol Secure (HTTPS)**. These are often used when there is a need for increased security, such as in online credit card purchases or online banking. S-HTTP provides strong security for HTTP-transported information, but it is used by only some vendors' applications. This is because it is used primarily in native HTTP communications and does not encrypt data in IP-level communications. For this reason, Mozilla (Firefox) and Microsoft have implemented HTTPS to protect data transported via their Web browsers. Today HTTPS is used much more commonly than S-HTTP.

Internet Control Message Protocol (ICMP)

Internet Control Message Protocol (ICMP) works behind the scenes to help IP track error conditions. One of the most common conditions it reports is when a node, router, or switch is unavailable. The *ping* utility that is used to test a network connection or the presence of a node uses ICMP. ICMP also can report when a TCP or UDP port is unavailable or when a destination network cannot be reached. It additionally reports when a network service cannot be accessed. Another example of the use of ICMP is to determine when a packet has timed out (exceeded the TTL limit in IPv4 or hop limit in IPv6) and the packet has been discarded.

Besides diagnostic uses, ICMP can be used by attackers to immobilize a computer. In Activity 3-10, you learn how to block ICMP tests to Mac OS X as a way to thwart attackers.

Activity 3-10: Closing ICMP Scanning for Security in Mac OS X

Time Required: Approximately 15 minutes
Objective: Block ICMP tests to Mac OS X Snow Leopard and Lion.

Description: Attackers can use ICMP to send hundreds of tests to slow or immobilize a computer (particularly a server) or to randomly search for a live computer to attack. Although ICMP does not technically use a TCP or UDP port, it is often used to accompany a malicious port scan to find a live computer to attack. If there have been attacks on your network, one way to help protect a Mac OS X computer is to block ICMP tests, which you learn how to do in this activity. You need access to an account with Administrator privileges to complete this activity.

1. Click the **System Preferences** icon in the Dock or click the **Apple** icon in the menu bar and click **System Preferences**.

2. In the System Preferences window under Personal, click **Security** (in Lion, click **Security & Privacy**).

3. Click the **Firewall** tab if it is not already selected.

4. If it is locked, click the **lock** in the lower left corner, and if requested, provide your account name and password and click **OK**.

5. On the Firewall tab, if the Firewall is turned off, click **Start**.

6. On the Firewall tab with the firewall started, click the **Advanced** button.

7. Click the box for **Enable stealth mode**, which blocks ICMP tests including *ping* (see Figure 3-18). Also, notice there is an option to Block all incoming connections, which can be used to block many exposed TCP and UDP ports, except those needed for essential Internet communications. Click **OK**.

8. Click **System Preferences** in the menu bar and click **Quit System Preferences**.

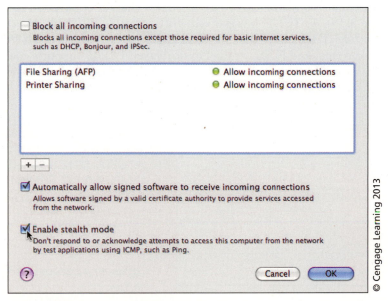

Figure 3-18 Blocking ICMP tests in Mac OS X

VoIP

Voice over IP (VoIP) is a network technology that enables telephony communications over an IP network. VoIP enables an organization to implement its own telephone system using an IP-based network and VoIP devices. Using VoIP can save an organization money because the organization can use its existing network for its internal telephone service and for long distance calls. VoIP services are also available to residences and businesses through cable TV, satellite, smartphone/cell phone, and private VoIP providers.

A VoIP network generally consists of at least three types of devices. First, there is a telephone device (for example, a VoIP-capable computer, telephone handset, cell phone, or smartphone) that is used to convert voice sounds into binary (ones and zeros) and then into IP packets. The telephone device communicates with a second type of device, a call processor or call server, that is able to:

- Set up and terminate calls
- Route calls
- Manage a calling session
- Translate telephone numbers or IDs into IP addresses

When the VoIP telephony system needs to be connected to the outside world, a third type of device is used—a specialized gateway that is used to convert the IP packetized voice data into a signal that can be transmitted over a public switched telephone network (PSTN), for regional, long-distance, or both voice communications. The same type of gateway is also used to connect a VoIP telephony system to a private telephone system, such as a private automatic branch exchange (PABX).

IP addresses are converted to telephone numbers and vice versa using the ITU E.164 standard used by PSTNs.

TCP/IP and the OSI Reference Model Compared

The TCP/IP components you have learned about in this chapter correspond to the OSI reference model (see Figure 3-19). As TCP/IP has evolved, portions of TCP/IP have moved closer to adherence to the OSI model. For example, the Physical and Data Link levels of TCP/IP are compatible with Ethernet, token ring, and FDDI. At the Physical layer, TCP/IP supports coaxial, twisted-pair, and fiber-optic cable, plus wireless communications. And at the Data Link layer, it is compatible with the IEEE 802.2 logical link control standard and MAC addressing.

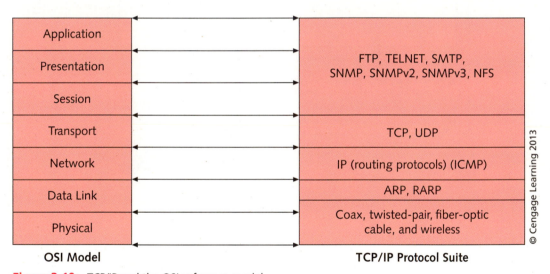

Figure 3-19   TCP/IP and the OSI reference model

The Network layer equivalent in TCP/IP is IP. The next compatible layer is the Transport layer, and both TCP and UDP operate at this level. The upper layers of the OSI model are represented by the TCP/IP applications protocols. For instance, Telnet operates at the equivalent of the Session, Presentation, and Application layers. SMTP and FTP operate at the equivalents of the Presentation and Application layers.

Transporting LAN Protocols over WANs

Before completing the discussion of protocols, it is important to examine several WAN protocols that are used for remote communications from LANs through WANs. Three of these protocols, Serial Line Internet Protocol (SLIP), Point-to-Point Protocol (PPP), and Layer Two Tunneling Protocol (L2TP), are used to encapsulate one or more LAN protocols, such as TCP/IP, for transmission over a WAN link. Another protocol, Signaling System 7 (SS7), is used to determine the fastest communications routes on telecommunications WANs.

SLIP

Serial Line Internet Protocol (SLIP) was originally designed for UNIX environments for point-to-point communications between computers, servers, and hosts using TCP/IP. SLIP is used, for example, when a user wants to communicate between a remote home computer and a UNIX/Linux computer that is on a LAN at the office. That user can employ a telephone line, for example, to connect to the UNIX/Linux computer, and then transmit packets using TCP/IP encapsulated within SLIP.

SLIP merely acts as the host WAN protocol, coordinating the connection session over the telephone wire and modems. After the protocol (with its data payload) reaches the destination, the SLIP header and trailer are removed, leaving TCP/IP.

Note that SLIP is an older remote communications protocol with more overhead than PPP (discussed in the next section). **Compressed Serial Line Internet Protocol (CSLIP)** is a more recent extension of SLIP that compresses header information in each packet sent across a remote link. CSLIP reduces the overhead of a SLIP connection by decreasing the header size and thus increasing the speed of communications. However, the header still must be decompressed at the receiving end.

Both SLIP and CSLIP are limited in that they do not support network connection authentication to prevent someone from intercepting a communication. They also do not support automatic setup of the network connection at multiple OSI layers at the same time for a faster connection. Another disadvantage is that SLIP and CSLIP are intended for asynchronous communications, as found, for example, in a modem-to-modem connection. They do not support synchronous connections, such as the creation of a connection strictly through the Internet from a modem to an ISP.

Many dial-up or remote communication services do not support SLIP or CSLIP because these protocols do not provide authentication. In addition, because of the lack of security, use SLIP only if necessary when the computer operating system you are configuring does not support PPP.

PPP

Point-to-Point Protocol (PPP) is used more commonly than SLIP or CSLIP for remote communications because it has lower overhead and greater capabilities and incorporates stronger security. PPP supports more network protocols than SLIP. It can automatically set up communications with several layers of the OSI model at once, and supports connection authentication and encryption for security.

Many operating systems, such as Windows 7 and most Linux systems, are configured to automatically use PPP for remote connections, such as broadband Internet connections.

PPP is supplemented by the newer **Point-to-Point Tunneling Protocol (PPTP)**, which enables remote communications to networks, intranets, and virtual private networks (VPNs; for more information on VPNs, see Chapter 7), and extranets by way of the Internet. Using PPTP, a company manager, for example, can access a report housed on that company's in-house intranet or VPN by dialing into the Internet from his or her home. Chances are that you already use PPP in Windows 7, Fedora, Red Hat Enterprise Linux, or Mac OS X.

An **intranet** is an IP-based private network that uses Web technologies for communications internal to an organization. An **extranet** makes an organization's intranet technologies available through a public network, such as the Internet. For instance, a business might have a Web-based inventory system on its intranet and make that inventory system available to certain customers and parts suppliers through the Internet (creating an extranet to those customers and parts suppliers). A VPN is a private network that is secured for access through a larger network, such as the Internet, like a private tunnel for members only.

PPP and PPTP both support synchronous and asynchronous communications, enabling connectivity through analog and digital modems, dial-up telephone lines, leased lines, and most forms of high-speed WANs.

PPP is recommended on networks where users connect using TCP/IP. Table 3-11 compares PPP to SLIP.

Table 3-11   PPP and SLIP compared

Feature	PPP	SLIP
Network protocol support	Supports multiple protocols including TCP/IP	Supports only TCP/IP
Asynchronous communications support	Yes	Yes
Synchronous communications support	Yes	No
Simultaneous network configuration negotiation and automatic connection with multiple levels of the OSI model between the communicating nodes	Yes	No
Support for connection authentication to guard against eavesdroppers	Yes	No

© Cengage Learning 2013

When you use PPP or PPTP, many Windows-based, UNIX/Linux, and Mac OS X systems offer the ability to perform password authentication and data encryption, functions that are not available in SLIP or CSLIP. For example, PPP and PPTP support **Password Authentication Protocol (PAP)**, which is used to verify the password entered to access a server over a WAN.

PAP alone can authenticate passwords, but it does not encrypt them. The **Challenge Handshake Authentication Protocol (CHAP)** can be used in conjunction with PAP to encrypt passwords so that they are difficult for a network intruder to intercept and decipher. CHAP is designed for UNIX/Linux computers, but Microsoft has developed MS-CHAP, which is compatible.

The security features, such as PAP and CHAP, that can be used with PPP make PPP a much better choice than SLIP for communications over a WAN.

L2TP

The **Layer Two Tunneling Protocol (L2TP)** works similarly to PPTP, and like PPTP is used on VPNs. Like PPTP, L2TP encapsulates PPP and creates special tunnels over a public network, such as the Internet. Unlike PPTP, L2TP uses an additional network communications standard, called Layer Two Forwarding, that enables forwarding packets on the basis of MAC addresses in addition to IP addresses.

SS7

Signaling System 7 (SS7) is a WAN protocol established by the International Telecommunication Union (ITU) to set up the fastest communications route between different kinds of telecommunications-based WANs. An example of this is between local access and transport area (LATA) lines and long-distance or interexchange carriers (see Chapter 2 to review LATAs and IXCs). SS7 is currently used in voice communications to support services such as call roaming for cellular communications, voicemail applications, and redirection of 800 calls. SS7 can quickly route traffic across WANs and is adapted for T-carrier and other WAN communications.

To learn more about the ITU, visit the Web site *www.itu.int/en/Pages/ default.aspx.*

SS7 is able to maintain fast communications by (1) keeping databases of routing information at different strategic points throughout a WAN, (2) quickly directing a central site's query about the fastest route for a particular call to the database site that contains the relevant routing information, and (3) tracking every telecommunications call to determine the fastest route for that call and subsequently updating the appropriate database.

Putting It All Together: Designing a Network to Use TCP/IP and Application Protocols

The study of TCP/IP can be summarized easily. First, most networks use TCP/IP. No matter whether you are designing a home network, an office network, or a large enterprise network that spans continents, your network will employ TCP/IP. It is simply the universal language of networks. In addition to TCP/IP, you will likely use one or more protocols or applications in the TCP/IP suite. For instance, if your network design includes access to the Internet, you will use HTTP and possibly FTP. If you monitor your network, you will use SNMP. If your network is relatively larger, you will use DHCP to lease IP addresses. For a medium to large network, you will employ a DNS server for domain name and IP address resolution.

Consider a professional office building in which 78 physicians, nurses, and office support personnel are networked. There is also a connection to the Internet. The physicians regularly use the Internet for research and download articles and software. This is an example of a TCP/IP network in which HTTP and FTP are used. TCP/IP communications over the WAN that accesses the Internet involve transporting the TCP/IP data encapsulated in PPP or PPTP. When one physician sends e-mail to a physician in another city, SMTP is used to transport her e-mail. Each time a nurse accesses a folder of information about pharmaceuticals that is shared on the network via a server, the nurse is using DNS in the background to locate that server. For convenience, DHCP is used in the background by all users to automatically assign IP addresses to their workstations. Finally, the network administrator uses Telnet with SSH when he works on one of the building's servers from his home. When the network administrator monitors the network, he uses SNMP.

To accomplish all of this the network administrator has done the following in the design of the network:

- Configured workstations and servers to use TCP/IP, using automatic (DHCP-based) IP addressing

- Used DHCP to lease IP addresses to workstations, while giving all servers permanent IP addresses

- Configured a network management station and certain workstations to use SNMP for network monitoring

- Set up network browsers, such as Internet Explorer, to use PPP and PPTP for Internet communications

- Enabled FTP and HTTP to be used through firewalls set up on workstations that access the Internet

- Configured the e-mail system to employ SMTP

- Configured a primary DNS server and at least one secondary DNS server as its backup

Chapter Summary

- The language of a network is protocols. If you take the time to learn about this language, it pays off by having well-designed and smooth-running networks.

- IPX/SPX and NetBEUI are two legacy protocols sometimes used with older NetWare and Microsoft networks.

- AppleTalk is another legacy protocol used by older Macintosh systems that run Mac OS and Mac OS X.

- TCP/IP is a combination of two protocols that are nearly universally used on networks and the Internet. TCP establishes a communications session and helps to ensure communications are reliable. IP enables data transfer and routing on a network through the use of packet addressing. UDP is a protocol sometimes used with IP instead of TCP when applications require low overhead and communications reliability is of less concern.

- IPv4 is the IP version predominantly in use today, but it has the limitation that IPv4 addresses are almost entirely used up.

- IPv6 is the newest version of IP, but it is not yet employed on many networks, although operating systems such as Windows, UNIX/Linux, and Mac OS X support it.

- The TCP/IP suite includes a huge range of vital protocols and applications. Some of these are Telnet, SSH, FTP, SMTP, DNS, DHCP, ARP, ND protocol, SNMP, HTTP, and ICMP.

- VoIP is a network technology for telephony communications over an IP network.

- Basic protocols used for remote communications between LANs and WANs include SLIP, PPP, PPTP, and L2TP. SS7 is a WAN protocol used to establish the fastest route between two telecommunications WANs.

Key Terms

Address Resolution Protocol (ARP)   A TCP/IP-based protocol that enables a sending station to determine the MAC address of the intended receiving station.

anycast   Used in IPv6, a packet that goes only to the closest interface and does not attempt to reach other interfaces with the same address.

AppleTalk   A peer-to-peer protocol used on legacy networks for communications between Macintosh computers. AppleTalk is a routable protocol, but is not used on the Internet.

broadcast   One copy of each frame or packet is sent to all points on a network, regardless of whether or not a node has requested it.

Challenge Handshake Authentication Protocol (CHAP)   A protocol used to encrypt passwords, such as server account passwords that are transferred over a WAN.

Classless Interdomain Routing (CIDR)   An IP addressing method that ignores address class designations and that uses a slash at the end of the dotted decimal address to show the total number of available addresses.

Common Management Interface Protocol (CMIP)   A protocol that gathers network performance data and is part of the OSI standards for network management.

community name   A password used by network agents and the network management station so their communications cannot be easily intercepted by an unauthorized workstation or device.

Compressed Serial Line Internet Protocol (CSLIP)   An extension of the SLIP remote communications protocol that provides faster throughput than SLIP.

Data Encryption Standard (DES)   A network symmetric-key encryption standard developed by the National Institute of Standards and Technology (NIST) and ANSI.

DNS dynamic update protocol   A TCP/IP-based protocol that enables information in a DNS server to be automatically updated, such as a Windows 7 workstation updating its leased DHCP IPv4 or IPv6 address.

domain   A logical grouping of network resources such as computers, printers, and network devices.

Domain Name System (DNS)   A TCP/IP application protocol that resolves domain and computer names to IP addresses, and IP addresses to domain and computer names.

dotted decimal notation   An addressing technique that uses four octets, such as 10000110. 11011110.01100101.00000101, converted to decimal (for example, 134.222.101.005), to designate a network and individual hosts on the network.

Dynamic Host Configuration Protocol (DHCP)   A network protocol that provides a way for a server to automatically assign an IP address to a device on its network.

extranet   A network that makes an organization's intranet technologies available through a public network, such as the Internet, but usually only for specific users. *See* **intranet**.

File Transfer Protocol (FTP)   A TCP/IP application protocol that transfers files in bulk data streams and that is commonly used on the Internet.

forward lookup zone   A DNS zone or table that maps computer names to IP addresses.

host address (A) resource record   A record in a DNS forward lookup zone that consists of a computer or domain name correlated to an IPv4 (or 32-bit) address.

Hypertext Transfer Protocol (HTTP)   A protocol in the TCP/IP suite that transports information over the Internet for access by Web browsers.

Hypertext Transfer Protocol Secure (HTTPS)   A secure form of HTTP that uses Secure Sockets Layer to implement security.

International Corporation for Assigned Names and Numbers (ICANN)   An organization that coordinates domain naming (the Domain Name System) and guidelines for domain registration.

Internet Assigned Numbers Authority (IANA)   An organization that assigns Internet IP addresses.

Internet Control Message Protocol (ICMP)   A protocol that works behind the scenes to help IP to track error conditions, such as the inability to reach a node or router.

Internet Protocol (IP)   A protocol used in combination with TCP or UDP that enables packets to reach a destination on a local or remote network by using dotted decimal addressing.

Internetwork Packet Exchange (IPX)   A legacy protocol developed by Novell for use with its NetWare file server operating system.

intranet   An IP-based private network that uses Web technologies for communications internal to an organization.

IP version 4 (IPv4)   The current version of IP used on most networks.

IP version 6 (IPv6)   The next version of IP after IPv4 that enables more addresses than are available through IPv4. Compared to IPv4, IPv6 also has a longer header coupled with IP extension headers for special communications needs.

IPv6 host address (AAAA) resource record   A record in a DNS forward lookup zone that consists of a computer or domain name mapped to an IPv6 (or 128-bit) address.

jumbogram   A data payload of 4 GB minus one byte (4,294,967,295 bytes) that is an option provided through IPv6, but is not available in IPv4.

kernel   An essential set of programs and computer code built into a computer operating system to control processor, disk, memory, and other functions central to the basic operation of a computer.

latency   The time it takes for information to travel from the transmitting device to the receiving device.

Layer Two Tunneling Protocol (L2TP)   A protocol that transports PPP over a VPN, intranet, or the Internet. L2TP works similarly to PPTP, but unlike PPTP, L2TP uses an additional network communications standard called Layer Two Forwarding that enables forwarding on the basis of MAC addressing.

loopback address   An address used internally by a computer for diagnostics and testing and is usually 127.0.0.1 (or in the range 127.0.0.0 to 127.255.255.255) for IPv4 or is 0:0:0:0:0:0:0:1 for IPv6.

Management Information Base (MIB)   A database of network performance information that is stored on a network agent for access by a network management station.

multicast   A transmission method in which a server divides users who request certain applications, such as multimedia applications, into groups. Each data stream of frames or packets is a one-time transmission that goes to multiple addresses, instead of sending a separate transmission to each address for each data stream.

namespace   A logical area on a network that contains a listing of named objects, such as computers, and that has the ability to perform name resolution.

Neighbor Discovery (ND) protocol   Uses messages and other means to discover the physical addresses and much more about computers and routers on a network. ND protocol enables a more extensive range of information to be determined beyond the capabilities of Address Resolution Protocol. *See* **Address Resolution Protocol (ARP)**.

NetBIOS Extended User Interface (NetBEUI)   Developed by IBM and Microsoft in the mid-80s, this legacy protocol incorporates NetBIOS for communications across a network.

network agent   Managed device that runs agent software that is in contact with the network management station. Most devices connected to modern networks are agents. These include routers, repeaters, hubs, switches, bridges, PCs (via the NIC/WNIC), print servers, access servers, and uninterruptible power sources (UPSs).

Network File System (NFS) protocol   A TCP/IP file transfer protocol that transfers information in record streams instead of in bulk file streams.

network management station (NMS)   A computer with software that monitors networked devices that are equipped to communicate via SNMP.

Password Authentication Protocol (PAP)   A protocol that is used to authenticate an account password when accessing a server, host computer, or directory service over a WAN.

pointer (PTR) resource record   A record in a DNS reverse lookup zone that consists of an IP (version 4 or 6) address correlated to a computer or domain name.

Point-to-Point Protocol (PPP)   A widely used remote communications protocol that supports TCP/IP (and other legacy protocols such as NetBEUI and IPX/SPX) communications over WANs.

Point-to-Point Tunneling Protocol (PPTP)   A remote communications protocol that enables connections to networks, intranets, extranets, and VPNs through the Internet.

primary DNS server   A DNS server that is used as the main server from which to administer a zone, such as updating records in a forward lookup zone for a domain. A primary DNS server is also called the authoritative server for that zone.

Quality of Service   A measurement specification of the transmission quality, throughput, and reliability of a network system.

Remote Network Monitoring (RMON)   A monitoring standard that uses remote network nodes, such as workstations or network devices, to perform network monitoring, including gathering information for network protocol analysis. Probes can be located on remote sections of the network, such as across bridges or routers.

Reverse Address Resolution Protocol (RARP)   A protocol used by a network node or by a software application at a node to determine its own IP address.

reverse lookup zone   A DNS server zone or table that contains records, which map IP addresses to computer or domain names.

root server   DNS server that is on the Internet and is used to find top-level domains (TLDs), such as .com or .net. There are 13 root servers throughout the world that act as final authorities for finding a TLD.

route aggregation   A technique for organizing network routes hierarchically. It also enables routes to be summarized resulting in reduced router advertising of routes (equating to less network traffic from routers).

secondary DNS server   A DNS server that is a backup to a primary DNS server and therefore is not authoritative.

Secure Hypertext Transfer Protocol (S-HTTP)   A secure form of HTTP that often uses Cryptographic Message Syntax and MIME Object Security Services. S-HTTP is not as commonly used as HTTPS. *See* **Hypertext Transfer Protocol Secure (HTTPS)**.

Secure Shell (SSH)   A form of authentication originally developed for UNIX/Linux systems to provide authentication security for TCP/IP applications, such as Telnet and FTP.

Sequenced Packet Exchange (SPX)   An older Novell protocol that is used for network transport for application software, such as database information, when there is a particular need for data reliability. SPX is generally paired with IPX.

Serial Line Internet Protocol (SLIP)   Designed for UNIX environments for point-to-point communications between computers, servers, and hosts using TCP/IP.

service resource record (SRV RR)   A record in a DNS zone that is created to locate commonly used TCP/IP services. The SRV record is formatted to include information about the service that is provided by a server, the domain that is serviced by the server, and the protocol used by the server.

Signaling System 7 (SS7)   A WAN protocol for telecommunications networks that is used to set up the fastest route between two telecommunications carriers.

Simple Mail Transfer Protocol (SMTP)   A protocol in the TCP/IP suite used to transmit e-mail, such as over the Internet.

Simple Network Management Protocol (SNMP)   A protocol in the TCP/IP suite that enables computers and network equipment to gather standardized data about network performance.

sliding window   The agreed-upon number of data bytes transmitted in a packet when two nodes are communicating via TCP. The amount of data can be dynamically varied, hence the sliding window, on the basis of network traffic conditions and available buffer space at each node.

source routing   A routing technique in which the sender of a packet specifies the precise path the packet will take to reach its destination.

start of authority (SOA) resource record   The first record in a DNS zone, it indicates if a server is authoritative for the current zone.

stateful autoconfiguration   Uses dynamic addressing for an IPv6 host by obtaining the IPv6 address through DHCPv6 and a DHCPv6 server.

stateless autoconfiguration   When a network host assigns its own IPv6 address without obtaining it from a DHCPv6 server.

subnet mask   A subnet mask is a designated portion of an IP address that is used to indicate the class of addressing on a network and to divide a network into subnetworks as a way to manage traffic patterns.

TCP port   Functioning like a virtual circuit, a TCP port enables communication between individual processes at two communicating nodes or devices. Each communicating process has its own port, and one or more ports can be used simultaneously to handle many communicating processes.

Telnet   A TCP/IP application protocol that provides terminal emulation.

terminal   A device that consists of a monitor and keyboard, used to communicate with host computers that run the programs. The terminal does not have a processor to use for running programs locally.

terminal emulation   Using software to make a computer, such as a PC, behave as though it were a terminal.

Transmission Control Protocol (TCP)   This transport protocol, which is part of the TCP/IP suite, establishes communication sessions between networked software application processes and provides for reliable end-to-end delivery of data by controlling data flow.

Trivial File Transfer Protocol (TFTP)   A TCP/IP file transfer protocol that is designed for the transfer of files that enable a diskless workstation to boot.

unicast   One copy of each frame or packet is sent to each destination point.

User Datagram Protocol (UDP)   A protocol used with IP, as an alternative to TCP, for low-overhead connectionless communications.

Voice over IP (VoIP)   A network technology that enables telephony communications over an IP network.

X.400   A set of standards for global message handling for e-mail.

zone   A partition in a DNS server that contains specific kinds of records in a lookup table, such as a forward lookup zone that contains records in a table for looking up computer and domain names to find their associated IP addresses.

Review Questions

1. Which of the following are properties of a LAN protocol? (Choose all that apply.)

   a. handles source and destination node addressing

   b. follows standards, such as the IEEE 802 standards

   c. has the ability to transport data in 8 GB packets or larger for network efficiency

   d. enables reliable network links

2. The workstation used by the marketing director in your company has been successfully hacked through the open Telnet port, even though she does not use Telnet. What step should be taken to thwart future attacks?

   a. Close all TCP ports.

   b. Reduce the Telnet port's bandwidth.

   c. Close TCP and UDP port 23.

   d. Configure Telnet so that it cannot be used in the background mode.

3. Since it has lower overhead, why is UDP not used for all communications along with IP?

   a. Unlike TCP, UDP is chatty.

   b. TCP has a higher level of reliability for times when important data is transmitted.

   c. UDP is only supported for WAN communications.

   d. UDP does not work with IPv6.

4. The subnet mask is used for which of the following? (Choose all that apply.)

   a. to disguise servers so they appear to be workstations

   b. to create subnetworks

   c. to bridge AppleTalk with TCP/IP

   d. to show the class of addressing

5. Your company's network segment that is used by the Research Department experiences many broadcasts from various devices. What can you, as network administrator, do to control the broadcasts so that they are not sent to other network segments?

   a. Configure the router that connects the Research Department segment so that broadcasts are not forwarded to other network segments.

   b. Configure the Research Department devices so that broadcasts are sent only using the 272.0.0.0 IPv4 address so that they are ignored by workstations.

   c. Configure the devices to send broadcasts to a DNS server and configure a pointer record at the DNS server to drop the broadcasts.

   d. Configure the devices to use only IPv4 instead of IPv6, because IPv4 does not support broadcasts.

6. Your network is very busy and you decide to monitor the network traffic. Which of the following can be a significant source of extra traffic on a network?

   a. padding in an IPv4 packet

   b. setting the timing bit for a packet transmission

   c. creating packet flags

   d. TCP acknowledgements

7. Your company's network uses DHCP to lease IPv4 addresses. When an employee gets a new computer and it is necessary to configure the IPv4 network connectivity, which of the following should you use in Windows 7? (Choose all that apply.)

   a. the VTAM port

   b. the routing port

   c. obtain an IP address automatically

   d. disable gateways

8. A new office assistant in your company has said that he is experienced in setting up Windows Server 2008 R2. You discover that he is planning to manually assign the IPv4 address 127.0.0.100 to the server. What is the problem with this assignment?

   a. Server addresses must have five octets.

   b. The address 127.0.0.100 is among a group of IPv4 addresses that are reserved and should not be assigned.

   c. The last octet assigned to a server must be between 1 and 10.

   d. There is no problem; IPv4 address 127.0.0.100 is a perfectly valid permanent address for a server.

9. You manage a medium-sized network that is on two floors in a building. You have a network monitoring station and want to set up a network agent on each floor. Which of the following devices are candidates for network agents? (Choose all that apply.)

   a. switches

   b. servers

   c. workstations

   d. network cable

10. The IPv6 address 0102:07cc:6218:0000:0000:0000:4572:4ebd can also be rewritten as which of the following? (Choose all that apply.)

    a. 0102:07cc:6218:3x00:4572:4ebd

    b. 0102:07cc:6218::4572:4ebd

    c. 0102:07cc:6218:4572:4ebd

    d. 0102:07cc:6218:0:0:0:4572:4ebd

11. You are debating with a colleague about whether to use PPTP or L2TP for remote communications. Which of the following is an advantage of using L2TP?

    a. PPTP uses a compressed packet that takes time to compress and decompress, whereas L2TP does not.

    b. L2TP forces the network to use a special carrier signal, which is faster than the carrier signal used by PPTP.

    c. L2TP can tunnel in more directions, including in reverse.

    d. L2TP can take advantage of MAC addresses, but PPTP cannot.

12. An online stock brokerage has had reports of hackers obtaining information about accounts while customers are online. The firm discovers that an inadvertent programming change in its new software has omitted use of which of the following security methods?

    a. HTTPS

    b. Source Security

    c. Secure NetBEUI

    d. UDP Security

13. You are designing a new network for a mail order company of 284 employees. Network reliability is a must for a successful business strategy. When you set up DNS, which of the following should you do?

    a. Use only a reverse lookup zone.

    b. Set up three primary DNS servers.

    c. Configure a primary and a secondary DNS server.

    d. Employ IPv6 host address resource records for lower cost of operations.

14. When a server crashes and goes offline on a network, which of the following helps to determine that the server is unavailable?

    a. ICMP

    b. DNS

    c. SMTP

    d. NFS

15. In IPv6 the flow label field is used for what service?

    a. directory service

    b. Quality of Service

    c. Acknowledgement Service

    d. Authentication Service

16. Your company wants to migrate to IPv6 because of its improved security features. One important security feature that is required for IPv6 and that is not required for IPv4 is which of the following?

    a. source routing

    b. CIDR

    c. ICMP

    d. IPsec

17. What protocol does IPv6 use to discover the physical addresses of nodes on a network?

    a. Address Resolution Protocol (ARP)

    b. Neighbor Discovery (ND) Protocol

    c. Secure Shell (SSH) Protocol

    d. Network File System (NFS) Protocol

18. You are consulting for a business for which the beginning IPv4 octet used on its network is 222, which makes this a Class C network. What is the maximum number of addressable nodes that this business can have using traditional IPv4 addressing?

    a. 512

    b. 392

    c. 254

    d. 124

19. You are in a management meeting for your company in which the current topic is the TCP/IPv4 network. One of the managers is concerned that when someone turns off a workstation, information keeps circulating around the network, making communications slower and slower. What is your answer?

    a. This is a problem, but Windows 7 and Windows Server 2008/Server 2008 R2 have programs that automatically delete lost packets at regular intervals.

    b. NICs on servers can periodically reset a network to clear the bandwidth of circulating packets.

    c. Packets that are on the network for over a minute are automatically fragmented so they take up virtually no bandwidth.

    d. An IPv4 packet contains a Time to Live field that enables these kinds of packets to be discarded.

20. Your university has decided to migrate to IPv6 and in the process enable its CAN to use both IPv4 and IPv6. In a meeting, one of the application programmers in the IT department states a concern about there being network confusion in differentiating between IPv4 and IPv6 packets. What is your comment to address this concern?

    a. Both IPv4 and IPv6 contain a version number at the beginning of each packet so that it is clear which is an IPv6 packet and which is an IPv4 packet.

    b. There is no problem because routers can be configured to place an IP identifier at the end of each packet.

    c. An easy solution is to configure a dedicated IP server to properly route IPv4 and IPv6 packets according to the IP version.

    d. The application programmer is correct in that there is a flaw in the plan because the CAN must use only IPv4 or IPv6, but cannot use both.

21. Your network needs 2^8 host identifiers for 256 nodes. Which of the following formulas help you calculate the number of bits needed for the network identifier?

    a. $64 - 8 = 56$

    b. $8 + 24 = 32$

    c. $32 - 8 = 24$

    d. $8 / 2 = 4$

Case Projects

Nishida Kitchens is a medium-sized company that makes packaged Japanese foods including noodle and sauce combinations. Their foods are distributed to grocery stores and specialty food stores throughout Canada, Europe, and the United States. The company is moving into a new building and has hired Network Design Consultants to help them create a new network. Before the move, their head network administrator accepted a job with another company and his inexperienced assistant has been promoted as the head network administrator.

Nishida Kitchens has a business and sales unit of 42 computer users. The plant in which the foods are produced, packaged, and shipped has 45 computer users. The company has both Windows Server 2008 R2 and Red Hat Enterprise Linux servers. The business and sales unit uses Windows 7 workstations. The plant users have a combination of Windows 7 and Red Hat Enterprise Linux computers on user's desktops. The company plans to have Internet connectivity available to all network users. Nishida Kitchens has an outlet store across town, which provides the public with direct sales of its products. The outlet store also has Internet connectivity on a small network of 12 computers that are running Windows 7.

Case Project 3-1: Choosing a Network Protocol

What protocol do you recommend for this network, and what are its advantages?

Case Project 3-2: IPv6 Advantages

Nishida Kitchens wants to explore the value of converting to IPv6 over the next two years. Prepare a report or slide presentation that outlines the advantages of IPv6.

Case Project 3-3: Monitoring the Network

Nishida Kitchens wants the ability to monitor its network to keep the network stable and to troubleshoot problems. What should Nishida Kitchens implement to accomplish network monitoring at the main location and the outlet store? How can network monitoring be made secure?

Case Project 3-4: Establishing an E-Mail Server

Nishida Kitchens is considering the implementation of its own e-mail server so that employees can exchange e-mail with one another and with others over the Internet. What element is important to implement in the e-mail server so that messages can be transported over the Internet? How does this element work?

Case Project 3-5: Choosing a WAN Communications Protocol

For WAN communications, such as over the Internet connection, what protocol should be used by the Windows 7 and Red Hat Enterprise Linux workstations? What are the advantages of this protocol?

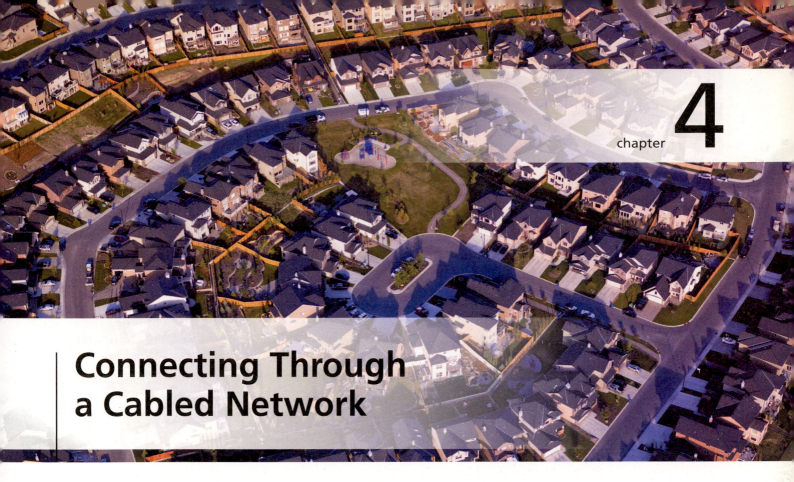

Connecting Through
a Cabled Network

A solid network cable implementation is not just the "tie that binds" users on many networks; it can be the difference between communications and no communications at all. If you want to build a solid cable installation, it is important to understand and carefully follow industry specifications.

After reading this chapter and completing the exercises, you will be able to:

- Explain network cable media, including coaxial, twisted-pair, and fiber-optic media, and identify which to use in a particular network configuration

- Discuss high-speed cable-media technologies for 100 Mbps, 1 Gbps, 10 Gbps, 40 Gbps, and 100 Gbps communications

- Explain the use of a NIC for connecting devices to cabled networks

- Design a cabled network

Communications media make LANs, MANs, CANs, and WANs possible.

The infrastructure of today's networks consists of a vast array of copper-based and fiber-optic cable media as well as wireless connections. In this chapter, you learn about the full range of communications cable, from the coaxial cable that was used on early networks to the state-of-the-art fiber-optic media used today. You explore high-speed technologies that include Fast Ethernet, Gigabit Ethernet, 10 Gigabit Ethernet, 40 Gigabit Ethernet, and 100 Gigabit Ethernet. You also explore the role network interface cards play in connecting computers and network devices.

Communications Media Types

The most basic level of communications is accomplished at the OSI Physical layer, or Layer 1, which includes communications media and interfaces. Communications media include copper wire communications cable, glass (or sometimes plastic) communications cable, and radio or microwaves. Interfaces are devices to which the communications media connect, such as network interface cards.

There are several basic communications media types:

- Coaxial cable

- Twisted-pair cable

- Fiber-optic cable

- Hybrid fiber/coax

- Wireless technologies

Coaxial and twisted-pair cables are based on copper wire construction. Fiber-optic cable is glass (usually) or plastic cable. Hybrid fiber/coax is a combination of coaxial and fiber-optic cables. Wireless media are radio or microwaves. In the next sections, you learn about the cable media. For each cable medium, you learn wiring specifications and the medium's advantages and disadvantages. (In Chapter 6, "Connecting Through a Wireless Network," you explore wireless communications.)

The characteristics of each communications medium make it suitable for particular types of networks. The most commonly used cabling in LANs is twisted pair. Coaxial cable is used mainly in older LANs and in LANs in areas with strong sources of signal interference. Coaxial cable is also used to connect some types of wireless antennas to network devices, such as a satellite dish to a digital modem. Fiber-optic cable is usually used to connect computers that demand high-speed LAN and WAN access and to connect networks between different floors and buildings in situations where there is significant electrical interference and where security is a concern. Wireless technologies are used in situations where it is difficult or too expensive to use cable and in situations in which flexibility to move network hosts and devices is a requirement.

When choosing the best medium for a LAN or WAN, it is important to consider the capabilities and limitations of each type, including factors such as:

- Data transfer speed

- Use in specific network topologies

- Distance requirements

- Cable and cable component costs

- Additional network equipment that might be required

- Flexibility and ease of installation

- Immunity to interference from outside sources

- Upgrade options

- Security

Before discussing network cable types, it is useful to consider several terms that apply to network cable. For instance, **backbone cabling** is cable that runs between network equipment rooms, floors, and buildings and is often used to link network devices, such as linking switches between floors or buildings. Backbone cabling is what forms the basis of a network backbone as introduced in Chapter 1, "Networking: An Overview."

In some locations, network cable is run through a **plenum area**, such as the space in a false ceiling through which circulating air reaches other parts of a building. Network cable often has a polyvinyl chloride (PVC) jacket or covering, and it is known that PVC can emit a toxic vapor in a fire. Consequently, it is safer (and often required by local fire codes) to use plenum cable in these areas. **Plenum cable** is Teflon-coated and does not emit a toxic vapor when burned.

When you install cable, check your local building codes and plan to use plenum cable in plenum areas, no matter what type of cable you install.

Copper-based network cables, such as coaxial and twisted-pair cables, have a measured **impedance** (in technical terms, resistance plus reactance). Impedance is the total amount of opposition to the flow of current and is measured in ohms. You should use cable that has the correct impedance according to the particular cable specifications. For example, the impedance for some types of twisted-pair network cable installations should be 100 ohms. Impedance is significant because it influences how fast a frame or packet can travel through the conductive material in optimal conditions. One simple step in troubleshooting a network is to use an ohm meter or a cable tester to measure the cable impedance.

Bus and star-bus hybrid networks use a terminator at the ends of network segments, which is most visible on networks using coaxial cable and is typically built into equipment on networks that use twisted-pair cable (depending on the topology). The terminator contains a resistor that absorbs each signal when it reaches the end of the network. Without a terminator, the segment violates IEEE specifications because signals can be mirrored back, or reflected, on the same path they just covered. You might think of this phenomenon as similar to looking into a pond in a certain light where you partially see your reflection mirrored back and you partially see the bottom of the pond. The signal reflection offsets network timing and can interfere with new signals being transmitted on the network.

Real-Life Networking

Faculty members at an engineering college installed cable (taken from a pile of cables in a research lab) to connect a workstation used for research to a network switch. The resulting network connection was extremely unreliable, and the faculty members called in a network administrator to help. The network administrator measured the cable impedance at 75 ohms, whereas the IEEE specification for that cable connection was 100 ohms. A 100-ohm cable matching IEEE specifications solved the problem. This example illustrates why it is always important to understand cable standards and to follow the standards or else face unwanted consequences.

A **baseband** transmission is one in which the entire channel capacity of the cable medium is used by one data signal. Thus, only one node transmits at a time. A **broadband** transmission employs several transmission channels on a single communications medium. This allows more than one node to transmit at the same time. The capacity of a channel to transmit data in terms of given speeds, such as 10 or 100 Mbps, is its **bandwidth**. Channels composing bandwidth on a cable might be compared to channels on a TV. In cable TV, you receive multiple television channels over a single wire, with the television tuner used to access a particular channel.

Technically, bandwidth is the transmission capacity of a communications medium, which is typically measured in bits per second (for data transmissions) or hertz (for data, voice, and video transmissions) and which is determined by the maximum minus the minimum transmission capacity.

Coaxial Cable

Coaxial cable (typically called coax) comes in two varieties, thick and thin. Thick coax cable was used in early networks, often as a backbone cable to join different networks. Coaxial cable was the first media type defined when Ethernet standards were established in the early 1980s. Thick coax is used infrequently today because there are better alternatives, such as fiber-optic cable. Thin coax cable has a much smaller diameter than thick coax cable and is used on networks to connect desktop workstations to LANs (although today there are few implementations of thin coax).

Thick Coax Cable   Thick coax cable is rarely seen on today's networks, but is briefly discussed here so that you are aware of it in case you run across it in an old installation. Thick coax cable (also called thickwire or thicknet) has a copper or copper-clad aluminum conductor as its core, as shown in Figure 4-1. Thick coax cable is relatively large with a 0.4-inch diameter, compared to thin coax cable, which has a 0.2-inch diameter. The conductor is surrounded by insulation, and an aluminum sleeve is wrapped around the outside of the insulation. A PVC or Teflon jacket covers the aluminum sleeve. This type of cable is also called RG-8 cable (RG means "radio grade").

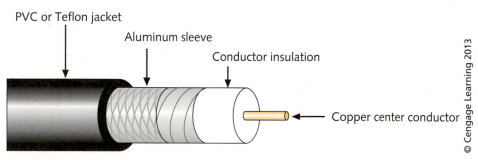

Figure 4-1   Thick coax (RG-8) cable

The cable jacket is marked every 2.5 meters to show where a network-connecting device can be attached. If you attach devices more closely than 2.5 meters, the signal can be impaired, and network errors may result. The connecting device is a media access unit (MAU) transceiver (transmitter/receiver) that is driven by a small amount of current (0.5 amperes) from the cable and that is equipped with a 15-pin **attachment unit interface (AUI)** connector.

The AUI connects via cable to a network node that has its own AUI connection to a network interface (as shown in Figure 4-2). A thick AUI cable can be up to 50 meters long, and a thin or office-grade AUI cable can be as long as 12.5 meters.

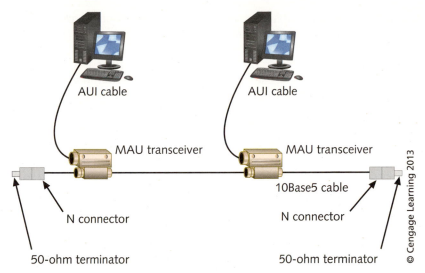

Figure 4-2   Connecting to thick coax cable

Thick coaxial cable is difficult to bend, so when using it, you must follow a minimum bend radius. On the plus side, this cabling has better EMI and Physical layer interference (RFI) immunity than thin coaxial because of the large-diameter conductor and aluminum shielding.

Thick coaxial cable works on bus networks that normally use transmission speeds of 10 Mbps, as shown in Table 4-1. According to IEEE standards, the maximum cable segment length, or run, is 500 meters. The shorthand for these specifications is **10Base5**. The 10 indicates that the cable transmission rate is 10 Mbps. Base means that baseband transmission is used instead of broadband. The 5 indicates 500 meters for the longest cable run.

Table 4-1   Thick coax cable (10Base5) properties for Ethernet applications

Property	Ethernet Specification
Impedance	50 ohms
Maximum length	500 meters (approx. 1650 ft)
Maximum number of taps into the cable	100 (including terminators)
Minimum distance between taps	2.5 meters (approx. 8.25 ft)
Maximum AUI cable length	50 meters (approx. 165 ft) for thick AUI cable and 12.5 meters (approx. 41.25 ft) for office-grade AUI cable
Maximum speed	10 Mbps
Band type	Baseband
Maximum number of connected segments	Five
Maximum number of segments containing nodes	Three
Maximum number of repeaters (times the signal is amplified and retimed)	Four
Maximum total length via repeaters	2500 meters (approx. 1.5 miles)

© Cengage Learning 2013

Thin Coax Cable   The use of thin coax cable is today replaced by twisted-pair cable, but there can be some niche uses for coax, such as in areas with extreme electrical interference. Thin coax cable resembles television cable. However, unlike television cable, the electrical characteristics of network cable are very precise and must meet the specifications established by the IEEE. The specifications for Ethernet require thin coax cable to have 50 ohms of impedance (as is the case with thick coax). Thin coax cable is labeled with the notation RG-58A/U (Radio Grade 58) to show that it is 50-ohm cable. Network administrators call the cable **10Base2** (or thinnet or cheapernet) because it has a maximum theoretical network speed of 10 Mbps, can have wire runs up to 185 meters (prior to 1990 it was 200 meters), and is used for baseband (Base) data transmission. However, these distinctions are blurred by the implementation of networking equipment, such as repeaters, that can amplify and retime signals for longer distances, as you learn in Chapter 5, "Devices for Connecting Networks."

Understanding the cable markings and properties is important in networking, or else when you buy cable you may end up with the wrong thing. This can be an expensive mistake if you discover you have the wrong cable after it is installed in your walls and ceilings—and your network does not work.

Thin coax cabling has a copper or copper-clad aluminum conductor at the core and an insulating foam material surrounding the core. A woven copper mesh, which, in high-quality cable, is surrounded by an aluminum foil sleeve, wraps around the insulating foam material, and the cable is covered with an outside PVC or Teflon jacket for insulation. It looks similar to the thick coax shown in Figure 4-1, but is much smaller in diameter. Thin coax cable comes in a variety of colors.

Thin coax cable is attached to a **bayonet nut connector (BNC)**, which is then connected to a T-connector. The middle of the T is connected to the NIC in the computer or network device. If that computer or device is the last node at the end of the cable, a terminator is connected to one end of the T-connector (see Figure 4-3).

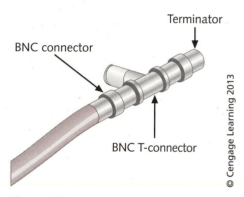

Figure 4-3   A BNC T-connector with a terminator at one end

Thin coax cable is easier and cheaper to install than thick coax, but twisted-pair cable is easier still to install and use because it is more flexible. An advantage of thin coaxial cable compared to twisted pair is that it is resistant to EMI and RFI. Coax is still found on some legacy networks and in places subject to very high EMI/RFI. Table 4-2 describes the properties of thin coax cable for Ethernet applications. In Activity 4-1 you compare different cable types, and in Activity 4-2 you compare cable connectors. Then, in Activity 4-3 you construct a thin coax cable.

Table 4-2   Thin coax cable (10Base2) properties for Ethernet applications

Property	Ethernet Specification
Impedance	50 ohms
Maximum length	185 meters (approx. 610.5 ft)
Maximum number of taps into the cable	30 (including terminators)
Minimum distance between taps	0.5 meters (approx. 1.65 ft)
Maximum speed	10 Mbps
Band type	Baseband
Maximum number of connected segments	Five
Maximum number of segments containing nodes	Three
Maximum number of repeaters (times the signal is amplified and retimed)	Four
Maximum total length via repeaters	925 meters (approx. 3052.5 ft)

© Cengage Learning 2013

Coax cabling is still used in areas that have extremely high EMI/RFI, such as in a machine shop or in a factory that has large motors or heavy electrical equipment. It is vital for network designers to understand older technologies like this, because they can offer a solution in some atypical circumstances that are not suitable for wireless or twisted-pair cable solutions.

Activity 4-1: Comparing Different Cable Types

Time Required: Approximately 10 minutes
Objective: Compare coax, twisted-pair, and fiber-optic cables.

Description: Even if you never install cable, you will better understand your network—including its capabilities and strategies for troubleshooting problems—if you understand the physical differences among cable types. You will also be better able to design a new network or upgrade a legacy network. In this activity, you compare the flexibility and appearance of coaxial, twisted-pair, and fiber-optic cables.

Exercise great care when handling fiber-optic cable to avoid the danger of glass shards entering the skin. Also, do not place the fiber-optic cable close to your eyes or rub your eyes immediately after handling the cable.

1. Obtain and examine cut sections of thick and thin coax cable. Notice the copper conductor, shielding, and jacket on each type of cable.

2. Obtain and examine cut sections of shielded and unshielded twisted-pair cable. (These types of cable are discussed in the next section.) Notice the shielding in shielded twisted-pair cable. Also, notice the wire pairs and their coloring.

3. Obtain and examine cut sections of single-mode and multimode fiber-optic cable. Determine if you can make out a fiber strand.

4. Examine cut sections of hybrid fiber/coax (HFC) cable. (You learn about HFC cable later in this chapter.)

5. Based on your observations, determine which cable type appears most flexible and easiest to install.

Activity 4-2: Comparing Cable Connectors

Time Required: Approximately 10 minutes
Objective: Compare connectors for different cable types.

Description: Each type of cable uses different kinds of connectors. This activity enables you to see the kinds of connectors used for different cable mediums.

1. Obtain and examine a BNC connector for thin coax cable.

2. Next, examine an RJ-45 connector for twisted-pair cable.

3. Last, examine SC, ST, and LC (and MT-RJ if one is available) connectors for fiber-optic cable.

4. Note the similarities and differences among these types of connectors.

Activity 4-3: Building a Thin Coax Cable

Time Required: Approximately 20–30 minutes
Objective: Experience how to construct a thin coax cable.

Description: A good way to understand the advantages and problems associated with different cable types is to build a cable. This activity gives you experience in attaching a BNC connector to thin coax cable, so that the BNC connector can later be connected onto one end of a T-connector. To complete the activity, you need a crimping tool and a wire stripper designed for use with coaxial cable, as well as a section of RG-58A/U cable and a BNC connector.

1. Use a high-quality crimping tool for the type of connector you use.

2. Use a wire stripper intended for RG-58A/U coaxial cable.

3. Use a high-quality gold-plated BNC connector.

4. Follow the directions of the manufacturer of the stripper to strip the coaxial cable (including setting the stripper for the cable type).

5. After the cable is stripped, ensure that all of the strands in the center conductor are wrapped tightly, with no ends sticking out.

6. Slide the crimping sleeve onto the cable.

7. Insert the center conductor into the center contact of the connector, ensuring that all of the braids are inside the center contact.

8. Use a crimping tool to crimp the center contact to the center conductor.

9. Carefully flare out the mesh braid away from its foam core.

10. Slide the BNC connector onto the foam core, ensuring that none of the braid is between the foam core and the sliding cylinder on the BNC connector, and maintaining the integrity of the aluminum foil as much as possible.

11. Slide the sleeve back up the cable so that it is flush with the bottom of the BNC connector.

12. Crimp the sleeve with a crimping tool.

Twisted-Pair Cable

Twisted-pair cable, which resembles telephone wire, was approved for networking by the IEEE in 1990 and has become a very popular cable communications medium. **Twisted-pair cable** is a flexible communications cable that contains pairs of insulated copper wires, which are twisted together for reduction of EMI and RFI, and covered with an outer insulating jacket. Twisted-pair cable is more flexible than coax cable and therefore better for running through walls and around corners. For most applications, the maximum run of twisted-pair cable is 100 meters (330 feet). Some types of twisted-pair cable can be used in high-speed 10 Gbps communications.

Although twisted-pair cable can be extended up to 100 meters, common practice is to limit runs to 90 meters or less to take into account extra wiring in network equipment and in wiring closets. Also, at this writing an application for twisted-pair cable for 40/100 Gbps is not on the horizon.

Twisted-pair cable is connected to network devices with RJ-45 plug-in connectors, which resemble the RJ-11 connectors used on telephones, as shown in Figure 4-4. These connectors are less expensive than T-connectors. They are also easy to connect and allow more flexible cable configurations than coax cable. There are two kinds of twisted-pair cable, shielded and unshielded. Unshielded cable is preferred because of its lower cost and high reliability.

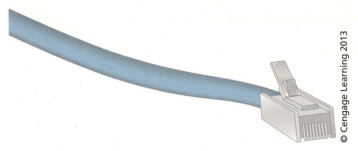

Figure 4-4   Twisted-pair cable with an RJ-45 plug-in connector

Shielded Twisted-Pair Cable   Shielded twisted-pair (STP) cable consists of pairs of insulated solid wire surrounded by a braided or corrugated shielding. Braided shielding is used for indoor wiring, and corrugated shielding is used for outside or underground wiring. Shielding reduces interference to the communication signal caused by RFI and EMI. Twisting the wire pairs also helps reduce RFI and EMI, but not to the same extent as the shield.

For effective RFI and EMI reduction, the interval of twists or lay length in each pair should be different. Also, connectors and wall outlets must be shielded for the best results. If the main shielding is torn at any point within the jacket, signal distortion is likely to be high. Another important factor in STP is to have proper grounding to have a reliable transmission signal reference point.

This type of cable is recommended in situations where heavy electrical equipment or other strong sources of interference are nearby. The top of Figure 4-5 shows an example of STP.

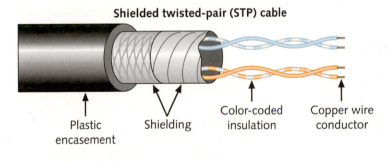

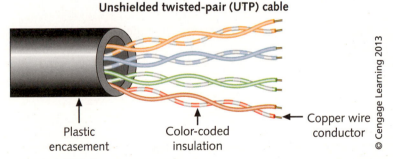

Figure 4-5   STP and UTP cables

Shielded cable and connectors along with the compatible network equipment are more expensive than unshielded cable.

Unshielded Twisted-Pair Cable   Unshielded twisted-pair (UTP) cable is the most frequently used network cable because it is relatively inexpensive and easy to install. UTP consists of wire pairs within an insulated outside covering and has no shielding material between the pairs of insulated wires twisted together and the cable's outside jacket. As with STP, each inside strand is twisted with another strand to help reduce interference to the data-carrying signal, as shown in the bottom of Figure 4-5. An electrical device called a media filter is built into the network equipment, workstation, and file server connections to reduce EMI and RFI; however, UTP is still susceptible to interference.

Earlier versions of UTP are Category 3 cable with a maximum transmission rate of 10 to 16 Mbps and Category 4 UTP with a maximum transmission rate of 20 Mbps. These are also known as **10BaseT** (for 10 Mbps, baseband, twisted pair) cables.

Category 5 has a 100 Mbps transmission rate and is used on 10BaseT and faster networks, such as Fast Ethernet (which you learn about later in this chapter). Category 5e (enhanced Category 5) has a 1 Gbps transmission rate, uses a better quality of copper, and has a higher twist ratio for more RFI/EMI protection than Category 5. In Category 6, the wire pairs are wrapped within a foil insulating layer for improved resistance to interference, and Category 6 has a fire-resistant plastic sheath. Category 6 supports a transmission rate of up to 1 Gbps. Category 6a is an improvement over Category 6 in that it is less subject to interference due to crosstalk and operates at a higher frequency (500 MHz). Category 6e is another enhanced version of Category 6 that supports transmissions higher than 1 Gbps as well as offering less crosstalk than Category 6, but typically operates at the same frequency as Category 6 (250 MHz). Category 6e is an older adaptation than Category 6a, and unlike Category 6a, Category 6e is not an official standard. Finally, in Category 7 each pair of wires is wrapped in a protective foil shield and all pairs are surrounded by another foil shield underneath the outer sheath. Category 7 is extremely resistant to EMI/RFI, but it requires special connectors and is not as flexible as other forms of twisted-pair cable. Category 7a is an amended standard for Category 7 that operates at frequencies of up to 1000 MHz, compared to 600 MHz for Category 7. Category 7a can be used in cable TV and telephone networks as well as on Ethernet networks. Category 7a can possibly be used for 40 and 100 Gbps applications, but at this writing test results are not conclusive and the IEEE is not currently proposing this medium for 40 or 100 Gbps communications.

Categories 6, 6a, 6e, 7, and 7a are more like STP because of their built-in shielding, but are still classified as UTP.

Table 4-3 shows the most frequently used twisted-pair cable categories as specified by the Electronic Industries Alliance/Telecommunications Industry Association (EIA/TIA) for Ethernet applications. UTP is generally preferred to STP because it has fewer points of failure, it has no shield that can tear (up through Category 5e), and connectors and wall outlets do not need shielding. Also, although proper grounding is important for UTP, it is not as critical to purity of the signal as for STP.

No matter what cable you use, absolutely ensure there is a true ground on all sections of cable. If one section is a true ground and one section has a different type of grounding, then handling both sections at the same time can result in a jolt strong enough to throw you off your feet.

Table 4-3   Ethernet twisted-pair cable standards

Twisted Pair as Defined in the EIA/TIA-568 Specifications for Horizontal and Backbone Cable	Shielding	Maximum Transmission Rate
Category 3	UTP	16 Mbps
Category 4	UTP	20 Mbps
Category 5	UTP	100 Mbps
Category 5e	UTP	1 Gbps (for assured handling of Gigabit Ethernet)
Category 6	UTP	1 Gbps (for assured handling of Gigabit Ethernet)
Category 6a	UTP	10 Gbps
Category 6e	UTP	10 Gbps
Category 7	UTP	10 Gbps
Category 7a	STP	10 Gbps (used in Ethernet, telephone, and cable TV applications)

Horizontal cabling, a term used in these tables, is defined by the EIA/TIA-568 standard as cabling that connects workstations and servers in the work area. Categories 5e, 6, 6a, and 6e twisted-pair cables are a popular choice for new horizontal cable installations because they have high-speed networking capabilities that make future equipment upgrades easier.

Tables 4-4 and 4-5 show the properties of twisted-pair cable for 10 Mbps Ethernet use (you learn about faster versions of Ethernet later in this chapter). In Activity 4-4 you build a twisted-pair cable.

> **NOTE** The tables for 10BaseT are provided because in general these specifications also hold for the more common 100BaseX, which is discussed later in this chapter. Even if you don't install cable yourself, these are important specifications for troubleshooting cable installed by someone else—such as when you use devices that "shoot" cable lengths.

Table 4-4   10BaseT (and in general 100BaseX) unshielded twisted-pair Ethernet specifications

Property	Ethernet Specification
Maximum length of one segment	100 meters (approx. 330 feet)
Maximum number of nodes per segment	Two nodes
Minimum distance between nodes	3 meters (approx. 9.9 feet)
Maximum number of segments	1024
Maximum number of segments with nodes	1024
Maximum number of daisy-chained hubs	Four
Impedance	100 ohms

© Cengage Learning 2013

Table 4-5   10BaseT (and in general 100BaseX) shielded twisted-pair Ethernet specifications

Property	Ethernet Specification
Maximum length of one segment	100 meters (approx. 330 feet)
Maximum number of nodes per segment	Two nodes
Minimum distance between nodes	3 meters (approx. 9.9 feet)
Maximum number of segments	1024
Maximum number of segments with nodes	1024
Maximum number of daisy-chained hubs	Four
Impedance	150 ohms

© Cengage Learning 2013

Real-Life Networking

The IT manager of a small company designed a network several years ago that used 10 Mbps devices (10BaseT) for communications. Because she had the fastest grade of twisted-pair cable installed in the walls of the building, and because she monitored the installation to ensure it met the specifications for 10BaseT, it was relatively easy for her company to later upgrade to 100 Mbps devices (100BaseX) and connect a server at 1 Gbps without the expense of installing new cable. She also had extra cable and cable connections installed so that as the company added new employees, giving them network access would be no problem. This example illustrates a good rule of thumb, which is to install the highest grade cable and provide room for expansion, so that you can take advantage of new technologies in the future.

Activity 4-4: Building a UTP Cable

Time Required: Approximately 20–30 minutes
Objective: Experience building a UTP cable.

Description: In this activity, you attach 4-pair UTP cable to an RJ-45 connector. You need the cable, a crimping tool (see Figure 4-6), a connector, and a wire stripper. These instructions and Figure 4-7 follow the EIA/TIA-568-B standard.

1. Lay out the wires on a flat surface in the arrangement shown in Figure 4-7.

2. Trim all the wires to the same length with a pair of wire cutters.

3. Insert the wires into the RJ-45 connector, ensuring that the connector is oriented the correct way (with the tab facing away when you insert the wires), with the first pair of wires (blue and white/blue) going to connectors 4 and 5 inside the RJ-45 connector, and connect the blue wire to connector 4 and the white/blue wire to connector 5, as shown in Figure 4-7.

4. Make sure the second pair of wires goes to connectors 1 and 2 and connect the white/orange wire to connector 1 and the orange wire to connector 2.

5. Make sure the third pair goes to connectors 3 and 6 and connect the white/green wire to connector 3 and the green wire to connector 6.

6. Make sure the fourth pair goes to connectors 7 and 8 and connect the white/brown wire to connector 7 and the brown wire to connector 8.

7. Make sure a portion of the cable jacket is inside the connector.

8. Insert the RJ-45 connector into the crimping tool and crimp the connector to the wires.

9. Test the installation by pulling the cable and connector in opposite directions to make sure your work does not come loose.

© Fotofermer/www.shutterstock.com

Figure 4-6 Crimping tool

After the cable is constructed, you can use an inexpensive cable tester (see Figure 4-8) to test the cable pairs for accuracy end to end. Also, although it is valuable to know how to set up a connector (you will also hear the term "connectorize") on twisted-pair cable, in most instances it is cheaper to purchase cable that is already connectorized and tested (and the cable is likely to be more reliable).

In Activity 4-4, you used the EIA/TIA-568-B standard, which is most common. EIA/TIA-568-A is the earlier standard that was used in the early and mid-1990s and is still used on some old networks. The EIA/TIA-568-B standard evolved to better accommodate PCs and faster

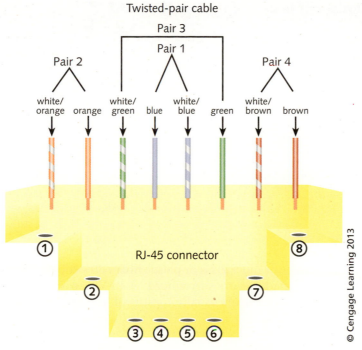

Figure 4-7   Twisted-pair cable connected to an RJ-45 connector

Figure 4-8   Network cable testers

twisted-pair cable. If you run into a situation in which you need a cross-over cable that connects to EIA/TIA-568-A on one end and EIA/TIA-568-B on the other end, you can use the following cable wiring scheme for the EIA/TIA-568-A end:

- Pin 1: white/green
- Pin 2: green
- Pin 3: white/orange
- Pin 4: blue
- Pin 5: white/blue
- Pin 6: orange
- Pin 7: white/brown
- Pin 8: brown

Real-Life Networking

If you are troubleshooting network cable because users are experiencing network slowdowns or network problems, look for places where the cable may be excessively bent, crushed under a table, or severely bent at the connector. In one organization, a twisted-pair cable was run through a doorway, instead of the wall, and network problems occurred each time someone completely closed the door and partially crushed the cable.

Fiber-Optic Cable

Fiber-optic cable consists of one or more glass or plastic fiber cores encased in a glass tube, called cladding. The fiber cores and cladding are surrounded by a PVC cover, as shown in Figure 4-9. Signal transmission along the inside fibers usually consists of infrared light.

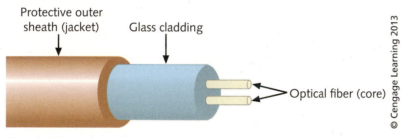

Figure 4-9   Fiber-optic cable

There are three commonly used fiber-optic cable sizes. The size is measured in microns (a micron is a millionth of a meter) and has two components, the core diameter and the cladding diameter. For example, 50/125-micron (μm) fiber cable has a core diameter of 50 microns and a cladding diameter of 125 microns. The other two commonly used sizes are 62.5/125-micron fiber cable and 100/140-micron cable. All three types of cable have multimode transmission capability, which means that multiple light waves can be transmitted on the cable at once. The most commonly used size for multimode cable applications is 62.5/125.

The cable core carries optical light pulses as transmitted by laser or light-emitting diode (LED) devices. The glass cladding is designed to reflect light back into the core. Fiber-optic cable is capable of handling high-speed network transmissions from 100 Mbps to over 100 Gbps. It is used in cable-plant backbones, such as between floors in a building, between buildings, and beyond. The fiber backbone between floors in a building is sometimes called a **fat pipe** because it has a wide bandwidth for high-capacity baseband and broadband communications. The most common use for fiber-optic cable in a campus environment is to connect different buildings to adhere to IEEE cabling specifications. Fiber-optic cable also is used in WAN and telecommunications systems to join LANs across large geographic areas. An advantage of fiber-optic cable is that its high bandwidth and low attenuation enable it to sustain transmissions over long distances.

Because the data travels by means of optical light pulses (on or off), there are no EMI or RFI problems associated with this fiber-optic cable, and data transmission is purely digital instead of analog. Compare this to copper wire–based coax and twisted-pair cable, both of which can experience problems with EMI or RFI, a distinct disadvantage of these mediums. However, both coax and twisted pair can be used for either analog or digital communications, which, in some situations, can be an advantage over digital-based, fiber-optic cable.

Another advantage of fiber-optic cable over coax and twisted-pair cable is that it is very difficult for someone to place unauthorized taps into fiber-optic cable; the cable is fragile, and installation requires a high level of expertise. Disadvantages of this cable are that it is very fragile, is relatively expensive, and requires specialized training to install.

The transmission of signals by light waves is related to the wavelength of the light. Some wavelengths travel through optical fiber more efficiently than others. Light wavelength is measured in nanometers (nm). Visible light, in the range of 400–700 nm, does not travel through fiber-optic cable with enough efficiency for data transfer. Infrared light, in the range of 700–1600 nm, travels efficiently enough for data transmission. Optical communications occur at three ideal wavelengths or windows: 850 nm, 1300 nm, and 1550 nm. High-speed transmissions typically use the 1300-nm window.

To be detected legibly, an optical signal transmission must have enough power when it reaches the receiver. **Attenuation**, or power loss, is the amount of signal that is lost as it travels through the communications medium from the source (transmitting node) to the receiving node. Attenuation in fiber-optic cable is measured in decibels (dB). Loss of optical power is directly related to the length of the cable along with the number of—and radius of—bends in the cable. Power loss also occurs as the wave passes through connectors and splices.

The wave must carry a minimum level of power when it leaves the transmitting device in order to be accurately translated at the receiving end. The minimum power level is called the power budget. The **power budget** for optical fiber cable communications is the difference between the transmitted power and the resulting signal strength, or sensitivity, at the receiver as measured in decibels. It is the minimum transmitter power and receiver sensitivity needed for a signal to be sent and received fully intact. For high-speed communications, the power budget must be 11 dB.

Fiber-optic cable comes in two modes: single-mode and multimode. **Single-mode fiber-optic cable** is used mainly for long-distance communications, has a central core diameter of 8–10 microns, and has a 125-micron diameter cladding. The central core diameter is much smaller than that of multimode cable. Only one light wave is transmitted on the cable at a given time.

Laser light is the communications signal for single-mode cable. The laser light source, contained in the sender's transmitting interface, coupled with a relatively large bandwidth, enables long-distance transmissions of up to 43 miles (70 kilometers) at high speeds. Single-mode fiber-optic cable does not have a determined speed limitation.

Multimode fiber-optic cable can support simultaneous transmission of multiple light waves for broadband communications. The diameter of multimode fiber-optic cable is between 50 and 115 microns. The transmission distance potential is not as great as that for single-mode cable—only up to 1.24 miles or 2 kilometers—because the available bandwidth is smaller and the light source is weaker. The transmission source for multimode cable is an LED device that is in the sending node's network interface.

Multimode cable comes in two varieties: step index and graded index. **Step-index multimode fiber-optic cable** reflects the light like a mirror within the cable, resulting in different signals arriving at different times and with an increased likelihood of distortion over longer cable runs. In **graded-index multimode fiber-optic cable**, light rays follow uniform curved routes inside the cable, resulting in signals that all arrive at the same time and with less long-distance distortion than step-index cable.

The types of connectors most often used with fiber-optic cable are subscriber connector (SC) and straight tip (ST) as shown in Figures 4-10 and 4-11. Both of these connectors meet EIA/TIA-568 standards. Generally, SC connectors can be used with either single-mode or multimode fiber-optic cable connections, and ST connectors are typically used with single-mode fiber-optic cable (although they can be used for multimode). Physically, SC connectors have a square shape and use a push-on-to-lock connection (also called a push-pull mechanism; it has the advantage that you can hear a click when it is in place). ST connectors have a round shape and use a bayonet-type locking attachment, similar to a BNC connector. The Lucent Connector (LC), developed by Lucent Technologies, is another frequently used connector that looks similar to an SC connector in that the LC connector has a square shape and uses a push-on-to-lock connection. LC connectors have the advantage that they are about half the size of regular connectors, which is a space-saving feature, often making it easier to add more cable runs in the future. Another type of connector, Mechanical Transfer Registered Jack (MT-RJ), is a newer connector that has grown in popularity and has a square-type end.

 Sometimes you hear the term "dark fiber"; this is fiber-optic cable that has been installed, but is not currently in use.

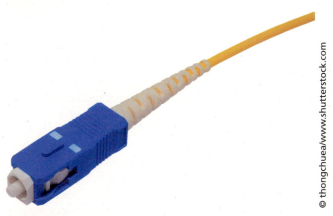

© thongchuea/www.shutterstock.com

Figure 4-10   SC connector

© tln/www.shutterstock.com

Figure 4-11   ST connector

An optical power meter (OPM) can be used for troubleshooting a fiber-optic cable installation. The OPM (see Figure 4-12) can be used to measure the average power of an optical signal and determine optical loss.

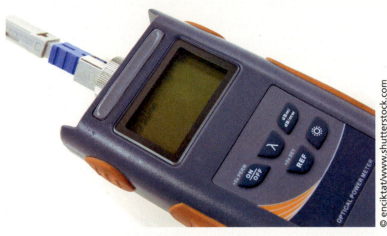

Figure 4-12   Optical power meter

Tables 4-6 and 4-7 summarize the properties of single-mode and multimode fiber-optic cables for the EIA/TIA-568-B specifications.

The EIA/TIA-568-B standard is most commonly used today and has small improvements over the earlier EIA/TIA-568-A standard. EIA/TIA-568-A and EIA/TIA-568-B are both suitable for Ethernet communications, but when Ethernet and telephone communications are combined, EIA/TIA-568-A is preferred because EIA/TIA-568-B is not fully compatible with some telephone wiring.

Table 4-6   EIA/TIA-568-B specifications for single-mode fiber-optic cable in a cable-plant backbone

Property	Value or Characteristic
Maximum length of one backbone segment	3000 meters (approx. 1.88 miles)
Maximum length of one horizontal segment (to the desktop)	Not recommended for horizontal wiring
Maximum number of nodes per segment	Two
Maximum attenuation	Less than 0.5 dB/km
Cable type	8.3/125 micron
Connector	ST, SC, LC, or MT-RJ connectors

© Cengage Learning 2013

Table 4-7   EIA/TIA-568-B specifications for multimode fiber-optic cable in a cable-plant backbone

Property	Value or Characteristic
Maximum length of one backbone segment	2000 meters (approx. 1.25 miles)
Maximum length of one horizontal segment (to the desktop)	100 meters (approx. 330 feet)
Maximum number of nodes per segment	Two
Maximum attenuation	3.75 dB/km for transmissions with a wavelength of 850 nm; 1.5 dB/km for transmissions at 1300 nm
Maximum number of segments	1024
Maximum number of segments with nodes	1024
Maximum number of daisy-chained hubs	Four
Cable type	62.5/125 micron
Connector	ST, SC, LC, or MT-RJ connectors

© Cengage Learning 2013

Hybrid Fiber/Coax Cable

Hybrid fiber/coax (HFC) cable networks have gained acceptance for use in existing telecommunications and broadband services. A hybrid fiber/coax cable consists of a single cable sheath that contains fibers and copper cables in different combinations for different implementations, ranging from backbone cables to single-site cable installations. Several factors must be taken into account when you use hybrid cables, such as the signal-level requirements at different locations in the network, noise tolerance requirements, distortion tolerance requirements, and power design.

Network solutions provided by cable networks and hybrid cables have grown to have a significant effect on the computer industry. Cable infrastructure based on hybrid-fiber backbones with coax to the home provides high bandwidth in the downstream direction and relatively high bandwidth in the upstream direction. Upstream bandwidth is usually lower than downstream because it is assumed that downloading files requires more speed and is done more frequently than uploading.

Cable TV was originally designed to send signals downstream using a high-bandwidth allocation. This design means there is less bandwidth available for upstream transmissions, usually 5 to 65 MHz, and the upstream band is shared by multiple customers. Today, the hybrid cables used in cable TV networks provide analog transmissions at 5 to 450 MHz downstream and digital transmissions at 450 to 1000 MHz. A disadvantage of cable TV communications is that some existing cable is poorly shielded coaxial cable, which means that data transmissions on older cable TV installations are subject to interference from electrical motors, CB radios, microwave ovens, DVRs, and television receivers.

To accommodate network and other new services, large cable networks today install hybrid fiber/coax cables. The fiber increases the upstream bandwidth and reduces noise, thus enhancing data communications, such as for cable modem hookups. In some areas hybrid fiber/coax cable is not fully installed, which limits networking options for cable customers. The installation of hybrid fiber/coax is expensive.

HFC cable has a bright future for WAN communications as more is installed in the cable TV infrastructure. Using HFC, cable operators can provide telephone service, multiple channels of interactive TV, and high-speed data services for PCs. A full HFC system can deliver:

- Plain old telephone service (POTS)
- Over 200 digital TV channels
- Over 400 digital point channels (customer-requested services)
- High-speed, two-way digital data link for PCs

High-Speed Technologies for Twisted-Pair and Fiber-Optic Cables

Newer high-speed LAN technologies have been developed for twisted-pair and fiber-optic cables that are designed to handle higher volumes of traffic over networks than the original 10-Mbps speeds. These include:

- Fast Ethernet
- Gigabit Ethernet
- 10 Gigabit Ethernet
- 40 and 100 Gigabit Ethernet

Fast Ethernet

The need for high-speed solutions led to the rapid development of Ethernet products capable of packet transfer rates of 100 Mbps over twisted-pair cable. Prompted by this broad interest, the IEEE standardized the high-speed Ethernet technologies generally called **Fast Ethernet**.

Two Fast Ethernet techniques evolved, because vendors were divided about how to implement it in the beginning. One vendor group, represented by Hewlett-Packard, led the way in the development of 100BaseVG or 100VG-AnyLAN. The other group, represented by Bay Networks (later purchased by Nortel Networks), Sun Microsystems (now part of Oracle Corporation), and 3Com (purchased by Hewlett-Packard), developed 100BaseX. Each of these approaches is described in the following sections.

The IEEE 802.3u Standard

The IEEE 802.3u standard for Fast Ethernet is called 100BaseX, which is the generic representation for several different Fast Ethernet transmission versions: 100BaseT, 100BaseTX, 100BaseT4, 100BaseT2, and 100BaseFX. With the exception of 100BaseT2, all of these Fast Ethernet versions use the CSMA/CD media access method for transmission of signals, as described in Chapter 2, "How LAN and WAN Communications Work." Other than 100BaseT2, all versions of Fast Ethernet propagate the signal in more than one direction on the network (unlike 100BaseVG/100VG-AnyLan). The exception, 100BaseT2, transmits signals in a timed-delay manner, timing the signals to avoid collisions.

Signal transmission is carried by twisted-pair or fiber-optic cable. In order to work, the 100BaseX algorithm requires that the signal cannot go through more than one Class I repeater or two Class II repeaters (such as devices that use repeater functions to amplify and retime the signal or any device that employs media translation; see Chapter 5 for more about repeaters).

The 100BaseX segment limitations for twisted pair are the same as those for 10BaseT: 100 meters per individual segment (again note that 90 meters is best to allow for wiring in network devices) and a maximum of 1024 segments with nodes, as shown in Table 4-8. A Class I repeater operates by translating line signals on the incoming port to a digital signal, thus allowing the media translation between different types of Fast Ethernet, such as between fiber-optic—100BaseFX—and twisted pair—100BaseTX. A Class I repeater introduces delays when performing the conversion, which means that only one Class I repeater can be put in a single, Fast Ethernet LAN segment.

Table 4-8   100BaseX communications options

100BaseX Implementation	Description	Distance
100BaseTX	Uses EIA/TIA type 1 or 1A 150-ohm shielded twisted-pair (two-pair) cable or Category 5, 5e, 6, 6a, 6e, 7, or 7a 100-ohm unshielded twisted-pair (two pairs) cable for 100-Mbps or faster communications	100 meters (approx. 330 feet)
100BaseT	Uses EIA/TIA 100-ohm Category 3, 4, 5, 5e, 6, 6a, 6e, 7, or 7a 100-ohm unshielded twisted-pair (two pairs) cable for 100-Mbps or faster communications	100 meters (approx. 330 feet)
100BaseT4	Uses EIA/TIA 100-ohm Category 3, 4, 5, 5e, 6, 6a, 6e, 7, or 7a 100-ohm unshielded twisted-pair (four pairs) cable for 100-Mbps or faster communications	100 meters (approx. 330 feet); does not support simultaneous sending and receiving (duplex), unlike all other versions of Fast Ethernet
100BaseT2	Uses EIA/TIA 100-ohm Category 3, 4, 5, 5e, 6, 6a, 6e, 7, or 7a 100-ohm unshielded twisted-pair (two pairs) cable for 100-Mbps or faster communications	100 meters (approx. 330 feet)
100BaseFX	Uses duplex (two-way) single-mode or multimode fiber-optic cable for 100-Mbps or faster communications	20 km (approx. 12 miles) for single-mode and 2 km (approx. 1.25 miles) for multimode
100BaseSX	Uses multimode fiber-optic cable for 100-Mbps or faster communications	500 meters (approx. 1800 feet)
100BaseBX	Uses single-mode fiber-optic cable (and a multiplexed signal to switch between send and receive) for 100 Mbps or faster communications	10 km (approx. 6 miles), 20 km (approx. 12 miles), or 40 km (approx. 25 miles)
100BaseLX10	Uses single-mode fiber-optic cable for 100 Mbps or faster communications	10 km (approx. 6 miles)

Real-Life Networking

Even a large organization that pays for an expensive cable installation can run into problems. One university contracted a cable installation, but the cable contractor did not precisely follow the 10/100BaseX specifications. As a result, when there was an early test of the cable installation, the testers found that computers either would not connect to the network or would intermittently connect and disconnect. When the testers used a device to test cable distances, they found that many were much longer than the distances allowed by the specification. The cable contractor was fired, and a new contractor was hired to remove cable from the walls and install new cable to follow the specifications.

A Class II repeater immediately repeats the signal from an incoming port to all the ports on the repeater. Typically Class II repeaters have all ports of the same Fast Ethernet medium type, such as all 100BaseTX. Very little delay is introduced by this quick movement of data across the repeater, which means two Class II repeaters are allowed per Fast Ethernet segment.

The high-speed communications of Fast Ethernet require that you precisely follow the standards in order to avoid having network problems.

As shown in Table 4-8, there are different ways to implement 100BaseX based on the communication medium.

Although it is possible to use cable other than Category 5 (or higher) or fiber-optic cable for Fast Ethernet communications, these higher-grade cables provide the best assurance of reliable high-speed communications.

The IEEE 802.12 Standard   Adopted by the IEEE as the 802.12 standard, the 100BaseVG/100VG-AnyLAN approach abandons the CSMA/CD transmission technique for one called demand priority. Demand priority ensures that the transmitted signal travels in only one direction. It is used in star networks, where workstations are linked by a central switch (you learn more about switches in Chapter 5, "Devices for Connecting Networks"). In this scheme, each node sends the switch a request to transmit. Requests are granted one by one. Incoming packets are examined for their destination address and sent directly to the recipient node on the star. Thus none of the other nodes see the packet, as shown in Figure 4-13.

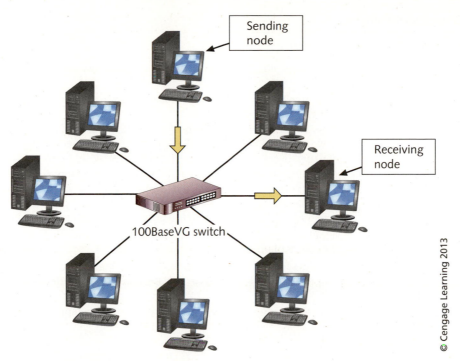

Figure 4-13 Using demand priority

Demand priority enables packets to travel up to 100 Mbps by eliminating the possibility of collisions. Besides fast transmission, demand priority has two important benefits. One is security. Because only the receiving node sees the transmitted packet, data cannot be viewed and decoded at any other node. Not many transmission modes can guarantee this type of network security. The other benefit of demand priority is its ability to handle multimedia and time-sensitive transmissions. The highest priority can be given to these transmissions, so that voice and video are transmitted within appropriate time sequences to prevent excessive distortion. Another advantage of 100BaseVG/100VG-AnyLAN is that it runs on Category 3 or higher twisted-pair cable with four pairs. Category 3 cable utilization is viable, because 100BaseVG/100VG-AnyLAN can divide data transmissions among all four pairs at the same time, sending up to 30 Mbps on any of the four pairs (but not exceeding a total of 100 Mbps on all four pairs).

Gigabit Ethernet

Gigabit Ethernet (or **1000BaseX**), which provides data transfer of up to 1 Gbps (gigabits per second), is intended to provide an alternative for backbone LAN congestion when Fast Ethernet cannot provide enough bandwidth for the demand. Gigabit Ethernet is true Ethernet in that it uses CSMA/CD, and it is designed to be an immediate upgrade path for virtually any existing 100BaseX Ethernet network that meets all of the established Gigabit Ethernet standards. The Gigabit Ethernet designers also intended it to attract existing token ring users who have star-based physical topologies that can be converted to a combination of Fast Ethernet and Gigabit Ethernet to provide increased bandwidth for growing client/server, multimedia, and VPN applications. The development of Gigabit Ethernet was hastened through the efforts of the Gigabit Ethernet Alliance, consisting of over 120 companies.

Gigabit Ethernet is particularly targeted for installations that use Network layer, or layer 3, routed communications. The first Gigabit Ethernet standard established was the IEEE 802.3z standard for fiber-optic multimode and single-mode cables. Following that standard, the IEEE 802.3ab standard was adopted for twisted-pair cable. Next, the IEEE 802.3ah standard was added for additional fiber-optic applications. Table 4-9 shows the current Gigabit Ethernet specifications.

Table 4-9   Gigabit Ethernet specifications

Gigabit Ethernet Implementation	Description
1000BaseBX10 (send and receive use different wave lengths)	Uses single-mode fiber-optic cable for up to 10 km (approx. 6 miles)
1000BaseCX (short-haul connection between switches)	Uses shielded copper twinaxial (coax) cable for a distance up to 25 meters (82.5 feet) to connect two switches
1000BaseLX (long-wave laser)	Uses 62.5/125 micron multimode fiber-optic cable for a distance of up to 550 meters (1815 feet), 50/125 micron multimode fiber-optic cable for up to 550 meters, and 10 micron single-mode cable for up to 5000 meters (16,500 feet)
1000BaseLX10 (long-wave laser)	Uses single-mode fiber-optic cable for up to 10 km (approx. 6 miles)
1000BaseSX (short-wave laser)	Uses 62.5/125 micron multimode cable for up to 220 or 275 meters (726 or 907.5 feet, depending on the frequency of the cable) and 50/125 micron multimode cable for 500 or 550 meters (1650 or 1815 feet, depending on the cable frequency)
1000BaseT (twisted pair)	Employs four-pair, Category 5, 5e, 6, 6a, 6e, 7, and 7a twisted-pair cable on segments of up to 100 meters
1000BaseTX (twisted pair)	Employs four-pair, Category 5, 5e, 6, 6a, 6e, 7, and 7a twisted-pair cable on cable segments of up to 100 meters (but never caught on with network equipment providers)
1000BaseZX (very long distance)	Uses single-mode fiber-optic cable for up to 70 km (approx. 43 miles)

© Cengage Learning 2013

Twinaxial or twinax cabling is coaxial cabling that has two main cores.

10 Gigabit Ethernet

10 Gigabit Ethernet (or **10GBaseX**), which is represented by the IEEE 802.3ae, 802.3ak, 802.3an, 802.3aq, and 802.3ap standards, is a high-speed networking protocol that is positioned to compete with other high-speed MAN, CAN, and WAN technologies, particularly SONET (discussed in Chapter 9, "Understanding WAN Connection Choices"). Also, it is designed to provide fast backbone networking in LANs. This standard is true Ethernet, but it operates only at full duplex—transmitting both ways on the communication medium at once—which means that it does not need to employ CSMA/CD because there are no packet collisions by design.

10 Gigabit Ethernet has been promoted by the 10 Gigabit Ethernet Alliance, an organization of over 120 members that was founded by 3Com, Cisco, Extreme Networks, Intel, Nortel, Sun Microsystems, and World Wide Packets. Table 4-10 shows the current 10 Gigabit Ethernet standards. Some of the standards have the same distances and general cable types, such as 10GBaseSR and 10GBaseSW, but they are different specifications because they use different types of interfaces and transmission characteristics.

Table 4-10   10 Gigabit Ethernet specifications

10 Gigabit Ethernet Implementation	Description
10GBaseCX4	Four-pair twinaxial (coax) copper cable for distances up to 15 meters (about 50 feet)
10GBaseER	9/125 micron single-mode fiber-optic cable for distances up to 40,000 meters (about 25 miles)
10GBaseEW	9/125 micron single-mode fiber-optic cable for distances up to 40,000 meters (about 25 miles)
10GBaseF	Four-pair Category 6, 6a, 6e, 7, and 7a twisted-pair cable for distances up to 100 meters (330 feet)

Table 4-10   10 Gigabit Ethernet specifications *(continued)*

10GBaseLR	9/125 micron single-mode fiber-optic cable for distances up to 10,000 meters (6.25 miles)
10GBaseLRM	62.5/125 micron multimode fiber-optic cable for distances up to 220 meters (720 feet)
10GBaseLW	9/125 micron single-mode fiber-optic cable for distances up to 10,000 meters (6.25 miles)
10GBaseLX4	62.5/125 micron multimode fiber-optic cable for distances up to 300 meters (990 feet)
10GBaseSR	50/125 micron multimode fiber-optic cable for distances up to 65 meters (214.5 feet)
10GBaseSW	50/125 micron multimode fiber-optic cable for distances up to 65 meters (214.5 feet)
10GBaseT	Category 6, 6a, 6e, 7, and 7a for distances up to 100 meters (330 feet)

© Cengage Learning 2013

NOTE 10GBaseCX4 and 10GBaseF use relatively short distances because these specifications are intended to connect servers, switches, and other network devices in close proximity. Using copper cable offers a cost savings over fiber-optic cable connections.

40 and 100 Gigabit Ethernet

Both **40 Gigabit Ethernet** (or **40GBaseX** and also called **40GBaseE**) and **100 Gigabit Ethernet** (or **100GBaseX/100GBaseE**) are relatively new high-speed Ethernet options ratified in the IEEE 802.3ba and IEEE 802.3bg standards. These standards were developed by the High Speed Ethernet subcommittee of the **Ethernet Alliance** with contributions from over 150 organizations representing companies, institutions, and governments all over the world. The Ethernet Alliance works to advance Ethernet standards and consists of users, vendors, educators, and government representatives. See *www.ethernetalliance.org* for more information about the Ethernet Alliance.

NOTE As separate organizations, the Gigabit Ethernet Alliance and the 10 Gigabit Ethernet Alliance have reached their goals to establish these standards and are now dissolved. The Ethernet Alliance remains after over 30 years as a voice in support of Ethernet technologies, including 40 and 100 Gigabit Ethernet.

40/100 Gigabit Ethernet is intended to serve two purposes: (1) enable faster computing services, such as through faster backbone speeds, and (2) provide faster communications for network aggregation points, such as within areas that aggregate network links to servers and network storage.

In terms of providing faster backbone speeds, this goal is intended to acknowledge that computing resources are doubling every two years in some organizations. Also, desktop and laptop computers are faster; there is more sharing of resources; and those resources, such as multimedia, **Internet Protocol television (IPTV)** and streaming media are growing at a rapid pace. IPTV is broadcasting television services over an IP network, particularly the Internet, in contrast to using cable and satellite communications. **Streaming media** is sending audio, video, or a combination of both over an IP network so that the contents of the media files can be played before the entire file is received. For example, radio station broadcasts and movies can be streamed over a network.

In terms of network aggregation, this situation refers to central resources such as servers and network storage in computer rooms. For example, servers continue to work faster because of advancements made possible by the use of multiple processors and faster processors and in clustering multiple servers to appear as one. Also, network storage, such as arrays of hard disks on storage area networks, is constantly growing and must be accessed faster. There is a need to aggregate links to all of these resources within a computer or network equipment room so there are no bottlenecks. 40/100 Gigabit Ethernet is intended to remove network transport bottlenecks surrounding these aggregated resources.

40/100 Gigabit Ethernet applies a range of new specifications and interfaces to accomplish faster data transmission. These capabilities include use of twinax cable and fiber-optic cable and communications across backplanes in computer equipment. 40/100 Gigabit Ethernet also includes the ability to link together 10 Gigabit Ethernet connections to appear as one 40 or 100 Gigabit Ethernet connection.

A **backplane** is a circuit board with many slots to support plugging in other circuit boards into one unit or chassis. Typically the chassis provides one or more power supplies (including backup power supplies) and circuits for data signals, and the chassis can even provide one or more forms of network connectivity. For network devices, a backplane can have many slots for circuit boards providing different network technologies.

One category of new options is the use of laser-optimized fiber-optic multimode cable, which is a relatively new type of multimode fiber-optic cable (since 2006) generally used for short runs to link network devices in a computer or network equipment room. This cable fulfills the need for aggregating network links at high speeds, which is part of the intended use of 40/100 Gigabit Ethernet. At this writing, the initial offerings of this cable start at version 3, which is formally called laser-optimized multimode fiber-optic cable version 3 (OM3). The newest version is laser-optimized multimode fiber-optic cable version 4 (OM4). OM4 extends the distance capabilities by about one quarter as a way to provide more device spacing options in a computer or network equipment room.

Tables 4-11 and 4-12 summarize the 40 and 100 Gigabit Ethernet physical specifications at this writing. Notice that the physical specifications for 40 and 100 Gigabit Ethernet are identical with the exception of the speed (40 versus 100 Gbps) and that there is no 100GBaseCR specification.

Table 4-11   40 Gigabit Ethernet specifications

40 Gigabit Ethernet Implementation	Description
40GBaseCR	Four-pair twinaxial (coax) copper cable for distances up to 7 meters (about 23 feet)
40GBaseFR	Serial single-mode fiber-optic cable communications for distances exceeding 2 km (about 1.24 miles)
40GBaseKR4	Transport across a backplane in a network device for up to 1 meter in distance and using four traffic lanes within the backplane
40GBaseLR4	Single-mode fiber-optic cable communications for distances up to 10 km (about 6.25 miles) using four different wave lengths
40GBaseSR4	Laser-optimized multimode version 3 (OM3) fiber-optic cable for distances up to 100 meters (approx. 330 feet) and laser-optimized multimode version 4 (OM4) fiber-optic cable for distances up to 125 meters (approx. 410 feet)

© Cengage Learning 2013

Table 4-12   100 Gigabit Ethernet specifications

100 Gigabit Ethernet Implementation	Description
100GBaseFR	Serial single-mode fiber-optic cable communications for distances exceeding 2 km (about 1.24 miles)
100GBaseKR4	Transport across a backplane in a network device for up to 1 meter in distance and using four traffic lanes within the backplane
100GBaseLR4	Single-mode fiber-optic cable communications for distances up to 10 km (about 6.25 miles) using four different wave lengths
100GBaseSR4	Laser-optimized multimode version 3 (OM3) fiber-optic cable for distances up to 100 meters (approx. 330 feet) and laser-optimized multimode version 4 (OM4) fiber-optic cable for distances up to 125 meters (approx. 410 feet)

© Cengage Learning 2013

Connecting Computers to a Cabled Network

A network interface card (NIC) is what enables a computer or network device to connect to a cabled network, opening the door to vast communications options. NICs are designed to match particular network transport methods, computer bus types, and network media. The network connection requires four components:

- An appropriate connector for the network medium
- Hardware and protocol control firmware and drivers
- A transceiver
- A controller to support the MAC sublayer of the Data Link layer

The NIC Connector

The connector and its associated circuits are designed for a specific type of medium, such as coax, twisted-pair, or fiber-optic cable, or wireless. Some older combination NICs are made with multiple connectors so they can be used with different media, such as twisted pair and thin coax. Today, a more common type of combination NIC has a single connector for either 10BaseT or 100BaseX cable—and some combinations also include 1000BaseTX.

A combination NIC with multiple connectors may support two or more media, but only one medium should be attached at a time, or the NIC cannot function properly.

The Role of Firmware and NIC Drivers

The network communications of a NIC are supported by **firmware**, which is software that is stored on a programmable chip on the NIC circuit board. The communications are also managed by a NIC **driver**, which is software—available on a DVD or CD-ROM, for example—that is used to manage network communications and how frames or packets are sent using a protocol. In a combination NIC, the firmware or driver may automatically detect the media type, such as 10BaseT or 100BaseX. In some operating systems, such as Windows 7 and Windows Server 2008/Server 2008 R2, hardware drivers including NIC drivers can be signed. **Driver signing** means that a digital signature is placed in the driver. The digital signature helps ensure that the driver is tested to be compatible with the operating system, that during installation the driver cannot overwrite a newer driver, and that the driver is tested to be free of defects or viruses. Try Activity 4-5 to examine the NIC driver configuration in Windows 7 and Windows Server 2008/Server 2008 R2. Next, try Activity 4-6 to configure a NIC in UNIX/Linux. Activity 4-7 enables you to view (and learn how to manually set up) the NIC driver configuration for the network medium in Mac OS X Snow Leopard or Lion. In Activity 4-8, you learn about confirming driver signing for a NIC in Windows 7 and Windows Server 2008/Server 2008 R2. Finally in Activity 4-9, you learn how to use the Internet to obtain the most recent driver for a NIC.

In some Windows 7, Server 2008, or Server 2008 R2 projects, you may see the User Account Control (UAC) box, which is used for security to help thwart intruders. The UAC box asks for permission to continue with an action or asks for the administrator password. If you see this box, click **Continue**. Because computer setups may be different, the box is not mentioned in the actual project steps.

Activity 4-5: Determining NIC Driver Settings in Windows 7 and Windows Server 2008/Server 2008 R2

Time Required: Approximately 10 minutes
Objective: View the NIC settings in Windows 7 and Windows Server 2008/Server 2008 R2.

Description: Many NIC drivers enable you to configure the NIC for the type of network medium, such as 10BaseT and 100BaseX. In this activity, you view the NIC settings in Windows 7 or Windows Server 2008/Server 2008 R2. You need a computer that has a cable-ready NIC installed as a separate card or built into the motherboard. The NIC does not have to actually be connected to the network (such as when you also have a wireless NIC and the wireless NIC is the active connection). You need to log on using an account that has Administrator privileges.

1. Click **Start** and click **Control Panel**. In Windows 7 and Server 2008 R2, make sure that **View by** is set to **Large icons** or **Small icons** and click **Network and Sharing Center**. In Windows Server 2008, click **Start**, click **Control Panel**, use the **Classic View**, and double-click **Network and Sharing Center**.

2. In Windows 7 and Server 2008 R2, click **Change adaptor settings**. In Windows Server 2008, click **Manage network connections**.

3. Right-click **Local Area Connection**, which is a cabled connection (you can use this connection even if it is not active), and click **Properties**.

4. Click the **Configure** button for the NIC in the Local Area Connection Properties dialog box.

5. Click the **Advanced** tab (consult with your instructor, if your driver uses a different tab).

6. Select the option to set the speed for the communications cable, such as **Speed & Duplex** (the actual selection name will depend on the manufacturer of your NIC and the NIC driver software).

7. Click the down arrow in the list box for **Value**, as shown in Figure 4-14. What cable or cable speed options are displayed?

8. Click **Cancel** to close the NIC Properties dialog box. (Make sure you click **Cancel** so that you do not inadvertently change the NIC settings.)

9. Close the Local Area Connection Properties dialog box, if it is still open. Close the Network Connections window and the Network and Sharing Center window, if these are open.

Figure 4-14   Viewing a NIC's speed options in Windows 7

Activity 4-6: Configuring the NIC Media Type in UNIX/Linux

Time Required: Approximately 10 minutes

Objective: Configure the NIC media type in UNIX/Linux.

Description: UNIX/Linux systems enable you to configure the NIC connection for a particular media type. In this activity, you use the *ifconfig* command-line utility to configure the media type. Ask your instructor about what interface to specify, such as eth0 or em1, and what media type to use, such as 100BaseT. Note that you need to use the root account for this activity.

1. Open a terminal window from which to enter commands.

2. Type **su root** and press **Enter**. (When you use Fedora 15 Live Media or higher, you do not need to enter a root password. For other Linux distributions, enter the root password and press **Enter** at this point.)

3. Type **ifconfig**, followed by the interface name, the word **media**, and the media type. For example, if your NIC driver uses 100BaseT as the media type and your network interface card is em1, you could type **ifconfig em1 media 100baseT** (see Figure 4-15). Press **Enter**. (Not all NICs support this configuration option; thus, you may get an error message. If so, it is still useful to keep this command in mind for other NICs. Further, to learn the media types supported on your system, try typing **man ifconfig**, press **Enter**, and look for the options associated with the media parameter. Type **q** to exit the manual pages.)

4. Close the terminal window.

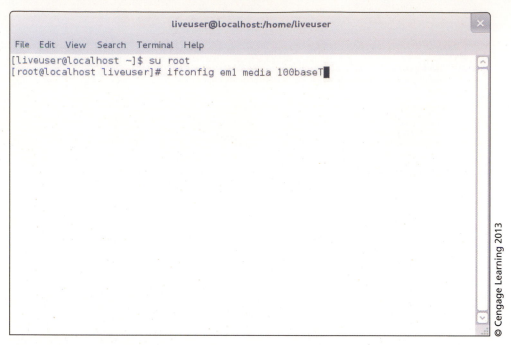

```
                    liveuser@localhost:/home/liveuser                    ✕

 File  Edit  View  Search  Terminal  Help
[liveuser@localhost ~]$ su root
[root@localhost liveuser]# ifconfig em1 media 100baseT█
```

© Cengage Learning 2013

Figure 4-15   Configuring the NIC media type in Fedora Linux

Keep in mind that UNIX/Linux commands also work in Mac OS X operating systems from a terminal window. When you use the *ifconfig* command in Mac OS X, the result shows the media setting for the NIC or WNIC, which can be autoselect or manual for choosing the media type. As in Linux, the Darwin UNIX distribution used in Mac OS X supports interface card and media parameters to configure the media type, such as *ifconfig eth0 media 100baseTX*. You can open a terminal window in Mac OS X by opening **Finder**, clicking **Go** in the menu bar, clicking **Utilities**, and double-clicking **Terminal**.

Activity 4-7: Determining NIC Driver Settings in Mac OS X

Time Required: Approximately 10 minutes

Objective: View the NIC driver settings for the cable medium in Mac OS X Snow Leopard and Lion.

Description: Mac OS X operating systems enable you to manually configure the NIC settings or to have the NIC driver automatically detect the network medium. In this activity, you view the NIC settings in Mac OS X Snow Leopard or Lion. You need a computer that has a cable-ready NIC installed as a separate card or built into the motherboard. The NIC does not have to actually be connected to a wired network (such as when you also have a wireless NIC and the wireless NIC is the active connection). You need to log on using an account that has Administrator privileges.

1. Click the **System Preferences** icon in the Dock or click the **Apple** icon in the menu bar and click **System Preferences**.

2. In the System Preferences window under Internet & Wireless, click **Network**.

3. Click **Ethernet** in the left pane, even if it is not connected.

4. Click the **Advanced** button in the Network window.

5. Click the **Ethernet** tab in Snow Leopard or the **Hardware** tab in Lion. (Note that in Snow Leopard you see the Ethernet ID and in Lion you see the MAC Address. The Ethernet ID and MAC Address refer to the same thing, which is also called the physical or device address assigned to a NIC or WNIC. See the "Data Link Layer" section in Chapter 2 to review the purpose of this address.)

6. On the Ethernet tab (in Snow Leopard) or Hardware tab (in Lion), click the **up/down arrows** for **Configure** and select **Manually** (if it is not already selected).

7. Click the **up/down arrows** for **Speed** and notice the media options. Record the options available on your computer (see Figure 4-16). Leave the default selection and reset **Configure** to **Automatically** (if that was the default when you started).

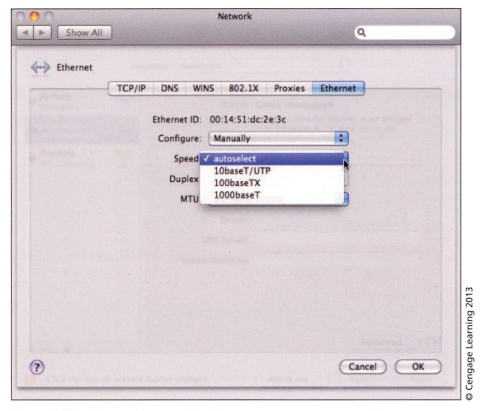

Figure 4-16   Viewing the NIC media options in Mac OS X Snow Leopard

8. Click **Cancel**.

9. Click **System Preferences** in the menu bar and click **Quit System Preferences**.

Activity 4-8: Confirming Driver Signing in Windows 7 and Windows Server 2008/Server 2008 R2

Time Required: Approximately 10 minutes
Objective: Confirm driver signing to ensure the use of a working and secure NIC driver in Windows 7 and Windows Server 2008/Server 2008 R2.

Description: In Windows 7 and Windows Server 2008/Server 2008 R2, you should use NIC drivers that are signed, if they are available from your NIC vendor (if they are not available consider using a different vendor for more assurance of compatibility). In this activity you learn how to determine if a NIC driver in Windows 7 or Windows Server 2008/Server 2008 R2 is signed. You need to log on using an account that has Administrator privileges. Also, your computer should have a NIC or WNIC installed. If the computer has both types of NICs, use the cabled NIC, even if it is not connected to the network with a cable.

1. In Windows 7 and Server 2008 R2, click **Start**, click **Control Panel,** and ensure that **View by** is set to **Large icons** or **Small icons.** Or in Windows Server 2008, click **Start,** click **Control Panel,** and use the **Classic View.** Click (in Windows 7 or Server 2008 R2) or double-click (in Windows Server 2008) **Network and Sharing Center.**

2. In Windows 7 and Server 2008 R2, click **Change adaptor settings.** In Windows Server 2008, click **Manage network connections.**

3. Right-click **Local Area Connection** and click **Properties** (if your computer does not have a cable-type NIC, you can right-click **Wireless Network Connection**).

4. Click the **Configure** button and click the **Driver** tab.

5. Look for a field that says Digital Signer (see Figure 4-17). What vendor do you see next to this field? If there is no vendor, then the driver is not signed.

6. While on the Driver tab, how would you begin an installation of an updated driver?

7. Click **Cancel** in the Properties dialog box for the NIC.

8. Close the Local Area Connection (or Wireless Network Connection) Properties dialog box, if it is still open. Close the Network Connections window and the Network and Sharing Center window, if these windows are open.

Figure 4-17 Driver signing for a NIC in Windows 7

Activity 4-9: Obtain the Most Recent Driver for a NIC

Time Required: Approximately 15 minutes
Objective: Learn how to obtain the most recent driver for your NIC.

Description: To ensure your network connection is working at its best, it is a good idea to check for a new NIC driver from time to time. In this activity, you discover how to obtain a NIC driver from a vendor's Web site. You need access to Firefox, Internet Explorer, or Safari, as well as an Internet connection.

The Web site page options and sequence may change over time. Use the Search or Site Map options to find Drivers and Downloads, if the Web page has changed since this writing. For Macintosh computers you can also use *download.cnet.com/mac/network-drivers/?tag=nav* in Step 2 and skip Steps 3 and 4.

1. Open Firefox, Internet Explorer, or Safari.

2. In the address line, enter **www.intel.com**.

3. Click or point to **Menu** and find the link or option for **Support** or **Support and Downloads**, and click **Download Latest Drivers**.

4. Notice that you can locate and download a driver for an Intel NIC from this Web page (you first need to know the name of the NIC). Or at this writing, select **Network Connectivity** as the product family, select **Intel® Desktop Adapters** as the product line, and select the NIC in the Select a product name box. Select an operating system for the NIC and select **Drivers** as the download type.

5. Close your Web browser.

Using a Transceiver

The cable connector is attached to the transceiver, which may be external to the NIC or built into it. A **transceiver** is a device that can transmit and receive, such as transmitting and receiving signals on a communications cable. For most computers, servers, and network equipment, the transceiver is built into the interface card. In some cases, most often in older network equipment, the transceiver is external to the card and a transceiver drop cable is used to connect the transceiver to the card.

The transceiver drop cable is necessary only when the transceiver is external to the NIC, and it should not be used when the transceiver is built into the NIC.

The Role of the MAC Controller Unit

The MAC controller unit and the firmware work together to correctly encapsulate source and destination address information—the physical addresses of the sending NIC and of the receiving or target NIC—the data to be transported, and CRC error control information (see the description of the OSI model in Chapter 2). The MAC controller works at the MAC sublayer of the OSI Data Link layer, formatting frames. The controller unit also works at the LLC sublayer of the Data Link layer by:

- Initiating the communications link between two nodes

- Working to ensure the communications link is not broken and remains reliable after it is established

- Ensuring that both NICs on the communicating nodes wait 9.6 microseconds between receipt of a frame and subsequent transmission of another frame, to provide a small pause or idle period, which allows each NIC to properly switch between receive and transmit modes

The MAC controller and firmware are customized for a particular type of network transport, which can be any one of the following:

- Ethernet

- Fast Ethernet

- Gigabit Ethernet

- 10 Gigabit Ethernet

- 40 Gigabit Ethernet
- 100 Gigabit Ethernet
- Token ring
- Fast token ring
- FDDI
- ATM

Token ring, fast token ring, and FDDI are network technologies that are rarely used today.

Half- and Full-Duplex NIC Communications

Many NICs are able to handle both half-duplex and full-duplex transmissions. Half duplex means that the NIC and network equipment are set up so they cannot send and receive at the same time. Full duplex is the capacity to send and receive simultaneously, which is possible because of buffering at the NIC (see Chapter 2, "How LAN and WAN Communications Work"). Full duplex is a good alternative on networks because it is usually faster. Buffering means that the NIC is equipped with memory to temporarily store information that it is not processing.

Before you configure a NIC for half duplex or full duplex, determine the setting of the communications device to which it is connected. For example, if a computer and its NIC are connected to a switch port, and that switch port is set for half duplex, then the NIC must also be set for half duplex. If a duplex mismatch occurs between the NIC and the communications device, they cannot communicate with each other.

Buses and NICs

NICs are customized for computer bus types. A **bus** is a pathway inside the computer that is used to transfer information to the CPU or to peripherals attached to the computer. Common types of buses in workstations and servers are:

- *Industry Standard Architecture (ISA)*: This is an older expansion bus design supporting 8-bit and 16-bit data transfer at a rate of 8 MB per second.

- *Extended Industry Standard Architecture (EISA)*: Designed as an alternative to IBM's patented Microchannel Architecture bus, EISA is based on ISA. EISA is capable of 32-bit communications and can use bus mastering, which is a process that reduces the reliance on the CPU for input/output activities.

- *Microchannel Architecture (MCA)*: This bus design is used in older IBM computers and has 32-bit communications capability.

- *Peripheral Computer Interface (PCI)*: This is a modern bus design that supports 32-bit and 64-bit communications. PCI uses a local bus design that enables the use of separate buses for network interfaces and for disk storage.

- *SPARC Bus (SBUS)*: This is a specialized bus in Sun Microsystems SPARC-based workstations and continued in Oracle Corporation's merger with Sun Microsystems.

- *Universal Serial Bus (USB)*: A bus standard that enables you to attach all types of devices—keyboards, printers, flash drives, cameras, pointing devices, telephones, and tape drives, for example—to one bus port on a computer.

Choosing a NIC

Every NIC is critical for effective communications on a network. When you purchase a NIC, consider the following questions:

- Is the NIC for a host computer, a server, or a workstation? Host computer and server NICs are often used to connect to a network at 1 Gbps or faster as a way to increase throughput, and these NICs must employ a fast bus type, such as PCI.

- What kind of throughput does the computer require? Workstation NICs may or may not require fast throughput depending on the applications served to the workstations. A 10/100 or 10/100/1000 Mbps NIC is a good choice for flexibility. Also, plan to use a PCI bus slot in the computer for the NIC.

- What network media and network transport method is in use? Different NICs are used for different media and transport methods, such as token ring NICs designed for token ring cable types and Ethernet NICs designed for Ethernet, Fast Ethernet, Gigabit Ethernet, 10 Gigabit Ethernet, and even 40/100 Gigabit Ethernet or a combination of these.

- Who manufactures the NIC? Purchase only brand-name, high-quality NICs—preferably with software that has driver signing—and take advantage of the fastest available expansion slot for the NICs, such as PCI.

- What is the computer or network equipment bus type? Make sure the NIC can be used with the existing expansion slots in the computer or network equipment.

- What operating system is used by the computer? All NICs require a driver that is compatible with the operating system running on the computer, for example, Windows 7, Windows Server2008/Server 2008 R2, Fedora or Red Hat Enterprise Linux, or Mac OS X Snow Leopard or Lion.

- Does the network use half-duplex or full-duplex communications? The NIC should have both half-duplex and full-duplex capabilities so it can be adapted for changes or upgrades to the network.

- If the card is for a special application, such as FDDI, how does it attach to the network? FDDI cards use either single or dual attachments. Also, some special applications use a NIC that does not have a built-in transceiver, which means the transceiver is obtained separately.

One of the best ways to prevent network problems is to purchase high-performance NICs for every station attached to the network. Also, it is critical to purchase NICs from vendors who regularly upgrade the NIC network driver to correct problems and to improve performance. Many NIC vendors offer a Web site from which to download updated drivers at no extra cost.

Real-Life Networking

A small business purchased nine Windows Vista workstations in which the cable-based NICs were built into the motherboard. When the business decided to upgrade to Windows 7, they discovered that the upgrade did not recognize the NICs because they were not from a mainstream vendor and used a specialized driver. The hardware vendor was unable to supply an updated driver for Windows 7. This illustrates that there can be unexpected problems when the NIC is nonstandard. As a solution, the company spent extra money on USB-connected wireless NICs and a wireless access point to connect to its network.

One source of network bottlenecks is a server NIC that is slow and in need of upgrading, such as an older server that has an EISA NIC instead of a PCI NIC. Another source of network slowdowns is a server that has a fast NIC, but a relatively slow CPU. In both cases, it appears to users that the network is slow, when the real problem is that the NIC, CPU, or both on the server are slow.

Putting It All Together: Designing a Cabled Network

There are lots of network cable options from which to choose, but most new cabled networks, large or small, are likely to involve the following choices:

- Use Ethernet as the transport method.

- Use twisted pair to the desktop, such as using UTP Category 5e, 6, 6a, 6e, 7, or 7a cable and 100BaseT or 100BaseT2 or faster.

- Employ fiber-optic cable (for the backbone) between floors in a building, such as using 1000BaseLX, 1000BaseSX, or 10GBaseSR or 10GBaseSW (and consider using an option that can later be upgraded to 100GBaseX, if needed).

- Connect servers to the network using 1 or 10 Gbps connectivity, such as 1000BaseTX or 10GBaseF.

- When you design a network, use the best and fastest options that your budget can afford. You might not need all of this capability at the start, but as you know, computing technologies evolve quickly and you could well need the extra capability a few years (or even months) down the road. This guideline particularly applies to servers, network cable, and network devices.

- Consider a small office of seven software programmers who work for a firm that creates specialty software for shopping malls. All of the programmers work in office cubicles within the same large room in a single-story building. A cabled network design for this office might use UTP Category 6a, 6e, 7, or 7a cable to link each workstation to a network switch via 100BaseT—using a star-bus hybrid topology. The firm also uses a Linux server that could be connected to the switch using 100BaseT.

- Another example is a small credit union that employs 28 people and is moving to a new two-story building planned for future growth of the business. The star-bus hybrid topology network design in the new building would include running 100BaseT to the computers on both floors of the building. Fiber-optic (1000BaseSX or 10GBaseLX4) cable would be run for the backbone (for a fat pipe) between floors. The credit union's two Windows Server 2008 R2 servers, which are accessed by all users, would be connected to the backbone using 1000BaseTX or 10GBaseF (see Figure 4-18). The design in Figure 4-18 includes some fault tolerance measures such as isolating the servers on the backbone and using multiple switches. (You learn more about fault tolerance in later chapters. The design shown in Figure 4-18 does not include a router; designing a network with routers is discussed in Chapter 5.)

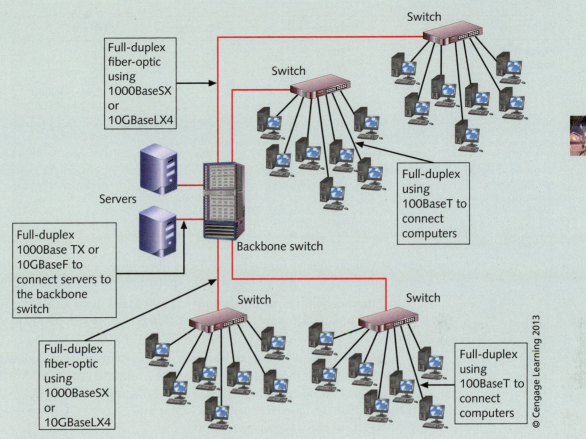

4

Figure 4-18 Designing a network for a small credit union

© Cengage Learning 2013

Chapter Summary

- The different specifications and uses of network communication cables probably seem a little confusing at this point. Table 4-13 is provided to give you a quick summary of the cable types so that you can view them all in one place.

Table 4-13 Review of cable types and characteristics

Cable Type	Coax	Twisted-Pair	Fiber-Optic	Hybrid
Specification	10Base5 10Base2 1000BaseCX 10GBaseCX4 40GBaseCR	10BaseT 100BaseT 100BaseTX 100BaseT2 100BaseT4 100BaseVG/100V 1000BaseT 1000BaseTX 10GBaseF 10GBaseT	10BaseF 100BaseFX 1000BaseBX10 1000BaseLX 1000BaseLX10 1000BaseSX 1000BaseZX 10GBaseER 10GBaseEW G-Any LAN 10GBaseLR 10GBaseLRM 10GBaseLW 10GBaseLX4 10GBaseSR 10GBaseSW 40/100GBaseFR 40/100GBaseLR4 40/100BaseSR4	N/A

(continues)

Table 4-13 Review of cable types and characteristics (*continued*)

Cable Type	Coax	Twisted-Pair	Fiber-Optic	Hybrid
Physical topology	Bus	Star Ring Star-bus hybrid Star-ring hybrid	Star Star-bus hybrid	Bus Star Ring Star-bus hybrid Star-ring hybrid
Speed	10 Mbps, 1 Gbps, 10 Gbps, 40 Gbps	10 Mbps, 100 Mbps, 1 Gbps, 10 Gbps	10 Mbps to multiple Gbps	10 Mbps and above, depending on the composition and network application
Flexibility	Not very flexible	Very flexible	Fragile	Not very flexible to fragile
Upgrade options to high-speed networking and WANs	Limited (but some versions are available for broadband transmissions)	Often easily upgraded depending on the version installed, particularly Category 5 cable and above	Designed for high-speed communications and WANs	Designed for high-speed communications and WANs

© Cengage Learning 2013

- High-speed technologies for twisted-pair and fiber-optic cabling include Fast Ethernet, Gigabit Ethernet, 10 Gigabit Ethernet, 40 Gigabit Ethernet, and 100 Gigabit Ethernet.

  - Fast Ethernet involves communications at 100 Mbps using either the 802.3u or the 802.12 standard. Of these, the 802.3u standard is more commonly used and is based on CSMA/CD. The 802.12 standard uses demand priority.

  - Gigabit Ethernet provides even faster network communications and is particularly important for backbone architectures. Gigabit Ethernet uses CSMA/CD.

  - 10 Gigabit Ethernet offers very high-speed communications. Unlike traditional Ethernet, 802.3u Fast Ethernet, and Gigabit Ethernet, 10 Gigabit Ethernet does not use CSMA/CD as the transmission method.

  - The newest Ethernet versions, 40 and 100 Gigabit Ethernet, are intended to enable faster computing through faster network backbones and to enable network aggregation, such as in computer and network equipment rooms.

- NICs have an important role on networks because these devices connect computers and network devices to network cable. Important NIC components on a cabled network include a connector, firmware and drivers, a transceiver, and a MAC controller.

Key Terms

10Base2 Used to designate a thin coax or thinnet network transmitting at 10 Mbps.

10Base5 Designates a thick coax or thicknet network transmitting at 10 Mbps.

10BaseT A network transmission approach for 10 Mbps communications using twisted-pair cable.

10GBaseX The generic reference for 10 Gigabit Ethernet versions, transmitting at 10 Gbps. *See* **10 Gigabit Ethernet**.

100BaseVG/100VG-AnyLAN Also called the IEEE 802.12 standard, a network transmission approach that uses demand priority instead of CSMA/CD. *See* **demand priority**.

100BaseX The generic representation for different Fast Ethernet transmission versions, transmitting at 100 Mbps and using the IEEE 802.3u standard. *See* **Fast Ethernet**.

1000BaseX The generic representation for Gigabit Ethernet versions, transmitting at 1 Gbps. *See* **Gigabit Ethernet**.

40GBaseX or 40GBaseE The generic reference for 40 Gigabit Ethernet versions, transmitting at 40 Gbps. *See* **40 Gigabit Ethernet**.

100GBaseX/100GBaseE The generic reference for 100 Gigabit Ethernet versions, transmitting at 100 Gbps. *See* **100 Gigabit Ethernet**.

10 Gigabit Ethernet   The IEEE 802.3ae, 802.3ak, 802.3an, 802.3aq, and 802.3ap standards for Ethernet communications at 10 Gbps. *See* **10GBaseX**.

40 Gigabit Ethernet   The IEEE 802.3ba and 802.3bg standards (for both 40 and 100 Gigabit) for Ethernet communications at 40 Gbps. *See* **40GBaseX**.

100 Gigabit Ethernet   The IEEE 802.3ba and 802.3bg standards (for both 40 and 100 Gigabit) for Ethernet communications at 100 Gbps. *See* **100GBaseX**.

attachment unit interface (AUI)   A network interface that connects coax, twisted-pair, or fiber-optic backbone cable to a network node, such as a hub, switch, or workstation. The interface consists of AUI standards for connectors, cable, interface circuits, and electrical characteristics.

4

attenuation   The amount of signal that is lost as it travels through a communications medium from its source (transmitting node) to the receiving node.

backbone cabling   As defined by the EIA/TIA-568 standard, cable that runs between network equipment rooms, floors, and buildings.

backplane   A circuit board with many slots to support plugging in other circuit boards into one unit or chassis. Typically the chassis provides one or more power supplies (including backup power supplies) and circuits for data signals, and the chassis can even provide one or more forms of network connectivity. For network devices, a backplane can have many slots for circuit boards providing different network technologies.

bandwidth   The transmission capacity of a communications medium, which is typically measured in bits per second (for data transmissions) or hertz (for data, voice, and video transmissions) and which is determined by the maximum minus the minimum transmission capacity.

baseband   A type of transmission in which the entire channel capacity of the communications medium (such as cable) is used by one data signal, enabling only one node to transmit at a time.

bayonet nut connector (BNC)   A connector that is used for thin coax cable and that has a bayonet-like shell. The male BNC connector has two small knobs that attach to circular slots in the female connector. Both connectors are twisted on for a connection. (Different renderings of what BNC stands for are bayonet navy connector, bayonet nut connection, and British naval connector.)

broadband   A type of transmission in which there are several transmission channels on a communications medium, allowing more than one node to transmit at the same time.

bus   A pathway inside the computer that is used to transfer information to the CPU or to peripherals attached to the computer.

coaxial cable   Also called coax, a network cable medium that consists of a copper core, surrounded by insulation. The insulation is surrounded by another conducting material, such as braided wire, which is covered by an outer insulating material.

demand priority   A data communications technique that transmits a packet directly from the sending node, through a hub, and to the receiving node, without passing through other network nodes.

driver   Software that enables a computer to communicate with devices such as NICs, printers, monitors, and hard disk drives. Also, a NIC driver enables the NIC to communicate with a network. Each driver has a specific purpose, such as handling Ethernet network communications.

driver signing   A process in which a digital signature is placed in a driver for a device. The digital signature helps ensure that the driver is tested and is compatible with the operating system and device for which it is written.

Ethernet Alliance   An international body that works to advance Ethernet standards and consists of users, vendors, educators, and government representatives.

Fast Ethernet   Ethernet communications at speeds up to 100 Mbps as defined under the IEEE 802.3u standard. *See* **100BaseX**.

fat pipe   Fiber-optic cable used on a network backbone for high-speed communications, such as between floors of a building.

fiber-optic cable   Communications cable that consists of one or more glass or plastic fiber cores inside a protective cladding material, covered by a plastic PVC outer jacket. Signal transmission along the inside fibers typically uses infrared light.

firmware   Software that is stored on a chip in a device, such as in a ROM, and that typically composes some type of system software.

Gigabit Ethernet   Refers to the IEEE 802.3z, IEEE 802.3ab, and IEEE 802.3ah standards for Ethernet communications at speeds up to 1 Gbps. *See* **1000BaseX**.

graded-index multimode fiber-optic cable   A type of multimode fiber-optic cable in which the light-based signals follow uniform curved routes inside the cable, resulting in signals that all arrive at the same time and with less long-distance distortion than step-index cable.

horizontal cabling   As defined by the EIA/TIA-568 standard, cabling that connects workstations and servers in the work area.

hybrid fiber/coax (HFC) cable   A cable that consists of a single cable sheath containing a combination of fibers and copper cables.

impedance   The total amount of opposition to the flow of current.

Internet Protocol television (IPTV)   Broadcasting television services over an IP network, particularly the Internet, in contrast to using cable and satellite communications.

multimode fiber-optic cable   Used for shorter distances than single-mode fiber-optic cable, this type of fiber-optic cable can carry several signals at the same time.

plenum area   An enclosed area, such as a false floor or ceiling, in which pressure from air or gas can be greater than the pressure outside the enclosed area, particularly during a fire. Plenum areas in buildings often extend to multiple rooms or extend throughout an entire floor and contain ventilation and heating ducts.

plenum cable   Teflon-coated cable that is used in plenum areas because it does not emit a toxic vapor when burned.

power budget   For fiber-optic cable communications, the difference between the transmitted power and the receiver sensitivity, as measured in decibels. It is the minimum transmitter power and receiver sensitivity needed for a signal to be sent and received fully intact.

shielded twisted-pair (STP) cable   Network cable that contains pairs of insulated wires that are twisted together, surrounded by a shielding material for added EMI and RFI protection, all inside a protective jacket.

single-mode fiber-optic cable   A form of fiber-optic cable that supports only one signal transmission at a time and that is used mainly for long-distance communications.

step-index multimode fiber-optic cable   A type of multimode fiber-optic cable that reflects the light-based signals like a mirror within the cable, resulting in different signals arriving at different times and with an increased likelihood of distortion over longer cable runs.

streaming media   Sending audio, video, or a combination of both over an IP network so that the contents of the media files can be played before the entire file is received.

transceiver   A device that can transmit and receive, such as transmitting and receiving signals on a communications cable.

twinaxial or twinax cable   Coaxial cabling that has two main cores.

twisted-pair cable   A flexible communications cable that contains pairs of insulated copper wires that are twisted together for reduction of EMI and RFI and covered with an outer insulating jacket.

unshielded twisted-pair (UTP) cable   Communications cable that has no shielding material between the pairs of insulated wires twisted together and the cable's outside jacket.

Review Questions

1. There is a portion of an old network in your building that has backbone cable marked as RG-8. When you measure the impedance of the cable, what should be the result showing that the cable is in good working condition?

    a. 50 ohms

    b. 35 ohms

    c. 22.5 ohms

    d. 18 ohms

2. Which of the following transmissions uses several transmission channels on a single communications medium?

    a. bursty

    b. baseband

    c. multicapacity

    d. broadband

3. You are installing UTP cable in a building to ensure up to 1 Gbps to the desktop. Which of the following cable types provide assured handling of 1 Gbps? (Choose all that apply.)

    a. Category 3

    b. Category 5

    c. Category 5e

    d. Category 6a

4. Gigabit Ethernet uses which of the following? (Choose all that apply.)

    a. headend termination

    b. fiber-optic, twisted-pair, and coax cable options

    c. CSMA/CD

    d. Application Layer padding

5. What type of communications cable is used by 10GBaseF?

    a. fiber-optic

    b. thick coax

    c. twisted pair

    d. thin coax

6. You have a new computer and a newly released NIC, but when you try to connect to your school's network, your computer frequently loses the network connection. Which of the following might be the problem? (Choose all that apply.)

    a. Your NIC is in the PCI slot, which does not offer fast enough communications with the computer.

    b. Your school uses a ring network, and this is a common problem with these networks.

    c. You forgot to disable the firmware chip for the PCI slot, which interferes with the firmware chip in the NIC.

    d. The driver for the new NIC has some software bugs, and you should download a more recent driver in which the bugs are fixed.

7. Hybrid fiber/coax cables are typically used for which type of installation?

    a. cable to the desktop

    b. the NIC's cable connection to a computer's motherboard

    c. networks that use token timing

    d. cable TV infrastructure

8. You are consulting for a real estate holding company that is considering the purchase of an office building in which there is 100BaseT cable and network equipment installed to each of the offices. You report to the real estate holding company that the speed of transmissions to the network sockets in each office is which of the following?

    a. 100 Kbps

    b. 100 Mbps

    c. 100 Gbps

    d. 100 Tbps

9. Which type of fiber-optic cable is best for long-distance communications of up to 40 miles or even more?

    a. single-mode

    b. multimode

    c. thicknet

    d. distance-modulated

10. Which of the following are the roles played by the MAC controller unit combined with the firmware of a NIC? (Choose all that apply.)

    a. correctly encapsulating the source and destination address information in packets

    b. detecting whether communications are duplex or nonduplex

    c. adjusting the signal tone of packets

    d. setting CRC error control information

11. You work as a security consultant for federal government agencies, such as the FBI, and you need to make sure that your work computer running Windows 7 is secure. One step that you can take is to do which of the following in relation to your computer's NIC driver?

    a. Make sure you use a 32-bit driver.

    b. Use a fast wireless connection so that it is harder for intruders to capture data from your computer.

    c. Confirm proper driver signing for the NIC driver.

    d. Use only a NIC integrated on the motherboard because this type of NIC is from a secure manufacturer.

12. When you install a 100BaseX twisted-pair cable segment, what should be the length of cable in order to allow for wiring in network devices and also ensure you are within the wiring specifications?

    a. 330 meters

    b. 225 meters

    c. 124 meters

    d. 90 meters

13. Step index applies to which type of cable?

    a. graded serial single-mode fiber-optic cable

    b. multimode fiber-optic cable

    c. thicknet

    d. thinnet

14. One of the users that you support in your company has purchased a new laptop. He purchased the computer at a computer outlet store, and a salesperson manually configured the

NIC for half-duplex communications. When he attaches the laptop to the network, it does not properly communicate. What might you do first to fix the problem?

   a. Set the NIC for 805.ab communications, which is required to use half duplex.

   b. Purchase a transceiver to use between the NIC and the network cable.

   c. Reset the computer to use full-duplex communications, because that is used by connecting devices on the network.

   d. Recommend that he take the laptop back to the store, because modern networks no longer use duplex communications.

15. Which of the following are the types of connectors you might find used with fiber-optic cable? (Choose all that apply.)

   a. fiber-tip BNC

   b. subscriber connector (SC)

   c. Lucent Connector (LC)

   d. Mechanical Transfer Registered Jack (MT-RJ)

16. Which of the following versions of Fast Ethernet use CSMA/CD? (Choose all that apply.)

   a. 100BaseFX

   b. 100BaseT4

   c. 100BaseT2

   d. 100BaseTX

17. 10 Gigabit Ethernet operates only at which of the following?

   a. full duplex

   b. 142 MHz

   c. singleplex

   d. 10.5482 Gbps

18. Which of the following cable types are used with 100GBaseSR4? (Choose all that apply.)

   a. OM3

   b. OM4

   c. UTP Cat 7r

   d. UTP Cat 9SC

19. The president of your company has replaced her two-year-old Microsoft computer with a newer one and wants you, as the network consultant, to set up her old computer for her administrative assistant. You realize that the NIC in the president's old computer, which is in the EISA slot, is damaged, and so you decide to replace the NIC. What type of slot for a NIC in the computer should you look for before ordering a new NIC?

   a. VL-bus

   b. NuBus

   c. SBus

   d. PCI

20. The IT manager in your company wants you to be able to build twisted-pair cable so there is an alternative if the company unexpectedly runs out of prebuilt cable. Plus the IT manager believes this will be good knowledge for cable troubleshooting. What cable connectors should you order to go with the twisted-pair cable?

   a. RG-58

   b. RJ-11

   c. RJ-45

   d. RG-58 A/U

Case Projects

CASE PROJECTS

Prairie Press is a publishing company that produces books of fiction. The company employs 32 people and has offices on three floors in a downtown building. Each employee uses Windows 7 Professional on a desktop or laptop computer. Prairie Press has two servers running Windows Server 2008 plus a Linux Web server. Currently, each floor in its building is wired using Category 5e UTP cable. The company's communications devices are outmoded half-duplex hubs and switches employing 10BaseT throughout the building—on each floor and between floors. The building is scheduled for renovations, and Prairie Press hires you through Network Design Consultants to assist in a new network design for a cabled network. Prairie Press wants to have a cabled network because it has already been determined that wireless communications would be unreliable due to nearby interference from radio and microwave broadcast devices.

Case Project 4-1: Desktop Cabling

What speed of communications to the desktop and laptop computers on each floor do you recommend? What cable medium can be used?

Case Project 4-2: Fat Pipe Cabling

What cabling do you recommend for linking the networks on each floor of the building? What are the advantages of the cabling that you recommend?

Case Project 4-3: Connecting the Servers to the Network

What cabling options do you recommend for connecting the three servers to the network? Are there any recommendations you have in terms of the server hardware?

Case Project 4-4: Workstation NICs

Many of the workstations were purchased a few years ago and have older NICs. Do you have any recommendations to assure good workstation connectivity when the new network is in place?

Case Project 4-5: Solving a NIC Communications Problem

During one of your visits to Prairie Press, a managing editor is having problems connecting her laptop computer to the 10BaseT network already in use. She is using Windows 7. Outline the steps you would take to troubleshoot this problem.

chapter 5

Devices for Connecting Networks

Designing a good network involves knowing the right device for the job. With the right device you can transform a slow network that frustrates users into a fast network that draws high praise.

After reading this chapter and completing the exercises, you will be able to:

- Describe how LAN network transmission equipment works, including repeaters, MAUs, hubs, bridges, routers, switches, and gateways

- Describe how WAN network equipment works, including modems, ISDN adapters, cable modems, DSL modems and routers, access servers, and remote routers

- Design a router-based network

Networks are more than communications cable, radio waves, and interfaces.
They are shaped into a functional topology by a rich variety of network transmission equipment. Without specialized transmission equipment, LANs would be limited to just a few nodes, and WANs would be virtually nonexistent. Network transmission devices are often hidden in wiring closets or in computer machine rooms, but they perform a vital role in making sure that e-mail goes to the right place, that a critical database can be accessed from another office, or that a file is successfully transmitted to another country.

This chapter describes network transmission equipment that is used on LANs, MANs, CANs, and WANs. Some of this equipment, such as modems, is already familiar to you. Other equipment, such as switches, routers, gateways, and access servers, may be new to you.

LAN Transmission Devices

LAN transmission equipment is used to connect devices on a single network, to create and connect multiple networks or subnetworks, and to set up some enterprise networks. The transmission equipment used on LANs can connect just a few computers, such as in a home or small office, or interconnect hundreds of computers in a large organization. These devices, discussed in the next sections, include:

- Repeaters
- MAUs
- Hubs
- Bridges
- Routers
- Switches
- Gateways

Some older devices, such as repeaters, MAUs, hubs, and bridges, are mentioned only briefly so you know what they are or so that you can understand how their capabilities have been incorporated into more modern devices.

Repeater

A **repeater** connects two or more cable segments and retransmits any incoming signal to all other segments. A cable **segment** is one cable run within the IEEE specifications, such as an Ethernet segment in a star-bus hybrid topology. A repeater is an inexpensive solution that operates at the OSI Physical layer—because it works with the electrical signal—and enables a network to reach users in distant portions of a building that are beyond the IEEE specifications for a single cable segment. The repeater can perform the following Physical layer functions:

- Filter out signal disturbance or noise caused by EMI and RFI
- Amplify an incoming signal and reshape it for more accurate retransmission
- Retime the signal (in Ethernet applications)
- Reproduce the signal on all cable runs

Retiming helps to avoid packet collisions on an Ethernet network once the signal is placed on the cable. Repeaters are used to:

- Extend a cable segment
- Extend a wireless signal
- Increase the number of nodes beyond the limit of one segment
- Sense a network problem and shut down a cable segment
- Connect to components in other network devices, such as hubs and switches, and amplify and retime signals

- Connect segments that use different media, such as connecting a 100BaseT segment to a legacy 10Base2 segment
- Extend backbone cable segments in LANs, CANs, and MANs
- Extend long, fiber-optic cable segments
- Increase the communication distance of T-carrier lines, as when reaching an office that is out of town

When a repeater retransmits a signal along more than one additional cable segment, it is called a multiport repeater. For instance, one repeater may have ports for two to eight additional cable segments. The cable that is run from a port is treated by the network as a normal cable segment.

Depending on the network topology and media, a single packet can travel through as many as four repeaters. When there are four repeaters between two nodes, at least two of the repeater segments must not have computers attached to them, to reduce the size of the collision domain. A **collision domain** consists of segments of an Ethernet network in which two or more computers can transmit at the same time, causing a collision (and slowing network transmissions). Segments of a network that are connected by repeaters form a collision domain. By following this guideline for connecting repeaters, you help ensure the signal strength conforms to the IEEE 802.3 specifications and you reduce the size of the collision domain (fewer computers means less collisions). Keep in mind that as you connect more repeaters and increase the collision domain, you create a less efficient network. This is one reason why switches, bridges, and routers are used instead of dedicated repeaters, because they can filter communications and manage network traffic.

Repeaters are used on WANs as well as on LANs, CANs, and MANs. For example, a T-1 WAN can be extended by placing a repeater every 2.2 kilometers (about 1.4 miles). In another example, a wireless MAN in the city can be extended to users in the outlying rural areas through the use of a repeater.

In the IEEE 802.3u specifications for Fast Ethernet, there are two kinds of repeaters, Class I and Class II. A Class I repeater is slower than a Class II repeater, and therefore only one Class I repeater can be used in a collision domain (when the cable segments connected to the repeaters are the maximum length of 100 meters, which is about 330 feet)—thus only one Class I repeater can be used between any two end nodes. This means that the total length of the network is shorter when Class I repeaters are used.

A network that uses Class II repeaters can have more than one repeater in the collision domain, but there should be no more than two Class II repeaters between any two end nodes. When two repeaters are connected on an IEEE 802.3u network, the maximum distance of the cable between them is 5 meters (about 16.5 feet), with each repeater supporting cable connections of up to 100 meters (for a total distance of 205 meters—about 676.5 feet).

Although Class I repeaters are slower than Class II repeaters, they are vital for connecting a network that uses different media types, such as connecting a 100BaseT4 cable segment to a 100BaseTX segment. In this design, the Class I repeater provides enough time to complete the packet translation between segments.

Repeaters can have ports for several types of cable connections, such as the following inbound to outbound connection examples for twisted pair and fiber optic:

- Twisted pair to twisted pair
- Twisted pair to fiber optic
- Fiber optic to fiber optic
- Fiber optic to twisted pair

Repeaters constantly check each outbound cable segment for problems. If a problem is detected, the repeater halts the transmission of data to that segment. This method of closing down a segment is called **partitioning**. For example, a segment may be partitioned if a terminator is missing or is defective, if there is a break in the cable, or if a workstation's NIC is malfunctioning and sending excessive packet traffic. When a segment is partitioned, all nodes on the segment are unable to communicate. The segment can be reset at the repeater to resume transmission as soon as the network problem is fixed. Activity 5-1 gives you experience with a partitioned segment.

Today you are unlikely to purchase a stand-alone repeater for a cabled network, because repeater functions are often built into other network devices such as hubs, switches, and routers. Before connecting one of these devices to a network, check the documentation to determine if some or all ports have repeater functionality. Also, if the ports act as repeaters, find out if they are Class I or Class II repeaters. Keep this information in mind, because the standards that apply to repeaters apply to these devices that have repeater functions.

You may, however, decide to purchase a repeater for a wireless network as one option for extending the network signal to computers that experience a weak signal from the main wireless router or access point (see Figure 5-1). Wireless repeaters (also called extenders) are used in particular on LANs, CANs, and MANs. For example, a WiMAX wireless MAN may use a repeater to extend a wireless signal to homes or businesses in a rural area that is surrounded by hills.

A wireless repeater also can have cable connections for twisted-pair or fiber-optic cables, with built-in twisted-pair cable ports that are particularly common. This means that a wireless repeater can intercept a signal from a main wireless access point and amplify and retransmit that signal to 10 nearby computers that have WNICs as well as to four computers that are connected to the wireless repeater through twisted-pair cable and traditional NICs at the recipient computers.

You learn more about wireless networks, including WiMAX, in Chapter 6, "Connecting Through a Wireless Network."

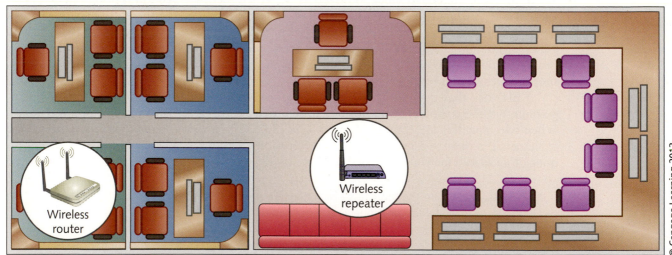

Figure 5-1   Using a wireless repeater to extend the coverage of a wireless router

© Cengage Learning 2013

In some Windows 7, Server 2008, or Server 2008 R2 projects, you may see the User Account Control (UAC) box, which is used for security to help thwart intruders. The UAC box asks for permission to continue with an action or asks for the administrator password. If you see this box, click **Continue**. Because computer setups may be different, the box is not mentioned in the actual project steps.

Activity 5-1: Partitioning a Segment

Time Required: 10 minutes
Objective: Learn to reset a partitioned segment.

Description: In this activity, you learn about a partitioned segment on a hub, switch, or router. You need a simple 10BaseT or 100BaseT hub/switch/router (or one that combines UTP connections and wireless), such as one you might use on a home network, a PC, a section of UTP cable that is connectorized, and another section of connectorized UTP cable that is defective. Make sure that both sections of UTP cable are 3 meters (about 9.9 feet) or longer. (If you do not have some defective cable, you can make it by using wire cutters to cut one of the wires going into the cable connector. Ask your instructor for help and for permission to make the cable defective before starting.)

1. Place the hub/switch/router and PC close to one another.

2. Make sure the hub/switch/router is not turned on and is unplugged from electrical power.

3. Attach one end of the defective cable to a port on the hub/switch/router and attach the other end to the NIC in the PC.

4. Plug in the hub/switch/router and the PC and make sure both are turned on. Observe the partition light (or other partition indicator) on the hub/switch/router to determine if that partition is defective. Press the reset button (if there is one) to determine if the partition can be reset.

5. Turn off and unplug the hub/switch/router and PC.

6. Use the good UTP cable to connect the PC to the hub.

7. Plug in and power on the hub/switch/router and PC. Now notice if the partition light (or indicator) is on. With the new cable, the segment should not be partitioned and should be fully functional.

8. If you want to further test your connection and your PC has Windows 7 with a shared folder, click **Start**, click **Computer**, click **Network** in the left pane, double-click a computer in the right pane in the Network window, and look for a shared folder that is displayed as a "Share." Close all windows when you are finished.

On some devices, the reset button is recessed in a small hole so that it is more difficult for the button to be pressed inadvertently. In this situation, use a pencil or pen to press the reset button inside the small hole.

Multistation Access Unit

As you have learned earlier in this book, token ring networks are rare today as are devices used on token ring networks. The multistation access unit is mentioned briefly in this section to complete your knowledge of network devices.

A **multistation access unit (MAU** or **MSAU)** acts as a central hub on a token ring network. This device is also referred to as a **smart multistation access unit (SMAU)**, when intelligence is built in to detect problems at a connected workstation and to isolate that workstation from the rest of the network. Used exclusively on token ring networks, MAUs can perform the following tasks:

- Connect workstations into a logical ring through a physical star topology

- Move the token and frames around the ring

- Amplify data signals

- Connect in a daisy-chained manner to expand a token ring network

- Provide for orderly movement of data

- Shut down ports to malfunctioning nodes

The MAU passes frames from one node to the next using a physical star topology, but transports frames as though they were going around a logical ring. Operating as a central hub, a MAU functions at the OSI Physical and Data Link layers.

MAU technology evolved into newer devices, such as the **controlled access unit (CAU)**, which allows several connected, stackable units to count as one MAU on a token ring network. CAUs also come with options for gathering information used in network performance management.

Hub

A **hub** is a central network device that connects network nodes, such as workstations and servers in a star topology (see Figure 5-2). A hub may also be referred to as a **concentrator**, which is a device that can have multiple inputs and outputs all active at one time. Hubs can:

- Provide a central unit from which to connect multiple nodes into one network
- Permit large numbers of computers to be connected on single or multiple LANs
- Provide multiprotocol services, such as Ethernet-to-FDDI connectivity
- Consolidate the network backbone
- Provide connections for several different media types (for example, coax, twisted pair, or fiber optic)
- Enable centralized network management and design

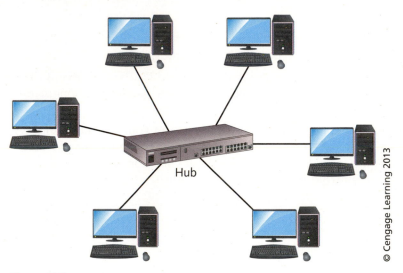

Hub

© Cengage Learning 2013

Figure 5-2   Simple hub connecting networked computers

Hubs were once commonly used because, historically, switches were more expensive than hubs. Today, prices for switches have come down significantly and switches provide better network traffic management, resulting in nearly universal use of switches. However, hubs are still used for temporary purposes, such as to enable a network analyzer to connect to a network. Hubs are also sometimes used in home and small office networks. However, hubs are generally a device of the past and are rarely used today in comparison to switches.

There are different types of network hubs. The simplest hubs provide central network connectivity by enabling a logical Ethernet bus network to be physically connected as a star. These are called **unmanaged hubs** and are for very small networks of up to 12 nodes (in some cases slightly more). Unmanaged hubs do not have management software or protocols to provide network management information or functions. Unmanaged hubs may be active or passive, but active hubs are used most frequently. A **passive hub** does no signal amplification as the data signal moves from one node to the next through the hub. An **active hub**, because it regenerates, retimes, and amplifies the carrier signal, functions like a multiport repeater. Both passive and active hubs operate at the Physical layer of the OSI model.

Many hubs are equipped with some level of intelligence, or software, which means that the hub can be used to perform network management functions. These are called **intelligent hubs** or **managed hubs**.

Some hubs have ports that can operate at either 10/100 or 10/100/1000 Mbps, offering multiple speed capabilities. The ports on most of these hubs are able to automatically sense the speed at which the devices connected to them are operating. Also, some multiple-speed hubs can divide the ports at each speed into separate collision domains, for more network efficiency.

Similar to repeaters, hubs can partition network segments that are experiencing problems. Most hubs have a light or light-emitting diode (LED) that indicates if a segment is partitioned. Also, there is typically a button or switch that can be pressed to bring that segment back into service after the problem is corrected. Before you press a reset button, make sure that you know how it impacts users on nonpartitioned segments, because on some simple hubs all segments are reset, regardless of whether they were partitioned.

On twisted-pair Ethernet networks, the hubs in the middle of the star topology used in these networks are essentially multiport repeaters. When you are using hubs (or switches), determine from the manufacturer's specifications whether ports on those hubs count as repeaters, so that your implementation follows the specifications for repeaters on the network. For example, if you are using stackable 100BaseTX hubs, determine how many hubs stacked together represent a repeater and whether those hubs constitute a Class I or Class II repeater.

Bridge

A **bridge** is a network device that connects one LAN segment to another. Bridges are used to:

- Extend a LAN when the maximum connection limit, such as the 30-node limit on an Ethernet bus segment, has been reached
- Extend a LAN beyond the length limit, for example, beyond 185 meters (about 610.5 feet) for a thinnet Ethernet segment
- Segment LANs to reduce data traffic bottlenecks
- Prevent unauthorized access to a LAN

Bridging functions are very popular on Ethernet II/IEEE 802.3 networks, but devices that perform only bridging have rapidly been replaced by those that can perform bridging and routing or bridging and switching functions (see the "Router" and "Switch" sections of this chapter). Bridges are explained here so that you can understand how traditional bridges are now replaced by routers and switches with bridging functions.

Because their implementation is invisible to users, the term "transparent bridge" is commonly used. Bridges are described as operating in **promiscuous mode**, which means they look at each frame's physical destination address before sending it on. This distinguishes a bridge from a repeater, which does not have the ability to look at frame addresses.

Bridges operate at the MAC sublayer of the OSI Data Link layer, because they read the source and destination physical address information in a frame. A bridge intercepts all network traffic and reads the destination address on each frame to determine if the frame should be forwarded to the next network. When a bridge is in operation, it examines the MAC address of the frames that flow through it to build a table of known destinations (the function of the bridging table is explained later in this section). If the bridge knows that the destination of a frame is on the same segment as the source of the frame, it drops the frame because there is no need to forward it. If the bridge knows that the destination is on another segment, it transmits the frame only to that segment. If the bridge does not know the destination segment, the bridge transmits the frame to all segments except the source segment, a process that is called **flooding**. The primary benefit of bridging is that it limits traffic to certain network segments. The bridge can filter and forward at relatively fast speeds because it looks only at Data Link layer information and ignores information at higher layers.

If a bridge is not connected to an uninterruptible power supply (UPS) or does not have one that is built in, it can lose the information in its bridging table when there is a power interruption.

Bridges provide full network access for any single protocol or combination of protocols because they are protocol independent. They look only at the MAC address. A single bridge can forward different protocols on the same network, including different LAN and WAN protocols. Figure 5-3 illustrates a bridge handling NetBEUI, IPX, and TCP/IP on a legacy network.

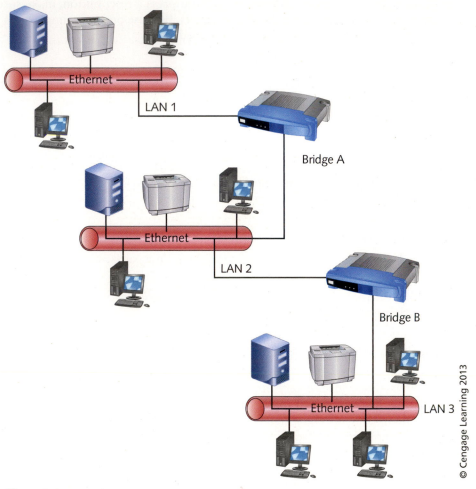

Figure 5-3   Cascade bridging

Bridges do not attempt to convert frames from one network protocol format to another, except for translational bridges. **Translational bridges** convert frames from one access method and media type to another, such as from Ethernet to token ring or vice versa. These bridges convert addressing information, by discarding token ring addressing information that is not used in Ethernet addressing, for example. The most common elements that are translated between token ring and Ethernet in a translational bridge are:

- Address bit order
- MAC address format
- Routing information differences
- Functions built into token ring frames that have no equivalent in Ethernet
- Token ring explorer packets, which are not used in Ethernet

A bridge performs three important functions: learning, filtering, and forwarding. When it is turned on, a bridge learns the network topology and addresses of devices on all attached networks. The bridge learns what is on the network by examining the source and destination addresses in the frames it receives, and it uses this information to build a bridging table that contains the address of every network node. Most bridges can store a large number of addresses in their bridging tables. The bridge uses its table as the basis for forwarding traffic.

A bridge may also contain instructions entered by the network administrator to not flood frames from specified source addresses or to discard certain frames instead of forwarding them. This filtering capability means that a bridge can be used for security, such as controlling access to a server used for company payroll.

Some bridges can link only two network segments. These bridges are used to cascade network segments. For example, in shown Figure 5-4, Bridge A connects LANs 1 and 2, and Bridge B connects LANs 2 and 3. A frame from LAN 1 has to go through both bridges to reach LAN 3.

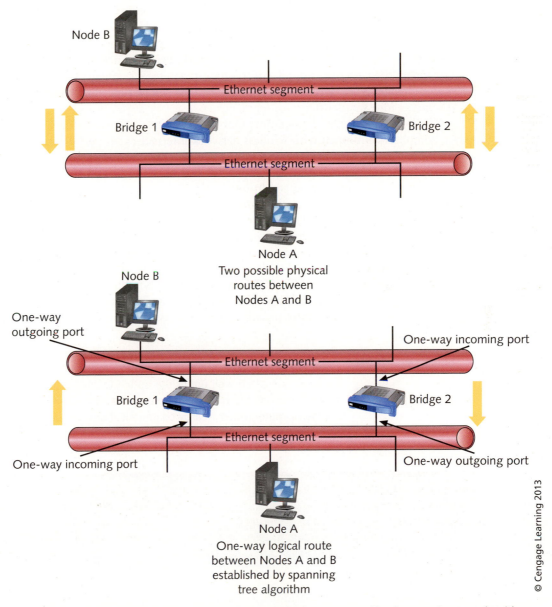

Figure 5-4   Possible physical routes compared to the logical route created by the spanning tree algorithm

© Cengage Learning 2013

There are also multiport bridges that can tie several segments into one network. Some multiport bridges have up to 52 ports or interfaces. Using the previous example, if Bridge A were a multiport bridge, it would have three ports to connect to LANs 1, 2, and 3. A frame from any one of these LANs would travel through only one bridge to reach its destination; the bridge's table would contain the addresses of all the nodes on each LAN.

Bridges can greatly enhance the performance of a network because they offer the ability to segment network traffic, limiting traffic to those networks where it belongs. This is in sharp contrast to repeaters and hubs, which retransmit all frames onto all connected segments. Another advantage of a bridge is that it can be used as a firewall to keep intruders out of a network. A **firewall** is software or hardware that secures data from being accessed outside a network and that can also prevent data from leaving the network through an inside source.

In general, there are two types of bridges: local and remote. A **local bridge** is used to directly connect two LANs in close proximity, such as two Ethernet LANs. It is also used to segment network traffic for the purpose of reducing bottlenecks. For example, in one agricultural research company, a bridge was used to link the Business Department network with the research lab network to enable sharing of certain files and e-mail. The Business Department network created a high volume of traffic because of the number of reports generated from a database server in a client/server software application system. Once the high-volume traffic to the database server was identified, the bridge was set to filter frames bound for that server so that they would not be forwarded to the lab network.

On a college campus, mainframes, graphics workstations, diskless workstations, and PCs accessing file servers may share the same network. Performance on this high-traffic network can suffer unless the network is divided into separate strategic segments based on device and application use. Bridges or devices with bridging functions can be placed on the network to isolate high-traffic areas into smaller network segments.

Wireless bridges are access points that are a subclass of local bridges and that communicate with computers equipped with wireless network interface cards (WNICs). A wireless bridge—for example, an 802.11g/n bridge—can adjust the rate of communication with each WNIC so that it might be communicating at 48 Mbps with one WNIC and at 18 Mbps with another WNIC, depending on the transmitting conditions.

An 802.11a-compatible wireless bridge operating at 54 Mbps can handle up to 64 clients, and an 802.11b-compatible wireless bridge can operate at up to 11 Mbps, handling up to 256 clients. An 802.11g wireless bridge can operate at up to 54 Mbps, with up to 256 clients (and is backward compatible with clients that are using 802.11b WNICs). An 802.11n wireless bridge offers even greater client access at several hundred clients (depending on the broadcast conditions and software applications in use), because 802.11n uses channel bonding and packet aggregation and offers more reliable communications. Also, wireless bridges can be cascaded with other indoor or outdoor bridges, or both. You learn more specifics about wireless communications in the next chapter.

If you are using wireless communications, don't be surprised if your computer is not communicating at the maximum speed. Wireless communications are often well under the optimum speed because of several factors, such as the distance between the computer and the wireless bridge or router, other nearby communications on the same or similar radio frequencies, and the building materials through which the signal travels.

Real-Life Networking

As an example of indoor and outdoor bridges, consider the case of one intercity university that initially had a cable running out the window of one building, across an alley, and into the window of another building. Several times a week, the cable was damaged, and the connection failed when a tall garbage truck went through the alley. The university solved the problem by installing two outdoor wireless bridges between the LANs in each building.

An indoor bridge is one that is in the same building, and an outdoor bridge is one that is in a nearby building.

Remote bridges are used to join distant networks. To reduce costs, bridges can be joined by a serial line. This is one way to join networks in different cities or states and combine them into a single large network, but as you learn later in this chapter, a router is often a better choice for this function.

Spanning Tree Algorithm   Networks that contain two or more bridges use the **spanning tree algorithm** to bridge frames and to set up a system of checks performed by bridges. This algorithm is defined by the IEEE 802.1d standard. The spanning tree algorithm is designed to accomplish two goals. One goal is to ensure that a frame cannot be caught in an endless loop on the network. When many network segments are connected by bridges, it is possible for frames to travel in a loop and never reach their destination. At a minimum, this eventually causes some network congestion. A large volume of looping frames can result in so much traffic that they cause a broadcast storm. A **broadcast storm** is the saturation of network bandwidth by excessive transmissions from devices attached to the network that can result in a virtual standstill of traffic.

A second goal of the spanning tree algorithm is to forward frames along the most efficient route. Efficiency in this case refers to (1) the distance the frame must travel, and (2) the utilization of cable resources. The spanning tree algorithm deals with moving frames by creating a one-way path around the network. All bridges on the network communicate with each other to establish the direction in which frames are bridged. You might think of the spanning tree algorithm as like a traffic planner who gathers information about all of the routes in the downtown area of a busy city. The planner wants to be sure that a driver cannot get stuck going round and round in the same loop of streets and unable to reach certain locations because traffic is heavy. So the planner designates specific streets as one way only, to keep traffic flowing. Any driver can go downtown and follow the one-way traffic to get to any destination without the worry of getting caught in traffic and being unable to reach certain destinations because of heavy chaotic traffic.

The spanning tree algorithm protocol enables bridges to communicate with one another using **bridge protocol data units (BPDUs)**, which are reserved multicast frames (multicasts are introduced in Chapter 2, "How LAN and WAN Communications Work," in which one frame is sent to multiple destinations) that allow bridges to learn about each other.

BPDUs can be a source of excessive network traffic. Monitor the frequency at which they are transmitted and set a larger interval between BPDU transmissions, if necessary. You can monitor BPDUs by using network monitor software, such as Microsoft Performance Monitor that is included with Windows Server systems or Microsoft Network Monitor that can be downloaded from *www.microsoft.com*.

The spanning tree algorithm is important to a network, and if you research how it works in detail, it may seem complex. Simply keep in mind the following summary of the ways in which it improves network efficiency:

- The spanning tree algorithm allows only one path to each network segment in a bridged network. This means ports on bridges that use this algorithm are set up to work in one direction, like a one-way street, with some ports allowing only incoming frames and other ports allowing only outgoing frames, as shown in Figure 5-4, which compares the possible physical routes between two nodes and the logical one-way route established by the spanning tree algorithm.

- The spanning tree algorithm prevents frames from endlessly traveling around the network, because frames travel in one direction and are discarded if they are not picked up after traveling around the network one time. The hop count is used to determine when a frame should be dropped. If the maximum route around the network is three hops (three one-way trips through bridges), then a frame is dropped at a bridge in which the hop count would be changed to four. The bridge discards the frame rather than increment the hop count to four.

- The spanning tree algorithm enables bridges to send frames along the best route.

When the spanning tree algorithm is turned on in a bridge or switch, the timing required to check for looping may interfere with automatic assigning of IP addresses in Microsoft Windows-based systems. You can circumvent this problem by running the *ipconfig* utility at the command line in these operating systems, which manually forces an address assignment, or you can turn off the spanning tree algorithm at the bridge or switch. You learned how to use *ipconfig* in Activity 2-3 in Chapter 2.

Router

A **router** performs some of the same functions as a bridge, such as learning, filtering, and forwarding. Unlike bridges, however, routers have built-in intelligence to direct packets to specific networks, study network traffic, and quickly adapt to changes detected in the network. Routers connect LANs at the Network layer of the OSI model, which enables routers to interpret more information from packet traffic than bridges can. Figure 5-5 shows a router directing a packet to a specific network, rather than unnecessarily broadcasting that packet to all connected networks. In general, routers are used to:

- Efficiently direct packets from one network to another, reducing excessive traffic
- Join neighboring or distant networks
- Connect dissimilar networks
- Prevent network bottlenecks by isolating portions of a network
- Secure portions of a network from intruders by acting as a firewall

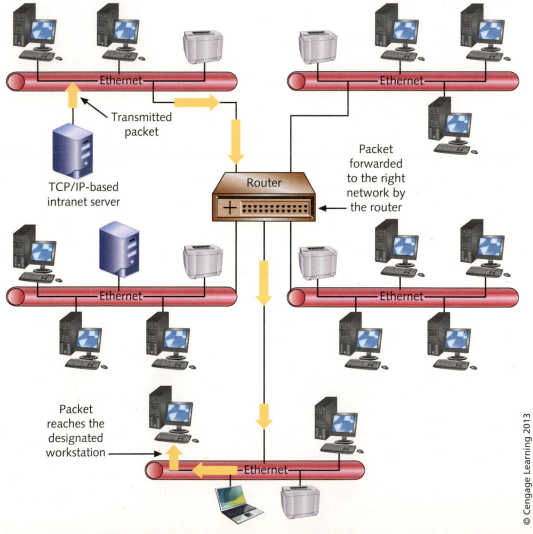

© Cengage Learning 2013

Figure 5-5   Router forwarding capabilities

Unlike bridges, routers can connect networks that have dissimilar data links. For example, an Ethernet network using the TCP/IP protocol can be connected to a packet-switched frame relay network that also uses IP (see Chapter 9, "Understanding WAN Connection Choices," to learn about frame relay). Some routers support only one protocol, such as TCP/IP. Multiple-protocol routers offer protocol conversion between dissimilar networks, such as between LANs and WANs. When equipped with the appropriate hardware and software, routers can connect to various networks, including:

- Ethernet
- Fast Ethernet
- Gigabit Ethernet
- 10 Gigabit Ethernet
- 40 Gigabit Ethernet
- 100 Gigabit Ethernet
- Different types of WANs (see Chapter 9)

Routers can keep track of network hops. A **hop** is the regeneration, amplification, and movement of a packet from one network onto another network by a router. For example, a packet that has traveled through three routers has made three hops. Hop information can be included in packets retransmitted by routers to help identify the fastest route to a particular destination and to detect packets that may be traveling through the network in an endless loop. For instance, consider a network in which there are two different routes that packets from node A can take to reach node B. One route involves going through two routers (two hops), and a second route involves going through three routers (three hops). When node A sends a packet to node B, that packet first goes through the router on its network segment. The router then determines that it can forward the packet on one route going through one more router or on a different route going through two routers. It chooses to send the packet the shortest way by using the route with only one more router between nodes.

One reason why many organizations create network diagrams is so that they can understand the number of hops from one point to another on the network. This can be invaluable information for network upgrades and troubleshooting. If you have a third party install or expand a network, also have them prepare a network diagram for you.

Also unlike bridges, which are transparent to other network nodes such as workstations and servers, routers receive regular communication from nodes confirming their address and presence. Routers are designed to send packets along paths with the lowest volume of traffic and with the lowest cost in terms of network resources. The route with the lowest cost is determined by such factors as distance or path length, load at the next hop, available bandwidth, and route reliability.

One or more of these factors are combined by software algorithms at the router into a single entity called a **metric**. A metric is used to determine the best route through a network. A metric can be calculated using any combination of the following:

- Number of incoming packets waiting to be processed at a particular port (connection) on the router
- Number of hops between the segment to which the transmitting node is attached and the segment to which the receiving node is attached
- Number of packets that the router can handle in a specific amount of time
- Size of the packet; if the packet is too large, the router has to divide it into two or more smaller packets
- Bandwidth (speed) between two communicating nodes
- Whether a particular network segment is available for use

Routers can also isolate portions of a network to prevent areas of heavy traffic from reaching the broader network system. This characteristic enables routers to prevent network slowdowns and broadcast storms. For example, consider a large and busy student computer lab in which students are learning to become network administrators. In this lab, students are frequently configuring different protocols, servers, and network devices, creating extremely large amounts of network traffic. Also, there are two lab instructors in the lab who need to have access to the main school network.

One way to manage the traffic created by this lab is to place a router between the lab's network segment and the school's main network. The router can be configured so that only communications from the two lab instructors are passed through to the main school network, while communications are blocked from the computers and the devices that the students are using for practice. Determining which communications go through and which are blocked can be done on the basis of Network layer IP addressing. Packets containing addresses from the instructors' computers are forwarded onto the main network by the router, while packets containing all other addresses are dropped at the router.

As a network grows in complexity, the need to ship packets along the shortest, most efficient path grows proportionally. Legacy bridges are often replaced by routers to ensure that growing network traffic is efficiently handled and network congestion is avoided. Also, when large networks must be joined, routers are more efficient than bridges. However, when you upgrade, take into account the packet-processing speed of the router compared to the frame-processing speed of a bridge. A bridge is inherently faster than a router, because it does not examine and handle routing information. To compensate, some routers are equipped with specialized processors to help them reach packet-processing speeds similar to the frame-processing speeds of bridges.

If you need routing services on your network, but either cannot afford or do not have a router, you can configure some computer operating systems to perform routing operations. Examples of operating systems that can be configured for routing include Windows Server 2008/Server 2008 R2 and UNIX/Linux. When you configure one of these systems for routing, you can, for example, route between two LANs or between a LAN and a WAN. If you route between two LANs, you will need to install two NICs, with one NIC connected to one network and one connected to the other network. To route between a LAN and a WAN, the server would have at least one NIC and a WAN adapter, such as for a DSL or ISDN WAN connection. Activities 5-2 and 5-3 enable you to learn where to configure routing in Windows Server 2008/Server 2008 R2 and in Linux. Activity 5-4 enables you to learn where to configure routing in Mac OS X Snow Leopard or Lion.

Activity 5-2: Configuring Windows Server 2008/ Server 2008 R2 as a Router

Time Required: 10 minutes
Objective: Learn where to configure Windows Server 2008/Server 2008 R2 as a router.

Description: A computer running Windows Server 2008/Server 2008 R2 can be configured to operate as a router. In this activity, you view where to configure routing services in Windows Server 2008/Server 2008 R2. You need access to an account that has Administrator privileges. In addition, Active Directory, Routing and Remote Access services, and DHCP services should already be set up on the server you access.

1. Click **Start**, point to **Administrative Tools**, and click **Routing and Remote Access**.

2. Right-click the computer name in the tree in the left pane and click **Properties.** Ensure that the **General** tab is selected. Notice that the server can be configured to act as an IPv4 or IPv6 (or both) router (see Figure 5-6). Click **Cancel** to close the Properties dialog box.

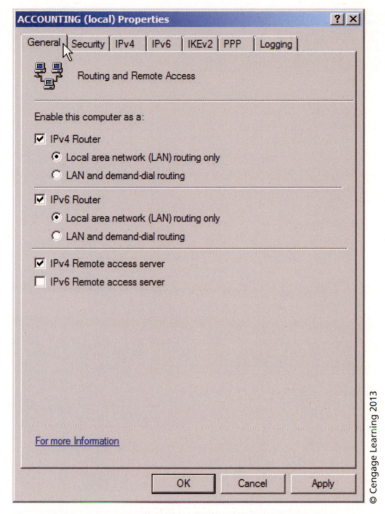

Figure 5-6 Options to configure Windows Server 2008 R2 to perform IPv4 and IPv6 routing

3. If necessary, click the **+ plus sign** in front of the server name in the left pane to expand the tree items under it. If necessary, click the **+ plus sign** in front of **IPv4** in the tree in the left pane. Click **IGMP** in the tree.

4. Right-click **Local Area Connection** in the right pane and click **Properties**. Be sure the **General** tab is selected. Notice that you can choose to Enable IGMP and to choose IGMP router as the Mode (see Figure 5-7). By choosing both of these options, you can configure routing for multicasts, such as those that are used by multimedia applications (for example, streaming video). Click **Cancel** in the Local Area Connection Properties dialog box.

Internet Group Management Protocol (IGMP) is a protocol employed by routers to create groups for multicasts. IGMP routing enables you to direct multicasts to a specific network while keeping them from going to another network, thus reducing its traffic.

5. Close the Routing and Remote Access window.

Figure 5-7   Options to configure IGMP routing in Windows
Server 2008 R2

Activity 5-3: Configuring UNIX/Linux as a Router

Time Required: 10 minutes

Objective: Learn where to configure Linux as a router.

Description: A computer running Linux, such as Fedora 15, can be configured as a simple router between two network segments, if the computer has two network interface cards. The Linux *route* command is used to configure the Linux operating system as a simple router and also enables you to view routing tables. In this activity, you use the *route* command to view routing table information and you read the *route* command *man* documentation, which explains how to configure a router. You need access to the root account.

1. Open a terminal window. (In the GNOME 3.x desktop in Fedora Linux 15 and higher, click **Activities** in the left side of the top Panel at the top of the desktop. Click **Applications** on the desktop to view icons of applications that can be opened. Click the **Terminal** icon to open a terminal window.)

2. Type **su root** and press **Enter**. (If you are using Fedora 15 Live Media or higher, you do not need to enter a root password. For other Linux distributions, enter the root password and press **Enter**.)

3. At the command line, type **route** and then press **Enter**. This action enables you to view the current routing table information (see Figure 5-8). The *route* command can also be used to set up routes between network segments.

The IP address listed under the Gateway column is the address of the network host(s), such as a router, through which a network is reached.

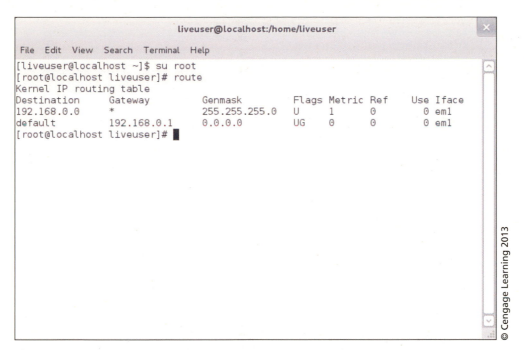

Figure 5-8   Using the *route* command in Linux

4. Type **man route** and press **Enter** to view the documentation associated with the route command. Notice that the *add* and *delete* options used with the *route* command are used to add or delete specific routes.

5. Type **q** to exit the documentation and then close the terminal window.

Activity 5-4: Configuring Routing in Mac OS X

Time Required: 10 minutes

Objective: Learn where to configure static routes in Mac OS X and view routing table information.

Description: A computer running Mac OS X, including Snow Leopard and Lion, can also use the *route* command in a way similar to computers running Linux. In Mac OS X, the *route* command can configure routing tables and static routes and set up default gateways for routes. However, the *route* command does not display routing tables as effectively as another command, *netstat*. In this activity, you view the *route* command documentation in Mac OS X and then you use the *netstat -rn* command to view routing table information. You learn more about *netstat* in Chapter 12, "Maintaining and Troubleshooting Your Network."

1. Click **Finder**, in the Dock if necessary to open Finder (or click in an open portion of the desktop). Click **Go** in the menu bar and click **Utilities**.

2. Double-click **Terminal** in the Utilities window.

3. At the command line, type **man route** and press **return** to view the online documentation for the *route* command. Press the **spacebar** to view the documentation a page at a time and briefly read the documentation so that you know this command also exists in Mac OS X. Press **q** when you are finished and to go back to the command-line prompt.

4. At the command line in the terminal window, type **netstat -rn** and press **return** to view the routing table information. Use the scroll bar to scroll up to see gateways and gateway IP addresses (see Figure 5-9).

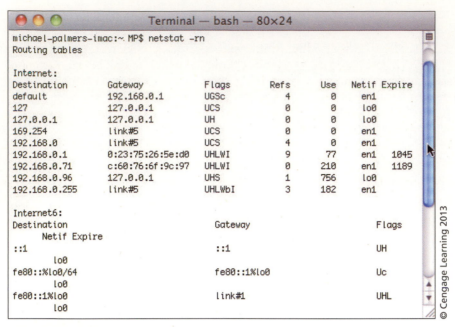

```
●●●              Terminal — bash — 80×24

michael-palmers-imac:~ MP$ netstat -rn
Routing tables

Internet:
Destination       Gateway         Flags     Refs    Use   Netif Expire
default           192.168.0.1     UGSc      4       0     en1
127               127.0.0.1       UCS       0       0     lo0
127.0.0.1         127.0.0.1       UH        0       0     lo0
169.254           link#5          UCS       0       0     en1
192.168.0         link#5          UCS       4       0     en1
192.168.0.1       0:23:75:26:5e:d0 UHLWI    9       77    en1   1045
192.168.0.71      c:60:76:6f:9c:97 UHLWI    0       210   en1   1189
192.168.0.96      127.0.0.1       UHS       1       756   lo0
192.168.0.255     link#5          UHLWbI    3       182   en1


Internet6:
Destination                       Gateway                   Flags
     Netif Expire
::1                               ::1                       UH
     lo0
fe80::%lo0/64                     fe80::1%lo0               Uc
     lo0
fe80::1%lo0                       link#1                    UHL
     lo0
```

Figure 5-9   Using the *netstat -rn* command in Mac OS X

© Cengage Learning 2013

The IP address or addresses listed under the Gateway column show the address(es) of the network host(s), such as routers, through which a network is reached.

5. Click **Terminal** in the menu bar and click **Quit Terminal**. Also, close any open windows, such as the Utilities window.

Some directory services, such as Microsoft Active Directory, create extra network traffic. The traffic is the result of frequent replication between multiple servers of the directory service data. A directory service is a large database of network resources, such as computers, printers, user accounts, and user groups. The database is replicated to all servers that are responsible for helping to manage network resources, such as authorizing users to log onto the network. One way to control the amount of traffic created by replication of the directory service database is to strategically place routers between remote servers. In addition, in Microsoft Active Directory, you can designate the routers as "site link bridges," so that the routers can direct replication traffic along the most efficient routes (designated as Active Directory "site links"). In Activity 5-5 you learn how to configure a site link bridge.

Activity 5-5: Configuring a Site Link Bridge in Windows Server 2008/Server 2008 R2

This activity is somewhat advanced and is included for students and classes who have an interest in Active Directory. If access to Active Directory is not available to you or you do not have the resources for this activity, simply make a mental note that configuring a site link bridge in Active Directory is a good way to enable a Windows Server network to operate more efficiently.

Time Required: 10 minutes

Objective: Learn where to configure a site link bridge in Windows Server 2008/Server 2008 R2.

Description: Microsoft Active Directory enables you to create a site link bridge between two or more networks. For example, the networks in Buildings A, B, and C might each be designated as individual sites, for a total of three sites. A single router might be used to link all three sites. The cables from each site into the router would be designated in Active Directory as site links.

An Active Directory administrator can control network traffic and set up fault tolerance (in case one site link is down), by enabling the router as a site link bridge (a site link bridge is a logical traffic director and not really a bridge). Although this sounds complex, the bottom line is that by setting up a site link bridge, you make a network of Windows servers work more efficiently and provide alternate communication routes, even when one link is down.

To perform this activity, Active Directory should be installed in Windows Server 2008/Server 2008 R2, and two site links should already be configured by your instructor. Also, you need an account with Administrator privileges.

1. Click **Start,** point to **Administrative Tools,** and click **Active Directory Sites and Services.**

2. Click the **+ plus sign** in front of **Sites** in the tree, if the objects under it are not already displayed.

3. Click the **+ plus sign** in front of **Inter-Site Transports** in the tree, if the objects under it are not displayed.

4. Right-click the **IP** folder in the tree.

5. Click **New Site Link Bridge**.

6. Enter a name for the site link bridge consisting of your initials and Bridge, such as JPBridge.

7. Click one of the site links (already created by your instructor) in the Site links not in this site link bridge option box.

8. Click the **Add** button (see Figure 5-10).

9. Click one other site link in the Site links not in this site link bridge option box.

10. Click **Add**.

11. How would you configure additional site links into the bridge?

12. Click **OK** and then close the Active Directory Sites and Services window.

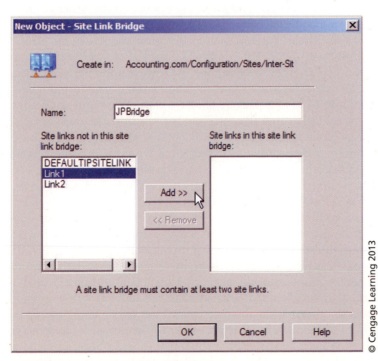

Figure 5-10   Creating a site link bridge

Static and Dynamic Routing

Routing can be either static or dynamic. **Static routing** requires routing tables, which are set up by the network administrator and which specify fixed paths between any two routers. The information in the tables is manually entered by the network administrator. The network administrator also intervenes to manually update routing tables when a network device fails. A router configured with static routes can determine that a network link is down, but it cannot automatically reroute traffic without intervention from the network administrator.

Dynamic routing occurs independently of the network administrator. Routers use dynamic routing protocols to automatically:

- Determine which other routers on other network segments they can reach
- Determine the shortest paths to other networks by using metrics
- Determine when the network path to a particular router is down or cannot be used
- Use metrics to reconfigure the best routes when a particular network path is unavailable
- Rediscover a router and network path after a network problem on that path has been solved

Routing Tables and Protocols

Routers maintain information about node addresses and network status in databases. Routing table databases contain the addresses of other routers. Routers that are configured for dynamic routing automatically update the routing tables by regularly exchanging address information with other routers.

Routers also regularly exchange information about network traffic, the network topology, and the status of network links. This information is kept in a network status database in each router.

When a packet arrives, the router examines the protocol destination address, such as the IP address in a TCP/IP packet. It decides how to forward the packet on the basis of the metrics it uses, such as network status information and a calculation of the number of hops required for the packet to reach its destination.

Routers that use a single protocol (such as TCP/IP) maintain only one address database. A multiprotocol router has an address database for each protocol it recognizes.

Routers exchange information by using a routing protocol. Routers use different techniques for communicating through a routing protocol. For example, a router may examine the status of all of its immediate links and send that information to other routers, using a link-state routing communication. Or a router might send a routing update to the other routers on the network, which consists of sending a part or all of the contents of its routing table.

Routers that are in a local system, such as within a single organization and on the same LAN, use two common protocols for communications: RIP and OSPF. **Routing Information Protocol (RIP)** is used by routers to determine the fewest hops between themselves and other routers, and this information is added to each router's table. The hop data is then used to help determine the best route to send a packet, similar to the use of hop counts by bridges. RIP is a less popular option because each RIP router sends a routing update message that contains the entire routing table as often as twice a minute. This can create excessive traffic on a network that contains several routers. The problem is exacerbated when designated servers are also configured to keep routing information and regularly send it through RIP.

RIP's usefulness is limited because this protocol uses only hop count as its metric. It cannot determine the best path to take when different options are available, such as Fast Ethernet versus Gigabit Ethernet or a high-traffic route versus a low-traffic route. Another limitation is that RIP is limited to 15 hops. A network over 15 hops away is treated as inaccessible. Still another limitation is that RIP communications can slow down on networks with links at different speeds, such as Fast Ethernet and Gigabit Ethernet. Despite these limitations, RIP continues to be used on small networks where a simple routing protocol is sufficient and where network traffic is not a significant problem. A RIP packet primarily consists of a header with command information; an IP address that provides information about associated networks; and a metric that is the distance, or the number of hops, from the broadcasting router to the network identified in the IP address.

The **Open Shortest Path First (OSPF) protocol** is more commonly used and offers several advantages over RIP. One advantage is that the router sends only the portion of the routing table that pertains to its most immediate router links, which is called the "link-state routing message." You might think of the link state as similar to taking the current blood pressure, temperature, and other vital signs of a network interface on a router. The link state information consists of:

- Router interface IP address
- Subnet mask

- Type of network connection (wired or wireless, for example)
- Other routers on the immediate network
- The router's relationship to other routers on the network (such number of hops to nearby routers)

OSPF version 2 (OSPFv2) is used with IPv4, and OSPFv3 is used with IPv6.

In OSPF, the most immediate router links are determined by setting up area border routers at either end of the network. For example, on a multiple-building business campus, you might divide the network of each building into a separate area and thus consider each building as a different network area. One large building (Building A) might house five routers and be considered Area A. One of the routers (a border router) in Area A connects to the network in Building B, which is Area B. And another router (also a border router) in Area A connects to the network in Building C, which consists of Area C. All five of the routers in Area A share routing table information using the OSPF protocol, as shown in Figure 5-11. You might consider these five routers

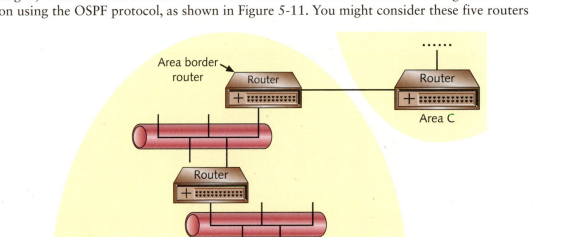
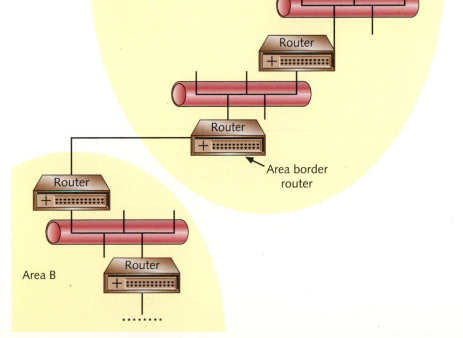

Figure 5-11   OSPF protocol border areas

as similar to neighbors in a block who regularly meet briefly over the fence or on the street to share information—starting off by asking, "How are you?" But because they are close by and familiar with one another, they don't have to reintroduce themselves and talk about their families from scratch. However, if someone has a new baby or is ill, this news comes up right away. The routers internal to each OSPF area are like the neighbors just over the fence and use area OSPF routing information exchanges in this way.

Several other advantages of the OSPF protocol over RIP are:

- It packages routing information in a more compact packet format than RIP.
- Only updated routing table information is shared among routers, rather than the entire routing table.
- There is no hop count limit as with RIP.
- It does not slow down on networks with different speeds.
- It enables better load balancing of network traffic than RIP.
- It enables better authentication security for routing information than RIP.

Because the OSPF protocol is more efficient than RIP, a router using the OSPF protocol can quickly build its routing table. When they are first turned on, routers that use the OSPF protocol begin determining the distance to the networks directly connected to them, which is called the distance vector. Next, using the distance vector data, the routers determine the link cost to each network. The farther away a network is from the router, the greater the link cost. When a network is moved, the router recalculates the link cost. Also, the OSPF protocol frequently checks for the addition of new networks so that these link costs can be calculated.

LAN-based routers that join networks within the same building or that link adjacent networks on a campus are local routers. For example, a local router might join two Ethernet networks on the same floor of a building or two networks in separate buildings. These routers continuously monitor their constituent networks so that routing tables are updated to reflect network changes. They monitor changes in line speeds, network load, network addressing, and network topologies.

Local routers are used to segment network traffic and to enforce security. A local router can be used to prevent certain types of packets from leaving a specific network segment, and it can be used to control which network nodes are able to reach a segment containing sensitive business information. When you employ a router for security, it acts like a firewall on your network, protecting the network from hackers and unwanted traffic.

Switch

Switches provide bridging capacity along with the ability to increase the bandwidth on existing networks. Switches used on LANs are similar to bridges, in that they operate at the Data Link MAC sublayer (Layer 2) to examine the device addresses of all incoming traffic. Also like a bridge, a switch keeps a table of information about addresses and uses that information to decide how to filter and forward LAN traffic. In addition, switches can use the spanning tree algorithm to manage network traffic.

Unlike a bridge, switches use switching techniques to increase the throughput of data and the bandwidth of installed media. A LAN switch typically uses one of two types of switching techniques, called the switching fabric: cut-through switching and store-and-forward switching.

Cut-through switching is accomplished by forwarding portions of frames before the entire frame is received. The frame is forwarded as soon as the MAC-level destination address is read, and the destination port is determined from the switch's table. This method affords relatively high transmission speeds, in part by forgoing error checking.

In store-and-forward switching (also called buffered switching), the frame is not forwarded until it is completely received. Once a frame is received by the switch, it is examined for errors, using the CRC, before being sent to the destination node. Next, the frame is buffered until an appropriate port and communications link are available (not busy with existing communications). Some switches (sometimes called routing switches) that use store-and-forward switching may also combine routing with switching and thus operate at the Network layer (Layer 3) to establish the fastest path to the destination. One advantage of switches that combine routing functions is that they offer more flexibility in segmenting network traffic to avoid broadcast storms, which can occur in Ethernet networks.

There are also switches that vendors have designed to operate at Layers 4 and above.

Store-and-forward switching has become more popular than cut-through switching, and some of these switches use a CPU to increase throughput. In ideal conditions, CPU-based switches are significantly faster than non-CPU switches. In some cases, though, CPU-based switches can become overburdened with incoming traffic, putting CPU utilization at 100% and actually causing the switch to be slower than those without a CPU. If a CPU-based switch is employed, it is important to check the capacity of the CPU to determine if it matches the anticipated load on the network.

One of the most common uses of switches is to reduce collisions and improve bandwidth on Ethernet LANs. Ethernet switches use their tables of MAC addresses to determine which port should receive particular data. Since each port is attached to a segment with only one node, that node and segment have the full bandwidth—10 Mbps, 100 Mbps, 1 Gbps, 10 Gbps, or 40/100 Gbps—because there are no other nodes, which reduces the likelihood of collisions.

Although in some circumstances IEEE specifications allow for two connected nodes on an Ethernet hub or switch segment, most network administrators attach only one node, to create a network design that can take advantage of improved bandwidth capabilities through switching.

By switching directly to the segment that is to receive the data, switches can significantly increase the bandwidth of a network without the need to upgrade the existing network medium. Consider, for example, an Ethernet hub that has eight attached 100 Mbps segments, but that has no switching capability. The capacity of this hub can never exceed 100 Mbps because it can retransmit data to only one segment at a time. If the hub is replaced by an Ethernet LAN switch, the total capacity of the network is increased by a factor of eight, for a total capacity of 800 Mbps (8 × 100 Mbps), because the switch can retransmit to each segment at nearly the same time. Since switches are cost effective compared with hubs, they offer an immediate way to improve performance on a high-traffic network.

Switches can be unmanaged or managed. An **unmanaged switch** is one that has a fixed configuration that you cannot change and that does not support network configuration or monitoring capabilities. A **managed switch** offers settings to configure the switch to use different options, to manage network traffic, and to help monitor the network. On most networks it is well worth any extra expense to purchase a managed switch for the configuration options to help manage network traffic and because it supports Simple Network Management Protocol (SNMP), thereby enhancing network monitoring and control.

Some examples of management options in managed switches include:

- Activating or deactivating specific ports
- Assigning priorities to ports
- Aggregating multiple links into one for higher bandwidth
- Using SNMP for monitoring
- Employing the spanning tree algorithm protocol
- Employing MAC filtering

Gateway

The term **gateway** is used in many contexts, but in general it refers to a software or hardware interface that enables two different types of networked systems or software to communicate. For example, you might use a gateway to:

- Convert commonly used protocols (for example, TCP/IP) to a specialized or proprietary protocol (for example, SNA used by legacy IBM mainframes or AppleTalk used by older Macintosh computers)
- Convert message formats from one format to another

- Translate different addressing schemes
- Link a host computer to a LAN
- Provide terminal emulation for connections to a host computer
- Direct e-mail to the right network destination
- Connect networks with different architectures

Because there are so many broad applications of gateways, they can function at any of the OSI layers. The most traditional type of gateway is a network device that translates one type of protocol to another that has a very different structural composition. This type of gateway operates at the Network layer of the OSI model. One example of this is a gateway that translates IBM's Systems Network Architecture (SNA) protocol for mainframe communications to another protocol, such as the more widely used TCP/IP. Another example is a gateway used to convert TCP/IP protocol communications to frame relay on a WAN (you learn about frame relay in Chapter 9). Yet another example is using a gateway to convert TCP/IP communications for use on a Fibre Channel **Storage Area Network (SAN)**. A SAN is a grouping of storage devices, such as hard disk arrays, that forms a subnet so that the storage devices are available to any server on the main network. **Fibre Channel** is a type of SAN that enables gigabit high-speed data transfer.

The problem with the traditional type of gateway for translating protocols is that it is relatively slow compared to other solutions, and as a result, the use of traditional gateways is becoming less frequent.

Another common use of the term "gateway" is for software that converts e-mail messages from one format to another.

Tables 5-1 and 5-2 summarize the LAN connectivity devices you have learned about so far, dividing these into older and current devices.

Table 5-1   Older LAN connectivity devices

Device	Function	OSI Layer	Uses
Repeater	Connects two or more cable segments; it amplifies and retimes a packet- or cell-carrying signal so that it can be sent along all outgoing cable segments attached to that repeater. Repeater functionality can be combined into other network devices, thus stand-alone repeaters are not commonly used other than to extend a wireless signal	Physical layer	• Extend cable segments • Increase the number of nodes • Connect segments that use different media • Extend backbone segments • Extend fiber-optic segments
Multistation access unit (MAU) and controlled access unit (CAU)	Functions as a central hub in a token ring network (when it is an active hub, it regenerates, retimes, and amplifies the retransmitted signal)	Physical and Data Link layers	• Connect workstations into a logical ring (with a physical star topology) • Expand a network through daisy-chaining
Hub	A central network device that connects network nodes in a physical star topology; an intelligent hub has network management functions	Physical layer	• Connect multiple nodes • Enable multiprotocol services between different types of LANs • Consolidate a backbone • Offer connections for different media types • Centralize network design

Table 5-2   Currently used LAN connectivity devices

Device	Function	OSI Layer	Uses
Bridge	Connects one LAN segment to another and performs functions such as learning, filtering, and forwarding; operates in promiscuous mode—even though stand-alone bridges are not common on cabled networks, bridging functions are used in routers and switches	Data Link layer (MAC sublayer)	• Extend a LAN • Segment LANs to reduce traffic bottlenecks • Prevent unauthorized access to a LAN • Translational bridges convert frames from one access method and media type to another
Router	As with a bridge, performs learning, filtering, and forwarding, but unlike a bridge can use routing to direct packets to a specific network	Network layer	• Direct packets from one network to another • Join neighboring and distant networks • Connect dissimilar networks • Manage network congestion • Secure networks by acting as a firewall
Switch	Provide bridging capacity along with the ability to increase the bandwidth on existing networks (Layer 2 switches); some switches have routing capabilities (Layer 3)	Data Link (for Layer 2 switches) or Network (for Layer 3 switches)	• Replace or use instead of hubs to reduce collisions and improve bandwidth • Provide options for network management (if a managed or intelligent switch)
Gateway	Enables two different types of networks (or software) to communicate	Any OSI layer, depending on the intended function of the gateway	• Convert common protocols to specialized protocols • Convert different message formats • Translate different addressing schemes • Link a host computer, such as a mainframe, to a LAN • Provide terminal emulation • Direct e-mail

© Cengage Learning 2013

WAN Transmission Devices

WAN transmission equipment is designed to work over Public Switched Telephone Networks (PSTN) and leased telephone lines such as T-carrier or Integrated Services Digital Network (ISDN). ISDN is a standard for digital data services over telephone lines that you learn more about in Chapter 9.

WAN transmission equipment may have an analog component, as is true for modems, or it may be completely digital, as for ISDN communications. Most WAN transmission equipment either converts a signal for long-distance communications or creates multiple channels within a single communications medium for higher bandwidth. There is not room here to discuss all of the varieties of WAN transmission devices, but there are several devices you are likely to work with:

- Analog telephone modems
- ISDN adapters
- Cable TV modems
- DSL modems and routers
- Access servers
- Remote routers

Analog Telephone Modems

Analog telephone modems have long played a role in making WANs possible, although their role is widely diminished because of faster alternatives, such as cable TV and DSL discussed later in this chapter. The term **modem** is a shortened version of the term "modulator/demodulator."

A modem converts a computer's outgoing digital signal to an analog signal that can be transmitted over a telephone line. It also converts the incoming analog signal to a digital signal that the computer can understand.

A modem is attached to a computer in one of two ways: internally or externally. An internal modem, the most commonly used variety, is installed inside the computer using an empty expansion slot on the main board. An external modem is a separate device that connects to a serial port on the computer. An external modem is attached with a cable designed for modem communications that matches the serial port connector on the computer.

There are three common types of connectors: an older style DB-25 connector that has 25 pins and resembles a parallel port for a printer (but does not use parallel communications); a DB-9 connector with nine pins; and a round PS/2 connector for serial communications, such as on an IBM PC. Universal serial bus (USB) connectors are also implemented for serial communications. USB is a standard for connecting all kinds of peripherals, such as keyboards, pointing devices, printers, modems, scanners, cameras, and backup and storage devices, and in many cases has replaced the use of traditional parallel and serial ports. Both internal and external modems connect to a telephone outlet through a regular telephone cable with RJ-11 connectors at each end.

The modem data transfer rate is measured in bits per second (bps), which is the number of binary bits (0s or 1s) sent in one second. Modems are currently capable of transmitting up to 56 Kbps. However, modems in conjunction with specialized ISP services can use data compression to effectively achieve 220 to 320 Kbps, and faster. If you use data compression for modem communications, be aware that files with digital images may reproduce at lower quality because of the compression/decompression algorithms used. Another strategy used to speed up modem communications is to join or bond two modems for twice the throughput.

The ITU has also developed standards for modem communications. The current most commonly used standard is V.92, which offers up to 56 Kbps transmission for downloads and up to 48 Kbps for uploads.

When a PC is connected to a modem, the data transfer speed of the PC is the data terminal equipment (DTE) communications rate. A DTE is a computer or device that prepares data to be transmitted over a telecommunications line. The speed of the modem is called the data communications equipment (DCE) communications rate. The DCE—such as a modem—is a device that converts data from a DTE—such as a computer—to be transmitted over a telecommunications line. The PC port setup for the modem (DTE rate) should be the same as or higher than the DCE rate of the modem. In Activity 5-6, you check the DTE rate in Windows 7 or Windows Server 2008/Server 2008 R2.

Modems use one of two communication formats: synchronous or asynchronous. Synchronous communications are continuous bursts of data controlled by a clock signal that starts each burst. Asynchronous communications occur in discrete units, each delimited by start and stop bits.

Activity 5-6: Configure the Port Speed for a Modem

Time Required: 5 minutes
Objective: Configure the port setup for a modem in Windows 7 or Windows Server 2008/Server 2008 R2.

Description: This activity enables you to check the modem port speed setup in Windows 7 or Windows Server 2008/Server 2008 R2. In Windows-based systems, it is important to make sure that the port speed (the speed set for the serial, USB, or parallel port to which the modem is connected) is the same as or higher than the speed capability of the modem. If it is not, then you are not using the full speed capability of the modem. Before you start, ask your instructor about the speed of the modem installed in the computer(s) that you use in this activity.

1. In Windows 7 and Server 2008 R2, click **Start**, click **Control Panel**, ensure **View by** is set to **Large icons** or **Small icons**, and click **Phone and Modem**. In Windows Server 2008, click **Start**, click **Control Panel**, ensure you are in the **Classic View**, and double-click **Phone and Modem Options**.

2. If you see the Local Information dialog box from which to specify the country/region, the local area code, and other communications information, provide the applicable information for your locale and click **OK**.

3. Click the **Modems** tab in the Phone and Modem (in Windows 7 and Server 2008 R2) or the Phone and Modem Options (in Windows Server 2008) dialog box.

4. Select a modem (if there is more than one option). Click the **Properties** button.

5. Click the **Modem** tab.

6. What is the value in the Maximum Port Speed box? Is it higher than the actual speed of the modem?

7. How can you change the port speed?

8. Click **Cancel** to close the Modem Properties dialog box. Click **Cancel** to close the Phone and Modem or Phone and Modem Options dialog box. Close any remaining open windows.

ISDN Adapters

ISDN WAN access has largely been replaced by DSL and cable TV, but ISDN is still available in some nonmetropolitan areas that don't offer more modern WAN technologies. ISDN lines require the use of a digital modem-like device called a terminal adapter (TA) to connect a PC. ISDN TAs are available for about the same cost as a high-quality asynchronous or synchronous modem, but have higher data-transfer capabilities (for example, 128 to 512 Kbps). A TA converts a digital signal to a protocol that can be sent over a digital telephone line. TAs typically include analog telephone jacks so you can plug in a conventional telephone or modem for use over the digital line. With most ISDN hardware, you connect to a single telephone line of copper pair (the same kind of wire that brings telephone service into your home or office consisting of one or two pairs of two wires twisted together), but you get separate channels for computer data and for analog telephone lines. You can use one analog line and one data line simultaneously, or two digital lines, or two analog lines.

ISDN is still viable in rural areas that don't offer cable or DSL and is used for broadcast services and credit card verification. Telephone company representatives often do not know of ISDN, and so you have to ask the local technical personnel if ISDN is available. If the local switches handle call forwarding, call waiting, and answering services, they are also likely to be equipped for ISDN.

Cable TV Modems

In many areas, cable TV providers also offer data services to businesses and homes. A cable modem communicates using upstream and downstream frequencies (channels) that are already allocated by the cable service. The upstream frequency is used to transmit the outgoing signal over a spectrum (contiguous range) of frequencies that carry data, sound, and TV signals. The downstream frequency is used to receive signals and is also blended with other data, sound, and TV downstream signals. Depending on the modem, upstream and downstream data rates may or may not be the same. For example, one vendor's services provide a 10 Mbps maximum upstream rate and a 50 Mbps maximum downstream rate. Another cable provider offers 10 Mbps for both the upstream and downstream rates. However, even though cable modems are built for high speeds and cable providers advertise their maximum speeds, at this writing, a single modem user is likely to have realistic access (bandwidth) in the range of 256 Kbps to about 6 Mbps for downloads and 1 to 6 Mbps for uploads. The actual speed is partially dependent on how many of your neighbors are using their cable modems at the same time. This is because one cable run that connects a group of subscribers to the cable hub can handle a maximum of 343 Mbps of bandwidth (in North America or about 445 Mbps in Europe). The cable service provider may establish a limit on your bandwidth (how fast you can transmit and receive) so that the provider can give more users access to the cable network.

The cable modem industry has been working to provide a set of standards with accompanying certification to govern cable modem communications in a project called the **Certified Cable Modem Project**. This project is more commonly referred to as **Data Over Cable Service Interface Specification (DOCSIS)**. Most cable communications companies support this project and have replaced older cable modems with modems certified to meet the DOCSIS standards. The following DOCSIS standards are in use:

- *DOCSIS 1.0*: Accepted in 1999, this standard enables 5 Mbps upstream and downstream communications for standard Internet access.

- *DOCSIS 1.1*: Accepted in 2001, this standard doubles the speed of DOCSIS 1.0 to achieve 10 Mbps, plus it includes data encryption security.

- *DOCSIS 2.0 (also called Adv PHY)*: Accepted in 2002, this standard is especially targeted for direct point-to-point communications, such as between two organizations. It is intended to compete with current T-carrier telecommunications applications. DOCSIS is capable of three times the upstream speed of DOCSIS 1.1 (up to 30 Mbps) and provides better insurance against sources of signal interference.

- *DOCSIS 3.0*: Accepted in 2006, this standard enables cable channels to be bound together (also called bonding) to achieve higher speeds. The DOCSIS standard specifies that at least four channels most be bonded. Not all cable providers offer DOCSIS 3.0, but the larger cable providers do offer it. At this writing, larger providers offer up to 100 Mbps through DOCSIS 3.0 and some providers are working to implement equipment to provide even faster throughput.

Cable modems can be either internal or external devices. An internal device looks similar to a modem card that fits into an expansion slot in your computer. External cable modems are more common and typically connect to your computer in one of three ways. One way is to connect the cable modem directly to a conventional network interface card that is already in your computer using twisted-pair wire (similar to telephone wire), an RJ-45 connector, and Ethernet communications. The second type of cable modem connects directly to a USB port on your computer. Once the cable modem is installed at the computer, the other end is connected to broadband coaxial wire used for cable TV communications. The third type of cable modem offers wireless connectivity in which the modem connects to the cable network and broadcasts wireless network services to nearby computers that have wireless NICs.

If you are purchasing a cable modem, make sure you purchase one that is certified to meet at least the DOCSIS 1.1 standard, and if you have a cable modem that is not certified or that is certified for DOCSIS 1.0, strongly consider upgrading to one that is certified for the DOCSIS 1.1 standard or higher. Besides the extra speed built into a DOCSIS 1.1–certified cable modem, you also get encryption security, which helps prevent others from having access to your data.

To ensure that a DOCSIS-certified modem will work on your cable system, the cable provider must have certified Cable Modem Termination Systems (CMTSs) at the headend (centralized cable operator's site). Most cable operators have CMTSs.

The advantage of cable modem communications is that currently unallocated bandwidth can be allocated to you, even for a millisecond or two, when you are downloading a large file, for example. This means that even when the cable is busy handling your and your neighbors' TV, radio, or computer communications, the system is always dynamically allocating unused cable bandwidth. If your neighbor is connected via her cable modem, but is not sending or receiving, then you can be allocated some of her bandwidth when you are downloading a file, for example.

Because you share the same cable with your neighbors, it is possible for a knowledgeable user to view or access the files on your computer, particularly if your modem is not certified or only certified for DOCSIS 1.0. For this reason, if you use a cable modem, it is vital that you protect your files and access to the computer through file security and personal firewalls. Windows 7, Windows Server 2008/Server 2008 R2, and Linux, for example, enable you to set up a personal firewall via built-in software functionality. For even more security help with Windows operating systems, visit the Microsoft Web site at *www.microsoft.com*. For more information on cable security, visit *www.cablelabs.com*, which is the Web site of CableLabs, a consortium of cable telecommunications companies that engages in research and development of cable telecommunications technologies.

DSL Modems and Routers

Another high-speed digital data communications service that has gained popularity is **Digital Subscriber Line (DSL)**. DSL, which is described in more detail in Chapter 9, is a digital technology that works over copper wire that already goes into most residences and businesses for telephone services (newer forms of DSL can be used over fiber-optic telephone lines). To use DSL, you can install an intelligent adapter in your computer that is to be connected to the DSL network. Another option is to connect a cabled or wireless DSL router to a DSL telephone line and provide cabled or wireless network access to nearby computers equipped with NICs or WNICs.

An intelligent adapter can be a card similar in appearance to a modem, but that is fully digital, which means it does not convert the DTE's (computer or network device's) digital signal to analog, but instead sends a digital signal over the telephone wire. Two pairs of wires are connected to the adapter and then out to the telephone pole. Communication over the copper wire is simplex, which means that one pair is used for outgoing transmissions, and the other pair for incoming transmissions, thus creating an upstream channel to the telco (telephone company) and a downstream channel to the user. The maximum upstream and downstream transmission rates are 200 Mbps for DSL communications. Also, the maximum distance from user to telco without a repeater (to amplify and extend the distance of the signal) is 5.5 kilometers (3.4 miles, which is similar to ISDN).

The actual transmission rate is determined by several factors, including the type of DSL service used, the condition of the cable, the distance to the telco, and the bus speed in the user's computer. Also, it is common even for telephone company representatives to call DSL adapters modems, although these adapters are not technically "modulator/demodulators," because they use a digital signal.

Like a cable modem, a DSL adapter or cabled/wireless router offers high-speed data transmissions, but it also has some advantages over a cable modem. For example, a cable modem uses a line shared by other users, which means its signal can be tapped and read by another user. A DSL line is dedicated to a single user, which means that there is less likelihood that the signal can be tapped without the telco being alerted. Also, the DSL user employs the full bandwidth of his or her line, in contrast to the cable modem user who shares bandwidth with others.

On networks, DSL can be connected by means of a combined DSL adapter and router, which is connected to the DSL line and that may be cabled to the user's internal network and may offer wireless user connectivity or a combination of both wireless and cabled connections. This means the device can be used to direct network traffic and to create a firewall so that only authorized users can access the network services. This type of connection enables multiple users to access one DSL line through their existing network, and it protects the network from intruders over the DSL line. Usually this type of connection comes with management software that enables you to monitor the link and perform diagnostics, such as with Motorola's software (see Figure 5-12). In Activities 5-7 and 5-8, you learn how to configure broadband access in Windows Server 2008/Server 2008 R2 and Windows 7. In Activity 5-9, you learn where to configure DSL access in Linux using the Network Connections utility in GNOME 3.x. Finally, in Activity 5-10, you learn where to configure DSL connectivity in Mac OS X.

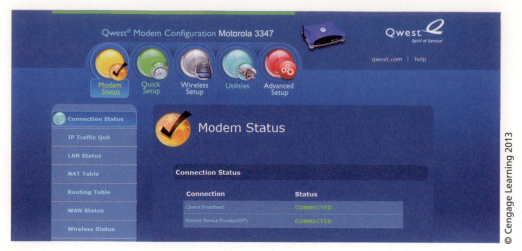

Figure 5-12   DSL monitoring and management software

Activity 5-7: Configure Windows Server 2008 for Shared Broadband Access

Time Required: 10–15 minutes
Objective: Configure Windows Server 2008 to access and share a broadband connection, such as through a cable modem or DSL.

Description: A home or small office server can be ideal for sharing high-speed Internet access on a small network via a cable modem or DSL connected to or installed in the server. The first step is to install or connect the cable modem or adapter with your PC turned off. (Consult your vendor or ISP for instructions about physically installing the cable modem or DSL adapter; or you can practice the steps without first installing a broadband device.) Next, configure the shared broadband access, which you learn in this activity. You need an account that has Administrator privileges. (These steps also work for Windows Vista. Further, if you have a wireless cable or DSL router for Internet connectivity, still choose the Broadband (PPPoE) option in Step 5 for practice sharing through an adapter in a computer, because the wireless router is likely already shared for multiple computers in range.) Finally, note that in some cases sharing a DSL or cable modem connection in Windows Server 2008 may not fully work when Active Directory is installed.

1. Click **Start**, click **Control Panel**, ensure **Classic View** is selected, and double-click **Network and Sharing Center**.

2. In the left portion of the Network and Sharing Center window, click **Set up a connection or network**.

Real-Life Networking

A small business that produces mountain bike parts originally had five telephone lines and five modems in workstations used for Internet access. When its telephone company made DSL available, it purchased a DSL router with a built-in adapter and connected the router to its small business network. Each Internet user now has faster Internet access, and the company saves money because one DSL line is much less expensive than five telephone lines. An added plus is that more employees now have Internet access.

3. Click **Connect to the Internet** (see Figure 5-13) and click **Next**.

4. If you are already connected to the Internet and see a message window confirming you are already connected, click **Set up a new connection anyway**.

5. In the How do you want to connect? window, select **Broadband (PPPoE)** and click **Next**.

6. In the Connect to the Internet window, provide a username and password for the Internet service provider connection. Reenter the password to confirm it. (If you don't have a user-name and password, enter fictitious information for practice.) Give the connection a name, such as Test plus your initials (for example, *TestJP*). Ensure that the box is checked for **Allow other people to use this connection**. Click **Connect** (or click **Cancel** if an Internet connection is already set up as previously indicated in Step 4).

7. Since this is practice, if you see a window showing the connectivity test was unsuccessful (such as because you already have a connection or you do not have access to the Internet), click **Set up the connection anyway**.

8. In the Connection to the Internet is ready to use window, click **Close**. (If you created a prac-tice connection and now want to delete it, with the Network and Sharing Center window still open, click **Manage network connections**, right-click the connection you created, click **Delete**, and click **Yes**. Close the Network Connections window.) Close the Network and Sharing Center window.

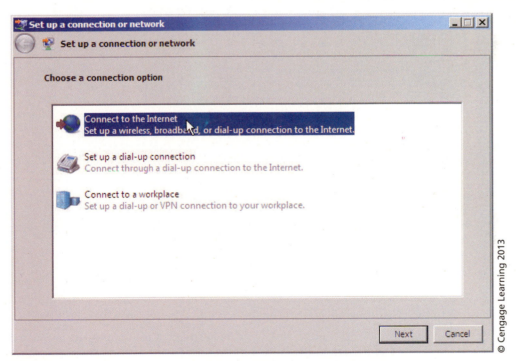

Figure 5-13 Configuring an Internet connection in Windows Server 2008

Activity 5-8: Configure Windows 7 or Windows Server 2008 R2 for Shared Broadband Access

Time Required: 10–15 minutes
Objective: Configure Windows 7 or Windows Server 2008 R2 to access and share a broad-band connection, such as a DSL or cable modem Internet connection.

Description: If your home or small office network does not have a server, you can set up a broad-band connection and share it using a network computer running Windows 7. Or, if you are using Windows Server 2008 R2, you can also set up a broadband connection to share. After you have installed the DSL adapter or cable modem for this activity (or you can practice the setup steps without one), you configure and share the broadband connection. You need an account that has Administrator privileges. (If you have a wireless cable or DSL router for Internet connectivity, still choose the Broadband (PPPoE) option in Step 5 for practice sharing through an adapter in a computer, because the wireless router is likely already shared for multiple computers in range.) Finally, note that in some cases sharing a DSL or cable modem connection in Windows Server 2008 R2 may not fully work when Active Directory is installed.

1. Click **Start**, click **Control Panel**, make sure **View by** is set to **Large icons** or **Small icons**, and click **Network and Sharing Center**.

2. In the Network and Sharing Center window, click **Set up a new connection or network**.

3. In the Choose a connection option window, click **Connect to the Internet** (see Figure 5-14). Click **Next**.

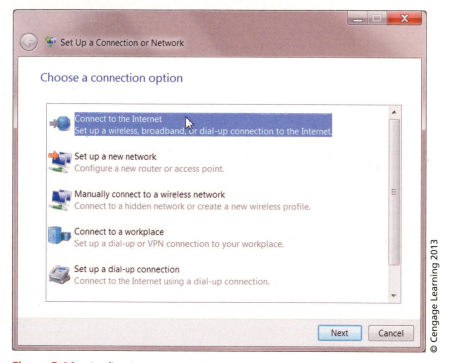

Figure 5-14   Configuring an Internet connection in Windows 7

4. If you are already connected to the Internet and see a message window confirming you are already connected, click **Set up a new connection anyway**.

5. In the How do you want to connect? window, select **Broadband (PPPoE)** and click **Next**.

6. In the Connect to the Internet window, provide a username and password for the Internet service provider connection. Reenter the password to confirm it. (If you don't have a username and password, enter fictitious information for practice.) Give the connection a name, such as Test plus your initials (for example, *TestJP*). Ensure that the box is checked for **Allow other people to use this connection**. Click **Connect** (or click **Cancel** if an Internet connection is already set up as previously indicated in Step 4).

7. Since this is practice, if you see a window showing the connectivity test was unsuccessful (such as because you already have a connection or you do not have access to the Internet), click **Set up the connection anyway**.

8. In The connection to the Internet is ready to use window, click **Close**. (If you created a practice connection and now want to delete it, ensure the Network and Sharing Center window is still open, click **Change adapter settings**, right-click the connection you created, click **Delete,** and click **Yes**. Close the Network Connections window.) Close any open windows, such as the Network and Sharing window.

Activity 5-9: Configure Linux for DSL Connectivity

Time Required: 10 minutes

Objective: Learn where to configure a DSL internal adapter in Linux using the GNOME desktop.

Description: You can purchase a DSL adapter card to install in a computer running Linux and use the Network Connections utility through the GNOME 3.x desktop to configure DSL communications. In this activity, you learn from where to configure DSL. You do not need a DSL adapter installed.

1. Click **Activities** in the top Panel, click **Applications,** and click **Network Connections.**

2. In the Network Connections window, click the **DSL** tab (see Figure 5-15).

Figure 5-15   Configuring a DSL connection in Linux

3. Click the **Add** button from the DSL tab.

4. You can use the DSL tab in the Editing DSL connection dialog box to configure the DSL service, account name, and password for connecting to the DSL provider.

5. After you have examined the DSL tab, click each of the **Wired, PPP Settings,** and **IPv4 Settings** tabs to view the options that can be configured on each tab. Record your observations.

6. Click **Cancel** in the Editing DSL connection dialog box.

7. Click **Close** in the Network Connections window.

Activity 5-10: Configure Mac OS X for DSL Connectivity

Time Required: 10 minutes

Objective: Learn where to configure a DSL internal adapter connection in Mac OS X Snow Leopard or Lion.

Description: A DSL adapter connection can be used with Mac OS X and configured through System Preferences. In this activity, you learn where to configure a DSL connection in Mac OS X Snow Leopard or Lion. You do not need a DSL modem card for this activity, but you do need to log on using an account that has Administrator privileges.

1. Click the **System Preferences** icon in the Dock or click the **Apple** icon in the menu bar and click **System Preferences.**

2. Under Internet & Wireless in the System Preferences window, click **Network.**

3. Ensure the lock is unlocked in the bottom left corner of the Network window (if it is locked, click the **lock,** provide your account name and password, and click **OK**).

4. Click the **Assist me** button in the bottom of the Network window.

5. Click **Assistant** to start the Network Setup Assistant.

6. Click **Continue** in the Network Setup Assistant window.

7. Click the option button for **I use a DSL modem to connect to the Internet** (see Figure 5-16). From here you can click **Continue** and enable Mac OS X to complete the steps for setting the connection.

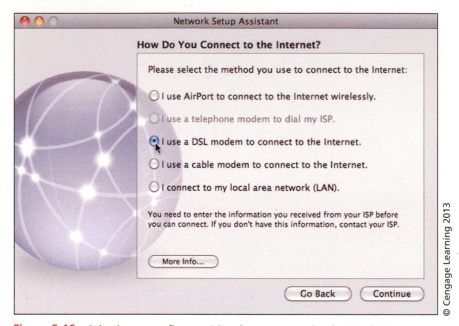

Figure 5-16   Selecting to configure a DSL adapter connection in Mac OS X

8. Because a DSL adapter is not required for this activity, close the Network Setup Assistant window at this point to discontinue the setup.

9. Click **System Preferences** in the menu bar and click **Quit System Preferences**.

Access Servers

An **access server** combines several types of WAN communications into one device. For example, one access server might combine transmission capabilities for modems, DSL, T-1, T-3, ISDN, and frame relay. Some access servers are designed for small to mid-sized applications.

**Real-Life
Networking**

A community college had an area in its machine and communications room that was filled with modems, wires, and devices for T-3 communications, and more wires and devices for a frame relay WAN connection. It replaced it all by using an access server to organize and manage WAN communications in one place. The access server has redundant power supplies and backplanes (to insert WAN communications modules) for fault tolerance. A cost-saving feature is that it can be expanded or reconfigured for changes in WAN services, such as retiring modems and using DSL.

Those servers have one Ethernet NIC to connect to the network. They also have a combination of synchronous and asynchronous communication ports, for terminal, modem, public telephone, DSL, and frame relay connectivity. Smaller access servers typically have 8 or 16 asynchronous ports and one or two synchronous ports. Larger access servers are modular with slots (perhaps 10 to 20) for communications cards, as shown in Figure 5-17. For example, one card may have eight asynchronous ports and one synchronous port. Another card may be for T-1 communications and yet another for DSL communications. There may also be modular cards with built-in modems, with possibly four modems per card. Some modular access servers contain nearly 70 modems. These servers may also have redundant power supplies for fault tolerance.

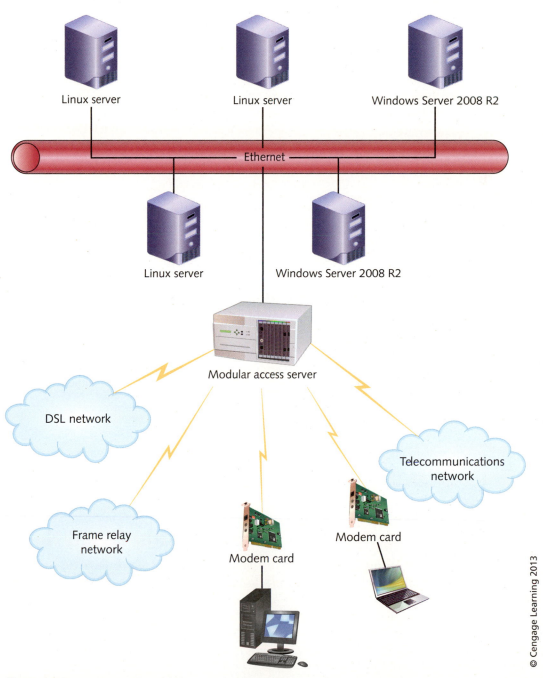

Figure 5-17 Using an access server

© Cengage Learning 2013

Remote Routers

As you learned earlier, a local router is used on LANs. A **remote router**, which performs the same kind of routing functions, enables networks to be connected into WANs over long distances, say from New York to Los Angeles. A single router in Los Angeles might connect a business in that city to remote business routers in Vancouver and Toronto, Canada, and New York. Or, a remote router might connect a state university campus with corresponding routers at satellite campuses throughout the state.

Remote routers connect WANs, such as frame relay, high-speed serial, and other WAN networks. As with a local router, a remote router can support multiple protocols, enabling communication with many kinds of distant networks. Also similar to a local router, a remote router can be set up as a firewall to restrict access to particular network resources.

Some remote routers are modular, so that different kinds of interfaces can be installed in expansion slots, such as an interface for ISDN and a different interface for frame relay. The advantage of a modular router is that it can be gradually adapted to meet the growth in communications that many organizations experience. Most routers connect to the WAN telecommunications line through a serial-type interface, such as a CSU/DSU for T-carrier communications or a modular adapter for other high-speed connections. A **channel service unit (CSU)** is a physical interface that connects with the T-carrier line. A **data service unit (DSU)** is like a digital modem that converts the signal received by the CSU to one that can be placed on a network and be received by a computer. The CSU/DSU typically combines both devices into one box with the appropriate ports for connections.

Table 5-3 summarizes the WAN connectivity devices you have learned about in this chapter.

Table 5-3   WAN connectivity devices

Device	WAN Connectivity Function
Telephone modem	Modulates and demodulates signals from digital to analog and vice versa to enable a computer to connect to and communicate over a telephone line
Terminal adapter	Enables a computer to connect to an ISDN line for digital communications
Cable TV modem	Connects a computer to a TV communications cable for digital communications
Cable TV modem combined with a cabled/wireless router	Connects to the TV cable and offers cabled, wireless, or both types of connectivity for multiple authorized computers as well as offering router and firewall functions
DSL adapter	Connects a computer to a DSL telecommunications line
DSL adapter combined with a cabled/wireless router	Connects to a DSL telecommunications line and provides cable, wireless, or both connections for Internet access to authorized computers as well as providing routing and firewall capabilities
Access server	Combines different WAN connectivity equipment into one device, such as for DSL, ISDN, T-carrier, frame relay, and analog modem connectivity
Remote router	Connects WAN technologies over long distances and provides routing capabilities

© Cengage Learning 2013

Putting It All Together: Designing a Router-Based Network

You have learned about many different kinds of network devices, so how do you put it all together? As you design a network, consider a few basic guidelines:

- Use the most effective devices for your application, such as using workgroup switches instead of hubs to connect users—because switches are faster.
- Understand which devices have repeater functions and stay within the accepted limits for the number of repeater-type devices between computers and networks (no more than four).
- Use routers to segment network (IP) traffic on mid-sized and large networks to reduce congestion.

- Use routers on networks, even small networks, for a firewall between you and the outside world—this helps keep intruders out and important information in.

- If you share an Internet connection on a small network, bring the WAN connection (DSL, ISDN, cable modem) into a router, if possible. If this is not possible, consider sharing the connection via a server (using ICS) and configuring the server with router functions (but know this may slow down the server, depending on the hardware).

- On a larger network, consider using an access server for multiple Internet connection options and connect the access server to a router.

- Internet connectivity can be important to home and business users. Purchase the best connectivity you can afford. DSL is often a good choice for security, reliability, speed, and cost. If you are in a rural area with few choices, ISDN is relatively expensive but faster than a modem. An ISDN line is often about twice the cost of basic telephone service (which is typically higher in rural areas anyway because of distance costs).

Consider a situation in which you are designing a network for a single-story office building. One portion of the building houses business offices for a small company of eight real estate appraisers. In another part of the building are offices for a local community unit of six social workers. Both groups want to share the cost of a DSL Internet WAN connection, because there are usually no more than two or three people on the Internet at one time. When you design this network, you might do the following:

- Bring the DSL connection into a router.

- Put all of the appraisers on one workgroup switch.

- Put all of the social workers on a different workgroup switch.

- Connect both switches to the router and use the router to segment traffic so that communications on one switch do not go through the other.

- Use the router as a firewall between both groups of users and the outside world on the DSL line.

- Enable both groups of users to access the DSL line through the router.

Figure 5-18 illustrates this basic network design.

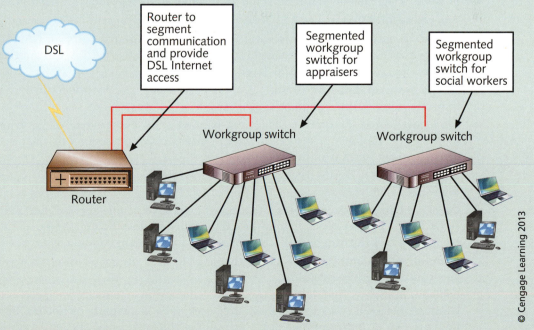

Figure 5-18   A router-based network

Chapter Summary

- Early networks and some wireless networks use repeaters as a way to expand network communications when the IEEE limits are reached or to extend the range of wireless communications. Also, some network devices incorporate repeater functions as they implement more complex network options such as filtering and forwarding packets and frames.

- Routers and switches incorporate some bridging functions for networking. Also, routers and switches are used in centralized star-based networks to link individual segments and to link networks to one another. These devices can be equipped with intelligence to help in collecting network data and for centralized network management.

- Routers are especially popular because they can control traffic patterns and because they can play a dual role providing both LAN and WAN connectivity. Switches are also popular because they are faster than hubs and can operate as Layer 2 (bridging) or Layer 3 (routing) devices. Routers and switches are extensively employed to reduce network bottlenecks.

- Analog modems used over PSTN lines have been used for many years, but analog modems are in far less use today with the advent of other faster WAN communications solutions. For example, digital adapters, including ISDN TAs and DSL adapters, provide much faster communications than analog modems, but require subscribing to ISDN or DSL services. Cable modems also have a widespread presence because they can be used over existing cable TV lines and offer high-speed access. Most cable operators emphasize using certified cable modems to guarantee compatibility.

- Access servers provide a single unit in which to combine all types of telecommunications connectivity, including modems, T-1, ISDN, and DSL. Finally, remote routers are used to join LANs at remote sites into WANs.

Key Terms

access server   A unit that connects synchronous and asynchronous devices to a network, providing routing for both types of communications.

active hub   A network transmission device that connects nodes in a star topology regenerating, retiming, and amplifying the data signal each time it passes through the hub.

asynchronous communications   Communications that occur in discrete units, in which the start of a unit is signaled by a start bit at the front, and a stop bit at the back signals the end of the unit.

bits per second (bps)   The number of binary bits (0s or 1s) sent in one second.

bridge   A network transmission device that connects different LANs or LAN segments using the same access method. An example is connecting one Ethernet LAN to another Ethernet LAN. Bridges operate at the Data Link layer.

bridge protocol data unit (BPDU)   A specialized frame used by bridges to exchange information with one another.

broadcast storm   Saturation of network bandwidth by excessive traffic, as when a large number of computers or devices attempt to transmit simultaneously or when computers or devices persist in transmitting repeatedly.

cable modem   A digital modem device designed for use with the cable TV system, providing high-speed data transfer.

Certified Cable Modem Project   Also called Data Over Cable Service Interface Specification (DOCSIS), a project sponsored by the cable modem industry to provide a set of standards and equipment certification to provide stability to cable modem communications.

channel service unit (CSU)   A device that is a physical interface between a network device, such as a router, and a T-carrier line.

collision domain   Two network segments connected by one or more repeaters; or the network segments between two or more Layer 2 devices, such as switches or bridges. In a collision domain, two or more computers can transmit at the same time, causing a collision (and slowing network transmissions).

concentrator   A device that can have multiple inputs and outputs all active at the same time.

controlled access unit (CAU)   Stackable hubs that count as one MAU and connect nodes on a token ring network.

cut-through switching   A switching technique that forwards portions of a frame before the entire frame is received.

data communications equipment (DCE)   A device that converts data from a DTE, such as a computer, to be transmitted over a telecommunications line. *See* **data terminal equipment.**

Data Over Cable Service Interface Specification (DOCSIS)   *See* **Certified Cable Modem Project.**

data service unit (DSU)   A device used with a channel service unit (CSU) for communications over a WAN connection, such as a T-carrier line. The DSU converts data to be sent over the line and converts data received from the line into a format for the receiving network.

data terminal equipment (DTE)   A computer or computing device that prepares data to be transmitted over a telecommunications line to which it attaches by using a DCE, such as a modem. *See* **data communications equipment**.

Digital Subscriber Line (DSL)   A technology that uses advanced modulation technologies on existing telecommunications networks for high-speed networking between a subscriber and a telco and that has communication speeds of up to 200 Mbps.

directory service   A large database of network resources, such as computers, printers, user accounts, and users groups. The database is replicated to all servers that are responsible for helping to manage network resources, such as authorizing users to log onto the network.

dynamic routing   A routing process in which the router constantly checks the network configuration, automatically updates routing tables, and makes its own decisions (often based on guidelines set by the network administrator) about how to route packets.

Fibre Channel   A type of SAN that enables gigabit high-speed data transfer. *See* **Storage Area Network (SAN)**.

firewall   Software or hardware that secures data from being accessed outside a network and that can also prevent data from leaving the network through an inside source.

flooding   When a network device, such as a bridge, retransmits a frame or packet to all of its outgoing ports.

gateway   A network device that enables communications between two different types of networked systems, for example, between complex protocols or between different e-mail systems.

hop   The movement of a frame or packet, point to point, from one network to the next.

hub   A central network device used in the star topology to join networks.

intelligent hub   Also called a managed hub, a hub that can be used to perform network management functions using the Simple Network Management Protocol (SNMP).

Internet Group Management Protocol (IGMP)   A protocol employed by routers to create groups for multicasts, such as for multimedia streaming video.

local bridge   A network device that connects networks in close proximity and that can be used to segment a portion of a network to reduce heavy-traffic problems.

local router   A router that joins networks within the same building or between buildings in close proximity such as on the same business campus.

managed hub   *See* **intelligent hub.**

managed switch   Has options to configure the switch, manage network traffic, and help monitor the network through SNMP. *See* **unmanaged switch.**

metric   A value calculated by routers that reflects information about a particular transmission path, such as path length, load at the next hop, available bandwidth, and path reliability.

modem   A modulator/demodulator that converts a computer's outgoing digital signal to an analog signal that can be transmitted over a telephone line. It also converts the incoming analog signal to a digital signal that the computer can understand.

multistation access unit (MAU or **MSAU)**   A central hub that links token ring nodes into a topology that physically resembles a star but in which data signals are transferred in a logical ring pattern.

Open Shortest Path First (OSPF) protocol   A routing protocol used by a router to communicate to other routers information about its immediate links to other nodes.

partitioning   To shut down a cable segment because a portion of the segment is malfunctioning.

passive hub   A network transmission device that connects nodes in a star topology, performing no signal amplification as the data signal moves from one node to the next through the hub.

promiscuous mode   Mode in which network devices read frame destination address information before sending a frame on to other connected segments of the network.

remote bridge   A network device that joins networks across the same city, between cities, and between states to create one network.

remote router   A router that joins networks in WANs across large geographic areas, such as between cities, states, and countries.

repeater   A network transmission device that amplifies and retimes a packet- or cell-carrying signal so that it can be sent along all outgoing cable segments attached to that repeater.

router   A network device that connects networks having the same or different access methods and media, such as Ethernet to token ring. It forwards packets to networks by using a decision-making process based on routing table data, discovery of the most efficient routes, and preprogrammed information from the network administrator.

Routing Information Protocol (RIP)   A protocol routers use to communicate the entire contents of routing tables to other routers.

segment   One cable run within the IEEE specifications, such as one run of 10Base2 cable that is 185 meters (610.5 feet) long and that has 30 nodes or fewer (including terminators and network equipment).

smart multistation access unit (SMAU)   A multistation access unit with intelligence built in to detect problems at a connected workstation and to isolate that workstation from the rest of the network.

spanning tree algorithm   Software that ensures that frames are not transmitted in an endless loop and that enables frames to be sent along the most cost-effective network path.

static routing   A routing process that involves control of routing decisions by the network administrator through preset routing instructions.

Storage Area Network (SAN)   A grouping of storage devices, such as hard disk arrays, that forms a subnet so that the storage devices are available to any server on the main network.

store-and-forward switching   A switching technique in which a packet is buffered and not sent until it is completely received and there is an open channel on which to send it.

switch   A device that links network segments and that forwards and filters frames between segments. Originally, switches operated primarily at OSI Layer 2, forwarding on the basis of physical or device addresses, but newer switches also function at OSI Layer 3 and higher.

synchronous communications   Communications of continuous bursts of data controlled by a clock signal that starts each burst.

terminal adapter (TA)   A device that connects a computer or a fax to an ISDN line. A TA simply converts a digital signal to a protocol that can be sent over a digital telephone line.

translational bridge   A bridge that converts frames from one access method and media type to another, such as from Ethernet to token ring or vice versa.

universal serial bus (USB)   A standard for connecting all kinds of peripherals, such as printers, modems, and tape drives, that has generally replaced the use of traditional parallel and serial ports.

unmanaged hub   A simple hub on a network that does not have built-in intelligence for network monitoring and management.

unmanaged switch   A switch that has a fixed configuration and that does not support network monitoring through SNMP.

Review Questions

1. Which of the following can be taken into account by a router when the router determines the route with the lowest cost? (Choose all that apply.)

    a. manufacturer of the nearest routers

    b. number of IP leases already in use by the DHCP server

    c. load at the next hop

    d. available bandwidth

2. The partition light is displayed on a switch used on your office network, and none of the users are currently able to use the network. What should you do first?

    a. Have all users turn their computers off and then on.

    b. Install new cable between each switch port and its corresponding computer.

    c. Push the reset button on the switch.

    d. Replace the switch with a new one.

3. When a bridge does not know the destination segment for a frame, which of the following is the result?

    a. It floods all but the source segment with that frame.

    b. It floods all segments with the frame, including the source segment.

    c. It flags the frame as unknown and sends the frame back to the source segment.

    d. It routes the frame to a DNS server.

4. Your network currently uses four unmanaged workgroup switches. There is an unmet need to periodically deactivate specific ports on the switches and also to monitor network activity at the switches. Which of the following should you consider?

    a. Replace the switches with hubs.

    b. Replace the switches with MAUs.

    c. Upload port access software in each switch.

    d. Upgrade to managed switches.

5. You have purchased a new router. When you implement it on your network, which routing protocol would you use on the router to ensure the most efficient router communications?

    a. Bridged Urgent Routing Protocol (BURP)

    b. IP network bridging protocol (IPNETB)

    c. Routing Information Protocol (RIP)

    d. Open Shortest Path First (OSPF) protocol

6. Your small five-person company needs Internet access for each employee. All of the employees' Windows 7 computers are connected to a small network; however, only your computer has a DSL adapter installed inside the computer. Which of the following is the most economical step you can take to extend DSL Internet access to your employees?

    a. Install a wireless DSL router.

    b. Provide USB DSL sticks for each computer.

    c. Configure the DSL broadband connection at your computer to be shared with others.

    d. Install an antenna on the DSL adapter in your computer to provide wireless access to the other computers.

7. Your network contains multiple managed switches, but you have noticed that often the network slows down because of looping frames. Which of the following is a solution?

   a. Ensure each port has a looping terminator.

   b. Enable the spanning tree algorithm on all of the switches.

   c. Enable forward switching.

   d. Ensure no more than two switches are designated as primary switches.

8. Which of the following are Physical layer functions performed by repeaters? (Choose all that apply.)

   a. retime a signal

   b. amplify a signal

   c. reproduce a signal on all cable runs on a cabled network

   d. filter out signal disturbance

9. Bridge protocol data units are used by which of the following?

   a. spanning tree algorithm

   b. SNMP monitoring

   c. repeaters to reform signal transmissions

   d. brouters to install a UDP firewall

10. Your home office is in a rural area that does not have cable TV or DSL. However, you do have conventional telephone service. Which of the following are options you can consider for Internet access? (Choose all that apply.)

    a. an Internet hub

    b. an analog telephone modem

    c. ISDN through an ISDN TA

    d. a WAN access server

11. You have determined that there is network congestion caused by the portion of your organization's network that is used by research engineers. What device can help you reduce the congestion between the research engineers' network and the rest of the organization's network?

    a. a workgroup hub

    b. a passive switch

    c. a repeater

    d. a router

12. Which of the following types of inbound to outbound cable connections can be used with a repeater? (Choose all that apply.)

    a. twisted pair to fiber optic

    b. fiber optic to fiber optic

    c. wireless to twisted pair

    d. twisted pair to twisted pair

13. You are expanding your cabled network and have proposed the purchase of four new switches. Your boss recently found four hubs in storage that were purchased several years ago, but have never been used. He suggests you use these hubs instead of purchasing the new switches. What is your response?

    a. Using the hubs will be fine, but the ports on the hubs will need to be configured for duplex.

b.   Hubs are not compatible with Ethernet, and so you will have to purchase the switches.

    c.   Unlike these older hubs, switches have a bridging capability and the ability to improve bandwidth for a more efficient network.

    d.   The hubs will be as good a solution as new switches and will save money.

14. A bridge looks at what type of address?

    a.   IP

    b.   UDP

    c.   TCP

    d.   MAC

15. Which of the following devices can work at the Network layer of the OSI model? (Choose all that apply.)

    a.   router

    b.   repeater

    c.   bridge

    d.   hub

16. Your accounting business with nine employees already has access to a cable TV line, and you want to provide Internet access for all employees using a cable-based wireless router. The cable company offers to give you 100 Mbps throughput using channel bonding. Which of the following will you need to purchase to ensure you can take advantage of the 100 Mbps throughput?

    a.   a combined wireless router and cable modem that is certified for DOCSIS 3.0

    b.   an Adv PHY compatible wireless router combined with a cable modem

    c.   an asynchronous analog wireless router combined with a cable modem

    d.   a point-to-point wireless router and cable modem

17. You are consulting for a large charitable organization that needs to have a combination of T-3, DSL, and frame relay WAN access. Which of the following devices enables you to consolidate these types of access into one modular box?

    a.   a loopback switch

    b.   an access server

    c.   an Ethernet joiner

    d.   a combination terminal

18. Which of the following switching methods forwards a frame only after all of the frame is received and checked for errors?

    a.   examination switching

    b.   cut-through switching

    c.   store-and-forward switching

    d.   spanned switching

19. Dynamic routing protocols can automatically accomplish which of the following? (Choose all that apply.)

    a.   Determine when a network path is down.

    b.   Restart a router that is offline.

    c.   Disable a switch that is causing a broadcast storm.

    d.   Determine the shortest paths to other networks.

20. Your company leases a T-1 line from a regional telecommunications provider. What type of interface is installed at your company's site to provide physical connectivity to the T-1 line?

    a. an analog modem

    b. a WAN carrier

    c. a repeater

    d. a CSU/DSU

Case Projects

CASE PROJECTS

Plains Research Institute is a private organization of 22 physical chemists and a business management staff of eight, including a computer support professional. The organization obtains research grants from corporations and government organizations to develop new or enhance existing chemical processes. For example, one group of chemists is researching the development of automotive engines to run on hydrogen. Another group of chemists is developing a better way to extract natural gas from coal-bed geologic formations and pump the natural gas to customers.

Plains Research Institute has leased a building on a university campus for five years, but now the university has other plans for that building, and so Plains Research Institute is purchasing a new building. They want to network the building and have hired you through Network Design Consultants. The building is a single-story building. All of the employees use either Windows 7 Professional or Fedora Linux on their workstations. The organization also has four Red Hat Enterprise Linux servers and one Windows Server 2008 R2 server. The old network in the university building contained a combination of unmanaged hubs and unmanaged switches. Because the Plains Research Institute president and management staff are very concerned about security, they have decided this will be a wired Ethernet network without a wireless component.

Case Project 5-1: Using Existing Devices

The computer support professional is charged with ordering new network devices. He asks you which existing devices can be reused on the new network and which should be retired. What is your recommendation?

Case Project 5-2: Connecting Workstations to the Network

What network devices do you recommend for connecting the workstations to the network?

Case Project 5-3: Internet and WAN Connectivity

Plains Research Institute currently can have DSL, cable modem, ISDN, or modem connectivity to the Internet. Also, it wants to install a T-3 line to connect to a network at a new remote research site. They ask you to create a short report or slide presentation that discusses how each of these, or a combination of them, can be connected to its network.

Case Project 5-4: Addressing Internet Security

In relation to Internet connectivity, both you and the chemists at Plains Research are concerned about security. What network device or devices can be used to address the concern about security?

Case Project 5-5: Managing Network Traffic

While in a planning meeting with Plains Research Institute, one of the experienced chemists mentions that the members of his team generate large volumes of network traffic. This has been a problem while in the university building. What do you recommend for the new network to manage network congestion? As an optional supplement to this assignment, consider creating a sample network diagram showing how, in general, this network might be designed.

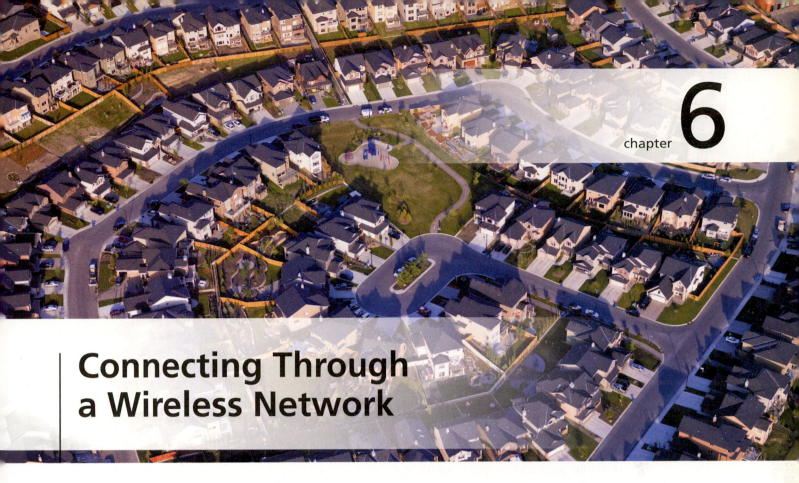

chapter 6

Connecting Through a Wireless Network

People are more productive in work and in play if they have freedom of movement. Wireless networking brings that freedom to homes and offices. Not only does it give you the freedom to roam, but it makes it easier to set up and use a network—helping you to capitalize even more on the potential of computers and networks.

After reading this chapter and completing the exercises, you will be able to:

- Explain current wireless networking technologies
- Discuss the history of wireless networks and their advantages
- Describe radio wave technologies
- Explain 802.11 radio wave networking
- Describe the Bluetooth and HiperLAN radio wave technologies
- Discuss infrared wireless technologies
- Explain wireless MAN networking through WiMAX and HiperMAN
- Explain cellular phone communications
- Describe terrestrial and satellite microwave technologies
- Consider design options for wireless networks

231

Wireless networks are everywhere—in homes, offices, airports, college campuses, and commercial work areas. In this chapter, you learn about many types of wireless network communications. First, you learn about current forms of wireless networking. Next, you follow a brief history of wireless networking and discover the advantages of this technology. You get an introduction into radio wave wireless networking and then explore the popular IEEE 802.11 wireless networking standards. You also learn about alternative radio wave technologies for LANs, including Bluetooth and HiperLAN. Next, you learn about diffused infrared technologies and wireless MANs. Finally, you explore cellular communications and land-based and satellite microwave technologies, and you put together what you have learned for designing wireless networks.

Current Wireless Networking Technologies

Just a decade ago, most computer users had to deal with a "spaghetti soup" of wires coming out of their computers for the keyboard, mouse, network connection, printer, speakers, and so on (and some still do). In addition, networks often involved the expense and effort of pulling wires through walls, ceilings, and floors. Today, wireless technologies have skyrocketed in popularity because they provide a measure of freedom from wires—and new, faster wireless technologies are constantly evolving. You can purchase wireless keyboards, mice, printers, and other devices. Fortunately, you can also design a network to be partially or totally wireless.

Current wireless networking technologies include the following:

- Radio wave technologies, including cellular

- Infrared technologies

- Terrestrial and satellite microwave technologies

Radio waves, infrared, and microwaves are all parts of the electromagnetic spectrum, which includes visible light, ultraviolet light, radio waves, infrared, X-rays, microwaves, and gamma rays. All of these are forms of electromagnetic radiation. Electromagnetic radiation is propagated through the Earth's atmosphere and through space.

See the Web sites *imagine.gsfc.nasa.gov/docs/science/know_l1/emspectrum .html* and *imagine.gsfc.nasa.gov/docs/science/know_l2/emspectrum.html* for more information about the electromagnetic spectrum.

Radio wave technologies are very popular and represent a fast growing sector of wireless networking. The radio wave technologies include the 802.11 wireless LAN standards and alternative industry-endorsed approaches, including Bluetooth and HiperLAN. WiMAX and HiperMAN are examples of wireless MAN technologies. Cellular technologies, such as 3G and 4G, also use radio wave technologies.

Infrared technologies are not as popular as radio wave approaches, but infrared offers some advantages because it is a relatively more secure form of wireless networking, in the sense that it is harder to tap into the infrared light signal without someone noticing. Infrared technologies are used for short distance communications such as within an office. Radio wave communications are used for short and longer distances from close range office communications, to communications between buildings, to communications over several miles as in the case of wireless MANs and CANs.

Microwave technologies are used for longer distances, including sending transmissions across continents via satellite.

You learn about each of these technologies in this chapter. First, however, it is worthwhile to set the stage by learning the history of wireless networks, their advantages, and about organizations that support wireless networking.

A Short History of Wireless Networks

Wireless networking has informal and formal roots. The informal beginning of wireless networking is in amateur radio. The formal roots are in the parallel development of standards for wireless networking by governmental and professional groups.

Amateur radio operators (also called hams) are licensed by the U.S. Federal Communications Commission (FCC) to transmit voice, Morse code, data, satellite, and video signals over radio waves and microwaves. In the 1980s, licensed amateur radio operators received permission from the FCC to transmit data on several radio frequencies above those used on personal radios. Most people are familiar with radio frequencies via the music played on AM and FM radio stations. These frequencies are only a small part of the possible radio frequencies through which a signal can be transmitted. Hertz (Hz) is the main unit of measurement for a radio frequency. Technically, one Hertz represents a radiated alternating current or emission of one cycle per second.

Radio frequencies (RFs) are the range of frequencies above 20 kilohertz through which an electromagnetic signal can be radiated into space.

Shortly after IBM introduced the personal computer in the early 1980s, amateur radio operators experimented with networking PCs over radio waves. They accomplished this by creating a device called a terminal node controller (TNC), which was placed between a computer and a radio transceiver (a combination transmitter and receiver). The TNC converted the computer's digital signal to an analog signal that was amplified by the transceiver and broadcast out through an antenna. The resulting technology was called packet radio (packet radio is also discussed in Chapter 2, "How LAN and WAN Communications Work"). Packet radio uses datagrams and wireless packet switching to send data in a digital packet through radio waves. The use of datagrams in packet radio works similarly to the use of datagrams on cabled networks and the Internet. Packet radio helped set the stage for today's wireless and cellular phone networks and soon caught the interest of commercial wireless networking companies as well as telecommunications companies.

In a parallel development, in 1985 commercial options for wireless computer networking were opened by the FCC on selected frequencies called the Industrial, Scientific, and Medical (ISM) band for nonlicensed public use. In the Telecommunications Act of 1996, the U.S. Congress further set the stage for wireless communications by implementing wireless communications "siting" (location) and emission standards and by providing incentives for future development of telecommunications technologies, including wireless communications (see *www.fcc.gov/telecom.html* for more information). Not long afterward, the Institute of Electrical and Electronics Engineers (IEEE) initiated the 802.11 wireless networking standards group, which was responsible for the first 802.11 standard set in 1997. Besides the IEEE, a sampling of other national and international organizations that influence wireless networking standards around the world includes the following:

- European Telecommunications Standards Institute (ETSI)
- International Engineering Task Force (IETF)
- International Multimedia Teleconferencing Consortium (IMTC)
- International Telecommunications Union (ITU)
- IPv6 Forum
- International Organization for Standardization (ISO)
- The Open Group
- World Wide Web Consortium (W3C)

For example, the ETSI has contributed to the HiperLAN standards that are used in Europe and other countries. Bluetooth is another wireless technology that, in part, grew out of Europe via the Scandinavian company, Ericsson (Ericsson has also contributed to the HiperLAN standards).

Along with the informal development of wireless networking technologies and the implementation of formal networking standards, more and more people in homes, schools, and offices around the world began using computers and wanting to connect them to networks. These trends and developments, and the many advantages of wireless networking, set the stage for the exponential growth of wireless networking technologies in the early 2000s.

Advantages of Wireless Networks

Today, wireless networks are designed and installed to accommodate all types of needs, which include the following:

- Enabling communications in areas where a wired network would be difficult to install
- Reducing installation costs
- Providing "anywhere" access to users who cannot be tied down to a cable
- Enabling easier small office and home office networking
- Enabling data access to fit the application

Providing an Alternative to Wired Networks

A wired network can be difficult or even impossible to install in some situations. Consider this scenario: Two buildings must be networked, but an interstate highway separates them. There are different alternatives for setting up a network in this situation. One is to dig a trench under the concrete highway, resulting in great expense and traffic delays while the trench is dug, the cable is laid, the trench is filled in, and the roadway is completely restored. A second option is to create a MAN to connect the two buildings. Both buildings might be connected to T-1 lines or to an Optical Ethernet MAN via a public network carrier or regional Bell operating company (RBOC). This involves less cost than laying new cable, but there is still the ongoing fee to lease the telecommunications lines. A third alternative is to install a wireless network, which involves the one-time cost of the equipment and the ongoing network management costs—all of which are likely to be the most cost effective over the long term.

Consider this second scenario: A renter of a large office needs to set up a network for her 77 employees. Installing a permanent cable plant is prohibited by the building owner. She likes this particular office because it is in a prime downtown location for her advertising business. The rent for this office is lower than that for any of the other locations that she investigated. She solves the networking problem by setting up a wireless network.

Consider this third scenario: A public library moved to a building in the historic business district of downtown. Even though the library is owned by the city, strict public and private covenants restrict the library management from obtaining the necessary permits to install network cable. Further, the library has experienced budget cuts. The library management addresses the need by installing an economical wireless network, which enables them to preserve the integrity of the building and to follow all of the covenants.

Saving Money and Time

Installing a wireless network may be less expensive and faster than installing a cable-based network. For example, consider a university foundation office that initiated a $15 million fundraising campaign. They hired an expensive consulting firm that assigned five people to the project and implemented 18 new staff members, for a total of 23 new people. A few days before going into operation, the foundation office realized they did not have network connections for the new staff and consultants. Installing new wiring was an expensive proposition and would not be possible for several months because the university's IT Department was already overworked. The solution was to implement a wireless network, which was set up in record time and cost less.

Installing a wireless network can be safer as well as cost effective in older buildings and other areas containing hazardous materials. These may include downtown office buildings, buildings on college campuses, and historic buildings. Besides safety and cost, a wireless network helps preserve the historic character of these buildings by eliminating the need to alter walls and ceilings to run cable.

Real-Life Networking

One university faced networking an old law school building in which there were old maintenance tunnels containing trace amounts of chlorine gas from leaky old air-conditioning lines and asbestos. The tunnels were no longer in use, and one option was simply to seal them. Another was to begin an expensive hazardous materials abatement program so that the tunnels could be used for network cable. The university found it was much cheaper and safer to seal the tunnels and to use wireless networking instead of running cable.

Providing Access Anywhere

Some computer users require network access from almost anywhere. For example, consider a large auto parts warehouse in which it is necessary to perform regular inventories using bar code scanners that can communicate with a network. Wireless networking gives the users of these scanners "anywhere" access so they are not restricted by dragging along a cable. In another example, wireless connectivity makes it possible for a hospital physician to carry a small mobile wireless computer from which to update a patient's records, order tests, or arrange surgery.

Simplifying Networks for Novices

In terms of small office and home office computing, wireless networking takes the hassle out of running cable. These environments can be frustrating because the installations are usually not done by professionals. As a result, the wrong cable might be used and cable might be run through areas of EMI or RFI or unintentionally damaged, such as by crushing it under a chair, behind a desk, or through a doorway. In addition, the small or home office user may spend many unproductive hours trying to determine why his or her network does not work. A wireless network can be much easier to install and maintain in this situation. Wireless networking is now so popular that most computers purchased online or in office supply stores come with both cabled and wireless NICs, and wireless access points, routers, and extenders (repeaters) are commonly sold through these outlets.

The advantage of wireless networking for home and small office users is that the costs of wireless devices are now very reasonable. Implementing a wireless network along with using the automated IP addressing options in operating systems such as Windows 8, Windows 7, Windows Server 2012, Windows Server 2008/Server 2008 R2, and Mac OS X means that a complete home network can be set up with little or no prior experience.

Enhancing Data Access

Access to some types of data and software applications can be significantly enhanced through wireless networking. Consider a large company that permanently employs 10 internal auditors. The auditors visit several departments and locations each day and need to access the financial data, reports, and other information kept by those departments. An auditor can easily go to several different locations and still access any financial data by carrying a laptop computer equipped with a wireless NIC. In another example, a chemical engineer might need to work in several locations in a chemical plant. In one location she might monitor data while a reaction is taking place in production. From another location, she might need to view the inventory of chemicals to be sure there is adequate inventory to start a different production process. And from yet another location, she might need to access the company's online research library. Wireless access allows her to accomplish all of these tasks with ease.

Wireless Network Support Organizations

Several organizations exist to promote wireless networking. One of the most recognized organizations is the Wi-Fi Alliance that promotes wireless networking for LANs. The Wi-Fi Alliance also offers a certification program to vendors, which tests wireless devices so that they can be certified to meet IEEE 802.11 standards as well as accepted security practices. Devices that pass the testing can display the Wi-Fi CERTIFIED insignia. In Activity 6-1 you visit the Wi-Fi Alliance Web site to learn about its resources.

Activity 6-1: Learning About the Wi-Fi Alliance

Time Required: 10 minutes
Objective: Learn about the Wi-Fi certification and the resources available through the Wi-Fi Alliance.

Description: The Wi-Fi Alliance works to encourage even more widespread use of wireless networking and to help ensure that wireless device vendors follow accepted standards so that devices can interoperate. In this activity, you visit the Wi-Fi Alliance Web site to learn about the certification program and resources that are made available.

1. Open a Web browser and point the browser to *www.wi-fi.org*.

2. What links are available through the tabs and buttons on this Web site?

3. Point to the **Certification** tab and click **Benefits of Wi-Fi CERTIFIED** (or if the Web site has changed, look for a link about the benefits of certification). What are some of the benefits?

4. Return to the About or main page.

5. Click the **Discover and Learn** link or **Knowledge Center** (or other appropriate learning links if the Web site has changed) and explore the learning resources available. Record your observations.

6. Leave your Web browser open for the next activity.

The University of New Hampshire with sponsorship from the WLAN Consortium (of vendors that make wireless devices) hosts the Interoperability Lab (iol) providing precertification to help speed up the process of Wi-Fi certification. You can learn more about the iol at *www.iol.unh.edu/services/testing/wireless*.

Another support organization is WINLAB, which is a research consortium of universities for wireless networking and is located at Rutgers University. WINLAB is sponsored by the National Science Foundation and has been in operation since 1989. Try Activity 6-2 to learn about the most recent areas of research undertaken by WINLAB.

Activity 6-2: WINLAB Project

Time Required: 10 minutes
Objective: Learn how WINLAB is exploring new wireless technologies.

Description: In this activity, you learn about the current focus projects of WINLAB, the research consortium for wireless networking.

1. Open a Web browser, if one is not already open, and point the browser to *www.winlab.rutgers.edu/pub*.

2. Click the link for **Focus Projects**.

3. What projects are currently under way as focus projects? Record your observations.

4. Go back to the home page.

5. Click the link for **About WINLAB**. Take a moment to read about the purpose of WINLAB.

6. Record your observations and close your Web browser.

Radio Wave Technologies

Network signals are transmitted over radio waves in a fashion similar to the way your local radio station broadcasts, but network applications use much higher frequencies. For example, an AM station in your area might transmit at a frequency of 1290, which is 1290 kilohertz (kHz), because the AM broadcast range is 535–1605 kHz. The FM range is 88–108 megahertz (MHz). In the United States, network signals are transmitted at much higher frequencies, including 902–928 MHz, 2.4–2.4835 GHz, or 5–5.825 GHz.

Each of these ranges is also called a band—the 902 MHz band, the 2.4 GHz band, and the 5 GHz band. The 902 band is primarily used in older nonstandardized wireless devices and is not discussed further in this book.

In radio network transmissions, a signal is transmitted in one or multiple directions, depending on the type of antenna that is used. For example, in Figure 6-1, the signal is directional because it is transmitted from the antenna on one building to the antenna on another. The wave is very short in length with a low-wattage transmission strength (unless the transmission operator has a special license from the FCC for a high-wattage transmission), which means it is best suited to short-range **line-of-sight transmissions**. A line-of-sight transmission is one in which the signal goes from point to point, following the surface of the Earth, rather than bouncing off the atmosphere to skip across the country or across continents. A limitation of line-of-sight transmissions is that they are interrupted by tall land masses, such as hills and mountains. A low-power (1–10 watts) radio wave signal has a data capacity in the range of 1 megabit per second (Mbps) to over 300 Mbps.

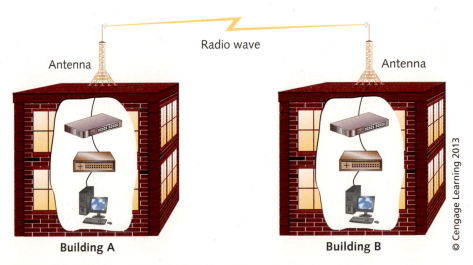

Figure 6-1   Wireless communications by radio waves

Most wireless radio wave network equipment employs **spread spectrum technology** for packet transmissions. This technology spreads the transmission over one or more adjoining frequencies, using greater bandwidth to transmit the signal. Spread spectrum frequency ranges are very high, in the 902–928 MHz range and much higher. Spread spectrum transmissions typically send data at a rate of 1–600 Mbps.

The 902 MHz, 2.4 GHz, and 5 GHz spread spectrum frequencies are offered by the FCC as unlicensed frequencies available for many kinds of wireless activity including wireless phones, wireless networking, and Bluetooth devices. You learn about Bluetooth in the "Bluetooth" section later in this chapter.

Radio wave communications can save money where it is difficult or expensive to run cable. Radio wave installations are also useful in situations where portable computers are used and need to be moved around frequently. Compared to other wireless options, they are relatively inexpensive and easy to install.

There are some disadvantages to radio wave communications. One is that wireless networks are more susceptible to interference than cabled networks, such as interference caused by certain building materials and by surrounding electrical devices. Such interference can reduce the speed of communications, cause communications to be intermittent, or prevent communications altogether. Another disadvantage is that some of the wireless frequencies are shared by amateur radio operators, the U.S. military, and cell phone companies, which means these frequencies can experience competing interference from these sources. Natural obstacles, such as hills, also can diminish or interfere with the signal transmission. Further, although wireless security is greatly improved, it cannot guarantee the same level of security as a fully enclosed cable system in which access to the cable (and to outside sources) is carefully restricted. (However security on any network is only as strong as the weakest link—all it takes is one unsecure computer or network segment to breach security for the whole network.)

One of the main radio wave wireless technologies is based on the IEEE 802.11 family of standards. Other radio wave technologies include Bluetooth, HiperLAN, Infrared, WiMAX, HiperMAN, and cellular phone. You learn about these technologies in later sections of this chapter.

IEEE 802.11 Radio Wave Networking

There are different types of radio wave wireless communications in use, but the type that offers significant advantages in terms of compatibility and reliability follows the IEEE 802.11 standards. The original standard was 802.11 (without a following letter), but the standards that are most popular today are 802.11a, 802.11b, 802.11g, and 802.11n. 802.11ac and 802.11ad are newer, emerging standards at this writing. You will learn more about all of these standards later in the chapter.

Many wireless network users deploy IEEE 802.11 devices because these devices do not rely on proprietary communications, which means that 802.11 devices from different vendors can be intermixed. Because 802.11 devices are not proprietary, different manufacturer's devices are more likely to interoperate, and upgrades to newer wireless features are easier to implement. Thus, understanding the IEEE 802.11 standards for wireless networking and the devices that use these standards is important for designing wireless networks.

The original IEEE 802.11 standard is also called the IEEE Standard for Wireless LAN Medium Access Control (MAC) and Physical Layer (PHY) Specifications. The 802.11 family of standards encompasses wireless data communications stations that are either fixed or mobile. Note that a fixed station is one that is not in motion, such as one in a building (including a stationary laptop); a mobile station is one that is traveling, such as a wireless computer (or computer device) in a car or one carried by a person who is walking.

The 802.11 standards involve two kinds of communications. The first is asynchronous communications (see Chapter 5, "Devices for Connecting Networks"), in which communications occur in discrete units with a start bit at the front and a stop bit at the back. The second type consists of those governed by time restrictions, in which the signal has a given amount of time to reach its destination or is considered lost or corrupted. The element of time restrictions makes the 802.11 standards similar to the 802.3 (Ethernet) standard, in which a signal must also reach a given destination within a given time. The 802.11 standards include support for network management services, such as the SNMP protocol that is used with management software for managing and monitoring a network. They also include support for network authentication.

The 802.11 standards for wireless devices deal primarily with the bottom two OSI layers: the Data Link and Physical layers. Focusing wireless specifications on the lower two layers allows other network applications such as network operating systems or LAN applications to run on an IEEE WLAN without modification. The Data Link layer formats data into frames and performs error checking. The Physical layer deals with the actual transmission of data over the medium, in this case over the airwaves. IEEE 802.11 divides the Data Link layer into two sublayers: the MAC and LLC sublayers, where standards are defined for the access method (which you learn later in this chapter), for addressing, and for data validation through a cyclic redundancy check (CRC). At the Physical layer, the 802.11 standards define data transmission rates over specified frequencies. The standards also provide for methods, such as spread spectrum technologies, for placing a data signal onto radio waves and infrared.

In terms of operating environments, the 802.11 standards recognize indoor and outdoor wireless communications. An indoor operating environment might be an office building, a manufacturing area, a retail store, or a private home—all areas in which the wireless communications take place inside a single building. An outdoor area can be a university campus, a sports field or complex, or a parking area, in which wireless communications occur outdoors or between buildings.

In the next sections, you learn some specifics about how IEEE 802.11 wireless networks function:

- The wireless components used in IEEE 802.11 networks
- Wireless networking access methods
- How data errors are handled
- Transmission speeds used in IEEE 802.11 networks
- Security techniques
- How authentication is used to disconnect
- 802.11-based topologies
- How to use multiple-cell wireless LANs

Wireless Components

Wireless communications usually involve three main components: a card that functions as a transmitter/receiver (transceiver), an access point, and antennas.

The transceiver card is a **wireless NIC (WNIC)** that functions at both the Physical and Data Link layers of the OSI model. A WNIC can be an internal PCI (Peripheral Computer Interface) or miniPCI card, a removable CardBus or PCMCIA (Personal Computer Memory Card International Association) card, or a USB (Universal Serial Bus) key fob or stick. A WNIC can be added to either a laptop or desktop computer, and many of these now come with a built-in WNIC (or built-in cable-based NICs and WNICs).

Most WNICs are compatible with the Microsoft **Network Driver Interface Specification (NDIS)**. NDIS is a network driver specification and application programming interface (api) for creating and using network interface card drivers that work with many network protocols. As an api, NDIS consists of a library of small programs or subroutines used for network communications. This library of programs is facilitated through the ndis.sys system file along with other related system files. In Microsoft operating systems, NDIS is essential to the function of NICs and WNICs. NDIS is also supported in Linux through "wrapper driver" initiatives.

Attackers have written malware that has replaced or attached to NDIS software files for the purpose of intercepting network traffic from individual computers. Be cautious when receiving messages to replace or fix your NDIS or network drivers.

An **access point** is a device that can optionally attach to a cabled network and that services wireless communications between WNICs and the cabled network. An access point is usually a bridge, switch, or router. For connecting to a cabled network, an access point may have one or more of the following types of network interfaces (see Chapter 4, "Connecting Through a Cabled Network" to review AUI through 100 GB Ethernet technologies):

- Attachment unit interface (AUI)
- 10Base2
- 10BaseT
- 100BaseTX, 100BaseT, 100BaseT2, and 100BaseT4
- 1000Base technologies
- 40 GB Ethernet technologies
- 100 GB Ethernet technologies
- FDDI
- Cable modem port
- DSL telecommunications port

Modern access points typically have routing capabilities.

An **antenna** is a device that sends out (radiates) and picks up radio waves. Both WNICs and access points employ antennas. Most wireless network antennas are either directional or omnidirectional.

When you purchase 802.11 devices, make sure they are certified by the Wi-Fi Alliance, to ensure that one vendor's devices work with those of another vendor and that devices using different 802.11 standards can interoperate.

Directional Antenna   A directional antenna sends the radio waves in one main direction and generally can amplify (strengthen) the radiated signal to a greater degree than an omnidirectional antenna. Amplification of the radiated signal is called **gain**. In wireless networking, a directional antenna is typically used to transmit radio waves between antennas on two buildings connected to access points, as shown in Figure 6-2. In this type of application, the directional antenna offers longer reach than an omnidirectional antenna because it is more likely to radiate a stronger signal—a signal that has more gain—in one direction. Notice in Figure 6-2 that the antenna does not truly radiate the signal in only one direction because portions of the signal are radiated out a small distance along the way.

A common problem for a wireless access point in a home or small office is that some computers receive a low signal because of their distance away from the access point. If all computers are in the same direction away from the access point, one solution is to replace the omnidirectional antenna on the access point with a directional antenna for greater signal strength in the direction of the client computers.

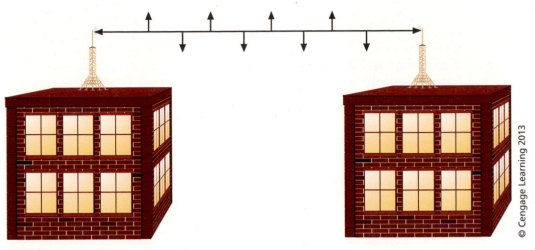

Figure 6-2   Directional antennas

Omnidirectional Antenna

An omnidirectional antenna radiates the radio waves in all directions. Because the signal is diffused more than the signal of a directional antenna, it is likely to have less gain than that of a directional antenna. In wireless networking, an omnidirectional antenna is often used on an indoor network, in which users are mobile and need to broadcast and receive in all directions. In addition, the signal gain in an indoor network often does not have to be as high as that for an outdoor network, because the indoor distances between wireless devices are shorter. Figure 6-3 illustrates a wireless network using omnidirectional antennas.

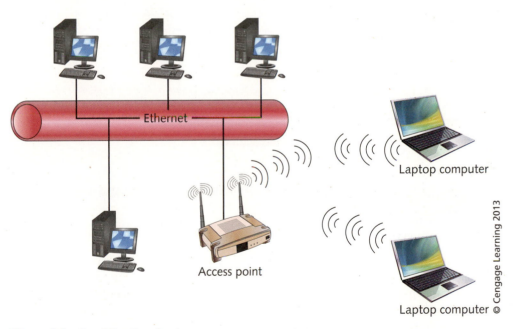

Figure 6-3   Omnidirectional antennas

On portable devices, such as laptop computers and larger tablet computers, the WNIC may use a small snap-on omnidirectional antenna, but more likely the antenna is built into the computer or device so that you do not see it. In modern cell phones, smartphones, eReaders (such as the Kindle), and smaller tablet PCs (such as the Apple iPad, Android Xoom, or Android XYBoard), typically the antenna is omnidirectional and built into the device (see Figure 6-4 for a sample Kindle Wi-Fi settings screen). An access point used for a local indoor network may have a snap-on omnidirectional antenna, or it may have an omnidirectional antenna that connects to the access point using a cable. An access point for an outdoor network that connects two buildings is likely to use a high-gain antenna that connects to the access point using a cable. In Activity 6-3 you view the components used in wireless communications. In Activity 6-4 you learn how to install the Wireless LAN Service in Windows Server 2008/Server 2008 R2, which must be installed before you can use a WNIC for a wireless network. In Activity 6-5 you learn how to manually configure a WNIC in Windows 7 and Windows Server 2008/Server 2008 R2. Finally, in Activity 6-6 you learn from where to configure a WNIC in Mac OS X Snow Leopard or Lion.

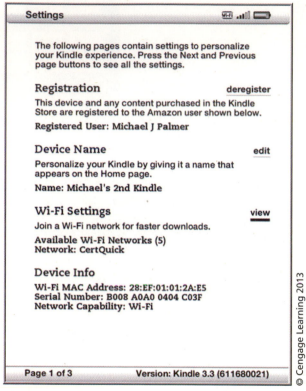

Figure 6-4   Kindle eReader setup screen with Wi-Fi settings

Activity 6-3: Wireless Networking Components

Time Required: 10 minutes
Objective: View wireless networking components.

Description: The main components used in wireless communications are WNICs, access points, and antennas. In this activity, you have an opportunity to view each type of component, provided by your instructor or by a lab instructor (or you can view these devices on a home or small office network).

 If you don't have access to devices to examine, consider searching for each device on the Internet to view pictures. Search for wireless access point, wireless network adapter, and Wi-Fi antenna.

1. Obtain a WNIC and examine it. What type is it, and how does it connect to the computer or other wireless device? What standard or standards does it use?

2. Next, obtain an access point, such as a wireless bridge or router, and examine it. Check out the documentation for the access point, if it is available. To what standard does it conform?

3. Last, examine the antennas that are used with the WNIC and with the access point. What types of antennas do they use?

4. Record your observations in a lab journal or in a word-processed document.

In some Windows 7, Server 2008, or Server 2008 R2 projects, you may see the User Account Control (UAC) box, which is used for security to help thwart intruders. The UAC box asks for permission to continue with an action or asks for the administrator password. If you see this box, click **Continue**. Because computer setups may be different, the box is not mentioned in the actual project steps.

Activity 6-4: Install the Wireless LAN Service in Windows Server 2008/Server 2008 R2

6

Time Required: 10 minutes
Objective: Use Server Manager to install the Wireless LAN Service in Windows Server 2008/Server 2008 R2.

Description: Before you can configure a WNIC in Windows Server 2008/Server 2008 R2, it is necessary to install the Wireless LAN Service. In keeping with Microsoft's initiative to increase security, the Wireless LAN Service is not installed by default and you have to manually install it to enable wireless communications on a server. For this activity, the Wireless LAN Service should not already be installed and you need access to an account that has Administrator privileges.

1. For Windows Server 2008/Server 2008 R2, if Server Manager is not already open, click **Start,** point to **Administrative Tools,** and click **Server Manager.**

2. Make sure that **Server Manager** (*computer name*) is selected in the tree in the left pane (see Figure 6-5).

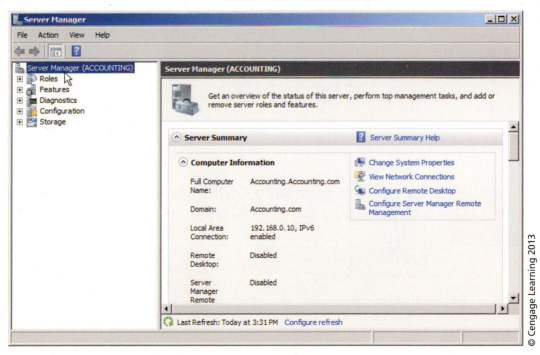

Figure 6-5   Using Server Manager in Windows Server 2008 R2

3. Scroll to the Features Summary section in the right pane and click **Add Features**.

4. In the Select Features window, scroll to the bottom of the listing of features and click the box for **Wireless LAN Service** (see Figure 6-6).

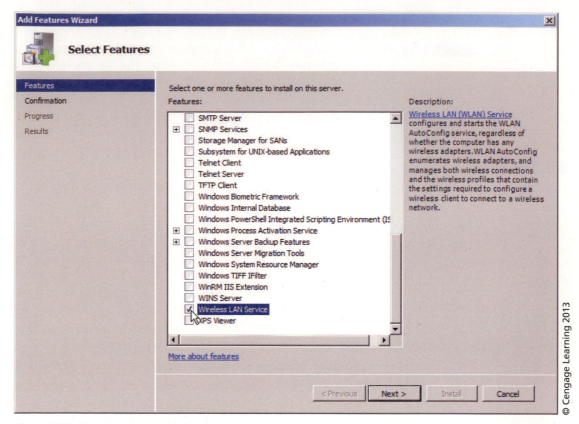

Figure 6-6   Selecting to install Wireless LAN Service in Windows Server 2008 R2

5. In the Select Features window, click **Next**.

6. In the Confirm Installation Selections window, click **Install**.

7. In the Installation Results window, click **Close**.

8. Close Server Manager.

Activity 6-5: Manually Configuring a WNIC in Windows 7 and Windows Server 2008/Server 2008 R2

Time Required: 10–15 minutes
Objective: Learn how to configure a wireless NIC in Windows 7 and Windows Server 2008/Server 2008 R2.

Description: In many cases, when you install a WNIC, Windows 7 and Windows Server 2008/Server 2008 R2 can automatically configure the hardware through their Plug and Play (PnP) capability. If the hardware is not detected by PnP or you want to configure it yourself, you can configure it manually, as you learn in the steps that follow (but you don't complete the installation, so you can perform this activity regardless of whether you have a WNIC). You need access to an account that has Administrator privileges. Also, the Wireless LAN Service should not already be installed as a feature in Windows Server 2008/Server 2008 R2.

To install a WNIC in Windows Server 2008:

1. Click **Start** and click **Control Panel**.

2. If necessary, click **Classic View** in the Control Panel window.

3. Double-click **Add Hardware**.

4. Click **Next** in the Welcome to the Add Hardware Wizard window.

5. In the next window, you can have the operating system search for the hardware and try to install it via PnP, or you can select to install the hardware manually by selecting it from a list (see Figure 6-7).

6. Click **Cancel**, so that you do not complete the installation.

7. Close the Control Panel window.

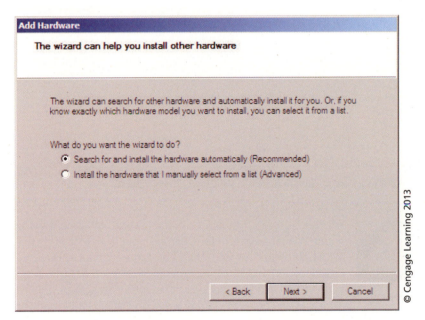

Add Hardware

The wizard can help you install other hardware

The wizard can search for other hardware and automatically install it for you. Or, if you know exactly which hardware model you want to install, you can select it from a list.

What do you want the wizard to do?

- ⊙ Search for and install the hardware automatically (Recommended)
- ○ Install the hardware that I manually select from a list (Advanced)

[< Back] [Next >] [Cancel]

© Cengage Learning 2013

Figure 6-7   Using the Add Hardware Wizard in Windows Server 2008

To install a WNIC in Windows 7 or Server 2008 R2:

1. Click **Start** and click **Control Panel**. Make sure that **View by** is set to **Large icons** or **Small icons**.

2. Click **Devices and Printers** in the Control Panel window.

3. Notice the button for *Add a device*, which you can use to install a new device (see Figure 6-8, which also shows a WNIC that needs to be installed manually because Plug and Play did not automatically install it as indicated by the exclamation point in the figure).

4. Close the Devices and Printers window.

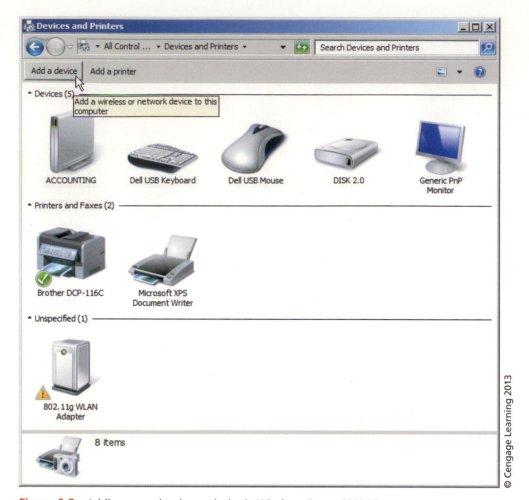

Figure 6-8 Adding a new hardware device in Windows Server 2008 R2

In Linux, you can manually configure a WNIC by using the *ifconfig* command in a terminal window. For example, if the WNIC is the only NIC in the computer (wlan0), then you can assign an address by entering *ifconfig wlan0 192.168.0.4 netmask 255.255.255.0*, for example (your IP address and subnet mask will differ). Next, to activate the WNIC enter *ifconfig wlan0 up*. Mac OS X is based on Darwin UNIX, and you can also use the *ifconfig* command in Mac OS X to configure a WNIC or NIC.

Activity 6-6: Configuring a WNIC in Mac OS X Snow Leopard and Lion

Time Required: 10 minutes

Objective: Learn from where to configure a WNIC in Mac OS X Snow Leopard and Lion.

Description: WNICs that are compatible with Mac OS X Snow Leopard and Lion will be automatically detected by the operating system. When you install a new WNIC, you can make sure it is properly configured via the Network option in the System Preferences window. In this activity, you learn from where to configure a WNIC such as AirPort. Your computer should already have a WNIC installed.

1. Click the **System Preferences** icon in the Dock, or click the **Apple** icon in the menu bar and click **System Preferences**.

2. Click **Network** in the Internet & Wireless section of the System Preferences window (see Figure 6-9).

Figure 6-9   Selecting Network in System Preferences in Mac OS X Lion

3. In the Network window, if there is a green dot to the left of the WNIC, such as AirPort or Wi-Fi, this indicates the WNIC is connected and working. Click the WNIC, if necessary, to select it.

4. Click the **Advanced** button.

5. Notice the tabs available for configuring the WNIC. Record the names of the tabs.

6. Click **Cancel** and close the Network window.

Wireless Networking Access Methods

There are two access methods incorporated into the 802.11 standard: priority-based access and Carrier-Sense Multiple Access with Collision Avoidance (CSMA/CA). Both access methods are Data Link layer functions.

In **priority-based access**, the access point device also functions as a point coordinator. The point coordinator establishes a contention-free period, during which stations cannot transmit (other than the point coordinator), unless first contacted by the point coordinator. The point coordinator polls stations during the contention-free period. If a station indicates through a single short transmission that it is pollable because it has a message to send, the point coordinator places that station on its polling list. If a station is not pollable, the point coordinator sends a beacon frame to indicate how long the station must wait until the next contention-free period. Stations on the pollable list are next granted access to communicate, one at a time. After the stations on the polling list have all had an opportunity to transmit, there is another contention-free period during which the point coordinator again polls each station to determine if it is pollable and wants to transmit.

Priority-based access is intended for communications that are time sensitive. Time-sensitive communications typically include voice, video, and videoconferencing, all of which are applications that work best with uninterrupted throughput. Priority-based access is also called **point coordination function** in the 802.11 standard.

Carrier Sense Multiple Access with Collision Avoidance (CSMA/CA) is a more commonly used access method in wireless networking and is also called the **distributed coordination function**. In CSMA/CA, a station waiting to transmit listens to determine if the communication frequency is idle. It determines if the frequency is idle by checking the Receiver Signal Strength Indicator (RSSI) level. The point at which the transmission frequency is idle is when there is the most risk of collisions by two or more stations that want to initiate a transmission at the same time. As soon as the frequency is idle, each station listens for DIFS seconds to make sure the frequency remains idle. DIFS is the distributed coordination function's intraframe space, which is a predefined mandatory idle or delay period.

If the frequency remains idle for DIFS seconds, stations avoid a collision because each station needing to transmit calculates a different amount of time to wait or a "backoff time" until checking the frequency again to see if it is idle. If the frequency remains idle, the station with the shortest backoff time (delay time) transmits. If the frequency does not remain idle, stations that need to transmit wait until the frequency is idle and then wait again according to the backoff time they have already calculated.

The backoff time is determined by multiplying a predetermined slot-time by a random number. The slot-time is a value stored in a management information base (MIB) table kept by each station. The random number is any number between 0 and the maximum collision window size. The maximum collision window size is also stored in the station's MIB. Thus, there is a unique backoff time for each station that needs to transmit, enabling stations to avoid collisions. (See the information about SNMP and MIB in Chapter 3, "Using Network Communication Protocols.")

Handling Data Errors

Wireless network communications are subject to interference from weather conditions, solar flares, competing wireless communications, physical obstacles, and other sources. Any of these forms of interference can corrupt the successful reception of data. The automatic repeat-request (ARQ) characteristic in the 802.11 standard helps wireless devices take these possibilities into account.

With ARQ, if the station sending a packet does not receive an acknowledgment (ACK) from the destination station, the sending station automatically retransmits the packet. The number of times that the sending station retransmits before assuming that the packet cannot be delivered depends on the size of the packet. Each station keeps two values, one that specifies the maximum size of a short packet and one that specifies the size of a long packet. Each station also keeps two additional values, one to show how many times to retry sending a short packet and one to indicate how many times to retry sending a long packet. A station ceases trying to retransmit a packet on the basis of these values.

As an example of ARQ error handling, assume that a station defines a short packet as having a maximum size of 776 bytes and the retransmit limit for a short packet is 10 times. Assume also that the station transmits a 608-byte packet, but does not receive an ACK from the destination station. This means that the sending station will retry sending the same packet up to 10 times without an ACK. After 10 unacknowledged attempts, it will stop trying to retransmit that packet.

Transmission Speeds

The 802.11 wireless transmission speeds and related frequencies are defined through four standards: 802.11a, 802.11b, 802.11g, and 802.11n. The transmission speeds in these standards correspond to the Physical layer of the OSI model.

At this writing, there are two newer very-high-speed wireless LAN standards under development for release in the near future: 802.11ac and 802.11ad. All of these standards are discussed in the next sections.

802.11a   The 802.11a standard outlines the following speeds in the 5 GHz range for wireless networking:

- 6 Mbps
- 9 Mbps
- 12 Mbps
- 18 Mbps
- 24 Mbps
- 36 Mbps
- 48 Mbps
- 54 Mbps

All devices that conform to the 802.11a standard must be able to transmit at 6, 12, and 24 Mbps.

The 802.11a standard uses **Orthogonal Frequency Division Multiplexing (OFDM)** to radiate the data signal over radio waves and is performed at the Physical layer of the OSI model. OFDM functions by dividing the 5 GHz frequency range into a series of 52 subcarriers or subchannels. It then splits data to be sent over the 52 subcarriers and transmits the data over all 52 subcarriers at the same time, called transmitting in parallel. Four of the subcarriers are used for information to control the transmission, and 48 of the subcarriers host data.

Devices for the 802.1a standard are not as widespread as those for the 802.1b standard, which reached the market about two years earlier. Both standards have been largely superseded by the more recent 802.11g and 802.11n standards.

While the top speed of 802.11a is 54 Mbps, the average throughput is really about 27 Mbps.

802.11b

The **802.11b** standard is used in the 2.4 GHz frequency range and offers data transmission speeds that include:

- 1 Mbps
- 2 Mbps
- 5.5 Mbps
- 10 Mbps
- 11 Mbps

The 802.11b standard uses **Direct Sequence Spread Spectrum (DSSS)**, which is a Physical layer method for radiating a data-carrying signal over radio waves. DSSS first spreads the data across any of up to 14 channels, each 22 MHz in width. The exact number and frequency of the channels is related to the country in which the transmission takes place. In Canada and the United States, the actual number of channels used in the 2.4 GHz frequency range is 11. In Europe, 13 channels are used, except in France, which uses only four channels. The data signal is sequenced over the channels and is amplified to have a high gain to combat interference. For speeds of 5.5 Mbps and above, 802.11b also uses Barker Code and Complementary Code Keying (CCK), which enable DSSS to send more information per transmission.

Many 802.11b networks typically operate at 4–5 Mbps, once all transmission factors are taken into account, such as RFI and distances between devices.

802.11g

The **802.11g** standard was developed after the 802.11a and 802.11b standards and supports three transmission technologies on the 2.4 GHz band: OFDM, CCK, and Packet Binary Convolution Code (PBCC).

OFDM is the native mode for 802.11g and works in the same way as it works for 802.11a, only at 2.4 GHz instead of 5 GHz. The transmission speeds available when using OFDM are:

- 6 Mbps
- 9 Mbps
- 12 Mbps
- 18 Mbps
- 24 Mbps
- 36 Mbps
- 48 Mbps
- 54 Mbps

802.11g can optionally use DSSS with CCK for backward compatibility with 802.11b, and in this mode it offers the following speeds:

- 1 Mbps
- 2 Mbps
- 5.5 Mbps
- 11 Mbps

Some manufacturers of 802.11g devices don't fully adhere to the 802.11g standard in that their devices don't really provide compatibility for 802.11b. When you purchase an 802.11g device to be used on a mixed 802.11g and 802.11b network, ensure that the manufacturer's specifications include 802.11b and look for the Wi-Fi CERTIFIED insignia on the box.

Pioneered by Texas Instruments (TI), Packet Binary Convolution Code (PBCC) is another option for compatibility with 802.11b (TI calls it 802.11b+). PBCC is not part of the 802.11b standard, but is an unofficial extension used with 802.11b by some vendors to enable faster speeds by performing faster error checking and sending larger packets. When using the optional PBCC mode, 802.11g offers the following speeds:

- 22 Mbps
- 33 Mbps

Devices that support 802.11g must all support at least 1, 2, 5.5, 6, 11, 12, and 24 Mbps according to the standard.

802.11g has a slightly shorter range than 802.11b, and so you may need to use more access points than with 802.11b—depending on the distances you need to cover. Also, unlike 802.11a and 802.11b, 802.11g has a smaller bandwidth at 90 MHz, which means that the prudent network administrator employs no more than three access points (using 30 MHz each) in a particular area.

The typical network running only 802.11g has an actual throughput of 20–25 Mbps.

One advantage of 802.11g is that you can combine 802.11g devices and 802.11b devices on the same LAN, enabling you to retain an earlier investment in 802.11b devices. At the same time, combining 802.11b and 802.11g devices can be a significant disadvantage, because your network performance will be much lower than if you use only 802.11g devices. The slow performance of a network combining 802.11b and 802.11g is caused by two factors. First, 802.11b has a top speed of 11 Mbps. If your 802.11g access point is communicating with a computer that has an 802.11b WNIC, then the top speed is 11 Mbps (and actually more like 4–5 Mbps). Other devices waiting to transmit, such as those using 802.11g, have to wait longer. This is like following a slow moving car on a two-lane highway with no passing. You may be following in a Ferrari, but you can't go any faster until the slow moving car turns off the road—and if there are two slow moving cars ahead, you'll have to wait even longer. Second, 802.11g has a slot-time (9 µsec) that is less than half that of 802.11b (20 µsec). As you recall from the earlier discussion of CSMA/CA, this means the backoff time is longer for 802.11b—which again means those devices using 802.11g are trailing that slow moving car. And, the more 802.11b devices that are on the network, the slower the overall performance.

When you set up a wireless network using 802.11b, 802.11g, or both, performance may be degraded by the presence of devices such as microwave ovens, radios, and cordless phones that operate in the 2.4 GHz band. This is because your wireless network devices use techniques to counteract RFI on the same frequency by lowering the rate of transmission. Also, if you have devices that are relatively far from your access point, they will transmit at slower speeds to compensate for the lower signal strength—once again, like the Ferrari following the slower car.

Real-Life Networking

A large furniture store hired a local office products company to install wireless communications between particular computers and computer-based cash registers within the store. The office products company had a supply of old unsold 802.11b devices and WNICs and a few newer 802.11n wireless devices that it installed for the furniture store. The furniture store discovered that the wireless network ran at a much slower speed (typically 4–6 Mbps) than its aging 10BaseT wired network. The furniture store would have experienced much faster network communications if only 802.11n devices and WNICs had been used.

802.11n   802.11n is one of the latest and fastest iterations of the 802.11 standards for wireless communications. 802.11n uses a technology called **multiple-input multiple-output (MIMO)** coupled with **spatial multiplexing**. MIMO involves using multiple antennas at the transmitting and receiving devices, and spatial multiplexing means a device can transmit and receive two or more data streams over one channel within a frequency. MIMO with spatial multiplexing is accomplished by using two or more transmitters (and antennas) and the same number of receivers (and antennas) for simultaneous transmission and reception. The result is that data transmissions can follow multiple paths to the point of reception. For example, one path might be a straight path with no objects between the transmitter and receiver. Another path might mean that the signal is bounced off the right side wall in a house and still another path is bounced off a left side wall.

802.11a/b/g experience reflections off of walls and objects as obstacles making communications less efficient. In contrast, 802.11n uses walls and obstacles to actually facilitate multiple communications paths for faster transmissions.

Another improvement in the 802.11n technology is in the use of aggregation of frames and ACK responses used to verify successful receipt of frames. In 802.11a/b/g, a 128-byte ACK is sent back from the receiver to the sender after a single frame is received as a way to show the frame has been successfully received. In 802.11n, the size of the ACK frame is reduced to 8 bytes and one ACK can be used to verify receipt of multiple frames (instead of just one frame). Also, in 802.11n multiple frames can be aggregated together in one transmission, and there is also the ability to verify receipt of multiple frames in what is called a block ACK. The 802.11n improvements in the use of frame aggregation and block ACKs can make the 802.11n technology much faster than its predecessors in two ways. First, more data is transmitted per session. This is like when you order eight items to be sent by surface mail. One way to send the order is to package each item separately and send one item each day (similar to the 802.11a/b/g technologies). Another method is to package all items in one box and send the one box as soon as possible (similar to the 802.11n technology). Clearly, the second method is much faster.

The second advantage of these improvements is related to channel acquisition. All 802.11 technologies experience delays in acquiring a transmission channel and in releasing a channel. Using frame aggregation and block ACKs as in 802.11n significantly reduces the number of times a channel must be acquired and released, because more information is sent with each transmission, resulting in far fewer channel acquisitions/releases.

Some vendors have chosen to omit the use of ACKs in 802.11a/b/g devices because of the extra overhead and as a way to make their devices faster. The downside is that such devices can result in more data errors, which can be a problem on networks requiring data accuracy. This can be one reason for retiring older wireless equipment. The implementation of 802.11n has meant that most vendors incorporate the use of ACKs in their devices, because 802.11n handles ACKs more efficiently.

802.11n can use 20 and 40 MHz channels within the 2.4 and 5 GHz bands. Currently, there can be up to four simultaneous data streams per 20 or 40 MHz channel for a top speed of 600 Mbps (on a 40 MHz channel within the 5 GHz broadcast frequency).

At present, there are about 128 broadcast speeds possible over 20 and 40 MHz channel communication, depending on the number of data streams. The slowest speed is 6.5 Mbps on a single stream on a 20 MHz channel, and the highest is 900 Mbps on a multistream 40 MHz channel.

At this writing, most 802.11n devices have a top speed of 300+ Mbps. However, it is also important to recognize that factors such as distance, obstacles, and electrical interference affect the actual throughput. Other factors that influence throughput include having to go through cabled portions of a network that operate at much lower speeds (for example, 100 Mbps) and the throughput of WAN connections, such as DSL or cable TV WAN connections. 802.11n devices are also mandated through Wi-Fi certification to be backward compatible with 802.11a/b/g devices, which can affect actual speeds as you learned in the 802.11g section of this chapter—mixing slower 802.11 devices on the same network as 802.11n devices can significantly slow a network.

802.11ac   Currently under development at this writing, 802.11ac is one of two approaches to achieve wireless transmissions in the 1 Gbps and higher range. 802.11ac is intended to use the 2.4 and 5 GHz bands for transmissions, with 2.4 GHz for backward compatibility with earlier standards and 5 GHz offering more capability for higher transmission rates.

802.11ac is designed around the tested technologies used by 802.11n, which include OFDM and MIMO. However, MIMO is expanded into multiuser MIMO or MU-MIMO, so that frames sent to and from multiple clients can be sent simultaneously on the same channel. Building on 802.11n, which operates within the 20 and 40 MHz channels, 802.11ac expands transmission capabilities to use the 80 MHz channel for even wider bandwidth, particularly within the 5 GHz band.

802.11ad   Also under development at this writing, the 802.11ad standard is targeted at accomplishing transmission speeds of roughly 7 Gbps. Like 802.11ac, 802.11ad is based on using OFDM, MIMO, and MU-MIMO. 802.11ad has backward compatibility with earlier standards in the 2.4 GHz range and more high-speed capabilities in the 5 GHz range. Unlike 802.11ac, 802.11ad operates using the 60 MHz channel.

At this writing, 802.11ad is designed for shorter transmission distances, such as within a room, because it is likely to be restricted by walls. Wireless device manufacturers view 802.11ad to be attractive for wireless components such as keyboards, pointing devices, and storage drives. Manufacturers are also looking at 802.11ad for Wi-Fi-based phone communications and HD movies on big-screen wireless TVs.

802.11a, 802.11b, 802.11g, 802.11n, 802.11ac, and 802.11ad Compared

The 802.11a, 802.11g, and 802.11n standards offer the advantage of speed over the 802.11b standard, with 802.11n offering the optimum speed at this writing and with 802.11ac likely to surpass 802.11n in the future for general wireless LAN communications. However, for 802.11a speed comes at the cost of shorter range. Currently, 802.11a devices transmit up to 18 meters (about 60 feet), while 802.11b devices can reach over 91 meters (about 300 feet). The transmission range of the 802.11g devices on the market, as of this writing, varies from 30 meters (about 100 feet) to under 100 meters (about 330 feet). 802.11n devices are generally capable of twice the upper limit of 802.11g devices or about 200 meters (about 650 feet). The takeaway message is that at this writing 802.11n is a much better and more versatile alternative than 802.11a, 802.11b, or 802.11g. However, it is good to remember that 802.11a/b/g/n all work in either the

20 or 40 MHz channels. Because 802.11n uses spatial multiplexing, it can occupy most of the bandwidth within 20 or 40 MHz, leaving little channel bandwidth for any surrounding wireless data devices competing for the same channels. Table 6-1 summarizes the characteristics of 802.11a, 802.11b, 802.11g, 802.n, 802.11ac, and 802.11ad.

Table 6-1 802.11a, 802.11b, 802.11g, 802.11n, 802.11ac, and 802.11ad characteristics

	Operating Frequency Range	Operating Speeds (bandwidth)	Communications Method	Current Practical Maximum Distance	Cost to Implement
802.11a	5 GHz	6, 9, 12, 18, 24, 36, 48, 54 Mbps	Orthogonal Frequency Division Multiplexing (OFDM)	About 18.18 meters (approximately 60 feet)	Relatively more due to the need for more access points
802.11b	2.4 GHz	1, 2, 10, 11 Mbps	Direct Sequence Spread Spectrum (DSSS) coupled with Complementary Code Keying (CCK)	About 91 meters (approximately 300 feet)	Relatively less using fewer access points
802.11g	2.4 GHz	6, 9, 12, 18, 24, 36, 48, 54 Mbps using OFDM; 1, 2, 5.5, and 11 Mbps using DSSS with CCK; and 22 and 33 Mbps using PBCC	Orthogonal Frequency Division Multiplexing (OFDM); Direct Sequence Spread Spectrum (DSSS) coupled with Complementary Code Keying (CCK); or Packet Binary Convolution Code (PBCC)	About 100 meters (approximately 330 feet), but some network devices really work at only up to approximately 30 meters (about 100 feet)	Until the introduction of 802.11n devices, the least expensive option
802.11n	2.4 and 5 GHz	At this writing, 6.5 up to 900 Mbps depending on the frequency and number of data streams	Orthogonal Frequency Division Multiplexing (OFDM) accompanied by multiple-input multiple-output (MIMO) technology using spatial multiplexing for the ability to transmit two or more data streams	About 200 meters (approximately 650 feet)	The least expensive option because of range, speed, and price
802.11ac	2.4 and 5 GHz	At this writing, up to 1 Gbps depending on the frequency and number of data streams	Orthogonal Frequency Division Multiplexing (OFDM) accompanied by multiple-input multiple-output (MIMO) technology using spatial multiplexing for the ability to transmit two or more data streams (and supporting multi-user MIMO or MU-MIMO)	Under development at this writing	Undetermined at this writing
802.11ad	2.4 and 5 GHz	At this writing, up to 7 Gbps depending on the frequency and number of data streams (this technology is currently targeted for wireless electronic components, phones, and TVs)	Orthogonal Frequency Division Multiplexing (OFDM) accompanied by multiple-input multiple-output (MIMO) technology using spatial multiplexing for the ability to transmit two or more data streams (and supporting multiuser MIMO or MU-MIMO)	Under development at this writing	Undetermined at this writing

Don't rely on your system to measure up to the optimum speeds. The actual speed will typically be considerably less because of factors such as surrounding RFI and EMI, distance between communicating nodes, transmission wattage, antenna gain, materials in separating walls, and other factors.

802.11 Deployment Tips

When you deploy an 802.11 wireless access point, bridge, or router, there are several steps you can take to increase the performance. These include:

- Avoid placing an access point against a wall or on the floor.

- If possible, locate the access point in a main or central location that is in the middle of the client computers.

- If the access point cannot be centrally located, consider extending the signal by using a wireless repeater (see Figure 5-1 in Chapter 5) or by replacing the omnidirectional antenna with a directional antenna pointed in the direction of the client computers.

- Avoid locating the access point on or inside a metal cabinet or shelf.

- Remove sources of interference, including microwave ovens, cordless phones, and objects that block the transmission path.

- Consider replacing internal WNICs that do not have external antennas, such as a WNIC built into a computer's motherboard, with WNICs that have external antennas, such as via a PCI card or USB external WNIC. Also, be sure that all WNIC drivers are up to date.

- Replace any 802.11a, 802.11b, and 802.11g devices and WNICs with 802.11n devices and WNICs (or with 802.11ac WNICs and devices as these become available).

- Use the 5 GHz band and 40 MHz channels for 802.11n access points. The 5 GHz band has a shorter wavelength, which generally has a longer broadcast reach. Also, more data streams are available in the 40 MHz channel range. As 802.11ac access points become available, use the 5 GHz band and 80 MHz channels.

- Purchase devices with multiple antennas for more data streaming capability.

802.11 Security Techniques

Security is just as important on wireless networks as on cable networks. Because wireless networks are now common, attacks on wireless networks are increasing. As you consider security for your network, begin by considering the methods attackers can use.

One of the first steps in an attack is locating wireless network targets. To do this, there are four main elements that an attacker may use:

- An antenna

- A wireless network interface card

- A GPS (global positioning system) device

- War-driving software

An attacker may use several kinds of antennas, depending on whether the goal is to find a network that uses omnidirectional communications (such as an inside network) or one that uses directional communications (such as a network that goes between buildings). Some attackers come equipped with an assortment of omnidirectional and directional antennas, some high gain and some low gain. The antenna is connected to a wireless network interface card. You might think of these attackers as similar to fishermen who go out equipped with different flies for different fishing conditions.

Another element in the attacker's arsenal is a GPS device. The GPS is connected to a computer and is used to determine the location of the target wireless network. Finally, attackers use war-driving software (driving refers to driving around in a vehicle) that can take the information obtained through the antenna and pinpoint the location of the network with a GPS. Not only can war-driving software determine the location of a network, but it can also determine whether the network is an IBSS or ESS topology (these topologies are described in the section "802.11 Network Topologies" in this chapter).

Real-Life Networking

There are companies that sell devices which can be used for an attack on a wireless network. One company makes a handheld antenna and reception device that resembles a gun, attaches to a specialized WNIC on a portable computer, and is used to scan wireless frequencies for activity. A wireless network configured without security, such as a network used in a food court on a college campus, makes an ideal target for an attacker in a car in a nearby parking lot. A coffee shop or airport offering wireless connectivity is another attraction for an attacker who looks like just another laptop computer user, but who is using a WNIC and war-driving software to intercept wireless transmissions.

 Some war-driving software uses Broadcast Probe Requests sent from wireless network devices. You can thwart these intrusions by disabling Broadcast Probe Requests on WNICs and access points. Of course there is war-driving software that uses other means to detect a wireless network, so your best defense is to configure wireless security as discussed later in this section.

After an attacker locates an interesting target network, she or he can use a wireless "network sniffer" customized for 802.11, Bluetooth, or HiperLAN/HiperMAN to capture packets. The goal of the attacker may be to capture account names and passwords or simply to spy on network communications, as when one company spies on another.

Some wireless networks are particularly susceptible to man-in-the-middle attacks. A **man-in-the-middle attack** occurs when the attacker is able to intercept a message meant for a different computer. The attacker is literally operating between two communicating computers and has the opportunity to listen to and modify communications.

Your best defense against attacks is to take advantage of wireless security options. The 802.11 standard provides for several security approaches: open system authentication and Wired Equivalent Privacy (WEP) protocol shared key authentication. Besides these options, in most operating systems, you can also use Wi-Fi Protected Access (WPA) and service set identifier (SSID). Another security method that can be used is 802.1X/802.11i, which is available for wireless and wired networks.

Open System Authentication

In **open system authentication**, any two stations can authenticate with each other. The sending station simply requests to be authenticated by the destination station or access point. When the destination station verifies the request, authentication is completed. Open system authentication provides very little security, and you should be aware that on many vendors' devices, it is used by default.

Shared Key Authentication and Wired Equivalent Privacy

Shared key authentication provides more security than open system authentication because it employs **Wired Equivalent Privacy (WEP)**. In shared key authentication with WEP, two stations, such as a WNIC and an access point, use the same encryption key generated by WEP services. A WEP encryption key is a 40- or 104-bit key that also includes a checksum and initialization information for a total actual encryption key length of 64 or 128 bits (consisting of the key, checksum, and initialization information). If you have a choice between using 64- or 128-bit encryption, choose 128-bit encryption, because a longer encryption key is harder for an intruder to break. Systems protected by WEP can store up to four keys in a key index. To authenticate using shared key authentication and WEP, one station contacts another, requesting authentication. The second station, which is the one that is contacted, sends back a specialized challenge text. The first station encrypts the challenge text using a WEP encryption key and sends the encrypted text back to the second station. Finally, the second station decodes the challenge text using the same encryption key and compares that text with the challenge text it sent originally. If the encrypted challenge text is identical to the original challenge text, the second station verifies the authentication for continued communications.

 There are many tutorials and free software available on the Internet for cracking WEP security, which can be done in a matter of seconds. This is why WPA and WPA2 security is recommended over WEP and why the Wi-Fi Alliance does not believe WEP to be secure.

Wi-Fi Protected Access   Wi-Fi Protected Access (WPA) uses encryption keys and a key index similarly to WEP, but in this method the encrypted keys are regularly changed. Changing the keys makes WPA a more secure technique than WEP. WPA2 is the newest version of WPA at this writing and is designed to use stronger encryption methods and offer compatibility with the 802.11i authentication described in the section "802.1X and 802.11i."

WPA2 uses Advanced Encryption Standard (AES), which was developed through the National Institute of Standards and Technology (NIST) and is considered "government grade security" by the Wi-Fi Alliance because it was adopted by the U.S. government in 2002 and by the IETF in 2003. AES uses a private-key block-cipher technique in which plain text data is divided into 128-bit blocks. The private key can be either 128, 192, or 256 bits in length. Using this encryption key range, the number of possible combinations used to thwart attackers is impressive:

- 3.4×10^{38} combinations for a 128-bit key
- 6.2×10^{57} combinations for a 192-bit key
- 1.1×10^{77} combinations for a 256-bit key

WPA2 is backward compatible with WPA, but cannot be used at the same time as WEP. WPA2 is required for the Wi-Fi CERTIFIED insignia on a wireless device.

Some wireless products and operating systems also offer WPA/WPA2 with an enhancement called preshared key (PSK). The preshared key option is targeted for home and small networks that do not have additional enterprise network security measures, such as accounts that are authenticated through a domain. Setting up PSK network security is simplified for the home or small office user. She or he enters a password or passphrase, which acts as a master key when installing an access point. After the passphrase is entered, WPA/WPA2 encryption is automatically set into motion. All wireless devices must use the same passphrase. To employ PSK, this option must be supported on your WNIC and wireless network devices. Also, keep in mind that WPA/WPS2 security with PSK is only as strong as the strength of the PSK passphrase shared between devices. A longer PSK passphrase with a combination of numbers, upper and lowercase letters, and symbols provides better security than just using 12345 or the first name of your cousin. The passphrase can be 8 to 63 ASCII characters or up to 64 hexadecimal digits in length. Some security experts recommend a passphrase of at least 20 characters, and others recommend 33 characters or more.

When you configure WPA or WPA2, there can be two options: personal and enterprise. *WPA/WPA2 personal* uses PSK. This form of security is typically used on a home, small office, or larger office network that does not use a Remote Authentication Dial-Up User Service server, also known as a RADIUS server. *WPA/WPA2 enterprise* uses 802.1X (described in the section "802.1X and 802.11i Security") and coordinates security through an enterprise-wide RADIUS server. A RADIUS server is used to configure authentication and access to enterprise networks that use a variety of access services such as wireless, internal network, virtual private network (VPN), dial-up, Internet, and remote access. RADIUS is the protocol used by such a server, and this protocol is employed to enforce access rules while the server offers software for administering the protocol and keeping access statistics. A Windows Server 2008/Server 2008 R2 server can be configured to be a RADIUS server on an enterprise network. In Activity 6-7 you learn how to configure security on a Windows 7 wireless workstation.

Depending on when you purchased wireless devices, some may support WPA and others may support both WPA and WPA2 with the newer 802.11i (discussed later in this chapter). If you configure to use 802.11i and discover some devices can't access the network, try configuring for WPA instead, because WPA is generally more backward compatible with older devices than 802.11i.

Activity 6-7: Configuring WPA in Windows 7

Time Required: 5–10 minutes
Objective: Learn where to set up WPA/WPA2 in Windows 7.

Description: In this activity, you learn where to configure security in a Windows 7 system that is equipped with a WNIC. The WNIC should already be installed, and it should support different security options, such as WEP and WPA/WPA2. Also, you need to already be connected to a wireless network, such as through an access point, and you need a Windows 7 account that has Administrator privileges.

1. Click **Start** and click **Control Panel**. Be sure that **View by** is set to **Large icons** or **Small icons**.

2. In the All Control Panel Items window, click **Network and Sharing Center**.

3. Click **Connect to a network**.

4. Right-click the network to which you are connected and click **Properties**. In the Properties dialog box, click the **Security** tab, if necessary (see Figure 6-10).

If you were not already connected to a network, at this point you would right-click a network to access, click **Connect**, enter the security code (if requested), such as for WEP or WPA/WPA2, and click **OK** to access the network. Once connected, you could follow the steps outlined here to further configure security.

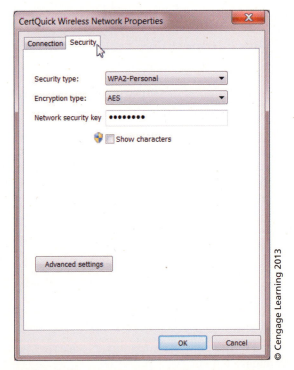

© Cengage Learning 2013

Figure 6-10   Security tab in Windows 7

5. Click the **down arrow** in the Security type box to view the different types of security that can be configured. Record the options that you see. Click in an open area of the dialog box to close the listing of security type options.

6. Notice that there is a box in which to provide a Network security key. Also, you can set AES or TKIP encryption in the Encryption type box. (The options you see on the Security tab can depend on the type of network connection, including the access point's or wireless modem's capabilities. In many instances, you will see the *Advanced settings* button that can be used to enable additional security, such as Federal Information Processing Standards compliance or configuration of 802.1X security described in the section "802.1X and 802.11i Security.")

7. Click **Cancel** in the Properties dialog box.

8. Close the Network and Sharing window.

Service Set Identifier   When you purchase wireless devices, ensure that they support a service set identifier (SSID). The SSID is an identification value that typically can be up to 32 characters in length. SSID is not truly a password, but rather a value that defines a logical network for all devices that belong to it. For example, the SSID might be a series of random characters, or it might be a string that actually describes the name or purpose of the network, such as "Atmospheric Research." Deploying an SSID is not likely to thwart a serious attacker, but it is wise to use one, as another block to make attacks a little more difficult. The SSID is also helpful on a home or small office network to enable local network users to distinguish a specific network from other networks in the area. The SSID is the network name that you see when you use the Windows Network and Sharing Center to view nearby wireless networks or when you click the *Currently connected to* applet at the right side of the Taskbar in Windows 7 and Server 2008/Server 2008 R2 to view wireless networks. When you purchase devices that use an SSID, often the SSID is configured to a default value by the vendor. As your first step, configure your wireless network devices to use the SSID and provide your own new value to replace the default (which attackers are likely to know). For enhanced protection, use an SSID value that is difficult to guess. In Activity 6-8 you learn from where to configure an SSID and security options in a UNIX/Linux system with the GNOME 3.x desktop.

Activity 6-8: Configuring the SSID and Wireless Security Options in UNIX/Linux

Time Required: 10 minutes
Objective: Learn from where to configure an SSID and wireless security options in the GNOME 3.x desktop used in UNIX/Linux systems.

Description: In this activity you learn where to configure the SSID and wireless security options in Linux using the GNOME 3.x desktop and the Network Connections applet. A WNIC should already be installed. If you are using Fedora Live Media Linux, it is not necessary to log into the root account. Also, you do not need a WNIC installed, or if a WNIC is installed on your computer but Linux does not recognize the WNIC, you can still proceed with this activity.

1. Log onto your account, such as liveuser.

2. Click **Activities** in the Panel at the top of the desktop.

3. Click **Applications**.

4. Click the **Network Connections** applet.

5. Click the **Wireless** tab in the Network Connections window.

6. Click the **Add** button in the Network Connections window.

7. Ensure the Wireless tab is selected in the Editing dialog box. Notice that you can provide an SSID in the SSID text box (see Figure 6-11).

Figure 6-11   Wireless tab in the Editing dialog box in Linux

8. Click the **Wireless Security** tab in the Editing dialog box.

9. Click the **down arrow** in the Security text box to view the options. Record the options that you see.

10. Click the pointer in a blank area of the Editing dialog box (to close the options listing) and then click **Cancel** in the Editing dialog box.

11. Click **Close** in the Network Connections window.

For some WNICs (depending on the WNIC driver and vendor), you can configure the SSID in Windows 7 and Windows Server 2008/Server 2008 R2 via the Device Manager. In Windows 7, click **Start**, right-click **My Computer**, and click **Manage**; or in Windows Server 2008/Server 2008 R2, click **Start**, point to **Administrative Tools**, and click **Computer Management**. Double-click **Device Manager** in the left pane and double-click **Network Adapters** in the right pane. Right-click the **wireless adapter** and click **Properties**. Click the **Advanced** tab and click **SSID**. Enter the SSID value and click **OK**. Click **Yes** to restart the computer, if necessary.

Some wireless vendors indicate in their promotional material or documentation that an SSID is a password. In one sense, it is similar to a password, because it is a value known to each wireless station. Also, access points can be configured to require the SSID in communications with clients. But, unlike a password, the SSID is used in all kinds of wireless communications, from beacon frames sent frequently by all access points to roaming requests to move from one access point to another. The bottomline is that there are plenty of communications that an attacker can examine to easily determine the SSID.

802.1X and 802.11i Security
802.1X is a wireless and wired authentication approach offered by the IEEE and is supported in modern operating systems, including Windows 7, Windows Server 2008/Server 2008 R2, many Linux distributions, and Mac OS X. This is a port-based form

of authentication, in which communications are defined to occur over a port (wireless port or LAN-based port). As you recall from Chapter 3, TCP uses ports for communications, such as for HTTP or FTP. The port over which the connection is made can act in two roles (but only one at a time). One role is as an uncontrolled port that allows communications regardless of whether authentication has taken place. The other role is as a controlled port that allows only authenticated communications. Here are the general steps used in 802.1X for authentication in wireless communications:

1. When a WNIC enters the reception range of an access point or another WNIC, it becomes a "supplicant," and the access point or other WNIC becomes the "authenticator."

2. The authenticator sends a request for verification of identity to the supplicant over an uncontrolled port.

3. If the supplicant does not send back the information, the port is closed and that is the end of the communication. If the supplicant does send back the required authentication information to the authenticator, then the authenticator contacts an authentication server to verify the supplicant's information (the authentication server may or may not be the same device as the authenticator).

4. The authentication server asks the supplicant for further identification.

5. If the supplicant provides the appropriate identification, the authentication server sends a special key to the access point.

6. The access point initiates a controlled port and sends a different key to the supplicant, concluding the authentication stage of the communication.

One problem with generic 802.1X is that the authentication transmissions are not encrypted. A relatively new standard for 802.11 wireless security is **802.11i**, which builds on the 802.1X standard. Not only is 802.11i compatible with 802.1X, but it also uses the **Temporal Key Integrity Protocol (TKIP)** for creating random encryption keys from one master key. TKIP creates a unique encryption key for each packet. Some encryption experts believe that this technique means that it would take an attacker over 100 years to decrypt a message. 802.11i further encrypts the data in a wireless packet using AES for encryption, which is described in the section, "Wi-Fi Protected Access." Another feature of 802.11i is the use of **Robust Secure Network (RSN)**, which is designed to create secure communications channels. Referring back to Activity 6-7, you noticed that there are configuration options for 801.1X, for AES, and for TKIP in Windows 7. Windows Server 2008 and Server 2008 R2 also have these security options that are configured using similar steps as in Windows 7. In addition, in Activity 6-8, you noticed that Dynamic WEP (802.1X) is a configuration option in Linux. In Activity 6-9, you view from where to configure 802.1X and the 802.1X settings option in Mac OS X Snow Leopard or Lion.

802.1X and 802.11i can slow down network communications a little, but the extra security is usually worth it.

Activity 6-9: Configuring 802.1X in Mac OS X Snow Leopard or Lion

Time Required: 10 minutes

Objective: Learn how to configure 802.1X in Mac OS X Snow Leopard or Lion.

Description: In this activity you learn from where to configure 802.1X in Mac OS X Snow Leopard or Lion. You need access to an account that has administrative privileges, and your computer should have a WNIC, such as AirPort or Wi-Fi (and an established wireless connection is helpful but not required).

1. Click the **System Preferences** icon in the Dock; or click the **Apple** icon in the menu bar and click **System Preferences**.

2. Click **Network** in the Internet & Wireless section of the System Preferences window (refer to Figure 6-9).

3. In the Network window, select the WNIC in the left pane, such as **AirPort** or **Wi-Fi**, and click the **Advanced** button.

4. Ensure the tab corresponding to your WNIC is selected, such as **AirPort** or **Wi-Fi**. If you have a network connection already established, in the Preferred Networks text box, notice the name of the active network and notice the security that is enabled, such as *WPA/WPA2 Personal* (see Figure 6-12).

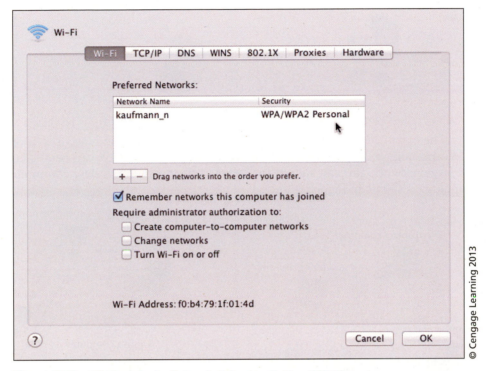

Figure 6-12   Wi-Fi tab in the Network dialog box in Mac OS X Lion

5. Click the **802.1X** tab. Record the settings that can be configured on this tab (your connection may not have 802.1X, in which case the settings will be inactive).

6. Click **Cancel** and close the Network window.

Using Authentication to Disconnect

Another function of the authentication process is disconnecting when a communication session is complete. The authentication process is important when disconnecting because two communicating stations cannot be inadvertently disconnected by another nonauthenticated station. Two stations disconnect when either station sends a deauthentication notice. The deauthentication notice results in an instant termination of communications.

802.11 Network Topologies

Two general topologies, or physical arrangements of wireless devices, are used in the 802.11 standard. The first topology, the **independent basic service set (IBSS) topology**, is the simplest, consisting of two or more wireless stations that can be in direct communication with one another. This type of network is relatively unplanned because stations are often added on an impromptu basis. The IBSS topology consists of ad hoc peer-to-peer communication between WNICs on individual computers, as shown in Figure 6-13.

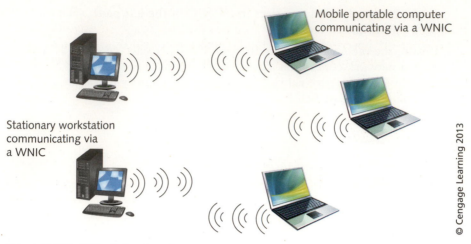

Figure 6-13 IBSS wireless topology

The **extended service set (ESS) topology** deploys a more extensive area of service than the IBSS topology by deploying one or more access points. An ESS can be a small, medium-sized, or large network and can significantly extend the range of wireless communications. The ESS topology is shown in Figure 6-14.

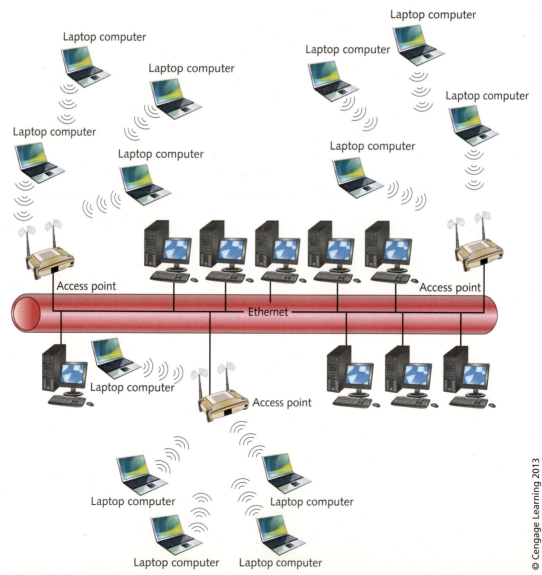

Figure 6-14 ESS wireless topology

As long as you stay with devices that are 802.11 compliant, it is easy to expand an IBSS network into an ESS network. However, avoid combining both networks in the same proximity, because the IBSS peer-to-peer communications are not stable in the presence of the access points used in an ESS network, and ESS network communications may be interrupted as well.

For more information about the IEEE 802.11 standards, visit the IEEE's Web site at *www.ieee.org*. You can order a complete copy of the standard from this Web site.

Multiple-Cell Wireless LANs

When an ESS wireless topology employs two or more access points, it becomes a **multiple-cell wireless LAN**. In this topology, the broadcast area around a single access point is a **cell**. For example, if there are five access points in an indoor network in the same building, then there are five cells. In addition, if all five cells are configured in the same way (same frequency, speed, and security parameters), a PC or handheld device equipped with a WNIC can move from cell to cell, which is called **roaming**. (You are probably familiar with cells and roaming because these same concepts are used in cellular phone networks.)

As an example of roaming on an ESS wireless topology, consider a law school that deploys wireless networking through five access points associated with cells I through V. Cell I might encompass the law library. Cells II and III might be in the areas housing the professors' offices. Cell IV might be for the administrative office area, and cell V might be in the mock courtroom where students practice arguing cases. By configuring all of the cells in the same way, any law student, professor, or office associate can carry a portable computer with a WNIC into any cell and be able to access the law school's network.

Although 802.11 does not specifically define a standard for a roaming protocol, one protocol developed by wireless vendors, called **Inter-Access Point Protocol (IAPP)**, does generally conform to the 802.11 standard. IAPP enables a mobile station to move from one cell to another without losing connection. IAPP encapsulates both the User Datagram Protocol (UDP) and IP for roaming communications.

As you learned in Chapter 3, UDP is a connectionless protocol that can be used with IP, instead of TCP, which is a connection-oriented protocol.

IAPP enables existing access points to be notified when a new access point is attached to a network, and it enables adjacent access points to share configuration information with one another. IAPP also enables an access point that has been communicating with a mobile station to automatically transfer information about the original connection (and any data waiting to be sent) to another access point when the mobile station moves from the cell of the first access point to the cell of the second access point.

Alternative Radio Wave Technologies

There are several wireless radio wave communication alternatives to 802.11 for LANs, but some of the most popular include the following:

- Bluetooth
- HiperLAN

Each of these is a wireless specification developed and supported by specific vendors and is described in the sections that follow.

Bluetooth

Bluetooth is a wireless technology defined through the Bluetooth Special Interest Group, used for short-range transmissions using Bluetooth-enabled devices. There are many kinds of wireless products that use Bluetooth, including PCs, wireless access points, tablets, keyboards, mice, cell phone and audio headsets, printers, home entertainment centers, gaming devices, medical devices, automotive devices, and others.

Bluetooth uses **Frequency Hopping Spread Spectrum (FHSS)** within the 2.4 GHz frequency range (2.4–2.485 GHz) designated by the FCC for unlicensed ISM transmissions. Frequency hopping means that transmissions hop among 79 frequencies for each packet that is sent. The advantage of frequency hopping is that it reduces the likelihood of interference when multiple devices are in use. Bluetooth operates at about 1600 hops per second using full-duplex communications.

By using high-wattage transmissions, Bluetooth can transmit up to 100 meters (about 330 feet), but in practicality, many Bluetooth devices transmit up to 10 meters (about 33 feet). Bluetooth version 2 typically uses asynchronous communications at 57.6 or 721 Kbps. Bluetooth devices that use synchronous transmissions operate at 432.6 Kbps, but these devices are less popular than those that use asynchronous communications.

Bluetooth version 3 offers the optional high speed (+HS) specification, which has a transmission capability of up to 24 Mbps.

Bluetooth version 4 offers three operating environments:

- *High-speed Bluetooth*: Implements Bluetooth version 3+HS communications at up to 24 Mbps at this writing (operates without using low-energy or classic Bluetooth).

- *Low-energy Bluetooth*: New as of Bluetooth version 4 and offers a low-energy mode for sensors such as in-home glucose monitors, pedometers, watches, and remote control devices. This technology can transmit at up to about 1 Mbps at a range of about 100 meters (33 feet) and can use optional 128-bit AES encryption.

- *Classic Bluetooth*: Encompasses the older versions of Bluetooth from 1.1 through 3.0 (excluding 3.0+HS), with a maximum data rate of approximately 1 Mbps.

Complementing these options, Bluetooth version 4 can operate in two modes:

- *Single mode*: Uses the full low-energy capability, but can communicate only with other devices that are in single mode

- *Dual mode*: Existing classic mode devices (Bluetooth versions 1.1 through 3.0) can be set up to use the low-energy capability

In terms of broadcast range, Bluetooth devices can generally be divided into three classes:

- *Class 1*: Up to about 100 meters (330 feet) typically used for network-type applications such as wireless access points

- *Class 2*: Up to about 10 meters or 33 feet typically used for wireless devices such as keyboards, mice, microphones, and audio devices and encompasses the most commonly used Bluetooth devices

- *Class 3*: Up to about 1 meter or 3 feet typically used for close range transmissions, such as medical monitoring devices, watches, and exercise monitoring

Some Bluetooth version 4 devices now focus on using an in-between Class 1 range of about 61 meters (about 200 feet). This includes wireless headsets for telephone and computer use.

Bluetooth uses **time division duplexing (TDD)**, which means that packets are sent in alternating directions using time slots. A transmission can use up to five different time slots, resulting in packets that can be sent and received at the same time in a process that resembles full-duplex communications. Up to seven Bluetooth devices can be connected at the same time (some vendors claim that their technologies offer up to eight devices, but this does not conform to the specifications). When devices are communicating, one device is automatically selected as the master device that sets up control functions such as clocking the time slots and managing the hops. In all other respects, Bluetooth communications represent peer-to-peer networking.

One of three encryption modes can be configured for a Bluetooth device:

- *Mode 1*: No encryption is used.

- *Mode 2*: Communications that are addressed (such as by using a node's IP address) are encrypted, but broadcast communications are not encrypted. Encryption employs a different 128-bit link (for the individual communications link) encryption key for each addressed communication.

- *Mode 3*: All communications are encrypted using a 128-bit encryption master key.

The actual encryption method used for Bluetooth is **stream cipher encryption**. In stream cipher encryption, every bit in a stream of data is encrypted, which makes this a highly secure encryption method.

Some users create a **Bluetooth personal area network (PAN)**, which is a capability enabled through Windows, Linux, and Mac OS X operating systems for linking Bluetooth devices to a computer and in some cases to one another. For example, consider a PAN network of personal devices in a small work area around a PC. The devices in the work area might include a keyboard, pointing device, printer, smartphone, camera, tablet PC, another computer, and other devices. Bluetooth is a common and convenient way of connecting such devices to create a wireless PAN. In a typical Bluetooth PAN setup, the connected devices are slaves and the main computer that connects them is the master, which coordinates the communications with the slaves. Besides through PC operating systems, another common Bluetooth PAN is within a vehicle. Car and truck manufacturers offer the option to have a Bluetooth PAN so that your Bluetooth-capable cell phone or smartphone automatically connects to the PAN for hands-free operation while you are in the vehicle.

You can configure Bluetooth devices and a Bluetooth PAN in Windows 7 and Server 2008/ Server 2008 R2 through the Network and Sharing Center (look for an option to configure Bluetooth devices in the left pane). In Linux with the GNOME 3.x interface, you can configure Bluetooth devices using the Network Connections application. Mac OS X Snow Leopard and Lion enable you to configure Bluetooth and a Bluetooth PAN through System Preferences, which includes the Bluetooth Setup Assistant. Of course, your computer must first have Bluetooth capability.

Table 6-2 summarizes Bluetooth version specifications.

You can find out more about Bluetooth by visiting its official Web site at *www.bluetooth.com.*

Table 6-2 Bluetooth version specifications

Bluetooth Version	Range	Data Rate	Encryption
1.2	• *Class 1*—Up to about 100 meters (330 feet) • *Class 2*—Up to about 10 meters (33 feet) • *Class 3*—Up to about 1 meter (3 feet)	Up to 1 Mbps	128-bit stream cipher
2.1 with Enhanced Data Rate (EDR)	• *Class 1*—Up to about 100 meters (330 feet) • *Class 2*—Up to about 10 meters (33 feet) • *Class 3*—Up to about 1 meter (3 feet)	Up to 3 Mbps	128-bit stream cipher
3.0 with High Speed (+HS)	• *Class 1*—Up to about 100 meters (330 feet) • *Class 2*—Up to about 10 meters (33 feet) • *Class 3*—Up to about 1 meter (3 feet)	Up to 24 Mbps	128-bit stream cipher
4.0	• *Class 1*—Up to about 100 meters (330 feet) • *Class 2*—Up to about 10 meters (33 feet) • *Class 3*—Up to about 1 meter (3 feet)	Up to 24 Mbps	128-bit stream cipher

HiperLAN

HiperLAN (High-Performance Radio Local Area Network) originated and is used primarily in Europe. This technology is now in its second version called HiperLAN2. HiperLAN2 can transmit at up to 54 Mbps in the 5 GHz range. Besides speed, an advantage of HiperLAN2 is its compatibility with Ethernet.

HiperLAN2 also supports **Data Encryption Standard (DES)**. The National Institute of Standards and Technology and ANSI developed DES. HiperLAN2 uses a public encryption key that is published for any network station to view and a private encryption key that is reserved only for the sending and receiving stations. Both keys are necessary to decrypt data.

HiperLAN2 supports Quality of Service (QoS), which provides an assured level of transmission for different classes of service, such as data or video. QoS is made possible because access points centralize and schedule the wireless communications.

HiperLAN2 operates in two modes. One is the direct mode, which is a peer-to-peer network mode (similar to the 802.11 IBSS topology) that consists of only communicating stations. The other mode is called the centralized mode, because it involves larger networks using access points that centralize and control the network traffic. Both modes use time division duplexing (TDD) as the communications method, which is the same method used by Bluetooth.

HiperLAN and HiperLAN2 have been used in Europe because they offer relatively fast wireless networking in the 5 GHz band. Some European countries have conflicts in the 2.4 GHz band, and so 5 GHz HiperLAN and HiperLAN2 have been appealing as an alternative. However, 802.11n has become increasingly popular in Europe because it is faster than HiperLAN2 and also works in the 5 GHz range. See Table 6-3 for a comparison of the alternative radio wave technologies.

Table 6-3   Alternative radio wave technologies

	Frequency	Transmission Method	Applications	Range	Data Rate
Bluetooth	2.4 GHz	Time division duplexing (TDD)	Used for wireless networks and devices such as PCs, tablets, keyboards, mice, phone headsets, printers, audio and video devices, entertainment centers, gaming devices, medical devices, automotive devices, and others	• *Class 1*—Up to 100 meters (330 feet) • *Class 2*—Up to 10 meters (33 feet) • *Class 3*—Up to 1 meter (3 feet)	• Version 1.2— Up to 1 Mbps • Version 2.1— Up to 3 Mbps • Versions 3 and 4—Up to 24 Mbps
HiperLAN/ HiperLAN2	5 GHz	TDD	Used in European wireless networks	Up to about 50 meters (164 feet)	Up to 10 Mbps for HiperLAN and up to 54 Mbps for HiperLAN2

© Cengage Learning 2013

Infrared Technologies

Infrared light can be used as a medium for network communications. This technology is probably most familiar to you in the remote control devices for your television and stereo. Infrared is an electromagnetic signal, just as a radio wave is an electromagnetic signal, but it is closer to the range of visible electromagnetic signals that we call visible light.

Infrared can be broadcast in a single direction or in all directions, using an LED to transmit and a photodiode to receive. In terms of frequency at the Physical layer, it transmits in the range of 100 gigahertz (GHz) to 1000 terahertz (THz); in terms of the electromagnetic wavelength spectrum, it exists in the range of 700 to 1000 nanometers.

Like radio waves, infrared can be an inexpensive solution in hard-to-cable areas or where there are mobile users, with the advantage that the signal is difficult to intercept without someone knowing. Another advantage is that infrared light is not susceptible to interference from RFI and EMI.

There are also some significant disadvantages to this communications medium. One is that data transmission rates only reach up to 16 Mbps for directional communications, and they are less than

1 Mbps for omnidirectional communications. Another disadvantage is that infrared does not go through walls, as you discover when you take your TV remote control into another room and try it from there. Infrared also can experience interference from strong light sources. On the other hand, this disadvantage makes infrared transmissions more secure, because it has a limited reach.

Infrared technologies can use access points to extend the reach of communications and to create larger networks.

Diffused infrared transmits by reflecting the infrared light from the ceiling, as shown in Figure 6-15. The IEEE 802.11R standard is for 1 and 2 Mbps diffused infrared communications, enabling a transmission range of 9 meters (about 30 feet) and 18 meters (about 60 feet) depending on the height of the ceiling (the higher the ceiling the lower the transmission range).

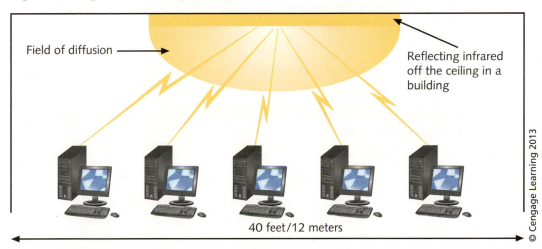

Field of diffusion

Reflecting infrared off the ceiling in a building

40 feet/12 meters

© Cengage Learning 2013

Figure 6-15   Diffused infrared wireless communications

Although diffused infrared is not subject to interference from EMI or RFI, windows in a building can create interference because infrared is sensitive to strong light sources. Consider the presence of windows before implementing diffused infrared on a wireless network. Infrared is also not appropriate for outdoor use.

The communication method used by the IEEE 802.11R standard is **pulse position modulation (PPM)**. In PPM, the binary value of a signal is related to the position of the light pulse within a range of positions in the electromagnetic light spectrum. In the 802.11R standard for 1 Mbps communications, there are 16 possible pulse positions (16-PPM), with each position representing four bits. In 2 Mbps communication, each pulse represents two data bits, and there are four possible pulse positions (4-PPM). A pulse in a particular position indicates a value is present, and no pulse in a position means no value is present. PPM is a symbolic coding scheme that resembles binary in that there are only zeroes and ones.

Wireless MANs

In many areas WiMAX wireless services are available. **WiMAX** is another name for the IEEE **802.16** standard for wireless MANs. WiMAX is sometimes called a connection for the "last mile," because it can be used to provide wireless connectivity between an office or home and a wired network provider, such as one providing access to the Internet. For example, you might have an office in a part of a city or in a rural area that is several miles from a network provider or a telecommunications company—or from the main building of your company. One way to connect your office is for the network provider (or your own company) to install wireless communications at its location and an omnidirectional or directional antenna (depending on the application). This antenna might be placed at the top of a tall building, on a hill, or on a mountainside. As a user who is several miles away, you would have a directional antenna pointed at the provider's antenna, and your antenna would be connected to a wireless router in your office or home.

WiMAX operates in the 2 to 66 GHz range. Although WiMAX can work over unlicensed and licensed frequencies, most commercial applications are licensed. In the United States, most WiMAX networks operate at the 2.3, 2.5, 3.5, 3.65, and 5.8 GHz frequencies, with most using 2.5 GHz. Internationally, the 3.5 GHz frequency is more commonly used. Using licensed frequencies enables WiMAX providers to use a higher broadcast wattage for a stronger signal and greater distance.

The IEEE 802.16 standard provides connectivity up to 75 Mbps and has a reach of up to 48 kilometers (about 30 miles). In many installations, though, the actual distance is less than this, 8 to 16 kilometers (5 to 10 miles), depending on the devices in use. WiMAX can be a cost-effective way to create a network over several miles.

WiMAX offers a convenient alternative to wireless hotspots (discussed in the next the section) and is being deployed by cities, organizations, and major wireless communications providers.

A European alternative to WiMAX is HiperMAN (High-Performance Radio Metropolitan Area Network). HiperMAN is a standard from the European Telecommunications Standards Institute (ETSI), developed in coordination with WiMAX so that they can interoperate. A main difference is that HiperMAN transmits between 2 and 11 GHz, instead of up to 66 GHz as for WiMAX. Another focus of HiperMAN is the use of packet switching (see Chapter 2, "How LAN and WAN Communications Work," to review packet switching). Most applications for HiperMAN are targeted in the 3.5 GHz band, which is the wireless MAN frequency emphasized internationally for licensing.

Wireless Hotspots

At one time a wireless hotspot basically meant a specific location, such as an Internet coffee shop or café, where wireless access is available. With 3G and 4G networking, individuals now have other alternatives for wireless network access, as you learn in the next two sections.

Stationary Wireless Hotspots

Wireless networking has found its way into all types of public areas to enable Internet and network access, particularly for mobile users. An area with public wireless access is called a hotspot, which is simply a location that provides one or more public access points to users. Examples of places in which you might find a hotspot include the student union or library in a school, a public library, an airport, a coffee shop, or a hotel.

There are several Web sites for finding wireless hotspots in specific areas. One such site is *www.wi-fihotspotlist.com.* Use your Web browser and search on "wireless hotspots" to find other Web sites with hotspot listings.

Before using a wireless hotspot, be absolutely certain that you have configured security measures on your computer and use any security supported by the hotspot, such as WEP or WPA/WPA2. Also, have a firewall configured on your wireless connection. Hotspots are targets for "war drivers" and "war walkers"—computer attackers in a vehicle or on foot who are attempting to find, monitor, and possibly intrude on wireless communications. Avoid transmitting credit card, sensitive account, or other personal information from hotspots, unless you are certain about the security measures.

If you set up a hotspot for an organization, consider implementing WPA2 for security. You can tell public users how to configure the security on their computers by directing them to a Web page from your organization that has instructions about acceptable use of the hotspot and how to configure security.

Mobile Hotspots

3G and 4G networks make it possible for individuals to create their own wireless hotspots from any location that is also accessible by cell phone. There are two ways to create such a **mobile hotspot**. The first way is to purchase a 3G/4G USB digital modem that can be plugged into an individual computer and is intended for one user. 3G/4G digital modems are Plug and Play for fast setup, and some also double as a flash drive for extra storage. Some also come with a meter to monitor usage, which can be important to help ensure the user stays within his or her wireless data service plan. The connection to the 3G/4G network typically requires a password.

A second option is to purchase a 3G/4G mobile wireless hotspot device (see Figure 6-16). The 3G/4G mobile hotspot wirelessly connects to the 3G/4G network similar to the 3G/4G USB modem or a cell phone with a wireless data connection. The hotspot is a small portable device about the size of a smartphone and weighing just a few ounces. Mobile hotspots can connect up to about five users (depending on the device and 3G/4G wireless service provider) from about 12–15 meters (40–50) feet away. Hotspot clients can be PCs, eReaders, smartphones, MP3 players, and other similar devices that are equipped with 802.11b/g/n/ac compatible WNICs (803.11a is omitted from most 3G/4G hotspot support). 3G/4G hotspots can also operate on a battery with a battery life of several hours.

Courtesy Verizon Wireless

Figure 6-16   4G mobile hotspot

At this writing, mobile hotspots require a data service plan with a wireless service provider, which is often similar to monthly data plans for smartphones or tablets. Because data service plans can be expensive, users typically are careful about downloading too many large files, such as photos, streaming video, and music.

When you purchase a wireless modem or hotspot, ensure that it is compatible with 4G or can be upgraded for 4G, because 4G is faster than 3G resulting in better service for users and more data access for the dollar.

Cellular Phone Communications

Cellular phone communications work on the basis of packet radio, which was described earlier in this chapter as a wireless data transmission technology that employs wireless packet switching to send digital radio signals. (See Chapter 2 to review how 2G, 3G, and 4G networks work.) Your smartphone or cell phone (and 3G/4G tablet PC) is basically a radio transmitter and receiver (transceiver) equipped with an omnidirectional antenna. It uses packet radio communications to transmit to a nearby cell tower, which forms a cell similar to the concept of a cell in a wireless LAN. The range of a cell for telecommunications can be a few city blocks or up to about 250 miles, depending on the technology. The cell tower is connected to a service box that is often buried underground. The combination of the cell tower and the service box forms a base station.

The base station is connected to an underground or aboveground cable that connects it to a call switching center (also called a mobile telephone switching office or MTSO) that switches the call to the appropriate telecommunications system from which to communicate with other cell phones or landline phones—plain old telephone service (POTS) or public switched telephone networks (PSTN) as described in Chapter 2 (see Figure 6-17). The cell phone negotiates with the base station to determine an unused radio frequency channel for communications. Because most cell phones are now equipped with a GPS, the base station identifies not only the cell phone but also its location.

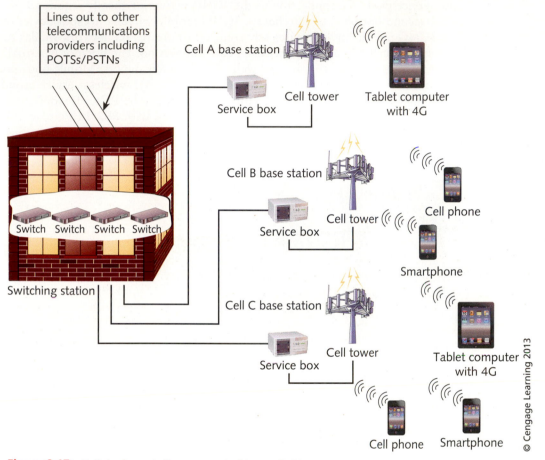

Figure 6-17   Cellular base stations connected to a switching center

The frequencies used by cell phone carriers depend on the carrier and the technology in use, but are higher than those for FM radio transmissions and lower than those for microwave transmissions. Chapter 2 describes the frequencies in use for 3G and 4G cellular communications.

Microwave Technologies

Microwave systems work in one of two ways: terrestrial microwave and satellite microwave. Microwave communications are interesting to follow because the technology is constantly evolving. It offers lots of promise because microwave transmissions have a theoretical bandwidth of up to 720 Mbps and beyond—although there are no current implementations that offer this kind of bandwidth.

Terrestrial Microwave

Terrestrial microwave transmits the signal between two directional parabolic antennas, which are shaped like dishes as shown in Figure 6-18. These transmissions are performed in the frequency ranges of 4–6 and 21–23 GHz and require the operator to obtain an FCC license. These data communications systems generally offer communications at 1 and 10 Mbps, depending on the power of the transmitter.

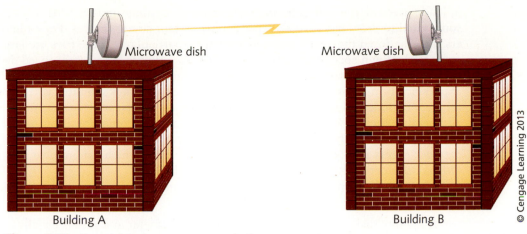

Figure 6-18   Terrestrial microwave communications

As with other wireless media, microwave solutions such as terrestrial microwave are sometimes applied where cabling costs are too high or where cabling and wireless options are not possible. For example, terrestrial microwave might be a good solution for communications between two large buildings in a city.

Satellite Microwave

Satellite microwave transmits the signal between three antennas, one of which is on a satellite in space, as shown in Figure 6-19. Satellite microwave is one solution for joining business, educational, or military networks across a country or between two continents—but this can be an expensive solution. However, ISP satellite services are available for home and office users at a reasonable cost (but usually more than that for cable modem or DSL services).

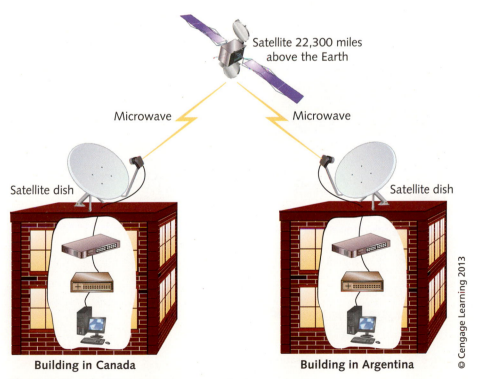

Figure 6-19   Satellite microwave communications

Satellite networks for Internet access are available in more and more rural areas and in metropolitan areas that do not offer ISDN, cable modem, or DSL services. The marketed connection speeds through a satellite network are currently up to about 2–3 Mbps for download and upload speeds with some offering new systems providing up to 12 Mbps for downloads—but some satellite providers throttle speeds under certain circumstances. For example, some providers throttle down the speed for uploading files, particularly if the files are large. Other providers throttle down speeds as more users are on the satellite. The actual speed depends on factors such as weather; signal strength of the user's equipment; and, most particularly, amount of use experienced on the satellite. For example, the use of some satellites is divided between military and commercial communications. If military communications are heavy at particular times, and because they take precedence over commercial uses, communications may be slower for the commercial user at those times. Some satellite network providers offer equipment that combines network access with satellite TV access using one dish, which can involve high initial expenses. Others offer network access using a dedicated dish.

The user equipment needed for satellite communications typically includes the following (also see Figure 6-20):

- A satellite dish about 1 meter (2 or 3 feet) in diameter and that is usually a little larger than a dish used for satellite TV

- A digital modem to transmit the signal and another digital modem to receive the signal (these may be in separate boxes or both housed on one box)

- Coaxial (TV-like) cables from the modems to the dish

- A USB cable from the modems (usually attached to the receiving modem) that connects to a USB port on your computer (or it can connect to a router on a network for sharing the satellite access)

- Software from the satellite provider to enable the computer setup (in some cases it is also necessary to have an analog modem for the initial setup because the installation software "provisions" or verifies the satellite connection with the satellite provider via a one-time modem/telephone line communication)

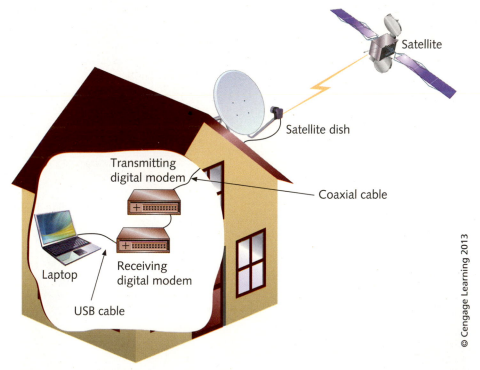

Figure 6-20   Satellite communications setup

Many communications satellites are in geosynchronous orbits at 22,300 miles above the Earth. These are often called **geosynchronous satellites**. Geosynchronous means that the orbit of these satellites enables them to maintain a position that is stationary with respect to the Earth. The extreme distance of the satellites and high-atmospheric disturbances can cause transmission delays that are unacceptable for time-sensitive communications involving data transfers and multimedia. Some companies have deployed newer **low Earth orbiting (LEO) satellites**, which

6

orbit at a distance of between 435 and 1000 miles above the Earth's surface, resulting in faster two-way transmission of signals. LEO satellites are used for both broadband computer and satellite phone communications. A satellite phone sends and receives a signal directly to a constellation of LEO satellites that register the phone for the current satellite phone communication. After the call is initiated, it can be directed through satellite microwave communications back to Earth to a POTS/PSTN or cellular phone network on Earth.

Currently, satellite networks are used for:

- Broadband (high-speed) Internet communications
- Satellite phone communications
- Worldwide video conferencing
- Classroom and educational communications
- Other communications involving voice, video, and data

A limitation of satellite communications is that they can experience interference during severe rain and snow storms. For snow storms, the remedy is often to brave the elements and simply clear the snow from your dish. See Table 6-4 to compare different wireless communications technologies.

Table 6-4 Advantages and disadvantages of different forms of wireless communications

	Radio Wave	Infrared	Terrestrial Microwave	Satellite Microwave
Advantages	• An inexpensive alternative to installing communications cabling • An option for portable communications • Usually no licensing requirements	• Signal is difficult to intercept	• An inexpensive alternative where communications cabling cannot be installed easily, particularly over long distances • May be less expensive in the long run than leasing telecommunications lines	• Can be a good alternative in areas where cable or other wireless communications are not available • A good alternative for very long distances, such as across a country or spanning continents
Disadvantages	• Subject to interference from portable phones and other wireless devices that operate at the same frequencies • Subject to interference from natural obstacles	• May not be feasible when high-speed communications are needed • Subject to interference from other light sources • Does not go through walls • Does not offer as many device choices as other forms of wireless networking	• Expensive to install and maintain • Subject to interference from rain, snow, fog, and atmospheric conditions	• Some providers throttle transmission speeds; find out the actual transmission rates and limitations before you buy • Subject to interference from rain, snow, fog, and atmospheric conditions

Putting It All Together: Designing a Wireless Network

There are lots of wireless options, so how do you sort them out? The wireless options that you use will ultimately depend on what you want to accomplish. Here are some guidelines for designing wireless networks:

- For home and office installations use 802.11n or 802.11ac (as it becomes available).
- If you have the choice to use a wireless bridge, switch, or router for your access point, choose the wireless router. A wireless router can manage network traffic and act as a firewall by filtering IP addresses.

- When you design a wireless network, carefully consider the number of computers that must be connected and the distances. Your network will run faster if you use more access points and shorter distances between computers and access points.

- Avoid implementing a combination of wireless device technologies on a network, such as 802.11g and 802.11n, because this will reduce the potential speed. If you must combine different technologies, develop a plan to steadily phase out the older ones, such as 802.11g devices and WNICs.

- For creating networking applications that span several miles, consider WiMAX (802.16) as a possibility. It can be a cost-effective way to create an Ethernet MAN in a city or to extend network options into rural areas.

- The number of war drivers and walkers is growing. Ensure that your wireless network is protected by WPA or WPA2. Also, plan to use 802.1X/802.11i for security, if these are supported on your systems. Don't leave your security configuration at the defaults. Check the configurations of all access points and WNICs to configure security, because the default may be no security.

- Always configure the SSID for your wireless network for a little extra security—it can only help.

Designing for a Home or Small Office

The 802.11n (or 802.11ac as devices become available) standard is a great option for a home or small office. Consider a home with four people in which there is one desktop computer used by the parents and two laptop computers, one used by a high school student and the other by a junior high school student—all using Windows 7. Also, there is a cable TV connection, and members of the household want to share Internet access through the cable. This situation offers the following options:

- Simply equip all of the computers with WNICs and connect a cable modem for Internet connectivity to the desktop computer. The desktop computer is used to share the Internet connection via ICS (Windows Internet Connection Sharing). This is the IBSS topology shown earlier in Figure 6-13.

- Another, more expensive option is to purchase an 802.11n (or 802.11ac when available) combined wireless router (and access point) and cable modem. In this scenario, the family connects the TV cable to the router for a shared wireless Internet connection. The router is placed in a central location in the home, such as in an office, bedroom, or the kitchen. All of the computers, of course, are outfitted with WNICs. This option, which uses the ESS topology, is a little more costly, but it provides more assured connectivity and security.

Now, consider a small office of eight architects. Each architect has a laptop computer. The network design for this office is similar to option 2 for the home scenario. The office might purchase an 802.11n (or 802.11ac) wireless router combined with a cable or DSL modem (or possibly a satellite connection, if cable or DSL are not available). In this context, configuring all security options, such as a combination of WPA2 and 802.1X and 802.11i (depending on what your systems support), is important, because the office handles confidential information as well as financial information. The router is also a must to act as a firewall between the office and the outside world.

Designing for a Large Organization

A large organization that already has cabled networks might use wireless networking designs in several ways. Consider a large outdoor outfitting company that has a business campus with buildings that house business offices, a manufacturing center, and a warehouse. In the same city about 7 miles away, the company has a large customer outlet store on an interstate highway. When developing a network design, this company might:

- Install 802.11n (or 802.11ac) wireless networks to coexist in areas that are already cabled, as shown in Figure 6-14. In this way, when new employees are added or when new offices are built, these might be connected through wireless access points that are connected to the cabled network.

- Use 802.11n (or 802.11ac) wireless networking via access points in the outlet store, so that customer service representatives can carry handheld computers for checking on the location of items, determining if items are in stock, finding detailed information about specific items, and taking inventory while roaming in the store.

- Set up wireless access in the manufacturing and warehouse centers for employees who use laptop or tablet computers to roam from one location to the next. Wireless access in these locations is also useful for taking inventory of manufactured stocks and for tracking the use of raw materials for manufacturing.

- Use 802.16 for wireless communications between buildings on the main campus and to the outlet store that is 7 miles away as illustrated in Figure 6-2, using directional antennas for better security and reach.

Chapter Summary

6

- The wireless networking technologies that are currently used include radio waves, infrared, microwave, and satellite wireless networks.

- Today, wireless networks are used for many purposes. For example, they are used in areas where wired networks are difficult to install. In addition, they are used to reduce network installation costs and to enable mobile computing.

- Radio wave technologies typically use line-of-sight communications that send a signal from one point to another along the Earth's surface, rather than bouncing a radio signal off the Earth's atmosphere. Radio wave technologies also use spread spectrum communications, which means that radio waves are carried across several contiguous frequencies.

- The IEEE 802.11 standards are currently used for many forms of radio wave network communications. These standards involve three main components: a WNIC, access points, and antennas. The well-established standards within 802.11 are 802.11a, 802.11b, 802.11g, and 802.11n. Standards in development at this writing are 802.11ac and 802.11ad.

- Radio technology alternatives to the 802.11 standards include Bluetooth and HiperLAN.

- The 802.11R standard uses diffused infrared light transmissions for small, relatively secure networks housed in a somewhat confined office or work area.

- Wireless MANs use the 802.16 (WiMAX) standard for wireless communication up to about 48 kilometers (30 miles). Europe also offers HiperMAN, which is compatible with 802.16, for wireless MAN connectivity.

- Wireless mobile hotspots can be established using a 3G/4G modem for a single computer or a 3G/4G mobile hotspot to connect multiple Wi-Fi capable computers to the 3G/4G mobile hotspot through their WNICs.

- Cellular phone communications use base stations for each cell and connect base stations to call switching centers to direct calls to the desired cellular or landline service.

- Microwave networking comes in two forms: terrestrial microwave and satellite microwave. Of these, satellite microwave can be very expensive because of the cost of sending a satellite into space.

Key Terms

802.11a   An IEEE standard for wireless networking at 5 GHz with a top speed of 54 Mbps.

802.11ac   An IEEE standard for wireless networking under development at this writing that operates at 2.4 and 5 GHz with a top speed of 1+ Gbps.

802.11ad   An IEEE standard for wireless networking under development at this writing that operates at a top speed of about 7 Gbps and is primarily targeted for wireless computer components, phones, TVs, and other short-range wireless devices.

802.11b   An IEEE standard for wireless networking at 2.4 GHz, with a top speed of 11 Mbps.

802.11g   An IEEE standard for wireless networking at 2.4 GHz, having backward compatibility with 802.11b and a top speed of 54 Mbps.

802.11i   A standard for wireless and wired security that builds on the 802.1X standard and implements the Temporal Key Integrity Protocol (TKIP) for creating random encryption keys from one master key. 802.11i also employs Robust Secure Network (RSN) for creating secure communications channels. *See* **Temporal Key Integrity Protocol (TKIP)** and **Robust Secure Network (RSN)**.

802.11n   An IEEE wireless networking standard at 2.4 and 5 GHz with a top speed of 300+ Mbps.

802.16   Also called WiMAX, an IEEE standard for wireless MANs that can reach up to 48 kilometers (about 30 miles) and transmit up to 75 Mbps. *See* **WiMAX**.

802.1X   A wireless and wired authentication standard offered by the IEEE that is a port-based form of authentication.

access point   A device that attaches to a cabled network and that services wireless communications between WNICs and the cabled network.

Advanced Encryption Standard (AES)   An encryption standard that uses a private-key block-cipher technique in which plain text data is divided into 128-bit blocks. The private key can be either 128, 192, or 256 bits in length. WPA2 uses AES encryption. *See* **Wi-Fi Protected Access (WPA)**.

antenna   A device that sends out (radiates) and picks up radio waves.

automatic repeat-request (ARQ)   An 802.11 error-handling technique that helps to reduce communication errors created by sources of interference, such as adverse weather conditions.

Bluetooth   A wireless networking specification that uses the 2.4 GHz band that is defined through the Bluetooth Special Interest Group.

Bluetooth personal area network (PAN)   A network of personal devices used in a small area, such as around a PC or in an automobile. In a work area, this might include a keyboard, pointing device, printer, smartphone, camera, tablet PC, and another computer. In a car, devices might include a cell phone, GPS, and headset. Bluetooth is a common and convenient way of connecting such devices to create a wireless PAN. *See* **Bluetooth**.

Carrier Sense Multiple Access with Collision Avoidance (CSMA/CA)   Also called the distributed coordination function, an access method used in 802.11 wireless networking that relies on the calculation of a delay or backoff time to avoid packet collisions.

cell   In wireless LAN networking, the broadcast area around an access point. In cellular phone communications, the broadcast area around a base station.

Data Encryption Standard (DES)   An encryption standard created by the National Institute of Standards and Technology and ANSI. DES uses both a public and a private encryption key.

diffused infrared   Reflecting infrared signals off of a ceiling inside a building. Diffused infrared is used by the 802.11R standard for wireless communications.

Direct Sequence Spread Spectrum (DSSS)   An 802.11b/g wireless communication technique that spreads the data across any of up to 14 channels, each 22 MHz in width. The data signal is sequenced over the channels and is amplified to have a high gain to combat interference.

distributed coordination function   *See* **Carrier Sense Multiple Access with Collision Avoidance (CSMA/CA)**.

extended service set (ESS) topology   A wireless topology that uses one or more access points to provide a larger service area than an IBSS topology.

Frequency Hopping Spread Spectrum (FHSS)   Used in the Bluetooth, a wireless technology in which transmissions hop among 79 frequencies for each packet that is sent.

gain   Ability of an antenna to amplify a radiated signal.

geosynchronous satellite   Satellite in geosynchronous orbit at 22,300 miles above the Earth. Geosynchronous means that the orbit of such satellites enables them to maintain a position that is stationary with respect to the Earth.

Hertz (Hz)   The main unit of measurement for a radio frequency; one Hertz represents a radiated alternating current or emission of one cycle per second.

HiperLAN   Popular in Europe, a wireless specification compatible with Ethernet and ATM communications and that uses the 5 GHz band.

HiperMAN   A European standard for wireless MAN communications and that is compatible with WiMAX while operating between 2 and 11 GHz. *See* **WiMAX.**

hotspot   A public location that provides an access point for Internet and network users, such as a coffee shop or airport. Alternatively, a 3G/4G device that can connect up to 5 client computers through WNICs.

independent basic service set (IBSS) topology   An 802.11 wireless topology that consists of two or more wireless stations that can be in communication; IBSS does not use an access point.

infrared   An electromagnetic signal that transmits in the range of 100 gigahertz (GHz) to 1000 terahertz (THz).

Inter-Access Point Protocol (IAPP)   A roaming protocol for wireless networks that enables a mobile station to move from one cell to another without losing connection.

line-of-sight transmission   A type of radio wave signal transmission in which the signal goes from point to point, rather than bouncing off the atmosphere to skip across the country or across continents. Line-of-sight transmissions follow the surface of the Earth.

low Earth orbiting (LEO) satellite   A satellite that orbits at a distance of between 435 and 1000 miles above the Earth's surface, resulting in faster two-way transmission of signals.

man-in-the-middle attack   The interception of a message or data transmission meant for a different computer, by an attacker who is literally operating between two communicating computers.

mobile hotspot   Wireless connectivity through a 3G/4G network, such as through a USB digital modem for a single computer or a mobile wireless hotspot device that can host multiple users.

multiple-cell wireless LAN   An extended services set (ESS) wireless topology that employs two or more access points.

multiple-input multiple-output (MIMO)   A communication technology used in 802.11n/ac/ad and in 4G communications that involves using multiple antennas at the transmitting and receiving devices in wireless communications. It can be coupled with spatial multiplexing. *See* **spatial multiplexing.**

Network Driver Interface Specification (NDIS)   A network driver specification and application programming interface (API) for creating and using network interface card drivers that work with many network protocols.

open system authentication   The default form of authentication in 802.11 in which any two stations can authenticate with each other. There is no elaborate security, only the mutual agreement to authenticate.

Orthogonal Frequency Division Multiplexing (OFDM)   Used in 802.11a/g/n/ac/ad wireless network communications, a multiplexing technique that divides a frequency range into a series of small subcarriers or subchannels and transmits information all at once over all of the subcarriers.

point coordination function   *See* priority-based access.

preshared key (PSK)   An enhancement available for Wi-Fi Protected Access (WPA) intended for home and small office users that employs a password along with frequently changing encryption keys through WPA. *See* **Wi-Fi Protected Access (WPA).**

priority-based access   Also called the point coordination function, an access method in 802.11 wireless communications in which the access point device also functions as a point coordinator. The point coordinator gives each station that has been polled an opportunity to communicate, one at a time, thus ensuring that only one device communicates at a given moment.

pulse position modulation (PPM)   A communications method used in diffused infrared communications in which the binary value of a signal is related to the position of the pulse within a range of possible positions.

radio frequencies (RFs)   A range of frequencies above 20 kilohertz through which an electromagnetic signal can be radiated through space.

RADIUS server   A server that employs the RADIUS protocol and that is used to configure the protocol in order to manage authentication and access to enterprise networks that use a variety of remote access services including wireless, internal network, virtual private network (VPN), dial-up, Internet, and other forms of remote access. RADIUS servers also keep access statistics. *See* **Remote Authentication Dial-Up User Service (RADIUS)**.

Remote Authentication Dial-Up User Service (RADIUS)   A protocol used by a RADUIS server to enforce rules governing remote access to network services and servers. *See* **RADIUS server**.

roaming   On a wireless network, moving a laptop computer, tablet, handheld device, or other mobile device from cell to cell.

Robust Secure Network (RSN)   A security method used in 802.11i, which is designed to create secure communications channels.

satellite microwave   Microwave transmissions between ground-based units and a satellite.

service set identifier (SSID)   Used on wireless devices, an identification value that typically can be up to 32 characters in length, and its purpose is to define a logical network for member devices (each device is configured to have the same SSID).

shared key authentication   A wireless 802.11 authentication technique in which two stations use a shared WEP encryption key to encrypt and decrypt a unique challenge text. Authentication is accomplished if the sending and receiving stations properly encrypt and decrypt the challenge text.

spatial multiplexing   Enables a wireless device to transmit and receive two or more data streams over one channel within a frequency. Spatial multiplexing is used with MIMO in 802.11n/ac/ad communications. *See* **multiple-input multiple-output (MIMO), 802.11n, 802.11ac,** and **802.11ad**.

spread spectrum technology   Communications technology that is used by wireless networks for very-high-frequency communications between networks. In spread spectrum, one communication involves using several adjoining frequencies.

stream cipher encryption   An encryption method in which every bit in a stream of data is encrypted.

Temporal Key Integrity Protocol (TKIP)   Designed for creating random encryption keys from one master key, TKIP creates a unique encryption key for each packet. *See* **802.11i**.

terrestrial microwave   Microwave transmissions between two directional parabolic antennas located on the Earth's surface.

time division duplexing (TDD)   A communications method used by Bluetooth in which packets are sent in alternating directions using time slots. A transmission can use up to five different time slots, resulting in packets that can be sent and received at the same time in a process that resembles full-duplex communications.

Wi-Fi Alliance   An organization that promotes wireless networking for LANs. The Wi-Fi Alliance also offers a certification program to vendors, which tests wireless devices so that they can be certified to meet IEEE 802.11 standards as well as accepted security practices.

Wi-Fi Protected Access (WPA)   A wireless authentication and encryption method that uses encryption keys that are regularly changed to foil attackers. The current version is WPA2. *See* **preshared key (PSK)**.

WiMAX   The IEEE 802.16 standard for wireless MANs that can reach up to 48 kilometers (about 30 miles) and transmit up to 75 Mbps. *See* **802.16** and **HiperMAN**.

Wired Equivalent Privacy (WEP)   A security method that involves using the same encryption key at both stations that are communicating. This method is less secure than WPA/WPA2.

wireless NIC (WNIC)   A network interface card that has an antenna and is used for wireless communications with other WNICs or with access points on a wireless network.

Review Questions

1. You are consulting for a small office of field biologists who are experiencing intermittent problems with accessing their network. You notice that the wireless access point they all use for connectivity is located on the floor next to a wall in their office. Also, the access point has two antennas. What do you recommend to help address their intermittent access problems? (Choose all that apply.)

   a. Turn the amperage up on the access point.

   b. Move the access point off of the floor, such as placing it on a table that has no obstructions.

   c. Move the access point away from the wall.

   d. Remove one of the antennas to prevent antenna interference.

2. At which OSI layer(s) does a wireless NIC (WNIC) function? (Choose all that apply.)

   a. Wireless

   b. Transactional

   c. Data Link

   d. Physical

3. As you set up a wireless network, you are concerned about having the ability to monitor your wireless network. Which of the following protocols can you use over a wireless network for network management and monitoring?

   a. 802.3

   b. SNMP

   c. Telnet

   d. UDP

4. How does 802.11n handle the use of ACKs?

   a. It uses block ACKs, which make communications faster.

   b. It uses split ACKs so that ACKs can be split and sent with different frames.

   c. It uses asynchronous ACKs for more accuracy.

   d. It does not use ACKs as a way to double the throughput.

5. You are designing a new network and want to go wireless for part of the network. Your design specifications call for a wireless technology that can use the 5 GHz band at up to 100 Mbps. Which of the following is the best fit for your network?

   a. 802.11n

   b. 802.11g

   c. 802.11b

   d. 802.11a

6. You are planning to work while on a business trip to a college campus in Germany. When you ask about wireless connectivity, you are told that the college uses HiperMAN. What technology offered in North America can interoperate with HiperMAN?

   a. 802.11q

   b. PPM

   c. WiMAX

   d. token wireless

7. When Bluetooth is configured for Mode 1 encryption, this means which of the following? (Choose all that apply.)
   a. Only broadcast communications are encrypted.
   b. Only addressed communications are encrypted.
   c. All communications are encrypted.
   d. No communications are encrypted.

8. Terrestrial microwave for networking uses what kind of antennas? (Choose all that apply.)
   a. parabolic
   b. roaming
   c. topographic
   d. directional

9. As you are considering wireless security for your network, you decide that you would like to employ 802.1X; however, a colleague mentions that it does not use random encryption keys. What compatible solution do you choose?
   a. cell encryption for 802.1X
   b. 802.11i with TKIP
   c. 802.11xx
   d. AER encryption for 802.1

10. You have just installed a new access point for your small office network, and when you look for your network in Windows 7, you see the name of the vendor who made the access point. You want to change the name to the name of your company. What option in the access point's setup do you change?
    a. access name (AN)
    b. frequency name (FN)
    c. network ID (net_ID)
    d. service set identifier (SSID)

11. Your business has just purchased a satellite Internet connection through an ISP. Which of the following is equipment you can expect to install? (Choose all that apply.)
    a. a dish
    b. digital modems for sending and receiving
    c. fiber-optic cable for connecting devices
    d. a satellite-tracking device to follow the satellite across the sky

12. Which of the following operates at 5 GHz? (Choose all that apply.)
    a. 802.11n
    b. 802.11g
    c. 802.11a
    d. 802.11b

13. The wireless networks on your business campus all use a RADIUS server to coordinate wireless security. When users configure wireless security on their computers, which of the following should they configure?
    a. WPA2 enterprise
    b. WPA2 vpn
    c. WEP personal
    d. WEP private

14. When you stay at a motel and use the motel's wireless Internet, you see a message that this is an unsecure network, because that network has the lowest level of authentication. What authentication is in use?

    a. 802.1X unsecure

    b. WEP with no password

    c. WPA1

    d. open system

15. How does the CSMA/CA wireless access method determine if its transmission frequency is idle (no one is sending)?

    a. by testing the frame signal strength

    b. by counting the number of ACKs

    c. by checking the Receiver Signal Strength Indicator level

    d. by sending one all-clear packet and waiting for the response of the access point

16. In most wireless networking situations, there is generally some amount of interference, such as from physical obstacles or other wireless communications. The 802.11 standard is designed to help compensate for some interference through which of the following?

    a. hotspot detection

    b. automatic repeat-request

    c. automatic wattage increase

    d. frame echoing

17. Bluetooth uses which of the following communications techniques?

    a. frequency hopping

    b. half-duplex multiplexing

    c. channel dividing

    d. channel mixing

18. When you design a wireless network around an access point, what topology is in use?

    a. independent basic service set

    b. cell roaming

    c. hybrid ring

    d. extended service set

19. As you are pulling up to park across the street from your business, you see a man in a car who initially looks like he is just parked and using his laptop computer. However, you notice that on the car seat there are several types of antennas. In this situation you might suspect that the man is doing which of the following?

    a. accessing a 3G network

    b. using HyperLAN

    c. war driving

    d. tuning his WNIC

20. Orthogonal Frequency Division Multiplexing, which divides a frequency range into subchannels, is used by which of the following 802.11 wireless technologies? (Choose all that apply.)

    a. 802.11n

    b. 802.11g

    c. 802.11b

    d. 802.11a

Case Projects

You are working on assignments for two customers: Thomas Jefferson Community College in Virginia and the Tasty Pelican restaurant in Montréal. For the community college, you help it to design a wireless network for the financial resources team members in the administration building and you help it determine how to connect the administration building to the student services building. For the Tasty Pelican restaurant, you help design a small private wireless network for its restaurant and a public network for its adjoining coffee shop.

Case Project 6-1: Designing a Wireless Network for Roaming Team Members

Thomas Jefferson Community College uses a team approach for managing the financial resources of the college. The team members primarily work in the administration building, which houses the president's office, human resources, payroll, accounting, development, and the main IT office. Each area uses teams and team members who are often mobile, going between work areas. For example, the payroll supervisor is on both the payroll team and the human resources team. She also often attends meetings in the accounting area and serves as a backup accounting supervisor. In another example, the IT manager of applications development spends equal amounts of time in the president's office, human resources, payroll, accounting, development, and IT areas. Currently it is difficult for any team member to access networked computer resources when not in the office. How might you design a wireless networking alternative for this environment?

Case Project 6-2: Creating a Network Diagram to Supplement Your Recommendation

Create a diagram to help upper management understand the wireless network alternative you are proposing.

Use network drawing software such as Visio, AutoCad, or another drawing package. If a network drawing package is not available, use Microsoft Paint with networking icons obtained from your instructor.

Case Project 6-3: Connecting the Administration Building to Student Services

The network in the Thomas Jefferson Community College administration building is connected to the network in the student services building only via five old dial-up modem connections in an access server because a river separates the buildings. DSL and cable modem options are not available in this area. What wireless alternatives exist for the college to link these buildings? Which of the alternatives do you recommend?

Case Project 6-4: Wireless Options for a Restaurant and Coffee Shop

The Tasty Pelican is an upscale restaurant in Montréal that services up to 55 customers per evening. The management of the Tasty Pelican wants to speed the processing of food orders by equipping its waitpersons with handheld devices. Also, the Tasty Pelican has an adjoining coffee shop, and it wants to offer public wireless Internet access in the coffee shop. What wireless options do you recommend for the restaurant and the coffee shop?

Case Project 6-5: Security Measures

What security measures are available for wireless solutions that might be applied to the Thomas Jefferson Community College and the Tasty Pelican designs?

chapter 7

Sharing Resources on a Network

S haring network resources, such as files, multiplies the value of those resources many times over. It is similar to writing a song or a poem and publishing it for others to use and enjoy.

After reading this chapter and completing the exercises, you will be able to:

- Explain how to use peer-to-peer networking in a home or office
- Configure Windows 7 UNIX/Linux and Mac OS X for peer-to-peer networking
- Configure user accounts
- Configure folder and file sharing
- Configure printer sharing
- Use Internet connection sharing
- Explain cloud computing
- Explain virtual private networks
- Explain storage area networks
- Design a peer-to-peer office network to share resources

Networks thrive through sharing resources. Today many people are discovering the simple yet powerful capabilities of peer-to-peer networks and resource sharing. Peer-to-peer networks provide an entry-level networking experience that can match the needs of homes and small offices, enabling the sharing of multiple computer resources. In this chapter, you learn the advantages and disadvantages of peer-to-peer networks. You learn how to configure peer-to-peer networking, share folders, and share printers. Also, for sharing on larger networks you learn about cloud computing, virtual private networks, and storage area networks.

What Is Peer-to-Peer Networking?

A peer-to-peer network is one of the simplest ways to configure a network, often used for home offices and small businesses. On a peer-to-peer network, workstations are used to share resources such as files and printers and to connect to resources on other computers. Windows 7, UNIX/Linux, and Mac OS X Snow Leopard and Lion are examples of operating systems that can be used for peer-to-peer network communications. Files, folders, software, printers, and peripherals on one computer can be shared and made available for others to access. No special host computer, such as a server, is needed to enable workstations to communicate and share resources, although in some cases a server can be used as a powerful workstation. Figure 7-1 illustrates a peer-to-peer network. Another example of a peer-to-peer network is Bluetooth PAN, such as when a laptop computer is wirelessly connected to one or more small tablet PCs through a Bluetooth connection.

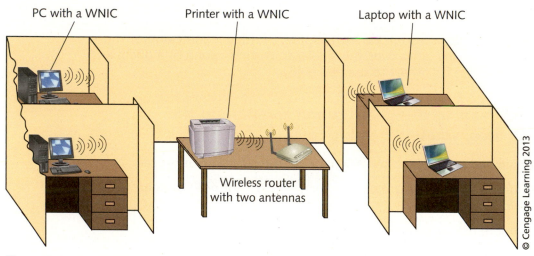

Figure 7-1   A simple peer-to-peer network in a small office

Peer-to-peer networking can be effective for very small networks for the following reasons:

- It enables people to be instantly productive in terms of sharing resources.
- It is relatively easy to set up.
- It is inexpensive to maintain.
- It is simple in concept, so that no one has to learn to manage a server or complex host computer.

On the other side of the coin, there are some disadvantages associated with peer-to-peer networking. With this approach, management of network resources is decentralized. As the network increases in size and the number of shared network resources increases, coordination and administration of resources becomes more and more difficult.

The security of the resources is another important issue. Each of the users is responsible for the security of his or her own resources and must know how to set up the proper security.

Real-Life Networking

A sometimes overlooked task on a home or small office network with shared resources is installing and using a virus checker. On the home computer of an enthusiastic 14-year-old Internet game player, a virus was introduced. The computer had no virus checking software, and the virus soon spread to other networked computers through shared folders. His mother, who used the same laptop at home and at work, unknowingly ported the virus to work. A virus checker is an easy and inexpensive way to prevent these problems. Also, some workplaces have established rules enforced through their servers to help ensure that all clients have at least a minimum set of security measures in place, or the client cannot log onto a the workplace network. Windows Server 2008/Server 2008 R2 can enforce such measures when configured as a Network Policy Server that enforces a Health Policy.

Also, a workstation operating system is not designed to handle a growing load of clients in the same way as a server operating system.

Peer-to-peer networks are generally effective for up to about 10–20 workstations in Windows 7. A peer-to-peer network of UNIX/Linux or Mac OS X workstations can handle more than 10 (depending on the hardware), but are still limited in scope compared to a server operating system. As the number of workstations increases, the peer-to-peer network model becomes less effective for the following reasons:

- Peer-to-peer networking offers only moderate network security, as user account information must be managed on each workstation.

- There is no centralized storage of information for account management. When the number of computers and users grows, so does the need to have a central place to store and manage information. It is much easier to manage files by locating them on a central file server.

- Network management becomes more difficult because there is no central administrative software from which to manage computers and network access authorization and coordinate backing up important files and establishing other fault tolerance operations.

- Peer-to-peer networks can experience slow response because this model is not optimized for multiple users accessing one computer. If many homegroup or workgroup members access one shared folder at the same time, for example, all are likely to experience slow response. On Microsoft networks, a **homegroup** or **workgroup** is well suited for small networks that consist of users who have common needs for sharing resources, such as files and printers. In addition, a homegroup or workgroup is an alternative to creating a more complex centralized domain, which is intended for larger networks. A **domain** centralizes control of network resources into a logical grouping of user accounts, computers, printers, and network devices and can manage thousands of computers.

You can also create a server-based network using only workgroups and no domain, which retains elements of the peer-to-peer approach coupled with some ability to centralize administration, such as through user accounts. The advantage of this approach is that, depending on the server hardware, a server system enables hundreds of users to access the same resources at the same time. You learn more about applications of server systems in Chapter 8, "Using a Server."

Peer-to-Peer Networking for Home Use

Many people set up a peer-to-peer network for home use. Even if your home has only two computers, a peer-to-peer network can make sense for sharing a printer, an Internet connection, and files. When there are more computers in your home, a network makes even more sense for the same reasons plus others, such as keeping backup copies of financial files on two computers.

Many computer users also use digital cameras, smartphones, or tablet PCs to take pictures and want to load the pictures onto their main computer to make photo albums. To share particular pictures with other family members, some people burn copies on DVDs/CDs, creating the expense and clutter of extra DVDs/CDs. With a network, it is easy to make pictures available to other family members without creating DVDs/CDs.

Consider a married couple, both attorneys, who often take work home on laptop computers. They frequently need to print documents for the court, such as briefs. Also, they use the Internet for research. A home network can make their lives easier through sharing a network printer and an Internet connection.

As you learned in Chapter 6, "Connecting Through a Wireless Network," creating a home peer-to-peer network can be accomplished by purchasing a wireless switch or router—eliminating the need to run network cable. For example, with two computers equipped with WNICs, a network printer with a WNIC, and a wireless router, a home network can be up and running very quickly. The advantages of a wireless home network can still be multiplied by adding wireless tablet PCs, smartphones, and network-enabled TVs and entertainment centers.

Microsoft Windows 7 offers a wizard to guide users through setting up a home or office network—wired or wireless—that you can start in the Network and Sharing Center from the *Set up a new connection or network* option. This option starts the Set Up a Connection or Network Wizard (see Figure 7-2) to help the user automatically configure TCP/IP and connect to other computers through a network device, such as a switch or wireless router.

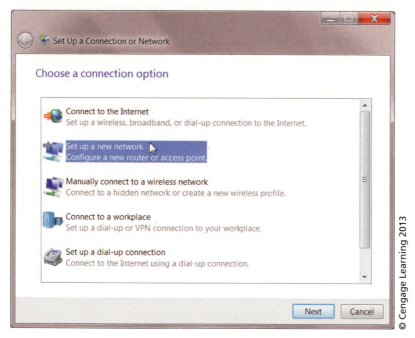

Figure 7-2   Windows 7 Set Up a Connection or Network Wizard

When you configure a peer-to-peer network in Windows 7, there are four options for the network location:

- *Home network*: Which consists of computers in a home that are used by individuals who are trusted in terms of security and enables you to create a homegroup for sharing resources. Network discovery, which makes computers on the home network visible to other home network computers, is turned on by default for a home network.

- *Work network*: Which consists of computers that are all peers that can be viewed by other computers through network discovery; uses a workgroup (see the "Using Workgroups in Windows" section in this chapter) to manage shared resources; consists of computers on the same subnet; and has up to about 20 computer members. A homegroup cannot be used when the network location is configured as a work network.

- *Public network*: Which is a network for public or customer use in a motel, coffee shop, train station, airport, or similar public place and on which network discovery is turned off so that no one can view that your computer is connected to the network. Homegroup and workgroup options do not work from a public network. (See Figure 7-3, which shows Home, Work, and Public network options on a peer-to-peer network that does not have a domain, and so only these three options are listed.)

- *Domain network*: Which is the only option offered if you are connecting to a network that is managed by one or more servers (not a peer-to-peer network) and has an established domain that is a concept used to manage network resources through a medium-sized or enterprise network (see Chapter 8). (Home and small office users as well as public places such as coffee shops are not likely to have a domain.)

Figure 7-3 Network location options in Windows 7 on a network that does not have a domain

Network discovery is a Windows option that manages how computers are seen on a Windows network. There are three network discovery states:

- *Off*: An individual computer configured to use a homegroup or workgroup cannot view other computers or devices such as a printer on the network, and other computers cannot view the computer in the homegroup or workgroup.

- *On*: An individual computer or computers in a homegroup or workgroup can view other computers and devices on the network.

- *Custom*: A network administrator on a server-based network can configure specific network discovery rules, such as discovering routers and subnets or blocking discovery of certain computers or resources on the basis of firewall rules.

For simple peer-to-peer network sharing, Windows 7 offers the homegroup concept. When you set up a network and network access in Windows 7, as illustrated in Activity 7-1, a home-group is automatically created; or if a homegroup already exists you have the option to join the homegroup when you set up a Windows 7 computer for networking. Access to a homegroup is secured through a password that each member must provide. Each category of shared resources is shared through a library and includes libraries for:

- Pictures
- Documents
- Music
- Videos

Printers can also be shared through a homegroup.

By default, libraries are shared so that members can only view, read, or listen (for audio files) to items in the library. Specific homegroup members can be granted additional access to change the content of libraries. In Windows 7 a library is different from a folder because it enables a single view of folders shared through libraries. To view and manage libraries in a homegroup, click Start, click Documents, and Homegroup in the left pane of the Documents window, and click View homegroup settings, if necessary (see Figure 7-4 in Activity 7-1).

Using a homegroup is one of the easiest ways to set up and use resource sharing on a peer-to-peer home network or even on a small office network. In Activity 7-1, you learn how to start the Set Up a Connection or Network Wizard in Windows 7 to create a new network or join an existing network, and you learn about the options to configure for a homegroup.

In some Windows 7 or Server 2008/Server 2008 R2 projects, you may see the User Account Control (UAC) box, which is used for security to help thwart intruders. The UAC box asks for permission to continue with an action or asks for the administrator password. If you see this box, click **Continue**. Because computer setups may be different, the box is not mentioned in the actual project steps.

Activity 7-1: Starting the Windows 7 Set Up a Connection or Network Wizard and Configuring a Homegroup

Time Required: 10 minutes

Objective: Learn how to start the Set Up a Connection or Network Wizard and where to configure a homegroup.

Description: Windows 7 contains wizards to guide users through configuring network connections and peripherals. In this activity, you learn how to start the Windows 7 Set Up a Connection or Network Wizard for a home or small office. You also learn where to configure a homegroup. You need a computer that has a NIC or WNIC already installed and access to an account that has Administrator privileges.

1. Click **Start** and click **Control Panel**.

2. Be sure **View by** is set to **Large icons** or **Small icons** and click **Network and Sharing Center**.

3. In Network and Sharing Center, click **Set up a new connection or network**.

4. After the Set Up a Connection or Network Wizard starts in the next dialog box, you can click *Set up a new network* (do not actually click it now; refer to Figure 7-2), which can be used to set up a home or small office network. For a home or small office that has a wireless router or access point, the wizard will automatically detect the device and enable you to configure the network using that device. When you configure a home network through the steps in this option, you can create a homegroup at the same time. Click **Cancel**.

5. In the Network and Sharing Center, click **HomeGroup** in the left pane of the window.

6. Click **Create a homegroup**. Notice the settings that can be configured for a homegroup (see Figure 7-4), such as sharing picture and music libraries or sharing a printer with other members of the homegroup. How can you change the homegroup password? What selection enables you to stream videos over the home network?

7. Click **Cancel** in the HomeGroup window. Click **Cancel** again.

8. Close the Network and Sharing Center window.

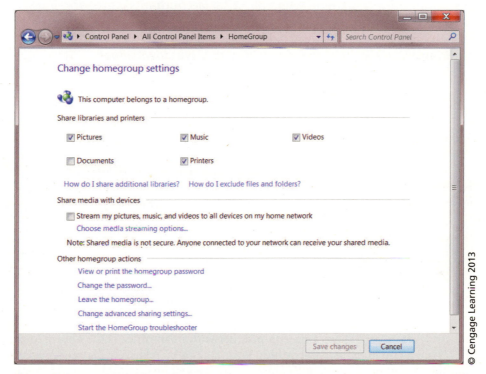

Figure 7-4   Homegroup configuration options in Windows 7

Peer-to-Peer Networking for Office Use

Peer-to-peer networking can make sense for a small office for many of the same reasons as for a home—to share resources. Also, peer-to-peer networking can be valuable in a small office to help make users much more productive, enabling them to share information without having to walk from one desk to another to exchange a DVD/CD or flash drive.

Some brief examples of small office implementations include the following:

- A travel agency of five people uses a peer-to-peer network to share an Internet connection for researching and booking reservations.

- An office of two physicians, two nurses, and two office assistants is networked to track patient information, send prescriptions to pharmacies through the Internet, and share two laser printers.

- A small office of three hydrologists shares files, a printer, a plotter, and Internet access in their business of locating and tracking water resources.

- A small retail book store has a networked cash register and a Windows 7 computer to track sales and tax reporting information.

- A financial advising firm of four associates and one receptionist shares customer files, contacts its parent company through a shared Internet connection, and downloads financial allocation models.

Real-Life Networking

A tax accounting firm created a computer network and configured it to share files from one Windows workstation. During tax time when all 12 tax accountants were working with clients, access to the shared files on that computer was extremely slow—which was costly because it extended the work time with clients and delayed scheduled appointments. The solution was to replace the Windows workstation that was used to share files with a Windows server.

As in a home, peer-to-peer networking can be appealing in a small office because this model is simple to configure and maintain, while yielding large gains in productivity. When you set up a small office peer-to-peer network, the key is to keep the network small, such as under about 20 computers for a network location configured as a work network in Windows operating systems. Also, peer-to-peer networks are most efficient when the resources are spread between multiple computers, so one computer is not the target of most of the sharing.

To determine how many computers you can have for a particular Windows operating system, such as Windows 7, click **Start**, click **All Programs**, click the **Accessories** folder, right-click **Command Prompt**, click **Run as administrator**, at the command line type **net config server**, and press **Enter**. Check the value for Maximum Logged On Users.

Another advantage of a peer-to-peer network in an office is the ability to back up important files, such as financial and client files. Backups can be relatively fast and performed regularly, so that the important files on one computer are backed up on another computer. In one physician's office each physician uses voice recognition software to dictate a letter after each patient's visit. The letter summarizes the office visit and is mailed to the patient. A copy of the letter is kept as a record of the visit. Every evening the physicians back up the newly written letters from their computers to the computer used by the office manager.

Configuring Windows-Based Computers for Peer-to-Peer Networking

In Windows 7 (and Windows Server 2008/Server 2008 R2), important elements for peer-to-peer computing include ensuring that:

- Client for Microsoft Networks is installed.
- TCP/IP is installed and configured.
- File and Printer Sharing for Microsoft Networks is set up.
- A homegroup or workgroup is configured.

The Set Up a Connection or Network Wizard can be used to help you configure these elements. Another option is to configure them manually, which can be useful so that you understand the steps involved in configuring peer-to-peer networking. The following sections explain each element along with configuration information.

An important reason for understanding these elements is so you can troubleshoot problems when a computer fails to connect properly.

Client for Microsoft Networks

Client for Microsoft Networks enables your computer to access the resources shared on the network. This service comes installed automatically in Windows 7 (see Figure 7-5). When you run the Set Up a Connection or Network Wizard, the wizard checks to ensure Client for Microsoft Networks is installed (or it will install it).

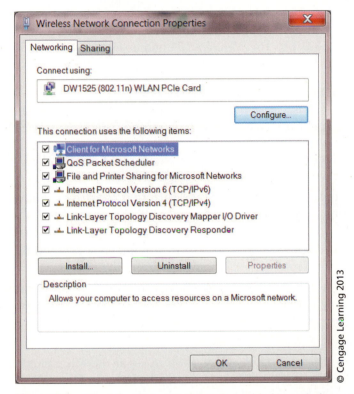

Figure 7-5 Client for Microsoft Networks enabled in a wireless network connection in Windows 7

If Client for Microsoft Networks has been disabled for some reason, the general steps to enable it in Windows 7 or Server 2008/Server 2008 R2 are:

1. Click Start and click Control Panel. Ensure that View by is configured for Large icons or Small icons in Windows 7 and Server 2008 R2, or use Classic View in Windows Server 2008.

2. Click or double-click (for Windows Server 2008) Network and Sharing Center.

3. In Windows 7 and Server 2008 R2, click Change adapter settings in the left pane of the Network and Sharing Center. In Windows Server 2008, click Manage network connections.

4. Right-click the network connection you want to configure, such as Local Area Connection or Wireless Network Connection, and click Properties.

5. In the Connection Properties dialog box and under *This connection uses the following items*, ensure that there is a checkmark in the box for *Client for Microsoft Networks* (refer to Figure 7-5). If the box is not checked, click it.

6. Click OK in the Connection Properties dialog box.

7. Close the Network Connections window, and if requested, click Yes to reboot your computer.

TCP/IP Configuration

TCP/IP should be installed and configured on your computer to ensure it can access a peer-to-peer network. As you learned in Chapter 3, "Using Network Communication Protocols," you can configure to use an IP address and subnet mask, or you can select to obtain the IP address configuration automatically. In Chapter 3, you learned about tools for viewing IP address information in Windows, Linux, and Mac OS X. You can use the same tools to configure TCP/IP—Control Panel in Windows, *ifconfig* in UNIX/Linux, and System Preferences (or *ifconfig* in a terminal window) in Mac OS X.

For a peer-to-peer network, one of the simplest options is to configure TCP/IP to obtain the IP address automatically. When a computer that is configured to automatically obtain an IP address is switched on, it tries to find a DHCP server to obtain an IP address. As discussed in Chapter 3, a DHCP server is a server that uses software and DHCP to automatically assign an IP address from a pool of possible addresses. If there is no DHCP server available, such as on a peer-to-peer network, the computer automatically assigns itself an IP address from the reserved range of 169.254.0.1 to 169.254.255.254 and a subnet mask of 255.255.0.0. This is called **automatic private IP addressing** (**APIPA**, pronounced "ah–pip–ah").

File and Printer Sharing for Microsoft Networks

In Windows 7 and Server 2008/Server 2008 R2, File and Printer Sharing for Microsoft Networks should be installed and enabled, which is the default setting. This is the service that enables you to share files and printers on a network.

When File and Printer Sharing for Microsoft Networks is not installed, you can install it through the following general steps:

1. Click Start and click Control Panel. Make sure that View by is configured for Large icons or Small icons in Windows 7 and Server 2008 R2; or use Classic View in Windows Server 2008.

2. Click (for Windows 7 and Server 2008 R2) or double-click (for Windows Server 2008) Network and Sharing Center.

3. In Windows 7 and Server 2008 R2, click Change adapter settings in the left pane of the Network and Sharing Center. In Windows Server 2008, click Manage network connections.

4. Right-click the network connection to configure, such as Local Area Connection or Wireless Network Connection, and click Properties.

5. In the Connection Properties dialog box, look to see if there is a checkmark in the box for File and Printer Sharing for Microsoft Networks (refer to Figure 7-5). If the box is not checked, then click the box to place a checkmark in it.

6. Click OK in the Connection Properties dialog box.

7. Close the Network Connections window. Click Yes if asked to reboot the computer.

In Windows 7 and Server 2008/Server 2008 R2, the Windows Firewall, which controls security for the services that can be used between a computer and the network, is automatically enabled when File and Printer Sharing for Microsoft Networks is newly enabled. The ability to share files and printers through Windows Firewall is also automatically enabled as a firewall exception. However, if clients are having problems accessing shared files and printers from your computer and you have File and Printer Sharing for Microsoft Networks checked in the NIC's connection properties, then you should check the Firewall configuration as described in Activity 7-2.

Activity 7-2 is tailored for use with Windows Firewall. If your computer uses virus checking and security software that takes over the functions of Windows Firewall, these steps likely will not apply. Consider accessing a different computer that has Windows Firewall in use.

Activity 7-2: Enabling File and Printer Sharing as an Exception in Windows Firewall

Time Required: 5–10 minutes
Objective: Ensure that File and Printer Sharing is allowed through Windows Firewall.

Description: When you want to share files, printers, or both using Windows 7 or Server 2008/Server 2008 R2, ensure that File and Printer Sharing is allowed as an exception to the security rules in Windows Firewall. You learn how in this activity. The Windows Firewall should be installed and active, and you need an account that has Administrator privileges.

1. Click **Start** and click **Control Panel**. Be certain that **View by** is configured for **Large icons** or **Small icons** in Windows 7 and Server 2008 R2; or use **Classic View** in Windows Server 2008.

2. In Control Panel, click (or double-click in Windows Server 2008) **Windows Firewall** (see Figure 7-6).

3. In the left side of the Windows Firewall window, click **Allow a program or feature through Windows Firewall** (or click **Allow a program through Windows Firewall** in Server 2008). If you are using Windows Server 2008, click the **Exceptions** tab in the Windows Firewall Settings window, if necessary.

4. If necessary, scroll to find File and Printer Sharing. Click the box to the left of **File and Printer Sharing**, if the box is not checked. (If you are using Windows Server 2008 R2, you can also configure checkboxes for the network location, which include Domain, Home/Work (Private), and Public.)

5. Click **OK**.

6. Close the Windows Firewall window and any other open windows.

Figure 7-6 Selecting Windows Firewall in Windows Server 2008 R2

A further step to ensure file and printer sharing in Windows 7 or Server 2008/Server 2008 R2 is to verify that network discovery and file and printer sharing are enabled through the Network and Sharing Center. The general steps to be certain they are turned on are:

1. Click Start and click Control Panel. In Windows 7 and Server 2008 R2, set View by to Large icons or Small icons; or in Windows Server 2008, use the Classic View.

2. Click or double-click Network and Sharing Center.

3. In Windows 7 and Server 2008 R2, click *Change advanced sharing settings*, if necessary, click the down arrow for the appropriate network location (click the down arrow for *Home or Work* or click the down arrow for *Public (current profile)*), and ensure that the *Turn on network discovery* and *Turn on file and printer sharing* option buttons are selected. In Windows Server 2008 look in the Sharing and Discovery section of the Network and Sharing Center window and ensure that *Network discovery* is set to *On* or *Custom* and that *File Sharing* and *Printer Sharing* are both set to *On*.

If you want to share files between Windows 7 and earlier operating systems—such as with users running Vista or XP—in Windows 7 ensure that *Turn off password protected sharing* is selected in Step 3 when changing the advanced sharing settings. Also, in Windows 7 give the appropriate access permissions, such as Read, to the Everyone group for the folders you want to share. You learn about permissions in the section, "Sharing Folders and Directories."

4. Close the open windows when you are finished.

Using Workgroups in Windows

Besides homegroups, Windows 7 uses workgroups to identify computers and other resources on a network. Workgroups are typically used in a network location that is specified as a *work network* as explained earlier in the section "Peer-to-Peer Networking for Home Use." In a peer-to-peer work network, computers in a specific workgroup can communicate with one another; and one computer can access shared resources on a different computer (with the right security clearance, of course). This is because computers in the same workgroup are considered peers with one another.

Windows Server 2008/Server 2008 R2 also support using workgroups, but this approach typically is used on smaller server-based networks that have one or two servers and that do not use a domain.

In Windows 7, the default workgroup is WORKGROUP. However, you can customize a different workgroup name for your network. In a larger office, you might configure more than one workgroup, particularly if users are divided into groups that have different functions, such as attorneys and office staff in a law firm.

Many users have wondered about the differences between using a homegroup and using a workgroup. Table 7-1 compares some of the differences to help you better understand which type of group to configure for your network. One of the most significant differences is in the ease of setting up security, which is simplified through homegroups. Work networks that use a workgroup typically have more sensitive information and more varied kinds of members, requiring a wider range of options for establishing security.

Computers in a homegroup are also members of a workgroup, even if it is the default WORKGROUP that is automatically set up when a computer is set up on a network. Sharing resources is still managed through the homegroup without the need to actually configure the shared resources in a workgroup. In this scenario, which is common for home networks, the workgroup is not actually used to manage the shared resources, it simply acts as a parent network management container for the homegroup, and so the workgroup is transparent to the home user. Security for a homegroup is handled by requiring the correct homegroup password to join the homegroup and access that homegroup's resources. Security for a workgroup is managed through carefully setting up security permissions for all folders.

Table 7-1   Comparing homegroup to workgroup characteristics

Homegroup	Workgroup
Only used in Windows 7 (which means all members must be Windows 7 computers)	Can combine different Windows operating systems, such as Windows XP, Windows Vista, Windows 7, and Windows Server systems
Ideally used for up to about 15–20 users on a peer-to-peer network (over 20 users can create management problems)	Ideally used for up to about 15–20 users on a peer-to-peer network (over 20 users can create management problems)
Enables automatic resource sharing and security measures through selecting libraries to share among members (refer to Activity 7-1)—intended for novice users	Setting up sharing and security is more complicated and involves specifying sharing and permissions for specific files and folders (which can create security conflicts that are more difficult to solve)—intended for intermediate users who understand security and managing permissions (see the sections in this chapter "Configuring Sharing and Share Permissions" and "Configuring NTFS Permissions")
The homegroup creator establishes a homegroup password that applies to all homegroup members (homegroups are on the same network or subnet)	A workgroup is not protected by a password, which means a new member can join by specifying only the workgroup name (workgroups are on the same network or subnet)

© Cengage Learning 2013

In Activity 7-3 you learn how to establish a workgroup name or join an existing workgroup.

Activity 7-3: Establishing or Joining a Workgroup

Time Required: 5 minutes
Objective: Create a new workgroup or join an existing one.

Description: Workgroups are important on Windows 7 peer-to-peer networks for accessing and securing resources. In this activity, you learn how to start a new workgroup or join a workgroup that is already in existence. You need access to an account with Administrator privileges. Also, your computer should be connected to a network containing at least one workgroup, and the computer should be configured as a member of a workgroup.

1. Click **Start** and click **Control Panel**. Ensure that **View by** is configured for **Large icons** or **Small icons** in Windows 7.

2. Click **System**.

3. In the left pane of the System window, click **Advanced system settings**.

4. In the System Properties dialog box, click the **Computer Name** tab, if it is not already selected.

5. What is your current computer name and workgroup?

6. Click the **Change** button.

7. You will see options for Domain or Workgroup in the *Member of* section. Ensure that the **Workgroup** option button is selected.

8. If you have permission from your instructor to change the workgroup, enter a new workgroup name consisting of your initials and the word "GROUP," such as *MPGROUP* (see Figure 7-7). If you don't have permission to change the workgroup, click **Cancel** and close all windows.

 The operating system will automatically change the workgroup name to all uppercase.

9. Click **OK** in the Computer Name/Domain Changes dialog box. If you see a box welcoming you because you have created a new workgroup, click **OK**.

10. Click **OK** in the box noting you will have to restart the computer (make sure your work is saved first).

11. Click **Close** in the System Properties dialog box.

12. Click **Restart Now**.

Figure 7-7   Entering a workgroup name in Windows 7

On a peer-to-peer network, you can use the Network window to view your computer and those of your fellow workgroup members. You do this in Activity 7-4.

Activity 7-4: Viewing the Members of Your Workgroup

Time Required: 5 minutes
Objective: View your workgroup members.

Description: In this activity, you view the members of your workgroup.

1. Click **Start**, click **Computer**, and click **Network** in the left pane of the Computer window.

2. What computers do you see? Are there any printers or other devices shown? Close the Network window.

Configuring UNIX/Linux Computers for Peer-to-Peer Networking

In UNIX/Linux, peer-to-peer networking is made possible by ensuring that TCP/IP is installed and properly configured. Use the *ifconfig* command as you learned in Chapter 1, "Networking: An Overview," to check the configuration. Also, you can use *ifconfig* to configure the TCP/IP connection, as you learned in Chapter 4, "Connecting Through a Cabled Network."

 To review the *ifconfig* command options, type *man ifconfig* and press Enter at the UNIX/Linux command line.

Directories and files are shared between UNIX/Linux computers through the Network File System (NFS, see Chapter 3), which is compatible with TCP/IP.

In a combined Windows 7 and UNIX/Linux peer-to-peer network, file sharing is made possible by a UNIX/Linux application called Samba. Many versions of UNIX and Linux (as well as the Mac OS X operating system) use the **Samba** software that supports **Server Message Block (SMB) protocol**. SMB is a resource-sharing protocol used in Windows-based networking. Samba employs SMB to contact and connect to Microsoft Windows operating systems. Linux distributions offer NFS and Samba.

NFS and Samba can be used on a typical Fedora Linux workstation, in Red Hat Enterprise Linux, or in most Linux distributions. In the GNOME desktop you can review which software packages are installed, such as Samba (and add and remove packages), by clicking Activities, clicking Applications, and clicking Add/Remove Software. If Samba is not installed, enter *samba* in the text box and click Find to view Samba packages you can install.

Configuring Mac OS X Computers for Peer-to-Peer Networking and Resource Sharing

Many Apple peer-to-peer networks use Apple's **AirPort** wireless approach, which is particularly appropriate for a home or small office network. AirPort networks use an AirPort Extreme Base Station or an AirPort Express Base Station. An AirPort Extreme Base Station is a wireless router that can have a connection to the Internet and can connect up to 50 users. A USB external hard drive can be connected to an AirPort Extreme Base Station so that Macintosh users connecting through the base station can share files on the base station's external hard drive. The AirPort Extreme Base Station can also have a built-in hard disk that is used for automatic backups through the network using the Mac OS X Time Machine backup software. The AirPort Extreme Base Station can use 802.11b/g/n at 2.4 or 5 GHz, depending on the 802.11n technology selected for use.

The AirPort Express Base station enables up to 10 users to wirelessly connect to the network by offering 802.11b/g/n wireless connectivity at 2.4 or 5 GHz. An AirPort Express Base station can receive music from Apple iTunes through a connected Mac OS X computer and can play music through compatible AirPort Express speakers, such as in another room. It is also possible to download applications (apps) for an iPhone or iPod Touch and use either of these devices to wirelessly manage an iTunes library on a network.

Mac OS X Snow Leopard and Lion offer the AirPort Utility to configure an AirPort Extreme or AirPort Express wireless network. For example, the general steps to configure a new wireless AirPort Express network are as follows:

1. Ensure Finder is open.

2. Click Go in the menu bar and click Utilities.

3. Double-click AirPort Utility as shown in Figure 7-8.

4. Choose the AirPort Express device and click Continue.

5. Configure the AirPort Express options, which include the name for AirPort Express and the password (and the option to remember the password in my keychain). Click Continue.

6. Select to create a new wireless network and click Continue.

7. Enter a network name (SSID) and configure the security, such as selecting to configure WPA/WPA2, WEP, or no security (WPA/WPA2 offers the best security). Click Continue.

8. Configure whether to use DHCP for automatically assigning IP addresses, such as through a DSL or cable modem using Internet connectivity. Click Continue.

9. Review the summary of your settings and click Update.

10. In the box that warns the device and network services will be temporarily unavailable, click Continue.

11. After the AirPort Express Base Station reboots, you will see a window that shows the setup is complete and a green bullet should appear to the right of the base station's name. Click Quit.

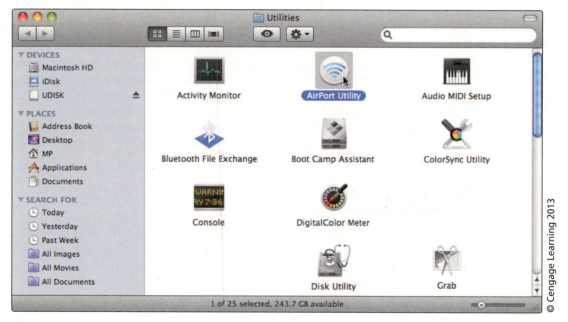

Figure 7-8   Selecting the AirPort Utility in the Mac OS X Utilities window

© Cengage Learning 2013

In Chapter 1, you learned that an Internet connection can be shared in Mac OS X Snow Leopard and Lion. Mac OS X offers many other resources that can be shared, but first you must enable which resources to share. The resources that can be shared are presented in Table 7-2.

Mac OS X Snow Leopard and Lion offer the Sharing utility from System Preferences to enable specific resource sharing services. In Activity 7-5 you learn how to access and use the Sharing utility.

Table 7-2   Resource services that can be shared in Mac OS X Snow Leopard and Lion

Resource Service	Explanation
DVD or CD sharing	The DVD/CD-ROM drive can be accessed and used by other computers.
Screen sharing	The computer can be viewed and controlled by another user, which is similar to Remote Desktop in Windows computers; can enable a remote support person to diagnose a problem or help a new user.
File sharing	Other computer users can access this computer's files through a network.
Printer sharing	Other computer users on the network can access one or more printers or fax devices connected to this computer.
Scanner sharing	This computer's scanner can be used by other computers on the network.
Web sharing	Web pages stored in the Sites folder under a particular user's Home folder on this computer can be accessed by other network computers.
Remote Login	This computer can be accessed by other network computers using SSH (Secure Shell, which is explained in Chapter 3).
Remote Management	Other computers can remotely use this computer using Apple Remote Desktop, which is an application that is sold separately by Apple.
Remote Apple Events	Remote computers can send commands to this computer from scripts as used through Apple Events software (a script is a file containing a list of commands to execute to accomplish specific actions).
Xgrid sharing	Xgrid is software that works through an external computer controller to remotely run specific tasks on an agent computer when Xgrid sharing is enabled on the agent. With Xgrid a remote computer with an Xgrid controller can run tasks or jobs on one or more other agent computers.
Internet sharing	Other computers can share the Internet connection on this computer.
Bluetooth sharing	Other computers with Bluetooth can share files on this computer (with Bluetooth). See Chapter 6 for more about Bluetooth PAN.

© Cengage Learning 2013

Activity 7-5: Using the Mac OS X Sharing Utility

Time Required: 10 minutes

Objective: Open and use the Sharing utility in Mac OS X Snow Leopard and Lion.

Description: In this activity, you learn how to use the Mac OS X Sharing utility that is accessed through System Preferences.

1. Click the **System Preferences** icon in the Dock, or click the **Apple** icon in the menu bar and click **System Preferences**.

2. In the System Preferences window under Internet & Wireless, click **Sharing**.

3. Notice the sharing services that can be configured as shown in Figure 7-9.

4. Click the box for **File Sharing**, if the box does not already contain a checkmark. This action turns on the file sharing service so that you can specify which individual files and folders to share with other network computers. Notice that you can click the **+** *plus sign* under the Shared Folders text box to specify which folders to share. Also, you can click the **+** *plus sign* under the Users text box to select users and groups that can access the shared folders. Next to each group or user are the permissions that determine the type of access. Mac OS X folder and file permissions are explained in the section "Sharing Folders and Directories."

5. Click the **Options** button in the Sharing window. Which option can you select to enable sharing files with Windows computers? Click **Done**.

6. Click **System Preferences** in the menu bar and click **Quit System Preferences**.

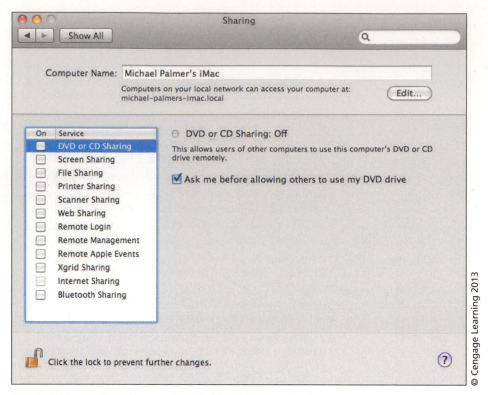

Figure 7-9   Sharing services options in Mac OS X

Configuring User Accounts

In most operating systems, including Windows, UNIX/Linux, and Mac OS X systems, access to shared resources is managed through user accounts. A **user account** on a computer might be compared to a bank account. A bank is a repository of resources that are accessed through bank accounts. It is the account number and security used by the bank that protects your money. When you need to access your money, you do so through your bank account. The same is true for computer resources, which you access through a user account. For all systems, the user account is central to **authentication** of users for access to specific resources. Authentication is the process of verifying that a user is authorized to access a particular computer, server, network, or network resource.

When you share resources over a network, you should first configure user accounts for people to access those resources. In the following sections, you learn how to configure user accounts in Windows 7, Linux, and Mac OS X Snow Leopard and Lion. In Chapter 8, you learn how to configure accounts in Windows Server 2008/Server 2008 R2 for a workgroup or domain context.

Configuring User Accounts in Windows 7

User accounts are configured and managed through the Windows 7 Control Panel's User Accounts tool. With the User Accounts tool you can:

- Create an account
- Modify an account, such as the password
- Delete an account

In Activity 7-6 you create an account, modify the password, and delete the account. Note that learning how to change an account's password is important, because when you manage user accounts, you will soon find out that users sometimes forget their passwords and need you to change the password. This is the most common user account management activity—changing passwords. On a user account, you cannot view a current password, for the sake of the security of the account holder. However, you can change the password at the user's request.

Activity 7-6: Creating and Managing a Windows 7 User Account

Time Required: 15 minutes
Objective: Create and manage a user account in Windows 7.

Description: User accounts enable access to shared resources on a network. In this activity, you create a user account, change the account's password, and then delete the account in Windows 7. You need an account with Administrator privileges for this activity.

1. Click **Start** and click **Control Panel**. Make certain that **View by** is configured for **Large icons** or **Small icons** in Windows 7.

2. Click **User Accounts**.

3. Click **Manage another account** to view the accounts that are already created. What user accounts are already created? Notice that one of the accounts is called Guest, which is a default account to enable a temporary or guest user. This account is turned off by default as a security measure. If you enable the Guest account for a temporary user, ensure that you establish a password, so there is no open "back door" into your system.

4. Click **Create a new account** in the Manage Accounts window.

5. In the Name the account and choose an account type window, enter the name for the account, such as your first name and last name plus the word "test"—for example, *Michael Palmertest*. Do not use your own name without adding additional characters, such as "test," so that when you delete the account you do not accidentally delete your own account. Also, ensure that the **Standard user** option button is selected (see Figure 7-10). Notice there are two kinds of accounts:

   • *Standard user*: Which is for users who manage their own resources, but not the computer or resources of other users.

   • *Administrator*: Which is for users who handle all computer administration including settings that affect all users and creating user accounts.

6. Click **Create Account**.

7. Notice that the new account now appears in the Manage Accounts window. Click the account you just created.

8. Click **Create a password** in the Change an Account window.

9. Enter a password and confirm the password. Enter a hint as a reminder of the password.

10. Click **Create a password**.

11. In the Change an Account window, notice that the account change options now include the option to change the password. Click **Change the password**. Enter a new password, confirm the password, and enter a password hint. Click **Change password**.

12. In the Change an Account window, click **Delete the account**. You can choose to keep the files associated with the account or to delete them. For this activity, click **Delete Files**.

13. In the Confirm Deletion window, click **Delete Account**. Your test account should now be gone from the Manage Accounts window.

14. Close the Manage Accounts window.

7

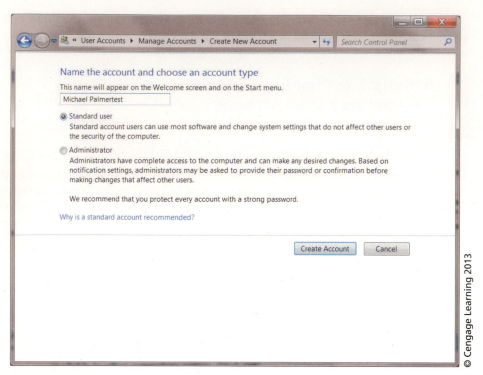

© Cengage Learning 2013

Figure 7-10 Creating a new account in Windows 7

Configuring Accounts in UNIX/Linux

Access to shared resources on a UNIX/Linux system is also managed through user accounts. Each user account in UNIX/Linux is associated with a **user identification number (UID)**. Also, users who have common access needs can be assigned to a group via a **group identification number (GID)**, and then the permissions to access resources are assigned to the group, instead of to each user. When the user logs on to access resources, the password file is checked to permit logon authorization. The password file (/etc/passwd) contains the following kinds of information:

- The user name
- An encrypted password or a reference to the **shadow file**, a file associated with the password file that makes it difficult for intruders to determine the passwords of others (if the shadow file capability is turned on)
- The UID, which can be a number that is theoretically in the millions (depending on the UNIX or Linux kernel version)
- A GID with which the user name is associated
- Information about the user, such as a description or the user's job
- The location of the user's home directory (a directory automatically assigned to the user for storing his or her files)
- A command that is executed as the user logs on, such as which shell (operating environment) to use

In many UNIX/Linux systems, including Fedora and Red Hat Enterprise Linux systems, any account that has a UID of 0 automatically has access to anything in the system. As account administrator, occasionally examine the /etc/passwd file to ensure that only the root account has this UID. You can view the contents of the /etc/passwd file from the root account (or an account with root privileges) by entering *more /etc/passwd* at the command line, and then pressing the Spacebar, Page Down, or Enter to view each page.

The shadow file (/etc/shadow) is normally available only to the system administrator. It contains password restriction information that includes the following:

- The minimum and the maximum number of days between password changes
- Information on when the password was last changed
- Warning information about when a password will expire
- Amount of time that the account can be inactive before access is prohibited

Information about groups is stored in the /etc/group file, which typically contains an entry for each group consisting of the name of the group, an encrypted group password, the GID, and a list of group members. In some versions of UNIX/Linux, including Fedora and Red Hat Enterprise Linux, every account is assigned to at least one group and can be assigned to more. User accounts and groups can be created by editing the password and shadow and group files, but a safer way to create them is by using UNIX/Linux commands created for this purpose. If you edit the files, you run the risk of an editing error that can create unanticipated problems. Also, it is important to make sure that each group has a unique GID because when two or more groups use the same GID, there is a serious security risk. For example, an obvious risk is that the permissions given to one group also inappropriately apply to the other.

In Fedora and Red Hat Enterprise Linux, the *useradd* command enables you to create a new user. The parameters that can be added to *useradd* include the following:

- *-c* gives an account description.
- *-d* specifies the user's home directory location.
- *-e* specifies an account expiration date (use the format YYYY-MM-DD).
- *-f* specifies the number of days the account can be inactive before access is prohibited.
- *-g* specifies initial group membership.
- *-G* specifies additional groups to which the account belongs.
- *-m* establishes the home directory if it has not previously been set up.
- *-M* means do not create a home directory.
- *-n* means do not set up, by default, a group that has the same name as the account (in Red Hat Enterprise Linux).
- *-p* specifies the account password.
- *-r* creates administrative accounts that have some root privileges.
- *-s* designates the default shell associated with the account.
- *-u* specifies the UID.

In Fedora and Red Hat Enterprise Linux, for example, the command *useradd -c "Lisa Ramirez, Accounting Department, ext 221" -p green$thumb -u 700 lramirez* creates an account called lramirez with a comment that contains the account holder's name, department, and extension; a password set to green$thumb; and a UID equal to 700 (see Figure 7-11).

In Fedora and Red Hat Enterprise Linux, a UID less than 500 is typically used for system-based accounts, and user accounts have a UID of 500 or more. The parameters set by default, because they are not specified, are to create a group called lramirez and to create the home directory /home/lramirez (with lramirez as owner). Home directories are areas on the computer in which users store data. If you do not want a group automatically created at the time you create an account, use the *-n* parameter with the *useradd* command. When you use the *-n* parameter, the account is automatically assigned to a general group called users (with GID 100), instead of to a newly created group with the same name as the account. Setting up a default group with a name that is the same as the account name is a characteristic of Linux, but is not generalized to all UNIX distributions.

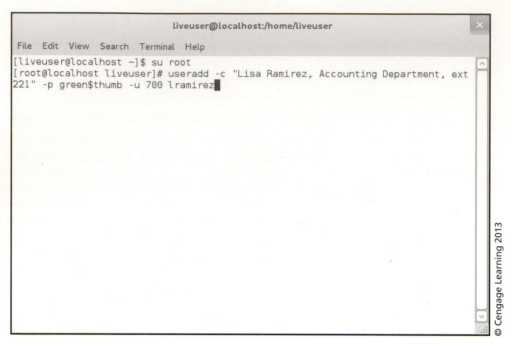

Figure 7-11   Creating an account in Fedora Linux

In many versions of UNIX/Linux, such as Fedora and Red Hat Enterprise Linux, if no password is specified at the time the account is created, then the account is disabled by default. Also, for some versions of UNIX/Linux, including Fedora and Red Hat Enterprise Linux, user names should be entered in lowercase.

The parameters associated with an account can be modified by using the *usermod* command. For instance, to change the password for the account lramirez, you enter *usermod -p applebuTTer# lramirez*. Account setup can be automated by writing a shell script (a file of commands) that contains prompts for the desired information. Accounts are deleted through the *userdel* command, which enables you to specify the username and (optionally) delete the home directory and its contents. In Fedora and Red Hat Enterprise Linux, to delete an account, the home directory, and all files in the home directory, use the *-r* parameter instead of specifying the home directory, such as entering *userdel -r lramirez*.

Useradd, *usermod*, and *userdel* generally work in all versions of Linux and most versions of UNIX. Also, installations of Fedora and Red Hat Enterprise Linux, such as those for servers, include a GNOME desktop option to configure user accounts. You can find this option in GNOME 3.x or above by clicking Activities, clicking Applications, and clicking Users and Groups, which opens the graphical User Manager application (see Figure 7-12).

Groups are used in UNIX/Linux for granting permissions to one user or a group of users to access specific resources (you learn about permissions later in this chapter). Information about groups is typically stored in the /etc/group file, and group security information is in the /etc/gshadow file. Groups are created using the *groupadd* command. There are typically two inputs associated with this command. The *-g* parameter is used to establish the GID, and the group string creates a group name. For example, to create the auditors group, you enter *groupadd -g 2000 auditors*. Once a group is created, it is modified through the *groupmod* command. Groups are deleted through the *groupdel* command. For the purposes of this book, simply keep in mind that a group with the same name as the user account is created at the time of the user account. The group provides a way to give access to the resources managed by a user account.

Activity 7-7 enables you to create and manage a user account in UNIX/Linux.

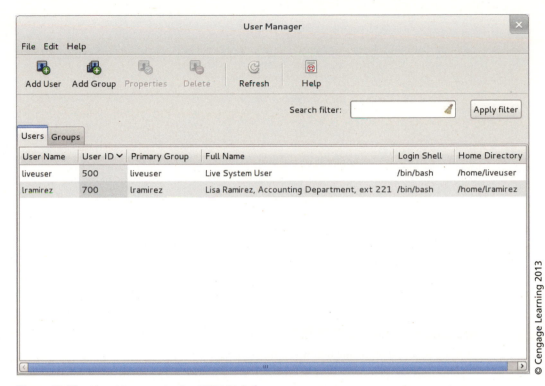

Figure 7-12   User Manager in the GNOME desktop

Activity 7-7: Creating and Managing a UNIX/Linux User Account

Time Required: 15 minutes
Objective: Create and manage a user account in Linux.

Description: This activity enables you to create a user account, change the password, and delete the account in Linux using the GNOME 3.x or higher desktop. You need to log onto the root account to perform this activity using the *su* (superuser) command.

1. In the GNOME 3.x desktop, click **Activities** in the left side of the top Panel on the desktop. Click **Applications** on the desktop to view icons of applications that can be opened. Click the **Terminal** icon to open a terminal window.

2. At the command line in the terminal window, type **su root** and press **Enter**. (Remember, if you use Fedora 15 Live Media or higher, you do not need to enter a root password. For other Linux distributions you will need to enter the root password at this point. If you do not know the root password, check with your instructor.)

3. When you set up the account, use your last name, plus the word "test." For example, type *useradd -c "Palmer, practice account" -p practice palmertest*, and press **Enter**. (Note that when you do not specify the UID, Fedora and Red Hat Enterprise Linux will use the next available number over 500. Also, use all lowercase for the user name.)

4. Type **more /etc/passwd** and press Enter to view the contents of the password file. Do you see the account that you created? (You may need to press the **spacebar** one or more times to go to the end of the file—you can press **q** to exit the file contents listing.)

5. Now use the *usermod* command to change the password of your new account, such as by typing *usermod -p newpassword palmertest* and pressing **Enter**.

6. Finally, delete your test account by using the *userdel* command, for example, type *userdel -r palmertest* and press **Enter** to delete the account and its home directory (see Figure 7-13).

7. Close the terminal window.

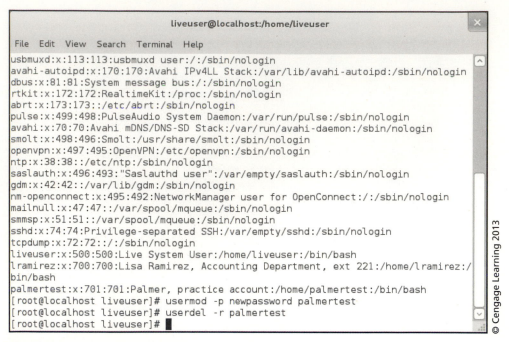

Figure 7-13   Managing a user account in Fedora Linux

Configuring Accounts in Mac OS X

Mac OS X Snow Leopard and Lion also can be configured for multiple accounts by using the Accounts utility in System Preferences. When Mac OS X is used in a home, public library, or other location with children, parental controls is a useful feature that can be configured. The parental controls feature enables access limitations to be placed on specific accounts as shown in Table 7-3.

Table 7-3   Parental controls settings in Mac OS X

Parental Control	Explanation
System	Limits the activities and applications that an account can perform
Content	Manages which Web sites can be accessed and manages access to the Dictionary
Mail & iChat	Manages e-mail correspondents and iChat partners
Time Limits	Manages which times of the day and night the account can be used and how long it can be used
Logs	Creates computer activity logs that can be viewed

© Cengage Learning 2013

There are several types of accounts that you can configure in Mac OS X Snow Leopard and Lion in addition to an account that has parental controls. The accounts you can configure include:

- *Administrator*: Used to manage the computer and operating system

- *Standard*: Grants access privileges for general users

- *Sharing only*: Grants access only to shared resources such as files and folders but does not come with privileges to run applications

- *Group*: Contains only other users or groups and is used to make it easier to assign access privileges to specific resources

- *Managed with parental controls*: Establishes parental controls on an account

Mac OS X includes a Guest account that is disabled by default as a security measure. If you plan to allow guests to access a Mac OS X computer, you can enable the Guest account and also choose whether to allow users of the Guest account to access shared folders. You configure these options by selecting the Guest account in the Accounts window opened through System Preferences.

Similar to Windows operating systems and UNIX/Linux, Mac OS X account holders can have home directories in which to store applications and personal files. Home directories are found under the main /Users directory and are accessed and managed by the account holder. Each home directory contains subdirectories in which to store documents, movies, pictures, music, public files for sharing, and other files. Activity 7-8 enables you to configure a new account in Mac OS X.

Activity 7-8: Creating a User Account in Mac OS X

Time Required: 15 minutes
Objective: Create and manage a Mac OS X user account.

Description: This activity enables you to create a user account, change the password, and delete the account in Mac OS X Snow Leopard or Lion. You need to log onto an account that has Administrator privileges.

1. Click **System Preferences** in the Dock, or click the **Apple** icon in the menu bar and click **System Preferences**.

2. Click **Accounts** (or **Users & Groups** in Mac OS X Lion) under System in the System Preferences window.

3. If necessary to open it, click the **lock icon** in the bottom left corner of the Accounts or Users & Groups window. If requested, provide your account name and password in the security box to enable changes to System Preferences and click **OK**.

4. Click the **+ plus sign** below the My Account text box (Snow Leopard) that lists current accounts. In Lion, click the **+ plus sign** below the left pane showing the Current User and Other Users.

5. Click the **up/down arrows** in the **New Account** box and record the types of accounts that can be configured. Ensure that **Standard** is selected.

6. Enter the full name of the account holder, such as *Jason Brown*. Next, enter the name for the user account, such as *jasonbrown* (the name provided by default). Enter a password for the account and verify the password. Include a password hint (see Figure 7-14).

Figure 7-14   Creating a new account in Mac OS X Lion

In Mac OS X Snow Leopard, there is a Turn on FileVault protection option enabling the user's home directory to be encrypted as an extra security measure. Leave the Turn on FileVault protection check box blank
for this activity The Turn on FileVault protection option is not displayed in
Mac OS X Lion, as shown in Figure 7-14.

7. Click **Create Account** (Snow Leopard) or **Create User** (Lion).

If you are provided the option to use automatic login, select to **Turn Off
Automatic Login**.

8. In the Accounts or Users & Groups window, ensure that the new account is selected. Click
the **Reset Password** button.

9. Enter a new password for the account and verify the password. Also, enter a new password
hint. Click **Reset Password**.

10. To delete the account you created, click the account in the left pane of the Accounts or
Users & Groups dialog box, and click the - **minus sign** under the My Account box.

11. Click the **Delete the home folder** option button and click **OK** (see Figure 7-15). (In Mac OS X
Lion there is an option to *Erase home folder securely*, which can be used to ensure that the
folder contents cannot be easily recovered.) Notice the account is deleted in the listing of accounts in the Accounts (or Users & Groups) window.

12. Click **System Preferences** and click **Quit System Preferences**.

Figure 7-15   Deleting an account and its home folder in Mac OS X Lion

Sharing Folders and Directories

Files and folders or directories can be set up for sharing over a network. Windows 7 (and
Windows Server 2008/Server 2008 R2), UNIX/Linux, and Mac OS X provide ways to share files/
folders/directories. In these systems there are two processes involved: configuring the resource
for sharing and setting security permissions to control who can access the shared resources. In
the following sections you learn how to do both.

Sharing Files and Folders in Windows 7

There are several elements to sharing and accessing files and folders in Windows 7:

- Configuring sharing and share permissions
- Configuring NTFS permissions
- Accessing a share folder

Each of these elements is described in the next sections.

Configuring Sharing and Share Permissions

In Windows 7 (and Windows Server 2008/Server 2008 R2), a folder or drive is shared through its properties. This is accomplished by accessing the folder or drive via the Computer or Documents window. Right-click the folder or drive and click Share with to configure sharing for a homegroup; for a workgroup, right-click the folder or drive, click Properties, and click the Sharing tab in the Properties dialog box.

When you configure sharing for a homegroup, the sharing options include (see Figure 7-16):

- *Nobody*: The file or folder is not shared with any homegroup member.

- *Homegroup (Read)*: Homegroup members can read the shared folder or file's contents, but cannot copy a new file to a shared folder or change the contents of a shared file.

- *Homegroup (Read/Write)*: Homegroup members can read the contents of shared folders and files and make changes such as adding a new file to a shared folder or changing the text in a shared file.

- *Specific people*: Only designated user accounts in the homegroup can access shared folders or files.

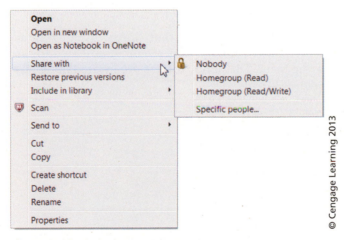

Figure 7-16   Homegroup sharing options

Traditional Windows share permissions for access by a workgroup are configured through the Advanced Sharing option in the properties of a folder or file. For example, right-click a folder, click Properties, click the Sharing tab, click Advanced Sharing, click Share this folder, and click Permissions (see Figure 7-17 and also try Activity 7-9 to use these steps). The available share permissions are:

- *Read*: Permits groups or users to read and execute files
- *Change*: Enables users to read, add, modify, execute, and delete files
- *Full Control*: Provides full access to the folder including the ability to take control or change share permissions

When you share a folder using the traditional share permissions, there is a caching option that enables you to set up a folder so that it can be accessed by a client, even when the client is

Figure 7-17   Configuring share permissions in Windows 7

not connected to the network. This capability is particularly useful for laptop users who travel away from the network. The contents of the folder can be stored on the client's hard drive while he or she is not on the network.

Windows 7 includes several public folders that can be used by an account holder to share documents. For security, these public folders are not configured for sharing by default. You must first enable sharing them. The public folders are located in the \Users\Public folder and include:

- Public Documents
- Public Downloads
- Public Music
- Public Pictures
- Public Recorded TV
- Public Videos

Configuring NTFS Permissions   For Windows 7, in addition to share permissions, there are also file and folder permissions that can be set. These are a more extensive set of permissions and are controlled by the NT File System (NTFS) used in Windows 7 (and Server 2008/Server 2008 R2).

NTFS permissions are set by accessing the file or folder, right-clicking it, clicking Properties, and clicking the Security tab (see Figure 7-18). The permissions that you can set are presented in Table 7-4.

NTFS and share permissions on the same folder are not cumulative. For example, if the Everyone default group in Windows 7 is granted NTFS Read access on a folder, but the share permissions for that folder are Full control for the same group, the Everyone group still has only Read access to that folder. A summary of the permissions rules are:

- NTFS permissions are cumulative with the exception that if an account or group to which the account belongs is denied access, this overrides other permissions.
- When a folder has both NTFS and share permissions, the most restrictive permissions apply.

Table 7-4   Windows 7 NTFS folder and file permissions

Permission	Description	Applies To
Full control	Can read, add, delete, execute, and modify files, plus change permissions and attributes, and take ownership	Folders and files
List folder contents	Can list (traverse) files in the folder or switch to a subfolder, view folder attributes and permissions, and execute files, but cannot view file contents	Folders only
Modify	Can read, add, delete, execute, and modify files, but cannot delete subfolders and their file contents, change permissions, or take ownership	Folders and files
Read	Can view file contents, view folder attributes and permissions, but cannot traverse folders or execute files	Folders and files
Read & execute	Implies the capabilities of both List Folder Contents and Read (traverse folders, view file contents, view attributes and permissions, and execute files)	Folders and files
Special permissions	Consists of your customized permissions combination. Click the Advanced button to configure special permissions.	Folders and files
Write	Can create files, write data to files, append data to files, create folders, delete files (but not subfolders and their files), and modify folder and file attributes	Folders and files

© Cengage Learning 2013

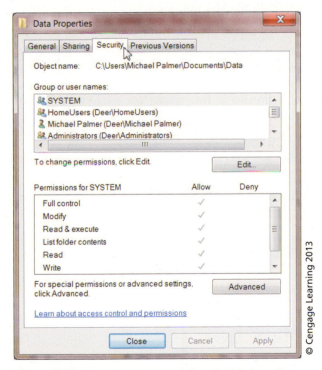

Figure 7-18   Setting NTFS permissions in Windows 7

NOTE   Medium-sized and large organizations often prefer to share drives and folders from a server because this enables stricter management of access and security to company information. Small offices may use a server or simply share resources from clients. No matter how resources are shared, it is important to use the security techniques described in this chapter and elsewhere in this book to ensure that documents do not end up in the wrong hands.

Activity 7-9 enables you to create a test folder and configure it for sharing in Windows 7.

Activity 7-9: Sharing a Folder in Windows 7

Time Required: 15 minutes

Objective: Share a folder in Windows 7 and configure its permissions.

Description: In this activity, you create a folder, share it, and configure its share and NTFS permissions.

1. Click **Start** and click **Documents**.

2. Click **New Folder** in the menu bar and enter your last name plus the word "test," such as *Palmertes*t for the folder's name and press **Enter**.

3. Right-click the folder you created and click **Properties**.

4. Click the Security tab.

5. Click a group or user listed under Group or user names (possibilities include *HomeUsers (yourcomputername\HomeUsers)*, *Administrators (yourusername\Administrators)*, or *Users (yourcomputername\Users)* in the box under *Group or user names*.

6. Notice that Read & execute, List folder contents, and Read are checked by default. Click the **Edit** button to edit the permissions.

7. In the *Permissions for* dialog box, ensure that the group or username you are working with is highlighted and then place a checkmark in the box for **Modify** in the **Allow** column (see Figure 7-19). Notice that Write is also now checked automatically. Click **OK**.

8. In the Properties dialog box, click the **Sharing** tab.

9. On the Sharing tab, click the **Advanced Sharing button**.

10. In the Advanced Sharing dialog box, click the box for **Share this folder**. Note that the *Share* name textbox now displays the name of your folder. Also, notice that *Limit the number of simultaneous users to* is set to 20 by default. You can limit the access to a certain number of users at the same time, such as to two or four users. You might do this in order to reduce the load on the computer sharing the folder. For this activity, leave the default at 20.

11. In the Advanced Sharing dialog box, click the **Permissions** button.

12. Click the **Allow** box for **Change** (which applies to the Everyone group that is composed of all user accounts on this computer).

13. Click **OK** in the Permissions for dialog box and click **OK** in the Advanced Sharing dialog box. Finally, click **OK** in the Properties dialog box.

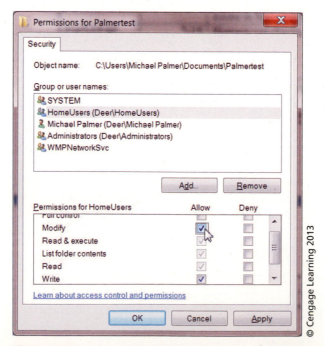

Figure 7-19   Selecting the Modify permission in Windows 7

Real-Life Networking

A small law office created a shared folder containing client information and payments on a Windows computer used by the office associates. NTFS and share permissions on the folder were set at *Full control* for all users. Each night the office was cleaned by one person from a janitorial service. One evening a member of the cleaning service brought a laptop computer, connected it to the network, and was obtaining the client records, including credit card and other personal information that could be used in identity theft—when he was interrupted by one of the attorneys who came back to work. The network intruder was prosecuted, and the law office tightened its network security. This is a good example of why it is important to restrict access to all folders through setting the appropriate permissions.

Accessing and Sharing Resources in Windows 7

When a folder is marked to share over a network, other computers can access that folder in Windows 7 (or Windows Server 2008/Server 2008 R2) through the Network window that is accessed by the following general steps:

1. Click the Start menu and click Computer.
2. Click Network in the left pane.
3. If you see a message to turn on network discovery, select to turn it on.
4. Double-click the computer on which folders are shared (enter an account name and password, if requested).
5. Double-click the shared folder you wish to access.

When a client regularly accesses a shared folder, there is the option to map the folder, making it look just like another local drive at the client. Mapping is a software process that enables a client workstation to attach to the shared folder of another workstation or server and assign it a drive letter. The network folder that is attached is called a mapped drive in Windows-based operating systems. In UNIX/Linux, a mapped drive is called a mounted volume. In Activity 7-10 you learn how to map a drive in Windows 7.

Activity 7-10: Mapping a Drive in Windows 7

Time Required: 10 minutes
Objective: Map a shared drive in Windows 7.

Description: In this activity, you map the shared folder you created in Activity 7-9 as a mapped drive on your computer.

1. Click the **Start** menu, right-click **Computer**, and click **Map Network Drive**.
2. Click the **Browse** button (see Figure 7-20 and note that the default drive letter you see may vary from the one in the figure).
3. Click the small **arrow** in front of the computer (in this case your computer) sharing the folder.
4. Click the shared folder that you created in Activity 7-9 and click **OK**.
5. Set the drive letter to which you want to map the network drive or leave the default selection.

6. Make sure the box for **Reconnect at logon** is checked. This option tells the operating system to reconnect to the same drive each time you log on and are connected to the network.

7. Click **Finish**. Close the open window for the shared drive.

8. To disconnect (unmap) the shared drive, click **Start** and click **Computer**. Notice that your shared drive is listed under Network Location in the Computer window.

9. Right-click the drive.

10. Click **Disconnect**.

11. Close the Computer window.

The same steps apply when you map a drive in Windows Server 2008/Server 2008 R2.

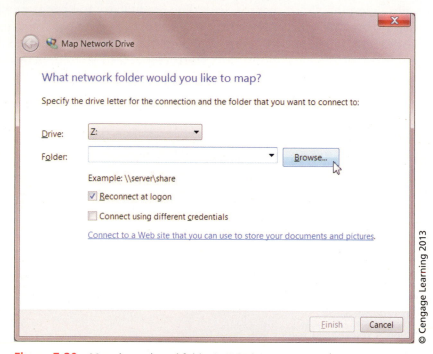

Figure 7-20   Mapping a shared folder in Windows 7

Configuring Sharing in UNIX/Linux

File and directory sharing in UNIX/Linux involve elements that include setting file permissions and using tools such as NFS and Samba. You learn about them in the next sections.

Configuring File Permissions   An important step for sharing UNIX/Linux files and directories is to set up file permissions. A directory or file can be assigned any combination of three permissions:

- Read
- Write
- Execute

The permission to read a file enables the user to display its contents and is signified by the letter *r*. Write permission entails the ability to modify, save, and delete a file, as signified by a *w*. The execute permission, indicated by an *x*, enables a user or group of users to run a program. For example, if you create a program to perform database queries of customer service information for a business and want a group of customer service representatives to be able to run that program, you need to give the group the *x* permission. Also, when a directory is flagged with an *x*, that means a user or group can access and list its contents. Therefore, although a directory can be given read and write permissions for a user or group, these permissions have no meaning unless the directory is given the execute permission for that user or group.

Executable programs can have a special set of permissions called Set User ID (SUID) and Set Group ID (SGID). When either of these is associated with an executable, the user or group member who runs it can do so with the same permissions as held by the owner. This provides more access permissions than when the file is executed simply by the user.

Permissions are granted in four categories:

- Ownership
- Group membership
- Other (or World)
- All (All is not used in every version of UNIX/Linux, but it is included in Fedora and Red Hat Enterprise Linux.)

The owner of the file or directory typically has all permissions, can assign permissions, and has the designation of *u*. Group members, designated by *g*, are users who may have a complete set of permissions, one permission, or a combination of two, such as read and execute. The designation "other," or *o* (sometimes referred to as World), consists of nonowners or nongroup members who represent generic users. Finally, the all or *a* designation represents the combination of *u* + *g* + *o*.

For example, the owner of a file has read, write, and execute permissions, by default. A particular group might have read and execute permissions, while others might have only read permissions, or perhaps no permissions. In another example, if there is a public file to which all permissions are needed for all users, then you would grant read, write, and execute permissions to all.

Permissions are set up by using the *chmod* command in UNIX/Linux. *chmod* has two different formats: symbolic and octal. The octal format is more complex than the symbolic format and is not discussed in this book.

In the symbolic format, you specify three parameters: (1) who has the permission, (2) the actions to be taken on the permission, and (3) the permission. For example, consider the command *chmod go -r-w-x* * that is used on all files (signified by the *) in a directory. The *g* signifies groups, and *o* signifies others. The - means to remove a permission, and *-r-w-x* signifies removing the read, write, and execute permissions (all three are removed; in some versions of UNIX/Linux, you might also enter *chmod go -rwx*). In this example, only the owner and members of the owner's group are left with read, write, and execute permissions on the files in this directory. In another example, to grant all permissions for all users to the data file in the /public directory, you would enter *chmod a+r+w+x /public/data* or *chmod a+rwx /public/data*. Activity 7-11 gives you experience assigning permissions in UNIX/Linux.

Activity 7-11: Assigning Permissions in UNIX/Linux

Time Required: 10 minutes
Objective: Assign permissions in UNIX/Linux.

Description: Permissions in UNIX/Linux are important for enabling access to files and directories. In this activity, you learn how to use the *chmod* command to assign permissions in Fedora and Red Hat Enterprise Linux. Log on using your personal account and not the root account.

1. Open a terminal window. (In the GNOME 3.x desktop, click **Activities**, click **Applications**, and click **Terminal**.)

2. Switch to your home or practice directory if you are not in this directory by default, such as by typing *cd /home/liveuser* or *cd /home/useraccountname* and pressing **Enter**.

3. Type **touch**, press the **spacebar**, and type your last name with the word "test" added onto your last name, such as *touch palmertest*. The *touch* command can be used to quickly create an empty file.

4. At the command prompt, type **chmod a+r+x** *filename* such as *chmod a+r+x palmertest* (see Figure 7-21) and press **Enter**.

5. Type *ls -l filename*, such as *ls -l palmertest*, and press **Enter** to view the contents of the directory. Notice the information in the left column that shows the assigned permissions for the file you created (see Figure 7-21).

6. Close the Terminal window.

Figure 7-21   Using the *chmod* command in Fedora Linux

Using NFS and Samba to Access Shared Directories

As you learned earlier, UNIX/Linux systems enable resource sharing by using NFS. NFS enables one computer running UNIX/Linux to mount a partition on another UNIX/Linux computer and then access file systems on the mounted partition as though they are local.

When a client mounts an NFS volume on a host, both the client and the host use **remote procedure calls (RPCs)**. An RPC enables services and software on one computer to use services and software on a different computer. To use NFS in Fedora or Red Hat Enterprise Linux, the following services must be enabled:

- *portmap*: Establishes and manages the remote connections through designated User Datagram Protocol (UDP) ports

- *rpc.mountd*: Handles the RPC request to mount a partition

- *rpc.nfsd*: Enables the Linux kernel to manage specific requests from a client

The security that controls which clients can use NFS on a hosting computer is handled through entries in two files. The /etc/hosts.allow file contains the clients that are allowed to use NFS, and the /etc/hosts.deny file contains computers that are not allowed to use NFS. Besides configuring the /etc/hosts.allow and /etc/hosts.deny files, the resources mounted through NFS are also protected by the permissions on the directories and files. You can use the *mount* command to mount an NFS volume. To learn more about the *mount* command, in a terminal window enter *man mount* and press Enter. You will likely need root privileges to mount a drive.

UNIX/Linux computers can access shared Windows-based drives through the use of Samba. Samba is configured in the /etc/samba/smb.conf file. You can access a shared drive from the GNOME 3.x desktop.

Configuring Sharing in Mac OS X

In Activity 7-5 you learned how to enable the file sharing service in Mac OS X Snow Leopard and Lion. After the file sharing service is enabled, you can select specific folders and files to share. For example, to share a folder you can display that folder's Info window using the *Get info* option and select to share the folder. Also through the Info window, you can set permissions for a folder. The permissions that can be set are described in Table 7-5. When permissions are established they are set to apply to three types of users (keep in mind that Mac OS X is built on UNIX and so the permissions are similar):

- *Owner*: The user account that has complete access to the folder or file, including the ability to modify it, delete it, and configure permissions for that folder or file.
- *Group*: A specific group of user accounts created to help manage permissions.
- *Everyone*: All other user accounts that can access the computer, including Guest.

Table 7-5   Mac OS X folder and file permissions

Permission	Description	Applies to
Read only	Can open folders and files to view their contents, but cannot make changes or save files	Folders and files
Write only (Drop Box)	Can save files, but cannot open them to view their contents	Folders and files
Read & write	Can open, modify, save, delete, and view the contents of files	Folders and files
No access	Cannot open files to view their contents and cannot save files	Folders and files

© Cengage Learning 2013

Activity 7-12 enables you to create a new folder, share the folder, and establish permissions for the folder's contents.

Activity 7-12: Folder Sharing and Permissions in Mac OS X

Time Required: 10 minutes
Objective: Share a folder and set the folder's permissions.

Description: Mac OS X Snow Leopard and Lion enable you to manage folder and file sharing through the Info window for a folder or file. In this activity, you create a new folder within your home directory, share the folder, and configure folder permissions. You do not need Administrator privileges, but you can use any standard or Administrator account.

1. Click the **Finder** icon in the Dock to open a window showing the contents of your home directory.
2. Click **File** in the menu bar and click **New Folder** in the File menu.
3. Type in the name of the new folder to include your last name and the word "test," such as *Palmertest*. Press **return**. You should now see the new folder in your home directory window.
4. Ensure that the new folder is highlighted, click the **File** menu in the menu bar at the top of the desktop, and click **Get Info**.
5. If necessary, click the **right-pointing arrow** next to **General** in the Info window to display the general information for the folder.
6. In the General section of the Info window, click the box for **Shared folder** (see Figure 7-22).
7. If necessary, click the **right-pointing arrow** next to **Sharing & Permissions** to view the information under this category.
8. Notice the permissions granted to your account, to groups on your computer, and to everyone. Record the permissions listed on your computer.

9. In the table showing assigned permissions in the Sharing & Permission section of the Info window, click the **up/down arrows** under the Privilege column for the permissions (Read only) assigned to **everyone**. Record the permissions that can be granted.

10. Select **Read & Write** to grant this permission to everyone.

11. Close the Info window and then close the window for your home directory.

Figure 7-22   Clicking the Shared folder box in the Info window in Mac OS X

Sharing Printers

Printer sharing can be an important asset on a peer-to-peer or server-based network. Network printing is often one of the most used resources, because the word processing, database, computer graphics, and other work performed by users often end with a printed document as the final product. Printed materials are used for reports, billing, important meetings, presentations, and information analysis, and in a huge realm of other activities. Printing information from the Internet can also be important for some organizations. In an investment company, Internet printing may be used regularly to print reports about a particular investment. At a car dealership, it may be used to research a particular vehicle by its VIN number and print a listing of known problems with that vehicle.

There are several common ways to implement network printing:

- By using a network-ready printer that has a WNIC or NIC

- By using a dedicated print server

- By sharing a printer through an operating system connected to the network

One of the simplest and most modern ways to enable network printing is by purchasing a printer that has a WNIC or NIC so you can connect it directly to the network and configure the printer to be shared. The printer in this case has print server functionality built in. A **print server** is a device with software that manages shared printing on a network, such as (1) receiving print jobs, (2) storing the print jobs until it is their turn to print, (3) queuing the print jobs, and (4) sending print jobs to the right printer. The advantage of this approach is that you do not have to purchase any extra devices, such as a specialized print server. Another advantage is that because the printer is not shared from a computer, you do not have to depend on a particular computer to be turned on before using the printer.

Printers that connect to a network require an IP address. The IP address can be configured through using an installation DVD/CD-ROM, through configuring and managing the printer through a computer operating system, by using a configuration menu on the printer, or by allowing automatic DHCP IP address assignment. If possible, it works best to assign a permanent IP address rather than a leased IP address through DHCP, because when an IP lease is expired and a new IP address is automatically assigned, users often have to reconfigure their computers to use the printer. It may take multiple tries in using the printer for users to finally determine they have to make a printer configuration change. This tip also applies to dedicated print servers.

A dedicated print server is a boxlike device that has a NIC (or WNIC) and one, two, or more ports for connecting printers, such as USB ports, as shown in Figure 7-23. It also contains

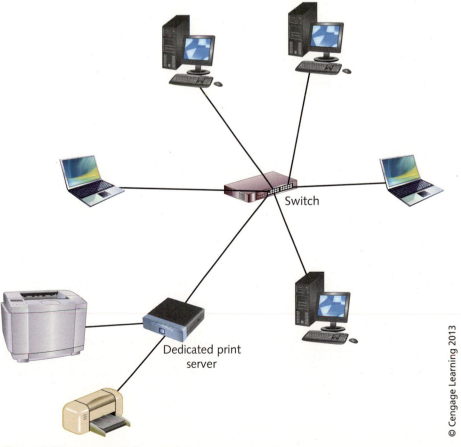

Figure 7-23 Using a dedicated print server

© Cengage Learning 2013

software to manage printing and ensure that a print job goes to the right printer. The advantage of this approach is that you can network one or more printers that do not have network interfaces, thus capitalizing on your prior investment in printers. Also, it provides a means to connect multiple printers using one device. The disadvantage is that if the dedicated print server malfunctions, all of the printers connected to it are out of service. Also, there is the time and expense of purchasing the dedicated print server and configuring its print services.

A workstation or server can also function as a print server. In this case, you connect one or more printers to the computer and configure the operating system to share the printer with others. This approach can be appealing if you already have printers without NICs or WNICs and they are working well for your needs. Also, there is no extra expense, as in purchasing a dedicated print server. You just use a printer and a computer that you have already purchased, which can be important for a home or small office budget. The disadvantage is that the computer with the printer must be left on, or no one can use the printer. Some offices handle this by placing a sign on the computer to remind everyone not to turn it off.

Configuring Shared Printing in Windows Systems

When you connect a printer to a Windows system, you can install it by using the installation DVD/CD-ROM that comes with the printer or by letting the Plug and Play capability of Windows 7 or Windows Server 2008/Server 2008 R2 automatically detect and configure the printer. Alternatively, you can manually install a printer by using the Add Printer Wizard. If you need to use the Add Printer Wizard, it is started through the following general steps:

1. In Windows 7 and Server 2008 R2, click Start, click Control Panel, set View by to Category, and click Hardware and Sound. In Windows Server 2008, click Start, click Control Panel, select to use the Classic View, and double-click Printers.

2. Click Add a printer.

3. Use the Add Printer Wizard to guide you through the remaining steps. Note that you can use the Add Printer Wizard to set up a local or network printer. A local printer is one attached to your computer and that you can share through the network. A network printer is a printer already shared through the network that you can configure to use from your computer. When you are configuring a local printer using the Add Printer Wizard, you have the ability to specify that the printer is to be shared.

After a printer is installed, you can go back and configure the printer for sharing, if you did not do this during the installation. Windows 7 and Server 2008/Server 2008 R2 offer the Print Management tool for configuring and managing printers. You can use the Print Management tool to configure a printer's properties for sharing and security. Also, before any printer is shared over a network, printer sharing must be turned on in Windows as is described earlier in this chapter in the section "File and Printer Sharing for Microsoft Networks."

 If the Print Management utility is not installed or available in a Windows operating system, you can also configure sharing from the Start menu Devices and Printers option in Windows 7 and Server 2008 R2 or the Printers option in the Windows Server 2008 Control Panel. Once you open the display of printers to configure, right-click a printer and click **Printer properties** or **Properties**.

When you configure a shared printer, make sure that you configure share permissions for the shared printer. Use the Print Management utility as presented in Activity 7-13. The Print Management utility is installed by default in Windows 7 (except in Windows 7 Home and Home Premium). In Windows Server 2008, the Print Management utility is installed when you use Server Manager (the main server management tool) to install the Print Services role. In Windows Server 2008 R2 it is installed through Server Manager when installing the Print and Document Services role.

For Windows 7 and Server 2008/Server 2008 R2, the following share permissions are checked for allow or deny:

- *Print*: Can send print jobs and manage your own jobs
- *Manage documents*: Can send print jobs and manage yours or those sent by any other user
- *Manage this printer* (in Windows 7/Server 2008 R2) or *Manage printers* (in Windows 2008): Can access the share, change share permissions, turn off sharing, configure printer properties, and delete the share
- *Special Permissions*: Shows whether special permissions are configured, and if they are allowed or denied

If you use the Add Printer Wizard to configure and share a printer, make sure you later examine that printer's properties to ensure that sharing permissions are configured appropriately in Windows operating systems.

After a printer is shared through a Windows workstation or server operating system, a Windows 7 client user on the same network can connect to the printer through the following general steps:

1. Click Start and click Computer.
2. Click Network in the left pane of the Computer window.
3. Double-click a computer or server that offers a shared printer.
4. Right-click the shared printer and click Connect.

Activity 7-13: Configuring a Shared Printer in Windows 7

Time Required: 10 minutes

Objective: Use the Windows 7 Print Management utility to configure sharing in a local or network printer that is already installed.

Description: A local or network printer that is already installed can be configured at any time. In Windows operating systems, a local printer is one that is connected to a computer through a cable, such as a USB cable. A network printer is a printer that is connected to the network either through a wireless connection, through a print server, or through a network cable to a switch. In this activity, you configure sharing for a local or network printer that is already set up in Windows 7. The printer should already be installed, but not shared. You need Administrator privileges to complete this activity.

If you are using Windows 7 Home or Home Premium or Windows Server 2008/Server 2008 R2 and do not have the Print Management utility as an Administrative Tools option, you can still perform this activity. In Windows 7 or Windows Server 2008 R2, click **Start**, click **Devices and Printers**, right-click a printer in the Devices and Printers window, and click **Printer properties**. Then continue from Step 6 in Activity 7-13. In Windows Server 2008, click **Start**, click **Control Panel**, double-click **Printers**, right-click a printer, click **Properties**, and continue from Step 6.

1. Click **Start** and click **Control Panel**. Set **View by** to **Large icons** or **Small icons**.
2. Click **Administrative Tools** in Control Panel.
3. In the Administrative Tools window, double-click **Print Management**.
4. In the middle pane, double-click **All Printers**.

5. Right-click a printer in the middle pane and click **Properties**.

6. Click the **Sharing** tab in the Properties dialog box.

7. On the Sharing tab, click the box for **Share this printer** and ensure that the box for **Render print jobs on client computers** is checked (see Figure 7-24). Notice that when a client shares this printer, the printer driver is also shared with the Windows client computer.

8. Click the **Security** tab in the Properties dialog box.

9. On the Security tab, click **Everyone** under *Group or user names* and notice that the permission for the Everyone group is (Allow) Print.

10. Click your account name and notice the permissions checked for your account. Record the permissions.

11. Click **OK** in the Properties dialog box. Close the Print Management window and close any other open windows.

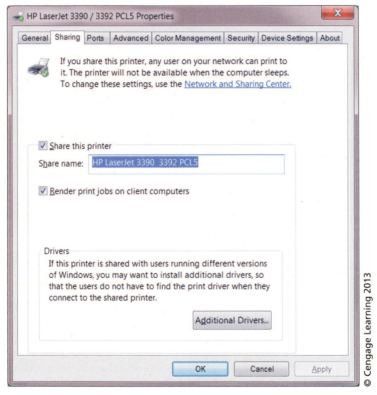

Figure 7-24   Configuring a shared printer in Windows 7

Configuring Shared Printing in UNIX/Linux

UNIX/Linux printing in a networked environment is essentially the process of logging in to a UNIX/Linux server and printing to one of its printers. Typically, when a UNIX/Linux server is accessed through network connectivity, it is set up to use the Berkeley Software Distribution (BSD) or the System V Release 4 (SVR4) spooling (print handling) systems. BSD uses three components for printing: the *lpr* print program, the *lpd* daemon, and the file /etc/printcap to specify printer properties. The file /etc/printcap is a text file that can be modified via a text editor. In SVR4, the printer system consists of the *lp* print program and the *lpsched* daemon. SVR4 printer properties are stored in the file /etc/printcap, which is modified by using the *lpadmin* utility.

If your version of UNIX/Linux can use either BSD or SVR4 printing services, note that administrators often consider BSD printing services to be more adaptable for network clients.

In Linux, you can also install a printer, configure sharing, and set up a print queue by using the GNOME 3.x printer configuration tool through the following general steps:

1. Click Activities, click Applications, and click Printing.

2. If a printer is not yet installed, use the Add button and follow the guided steps to install a printer and to adjust the firewall to allow network printing.

3. Select a printer and click the Printer menu option in the Printing window.

4. Place a check mark in the boxes for Enabled and Shared.

5. Click the Server menu and click Settings.

6. Configure the printer management options such as *Publish shared printers connected to this system* so that users can view shared printers over the network and *Allow users to cancel any job (not just their own)* if you want users to have this capability. Click OK.

7. Close the Printing window.

Configuring Shared Printing in Mac OS X Snow Leopard and Lion

The Mac OS X Print & Fax utility (Snow Leopard) or Print & Scan utility (Lion) enable you to manage printing (and fax or scanning) functions from one place. Using this utility you can add a local or network-connected printer, manage print jobs, and configure printer sharing. The Print & Fax or Print & Scan tools are accessed through System Preferences. Users who have Administrator account types can manage printers and print queues. Groups and Standard account type users can print and manage their own print jobs or can be designated for no access to a printer. Activity 7-14 shows you how to configure printing in Mac OS X Snow Leopard and Lion.

Activity 7-14: Sharing Printers in Mac OS X

Time Required: 10 minutes

Objective: Learn how to manage shared printing in Mac OS X Snow Leopard and Lion.

Description: This activity enables you to share a printer and configure printer sharing in Mac OS X. You also learn from where to add a local or network printer. Your computer should already have a local or network printer added, and you will need an account that has Administrator privileges.

1. Click **System Preferences** in the Dock or click the **Apple** icon in the menu bar and click **System Preferences**.

2. Click **Print & Fax** (Snow Leopard) or **Print & Scan** (Lion) under Hardware in the System Preferences window.

3. Notice that to add a local or network printer, you can click the **+ *plus sign*** under the Printers list.

4. If necessary, click to open the **lock icon** in the bottom left corner of the window so you can make changes.

5. In the Printers list, select the printer you want to configure.

6. If it is not already checked in the Print & Fax or Print & Scan window, click the check box for **Share this printer on the network** (see Figure 7-25).

7. In the Print & Fax or Print & Scan window, click the **Sharing Preferences** button.

8. Make sure that the check box for **Printer Sharing** is already checked in the Sharing pane and that **Printer Sharing** is highlighted.

9. If necessary, click the printer you want to configure in the Printers list.

10. What users or groups are listed under Users, and what is their access?

11. Click the **up/down arrows** for the access granted for a user or group listed under Users and record the options, but do not change the original settings.

12. Click **System Preferences** in the menu bar and click **Quit System Preferences**.

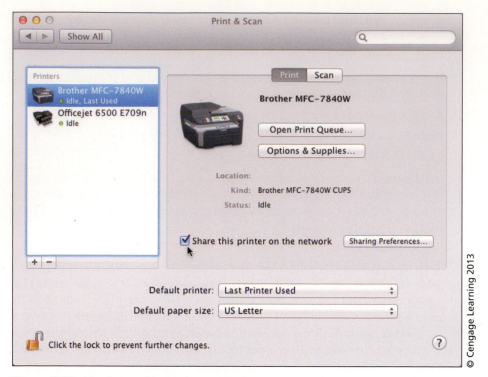

Figure 7-25 Sharing a printer in Mac OS X Lion

Shared Internet Access

In Chapter 1, you learned that Internet Access can be shared from a computer, and Activities 1-3 and 1-4 enabled you to configure shared Internet access in Windows and Mac OS X operating systems. Consider reviewing these activities as a review of Internet resource sharing.

As additional tips for Windows Internet sharing through the Internet Connection Sharing (ICS) capability in Windows, here are a few points to consider as offered by Microsoft:

- The computer configured for ICS needs an Internet connection, such as through a cable modem, DSL adapter, or satellite dish modem (note that a dial-up connection will likely be too slow to be effective).

- Ensure that file and printer sharing is enabled on the computer with ICS (check your Windows Firewall security).

- Plan to leave the computer with ICS on all of the time so that others always have access to the Internet.

- When you share a printer using a workstation or server, consider connecting that printer to the computer configured for ICS—in this way you have to leave only one computer on at all times.

- Do not configure ICS on a network that has servers running DHCP or DNS to avoid confusion about IP addressing.

Cloud Computing

Many organizations and vendors now enable widespread resource sharing through the use of cloud computing. **Cloud computing** involves providing a host of scalable Web-based applications and services over the Internet or a private network that are used by clients through Web browsers. The servers and resources available through the Web browser are depicted as available in a cloud, because there are many resources, but they appear as available from one unified resource (see Figure 7-26). You might compare this to using telephone services. There are many telephone companies and telephone technologies (such as land lines, satellite, and cell phones), but to the user they appear as one giant resource. In cloud computing, the user experiences programs and data as if they are installed on the user's computer, but in truth a small portion is on the local computer and all other resources are on servers and other devices in the cloud. Microsoft describes three types of cloud models:

- *Private cloud*: Computing resources are kept within an organization and used exclusively by that organization. For example, office applications like word processors, spreadsheets, databases, slide creation software, data storage devices, and network resources are all in a cloud that is transparent to the user. The resources are managed by the organization on the organization's premises. From the user's standpoint, the user simply runs the applications and stores data through Web-based software and the use of a Web browser. This model is considered most expensive, because the organization must still make the investment in equipment, a computer and network center, personnel, electricity, a building or buildings, and other resources.

- *Hosted private cloud*: Resources are made available through a third-party outsourcer, but are accessible only to users within a specific organization. In this model, specific resources are leased or owned by the organization, but are managed and often located at the site of the third-party outsourcer. This model is considered less expensive than the private cloud because the third-party outsourcer is believed to be able to consolidate expenses so that buildings, power costs, and personnel costs are consolidated among several customers.

- *Public cloud*: A variety of resources are available to any organization through a third party, and each organization subscribes only to specific resources, which may be shared by other organizations. This model is considered the least expensive because besides sharing personnel, building, and power costs, there is extensive sharing of equipment, because the same equipment and network devices can be shared among several customers.

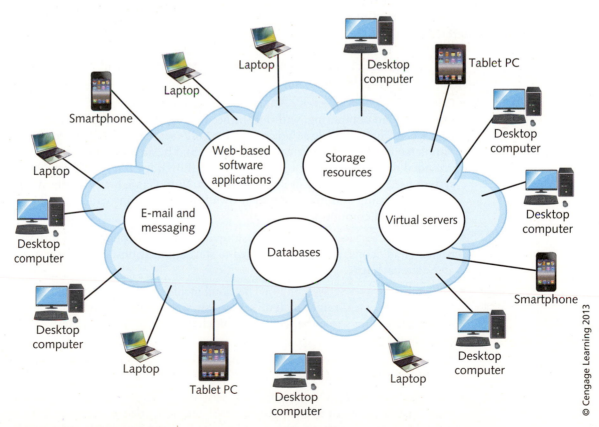

Figure 7-26 Cloud computing

© Cengage Learning 2013

Vendors including Apple, Microsoft, and Google offer public cloud services to organizational customers and to individual users. For example, individual users can use the Apple iCloud service to store and access personal resources from Macintosh computers, iPads, iPods, and iPhones including pictures, music, ebooks (iBooks), software, and documents. Users do not need to know about the network devices, servers, and other details of how the data is stored and transferred; they only need to know how to use their particular devices.

Google offers business applications through a public cloud in a service called Google Apps for Business. For a small business, Google offers email services, calendar applications, Google Docs for word processing, spreadsheets, slide presentations, and forms management. Google also offers storage in the cloud on which to save documents. In addition, Google offers Web site creation for business projects and internal business use. All of these cloud applications can be scaled up for medium and large businesses.

Microsoft offers Office 365 and Azure for cloud computing. Office 365 works through a public cloud in which users at a business use regular Microsoft Office software, such as Word, but through Microsoft cloud services. Office 365 also enables integration of services with mobile devices, such as cell phones and smartphones. It also provides for meetings through the cloud services. The basic idea is that businesses save on computer support expenses while workers can access their applications and data from any location that has Wi-Fi or 3G/4G communications. Storage of data and applications is on Microsoft's servers, and access for users is transparent through a cloud in a Web-like atmosphere.

Microsoft Azure is a set of cloud services that software developers in an organization can use to build customized business applications and databases that utilize Microsoft's cloud applications and storage in combination with those available within the organization. For example, a business that sells machine replacement parts to manufacturing facilities might use Azure to create a specialized inventory application. The inventory application might use a combination of Microsoft Office 365 Word and Excel while also using specialized Web-based software for tracking inventory and shipping. Some of the resulting data might be stored on in-house database servers, and some might be stored in Microsoft datacenters. To the user, the applications and location of the data make no difference, because they simply experience Web-based interfaces.

Part of understanding cloud computing is understanding the concepts and acronyms now associated with the cloud computing concept. Developing cloud computing concepts that are helpful to know are the following:

- **Communication as a Service (CaaS)**: Offering a unified range of communications services through cloud computing, without the need for users to purchase their own equipment and manage it. This can include Voice over IP (VoIP) services, VPN services (see the next section, "Implementing a Virtual Private Network"), and business telephone services as might be provided through a private branch exchange (PBX). A PBX is a privately owned telephone system used by a business or an organization. With CaaS, for example, a business can forgo purchasing and managing their own PBX and can instead subscribe to such a service through cloud computing.

- **Desktop as a Service (DaaS)**: The desktop is provided through the cloud, such as desktop background, icons, or menus provided to start applications, e-mail access, messaging access, and data backup.

- **Infrastructure as a Service (IaaS)**: The cloud includes devices that make up the "infrastructure." These devices might include servers, switches, routers, storage area networks with data storage arrays (see the section in this chapter, "Storage Area Networks"), firewalls, and other equipment.

- **Monitoring as a Service (MaaS)**: Monitoring software applications to ensure they are live and fully performing as needed.

- **Network as a Service (NaaS)**: Offering network services to the cloud and within the cloud, including the network infrastructure (IaaS) and network communications services (CaaS). Network communications services may include wired and wireless options, such as 4G.

- **Platform as a Service (PaaS)**: Buying, developing, testing, deploying, and managing software applications so the end user or organization does not have to worry about these tasks other than to use the software. Typically application features are tailored, to some extent, to the end-user's requirements, such as developing a specialized inventory system for a company and running that system through cloud computing.

- **Software as a Service (SaaS)**: Can overlap with PaaS and IaaS in that the cloud provider develops and provisions the software for the user, including providing servers on which the software runs. Further, the software is developed without giving the end user much say in the capabilities of the software. Also, SaaS software typically runs on demand through the cloud provider's servers rather than on the end user's workstation, such as running through remote desktop services or via a Web browser. Also, the cloud provider typically owns the software licenses and charges a subscriber fee.

- **Anything or Everything as a Service (XaaS)**: Includes a combination or all of the cloud services options, including CaaS, DaaS, IaaS, MaaS, NaaS, PaaS, and Saas.

Implementing a Virtual Private Network

For organizations, one problem with sharing resources is how to make them securely available to users who travel or work from home. Another problem is secure communications for resource sharing between a main business location and its branch offices, which is common for banks. One solution is the use of a virtual private network. A **virtual private network (VPN)** is a private network that is like a private tunnel through a larger network—such as the Internet, an enterprise network, or both—that is restricted to designated member clients only. Its purpose is to enable very secure networking for people connected through the Internet, such as an employee in New York accessing a company network in Oregon through the Internet. For the employee who is in New York on a business trip, the network access can be nearly the same as being at her desk in Oregon. From the standpoint of the company, the employee's access is secured through the VPN, which also helps to keep the company network safe from intrusions.

A VPN can use an Internet connection or an internal network connection to connect with a VPN server as shown in Figure 7-27. In Figure 7-27, users connect through DSL remote connections using secure VPN tunnels, which are indicated by the dotted lines. Users on the internal network also can connect through VPN tunnels, also indicated by the dotted lines. In this example, the users connect through VPN tunnels to a Windows Server 2008 R2 server running a combination of VPN and Web server services.

A VPN uses LAN protocols as well as tunneling protocols to encapsulate the data as it is sent across a public network such as the Internet. One of the benefits of using a VPN for remote access is that users can connect to a local ISP and connect through the ISP to a remote network or server. A VPN is used to ensure that any data sent across a public network, such as the Internet, is secure. Security is achieved by having the VPN create an encrypted tunnel between the client and a remote access server that is configured for VPN communications. A **remote access server (RAS)** is a specialized server that is located on a network for the purpose of enabling remote users to access the resources, such as servers and databases, of the main network. To create this tunnel, the client first connects to the Internet by establishing a connection using a remote access protocol. Once connected to the Internet, the client establishes a second connection with the VPN server. The client and the VPN server agree on how the data will be encapsulated and encrypted across the virtual tunnel. Information can then be sent securely between the two computers, because outsiders can't see into the tunnel.

The workhorse of a VPN connection is the remote access protocol, because it carries the network packets over a wide area network (WAN) link. One function of the remote access protocol is to encapsulate a packet, usually TCP/IP, so that it can be transmitted from a point at one end of a WAN to another point—such as between two computers with DSL adapters connected by a telecommunications line. TCP/IP is the commonly used transport protocol, and so it is most typically encapsulated in a remote access protocol for transport over a WAN.

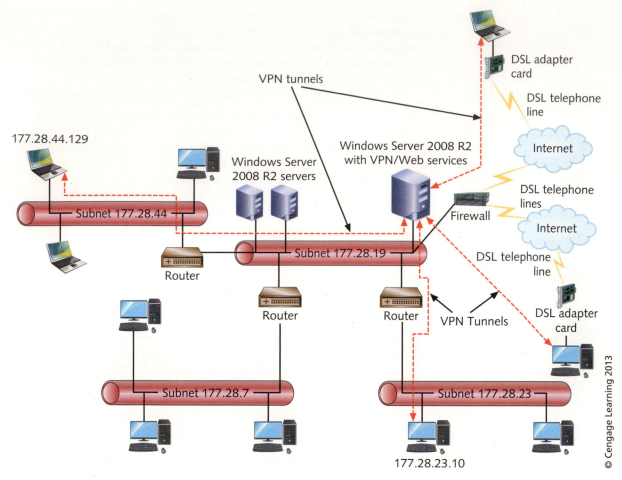

Figure 7-27 A VPN network

The most commonly used remote access protocol for security over a VPN is IP security (IPsec). IPsec is a set of IP-based secure communications and encryption standards created by the IETF to provide secure network communications. IPsec secures IP communications at the Network layer of the OSI model and is more fully explained in Chapter 11, "Securing Your Network." On some VPN networks, Layer Two Tunneling Protocol is used running inside IPsec for extra security. **Layer Two Tunneling Protocol (L2TP)** uses authentication techniques and can create special tunnels over a public network, such as the Internet. L2TP uses an additional network communications standard, called Layer Two Forwarding, that enables forwarding on the basis of MAC addressing (which is the physical address of the network interface) in addition to IP addressing.

A Windows Server 2008/Server 2008 R2 server can be configured as a RAS server offering a VPN. This is accomplished by installing the Network Policy and Access Services role through the Server Manager tool in Windows Server 2008/Server 2008 R2.

 Other remote access protocols are used on VPNs besides IPsec and L2TP, but according to the Virtual Private Network Consortium of vendors—such as Cisco, D-Link, Juniper Networks, NETGEAR—IPsec and L2TP are most typical.

Storage Area Networks

Some server-based networks centralize storage on a network in arrays of disk drives that are shared by users through network servers. This arrangement is called a **storage area network (SAN)**, which is a grouping of storage devices that forms a subnet. The storage devices are available to any server on the main network, and it appears to the users as though the storage is attached to the server they are accessing.

Typically, the subnet containing the storage devices uses Fibre Channel or iSCSI technology. **Fibre Channel** is a subnetwork technology originally developed for mainframes but now is used primarily for SANs and enables gigabit high-speed data transfers. **Internet Small Computer System Interface (iSCSI)** is another high-speed technology used in SANs that employs TCP/IP communications and **Small Computer System Interface (SCSI)** disk drives. SCSI is a 32- or 64-bit computer adapter that transports data between one or more attached devices, such as hard disks, and the computer or a SAN subsystem.

In terms of the physical device, a SAN usually looks like a large box or chassis enclosure containing disk drives, disk controllers, and an interconnection device, such as a switch, that connects to one or more servers (see Figure 7-28). The connection to a server is usually through an adapter card in the server that is tailored for the type of subnetwork technology, Fibre Channel or iSCSI.

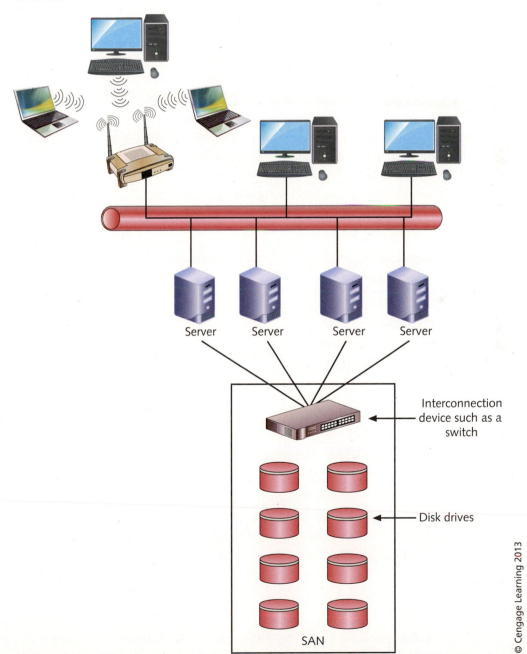

Figure 7-28   A basic SAN

The arrays of disks on a SAN are managed through SAN software on SAN connection devices and through an operating system. For example, Windows Server 2008/Server 2008 R2 both manage SANs through Microsoft Storage Manager for SANs. Individual drives in a SAN that uses SCSI disk drives can be identified and managed in Storage Manager for SANs through a logical unit number (LUN). Windows Server 2008/Server 2008 R2 also offers **Virtual Disk Service (VDS)** that enables management of disk volumes in multiple SANs through one interface on a single server—as a way to centralize and simplify SAN management.

Disks in a SAN can be configured in different combinations and used for different purposes, such as for:

- Main storage provided to network servers and workstations
- Data retrieval
- Data backup and archiving
- Restoring backed up or archived data
- Data duplication for fault tolerance, so that if a disk drive fails the data is still retained
- Disaster recovery, so that if all disks at one location are destroyed, the data is still available at another location
- Migrating data from one system to another system
- Storing data in a cloud, such as Apple's iCloud service, so that the data can be accessed through a network, Internet, or 3G/4G connection

In terms of planning a new SAN architecture for your network, it is important to know that Microsoft seems particularly interested in providing capabilities for iSCSI. This is because Microsoft recognizes the following advantages of iSCSI compared to Fibre Channel:

- More options for configuring topologies
- Less cost
- Fewer distance limitations
- Compatible with existing IPv4 and IPv6 networks over Ethernet
- Enables dynamic expansion
- Easier to configure
- More scalable
- More storage capacity
- Supports IPSec for security
- Easier to expand using equipment from different vendors

Putting It All Together: Designing a Peer-to-Peer Office Network to Share Resources

Peer-to-peer networking can be a straightforward and easy-to-maintain option for a small office network. If you are contemplating a peer-to-peer network, the following are some guidelines:

- Setup and maintenance is easier if you use operating systems from the same family, such as all Microsoft-based, Mac OS X, or all UNIX/Linux systems.
- If you are using Windows 7, keep the number of computers to 20 or less to assure faster response for shared resources. If you need to employ over 20 computers, consider implementing a server and server operating system, such as Windows Server 2008/Server 2008 R2.
- Use a higher version of Windows 7, such as Windows Home Premium, Professional, or Ultimate, for more versatility and security than Windows 7 Home for a peer-to-peer (or any other) Windows-based network.

- If you are purchasing one or more new printers, buy them network ready with NICs or WNICs built in. If you are using one or more older printers that are not network ready, you can connect these printers to a computer and still share them via Windows 7 or Mac OS X, for example.

- Configure share permissions (in Windows and Mac OS X operating systems) and file permissions (in all operating systems) on folders or directories before you share them over a network.

- In Windows 7, if your folder sharing is relatively simple, such as in a home or small office, you can use a homegroup for sharing files and other resources. For more complex sharing and security needs, consider using one or more Windows workgroups, such as in a small office with about 10 to 20 users.

Consider an auto dealership that wants to network the sales and business offices, which consist of Windows 7 Professional workstations and a wireless network. There are eight salespersons, a sales manager, a loan processor, and two business office workers who process the paperwork and vehicle titles. No one at the auto dealership has much technical experience with computers, but each one has a computer on her or his desk. This is a situation in which a peer-to-peer network can be of benefit.

The auto dealership's sales manager maintains a listing of new and used cars by stock number, which the salespersons access each time they work with a customer. The sales manager can set up a shared drive and use a workgroup to make this information available to all users on the network. Files that relate to finances might be secured so that only the sales manager, loan processor, and business office personnel can access them. Other files should also be secured through permissions.

There is one shared printer for the sales staff, which they use to print summary information from the sales manager's list. That printer is connected and shared through one of the salesperson's computers. The computer also has a DSL connection that is shared with all office staff using ICS. In addition, each salesperson maintains a record of customer contacts and shares this information with the other sales staff via a shared folder on her or his computer.

One member of the business office staff tracks the completed and open paper work and shares this information on the network via a folder. That information is also available to the loan processor. Further, the loan processor maintains records of closed loans that are periodically reviewed by the sales manager through a shared folder. The business office staff and loan processor share a printer that is connected to one of the business office computers, which is left on during work hours.

In this small office design:

- There are no more than 12 computers.

- No single shared folder experiences heavy access from more than two or three users at a time.

- The dealership saves money by sharing printers and an Internet connection.

- The Internet connection and shared printer in the sales area are on the same computer, which has a small sign to ensure it is left on during business hours.

- Security is set on the shared folders and printers to ensure that only authorized employees access them.

- The expense of the network is held to a minimum, plus the network is simple and easy to maintain by relatively inexperienced users.

Chapter Summary

- Peer-to-peer networking can be effective for home and small office networks, in part because it is relatively easy to set up and inexpensive to maintain.

- A peer-to-peer network becomes less advantageous as networks grow in size and require more centralized management of network resources.

- Important elements for configuring Windows-based peer-to-peer networks include ensuring that Client for Microsoft Networks is installed, using TCP/IP, enabling File and Printer Sharing for Microsoft Networks, and configuring a homegroup or workgroup.

- Implementing TCP/IP, NFS, and Samba is important for sharing and accessing shared files in UNIX/Linux. NFS enables UNIX/Linux computers to share directories and files with one another. Samba enables a UNIX/Linux system to access shared folders and files on Windows-based systems.

- Mac OS X supports peer-to-peer networks through AirPort devices and enables sharing resources through the Sharing utility. After a resource is enabled for sharing, such as a folder, you can specify which folders to share with which user accounts.

- Plan to configure user accounts in Windows 7, Windows Server 2008/Server 2008 R2, Mac OS X, and UNIX/Linux to have a way to manage who can own and who can access specific shared resources.

- Before you release folders, directories, and files for sharing, configure share permissions in Windows and Mac OS X systems and configure file permissions in Windows, Mac OS X, and UNIX/Linux systems.

- In Windows you can access shared folders by mapping a drive. In UNIX/Linux, shared directories are accessed in NFS by mounting a drive.

- Three basic ways to share a printer on the network include: (1) purchasing a printer with a built-in NIC or WNIC, (2) using a dedicated print server, and (3) connecting a printer to a computer and sharing it through the computer's operating system. Windows, Mac OS X, and UNIX/Linux all offer ways to set up and manage shared printing.

- Implementing Internet Connection Sharing (ICS) in Windows 7 can be an effective way to share an Internet connection on a peer-to-peer network. Mac OS X also offers the ability to share an Internet connection.

- Cloud computing enables sharing of resources and applications through Web-based tools and techniques that are transparent to the user.

- A virtual private network (VPN) enables remote users to access shared resources through secure "tunnels" on public and private networks, such as the Internet.

- A storage area network (SAN) can be used to group storage devices on a subnet for sharing storage among multiple servers without the need to have individual disk drives connected to individual servers.

Key Terms

AirPort   A wireless networking approach used on Apple computers that includes devices, such as WNICs and routers that operate using 802.11b/g/n networking.

Anything or Everything as a Service (XaaS)   Including a combination or all of the cloud services options: CaaS, DaaS, IaaS, MaaS, NaaS, PaaS, and Saas.

authentication   The process of verifying that a user is authorized to access a particular computer, server, network, or network resource.

automatic private IP addressing (APIPA)   A process in which a computer assigns its own IP address from the range 169.254.0.1 to 169.254.255.254 and assigns the subnet mask 255.255.0.0, when no DHCP server is present on the network.

cloud computing   A computing technology that provides a host of scalable Web-based applications and services over the Internet or a private network that are used by clients through Web browsers.

Communication as a Service (CaaS)   Offering unified communications services through cloud computing. This might include communications services such as VPN, VoIP, or private telephone services.

Desktop as a Service (DaaS)   Providing the desktop through cloud computing, such as desktop background, icons, or menus provided to start applications, e-mail access, messaging access, and data backup.

domain   A logical grouping of networking resources that centralizes management of elements such as user accounts, computers, printers, and network devices.

Fibre Channel   A subnetwork technology used primarily for SANs that enables gigabit high-speed data transfers. *See* **storage area network (SAN)**.

group identification number (GID)   A unique number assigned to a UNIX/Linux group that distinguishes that group from all other groups on the same system.

home directory   In UNIX/Linux, a user work area in which the user stores data on a server or other computer and typically has control over whether to enable other users to access her or his data.

homegroup   In Windows 7, a concept intended for home computer networks that enables sharing resources such as files, printers, music, and photos, using Windows 7 libraries.

Infrastructure as a Service (IaaS)   Providing the service equipment in cloud computing, which might include servers, routers, switches, storage arrays or SANs, and firewalls.

Internet Small Computer System Interface (iSCSI)   A high-speed technology used in SANs that employs TCP/IP communications and SCSI disk drives. *See* **storage area network (SAN)**.

Layer Two Tunneling Protocol (L2TP)   A protocol used in VPNs that employs authentication techniques and can create special tunnels over a public network, such as the Internet. L2TP uses an additional network communications standard, called Layer Two Forwarding, that enables forwarding on the basis of MAC addressing (which is the physical address of the network interface) in addition to IP addressing. *See* **virtual private network (VPN)**.

library   A Windows 7 element that enables a single view of multiple shared folders through a homegroup. *See* **homegroup**.

mapping   In Windows-based systems, the process of attaching to a shared resource, such as a shared folder, and using it as though it is a local resource. For example, when a workstation operating system maps to the drive of another workstation, it can assign a drive letter to that drive and access it as though it is a local drive instead of a remote one.

Monitoring as a Service (MaaS)   The cloud computing process of monitoring software applications to ensure the applications are live and fully performing.

mounted volume   A shared drive in UNIX/Linux.

Network as a Service (NaaS)   Offering network services to the cloud and within the cloud for cloud computing, including providing the infrastructure of equipment and communications services.

network discovery   A configuration option in Windows operating systems that determines whether computers and devices on a network can be viewed by other computers on the network.

Platform as a Service (PaaS)   When a cloud provider buys, develops, deploys, and manages software that is available to the end user.

print server   A device with software that manages shared printing on a network, such as (1) receiving print jobs, (2) storing the print jobs until it is their turn to print, (3) queuing the print jobs, and (4) sending print jobs to the right printer.

remote access server (RAS)   A specialized server that is located on a network for the purpose of enabling remote users to access the resources, such as servers and databases, of the main network.

remote procedure call (RPC)   Enables services and software on one computer to use services and software on a different computer.

Samba   Used by UNIX/Linux (and Mac OS X systems), this utility employs the Server Message Block (SMB) protocol, which is also used by Windows systems for sharing folders and printers. Samba enables UNIX/Linux systems to access shared Windows resources.

Server Message Block (SMB) protocol   A resource-sharing protocol used in Windows-based networking and that is employed by Samba software in UNIX/Linux systems for resource sharing with Windows-based computers.

shadow file   With access limited to the root user, a file in UNIX/Linux that contains critical information about user accounts, including the encrypted password for each account.

Small Computer System Interface (SCSI)   A 32- or 64-bit computer adapter that transports data between one or more attached devices, such as hard disks, and the computer.

Software as a Service (SaaS)   Providing software and software platforms through a cloud provider in which the end user has little say about the software features. SaaS also entails running the software on the cloud provider's servers, such as through terminal services or a Web browser.

storage area network (SAN)   A grouping of storage devices that forms a subnet. The storage devices are available to any server on the main network and appear to the user as though they are attached to the server they are accessing.

user account   On a network or in a computer operating system, a vehicle used to give a user access to resources through a user id and password (although it is possible to configure an account without a password). Information about a user is often associated with an account, such as the account password, access permissions, and information about the user.

user identification number (UID)   A number that is assigned to a UNIX/Linux user account as a way to distinguish that account from all others on the same system.

Virtual Disk Service (VDS)   Software in Windows Server 2008/Server 2008 R2 that enables management of disk volumes on multiple SANs through one interface at a server. *See* **storage area network (SAN)**.

virtual private network (VPN)   A private network that is like a private and secure tunnel through a larger network—such as the Internet, an enterprise network, or both—that is restricted only to designated member clients.

workgroup   As used in Windows-based networks, a number of users who share drive and printer resources in an independent (and decentralized) peer-to-peer relationship.

Review Questions

1. An automotive trade school maintains a staff of 15 professional recruiters who travel throughout the South to recruit students. The staff needs a secure way to access the school's network through the Internet while they are on the road. Which of the following do you recommend?

   a.   using a VPN

   b.   using only telephone Internet access to avoid wireless security problems

   c.   using Telnet

   d.   using Internet access permissions

2. A user account is like a key that enables a user to be _____ to a network for accessing resources.

   a.   timed

   b.   authenticated

   c.   sourced

   d.   linked to a MAC address

3. You are designing a SAN for your company and are considering the design options. Which of the following are examples of technologies that can be used for the SAN? (Choose all that apply.)

   a.   802.16 shared storage

   b.   iSCSI

   c.   ESIA

   d.   Fibre Channel

4. Which of the following are examples of common cloud computing models? (Choose all that apply.)

   a. dense cloud

   b. public cloud

   c. private cloud

   d. remote-optimized cloud

5. You are setting up a virtual private network and are implementing the remote access protocol to use. Which of the following are you most likely to choose for the remote access protocol?

   a. SLIP

   b. IPsec

   c. MAC2

   d. LLP

6. A small office of 19 hydrologists who provide water testing to help cities manage and protect their water sources needs to set up a network for file sharing. All of the hydrologists use Windows 7 Professional computers. What setting should they use for the network location when they set up the network for sharing resources?

   a. private network

   b. managed network

   c. work network

   d. public network

7. In Question 6, which of the following should the hydrologists use to share resources through the Windows 7 computers?

   a. homegroup

   b. workgroup

   c. managed group

   d. domain group

8. What tool is used to create an account in Windows 7?

   a. Workgroup Configuration

   b. Network Accounts

   c. Network and Sharing Center

   d. User Accounts

9. Which of the following can enable file sharing on a network that has both Windows 7 and Fedora computers? (Choose all that apply.)

   a. Server Message Block (SMB) protocol

   b. share tokens

   c. Samba

   d. Network File System (NFS)

10. You are creating an account in Windows 7 for the new office assistant to use on your computer to help you update spreadsheets. What type of account should you create?

    a. Standard

    b. Administrator

    c. File Manager

    d. Folder operator

11. In Windows 7, you have granted share permissions to a shared folder so that your business manager can view the files in the folder. However, although the business manager can view the contents of the files, she cannot modify the files as you have intended. Which of the following might be the problem?

   a.   The workgroup has expired.

   b.   File sharing is not permitted through wireless connections.

   c.   The share permission is set to *read* and should instead be set to *change*.

   d.   The share permission is set to *use* and should be reconfigured to *full control*.

12. One of the members of your office who uses a Windows 7 computer says he is tired of having to manually access a drive shared by your computer each time he logs on. What do you suggest?

   a.   He should create a desktop icon to access My Network Places.

   b.   He should simply leave his computer on when he leaves work, so he does not have to re-access the drive in the morning.

   c.   He should map the drive and configure it to reconnect each time he logs on.

   d.   He should set up automatic drive roaming.

13. When you set up a homegroup in Windows 7, shared objects, such as music and documents, are shared through which of the following?

   a.   group folders

   b.   trusts

   c.   libraries

   d.   homegroup grants

14. You have previously set up your personal printer connected to your Windows 7 computer so that it is shared with all of the employees in your small company over the network. Now you have purchased a wireless network printer and set it up, and you want to stop sharing your personal printer. Where in Windows 7 can you reconfigure your personal printer to stop sharing?

   a.   change the NIC configuration properties

   b.   use the *Turn off sharing* parameter in the Network window

   c.   change the printer's IP address to 127.0.0.1

   d.   use the Properties dialog box for that printer

15. When a UNIX/Linux system is set up to use BSD-based shared print handling, which of the following are likely to be components of the print handling setup? (Choose all that apply.)

   a.   *lpr*

   b.   *lpl* spooler

   c.   *lpd* daemon

   d.   use of the /etc/printcap file

16. In Linux, you have created a documents directory that contains programs for all users to execute, and that directory contains spreadsheets for users to read or update. After you switch to that directory, which of the following commands provides the necessary file permissions?

   a.   *chmod a+rwx* *

   b.   *chmod o+w+x a/*

   c.   *chmod g+r+x* *

   d.   *chmod o -rg*

17. In Linux, the shadow file is used for which of the following?

    a. keeping passwords secure

    b. monitoring the actions of users who access shared directories

    c. monitoring the actions of system administrators when they make changes to the system

    d. storing a backup copy of shared directories

18. You have created an account in Linux, but there seems to be a problem when you try to access that account. Which of the following might you try?

    a. Recreate the account without a GID.

    b. Recreate the account using a combination of upper and lowercase letters.

    c. Give the account a "Guest" designation for the account type.

    d. View the /etc/passwd file to ensure the account is created properly.

19. When you configure a new account in Mac OS X Snow Leopard or Lion, where is the new account's home directory located?

    a. /Users directory

    b. Accounts partition

    c. Home partition

    d. Mac OS X systems do not use home directories

20. There are four Mac OS X Lion computers in your home. All of the members in your home want to share music, documents, and photos through a wireless network. For this purpose you have purchased an AirPort Express 802.11n Base Station. What Mac OS X utility enables you to configure the AirPort Express wireless network?

    a. AirPort Utility

    b. AirPort Configuration option in System Preferences

    c. Control Panel Wireless Network option

    d. Network Manager

Case Projects

CASE PROJECTS

The Thomas Brown Foundation is a fundraising and development organization for the Alberta Symphony Orchestra and the Brown Art Museum. The Thomas Brown Foundation has a board of directors and eight full- and part-time staff members, including an executive director. The board has authorized the staff to move into larger quarters in an office building. One part of the move involves networking the computers used by the staff, which has not been done in the old office. The staff uses Windows 7 Professional.

Once a week, the chairperson of the board of directors drops into the present office to work for the Foundation and is expected to do the same in the future office. The executive director uses Mac OS X Lion on her laptop computer, and she wants to have a network connection available. The Foundation hires you through Network Design Consultants to assist with the network design.

Case Project 7-1: Recommending a Network Solution

The Foundation plans to share folders on the network along with other resources. You learn from talking with the executive director that the board currently does not plan to authorize the purchase of a server. With this information in mind, what type of network do you recommend? Discuss the advantages and disadvantages of what you recommend.

Case Project 7-2: Staff Training for Sharing Folders

The staff asks you to schedule a training session about sharing folders in Windows 7 Professional. What Windows 7 elements about folder sharing should be in your presentation?

Case Project 7-3: Reconfiguring a Network Connection

The executive director has heard about other organizations in which users have experienced problems when their network connectivity has been lost. She asks you to add to your presentation for Case Project 7-2 by including steps for reconfiguring a network connection.

Case Project 7-4: Enabling Shared Folder Access for the Board Chairperson

One of the staff has told the executive director that the board's chairperson cannot access shared folders offered by the Windows 7 Professional computers through her computer running Mac OS X Lion. Can you find a solution to make this possible, because it is a very sensitive matter for the executive director? If you know of a solution, briefly explain how it works.

Case Project 7-5: Connecting Two Printers

The board has authorized the purchase of two laser printers, one that can print in black and white and another that can print in color. What is your recommendation for connecting these printers for shared use on the Foundation's network?

Case Project 7-6: Cloud Computing

The Foundation is interested in exploring how it might take advantage of cloud computing for office software, fundraising software, and backing up its data. Prepare a brief report that explains how cloud computing might be of value to the Foundation.

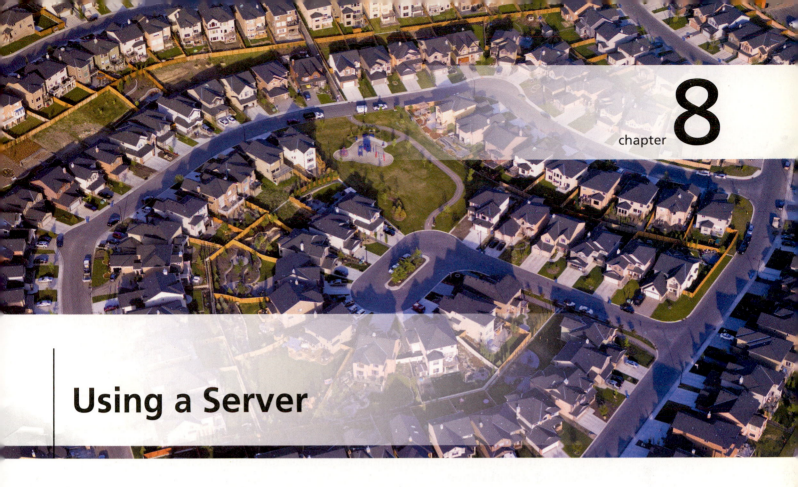

Using a Server

A workstation can be adapted to double as a user's main computer and to share resources with a few other users—but a server is built primarily for sharing resources and managing networks. Using a server compared to using a workstation is like driving a high-performance car compared to a regular sedan—if you are looking for speed and high capability for many users, a server is what you need.

After reading this chapter and completing the exercises, you will be able to:

- Explain how to use a server in a home or office network
- Install a server
- Explain server virtualization and virtual networks
- Understand typical management services provided by a server
- Understand new networking features for Windows Server 2012
- Set up a server
- Manage and monitor a server
- Design a server-based office network

Servers bring a network to a high level of capability and potential. They are an important solution when there are many resources to share and many users accessing those resources. In this chapter, you learn how a server can be used on a home or office network. You learn how to install a server using Windows Server 2008/Server 2008 R2 as an example. You also learn about using virtual servers and how to set up a server through creating user accounts. You learn to use management and monitoring tools in Windows Server, UNIX/Linux, and Mac OS X Server. Finally, you learn and review important elements for designing a server-based office network.

Using a Server in a Home Network

A server can benefit a home network in which there are many serious computer users or that uses a large range of multimedia and gaming applications over the network, for example. As you learned in Chapter 1, "Networking: An Overview," a server is a single computer that offers multiuser access. It provides a more robust environment than a workstation for storing, managing, and sharing resources. Some reasons to have a server on a home network are as follows:

- Store and play selections in a large music library
- Act as a versatile entertainment center for audio, video, and other entertainment applications
- Combine the needs of a home network and home office network
- Provide central management and storage for backing up all home network computers
- Share an Internet connection, providing better response for simultaneous use than one shared from a workstation

On a particular home network, a server might be used in one or a combination of these ways, or it might be used in more novel ways, such as managing home appliances.

Consider, for example, a home that uses one network for both home office and home entertainment purposes. An oil and natural gas pipeline inspector who runs his business from his home has such a network that uses Windows Server. By day, the network is used by the inspector and his wife, who is also his business partner. Federal and state regulations, procedure documents, client information, project results, and billing information are kept on their server, which they access from workstations in their home office. They also access the server while on the road using remote laptops, the Internet, and a virtual private network (VPN; see Chapter 7, "Sharing

Real-Life Networking

A family of five enjoys watching movies, sports, and news events from any location in their home. All of the family members have Android-based tablet PCs and smartphones that have Wi-Fi and 4G connectivity. Their large home is also equipped with a DSL-connected 802.11n wireless router for Wi-Fi access from any room. The family has a Windows Server to store important family files and to provide central backup services for their desktop PCs. The server is also loaded with software that organizes and streams content from Netflix, Hulu, Google, Amazon, TV station Web sites, and other Internet sources to their Android tablets and smartphones that are loaded with compatible apps. In this way, the Dad and Mom can watch the evening news on a tablet PC while making dinner, all family members can watch a movie or TV serial program on their tablet PCs or smartphones from anywhere in the house, and anyone can view a sporting event while relaxing in the backyard.

Resources on a Network"). They regularly back up all computers using backup software and media housed on the server. When their long workdays are over, they use the server to play music from their vast collection stored on the server.

In another example, a family implemented a server for their two sons who enjoy playing multiuser computer games. The parents have a say in what games are purchased and used, and their children invite friends for gaming activities at home. This approach enables the parents to provide a positive environment for their children and friends. It also frees up the shared Internet connection for the parents' use, because the children no longer use it for gaming.

Using a Server in an Office Network

A server can be ideal for all kinds of office uses, particularly when the number of users goes over 20. A server operating system is tailored for networking and sharing resources so that an office can easily scale up from a small operation to a large operation. With a server, multiple users can be connected and can use shared network resources with virtually no waiting. Some of the advantages of using a server in an office network are as follows:

- A server-based network can offer more powerful resource sharing with less delay than workstations on a peer-to-peer network.

- A server-based network enables central management of shared resources.

- A server-based network can be configured to offer very strong security for important shared resources, including providing centralized network authorization when users access the network.

- As the number of workgroups and users grows on a peer-to-peer network, so does the number of headaches in sorting out who can access what. Implementing a server can ease the headaches by bringing organization to users and the resources they access.

- As data files and databases grow in size, they require a server for efficient processing, management, and distributed access.

- A server has more networking tools available than a workstation.

Consider a veterinarian's office that started with one veterinarian, one technician, and one office receptionist. Originally, the veterinarian purchased three computers (one for each person) and created a peer-to-peer network. After a couple of years, she realized another veterinarian was needed in the office. Before long, the practice grew to five veterinarians, seven technicians, and a receptionist. At this point, sharing over the peer-to-peer network experienced significant delays. Information was scattered on different workstations, and the office needed better organization of computer resources. The veterinarian who started the practice hired a local computer company to install a server and to organize information into databases that all users could access. Backing up vital information also was centralized through the server, providing far more consistent and reliable backups.

In another example, the alumni and development office in a community college has a staff of 28 users in the office, which is separate from the main offices of the community college. They use a packaged software system that requires four servers. One server holds programs and utilities that users access and run from their workstations. A second server manages large alumni and donor databases. A third server contains a shadow copy of the databases on the second server and is used for creating and running reports or accessing the databases—so that updating processes on the main database server are not slowed down. The fourth server is used by the office's programmers to create and test new programs for the system, before they are implemented on the production servers. The fourth server is also used to test software updates and new software versions provided by the vendor of the software package, so these are also fully tested before going into production.

With the implementation of a virtual server, such as Microsoft Server 2008/Server 2008 R2 with Hyper-V, all four servers in the development office example could be placed on one well-equipped computer as four different virtual machines, thus saving money on equipment, power, and management costs. A virtual server is one computer that has software that enables you to run multiple operating systems. You learn about virtual servers and virtual machines later in this chapter.

Real-Life Networking

Programmers who develop software for an organization often are provided a test server. Not only can they test the programs on the server before placing them into production, they also can track changes to software. There is change control software that checks out programs (like checking out a book in a library) to programmers and then tracks the changes made. This reduces the chances that two or more programmers will work on the same program at the same time, possibly working at odds with one another or risking the loss of the changes made by one of the programmers. On financial systems, such change control software makes financial auditors happy, as it enables them to review changes made to programs, such as accounting or payroll programs.

Installing a Server

Before you install a server there are several factors to consider:

- What type of computer to use
- Where to locate a server
- Who should manage a server

What Type of Computer to Use

One option for choosing a computer as a server is to purchase one that a vendor has designed for that purpose and that comes with the server operating system installed. Another option is to use a computer that already has an operating system, such as Windows 7 Professional, and replace it with a server operating system. In either case, ensure that you use a computer that has adequate CPU, memory, and disk storage resources. There is not room in this chapter to go into all of the possibilities, because CPU, memory, and disk storage options are always expanding in the direction of faster and more. As a general rule, use a computer with the fastest CPU, most memory, and largest disk storage that you can afford. In addition, for disk space, calculate your present requirements and quadruple them (or more) to plan for the future. Once you estimate the space needed for users to store files or accommodate the projected growth of a database, you may need even more disk storage.

If you want to employ a virtual server, you need a CPU that is able to perform virtualization tasks. AMD CPUs implement this capability through AMD-V technology, and Intel enables virtualization through Intel Virtualization Technology (VT). Look for this capability in the specifications for the computer. You can also verify the CPU's virtualization technology in the setup for the computer (by pressing a function key, such as F2, when the computer boots).

If your budget is tight, another option is to use a computer you have already purchased and plan to purchase a larger system in a year or so. This approach enables you to implement a server now, gain experience with it, and based on that experience, purchase a computer in the future that better meets your needs.

Before you purchase a computer or try to convert an existing computer to be a server, check to ensure that you know the minimum requirements for the server operating system and that the server's components are compatible with the operating system. For example, Microsoft publishes minimum hardware requirements and hardware compatibility information at *www .windowsservercatalog.com*, and you can find requirements and compatibility information about UNIX/Linux systems on Web sites such as *www.redhat.com*. For Mac OS X Server requirements, go to *www.apple.com*. Furthermore, some hardware vendors display a logo on hardware to show that a particular system is designed to work with a specific server operating system, such as "Certified for Windows Server 2008 R2." Tables 8-1, 8-2, and 8-3 show the minimum and recommended hardware requirements for Windows Server 2008 R2, Red Hat Enterprise Linux version 6 for Servers, and Mac OS X Lion Server.

Microsoft offers the Microsoft Assessment and Planning (MAP) Toolkit that contains tools to assess and inventory an existing server and client environment for migrating to Windows Server 2008 R2. At this writing, you can visit *technet.microsoft.com/en-us/solutionaccelerators/ dd537573* to learn more about the MAP toolkit and to download it.

Tables 8-1, 8-2, and 8-3 refer to 32- and 64-bit processors. (These are also referred to as x32 or x64 processors.) 32- and 64-bit refers to the CPU's data bus size. A 64-bit CPU is faster than a 32-bit CPU because a 64-bit data bus can handle more data at one time.

Finally, when you plan a server, plan to bring a fast network connection to the server so that the network is not the bottleneck to the server. At the same time, it makes no sense to have a fast network and a fast NIC in the server, but a server computer that cannot keep up because it has a slow processor, not enough RAM, and slow disk drives. Purchase a computer that is well equipped to do the job as the server. The increased user productivity will make the server expense seem small by comparison.

Where to Locate a Server and Ensuring Power

When your organization has only one or two servers, the decision about where to locate them is relatively easy. Servers should be located in a place that is out of harm's way, such as away from traffic patterns in the office and preferably in an office or a room that can be locked at night. A server provides the most reliable service when it is not susceptible to being bumped or inadvertently unplugged. A location that can be locked is a good choice for security, but not if that location is a broom or utility closet that custodians access and use to store their equipment.

If the server or servers are housed in a small room or closet-sized area, make sure there is adequate cooling so the hardware does not overheat.

Purchase an **uninterruptible power supply (UPS)** for all servers (see Figure 8-1). A UPS ensures that servers remain working when there is a brief power outage or that there is time to properly shut down a server during a longer power outage. A UPS also helps to avoid hardware damage to a server when there are power outages, brownouts, or surges.

In a small organization, you might have one or two UPSs for your servers. In a larger organization that has many blade or rack-mounted servers, for example, you might have one large UPS that is really a cabinet that holds lots of interconnected batteries to support multiple servers.

Table 8-1 Minimum and recommended hardware requirements for Windows Server 2008 R2

Hardware	Standard Edition	Enterprise Edition	Web Server	Datacenter Edition	Itanium-Based Edition	Foundation Edition*	HPC Edition
CPU	1.4 GHz (64-bit) (2 GHz or faster is recommended)	1.4 GHz (64-bit) (2 GHz or faster is recommended)	1.4 GHz (64-bit) (2 GHz or faster is recommended)	1.4 GHz (64-bit) (2 GHz or faster is recommended)	Intel Itanium 2	1.4 GHz (64-bit) (2 GHz or faster is recommended, but note that this edition supports only one processor or one multicore processor at this writing)	1.4 GHz (64-bit) (2 GHz or faster is recommended)
Disk space	10 GB (40 GB or more recommended)	10 GB (40 GB or more recommended)	10 GB (40 GB or more recommended)	10 GB (40 GB or more recommended)	10 GB (40 GB or more recommended)	10 GB (40 GB or more recommended)	50 GB (100 GB or much more recommended)
RAM	512 MB (2 GB or more recommended)	512 MB (2 GB or more recommended)	512 MB (2 GB or more recommended)	512 MB (2 GB or more recommended)	512 MB (2 GB or more recommended)	512 MB (2 GB or more recommended, but unlike other editions there is a limit of 8 GB)	512 MB (2 GB or more recommended)
Drive	DVD	DVD	DVD	DVD	DVD	DVD	DVD
Display	Super VGA or better	Super VGA or better	Super VGA or better	Super VGA or better	Super VGA or better	Super VGA or better	Super VGA or better
Interactive devices	Keyboard and pointing device	Keyboard and pointing device	Keyboard and pointing device	Keyboard and pointing device	Keyboard and pointing device	Keyboard and pointing device	Keyboard and pointing device

*Unlike other editions, Foundation Edition has a user account limit of 15.

© Cengage Learning 2013

Table 8-2   Red Hat Enterprise Linux Version 6 Server hardware requirements

Hardware	Minimum	Recommended
CPU	Intel (32- or 64-bit processor) AMD64 IBM System z IBM Power	2 GHz or faster 64-bit processor (Intel, AMD64, IBM System z, or IBM Power)
RAM	512 MB (32-bit processor) 1 GB (64-bit processor) 2 GB (System z and IBM Power)	4 GB or more
Storage (Server)	1 GB	5 GB or much more depending on the applications to be used
Removable storage	DVD/CD-ROM drive or USB connection for installation or capability to run the OS from external media	Both a DVD/CD-ROM drive and multiple USB connections

© Cengage Learning 2013

Table 8-3   Mac OS X Lion Server hardware requirements

Hardware	Minimum	Recommended
CPU	Intel Core 2 Duo	Intel Core i3 or higher
RAM	2 GB	4 GB or more
Storage (server)	10 GB	15 GB or much more depending on the applications to be used
Removable storage	DVD/CD-ROM drive for installation	Both a DVD/CD-ROM drive and multiple USB connections

© Cengage Learning 2013

© Michael Biehler/www.Shutterstock.com

Figure 8-1   A UPS

A **blade server** (see Figure 8-2) is a modular server unit that looks like a card and that fits into a blade enclosure. The **blade enclosure** is a large box with slots for blade servers, and the box provides cooling fans, electrical power, connection to a shared monitor and pointing device, and network connectivity. A **rack-mounted server** (see Figure 8-3) is a CPU box mounted in a rack that can hold several such CPUs, each with its own power cord and network connection, and that often share one monitor and pointing device.

In medium and large organizations, decisions about where to place servers can influence who controls the servers, as well as the security for the servers. One of the most common discussions that organizations have about locating servers is whether to centralize them, decentralize them, or use a combination of both approaches. The final decision often reflects the culture of an organization.

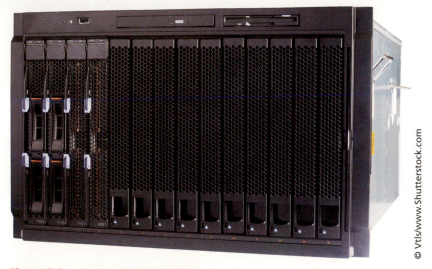

© Vtls/www.Shutterstock.com

Figure 8-2 Blade servers in a blade enclosure

© Spectral-Design/www.Shutterstock.com

Figure 8-3 Rack-mounted servers

8

Real-Life Networking

A small bank located a server in a hallway that was a shortcut between other bank offices. The server was on a table that was often bumped by people using the hallway, and the hallway was always left open for anyone to use. The bank decided to move the server to a more protected location after an employee dropped a stack of bank books and records on the server, causing it to fail and taking the bank tellers' access away.

Some organizations prefer centralizing their servers in a **server farm** (see Figure 8-4), to save money on management and resources. In this model, the servers are housed in a computer room or machine room. For the sake of security, the computer room is typically kept locked at all times, and admittance is strictly controlled. Other advantages of the centralized model are that the room is environmentally controlled to maintain a constant temperature and can be equipped with power-conditioning and UPS equipment that provides uninterrupted service during power fluctuations and outages.

Server farms can save money, since certain equipment—for example, power regulation equipment, backup devices, and an air conditioning system—can serve the entire location and need not be purchased for multiple server locations. The disadvantage is the high network traffic into and out of that portion of the network in which the server farm resides. Another disadvantage is that if there is a disaster, a tornado, for example, then all of an organization's servers might be damaged at the same time.

Some organizations prefer to decentralize or distribute servers to reflect the locations of offices, departments, or divisions. In decentralized situations, the servers are managed by server administrators at each location, so that management of particular servers is customized to the specific needs of that office, department, or division. Additional advantages of this approach are that it distributes the network traffic to servers, and if one location experiences a fire or flood, for example, the servers in other locations remain intact.

Figure 8-4   Server farm in a computer room

In the decentralized model, the physical security used for servers may vary widely from server to server and department to department. For example, one department may be well funded and have the resources to provide a secure, environmentally conditioned room for servers, and another department may be underfunded and provide only minimum physical security for its servers. Another disadvantage is that some departments may not have the funding for, or give a priority to, training server administrators.

The decentralized approach can also have drawbacks: security may not be a top priority for a particular office or department as it might be for centralized computer support staff.

As you plan where to locate servers in a medium-sized or large organization, consider the following:

- Guidelines that specify who can access the location
- Locked doors that are protected by cipher locks requiring a combination, identification card, or biometrics, such as a fingerprint or palm scan
- Cameras that monitor entrances and the computer equipment
- Motion sensors
- Power regulation devices
- Fire detection equipment, including smoke and flame sensors
- Fire suppression equipment

Who Should Manage a Server

In any organization there should be a designated server administrator to ensure that servers are consistently managed. A secondary or backup administrator is also important, because the main server administrator may have to be away from the office periodically, such as when she or he is on vacation. The primary goal is to ensure that servers are regularly maintained and monitored by the same people. Running a server by committee or by using whoever is around yields confusing and inconsistent results.

Server operating system training is important for those who administer servers. In a small office, the owner or office manager may prefer to manage a server and take server training. In medium-sized and large organizations, there are designated server administrators who are trained and often have certifications for managing the servers.

Installing Windows Server 2008 and Server 2008 R2

Each server system is installed using steps tailored for that server operating system. Providing installation steps for all of the server operating systems mentioned here is beyond the scope of this book, but this section presents the basic steps for installing Windows Server 2008/Server 2008 R2 as an example.

If you don't purchase a server with Windows Server 2008/Server 2008 R2 already installed, there are several ways to install the operating system on a computer, such as through the following methods:

- From the DVD installation disc(s)
- Using Windows Deployment Services (WDS, used to install multiple servers)
- As an upgrade from Windows Server 2003
- As a virtual server (using Microsoft Hyper-V, for example; virtual servers and Hyper-V are explained later in this chapter)

The very general steps provided in this chapter illustrate the DVD installation from scratch. This is the method you might use if you are installing the operating system on a new computer or converting a well-equipped Windows 7 computer to a server.

Before you install a server operating system over an operating system already on a computer, such as Windows 7, perform a backup of all files. For example, to open the backup tool in Windows 7, click **Start**, click **Control Panel**, set **View by** to **Large icons** or **Small icons**, click

Backup and Restore, and click **Back up now** to start a backup. In Fedora, use the *dump* or *tar* utilities to back up files via the command line. In Mac OS X, you can create a backup before upgrading to Mac OS X Server by using Time Machine, which can be started from the Dock or from the Applications window. If you don't have the resources to perform a backup of all files, consider taking the computer to a local computer support person who can perform the backup for you.

Configuring the BIOS First, ensure that your computer can boot from the DVD/CD-ROM drive. You need to configure the computer's **basic input/output system (BIOS)** to be able to boot from a DVD/CD-ROM drive. The BIOS is a program on a **nonvolatile random access memory (NVRAM)** chip that establishes basic communication with components such as the monitor and disk drives. The BIOS also performs memory and hardware tests when a computer is initially turned on. An NVRAM chip is a memory chip that does not lose its memory contents when the computer is turned off. For example, you can configure the boot priority from a DVD/CD-ROM drive, hard disk, or flash drive in the BIOS setup program of a computer. To boot from a DVD, you must set the priority to boot via the DVD/CD-ROM drive before booting from a hard disk. In Activity 8-1, you learn how to access the BIOS setup program on a computer.

Activity 8-1: Starting a Computer's BIOS Setup Program

Time Required: 15 minutes
Objective: Open the BIOS setup program on a computer.

Description: In this activity, you start the BIOS setup program so that you know where to set the disk boot priority on a computer. Some computers display a key combination for the BIOS setup on an initial boot screen just after turning on the computer. For other computers you must know which key or keys to press before you turn on the computer (consult the user's manual), because the computer does not display that information. Before starting, save any work and shut down your computer.

1. Turn on the computer and display your computer's BIOS Setup screen. How you do this varies with the computer, but common techniques are to press the **F1**, **F2**, or **Del** key as soon as the computer is turned on. Another way is to hold down any key on the keyboard while booting. The BIOS often sees the error and gives you the option to go into Setup. If none of these works, study your computer's documentation or carefully read all screens during system boot.

2. Look for settings for boot order. This usually involves using the cursor keys to position the cursor over a field and then pressing the space bar or Page Up/Page Down to step through the settings.

3. Step through the choices available on your computer.

4. If available, choose to boot from the DVD/CD-ROM drive before booting from the hard drive and save and exit the configuration screen (or make a note of how you would do this).

5. Use the appropriate option to save any changes and reboot the computer.

Operating System Installation from DVD The general steps for installing Windows Server 2008/Server 2008 R2 from scratch using a DVD installation are as follows:

1. Make sure the computer's BIOS is set to boot first from the CD/DVD drive (see Activity 8-1 to learn how to access the BIOS setup on a computer).

2. Insert the Windows Server 2008 or Server 2008 R2 installation DVD.

3. Turn off the power to the computer.

4. Turn on the computer and press any key to boot from the DVD/CD-ROM, if requested. The DVD might take a few moments to load.

5. When the Install Windows window appears, specify the language to install, such as English, in the *Language to install* drop-down box. In the Time and currency format box, make your selection, such as English (United States). In the Keyboard or input method box, make your selection, such as US.

6. Click Next.

7. The next window enables you to commence the installation. Before you get started, notice there is a link for *What to know before installing Windows* and you may see a link for *Repair your computer*. The *Repair your computer* link is designed to be used after Windows Server 2008/Server 2008 R2 is installed and a problem arises, such as when the computer won't boot after a power failure. You can use this link to repair problems with boot files.

8. Click the Install now button (see Figure 8-5).

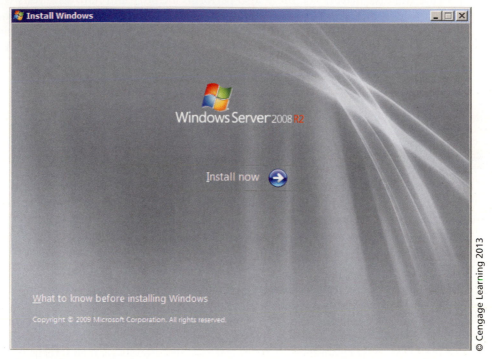

© Cengage Learning 2013

Figure 8-5   Install now button

9. Enter the Product Key.

10. Click Next.

11. In the next Install Windows window, you can select the operating system to install, such as Windows Server 2008 R2 Standard (Full Installation). Click Next.

12. Read the license terms, click the box for I accept the license terms, and click Next.

13. In the next window, you will select (click) the type of installation you want to perform from the following options (see Figure 8-6):

- Upgrade

  Keep your files, settings, and programs and upgrade Windows.

  Be sure to back up your files before upgrading.

- Custom (advanced)

  Install a clean copy of Windows, select where you want to install it, or make changes to disks and partitions.

  This option does not keep your files, settings, and programs.

If you are installing a virtual server in Hyper-V, the Upgrade option is likely to be disabled.

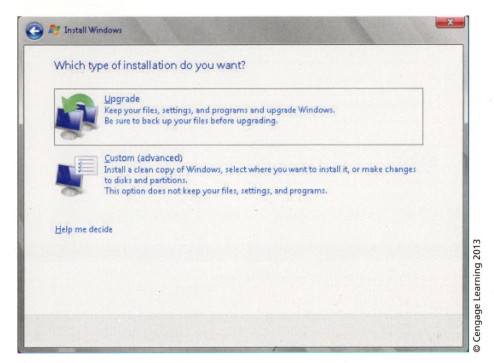

Figure 8-6 Selecting the installation type

14. Click Custom (advanced).

15. You might see the Compatibility Report window to report possible compatibility conflicts and direct you to check the Windows Server Catalog at *www.windowsservercatalog.com*, or if you have access to Microsoft TechNet visit *technet.microsoft.com/en-us/library/bb625087 .aspx* for more information.

16. The Windows Installation program displays disk partitions, including existing partitions and unallocated disk space. Select the disk partition or unallocated space you want to use. For example, click Disk 0 Unallocated Space on a new computer. (Note that the window displays an informational message at the bottom, if you highlight a partition that is too small or one that contains a non-NTFS partition. Further, there might be a *Load Driver* link at the bottom of the window, so you can install a more recent hard disk driver or a driver for a disk that is not properly recognized by Windows Server 2008/Server 2008 R2. You can click the *Load Driver* link or press F6 at this point to load a new driver.) Also, you might see a *Drive options (advanced)* link, which enables you to set up customized drive options. Figure 8-7 shows a disk with two partitions (both already allocated to NTFS), from which to select. Click Next after you have made your selection.

In Windows Server 2008 R2, there are four new options for setting up a drive, if you need them. In addition to the options in Figure 8-7, you can select to delete, format, and extend a drive. Also, you can set up a new drive.

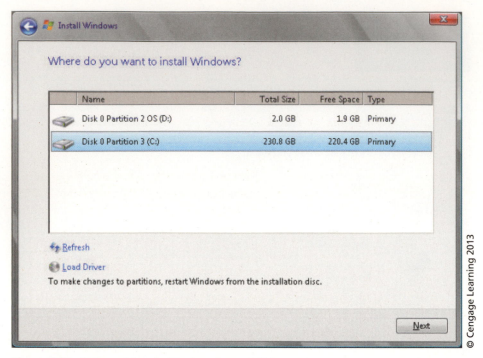

Figure 8-7   Disk partitions in Windows Server 2008

17. The installation program begins installing Windows Server 2008/Server 2008 R2 (you will see progress information about Copying files, Expanding files, Installing features, Installing updates, Completing installation).

18. The installation program restarts the computer. Let it boot from the hard drive.

19. You see the message: Please wait while Windows sets up your computer.

20. Next you see the Install Windows window in the Completing installation phase.

21. The system reboots again. Let it boot from the hard drive. (This might take a little extra time when performing an installation in Hyper-V or in another virtual server.)

Steps 20 and 21 are eliminated in Windows Server 2008 R2.

22. You see the message (a red circle with a white x in it) *The user's password must be changed before logging on the first time*. Click OK.

23. Enter a new password for the Administrator account and then enter the same password again to confirm the password. Click the blue circle with the white right-pointing arrow inside.

24. If you enter a password that is not a strong password, you see the message (with a white x in a red circle): *Unable to update the password. The value provided for the new password does not meet the length, complexity, or history requirements of the domain. Click OK and enter a different password.*

For a strong password, consider creating one that is at least eight characters long and that includes numbers; uppercase and lowercase letters; and characters such as $, !, and #.

25. When you see the message *Your password has been changed*, click OK.

26. At this point, the Windows desktop is opened and the Initial Configuration Tasks window is displayed. You can use the Initial Configuration Tasks window to start customizing your server.

From this point on, if you log off, you can log back on to the Administrator account using the password you entered in Step 23. The Administrator account has complete privileges to manage Windows Server 2008/Server 2008 R2.

Fedora Linux offers an installation guide for its operating systems. To access the installation guide for the current version of Fedora, go to *docs.fedoraproject.org/en-US/index.html* and select the link for Installation Guide.

For a Mac OS X Lion Server installation guide, go to *www.maclife.com/article/howtos/how_install_and_set_mac_os_x_lion_server* or to upgrade to Mac OS X Lion Server, go to *www.apple.com/macosx/server/docs/Upgrading_and_Migrating_v10.7.pdf*.

Virtualization

Virtualization is the ability to disguise the physical or individual hardware elements of computing to enhance or multiply resources. Through virtualization, one resource can be made to appear as many separate resources. For example, one computer can be virtualized to appear to the user as many computers or one storage device can look like multiple storage devices.

Several recognized forms of virtualization include:

- *Server virtualization*: Running multiple server operating systems on a single server computer (see Figure 8-8). For instance, this form of virtualization might include having two Windows Server 2008 R2 operating systems and one Linux operating system on one server computer. **Microsoft Hyper-V** is an example of server virtualization. VMware also sells a range of products for server, cloud, workstation, and application virtualization (visit *www.vmware.com* to learn about these products).

- *Workstation or PC virtualization*: Running multiple workstation operating systems, such as Windows XP, Windows 7, and Linux, on one computer.

- *Application virtualization*: Running single applications in their own virtual machine environments. On a Windows operating system, this means running applications to have their own file system and Registry. For example, if you are converting to a new accounting system, you might have the old accounting software in one virtualized application environment and the new accounting software in another virtualized application environment on the same physical computer. The old accounting software is used until the new software system is fully tested and operational.

- *Storage virtualization*: Setting up multiple networked disk storage units to appear as one unit. You have already learned about storage virtualization as Storage Area Networks (SANs) in Chapter 7, "Sharing Resources on a Network."

- *Hardware or CPU virtualization*: Using the CPU to perform virtualization tasks by having virtualization processes work inside a specially designed CPU. AMD implements this through AMD-V technology in some of its CPUs, and Intel does the same through Intel VT in some CPUs.

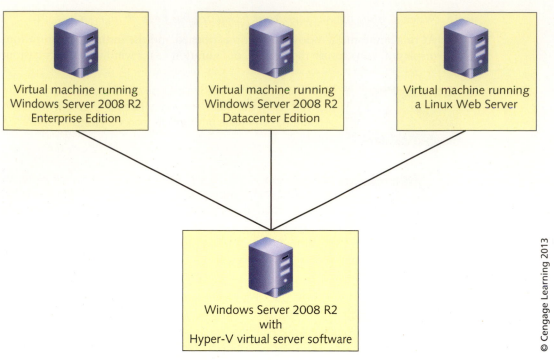

Figure 8-8   Virtual server housing three virtual machines in one computer

© Cengage Learning 2013

To learn more about AMD-V, visit *www.amd.com/us/products/ technologies/virtualization/Pages/virtualization.aspx* and for Intel VT, see *www.intel.com/technology/virtualization/technology.htm?wapkw=intel vt.*

- *Network virtualization*: Dividing a single network or network device, such as a NIC, into multiple channels or bandwidths so that the network appears as multiple networks or network pathways. On a virtual server, there might be one virtual NIC for each virtual machine. All of the virtual NICs can work through a single physical NIC in the computer, creating separate virtual pathways for each virtual server through the single NIC. (You might think of the physical NIC as operating in a similar fashion to a CPU that handles two or more software applications at the same time. To the user it looks like the CPU is running a word processor, Google search, and spreadsheet all at the same time. In the same way, to the network it looks like a single physical NIC but is actually three or four NICs in one on a virtual server.)

Of these options, server virtualization has aroused significant interest among those who work with server operating systems and is the focus of Hyper-V and VMware. Server virtualization involves turning a single server computing platform, such as an operating system or computer, into two or more virtual computing platforms. The popular application of this is to install software on one computer so that multiple operating systems can be run from that single computer. Instead of one operating system running at one time from one machine, two, three, or more operating systems can be running from a single machine. For example, if three operating systems are running on one physical machine, this means there are three virtual machines running through virtual server software on one computer. The **virtual server software**, such as Windows Server 2008 R2 running Hyper-V, is the software that enables a computer to house two or more operating systems. A computer running virtual server software is typically referred to as a **virtual server**. Each instance of an operating system running within the software is a **virtual machine**.

Reasons for Virtual Servers

One of the reasons why virtual servers are appealing is that they offer the ability to reduce the number of computers needed to run a business. Over time, businesses and organizations continue to add servers for new functions. For example, a business might add a Web server (or servers), additional DNS servers, and servers for new databases and software. The sprawl of servers is known as a server farm, because servers seem to sprout up everywhere.

Server proliferation requires more work in maintaining servers, resulting in the need to hire additional people to manage them. Locating space to store the servers is also a problem. As the number of servers grows, space can run out in an operations center or server room and it becomes necessary to invest in more space. Additional expenses are incurred for physical security, air conditioning, and heating to keep the servers in a secure, controlled environment. Further, the cost of electricity and fuel is rising, and more server hardware translates into higher electric, heating, and cooling bills.

The use of virtual servers enables an organization to consolidate servers into fewer physical computers, generally cutting the number of computers by two-thirds, three-fourths, or more depending on the hardware and applications. Server consolidation means that significant money can be saved on personnel, space, security, and energy costs.

Some organizations switch to virtual servers for the savings in electricity alone. Organizations report saving 40 to over 75 percent in the cost of electricity.

Real-Life Networking

Another reason for using virtual servers is that they enable businesses to keep older operating systems around as a way to continue using older software that fulfills particular needs. This is why it is estimated that Windows Server 2003 will remain active at many locations well after Microsoft discontinues support for it in 2014. As reported in a TechTarget survey, one CPA firm observes it has to keep 10 years of tax returns. The tax returns use older software on Windows Server 2003 and Windows XP computers. That firm can continue to access the old tax returns by using virtual server and virtual desktop software. In this way, the operating systems and software can be used within a virtual environment on new computers with new hardware and new drivers, so there is no need to continue maintaining older computer hardware.

Virtual Networks

A **virtual network** is a network on which virtual machines communicate through virtual links. Most virtual server software provides different options for configuring a virtual network. For each virtual machine in Hyper-V, you can configure one of three virtual networking options using Hyper-V Manager's Virtual Network Manager (see Figure 8-9):

- *External virtual network*: Offers communication between virtual machines and the physical network through a network interface card (and virtual machines can communicate with each other on the same virtual server)

- *Internal virtual network*: Enables communication between virtual machines and the host virtual server

- *Private virtual network*: Offers communications only between virtual machines on the same virtual server

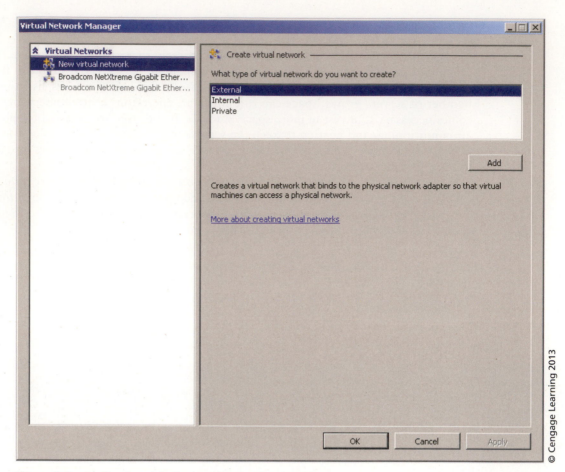

Figure 8-9 Configuring virtual networking options in Hyper-V

An external virtual network is commonly used for virtual machines that are in production for users to access. For an external virtual network, you can optionally specify a **virtual LAN identification number (VLAN ID)**. This is a unique number used for communication through the network adapter that distinguishes the virtual network from other networks. An external virtual network binds the network to a NIC in the virtual server, which in effect makes the NIC act like a virtual switch. When you set up an external network, Microsoft recommends (but it is not required) that you have a computer with two NICs, one for switching traffic through to the virtual network and one for all other external network traffic to the virtual server (computer) and its management operating system (Windows Server 2008/Server 2008 R2).

An internal virtual network is not linked with the NIC in the virtual server and is typically used in a test environment, such as when you are first experimenting with the use of virtual servers to develop how you will use them.

A private virtual network also does not use the NIC in the virtual server and is generally used to prevent network traffic from reaching virtual machines. This approach might also be used in a test environment or when you are upgrading virtual machines and want to make them unavailable.

Installing a Virtual Machine

The steps for installing a virtual machine (such as installing Windows Server 2008 R2 in Hyper-V or VMware) vary by the virtual server software. In general the steps for installing a virtual machine inside a virtual server are as follows:

1. Install the virtual server software on the computer, such as installing the Hyper-V role in Windows Server 2008 R2 or installing VMware.

2. Start the steps or wizard used to create a virtual machine in the virtual server software.

3. Specify the name of the virtual machine.

4. Allocate memory for the virtual machine.

5. Allocate disk space on which to create a virtual disk for the virtual machine.

6. Configure the virtual network, such as creating an external virtual network and specifying which NIC (or WNIC) to use for the virtual machine on the virtual network.

7. Insert the operating system installation DVD.

8. Follow the normal steps for installing the operating system on the virtual machine.

9. Associate the appropriate DVD/CD-ROM and flash drives with the virtual machine.

10. After the operating system is installed on the virtual machine, configure the operating system.

Review the operating system, application, and data storage requirements so that you know how much memory and disk space to allocate for a virtual machine, to ensure that the OS performs well within the virtual machine.

Appendix D, "A Step-by-Step Guide to Server Virtualization," gives detailed instructions for using server virtualization software to create virtual machines.

Server Functions in Windows Server, UNIX/Linux, and Mac OS X Server

As you learned earlier in this book, server operating systems are more robust than client operating systems. Server systems offer many specialized client, domain, and network management functions that are not available in client operating systems. Some typical management functions include:

- Directory services, such as Active Directory in Windows Server systems
- User account management with more extensive setup options and security
- E-mail server services
- DHCP and DNS server services
- Large-scale file and folder sharing services
- Database services
- Network security management
- Web server and Web applications
- Cloud services (see the "Cloud Computing" section in Chapter 7)

Typically, if your network uses mostly Windows client systems, then a Windows Server version is a good choice for managing clients. If the network clients are mostly Linux, then a Linux server is a good choice. And, if most clients run Mac OS X operating systems (and Apple devices such as iPhones, iPods, and iPads), then Mac OS X Server is a very compatible server selection. Each server system can also offer services to other types of clients; for example, a Windows Server can offer compatibility functions for UNIX/Linux and Mac OS X Server can use Samba for file sharing with Windows clients—but the most assured compatibility is to match the server operating system with the same family of client operating systems.

For example, consider the advantages of using a Mac OS X server for a mostly Apple device environment. Mac OS X Lion Server offers the following specialized server software for Apple devices:

- *Profile Manager*: Manages and enables setup of remote clients running Mac OS X Lion and iOS devices such as the iPad and iPhone.

- *Mail Server*: Provides e-mail services for clients and is particularly compatible with Mac OS X and iOS devices.

- *Xsan Admin*: Manages Xsan compatible Mac OS X disk volumes for storing information, such as on a Fibre Channel SAN connected to Mac OS X Server(s).

- *Wiki Server*: Offers a Wiki environment in which Apple device users can use and add to Wiki-based information from a Web site, including storing podcasts.

One area in which matching a server operating system to like client operating systems does not really apply is in the arena of Web servers. Windows Server Internet Information Services and Linux/Mac OS X Apache Web servers are nearly equally popular and are compatible with all kinds of clients, regardless of client operating system.

Looking Ahead: Windows Server 2012 on the Network

The newest Windows Server version, Windows Server 2012, has the following features that network and server administrators find of particular interest:

- Hyper-V 3.x with new features for replication and virtual switching

- New cloud computing options

- Ability to switch between Server Core (a command-line environment) and a GUI desktop, and moving the Server Manager interface from the server(s) to a remote console/workstation with the ability to manage multiple servers from one workstation with management software

- A visual database that works using network discovery for tracking all network IP addresses

Hyper-V 3.x is slated to have much improved ability to replicate virtual machines, including having the ability to compress and encrypt data within the replication process. This is good news for organizations that replicate virtual machines at remote locations for disaster recovery. If the main location becomes nonfunctional, such as because of a hurricane or flood, the replicated virtual machines can be started at the remote location with greater ease.

Hyper-V 3.x also offers an "extensible virtual switch," which can be used to optimize, monitor, and manage network traffic through a virtual server. The virtual switch means that network administrators can control Quality of Service (QoS) so that there is an assured level of throughput for specific types of virtual server and virtual machine communications. You learn more about QoS in Chapter 9, "Understanding WAN Connection Choices." The virtual switch also enables a network administrator to sample network traffic through a virtual server to determine how best to configure the virtual switch. As with hardware switches, the virtual switch enables filtering IP addresses and forwarding.

Also, Hyper-V 3.x can support as many as 32 **virtual CPUs** and up to 512 GB of memory, which translates into more computing power for each virtual machine. A virtual CPU simulates more CPUs than are actually in a computer, enabling applications to have their own processor. For example, a virtual CPU can be used by a virtual machine.

In terms of cloud computing, Windows Server 2012 enables an organization to build a private cloud that can also offer public cloud services. The cloud services can involve multiple servers that can offer any type of application to the user, including applications used from mobile devices like smartphones and tablet PCs. This capability, in part, is made possible because some versions of Windows Server 2012 can run on computers that have up to 160 logical CPUs and 32 virtual CPUs (in Hyper-V 3.x).

Windows Server 2012 additionally has the ability to switch between a GUI and non-GUI management interface. Windows Server 2008 introduced Windows Server Core, which is a non-GUI command-line server interface similar to what has been traditional on UNIX and Linux servers. The command-line interface is targeted at advanced server administrators who prefer using the command line for server management, particularly in an environment with many servers. However, other server administrators prefer to manage a server from a point-and-click GUI desktop. In Windows Server 2008/Server 2008 R2 a server installation is for either a GUI desktop or Server Core, but not both. Windows Server 2012 enables administrators to switch between the Server Core and GUI environments without having to reinstall the operating system. In addition, Windows Server 2012 is slated to enable moving the Server Manager tool from the server to a single workstation, from which the server administrator can manage multiple servers.

The Windows Server 2012 visual database of IP addresses means that a network administrator can quickly find unused addresses to assign to a new network device, such as to a switch, a new server, or a network printer. Windows Server 2012 IP address management uses network discovery to dynamically track all IP addresses on the local network for the network administrator to view and track in an automated database.

Setting Up a Server

After a server is installed, the next task is to set it up. There are several setup tasks, but some of the most important are as follows:

- Create user accounts.
- Optimize the performance of a server.
- Configure shared resources.
- Configure remote services.

You learn more about these setup tasks in the next sections.

Creating User Accounts

User accounts enable you to manage who accesses resources on one or more servers. In the following sections, you learn about creating accounts on a UNIX/Linux server, Mac OS X Server, and Windows Server.

Creating User Accounts in UNIX/Linux   In Chapter 7, "Sharing Resources on a Network," you learned how to configure user accounts in UNIX/Linux. The steps you learned for creating UNIX/Linux accounts can be used on a workstation or a server. For example, on a UNIX/Linux server you can use the command-line utilities *useradd*, *usermod*, and *userdel* in the same way as on a workstation.

There are also GUI tools that you can use to create and manage accounts, such as the User Manager tool in the GNOME 3.x desktop. The general steps for creating an account in User Manager via the GNOME 3.x desktop are as follows:

1. Log onto an account that has root privileges.

2. Click Activities.

3. Click Applications.

4. Click Users and Groups.

5. Ensure the Users tab is displayed.

6. Click Add user in the button bar.

7. Complete the information in the Add New User dialog box, including *User Name*, *Full Name*, *Password*, *Confirm Password*, *Login Shell* (shell in which to enter commands, with

the bash shell as the default, which you have been using in this book). Also, check the appropriate boxes for *Create home directory* (and include the Home Directory name, which is the user name by default), *Create a private group for the user*, *Specify user ID manually*, and *Specify group ID manually* (see Figure 8-10). Note that *Create home directory* and *Create a private group for the user* are checked by default.

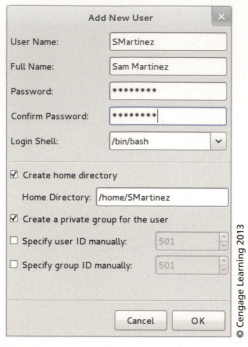

Figure 8-10   Creating an account in User Manager in Linux

8. Click OK to create the account.

9. If you see a message that the password is too weak, click Yes and reenter a password that is over seven characters and that combines uppercase and lowercase letters, numbers, and characters such as *, #, @.

10. Close User Manager when you are finished creating accounts.

 In Linux, a **shell** is an interface between the operating system and the user. A shell provides an environment in which to enter commands. The bash shell is popular and usually the default in Linux.

Creating User Accounts in Mac OS X   In Mac OS X Snow Leopard and Lion Server, user accounts are created in two ways. The first way is just after the Mac OS X Server is installed, the Server Assistant is launched. Server Assistant steps you through configuring the server including designating the type of configuration, configuring the Administrator account, setting up network connectivity, enabling server backup, using the mail server services, and adding new user accounts. When Server Assistant first starts, it offers three kinds of server configurations:

- *Standard*: The default configuration for a home office or relatively small office setting

- *Workgroup*: For medium or large organizations that use a directory service (such as Microsoft Active Directory discussed later in this chapter); enables Mac OS X Server to integrate with the existing directory service

- *Advanced*: For organizations that have experienced server administrators planning to use advanced networking, applications, and Internet services, and that want to highly customize the server

When you reach the point in Server Assistant used for setting up user accounts, for each account you provide the user name and password. Server Assistant automatically creates an e-mail account and chat address to go with each new account.

After your server is configured through Server Assistant and you want to create more accounts, you can do this from the Server Preferences utility. The Server Preferences utility is located in the /Applications/Server folder. To create an account, use these general steps:

1. Open Server Preferences.

2. Click Users under Accounts in the Server Preferences window.

3. Ensure the Account tab is selected in the Users window.

4. Click the + plus sign under the list of accounts to create a new account.

5. Enter the user name (the system will fill in the default short name for the account), the password, and verify the password. If the user is to be a server administrator, click the box for Allow user to administer this server.

6. Click the Create Account button.

7. After a user account is created, select the account (if necessary) in the Users window.

8. Click the Contact Info tab to provide contact information for the user, such as street address, phone information, Web site, and blog location.

9. Click the Services tab to configure services for the user, which include:
   - File sharing
   - iCal
   - Address Book
   - iChat
   - Mail
   - VPN (virtual private network)
   - Time Machine (to back up the user's home folder)

10. Click the Groups tab to assign the user to specific groups for accessing resources.

Creating User Accounts in Windows Server   Creating accounts in Windows Server is a different process from that on a workstation. There are two general environments for account setup in Windows Server:

- Accounts that are set up on a stand-alone server that does not have a domain or Active Directory installed

- Accounts that are set up in a domain when Active Directory is installed

When you set up a Windows Server, that server can be a stand-alone server or it can be part of a domain. A **stand-alone server** is one that does not have Active Directory installed. Instead, it manages user accounts and shared access locally through a workgroup. Clients that access a stand-alone server are members of the same workgroup as the server. This option is a good choice for a home or small business network. Unlike Windows 7, for example, a stand-alone server can efficiently manage well over 20 simultaneous users in a workgroup (depending on the hardware, it can manage hundreds of users).

The other option for managing accounts is to install Microsoft Active Directory and set up a domain. As you learned in Chapter 7, a domain centralizes control of network resources into a logical grouping of user accounts, computers, printers, and network devices. A domain is implemented through Active Directory, which is a directory service that houses information about all network resources such as servers, printers, user accounts, groups of user accounts, security policies, and other information. As a directory service, Active Directory is responsible for providing a central listing of resources and ways to quickly find and access specific resources—and for providing a way to manage network resources. When user accounts are created in a domain through Active Directory, those accounts can be used to access any domain server or resource.

Creating an Account on a Windows Stand-Alone Server   On a stand-alone server, new accounts are created by first installing the Microsoft Management Console (MMC) Local Users and Groups Snap-in. The MMC is a tool that can be customized by adding tool modules called "snap-ins" to manage different server functions, such as creating accounts or monitoring a server. If you have access to a Windows Server 2008 or Server 2008 R2 server that does not have Active Directory installed, try Activity 8-2 to create a user account on a stand-alone server using the MMC. If you have access only to a server that has Active Directory installed, try Activity 8-3 instead to use the MMC.

In some Windows 7 or Server 2008/Server 2008 R2 projects, you may see the User Account Control (UAC) box, which is used for security to help thwart intruders. The UAC box asks for permission to continue with an action or asks for the administrator password. If you see this box, click **Continue**. Because computer setups may be different, the box is not mentioned in the actual project steps.

Activity 8-2: Creating a User Account on a Stand-Alone Server

Time Required: 15 minutes

Objective: Create a user account on a Windows Server 2008/Server 2008 R2 server that does not have Active Directory installed.

Description: In this activity, you create a user account on a stand-alone server. The Windows Server 2008/Server 2008 R2 server that you use should not have Active Directory already installed. Also, you need an account that has Administrator privileges.

If you do not have access to a stand-alone Windows Server 2008/Server 2008 R2 server, you can follow the similar steps in Windows 7 to create an account.

1. Click **Start,** in the Start Search box (for Windows Server 2008) or in the Search programs and files box (for Windows Server 2008 R2); enter **mmc;** and click **MMC** under Programs.

2. Click the **File** menu and click **Add/Remove Snap-in.**

3. Under Available snap-ins, find and click **Local Users and Groups** as shown in Figure 8-11.

If Active Directory is already installed, Windows Server does not allow you to install the Local Users and Groups Snap-in; you must use the Active Directory Users and Computers Snap-in instead.

4. Click the **Add** button to make this a selected snap-in.

5. In the Choose Target Machine dialog box, leave **Local computer: (the computer on which this console is running)** selected and click **Finish.**

6. Click **OK** in the Add or Remove Snap-ins dialog box. Expand the console windows, if necessary.

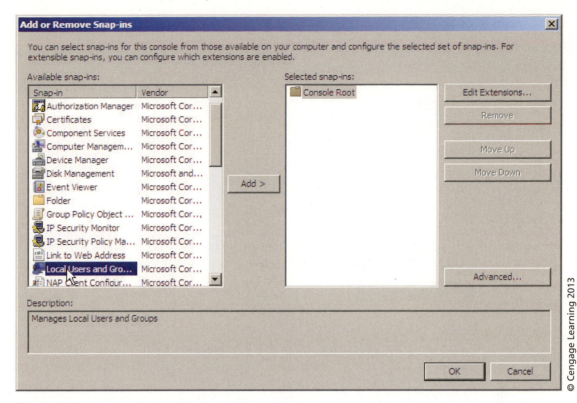

Figure 8-11   Opening the Local Users and Groups Snap-in

7. Double-click **Local Users and Groups** in the tree in the left pane.

8. Click the **Users** folder in the tree and then click the **Action** menu.

9. Click **New User** and complete the information to create the user account as shown in Figure 8-12 (enter a user name for the account, enter a full name, type a description, enter a password, and confirm the password).

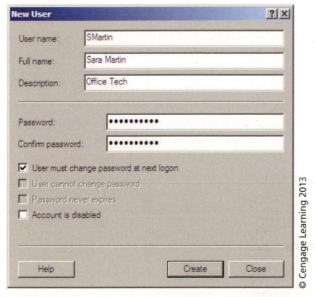

Figure 8-12   Creating a user account on a stand-alone Windows Server

10. Click **Create**. If you see a warning message that the password does not meet the password requirements, click **OK** and enter a new password that does meet the requirements, such as one that is over six characters long and that contains a combination of uppercase and lower-case letters and numbers.

Symbols that cannot be used in an account name in Windows Server are [ ] ; : < > = , + / \ ? * " | @. Also, each account name must be unique; no duplicates are allowed.

11. Create another account or click **Close** if you are finished creating accounts.

12. Close the MMC and click **No** so that you do not save the console settings.

An alternative to using the MMC Local Users and Groups Snap-in is to open the Computer Management tool. Click **Start**, point to **Administrative Tools**, click **Computer Management**, click **Local Users and Groups** in the left pane, click the **Users** folder, click the **Action** menu, and click **New User**.

Creating an Account in a Windows Domain   If a server is part of a domain, that means Active Directory is installed to provide directory services for managing domain objects such as servers and user accounts. Even though there are multiple computers in an organization, objects such as user accounts are managed from one place in a consistent fashion. Accounts are created and managed through the Active Directory Users and Computers tool. A set of user account policies can be established so that user accounts are managed in a consistent way and so that security policies are applied to all user accounts. Activity 8-3 enables you to create a user account on a Windows Server 2008/Server 2008 R2 server that is a member of a domain (this type of server is also called a domain controller).

Activity 8-3: Creating an Account in a Domain

Time Required: 20 minutes
Objective: Learn how to create a user account in a Windows Server domain.

Description: In this activity, you set up a new account in a Windows Server 2008/Server 2008 R2 domain using the Active Directory Users and Computers tool. You need to work from an account that has Administrator privileges. Also, the server you use should have Active Directory installed, which means it is a domain controller.

1. Click **Start**, in the Start Search box (for Windows Server 2008) or in the Search programs and files box (for Windows Server 2008 R2), enter **mmc**, and click **mmc** under Programs. Maximize the console windows, if necessary. Click the **File** menu and click **Add/Remove Snap-in**. Under the Available snap-ins, click **Active Directory Users and Computers** and click **Add**. Click **OK**.

2. In the left pane, click the **+ plus sign** in front of **Active Directory Users and Computers**, if necessary, to display the elements under it. Click the **+ plus sign** in front of the domain name, such as Accounting.com, to display the folders and organizational units (OUs) under it. An OU is a grouping of objects, including user accounts, within a domain that provides a means to establish specific policies for governing those objects. An OU also enables object management to be delegated, such as to a department head who manages accounts for those who work in her department.

3. Click the **Users** folder in the left pane. Are there any accounts already created? What objects are shown along with the accounts?

4. Click the **Action** menu or right-click **Users** in the left pane, point to **New**, and click **User**.

5. Type your first name in the First name box, type your middle initial (no period), and type your last name with the word "Test" appended to it in the Last name box (for example, *RyanTest*). Enter your initials with Test appended to them in the User logon name box (for example, *JRTest*) as shown in Figure 8-13. What options are automatically completed for you? Click **Next**.

New Object - User

Create in: Accounting.com/Users

First name: Jason   Initials: B

Last name: RyanTest

Full name: Jason B. RyanTest

User logon name:

JRTest   @Accounting.com

User logon name (pre-Windows 2000):

ACCOUNTS\   JRTest

< Back   Next >   Cancel

© Cengage Learning 2013

Figure 8-13   Creating a user account in a Windows Server domain

6. Enter a password and enter the password confirmation. Ensure the box is checked for **User must change password at next logon**. This option forces users to enter a new password the first time they log on, so that the account creator will not know their password. The other options include:

- *User cannot change password*: Means that only the account administrator can change the user's password

- *Password never expires*: Used in situations in which an account must always be accessed, such as when a program accesses an account to run a special process

- *Account is disabled*: Provides a way to prevent access to an account without deleting it

The Windows Server 2008/Server 2008 R2 default password requirements are enabled when you create an account. A password must be six characters or longer and cannot contain the account name or portions of the user's full name (beyond two characters of the name). Also, a minimum of three of the following four rules apply: includes numbers, includes uppercase letters, includes lowercase letters, and includes characters such as $, #, and !.

7. Click **Next**.

8. Verify the information you have entered and click **Finish**.

9. To continue configuring the account, in the right pane, double-click the account you just created, such as *RyanTest* (alternatively you can right-click the account and click **Properties**).

10. Notice the tabs that are displayed for the account properties and record them.

11. Click the **General** tab, if it is not already displayed, and enter a description of the account, such as **Test account**.

12. Click the **Account** tab to view the information you can enter on it.

13. Click the tabs you have not yet viewed to find out what information can be configured through each one.

14. Click **OK**.

15. Leave the Active Directory Users and Computers window open for the next activity.

The following is a brief summary of the account properties that can be set by right-clicking an account and clicking Properties in the Active Directory Users and Computers window (see Figure 8-14).

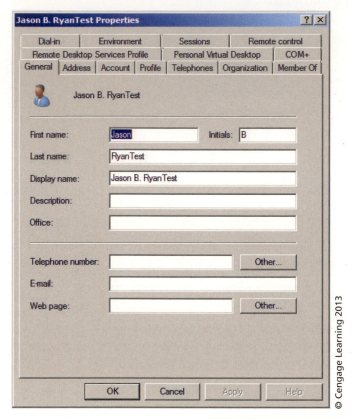

Figure 8-14   Domain user account properties

- *General tab*: Enables you to enter or modify personal information about the account holder that includes the first name, last name, and name as it is displayed in the console, description of the user or account, office location, telephone number, e-mail address, and Web page. There are also optional buttons to enter additional telephone numbers and Web page addresses for the account holder.

- *Address tab*: Used to provide information about the account holder's street address, post office box, city, state or province, postal code, and country or region.

- *Account tab*: Provides information about the logon name, domain name, and account options, such as requiring the user to change her or his password at next logon, and account expiration date, if one applies. A Logon Hours button on this tab enables you to set up an account so that the user logs onto the domain only at designated times, such as only from 8:00 AM to 7:00 PM Monday through Friday. Also, the Log On To button enables you to limit from which computer a user can log on to the server or domain.

- *Profile tab*: Enables you to associate a particular profile with a user or set of users, such as a common desktop. This tab also is used to associate a logon script and a home folder (directory) with an account. A logon script is a file of commands that are executed at logon, and a home folder is disk space on a particular server given to a user to store his or her files.

- *Telephones tab*: Enables you to associate specific types of telephone contact numbers for an account holder, which include one or more numbers for home, pager, mobile, fax, and IP phones.

- *Organization tab*: Provides a place to enter the account holder's title, department, company name, and the name of the person who manages the account holder.

- *Member Of tab*: Used to add the account to an existing group of users that have the same security and access requirements via security groups created to manage permissions. The tab also is used to remove the account from a security group.

- *Terminal Services Profile* (in Windows Server 2008) or *Remote Desktop Services Profile tab* (in Windows Server 2008 R2): Used to set up a user profile for a client that uses Terminal Services (renamed to Remote Desktop Services in Windows Server 2008 R2; these services enable a client to access a server and run applications on the server).

- *Personal Virtual Desktop* (in Windows Server 2008 R2): An account can be assigned to a specific virtual machine that provides a customized desktop for the account client computer.

- *COM+ tab*: Used to specify the COM+ partition set of which the user is a member.

- *Dial-in tab*: Permits you to control remote access from dial-in modems or from virtual private networks (VPNs).

- *Environment tab*: Enables you to configure the startup environment for clients that access one or more servers using terminal services (for running programs on the server).

- *Sessions tab*: Used to configure session parameters for a client using terminal services, such as a session time limit, a limit on how long a session can be idle, what to do when a connection is broken, and how to reconnect.

- *Remote control tab*: Enables you to set up remote control parameters for a client that uses terminal services. The remote control capability enables you to view and manipulate the client session while it is active, in order to troubleshoot problems.

 The information on some of these tabs can be extra work to maintain, such as when telephone numbers and office locations change. Keep this in mind as you enter information, so that you don't introduce more work than is necessary or required by your organization.

Sometimes users change their passwords or go several weeks without logging on—and forget their passwords. You do not have the option to look up a password, but you can reset it for the user. For organizations that have accounts that manage sensitive information, particularly financial information, it is advisable to have specific guidelines that govern the circumstances under which an account password is reset. For example, an organization might require that the account holder physically visit his or her account manager, rather than placing a telephone call because there is no way to verify the authenticity of the request by telephone. In Activity 8-4 you learn how to reset a user's password for an account in a domain.

Activity 8-4: Resetting an Account's Password

Time Required: 5 minutes
Objective: Reset the password on a Windows Server 2008/Server 2008 R2 user account.

Description: In this activity, you learn how to reset the password for a user.

1. Access the Active Directory Users and Computers window, or if it is closed, click **Start**, point to **Administrative Tools**, and click **Active Directory Users and Computers**.

2. Open the **Users** folder, if it is not already open.

3. Right-click the account you created in Activity 8-3.

4. Click **Reset Password**.

5. Enter the new password and then confirm it.

6. Ensure that the box is checked for **User must change password at next logon** (see Figure 8-15). Checking this box enables you to force the user to change the password you set, so that you will not know the new password, which is a best practice endorsed by Microsoft and often a requirement of financial auditors who scrutinize networks that handle financial information.

Figure 8-15   Resetting a password

7. Click **OK** in the Reset Password dialog box. Click **OK** in the information box.

8. Leave the Active Directory Users and Computers window open for the next activity.

Plan to practice good account management by deleting accounts that are no longer in use. If you don't, the number of dormant accounts may grow into a confused tangle of accounts, and you expose your company to security risks. When you delete an account, its globally unique identifier (GUID) is also deleted and is not reused even if you create another account using the same name. A GUID is a unique identification number associated with an account. In Activity 8-5, you delete an account.

Activity 8-5: Deleting an Account in a Domain

Time Required: 5 minutes
Objective: Practice deleting an account in Windows Server 2008/Server 2008 R2.

Description: In this activity, you delete the account that you created in Activity 8-3.

1. Access the Active Directory Users and Computers window, or open it if it is closed. To open the window, click **Start,** point to **Administrative Tools,** and click **Active Directory Users and Computers**.

2. If necessary, open the **Users** folder that contains the account you want to delete.

3. Right-click the account you created in Activity 8-3 and click **Delete**.

4. Click **Yes** to verify that you want to delete this account.

5. Close the Active Directory Users and Computers window and click **No** when asked to save the console settings.

Optimizing Server Performance

A server can be optimized for faster performance. Windows, UNIX/Linux, and Mac OS X servers offer ways to improve performance. Complete coverage of this complex topic is beyond the scope of this book, but this section outlines some basic tasks that can improve server performance.

Optimizing a Windows Server Performance and Configuring Data Execution Prevention   Processor scheduling allows you to configure how processor resources are allocated to programs. The default is set to Background services, which means that all programs running will receive equal amounts of processor time. The Programs setting refers to programs you are likely to be running at the server console, such as a backup program. Normally you will leave the default setting for Background services. Sometimes, though, you may need to give Programs most of the processor's resources, for instance, when you determine that a disk drive is failing and you want to back up its contents as fast as possible using the Backup tool. Another example when Programs is selected is when a server is used for terminal (or remote desktop services) in which remote users or processes run programs on the server.

An additional performance (and security) option that is good to know about is **Data Execution Prevention (DEP)**. When programs are running on the server, DEP monitors how they use memory to ensure they are not causing memory problems. This is intended to foil malware, such as computer viruses, Trojan horses, and worms. Malware sometimes works by trying to invade the memory space allocated to system functions. If DEP notices a program trying to use system memory space, it stops the program and notifies the system Administrator. Try Activity 8-6 to configure processor scheduling and DEP.

Activity 8-6: Configuring Processor Scheduling and DEP

Time Required: Approximately 10 minutes
Objective: Learn where to set up processor scheduling and Data Execution Prevention in Windows Server 2008/Server 2008 R2.

Description: Sometimes it is important to configure a server to optimize processor scheduling. Also, it is important to use DEP to protect how system memory is used. In this activity, you learn where to set the system resources for processor scheduling, and you learn to configure DEP.

1. Click **Start** and click **Control Panel**. In Windows Server 2008, ensure that **Classic View** is used, or in Windows Server 2008 R2 make sure that **View by** is set to **Large icons** or **Small icons**.

2. Double-click (in Windows Server 2008) or click (in Windows Server 2008 R2) **System**.

3. Click **Advanced system settings**.

4. In the System Properties dialog box, click the **Advanced** tab, if necessary.

5. In the Performance section, click the **Settings** button (see Figure 8-16).

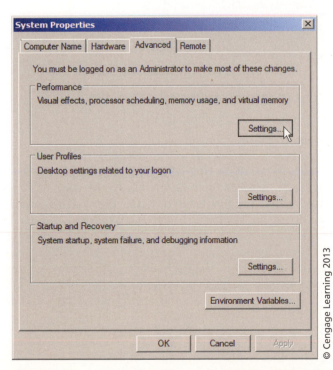

Figure 8-16   Selecting the Settings button in the Performance section

6. Click the **Advanced** tab in the Performance Options dialog box. Notice the options that can be set under Processor scheduling, which are *Programs* and *Background services*, which is the default setting.

7. Click the **Data Execution Prevention** tab. Ensure that **Turn on DEP for all programs and services except those I select** is enabled as shown in Figure 8-17.

Figure 8-17 Configuring Data Execution Prevention

8. Click **OK** in the Performance Options dialog box.

9. Click **OK** in the System Properties dialog box.

10. Close any remaining open windows.

Optimizing UNIX/Linux Through the File System Selection One of the best ways to optimize a UNIX/Linux server is by using the file system specifically designed for the operating system. UNIX and Linux support many different file systems, including file systems compatible with Windows operating systems. However, if you use an older UNIX/Linux file system or a Windows file system, such as NTFS, access to the files on your server will be slower than if you use the preferred (usually the default) file system for your UNIX/Linux operating system. For example, in all Linux installations use the extended file system version 4 (ext4), which has block sizes and speed improvements designed for Linux and enables very large files, from up to 16 GB to 16 TB depending on the Linux distribution. On many UNIX systems the UNIX file system (ufs) provides the best file access optimization.

Optimizing Mac OS X Server Mac OS X Server has many automated built-in functions that help to ensure performance. However, similar to Windows and UNIX/Linux systems,

Mac OS X Server uses virtual memory. **Virtual memory** is disk storage allocated to link with physical RAM to temporarily hold data when there is not enough free RAM. One way to ensure faster performance in Mac OS X Server as well as in other UNIX/Linux server systems and in Windows Server is to ensure that the disk housing the operating system has plenty of free space to allow for space the operating system needs to allocate to virtual memory. In Mac OS X and in other operating systems, this means regularly checking to ensure that the disk housing the operating system is never more than about two-thirds full. If there is not enough room left for virtual memory, there will be a degradation in performance.

Configuring Shared Resources on Windows, UNIX/Linux, and Mac OS X Servers

Shared resources in Windows, UNIX/Linux, and Mac OS X servers are configured in the same way as described in Chapter 7. In Windows Server, you configure a folder's properties for sharing and then configure share and NTFS permissions. In UNIX/Linux and Mac OS X, permissions are configured on directories and files that clients can access. Directories can be made available to be mounted via a network through NFS in UNIX/Linux. In Mac OS X Server, sharing specific resources, such as files and folders, is turned on through the Sharing utility as you learned in Chapter 7.

Managing Your Server

Windows Server, UNIX/Linux, and Mac OS X systems include tools for managing and monitoring a server. The following sections give you a small sampling of such tools.

Managing and Monitoring Windows Server

Task Manager is a Windows Server 2008/Server 2008 R2 management and monitoring tool that is several tools in one. It can be used to manage and monitor applications, processes, real-time performance, network performance, and users. For example, if an application is very CPU intensive, you can monitor this in Task Manager—and even close the application if necessary. Or, if a user's session is hung (no longer responding to user input), you can disconnect that user.

Another valuable tool is Performance Monitor. It is far more complex than Task Manager and is not discussed here. After you master Task Manager, consider reading the Microsoft help documentation about Performance Monitor. To do this click **Start**, click **Help and Support**, and search on **Performance Monitor**. Another option is to visit *www.microsoft.com* and search for documentation about Performance Monitor. You also learn about Performance Monitor for network monitoring in Chapter 12.

Managing and Monitoring Applications   You can use Task Manager to view applications running on the server by pressing Ctrl+Alt+Del while logged on to an account that has Administrator privileges. Click Start Task Manager, which displays a dialog box with six tabs: Applications, Processes, Services, Performance, Networking, and Users (an alternate way to start Task Manager is to right-click an open space on the taskbar and click Task Manager in Windows Server 2008 or Start Task Manager in Windows Server 2008 R2).

When you use the Applications tab, shown in Figure 8-18, you will see all of the software applications running from the server console. Any of the applications can be stopped by highlighting it and clicking the End Task button. If an application is hung, you can select that application and press End Task to stop the application and release server resources. The Switch To button brings the highlighted application to the front so you can work in it, and the New Task button enables you to start another application on the desktop by entering the program name in the Run dialog box (for Windows Server 2008) or the Create New Task dialog box (in Windows Server 2008 R2) and clicking OK. The status bar at the bottom of the screen shows information about the total number of processes, the CPU usage, and physical memory in use.

Figure 8-18 Task Manager Applications tab

If you right-click an application, several active options appear in a shortcut menu, as follows:

- *Switch To*: Takes you into the highlighted program.
- *Bring To Front*: Maximizes and brings the highlighted program to the front, but leaves you in Task Manager.
- *Minimize*: Causes the program to be minimized.
- *Maximize*: Causes the program to be maximized, but leaves you in Task Manager.
- *End Task*: Stops the highlighted program.
- *Create Dump File*: Creates a dump file to reflect activity by the application, which is stored by default in \Users\ADMINISTRATOR\AppData\Local\Temp as the file *program-processname*.DMP, then goes to the process on the Processes tab that is associated with the program. For example, if you make this selection for the Command Prompt program, the dump file is called cmd.DMP and the process on the Processes tab is cmd.exe. Creating a dump file is useful when you are having a problem with an application, for example, if the application crashes or freezes and you want to look for error information in the dump file as a clue to the problem.
- *Go To Process*: Takes you to the Processes tab and highlights the process associated with the program.

In Activity 8-7 you manage applications in Task Manager.

Activity 8-7: Working with Applications in Windows Task Manager

Time Required: Approximately 10 minutes
Objective: Use Task Manager in Windows Server 2008/Server 2008 R2 (and Windows 7) to monitor and manage applications.

Description: In this activity, you start an application and then use it to learn about Task Manager functions for controlling applications, including ending the application.

1. Click **Start**, point to **All Programs**, click **Accessories**, and click **Calculator**.
2. Press the **Ctrl+Alt+Del** keys at the same time. Click **Start Task Manager**.
3. Click the **Applications** tab, if it is not displayed already.
4. Right-click **Calculator** and notice the active options on the shortcut menu.
5. Click **Switch To**. What happens?
6. Click **Windows Task Manager** in the taskbar.
7. Click **Calculator**, if it is not still selected. Click **End Task** to close the Calculator application.
8. Leave Windows Task Manager open for the next activity.

Managing and Monitoring Processes

The Processes tab lists the processes in use by all running applications. If you need to stop a process, simply highlight it and click End Process. The Processes tab also shows information about each started process, as summarized in Table 8-4.

Table 8-4   Task Manager information on processes

Process Information	Description
Image Name	The process name, such as winword.exe for Microsoft Word
User Name	The user account under which the process is running
CPU	The percentage of the CPU resources used by the process
Memory (Private Working Set)	The amount of memory the process is using
Description	Full or formal name of the process, such as Client Server Runtime process

© Cengage Learning 2013

 Table 8-4 lists only the default information that is displayed on the Processes tab. You can change the display to view other information, such as page faults, base priority, and thread count (all described later in this chapter) by clicking the View menu and then clicking Select Columns.

Using the Processes tab within Task Manager you can increase the priority of a process (or processes) in the list so that it has more CPU priority than what is set as its default. Suppose, for example, that you want to increase the priority for Windows Explorer, which is process explorer.exe. To start, right-click explorer.exe, displaying a shortcut menu in which you can end the process, end the process tree (end that process and all subprocesses associated with it), or reset the priority. You click Set Priority to set the priority (see Figure 8-19).

Normally, the priority at which a process runs is set in the program code of the application, which is called the **base priority class**. If the base priority class is not set by the program, a normal (average) priority is set by the system. The server administrator always has the option to set a different base priority. As shown in Figure 8-19, the administrator can change the priority to any of six options: Low, BelowNormal, Normal, AboveNormal, High, or Realtime. You might think of these processes as being on a continuum, with Normal as the midpoint, which is 0. Low is –2, BelowNormal is –1, AboveNormal is +1, and High is +2. Realtime is given an extra advantage at +15. For example, a Low priority means that if a process is waiting in a queue—for example, for processor time, disk access, or memory access—all processes with a higher priority go first. The same is true for BelowNormal, except that processes

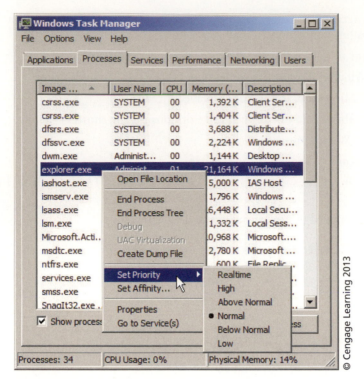

Figure 8-19 Setting the priority of a process

with this priority run before those set at Low, and so on. Activity 8-8 enables you to reset the priority of a process.

Activity 8-8: Managing Processes in Windows Task Manager

Time Required: 10 minutes

Objective: Use Task Manager in Windows Server 2008/Server 2008 R2 (or Windows 7) to monitor processes and to reset the priority of a process.

Description: In this activity, you use Task Manager to learn about how a process is functioning and then to reset the priority of that process.

1. Start the **Calculator** program, as you did in Activity 8-7.
2. Open **Task Manager**, if it is closed, and, if necessary, click the **Applications** tab.

Real-Life Networking

Use the Realtime priority only when necessary. If assigned to a process, that process may completely take over the server, preventing work by any other processes. For instance, a server administrator for a government office determined that a disk drive was failing on a server, and she decided to perform a fast backup of the day's work before the disk failed completely. She assigned the Realtime priority to the backup process and completed the backup.

3. Right-click **Calculator** and click **Go To Process**. What happens when you do this?

4. Right-click **calc.exe** and record the options.

5. On the shortcut menu, point to **Set Priority**.

6. Click **AboveNormal**.

7. Click **Change Priority** in the Windows Task Manager information box.

8. Position the Calculator program and Task Manager so that you can view both. Click several numbers on the Calculator and watch the CPU column for calc.exe. If you watch carefully, you will notice a temporary change in the CPU use, such as between 01 and about 04.

9. Click **calc.exe** and click **End Process**. Click **End Process** in the Windows Task Manager information box.

10. Close Task Manager.

Monitoring Services
The Services tab in Task Manager shows the services that are started, stopped, or paused. Compared to Server Manager and the Computer Management tools in Windows Server systems, this is a fast way to monitor server services, such as the PlugPlay service used to automatically recognize new hardware. From here you can start or stop a service by doing the following:

8

1. Right-click the service.

2. Click Start Service or Stop Service (see Figure 8-20).

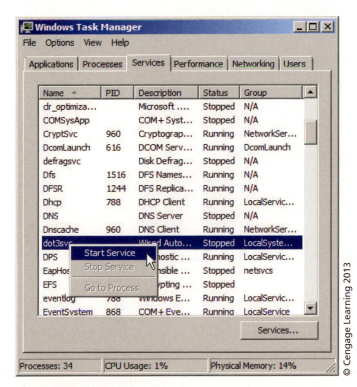

© Cengage Learning 2013

Figure 8-20   Starting a service

Because of display limitations, Task Manager does not use totally consistent names for services. For example, SamSs in Task Manager is shown as Security Accounts Manager in other server tools. PlugPlay in Task Manager is Plug and Play in other tools. If you are not sure about a service, maximize Task Manager and expand the Description column to view the description of a service.

The services on the Services tab might not be displayed in alphabetical order. You can put them in alphabetical order by clicking the Name column heading.

Monitoring Real-Time Performance   The Performance tab in Task Manager shows vital CPU and memory performance information through bar charts, line graphs, and performance statistics (see Figure 8-21). The CPU Usage and Memory bars show the current use of CPU and page file use. A **page file** is disk space, in the form of a file, for use when memory requirements exceed the available RAM—thus it is used for virtual memory. To the right of each bar is a graph showing the immediate history statistics. The bottom of the Performance tab shows more detailed statistics, such as those for handles and threads, which are described in Table 8-5. A **handle** is a resource, such as a file, used by a program and having its own identification so the program is able to access it. **Threads** are blocks of code within a program.

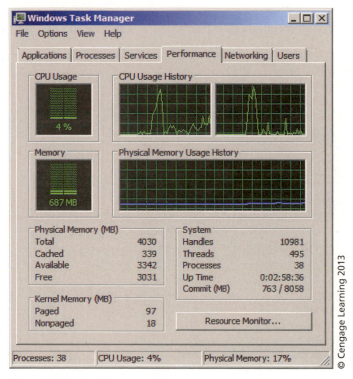

Figure 8-21   Performance tab

Monitoring Network Performance   The Networking tab in Task Manager enables you to monitor network performance on all of the NICs (and WNICs) installed in the server. A graphical representation shows the total network utilization, which is roughly the percentage of the network bandwidth in use.

The lower portion of the tab (see Figure 8-22) shows the network performance data across each NIC. It lists the name of the adapter (or connection), the network utilization detected by the adapter (from 0 to 100 percent), the speed of the network link (such as 100 Mbps), and the operational state of the adapter. This information can be valuable if you suspect there is a problem with a NIC in the server and you want an immediate determination if it is working. The information on the tab also can be an initial warning that something is causing prolonged high network utilization—80 to 100 percent, for instance.

Monitoring Users   The Users tab in Task Manager simply provides a listing of the users currently logged on. You can log off a user by clicking that user and clicking the Logoff button,

Table 8-5   Task Manager performance statistics

Statistic	Description
Physical Memory Total	The amount of RAM installed in the computer
Physical Memory Cached	The amount of RAM used for file caching
Physical Memory Available (in Windows Server 2008 R2 and Windows 7)	The amount of RAM currently not in use
Physical Memory Free	The amount of RAM available to be used
Kernel Memory Total	The amount of memory used by the operating system
Kernel Memory Paged	The amount of virtual memory used by the operating system
Kernel Memory Nonpaged	The amount of RAM memory used by the operating system
Handles	The number of objects in use by all processes, such as open files
Threads	The number of code blocks in use, in which one program or process may be running one or more code blocks at a time
Processes	The number of processes that are active or sitting idle
Up Time	The amount of time since the server was last booted
Page File (in Windows Server 2008)	Size of the page file
Commit (in Windows Server 2008 R2 and Windows 7)	Current page file size and maximum allocated size shown as a ratio

© Cengage Learning 2013

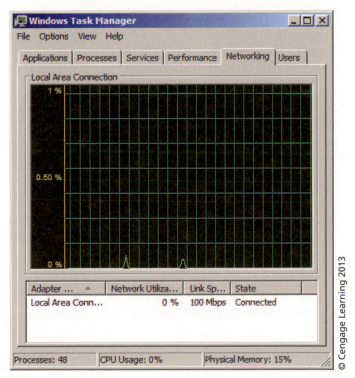

Figure 8-22   Networking tab

which ensures that any open files are closed before the user is logged off. For example, you might log off an inactive account at the end of the day before you backup a server. Another option is to Disconnect a user, which you might use if the Logoff action does not work because the user's connection is hung.

Managing and Monitoring UNIX/Linux

There are many management and monitoring utilities in UNIX/Linux. The following sections give you a snapshot of a few of these utilities.

Managing Processes with the *Top* Command   One of the most effective utilities for auditing system performance is the *top* command. The *top* command displays a listing of the most CPU-intensive tasks, such as the processor state, in real time (the display is updated every five seconds by default). This means that you can actually see what is happening inside the computer as it progresses.

Useful options for the *top* command are as follows:

- *-d* specifies the delay between screen updates.

- *-p* monitors the process with the specified process id (PID).

- *-s* allows the *top* utility to run in secure mode, which disables the interactive commands, such as *k* to kill a process (a good option for those not in charge of tuning the system).

- *-S* runs *top* in cumulative mode; this mode displays the cumulative CPU time used by a process instead of the current CPU time used.

While running, the *top* command supports interactive commands, such as *k*, which kills a running process. The *top* utility continues to produce output until you press *q* to terminate the execution of the program. Activity 8-9 enables you to use the *top* command.

Activity 8-9: Managing Processes with the *Top* Command

Time Required: 10 minutes
Objective: Use the *top* command in UNIX/Linux to manage processes.

Description: Sometimes your system might respond slowly or seem to have delays. In these conditions, it is useful to employ the *top* command to monitor CPU use by processes and other system information, as you learn in this activity. You can be in either your account or the root account to use the *top* command and the other UNIX/Linux utilities described in this section of the chapter, but it is recommended that you use your account when it is not necessary to be in the root account.

1. Open a terminal window to access the command line. (In GNOME 3.x click **Activities** in the top Panel, click **Applications**, and click **Terminal**.)

2. Display the CPU activity by typing **top** and then pressing **Enter**. Your screen should look similar to that shown in Figure 8-23. (Don't forget this display changes while on screen.)

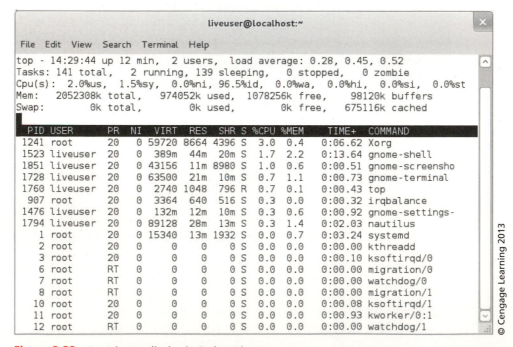

Figure 8-23   Sample *top* display in Fedora Linux

3. The processes are shown in the order of the amount of CPU time they use. After looking at the display for a short time, press **q** to exit from the *top* utility.

4. Run the *top* utility again. Notice the far-left column of information, labeled PID. This column lists the process id of each process shown. Notice the PID of the *top* command. (In Figure 8-23, the *top* command's PID is 1760. Yours is probably different.)

5. Press **k** to initiate the *kill* command. The *top* utility asks you to enter the PID to kill. Enter the PID of the *top* command. Press **Enter** to kill the process. (You might have to press **Enter** a second time to return to a command prompt.) Type **clear** and press **Enter** (you might have to execute **clear** more than once) to clear the lines from the screen. The *top* utility is no longer running.

6. Run the *top* utility in secure mode by typing **top -s** and pressing **Enter**.

7. Press **k** to initiate the *kill* command. Because top is running in secure mode, it displays the message "Unavailable in secure mode." Press **q** to exit the *top* utility.

8. Type **clear** and press **Enter** to clear the display for the next project.

9. Leave the terminal window open for the next activity.

Monitoring Memory Usage with the *free* Command A useful, though static, display of memory usage is generated by the *free* command. The *free* command displays the amount of free and used memory in the system. The *free* command also enables you to monitor the usage of your swap space. Swap space is disk space that acts like virtual memory and is configured when you install the operating system. (Swap space is also known as virtual memory.) By monitoring your system using the *free* command, you can determine if you have enough RAM for the tasks on your computer, and you can determine if your swap space is set properly. Unlike *top*, the *free* utility runs and then automatically exits.

Several useful options available with the *free* command are as follows:

- *-b* shows information in bytes (the default display is in kilobytes).
- *-m* shows information in megabytes.
- *-g* shows information in gigabytes.
- *-t* creates totals for RAM and swap memory statistics.

Activity 8-10 gives you experience with the *free* command.

Activity 8-10: Monitoring Memory with the *free* Command

Time Required: 5 minutes
Objective: Use the *free* command in UNIX/Linux to view memory use.

Description: Plan to periodically monitor memory use in your computer, particularly if the computer seems to run slowly when you use specific programs. In this activity, you use the *free* command to monitor memory.

1. Open a terminal window, if one is not open.

2. Type **free** and press **Enter**. The command displays the amount of total, used, and free memory. It also displays the amount of shared memory, buffer memory, and cached memory. In addition, the amount of total, used, and free swap memory is shown. By default, all amounts are shown in kilobytes.

3. Type **free -m** and press **Enter** to see the *free* command's output in megabytes.

4. Type **free -t** and press **Enter** to see memory use totals (see Figure 8-24).

5. Type **clear** and press **Enter**.

6. Leave the terminal window open for the next activity.

```
                              liveuser@localhost:~                          ✕

  File  Edit  View  Search  Terminal  Help
  [liveuser@localhost ~]$ free
                 total        used        free      shared     buffers      cached
  Mem:         2052308     1023296     1029012           0      105744      714420
  -/+ buffers/cache:        203132     1849176
  Swap:              0           0           0
  [liveuser@localhost ~]$ free -m
                 total        used        free      shared     buffers      cached
  Mem:            2004         999        1004           0         103         698
  -/+ buffers/cache:           198        1806
  Swap:              0           0           0
  [liveuser@localhost ~]$ free -t
                 total        used        free      shared     buffers      cached
  Mem:         2052308     1023652     1028656           0      105752      714972
  -/+ buffers/cache:        202928     1849380
  Swap:              0           0           0
  Total:       2052308     1023652     1028656
  [liveuser@localhost ~]$ █
```

© Cengage Learning 2013

Figure 8-24   Using the *free* command in Fedora Linux

Using the *df* and *du* Commands to Monitor Disk Usage

It is good practice to periodically monitor disk usage on a UNIX/Linux computer to ensure you are not running out of space and to determine how disk space is being used. The *df* and *du* utilities enable you to monitor the hard disks.

The *df* utility reports the number of 1024-byte blocks that are allocated, used, and available; the percentage used; and the mount point—for mounted file systems. The reports displayed are based on the command options entered. For example, Figure 8-25 shows the *df* information in megabytes for one file system (/dev/sr0, which is used for the live account in Fedora Live Media).

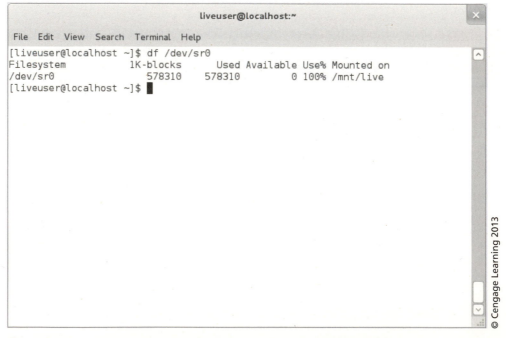

```
                              liveuser@localhost:~                          ✕

  File  Edit  View  Search  Terminal  Help
  [liveuser@localhost ~]$ df /dev/sr0
  Filesystem            1K-blocks       Used Available Use% Mounted on
  /dev/sr0                 578310     578310         0 100% /mnt/live
  [liveuser@localhost ~]$ █
```

© Cengage Learning 2013

Figure 8-25   Viewing information for one file system in 1K blocks in Fedora Linux

Some of the options you can use with *df* are as follows:

- *-h* displays information in human-readable format, such as using "29G" (G is for GB) instead of 29659208.

- *-l* displays only local file systems.

- *-m* displays sizes in megabytes.

- *-t* displays only the type of file system.

If you just enter *df* without specifying a file system, this shows information for all mounted file systems, including mounted DVDs, CD-ROMs, and flash drives. Also, note that the combined used and available disk space might not add up to the allocated space because the system uses some space for its own purposes.

The *du* utility summarizes disk usage. If you enter the command without options, you receive a report based on all file usage, starting at your current directory and progressing down through all subdirectories. File usage is expressed in the number of 512-byte blocks (default) or by the number of bytes (the *-b* option). Figure 8-26 shows the *du* command used to display information about the /dev directory in bytes.

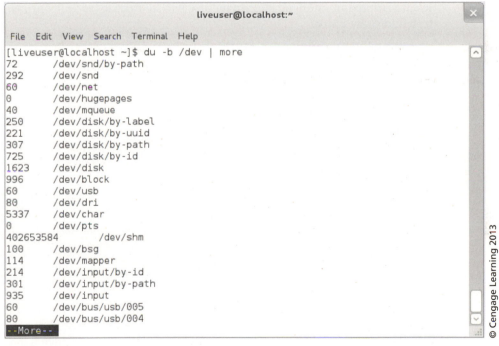

Figure 8-26   Viewing *du* information for the /dev directory in Fedora Linux

Valuable options to know for the *du* command include the following:

- *-a* displays information for files as well as for directories.

- *-b* displays information in bytes.

- *-c* creates a total at the end.

- *-S* omits the size of subdirectories in the totals for directories.

In Activity 8-11, you use both the *df* and *du* commands.

Activity 8-11: Monitoring Disk Space Using *df* and *du*

Time Required: 10 minutes

Objective: Use the *df* and *du* commands in UNIX/Linux to monitor disk space.

Description: In this activity, you use both the *df* and *du* commands to monitor disk space and disk usage.

1. With a terminal window open, type **df** and then press **Enter**.

   Notice that under the 1K-blocks column the display reports the number of blocks allocated for the file system. The Used column shows the number of blocks in use, and the Available column shows how many blocks are available. The Use% column shows the percentage of blocks in use, and the Mounted on column shows the mounted file systems. In some versions of UNIX/Linux, *df* also shows the statistics for mounted removable media, such as DVDs, CD-ROMs, and flash drives.

2. You can specify a file system as an argument. The statistics for that file system alone appear on the screen. Type **df /dev/sr0** if you are using Fedora Live Media (or another partitioned disk appropriate to your system, such as hda1) and press **Enter**. You see the disk statistics for that volume only.

3. The *-h* option causes the numbers to print in human-readable form. Instead of displaying raw numbers for size, amount of disk space used, and amount of space available, the statistics are printed in kilobyte, megabyte, or gigabyte format (as appropriate to the size). Type **df -h** and press **Enter**.

4. Type **clear** and press **Enter** to clear the display.

5. Ensure that you are in your home directory by typing **cd** and pressing **Enter**. To receive a report on disk usage, type **du | more** and then press **Enter**. (The results of the *du* command can be lengthy, so use the pipe expression "|" to pipe its output to the *more* command.)

6. The output shows the number of 512-byte blocks used in each subdirectory (including hidden subdirectories). Type **q** to exit the *more* command.

7. To view a similar report on disk usage by the number of bytes instead of by 512-byte blocks, type **du -b | more** and then press **Enter**.

8. Press the **spacebar** repeatedly to advance through the display of information, until you reach the command prompt.

9. Like the *df* command, the *du* command supports the *-h* option to display statistics in human-readable format. Type **du -h | more** and press **Enter**. Repeatedly press the **spacebar** to advance through the display or press **q** to go back to the command prompt. If you are working from a terminal window, close it.

Besides the *-h* option, the *du* command supports the *-x* option, which enables you to omit directories in file systems other than the one in which you are working, when more than one file system is mounted.

Monitoring Users with the *Who* and *Finger* Commands

To monitor who is logged in on a UNIX/Linux system, use the *who* command. On a server system, knowing who is logged in to the system is important because it allows the administrator to periodically verify authorized users and levels of use. Knowing who is logged in is also valuable for ordinary users, who can use that information to judge how busy the system is at a given time or who might want to contact another user.

Useful options for the *who* command are as follows:

- *am i* (type *who* in front, as in *who am i*) for information about your own session

- *whoami* (type whoami as all one word) to see what account you are using

- *-H* to show column headings
- *-u* to show idle time for each user
- *-q* for a quick list and total of users logged in
- *-b* is used by system administrators and others to verify when the system was last booted.

Another option on many UNIX/Linux systems (but not available in Fedora Live Media) is to employ the *finger* command for a display of users on a system. By default *finger* displays information about the user, such as the login name, user's full name, idle time, login time, and office information (if this information is available and associated with the user's account).

Remember that you can always read the online manual documentation for a command by entering *man* and the command name, such as *man who*.

Real-Life Networking

At a university, a UNIX system manager used the *top* command to monitor processes on a UNIX server because response was slow. He found that the server was slow because a user was running a CPU-intensive program. The system manager used the *finger* command and determined that the user was the university president's wife who was a statistician. This gave him the necessary information to call that user and report that her program was slowing the progress of other server users (although system operators warned against calling for political reasons). When he called this user, she was grateful, because her program was not responding, and she appreciated the help in killing it.

Managing and Monitoring Mac OS X

Because Mac OS X is built on Darwin UNIX, you can use many of the same management and monitoring commands as you learned in the last section for UNIX/Linux (except the *free* command). The following commands work from a terminal window in Mac OS X:

- *top* (but you cannot kill a process from within *top*)
- *du*
- *df*
- *who* (including *whoami*)
- *finger*

Besides the terminal window, Mac OS X offers the Network Utility from which you can run specialized Finger and Whois utilities through a GUI window. Activity 8-12 enables you to use both the terminal window and the Network Utility to execute network commands.

Activity 8-12: Using Command Line and Network Utility Commands from Mac OS X

Time Required: 15 minutes

Objective: Use the *top*, *du*, *df*, *whoami*, and *finger* commands from a terminal window and also use the Network Utility to execute Whois and Finger.

Description: Mac OS X and Mac OS X Server are versatile in that you can execute network commands in a terminal window as in UNIX/Linux or through the GUI-based Network Utility. In this activity, you use both the terminal window and the Network Utility to execute commands that are useful for managing a server, but that also work on a Mac OS X workstation.

1. Ensure that Finder is open by clicking **Finder** in the Dock or clicking an open area on the desktop.

2. Click **Go** in the menu bar and click **Utilities** in the Go menu.

3. Double-click **Terminal** in the Utilities window.

4. Type **top** in the command line and press **return**. Notice that the presentation of the *top* command (see Figure 8-27) is very similar to that for Linux (refer to Figure 8-23 to compare). What is the PID for the *top* command on your display (notice that the PID for *top* is 204 in Figure 8-27)?

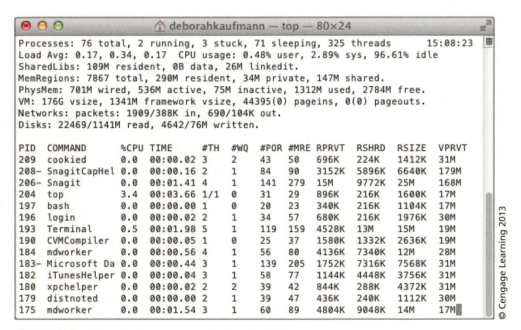

```
●●●                    ⌂ deborahkaufmann — top — 80×24
Processes: 76 total, 2 running, 3 stuck, 71 sleeping, 325 threads        15:08:23
Load Avg: 0.17, 0.34, 0.17  CPU usage: 0.48% user, 2.89% sys, 96.61% idle
SharedLibs: 109M resident, 0B data, 26M linkedit.
MemRegions: 7867 total, 290M resident, 34M private, 147M shared.
PhysMem: 701M wired, 536M active, 75M inactive, 1312M used, 2784M free.
VM: 176G vsize, 1341M framework vsize, 44395(0) pageins, 0(0) pageouts.
Networks: packets: 1909/388K in, 690/104K out.
Disks: 22469/1141M read, 4642/76M written.

PID  COMMAND      %CPU  TIME      #TH  #WQ  #POR #MRE RPRVT RSHRD RSIZE VPRVT
209  cookied      0.0   00:00.02  3    2    43   50   696K  224K  1412K 31M
208- SnagitCapHel 0.0   00:00.16  2    1    84   90   3152K 5896K 6640K 179M
206- Snagit       0.0   00:01.41  4    1    141  279  15M   9772K 25M   168M
204  top          3.4   00:03.66  1/1  0    31   29   896K  216K  1600K 17M
197  bash         0.0   00:00.00  1    0    20   23   340K  216K  1104K 17M
196  login        0.0   00:00.02  2    1    34   57   680K  216K  1976K 30M
193  Terminal     0.5   00:01.98  5    1    119  159  4528K 13M   15M   19M
190  CVMCompiler  0.0   00:00.05  1    0    25   37   1580K 1332K 2636K 19M
184  mdworker     0.0   00:00.56  4    1    56   80   4136K 7340K 12M   28M
183- Microsoft Da 0.0   00:00.44  3    1    139  205  1752K 7316K 7568K 31M
182  iTunesHelper 0.0   00:00.04  3    1    58   77   1144K 4448K 3756K 31M
180  xpchelper    0.0   00:00.02  2    2    39   42   844K  288K  4372K 31M
179  distnoted    0.0   00:00.00  2    1    39   47   436K  240K  1112K 30M
175  mdworker     0.0   00:01.54  3    1    60   89   4804K 9048K 14M   17M
```

© Cengage Learning 2013

Figure 8-27   Using the *top* command in Mac OS X Lion

5. Press **q** to exit the *top* information.

6. At the command line, type **df -h** and press **return** to view disk usage data in human-readable form (such as using 29G or 29 Gi for 29 gigabytes instead of 29659208).

7. Type **du | more** and press **return** to view a summary of disk usage by directory and subdirectory. Press the **spacebar** to view the results a window at time or press **q** to exit the display of data.

The *du* command in Darwin UNIX (and Mac OS X) does not support the *-b* option (to display information in bytes instead of in blocks) as is available for *du* in Linux. However, as true for Linux, you can view online documentation for a Darwin UNIX command by entering *man* plus the command, such as *man du*.

8. Type **du -h | more** and press **return** to see the size information in human-readable format. Press **q** to return to the command prompt.

9. Type **whoami** and press **return** to view the name of the account you are using.

10. Type **finger** and press **return** to view all accounts logged on. Notice that your account is listed twice, once as the account logged onto the local console and also as an account logged into the system.

11. If you have speakers connected, type **say I am good** and press **return** to learn a command not in Linux.

12. Click **Terminal** in the menu bar and click **Quit Terminal**.

13. Display the **Utilities** window (click it in the Dock if you shrank it) or open the Utilities window again, if it is closed (see Steps 1 and 2).

14. Double-click **Network Utility**.

15. Click the **Whois** tab in the Network Utility window. You can use the Whois utility to look up a user or domain. In the box for **Enter a domain address to look up its "whois" information**, type **apple.com** and click the **Whois** button. Scroll through the window to view the results.

16. Click the **Finger** tab. In the first box before the @ sign, enter the name of your account. You can leave the domain name blank, if you are not in a domain. Or if you are in a domain, enter the domain name. Click **Finger**. Notice that you see information showing when your account logged on (see Figure 8-28).

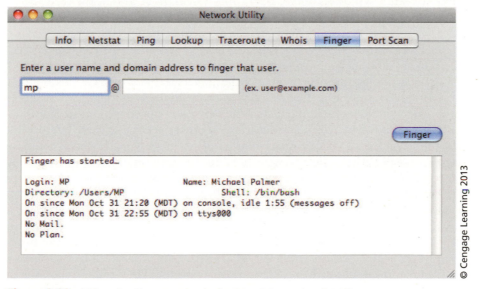

Figure 8-28   Using the Finger option in the Mac OS X Network Utility

17. Click **Network Utility** in the menu bar and click **Quit Network Utility**.

18. Close any remaining open windows.

Putting It All Together: Designing a Server-Based Office Network

As the number of network users increases, so do the reasons for implementing a server-based network. Some of the advantages of a server-based network over a peer-to-peer network are as follows:

- A server operating system is truly designed to be a multiuser system, whereas workstations on a peer-to-peer network are not designed for many simultaneous users.
- Servers offer industrial-strength capabilities for sharing resources.
- Servers come with many built-in monitoring and management tools.

- A server-based network enables you to centralize or decentralize network resources to match your organization's work culture.

- A server-based network enables an organization to more completely manage network security measures, resulting in better protection of data and resources than on a peer-to-peer network.

- A server-based network enables you to manage user accounts and network resources on a small level, such as through a stand-alone server or at a larger level through a domain—so that a network can be customized to very small or very large organizations.

- When a small organization grows larger, a server-based network offers growth potential so that it is easier to scale up the network resources to match growth in the organization.

Consider a medium-sized rural feed store in which there is an office staff of seven people and a sales staff of 10 people. The store has designated one Windows 7 workstation as the main computer from which to share files, with haphazard management. The problem is that when two or more salespersons check the warehouse inventory by accessing shared inventory files on the Windows 7 machine, response often slows to a crawl and causes impatient customers to wait. This is because three or four of the office staff are also often accessing shared files on the Windows 7 workstation. A possible solution in this context is to install a Windows Server operating system on the computer sharing the files, if the computer has hardware compatible with Windows Server. An even better solution is to purchase a new more powerful computer and equip it with a Windows Server operating system. In addition, the feed store should train one person to manage the server and train another person as a backup. They should also place the server in a secure location where it is not likely to be bumped or disconnected.

In a larger context, consider a firm that makes scientific instruments and employs 78 people. The firm has a business unit, a research unit, and a manufacturing unit. It also wants to offer a Web site to advertise its products and enable customers to place orders. This is a context that can use multiple servers, such as a Windows server for the business unit and two or more Linux servers for the research and manufacturing units. The Web server can employ either Windows Server or Linux, because there is robust Web server software for either operating system: Internet Information Services (IIS) for a Windows server or Apache for a Linux system. This context is certainly out of the realm of peer-to-peer networking and well suited for multiple servers to authenticate who logs onto the network, to efficiently share resources, and to provide strong security measures for the resources. For best management, it makes sense for this firm to train at least two people to administer the servers and to place the servers in a secure server room equipped with conditioned power and UPSs.

Finally, consider a firm of graphic artists who create specialized art for customers who host Web sites, such as the scientific instruments company just mentioned. The firm of graphic artists employs 12 people, all of whom use Mac OS X Lion workstations equipped with graphic arts and Microsoft Office software. All 12 people also use iPads and iPhones. Further, there are two part-time artists who connect to the firm's network using Windows 7. This firm can benefit from having Mac OS X Lion Server. All users can have accounts on the server and use it as central storage for their work files. The server also offers software to manage their iPads and iPhones for business use. Further, Mac OS X Lion Server and the Mac OS X Lion workstations can be configured to recognize network file sharing with the Windows 7 workstations.

Chapter Summary

- A server-based network can make sense for a home or office network when you have many shared applications and when the number of network users grows beyond 20 (or even beyond just a few users, depending on the type of computer use).

- Server-based networks can be an advantage over peer-to-peer networks because server-based networks offer more robust resource sharing, better security options, and centralized or decentralized management options for an organization.

- Before you install a server, consider factors such as what type of computer to use, where to locate a server, and who should manage a server.

- For creating a few servers, often the most effective method is to install directly from an installation DVD. To use the DVD installation method, you may need to configure the computer's BIOS to boot from a DVD/CD-ROM drive, if the computer is not already configured with this as a boot option.

- Setting up a server involves tasks such as creating user accounts and optimizing the server operating system.

- In Windows Server, you can choose to use a workgroup or a domain for managing user accounts. The choice you make affects the tools you use to create accounts. In UNIX/Linux you can use the same account creation tools as you learned in Chapter 7: *useradd*, *usermod*, and *userdel*. Another option in UNIX/Linux is to use the User Manager tool in the GNOME desktop. Mac OS X Server has two options for creating and managing user accounts: Server Assistant and Server Preferences.

- Windows Server systems offer many management and monitoring tools. Task Manager is a basic and useful tool to learn early on. Through Task Manager you can manage and monitor applications, processes, services, real-time and network performance, and users.

- As with Windows Server, UNIX and Linux systems offer a wide range of management and monitoring tools. Good tools to learn at first include *top* for managing processes, *free* for monitoring memory, *df* and *du* for monitoring disk use, and *who* and *finger* (for most Linux systems) for monitoring users.

- Mac OS X Server (Snow Leopard and Lion) is Darwin UNIX under the hood, so you can use UNIX management tools such as *top*, *df*, *du*, *who*, and *finger*. Mac OS X Server also has the Network Utility for managing network functions, including GUI tools for running Whois and Finger.

Key Terms

Active Directory   A directory service used in Windows Server that houses information about all network resources such as servers, printers, user accounts, groups of user accounts, security policies, and other information. As a directory service, Active Directory is responsible for providing a central listing of resources and ways to quickly find and access specific resources and for providing a way to manage network resources.

application virtualization   Running single applications in their own virtual machine environments.

base priority class   The initial priority assigned to a program process or thread in the program code.

basic input/output system (BIOS)   A program on a nonvolatile random access memory chip that establishes basic communication with components such as the monitor and disk drives. The BIOS also performs memory and hardware tests when a computer is initially turned on. On most computers you can update the BIOS. *See* **nonvolatile random access memory (NVRAM)**.

blade enclosure   A large box with slots for blade servers; the box provides cooling fans, electrical power, connection to a shared monitor and pointing device, and network connectivity.

blade server   A modular server unit that looks like a card and that fits into a blade enclosure.

Data Execution Prevention (DEP)   A security feature in Windows Server systems that monitors how programs use memory and stops programs that attempt to use memory allocated for system programs and processes. This is intended to foil viruses, Trojan horses, and worms that attempt to invade system memory.

external virtual network   A virtual network that offers communications between virtual machines and the physical network through a network interface card.

handle   A resource, such as a file, used by a program that has its own identification so the program is able to access it.

hardware or CPU virtualization   Using the CPU to perform virtualization tasks by having virtualization processes work inside a specially designed CPU.

internal virtual network   A virtual network that enables communications between virtual machines and the host virtual server.

Microsoft Hyper-V   Microsoft virtual server software that can be included with Windows Server 2008/Server 2008 R2 that enables running multiple operating systems on one physical computer.

Microsoft Management Console (MMC)   A Windows Server tool that you can customize by adding tool modules to manage different server functions, such as creating accounts or monitoring a server. (The MMC is also available in Windows 7.)

network virtualization   Dividing a single network into multiple channels or bandwidths so that the network appears as multiple networks.

nonvolatile random access memory (NVRAM)   Computer memory that does not lose its contents when the computer is turned off. One way to ensure nonvolatile memory is by connecting the memory to a battery.

page file   Disk space, in the form of a file, for use when memory requirements exceed the available RAM.

private virtual network   A virtual network that enables communications between virtual machines and the host virtual server.

rack-mounted server   A CPU box mounted in a rack that can hold several such CPUs, each with its own power cord and network connection, and that often share one monitor and pointing device.

server farm   A group of servers placed in the same location, as in a computer machine room.

server virtualization   Running multiple server operating systems on a single server computer.

shell   An interface between the operating system and the user. A shell provides an environment in which to enter commands. The bash shell is popular and usually the default in Linux.

stand-alone server   In Windows Server, this is a server that does not have Active Directory installed. Instead, it manages user accounts and shared access locally through a workgroup.

storage virtualization   Setting up multiple networked disk storage units to appear as one unit.

swap space   Disk space that acts like an extension of memory. *See* **virtual memory**.

thread   A block of program code executing within a running process. One process may launch one or more threads.

uninterruptible power supply (UPS)   A device built into electrical equipment or a separate device that provides immediate battery power to equipment during a power outage, surge, or brownout.

virtual CPU   A simulation of a CPU to have the equivalent of more CPUs than are actually in a computer, enabling applications, such as virtual machines to have their own processor.

virtualization   Ability to disguise the physical or individual hardware elements of computing to enhance or multiply resources. Through virtualization, one resource can be made to appear as many separate resources. For example, one computer can be virtualized to appear to the user as many computers, or one storage device can look like multiple storage devices.

virtual LAN identification number (VLAN ID)   A unique number used for communication through a network adapter that distinguishes the virtual network used by that adapter from other networks.

virtual machine   An instance of a discrete operating system running within virtual server software on one computer. Multiple virtual machines can run within the virtual server software on one computer.

virtual memory   Disk storage allocated to link with physical RAM to temporarily hold data when there is not enough free RAM. *See* **swap space**.

virtual network   A network on which virtual machines communicate through virtual links.

virtual server software   Software that enables a computer to house two or more operating systems.

workstation or PC virtualization   Running multiple workstation operating systems, such as Windows XP, Windows 7, and Linux, on one computer.

Review Questions

1. You are hired to consult for a new pharmaceutical company that will have 82 employees. The company plans to have a Web site and to use a database for tracking data on drug research. Which of the following do you recommend for this company? (Choose all that apply.)

   a. a peer-to-peer network because this will save money

   b. a server to house the research database

   c. a network with a domain to properly manage all of the user accounts

   d. a server for the Web site

2. Which of the following are advantages of using a virtual server? (Choose all that apply.)

   a. reduction in the number of computers needed

   b. lower energy costs

   c. less space required

   d. faster network throughput at the nearest router

3. Which of the following would best describe a blade server?

   a. a card that fits into an enclosure

   b. a stand-alone server on its own table

   c. a Web server used for a company wikis

   d. a server with a very fast CPU that is the managing server in a server cluster

4. Before you purchase and install a new computer for your company, which of the following should you consider? (Choose all that apply.)

   a. who will manage the server

   b. purchasing a UPS

   c. where to locate the server

   d. hardware compatibility

5. Your company uses Hyper-V for virtual servers. On a virtual database server used by many in the company, which of the following virtual network connections would be used to enable company-wide network access?

   a. external virtual network

   b. private virtual network

   c. domain virtual network

   d. internal virtual network

6. Your boss has purchased an Intel computer to use as a virtual server. However, when you attempt to install Hyper-V, there is a hardware error message. Which of the following is likely to be the cause?

   a. There is no BIOS.

   b. Active Directory must first be installed to coordinate hardware tasks.

   c. The boss didn't purchase a computer with a VT-capable CPU.

   d. The computer's NIC does not support multiple pathways.

7. The applications development manager for your company wants the programmers to develop a network time-card system to be used by 250 workers and the payroll office staff of 10. Because his budget is tight, he asks you to install Windows Server 2008 R2 on an older Intel computer that just meets the basic requirements for Windows Server 2008 R2 and to use this as the production server for the new time-card system. What is your reaction?

   a. This seems like an economical solution, as long as the server has 512 MB of memory.

   b. This solution will work effectively, but the computer should have a wireless network connection for fast throughput.

   c. This server is not likely to efficiently handle the load of the new system. A faster processor with more memory would be a better start.

   d. A time-card system of this magnitude really needs a mainframe.

8. Which tool can be used to create user accounts in Windows Server 2008 or Windows Server 2008 R2 when a server domain is present? (Choose all that apply.)

   a. Active Directory Users and Computers

   b. Local Users and Groups

   c. Domain Users

   d. System Setup

9. You are the server administrator for a company that relies on its Windows Server 2008 R2 server-based network. Because security is very important to this company, which of the following do you ensure is configured when you install a new server?

   a. Application Security Manager

   b. Data Execution Prevention

   c. Network Option Protection

   d. Secure Connection Translation

10. The applications development group in your company has just installed a new application for which there wasn't sufficient time to test. Now that the application is in production, you suspect it is slowing down Windows Server 2008. Which tool can you use to monitor the percentage of CPU resources required for the new application?

    a. Active Directory Manager

    b. Task Manager

    c. Device Manager

    d. System utility

11. You have received a report that a hacker may be logged onto a Windows Server 2008 R2 user account while that account holder is on vacation. Which tool can you use to view the users currently logged on?

    a. Control Panel Users utility

    b. System utility Accounts tab

    c. Task Manager Users tab

    d. Windows Firewall

12. What GNOME 3.x utility can be used to set up a new account in Linux?

    a. User Preferences

    b. *usermod*

    c. System Preferences

    d. User Manager

13. A user calls to report that he has hung a program on the Linux server you manage. Which of the following tools enables you to stop that program?

    a. *top*

    b. *off*

    c. *trof*

    d. *free*

14. Your new assistant is trying to install a new Linux server, but the computer is not booting from the installation disc when you turn it off and then on with the disc inserted. What should she try?

    a. Press and hold the button used to turn on the computer for 10 seconds.

    b. While turning off the computer, press and hold the Enter key to clear its memory and then turn on the computer.

    c. Reconfigure the BIOS to boot from the DVD/CD-ROM drive before booting from the hard drive.

    d. Reconfigure the computer to allocate more memory to the boot process.

15. Your Linux server seems to be running slower than you expect, and you want to check the swap space. Which of the following commands enables you to do this?

    a. *whatis*

    b. *free*

    c. *swap*

    d. *swapmem*

16. The IT manager wants you to produce information about the disk space occupied by users' home directories on a Linux server. What command enables you to determine this information?

    a. *du*

    b. *used*

    c. *free*

    d. *find*

17. It has been a long day, and you have worked on several Linux servers using different accounts. Right now, you don't remember what account you are logged into. What command can give you that information?

    a. *df*

    b. *whoami*

    c. *?*

    d. *user?*

18. You have been assigned to take over management of Mac OS X Lion Server. Which of the following tools can you use to create accounts for two new employees?

    a. Users and Computers Manager

    b. Users Utility

    c. Manager Assistant

    d. Server Preferences

19. You are configuring Mac OS X Server for your home office. Which of the following server configurations should you specify?

    a. Workgroup

    b. Homegroup

    c. Standard

    d. Advanced

20. You manage the Mac OS X Lion Server for your small office, and you need to determine if a specific user is logged on and if so how long that user has been logged on. Which of the following utilities do you use?

a. System Preferences Accounts option

b. Logon Utility Access tab

c. Network Utility Finger tab

d. Server Preferences Whois tab

Case Projects

Alberta Down Products is a company formed by the merger of two small outdoor products companies: Alberta Down Bags, which manufactures sleeping bags, and Polar Coats, which makes down parkas. Alberta Down Products is purchasing a new building in which to locate both companies. There will be 280 employees in the company who work in the business, marketing, manufacturing, and distribution departments of the company. Alberta Down Products is also opening an outlet store near the main company headquarters. The company hires you through Network Design Consultants to help with the changes in computer and networking services that will occur in the new main building and in the outlet store.

Case Project 8-1: Creating a Server for the Outlet Store

Alberta Down Products is working quickly to open the outlet store to sell remaining stocks of products that have labels from the two original businesses. There will be 20 networked computers in the outlet store. The company has provided the store with a computer to be quickly set up as a server. Describe what steps you would take in advance of installing Windows Server 2008 R2 on this computer and preparing a server for the outlet store.

Case Project 8-2: Using Virtual Servers

Alberta Down Products does not currently use any virtual servers. They are projecting a need for eight new servers. What are your recommendations in regard to the possible use of virtual servers?

Case Project 8-3: Creating Users

After the domain is installed, one of the server administrators is setting up accounts, but is not sure how to start the tool to create accounts in Windows Server 2008 R2. Explain what tool to use and how to start it.

Case Project 8-4: Solving a Problem on a Linux Server

As you are helping with the Windows servers, the Manufacturing Department, which is already up and running, calls about a problem with one of its Linux computers. The computer has issued a message that it is running low on disk space. What tool or tools can be used to determine the disk space, and how it is being used? Also, how can the department determine the number of users and what they are doing when this message is displayed?

Case Project 8-5: Testing a New Program

Alberta Down Products has purchased a new inventory program and is running a preliminary test with five users connected to a Windows Server 2008 R2 system. What tool can Alberta Down Products use to get basic performance information about the server while the program is running? Also, one user's session is hung. What tool can be used to disconnect that user?

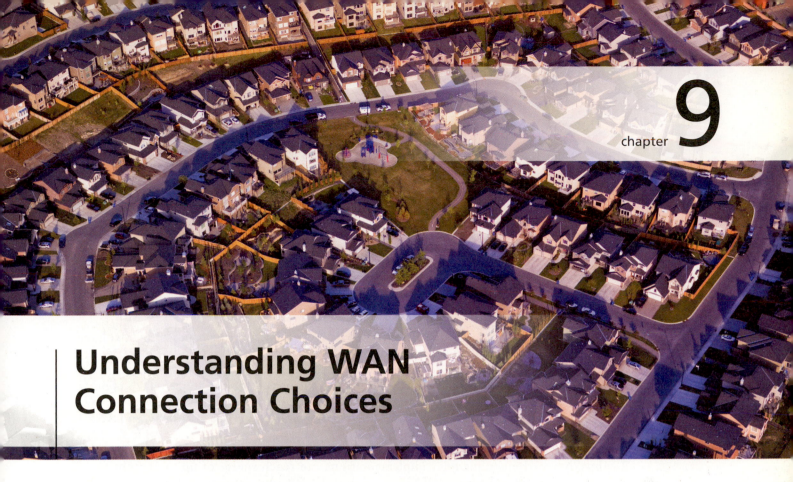

chapter 9

Understanding WAN Connection Choices

Twenty-five years ago, medical researchers working at different universities in the United States had only e-mail over BITNET as a means of quickly sharing information about their research findings. Today we take for granted that, thanks to fast WAN technologies, researchers can present an entire live video conference on their research to other scientists in the United States and overseas.

After reading this chapter and completing the exercises, you will be able to:

- Explain frame relay for use in WANs

- Describe ISDN communications for voice, data, and video networks

- Describe ATM for LAN and WAN implementations

- Describe DSL network communications for high-speed networking

- Explain how SONET works and how it is implemented

- Describe Optical Ethernet-based MANs

- Explain MPLS for WAN implementations

WAN technologies offer access to a wide realm of information for grade school, secondary school, and college students. Health professionals in remote rural areas use WANs to learn about new medical procedures. Corporations use WANs to join LANs at branch offices. Millions of people rely on WANs as much as on LANs, and in some cases rely on them more than LANs, particularly for Internet access.

In this chapter, you learn about the WAN technologies that have been in existence for many years and about others that are still evolving. You learn about frame relay and ISDN, which have been popular WAN technologies that have roots in the 1970s and 1980s and that came of age in the 1990s. Also, you learn about newer and often faster WAN technologies that include ATM, DSL, SONET, Optical Ethernet-based MANs, and MPLS.

Frame Relay

ITU-T standards for frame relay were proposed in 1984 to meet the demands of high-volume, high-bandwidth WANs. Additional standards have been approved to accommodate more demand for frame relay. Defined via the ITU-T I.451/Q.931 and Q.922 standards, frame relay has been a popular WAN option among some Fortune 1000 companies. Although frame relay's popularity is now diminishing as other WAN options have matured, it is still widely used because of its reliability and the ability to combine data and voice communications, such as between LANs in different locations.

Initially, the most common implementations of frame relay were at 56 Kbps and 2 Mbps, but current frame relay implementations can reach speeds of up to 45 Mbps over T-3/DS-3 links (see Chapter 2, "How LAN and WAN Communications Work," to review T-carrier for WAN communications). Frame relay is interoperable with faster technologies, such as SONET, for even faster communications speeds (see the section in this chapter, "SONET"). Frame relay is well suited for transporting IP and IP-related protocols over WANs.

Frame relay has grown out of an earlier WAN communications technology called X.25, which is an older, very reliable packet-switching protocol (see Chapter 2 to review packet switching) for connecting remote networks, such as remote LANs.

Frame relay defines communications between telecommunications network data terminal equipment (DTE) and data communications equipment (DCE) devices. A DTE on a frame relay network is terminating equipment on the customer premises, which may be housed in a router, switch, or communications controller (for a mainframe). A DCE is an internetworking device at the WAN provider's site that provides signal clocking and switching services. (DTEs and DCEs are also discussed in relation to analog modems in Chapter 5, "Devices for Connecting Networks.")

A frame relay network can transmit data packets using switched virtual circuits or permanent virtual circuits. A switched virtual circuit (SVC) is a two-way channel established from node to node, through a frame relay switch. The circuit is a logical circuit that is established only for the duration of the data transmission. After the transmission is completed, the channel can be made available to other nodes. An SVC is used for connections that have intermittent data transfers, such as a business that periodically transfers payroll data to a payroll processing center in a bank.

A permanent virtual circuit (PVC) is a logical communications channel that remains connected at all times. The circuit remains in place even when data transmission stops. A PVC is used for frequent data transfers, such as for a connection between a branch bank office and the main bank in which customer records are updated continuously throughout the day. Both switched and permanent virtual circuits are examples of packet switching.

As mentioned earlier, in frame relay a DTE might be a router, switch, mainframe communications controller, or computer at the customer site that is connected to a DCE, which is a network device, such as a switch that connects to the frame relay WAN as shown in Figure 9-1. A DCE is connected to a vendor's **packet-switching exchange (PSE)**, which is a switch in the frame relay WAN network located at the vendor's site. To convert packets, frame relay uses a **frame relay assembler/disassembler (FRAD)**, which is often a module in a router, switch, or chassis device (a device that combines different network devices such as switches and routers). A FRAD is a device that connects the customer's LAN to a frame relay network and is responsible for encapsulating (assembling) packets from the LAN so that they can be sent over the frame relay WAN. The FRAD also de-encapsulates (disassembles) frame relay–formatted data so that it can be read by the local network.

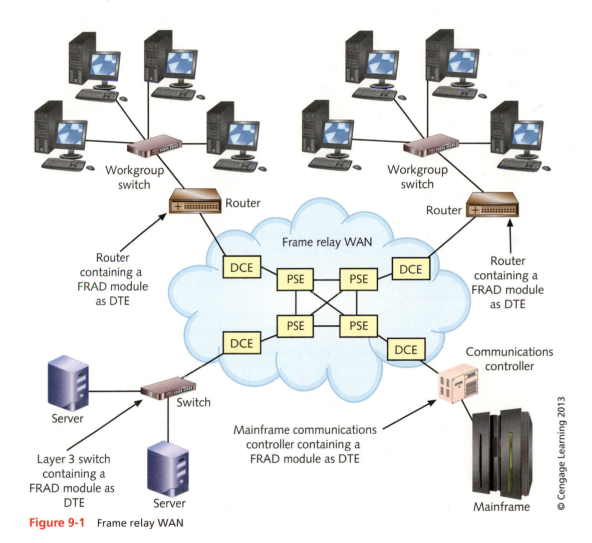

Figure 9-1 Frame relay WAN

Unlike its X.25 predecessor, frame relay is designed to interface with modern networks that do their own error checking. It achieves high-speed data transmission by assuming that newer network technologies have error checking on intermediate nodes, and therefore it does not incorporate extensive error checking, which means that it is a connectionless-oriented service (does not check to make sure data accurately reaches the receiving node). Because frame relay is used with TCP/IP-based LANs, it relies on TCP/IP to do most of the data transmission error checking. However, frame relay does look for bad frame check sequences. If it detects errors that were not discovered by intermediate nodes (PCs, server, switches, routers), it discards the bad packets. It also discards packets if it detects heavy network congestion, a disadvantage you should consider when evaluating this technology.

Frame Relay Layered Communications

Frame relay uses only two communications layers: the Physical layer and the **Link Access Protocol for Frame Mode Bearer Services (LAPF)**. These layers correspond to the OSI Physical and Data Link layers as shown in Figure 9-2.

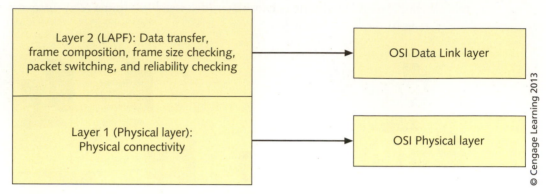

Figure 9-2 The frame relay communications layers compared to the OSI reference model

The Physical layer consists of interfaces, for example, an EIA-232C/D type of interface or adapter to connect to the frame relay network, and telecommunications lines, such as T-carrier lines, for communications on the wire. EIA-232C/D is a standard for serial interfaces (serial means sending one data bit at a time), such as were commonly used on computers before the USB interface. The Layer 2 LAPF is designed for fast communications services without the overhead associated with the older X.25 WAN networks, but it also includes an optional sublayer for situations requiring high reliability.

All frame relay communications implement the LAPF core protocol, which handles the basic communication services. The LAPF core protocol performs frame formatting and switching, measures the frame to make sure it is within the allowed length, and checks for transmission errors and line congestion. Frame relay communications can optionally use the LAPF control protocol for flow control on each virtual connection. The LAPF control protocol is managed from the receiving node.

Flow control is purposefully omitted from the required Level 2 functions to reduce overhead for faster service, which means that service is slower when the optional LAPF control protocol is implemented.

Switching and Virtual Connections

Frame relay uses multiple virtual connections over a single cable medium. Each virtual connection provides a data path between two communicating nodes. The virtual connections are a logical rather than a physical connection. As discussed earlier, two types of virtual connections exist within frame relay: PVCs and SVCs.

A frame relay PVC is a continuously available path between two nodes. The path is given a connection ID that is part of every transmitted packet. After the connection is defined, it remains open, so communication can occur at any time. Signal transmission is handled at the Physical layer, and virtual connections are part of the LAPF layer. A single cable medium can support multiple virtual connections to different network destinations.

A frame relay SVC requires the establishment of a transmission session. A call control signal is sent between the nodes to establish a session for communication. After the communication is finished, the call control signal issues a command for each node to disconnect. An SVC is designed to allow the network or T-carrier provider to determine the data throughput rate. It can be adjusted according to the needs of the application and network traffic conditions. Multiple switched virtual connections can be supported on a single cable from point to point. SVCs are a relatively newer technology within frame relay compared to permanent virtual connections.

Voice over Frame Relay (VoFR)

Frame relay includes an option, called **voice over frame relay (VoFR)**, to transmit voice signals over the network to reduce long-distance telephone costs between sites. Voice transmissions are accomplished by using one of two techniques: voice compression and silence suppression. Both techniques are used to increase the available bandwidth for data and voice.

Voice compression methods include:

- *Pulse code modulation (PCM)*: An audio communications technique that converts an analog audio signal into an 8-bit digital signal and is also used over the Internet for audio communications

- *Adaptive differential pulse code modulation (ADPCM)*: A form of PCM, but it transmits voice communications at less than half or one-fourth the speed of regular PCM communications

- *Sub-band adaptive differential pulse code modulation (SB-ADPCM)*: A variety of AD-PCM that is tailored to work over ISDN (see the section in this chapter, "Integrated Services Digital Network (ISDN)") and frame relay

All of these voice compression methods involve creating audio files that are created at the transmitting end and played at the receiving end.

Silence suppression is a technique that detects periods of silence between words or as a conversation shifts from one person to the other. Frame relay transmits data during the detected moments of silence. Voice quality over frame relay is likely to be lower for silence suppression than for voice compression, particularly in situations where the network is transmitting a high volume of voice and data traffic.

Voice over frame relay, with its companion ability to transmit faxes, has made this technology very appealing to corporate customers because it means they can achieve substantial savings by using combined data and VoFR, thus eliminating a significant portion of toll-based telecommunications services.

Vendor Services

Frame relay service providers, usually regional bell operating companies (RBOCs; see Chapter 2, "How LAN and WAN Communications Work") and long-distance telecommunications companies, typically offer a combination of three types of services:

- *Committed information rate (CIR)*: Provides a pledged minimum transmission rate, for example, T-1, fractional T-1, or T-3 (see Chapter 2). The problem with this service is that lines are not regularly monitored, and it is difficult for the customer to verify that he or she is always attaining this rate.

- *Permanent virtual connection (PVC)*: A continuous dedicated connection to a specific location, such as from a warehouse in Denver to a marketing center in Omaha. PVC services are likely to be the most appropriate because they establish a continuous communications path.

- *Port*: Based on purchasing access to a specific port or set of ports, such as a 56 Kbps or a T-1 port, on the vendor's telecommunications switch.

It is important for network administrators to fully understand these types of services when negotiating a frame relay implementation for their organization.

Integrated Services Digital Network (ISDN)

Integrated Services Digital Network (ISDN) was introduced in the 1970s to provide voice, data, graphics, and video digital services and was standardized in 1984 and 1988 by the ITU-T (at that time called the CCITT). These standards represent narrowband ISDN (N-ISDN) and when introduced were intended as a significant step up from commonly used 9.6 Kbps transmissions over telecommunications WANs. ISDN is a digital-based telecommunications standard with a current practical limit of 1.536 Mbps for transmitting a user's data and a theoretical limit of 622 Mbps.

ISDN is used less and less for WAN communications compared to other technologies, such as DSL, which are now more commonplace. ISDN, however, is still important to WAN users in rural areas who do not have easy access to alternatives other than slow modem communications or satellite Internet.

Individuals who need ISDN service to a residence can obtain a "single-line service" digital ISDN line from their local telco (telecommunications company). Single-line service enables the end user to connect several devices to the line, such as a fax, computer, and digital telephone. For example, some telcos offer connectivity for up to eight devices (the maximum for this type of ISDN service). Organizations that connect one LAN to another over an ISDN WAN generally do so through a T-carrier type of line.

ISDN has various applications, among them:

- LAN-to-LAN connectivity

- Home offices and telecommuting

- Off-site backup and disaster recovery for business computer systems

- Connecting a private telephone system to a public telecommunications company

- Transferring large image and data files

- LAN-to-LAN video and multimedia applications

- Backup for another primary and critical WAN service

Many major telecommunications and long-distance telephone companies offer ISDN services for homes, home offices, and businesses—although these services are barely advertised and more expensive compared to the more popular DSL (discussed later in this chapter). ISDN is still supported in Canada, Europe, and the United States because it provides an alternative to analog modem communications, particularly in rural and other areas that do not have DSL. The benefits of ISDN include the following:

- Provides voice, data, and video services over one network

- Has a layered protocol structure compatible with the OSI reference model

- Offers communications channels in multiples of 64, 384, and 1536 Kbps

- Has switched and nonswitched connection services

The general steps for setting up an ISDN broadband connection in Windows 7 are:

1. Click Start and click Control Panel.

2. Click Network and Sharing Center.

3. In the Network and Sharing Center window, click Set up a new connection or network.

4. Click Connect to the Internet and click Next.

5. Click Broadband PPPoE and click Next.

6. Provide the user name and password information for the Internet account through ISDN and click Connect.

Digital Communications Services

Two interfaces are supported in N-ISDN: basic rate interface and primary rate interface. Using a form of time division multiple access (TDMA) (also called time division multiplexing, see Chapter 2), the **Basic Rate Interface (BRI) ISDN** has an aggregate data rate of 144 Kbps. The BRI consists of three channels: two are 64-Kbps Bearer (B) channels for data, voice, and graphics transmissions; and the third is a 16-Kbps Delta (D, sometimes called Demand) channel used for communications signaling, packet switching, and credit card verification. The primary function of a D channel is for ISDN call setup and teardown, which is used for starting and stopping a communication session. BRI is used for:

- LAN-to-LAN connectivity
- Video conferencing
- Internet connectivity to an ISP
- High-speed connectivity for telecommuters and home offices

Multiple BRI channels can be "bonded" (sometimes called "trunked") together for even faster communications. For example, one BRI line with two 64-Kbps B channels is bonded to achieve a 128-Kbps connection for actual data throughput. With the 16-Kbps D channel added, plus 48 Kbps for maintenance and synchronization, the total rate is actually 192 Kbps. Another example is the bonding of three BRI lines consisting of 64-Kbps B channels for an aggregate actual data throughput speed of 384 Kbps.

Windows and many UNIX/Linux systems support bonding ISDN lines using Multilink PPP (see Chapter 3, "Using Network Communication Protocols," to review PPP). In addition, if you subscribe to BRI, some telecommunications companies have implemented download capabilities through the D channel, thus creating an additional 16 Kbps for downstream communications.

For those who are interested in using a Windows Server network, Activity 9-1 enables you to learn where to configure Multilink PPP in Windows Server 2008/Server 2008 R2.

In some Windows 7, Server 2008, or Server 2008 R2 projects, you may see the User Account Control (UAC) box, which is used for security to help thwart intruders. The UAC box asks for permission to continue with an action or asks for the administrator password. If you see this box, click **Continue**. Because computer setups may be different, the box is not mentioned in the actual project steps.

Activity 9-1: Setting Up Multilink PPP

Time Required: 15 minutes

Objective: Learn where to configure Multilink PPP in Windows Server 2008/Server 2008 R2.

Description: One way to enable telecommuters to dial into a LAN over a WAN is through a Windows Server configured as a Remote Access Service (RAS) server that has an installed TA and bonded ISDN lines. However, to enable bonding the ISDN lines, the server administrator has to configure the RAS server to use Multilink PPP. This activity enables you to view where to set up Multilink PPP. You need access to Windows Server 2008/Server 2008 R2 configured for RAS and an account that has Administrator privileges. Also, ask your instructor for the name of the RAS server.

1. Click **Start**, point to **Administrative Tools**, and click **Routing and Remote Access**.
2. In the tree in the left pane, right-click the server configured for RAS and click **Properties**.
3. Click the **PPP** tab (see Figure 9-3).

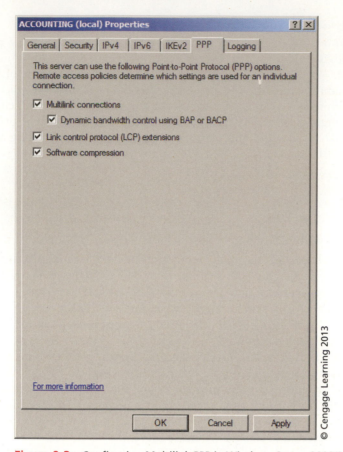

Figure 9-3   Configuring Multilink PPP in Windows Server 2008/Server 2008 R2

4. How can you enable Multilink PPP?

5. Notice that you can also configure to use Bandwidth Allocation Protocol (BAP) and Bandwidth Allocation Control Protocol (BACP). BAP enables the server to automatically increase the bandwidth to use as many of the bonded channels as necessary for a single user. BACP is used to have Multilink PPP select a preferred client for the maximum bandwidth when two or more clients vie for the same bandwidth.

6. Click **Cancel**.

7. Close the Routing and Remote Access window.

BRI ISDN is brought into the customer premises using four-wire twisted-pair telephone cable and can generally be connected in one of three ways. One way is to simply equip a computer with a terminal adapter (TA, see Chapter 5) that also contains an NT1 network terminator. The line connects into the server configured in this manner with an RJ-45 connector.

A second way is to connect the ISDN line into an external TA that is equipped with a U interface into which you plug in the ISDN line. A U interface enables full-duplex transmissions (see Chapter 2) between the TA and the ISDN provider's switch at the provider's site. The terminal adapter can be equipped with an RS-232 serial or USB port to connect to a computer and also a telephone port to connect to a regular telephone using RJ-11 connectors.

The third way is to bring the ISDN line into a network device called a **Network Termination Unit (NTU)**. The NTU is equipped with an ISDN U interface for an ISDN line that is connectorized with an RJ-45 connector. Multiple devices (up to eight), such as computers, fax machines, and telephones, can be connected to the NTU through S/T interfaces (at the NTU). An S/T interface is a four-wire interface between the device and the NTU (S and T are connection reference points in the interface). Computers equipped with ISDN-compatible NICs, fax machines, and telephones specifically designed to connect to ISDN are connected as shown in Figure 9-4.

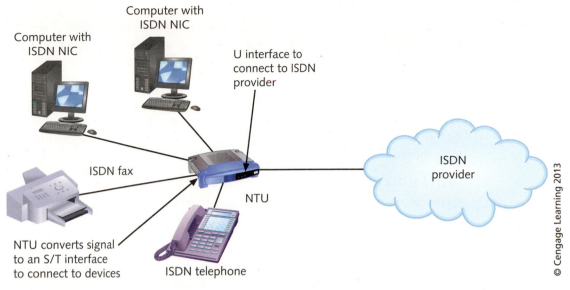

Computer with
ISDN NIC

Computer with
ISDN NIC

U interface to
connect to ISDN
provider

ISDN fax

ISDN
provider

NTU

NTU converts signal
to an S/T interface
to connect to devices

ISDN telephone

© Cengage Learning 2013

Figure 9-4　Connecting via an NTU

When you install a TA directly in a computer running a Windows operating system, you must configure the TA by telling it what type of ISDN switch is used at the telco, such as an AT&T switch (ATT). In most cases, when you install the TA, Windows operating systems automatically detect and configure it. After the TA is installed, click **Start** and then right-click **Computer**. On the shortcut menu, click **Manage**. Click **Device Manager** in the tree in the left pane. Double-click the TA in the right pane to configure it for the switch type; if the TA is not displayed in the right pane, double-click **Modems** and then double-click the TA under Modems to configure it for the switch type.

The **Primary Rate Interface (PRI) ISDN** supports faster data rates, with an aggregate of switched bandwidth equal to 1.536 Mbps. In the United States and Japan, PRI consists of twenty-three 64-Kbps channels and one 64-Kbps D channel for signaling communications and packet switching. European PRI ISDN consists of thirty 64-Kbps channels and one 64-Kbps signaling or packet-switching channel. The PRI is used for LAN-to-LAN connectivity, ISP sites, video conferencing, and, at corporate sites, support of telecommuters who use ISDN.

PRI connects into the customer premises by means of a multiplexer (as shown in Figure 9-5). A multiplexer (MUX) is a network device that can receive multiple inputs and transmit them to a single shared network medium or cable. The multiplexer may be an external device or a module in a router.

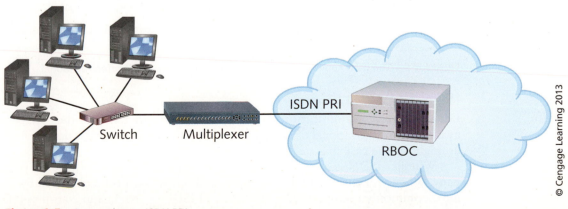

Switch　　Multiplexer

ISDN PRI

RBOC

© Cengage Learning 2013

Figure 9-5　Connecting to ISDN PRI

Multiple PRI trunks can be used at a single location, and in this case, it is possible to consolidate the number of D channels for signaling. For example, a company that has five PRI trunks for its telecommuting staff might purchase only one or two D channels (the second D channel could be used as a backup in case the first one malfunctions).

Broadband ISDN

Broadband ISDN (B-ISDN) is a 155 Mbps to more than 1 Gbps technology intended for compatibility with Asynchronous Transfer Mode (ATM) and synchronous optical network (SONET)—both discussed later in this chapter. B-ISDN never really got off the ground because other broadband telecommunications technologies, such as DSL replaced interest in B-ISDN.

ISDN and OSI Layered Communications

ISDN incorporates layered communications corresponding to the OSI reference model's Physical, Data Link, Network, and Transport layers as shown in Figure 9-6. ISDN Layer 1 provides for signal transmissions and contention detection—necessary because it is possible for two nodes to transmit at the same time. An echo bit is used to detect a collision and establish the priority of transmission. Layer 1 gives signaling information the highest priority. If there is contention between telephone and data communications, it gives telephone communications a higher priority. Layer 2 manages control signaling and ensures maximum detection of communication errors for highly reliable communications. Layer 3 handles call setup and teardown and establishes paths through circuit-switched and packet-switched connections. Layer 4 ensures the reliability of a connection path after it is established.

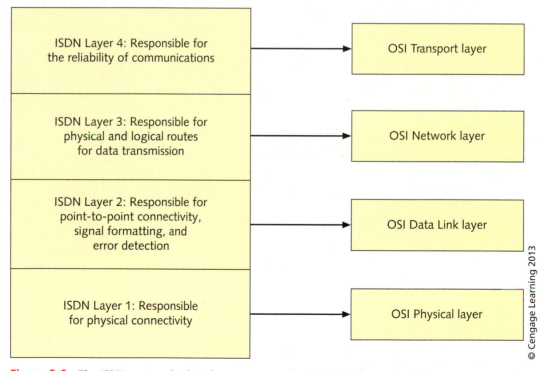

© Cengage Learning 2013

Figure 9-6   The ISDN communications layers compared to the OSI reference model

ISDN Considerations

ISDN is a telecommunications WAN option to consider when other WAN solutions are not available. Another appeal of ISDN is the ability to operate multiple devices over one connection, as might be the case in a small office.

Whether ISDN is available locally depends on the services offered by your telephone company. When you check on ISDN services, find out which protocol is used by your provider. The most commonly used protocols are National ISDN-1 (NI-1) and National ISDN-2 (NI-2). It is

Real-Life Networking

necessary to know which protocol is in use in order to configure customer premises communications equipment. NI-1 is commonly used by RBOCs or long-distance carriers, and many use NI-2, which is a later version of the ISDN protocol.

ISDN cabling can be twisted-pair copper wire or fiber-optic cable. Fiber-optic cable is preferred because it provides the best connectivity and high-speed options, particularly for PRI and B-ISDN. If twisted pair is used, consider the following three issues. First, the local wiring loop between the vendor site and the customer premises is limited to 5.5 kilometers (3.4 miles), unless a repeater is used to extend it. Second, cable installation should be high quality, with few sources of signal reduction such as noncompliant telephone cable or excessive cross-connects in telecommunications wiring closets. Third, existing line conditioners and analog signal noise reduction devices should be eliminated because they introduce distortion in digital signals.

Connecting to ISDN Through a T-Carrier

When you connect to ISDN without using a leased line, for example, through a T-carrier line, your provider is likely to offer circuit-mode services, packet-mode services, or both. **Circuit mode** means that your communications circuit lasts for the duration of the communications session and is used exclusively by the two connected devices until it is terminated. Circuit mode is most commonly employed in voice transmissions. **Packet mode**, used for data, means that several circuits can be used during a communications session, and each connected device is assigned an address and sequence number at the start of the session to ensure that data arrives at the correct destination. The advantage of packet mode is that it makes maximum use of the available bandwidth.

Asynchronous Transfer Mode (ATM)

Asynchronous Transfer Mode (ATM) is a high-speed network transport method for data, voice, video, and multimedia applications. ATM consists of an interface and a protocol that is able to switch both constant and variable bit rate traffic over a common transmission channel. ATM is also composed of hardware, software, and media that conform to ATM protocol standards. It is an integrated network access method supported by internetworking device manufacturers for LAN implementations and by RBOCs for WANs, providing organizations with very high-speed networking at costs related to the speed of the service. However, ATM's heyday was in the 1990s and early 2000s. ATM is still used, but its high overhead and relatively higher cost have made it a less frequently used technology compared to frame relay and DSL, for example. Another factor going against ATM is that it is relatively difficult to implement compared to other WAN technologies.

ATM provides a scalable backbone infrastructure to accommodate networks of various sizes, speeds, and addressing techniques. Figure 9-7 illustrates how ATM might be deployed for a combination LAN and WAN implementation.

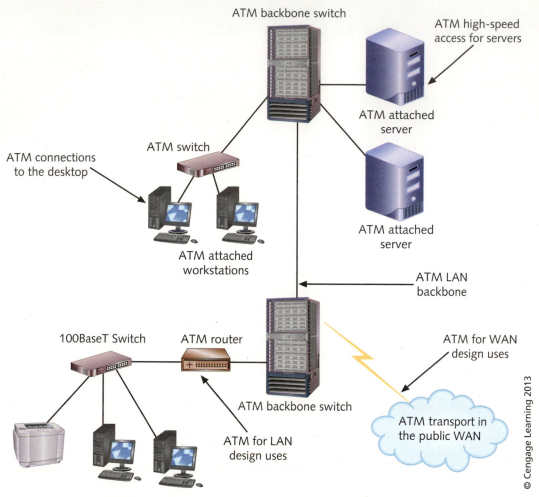

Figure 9-7   Sample ATM LAN and WAN application

Development of ATM began in the late 1960s at Bell Labs, where engineers experimented with cell switching as a high-speed alternative to packet switching. Their goal was to combine label-based switching, which is the basis for packet-switching networks, with time-division multiplexing (TDM, also called time division multiple access or TDMA).

Like some other WAN technologies, such as frame relay, ATM uses virtual circuits that are called channels. ATM channel speeds can be up to 40 Gbps. Information is transmitted in cells instead of packets. As used in WAN communications, a **cell** is a fixed-size data unit formatted for high-speed transmission. The fixed size of a cell means less delay at switches and routers than for packets. With an ATM cell, there is no delay for adjusting the window size and number of packets to send within a window (see Chapter 2). Also, there is no queue of packets waiting to be sent because of the window size.

The communications over ATM channels are accomplished by using **cell switching**, which places a short indicator, called a virtual channel identifier, at the beginning of each TDM time slot. This allows a device to place its bit stream onto an ATM communications channel asynchronously, making communications predictable and consistent, and thus providing a preset **Quality of Service (QoS)** for time-sensitive traffic, such as voice and video. QoS refers to providing an assured level of throughput and resources. In ATM, this means that a specific level of throughput and resources is set, using information provided in the ATM cell header for different types of transmissions of transported information. The information might be, for example, data or multimedia. The QoS capabilities of ATM offer two important advantages: (1) they make sure the proper network resources are assigned for successful transmission of a specified application, and (2) they reduce the likelihood that valuable network resources are underutilized on nonover-subscribed applications, which do not require them. QoS is configured in terms of attributes as shown in Table 9-1.

Table 9-1 ATM QoS service attributes

Service Attribute	Delay	Accuracy	Throughput
File transfer	High tolerance	Accuracy is important, and cell loss requires retransmission and lower throughput	Traffic occurs in bursts, and there is idle time between traffic bursts
Interactive point of sale	Low tolerance (requires transmissions of 100 milliseconds or less)	No cell loss tolerated	Low transfer rates, no bursts of traffic, low utilization
Interactive still image	Low tolerance (requires transmissions of 100 milliseconds or less)	Accuracy is important, and cell loss requires retransmission and lower throughput	Intermediate transfer rates and long periods of idle time
Real-time video	Extremely low tolerance	No cell loss tolerated	Consistent transfer rate and no bursts or idle time
Voice	Intermediate tolerance	Tolerance for high cell loss (up to 1 percent) before degradation in quality is noticed	Short bursts with predictable idle times

© Cengage Learning 2013

Although ATM was originally designed for use in WANs, it is also implemented in LANs. ATM is supported by several standards organizations, including ANSI, the IETF, the ETSI (in Europe), and the ITU-T.

Because ATM is a switch-based technology, it is easily scalable. As traffic loads increase or the network grows in numbers, you simply add more ATM switches to the network. ATM physical links operate over many cable types, including Categories 3 and above, UTP, STP, co-axial cable, and multimode and single-mode fiber-optic cables (with the appropriate speed for each type of cable). Possible ATM transmission speeds include 1.544 Mbps, 2 Mbps (wireless), 2.048 Mbps, 6.312 Mbps, 25.6 Mbps, 34.368 Mbps, 44.736 Mbps, 51.84 Mbps, 100 Mbps, 155.52 Mbps, 622.08 Mbps, 1.2 Gbps, 2.048 Gbps, 10 Gbps, and 40 Gbps. The lower speeds, 622.08 Mbps and below, are typically used for LAN implementations, and speeds above 622.08 Mbps are used for WANs. U.S. and international vendors have worked to ensure interoperability no matter who manufactures ATM devices. This makes ATM suitable for global WAN implementations.

Category 3 cable provides the minimum operation for ATM at 25.6 Mbps and may not be sufficiently reliable for most installations.

ATM is compatible with the following technologies:

- DSL
- Frame relay
- Gigabit and 10 Gigabit Ethernet

- SONET and SDH
- MPLS
- Wireless communications

Besides its use on LANs and connecting different LANs into a WAN, other common uses of ATM in countries that employ this technology include:

- Transporting ATM over SONET
- Connecting frame relay WANs using an ATM WAN

How ATM Works

ATM networks use virtual circuits to create pathways between sending and receiving nodes. As you learned in Chapter 2, a virtual circuit is a pathway between two nodes on a switched network—it appears as a dedicated point-to-point link and is transparent to the user. Three types of virtual circuits are employed by ATM: permanent virtual circuits, switched virtual circuits, and smart permanent virtual circuits.

An **ATM permanent virtual circuit (ATM PVC)** is a dedicated circuit that has a preassigned path and can have a fixed allocated bandwidth between two designated end points. This type of circuit is always up and active once it is created, thus eliminating delays caused by the setup and teardown of the circuit.

An **ATM switched virtual circuit (ATM SVC)** is set up and torn down on an as-needed basis. It is a temporary connection that is created by a request for transmission facility or by a device, such as a switch, at one end of a network. An ATM SVC is active only as long as the devices are communicating. After communication is complete, the circuit is torn down, and all of its resources are returned to the resource pool. The SVC is a dynamically established circuit that is created by signaling software and parameters defined by the device applications, communications equipment, and the ATM facilities. It requires no manual intervention.

ATM SVCs have the advantage of being transparent to the user for call setup and teardown. There is no manual setup of these circuits, and thus no intervention by the network administrator. A disadvantage is that there are delays caused by call setup and teardown, but the delays are transparent to users if the network is well designed.

An **ATM smart permanent virtual circuit (ATM SPVC)** combines the characteristics of PVCs and SVCs. An SPVC, like a PVC, must be manually configured, although only at the end devices. As with SVCs, each transmission has its own defined path to the switch or switches through which it must pass. In addition, as with PVCs, setup and teardown times are not a source of delay because the circuit is preconfigured manually. An SPVC also provides for alternate route fault tolerance similar to that of SVCs. Another advantage of an SPVC is that it provides a dedicated bandwidth; however, as with PVCs, that bandwidth is wasted during idle or low-use periods. A disadvantage is that SPVCs require administrative setup time and network administrator training.

ATM Layered Communications

ATM employs a four-layer architecture, called the ATM Protocol Reference Model, which enables multiple services to function at the same time on a single network. What sets ATM apart from other transport methods is the way that ATM functions at the equivalent of the OSI Data Link MAC sublayer. The ATM MAC equivalent sublayer operates independently of the upper layers, which enables it to avoid routing issues related to the Network layer, because the routing decisions are passed on to the upper layers. Nearly any type of upper-layer protocol can be placed within the ATM cell. The four ATM layers are shown in Figure 9-8, and two of these layers, the ATM layer and the ATM Adaptation layer (AAL), are the layers that specifically perform ATM functions.

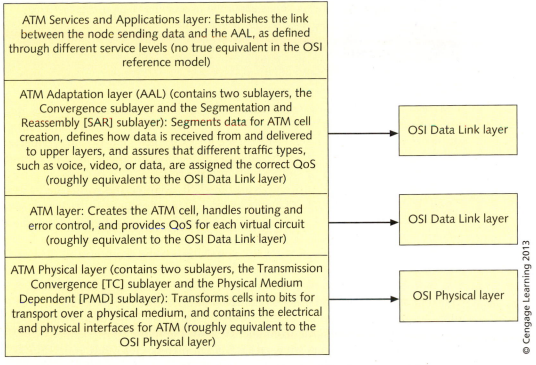

ATM Services and Applications layer: Establishes the link between the node sending data and the AAL, as defined through different service levels (no true equivalent in the OSI reference model)

ATM Adaptation layer (AAL) (contains two sublayers, the Convergence sublayer and the Segmentation and Reassembly [SAR] sublayer): Segments data for ATM cell creation, defines how data is received from and delivered to upper layers, and assures that different traffic types, such as voice, video, or data, are assigned the correct QoS (roughly equivalent to the OSI Data Link layer)

ATM layer: Creates the ATM cell, handles routing and error control, and provides QoS for each virtual circuit (roughly equivalent to the OSI Data Link layer)

ATM Physical layer (contains two sublayers, the Transmission Convergence [TC] sublayer and the Physical Medium Dependent [PMD] sublayer): Transforms cells into bits for transport over a physical medium, and contains the electrical and physical interfaces for ATM (roughly equivalent to the OSI Physical layer)

OSI Data Link layer

OSI Data Link layer

OSI Physical layer

© Cengage Learning 2013

Figure 9-8   ATM Protocol Reference Model compared to the OSI reference model

Visit the Broadband Forum at *www.broadband-forum.org* to learn more about ATM.

Digital Subscriber Line (DSL)

Digital subscriber line (DSL or **xDSL)** is a technology that uses advanced modulation technologies on existing telecommunications networks for high-speed networking between a subscriber and a telco, such as an RBOC. DSL supports transmission of data, voice, and video communications, including multimedia applications. Originally intended for telecommuters and small businesses, DSL is also used by medium-sized and large businesses and corporations as a "last mile" connectivity option from the business premises to a telco. The Telecommunications Act of 1996 was particularly influential in the development of DSL because that act encourages telecommunications and cable TV providers to develop interactive communications options over existing telephone networks. Today, DSL is used extensively in the United States and Europe.

DSL is useful for the following:

- Internet access, particularly for downloading and uploading files
- Residential lines for home use and telecommuting
- Office and small business WAN access
- Accessing multimedia over a network, including the latest music and movies
- Quickly transmitting a large image file, such as a map, from one location to another
- Taking an interactive class or seminar
- Implementing a distributed client/server application among geographically dispersed users
- Enabling telecommuters to work remotely
- Connecting to a business's intranet

To learn more about the Telecommunications Act of 1996, see *www.fcc.gov/telecom.html*.

DSL Basics

DSL is a digital technology that works over copper wire that already goes into most residences and businesses for telephone services. To use DSL, you must install an intelligent adapter in the device—computer, access server, or router, for example—that is to be connected to the DSL network. In a computer, the adapter can be a card similar in appearance to a modem, or in a router it may be a plug-in card or simply built into the router.

On a home or small office network, the DSL adapter and router may be combined into one small device about the size of a small switch. The adapter is fully digital, which means that it does not convert the DTE's (computer or network device's) digital signal to analog, but instead sends a digital signal over the telephone wire.

Generally, two pairs of wires are connected to the adapter and then out to the telephone pole. Communication over the copper wire is simplex for most DSL versions, which means that one pair is used for outgoing transmissions, and the other pair for incoming transmissions, thus creating an upstream channel to the telco and a downstream channel to the user. The maximum upstream and downstream transmission rates are 200 Mbps (although at this writing these speeds are not yet available from telcos). Also, the maximum distance, for most DSL versions, from user to telco without a repeater is 5.5 kilometers (3.4 miles, much like ISDN).

The actual transmission rate is determined by several factors, including the type of DSL service used, the condition of the cable, the distance to the telco, and the bus speed in the user's device.

When the connection is a card in a user's computer, a DSL adapter is similar to a cable modem in that it offers high-speed data transmissions, but it also has some advantages over a cable modem. For example, a cable modem uses a line shared by other users, which means its signal can be tapped and possibly read by another user. A DSL line is dedicated to a single user, which means that there is less likelihood that the signal can be tapped without the telco being alerted. In addition, the DSL user employs the full bandwidth of her or his line, in contrast to the cable modem user, who shares bandwidth with others and therefore may experience delays during times of heavy traffic. A disadvantage is that DSL is not quite as widely implemented as cable modem access.

Real-Life Networking

Before purchasing network equipment with DSL, check with your DSL provider. A new company decided to set up a small office downtown. The owner ordered a DSL line for shared Internet access and then went to a local office supply store to purchase a wireless router with a DSL port. When the owner connected the telephone cable to the DSL port, there was no Internet access. After researching the problem with his telephone company, he discovered the DSL capability on that particular wireless router was incompatible with the DSL connection and service from the telephone company. In most cases, you can search your telephony company's Web site for a list of compatible DSL adapters, access points, and routers.

DSL Service Types

There are nine main types of DSL services:

- *Asymmetric Digital Subscriber Line (ADSL)*: This is currently the most commonly used version of DSL. Aside from traditional data and multimedia applications, ADSL is also well suited for interactive multimedia and distance learning. ADSL permits voice transmissions to occur at the same time as data transmissions. In ADSL the downstream (download) rate is faster than the upstream rate.

- *G.lite Asymmetric Digital Subscriber Line (G.lite ADSL)*: This is a variation of ADSL that is developed for compatibility with Plug and Play (PnP), which enables computer operating systems and hardware to automatically configure new hardware devices.

- *Integrated Services Digital Network Digital Subscriber Line (IDSL)*: Many new residential and business areas deploy a telephone network device, called a Digital Loop Carrier, that is intended to improve the techniques used to physically distribute the telephone cable—but that interferes with DSL delivery. IDSL enables DSL communications in these areas.

- *Rate Adaptive Asymmetric Digital Subscriber Line (RADSL)*: This DSL version applies ADSL technology, but enables the transmission rate to vary depending on whether the communication is data, multimedia, or voice. RADSL is an advantage to customers because they pay only for the amount of bandwidth they need, and it helps the telco by allowing them to allocate unused bandwidth to other customers.

- *High Bit-Rate Digital Subscriber Line (HDSL)*: HDSL is designed for full-duplex communications over two pairs of copper telephone wires at a fixed sending and receiving rate. One limitation is that HDSL does not support voice communications as well as ADSL and RADSL do. HDSL was initially used by corporate DSL customers.

- *Symmetric High Bit-Rate Digital Subscriber Line (SHDSL)*: Also called G.shdsl, SHDSL can be used over one or two wires. When two wires are used, the maximum communications distance to the telco is longer than that for other DSL versions.

- *Very High Bit-Rate Digital Subscriber Line (VDSL)*: This DSL version, which is a form of ADSL, offers very high bandwidth and is intended as an alternative to networking technologies that use coaxial or fiber-optic cable, but its range from the telco is more limited than some other DSL versions. VDSL has typically been offered by telcos as a business version of DSL and can be combined with ATM.

- *Very High Bit-Rate Digital Subscriber Line version 2 (VDSL2)*: An upgrade to VDSL, VDSL2 is being introduced at this writing by many telcos in specific markets as a very

9

Real-Life Networking

When you employ ADSL or ADSL-derived versions of DSL for simultaneous computer and telephone use, it is necessary to place an inexpensive filtering device between the telecommunications line that comes in from the telco and the telephone. The filter, which has sockets at either end for a regular telephone cord connector, is used to block line noise that can diminish telephone conversations. However, do not place the filter between the incoming line and the DSL digital adapter. A new DSL small business customer placed the filter between the incoming line and a DSL digital adapter/router, causing problems when trying to use the DSL connection for Internet access. He placed several calls to the telco's customer service line until they determined the problem.

high-speed version of DSL. In these markets, telcos are offering VDSL 2 at speeds of 40 Mbps downstream and 20 Mbps upstream.

- *Symmetric Digital Subscriber Line (SDSL)*: SDSL is particularly useful for video conferencing and interactive learning because it uses symmetrical bandwidth transmissions. SDSL is often used by businesses because the download and upload speeds are the same, and telcos offer it with an uptime guarantee of 99.5 percent plus fast response if a problem occurs.

Table 9-2 summarizes the different kinds of DSL. In Activity 9-2, you learn where to configure DSL in Windows 7 and Windows Server 2008/Server 2008 R2. In Activities 9-3 and 9-4, you learn where to configure DSL in UNIX/Linux and Mac OS X Snow Leopard and Lion. Also, in Activity 9-5 you compare DSL services offered by RBOCs.

Table 9-2 Varieties of DSL

DSL Technology	Upstream Data Transmission Rate	Downstream Data Transmission Rate
Asymmetric Digital Subscriber Line (ADSL)	1 Mbps	Up to 9 Mbps
G.lite Asymmetric Digital Subscriber Line (G.lite ADSL)	Up to 500 Kbps	Up to 1.5 Mbps
Integrated Services Digital Network Digital Subscriber Line (IDSL)	Up to 144 Kbps	Up to 144 Kbps
Rate Adaptive Asymmetric Digital Subscriber Line (RADSL)	Up to 1 Mbps	Up to 7 Mbps
High Bit-Rate Digital Subscriber Line (HDSL)	Fixed rate at 1.544 Mbps or 2.048 Mbps	Fixed rate at 1.544 Mbps or 2.048 Mbps
Symmetric High Bit-Rate Digital Subscriber Line (SHDSL)	192 Kbps–2.3 Mbps	192 Kbps–2.3 Mbps
Very High Bit-Rate Digital Subscriber Line (VDSL)	1.5–2.3 Mbps	13–52 Mbps
Very High Bit-Rate Digital Subscriber Line version 2 (VDSL2)	Up to 200 Mbps	Up to 200 Mbps
Symmetric Digital Subscriber Line (SDSL)	1.544 or 2.048 Mbps	1.544 or 2.048 Mbps

© Cengage Learning 2013

To learn more about DSL, visit the DSL Forum Web site at *www.dslforum.com*.

Activity 9-2: Configuring DSL in Windows 7 and Windows Server 2008/2008 R2

Time Required: 10 minutes
Objective: Learn where to configure DSL in Windows 7 and Windows Server 2008/Server 2008 R2.

Description: In this activity, you learn where to configure a DSL adapter connection in Windows 7 or Windows Server 2008/Server 2008 R2. You do not need a DSL adapter for this activity, but you do need access to an account that has Administrator privileges.

1. In Windows 7 and Server 2008 R2, click **Start** and click **Control Panel**. Make certain that **View by** is set to **Large icons** or **Small icons**. In Windows Server 2008, click **Start** and click **Control Panel**. Use the **Classic View** in the Windows Server 2008 Control Panel.

2. Click (in Windows 7 and Server 2008 R2) or double-click (in Windows Server 2008) **Network and Sharing Center**.

3. In Windows 7 and Server 2008 R2, click **Set up a new connection or network**. In Windows Server 2008, click **Set up a connection or network**.

4. In Windows 7 or Server 2008/Server 2008 R2, click **Connect to the Internet** and click **Next**.

5. If you see a dialog box indicating you are already connected to the Internet, click **Set up a new connection anyway**.

6. Click the selection for **Broadband (PPPoE)** as shown in Figure 9-9 (if there is also a wireless access capability, you may see the Wireless option, which is a way to connect to a wireless router/DSL modem—but for this activity select Broadband (PPPoE)).

7. In the Type the information from your Internet service provider (ISP) dialog box, notice that you can provide a user name for your ISP account, a password, and a connection name.

8. Click **Cancel**.

9. Close the Network and Sharing Center window.

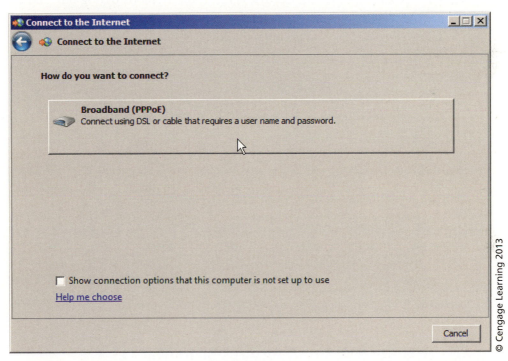

Figure 9-9 Configuring Windows Server 2008 R2 for a DSL connection

In Chapter 3, "Using Network Communication Protocols," Point-to-Point Protocol (PPP) was explained as a protocol that transports TCP/IP packets over WANs. **Point-to-Point Protocol over Ethernet (PPPoE)** is an addition to PPP that builds in the capability for virtual point-to-point connections (like virtual tunnels between two points) on an Ethernet network consisting of multiple end points. PPPoE is particularly well suited for communications through DSL networks. PPPoE is also used in Optical Ethernet networks (discussed later in this chapter in the section "Ethernet-Based MANs, CANs, and WANs (Optical Ethernet)").

Activity 9-3: Configuring DSL in UNIX/Linux

Time Required: 10 minutes

Objective: Learn where to configure DSL in UNIX/Linux using the GNOME 3.x desktop.

Description: In this activity, you learn where to configure a DSL adapter connection in Linux using the Network Connections tool in the GNOME 3.x desktop. You do not need a DSL adapter for this activity.

1. Log onto your account, such as liveuser.

2. Click **Activities** in the Panel at the top of the desktop.

3. Click **Applications**.

4. Click the **Network Connections** applet.

5. In the Network Connections window, click the **DSL** tab (see Figure 9-10).

6. Click the **Add** button, which you can use to configure a new DSL connection. Ensure the **DSL** tab in the Editing dialog box is selected and record the ISP account information that you can provide for a DSL connection.

7. Click the **PPP Settings** tab and click the **Configure Methods** button on the PPP Settings tab. Record the types of authentication that can be selected.

8. Click **Cancel** in the Allowed Authentication Methods dialog box and click **Cancel** in the Editing dialog box.

9. Close the Network Connections window.

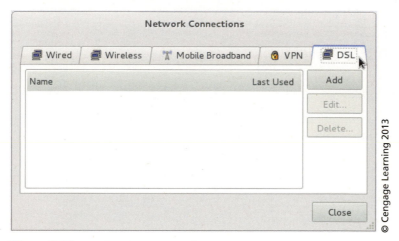

Figure 9-10   Configuring DSL in Linux

Activity 9-4: Configuring DSL in Mac OS X

Time Required: 10 minutes

Objective: Learn where to configure DSL in Mac OS X Snow Leopard or Lion.

Description: In this activity, you learn where to configure a DSL adapter connection in Mac OS X Snow Leopard or Lion. You do not need a DSL adapter for this activity, because you stop before completing the configuration. However, you do need access to an account that has Administrator privileges.

1. Click the **System Preferences** icon in the Dock, or click the **Apple** icon in the menu bar and click **System Preferences**.

2. Click **Network** in the Internet & Wireless section of the System Preferences window.

3. In the Network window, be sure the lock is unlocked in the bottom left corner; or to unlock it, click the **lock**, provide your account name and password, and click **OK**.

4. In the Network window, click the **Assist me** button.

5. Click **Assistant**.

6. Click **Continue**.

7. Click **I use a DSL modem to connect to the Internet** (see Figure 9-11). Click **Continue**.

8. In the Ready to Connect? window, assume you have a DSL modem and click **Continue**.

9. The How Do You Connect? window enables you to configure a PPPoE connection or to select other choices (see Figure 9-12).

10. At this point, close the How Do You Connect? window.

11. Close the Network window.

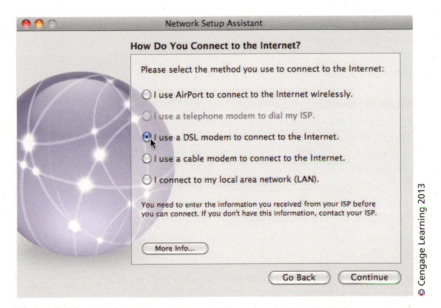

Figure 9-11   Selecting to configure a DSL modem in Mac OS X Lion

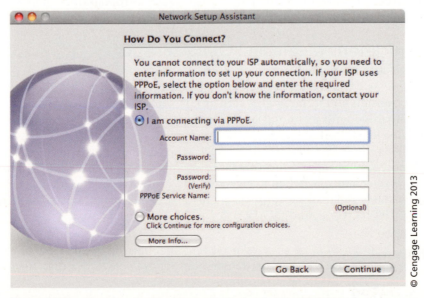

Figure 9-12   The How Do You Connect? window in Mac OS X Lion

Activity 9-5: Research the Availability of DSL

Time Required: 15 minutes
Objective: Determine the availability of DSL.

Description: DSL is a strong WAN technology competitor. In this activity, you research the availability of DSL services.

1. Access the Web page of the RBOC (telephone company) that serves your region (check a telephone book for the Web site).

2. Find out what DSL services are offered.

3. If possible, determine the cost or costs of the DSL services.

4. Create a document with your findings.

SONET

Synchronous optical network (SONET) is a fiber-optic technology that can transmit data at very high speeds. Many telephone companies offer SONET as one of their WAN service options. Bellcore and the Alliance for Telecommunications Industry Solutions (ATIS) developed the standard, which was proposed to ANSI in 1984 as an open, flexible, and affordable fiber-optic transmission standard. In 1986, the ITU-T began developing SONET-like transmission and speed recommendations, but these became a standard called **Synchronous Digital Hierarchy (SDH)**, which is used primarily in Europe. Today, SONET boasts data transmission rates of up to 39.813 Gbps.

One advantage of SONET is that it is nonproprietary, so point-to-point network equipment can be purchased from a variety of vendors. SONET can connect to interfaces for ATM, ISDN, routers, and other equipment to provide very high-speed communications. Another advantage of SONET is that high-speed communications are possible over very long distances, such as between cities or states. SONET is particularly useful for:

- Providing very high-speed data connectivity between distant networks (for example, between college campuses and research centers sponsored by private businesses)

- Video conferencing between distant sites

- Long-distance teaching

- High-quality sound and video reproduction

- High-speed transmission of complex graphics, such as topographic maps and images created through satellite photography

Communications Media and Characteristics

SONET high-speed communications use single-mode fiber-optic cable and T-carrier communications (starting at T-3). The main transport method occurs at the OSI Physical layer, which enables other transmission technologies, such as ISDN and ATM, to operate over SONET. SONET is most compatible with technologies that employ fixed cell lengths (such as ATM) instead of variable frame length technologies.

SONET operates at a base level of 51.84 Mbps or optical carrier level 1 (OC-1), and the electrical equivalent is called Synchronous Transport Signal Level 1 (STS-1). From here, the signal can be incrementally switched to higher speeds as needed for a particular type of service. The currently available range of speeds is shown in Table 9-3. The options most often used presently are OC-3, OC-12, OC-48, and OC-192.

STS, the electrical equivalent level, specifies the number of paths that SONET uses for transmission. For example, STS-1 uses one path, and STS-12 uses 12 paths.

Table 9-3   SONET transmission rates

Optical Carrier Level	STS Level	Transmission Rate (Mbps)
OC-1	STS-1	51.84
OC-3	STS-3	155.52
OC-9	STS-9	466.56
OC-12	STS-12	622.08
OC-18	STS-18	933.12
OC-24	STS-24	1244.16
OC-36	STS-36	1866.24
OC-48	STS-48	2488.32
OC-96	STS-96	4976.64
OC-192	STS-192	9953.28
OC-768	STS-768	39813.12

© Cengage Learning 2013

The ITU-T version, Synchronous Digital Hierarchy (SDH), is similar to SONET, but the basic SDH rate is 155.52 Mbps instead of 51.84 Mbps and is called Synchronous Transport Model Level 1 (STM-1). The SDH optical transmission rates are shown in Table 9-4.

Table 9-4   SDH levels compared to SONET

SDH Level	SONET Equivalent	Transmission Rate (Mbps)
STM-1	OC-3	155.52
STM-3	OC-9	466.56
STM-4	OC-12	622.08
STM-6	OC-18	933.12
STM-8	OC-24	1244.16
STM-12	OC-36	1866.24
STM-16	OC-48	2488.32
STM-32	OC-96	4976.64
STM-64	OC-192	9953.28
STM-256	OC-768	39813.12

© Cengage Learning 2013

SONET Network Topology and Failure Recovery

SONET travels in a ring topology and offers three possible methods of failure recovery (which method is implemented depends upon the architecture used by the WAN provider): unidirectional path switching, automatic protection switching, and bidirectional line switching. In unidirectional path switching there is only one fiber-optic ring. The data signal is transmitted in both directions around the ring. The receiving node determines which signal to accept. If there is a break in one path, the signal on the alternate path still reaches the destination node. The data sent along the alternate path warns the receiving node that only one path is open.

In automatic protection switching, if a failure is detected at some point on the SONET network, the data is directed to an alternate switching node where it is redirected to the assigned destination.

The third method of recovery, bidirectional line switching, provides the highest level of redundancy, up to 99 percent. It uses a dual-ring topology so there are always two paths to a node. Figure 9-13 shows bidirectional line switching. The data is sent to both rings, but in opposite directions. If there is a break along one path, the data on the second path still gets through.

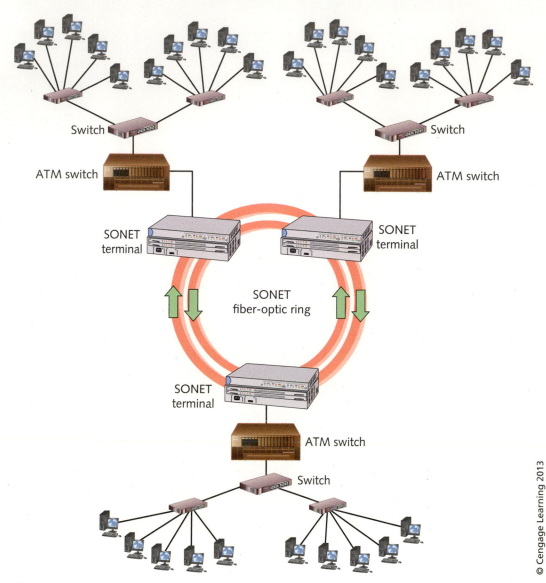

Figure 9-13   SONET bidirectional line switching with dual rings

SONET Layers and the OSI Model

Four protocol layers are used in SONET as shown in Figure 9-14, but only the bottom layer has an actual correspondence to the OSI model. The bottom layer is the Photonic layer, which corresponds to the Physical layer of the OSI model. It handles transportation and conversion of the transported signals. The transmitted electrical signals are changed into optical signals and placed onto the fiber-optic cable, and the received optical signals are changed back to electrical signals. This layer also monitors aspects of the signal transmission, including the optical pulse shape, transmission power levels, and wavelength of the transmitted signal.

The second layer is called the Section layer. This layer encapsulates data, ensures that data is sent in the correct order, ensures the timing of each frame, and checks for transmission errors.

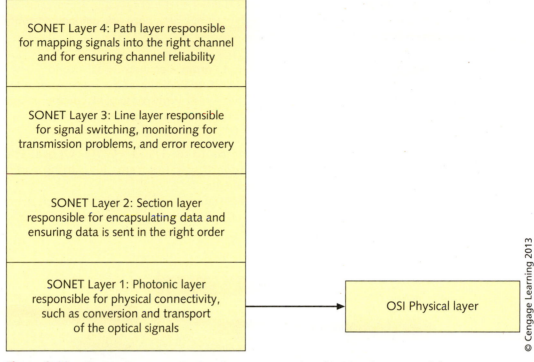

Figure 9-14   The SONET communications layers compared to the OSI reference model

Next is the Line layer, which monitors for problems and handles recovery switching if a problem is detected. It is also responsible for synchronizing and switching the signal and for ensuring that the entire frame reaches its destination.

The top or Path layer provides signal mapping into the communications channels. For example, it might map an ATM signal into one channel and an Ethernet signal into another. It also ensures the reliability of a channel from source to destination.

Ethernet-Based MANs, CANs, and WANs (Optical Ethernet)

High-speed Optical Ethernet technologies are alternatives to SONET and frame relay in Ethernet-based metropolitan area networks (MANs) over fiber-optic cable and can be less expensive than SONET, frame relay, or ISDN in a MAN/CAN. Optical Ethernet is also cost-effectively used in WAN implementations. Several companies provide Optical Ethernet for MANs/CANs and WANs. These networks generally consist of:

- A Gigabit or 10 Gigabit Ethernet backbone (40 and 100 Gigabit applications of Optical Ethernet are being explored by the IEEE at this writing)
- Multimode fiber-optic cable connections of up to six miles
- Single-mode fiber-optic cable connections of up to 43.4 miles

There are various terms used for Optical Ethernet, which include:

- *Optical Ethernet*: The general form of Optical Ethernet that transports Ethernet frames over a MAN, CAN, or WAN using an optical transport infrastructure (fiber-optic cable).
- *Carrier Ethernet* (also called *Metro Ethernet* or *Metro Optical Ethernet*): A concept developed by the Metro Ethernet Forum that defines subscriber services over carrier-grade Ethernet media and that consists of the following characteristics: is scalable, provides standardized services, is reliable and protected/secure, offers hard QoS, and enables service management. In Carrier Ethernet, the term hard QoS refers to providing a minimum level or guaranteed level of bandwidth.

- *Packet-Optical Transport*: Optical Ethernet that incorporates features of SONET/SDH, Ethernet switching equipment, SAN (storage area network), video communications, and other modern carrier technologies.

The **Metro Ethernet Forum** is an industry alliance to promote Carrier Ethernet. You can visit its Web site at *metroethernetforum.org*. For an example of services visit *www.centurylink.com/business/products/products-and-services/data-networking/metro-optical-ethernet.html*.

All forms of Optical Ethernet conform to the ITU-T's G.709 Optical Transport Network (OTN) standard. The G.709 OTN standard specifies frame formatting and how to transport data over wave lengths used in optical media.

Figure 9-15 illustrates the general design of Optical Ethernet, which is primarily based on linking LANs that use Fast Ethernet or Gigabit Ethernet to an Optical Ethernet MAN, CAN, or WAN that consists of Gigabit Ethernet or 10 Gigabit Ethernet.

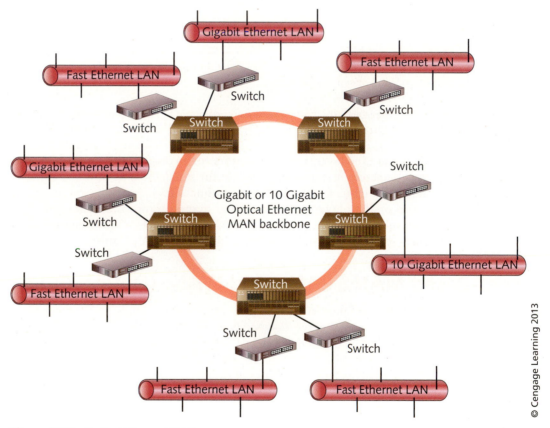

© Cengage Learning 2013

Figure 9-15   Optical Ethernet MAN

Each LAN that is connected to the Optical Ethernet backbone is assigned a class of service according to the type of contract that the customer has purchased. More expensive contracts offer classes of service that give the customer's traffic more priority and bandwidth. Less expensive contracts provide classes of service that give the customer's traffic less priority and less bandwidth.

Multiprotocol Label Switching (MPLS)

Many WAN providers offer **Multiprotocol Label Switching (MPLS)** as an alternative to SONET and frame relay or as a way to enhance SONET and frame relay services. In fact, MPLS has become attractive to many users on the basis of cost savings alone.

MPLS is a switching protocol for backbone or label edge routers to optimize IP packet exchange through creating labels that integrate the equivalent of Data Link and Network layer information. Understandably, this definition contains several concepts that need to be explored through explaining the basics of how MPLS works.

In MPLS, a label (like a packet header) is attached at the front of a packet so that the label contains the equivalent of both Data Link and Network layer information that MPLS switches and routers can use for quickly directing where the packet goes. Important information in the MPLS label includes (there is other label information not listed here):

- A label value (for directing the packet to the right place)
- A traffic class field (for QoS)
- A time-to-live (TTL) field (so that a packet is not stuck in an endless loop on the network)

The MPLS label is attached to a packet by a backbone or label edge router. The backbone router is a router that is on the customer's premises and is equipped for MLPS. A label edge router is an MPLS capable router in the "cloud" of the MAN/WAN provider (the first router encountered when a packet is received by the MAN/WAN provider from the customer's network).

In a MAN/WAN without MPLS, each time a packet goes through a router, the router examines the packet header, checks its routing table, and makes a decision about where to forward the packet. The router's decision time creates a slight delay, which when multiplied by every packet sent, reduces the speed of the network.

In a MAN/WAN with MPLS, after the backbone or label edge router assigns a packet label, all other routers quickly check the MPLS label of a packet. The router sends the packet toward its destination, without taking any time to look up the information in the router table and make a decision about how to forward the packet. The overall speed of the network is enhanced considerably by reducing delays through routers.

Regular Ethernet traffic can be sent through MPLS-equipped devices. Also, frame relay, SONET, and ATM traffic can be sent through MPLS, taking advantage of MPLS coupled with the individual WAN technology.

For some MAN/WAN customers, the lower cost and increased speed of MPLS is enough by itself—without combining MPLS with frame relay or using frame relay alone, for example. Besides cost, another advantage of MPLS over frame relay in some situations is that MPLS does not use PVCs or SVCs. Consider a shoe company that has a main headquarters and needs WAN services to connect each of its retail stores to the headquarters. All retail stores have constant communications with the headquarters. Also, there are times when one store is out of a pair of shoes and needs WAN connectivity to check the inventory at another store to see if the other store can quickly ship over that pair of shoes. In frame relay, each retail store can communicate with the headquarters over dedicated PVCs and SVCs, but cannot communicate with other retail stores (see Figure 9-16), unless it purchases separate PVCs between each store (in a mesh-like network). However, with MPLS, all retail stores can automatically communicate with headquarters and one another, because communications are not dedicated along specific virtual circuits, but instead use label information to be able to go to multiple places in the cloud (see Figure 9-17).

In Activity 9-6, you learn how any one or a combination of the WAN technologies discussed in this chapter are used in a business.

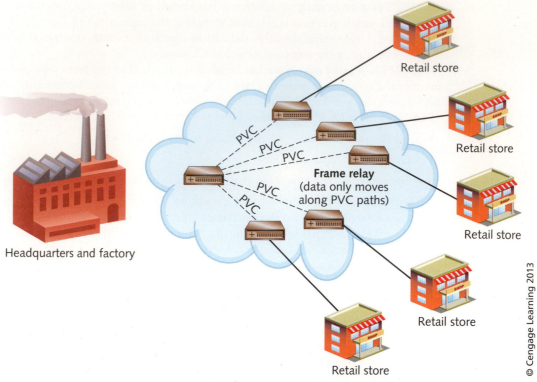

Figure 9-16   Shoe company connecting through frame relay

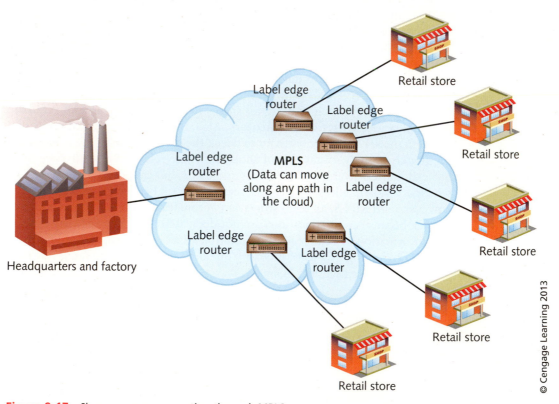

Figure 9-17   Shoe company connecting through MPLS

Activity 9-6: Determine the WAN Technologies Used by a Business

Time Required: 30 minutes or more
Objective: Find out how WAN technologies are used by a business.

Description: In this activity, you visit a local business that uses frame relay, ISDN, ATM, DSL, SONET, Optical Ethernet, MPLS or some combination of these; or your class might have a guest speaker from such a local business who has agreed to provide an in-class presentation.

1. Find out how the LAN(s) at the site connect(s) to the WAN.
2. Find out if the WAN connects to one or more remote LANs.
3. Ask about how the WAN services are used by the organization, for example, for e-mail, multimedia, business data sharing, conferencing, or other applications.
4. Ask about the available bandwidth.
5. Ask which protocols are transported from the LAN through the WAN.
6. Ask any other questions that seem relevant to what you are learning about WANs.
7. Record your findings.

Table 9-5 presents a summary of the WAN technologies covered in this chapter.

Table 9-5   Comparing WAN technologies

Technology	Frame Relay	ISDN	ATM	DSL	SONET/SDH	Optical Ethernet	MPLS
Speed	Up to 45 Mbps	16 Kbps to a theoretical 1 Gbps in B-ISDN	Up to 40 Gbps	Up to 200 Mbps downstream and upstream	Up to 39.813 Gbps	Up to 10 Gbps (with investigation into 40 and 100 Gbps)	Theoretically up to 100 Gbps or as fast as the technology provided by the MPLS provider
Usage considerations	Used particularly in corporate environments and merging with SONET applications	Used less and less in head-to head-competition with DSL, cable modems, and satellite communications	Complexity of setup and maintenance has discouraged many users, and so ATM has lost ground to Optical Ethernet and other options	Popular for home and small office Internet access	Provides great versatility for medium-sized and large organizations	A strong alternative for MANs and provides strong competition to ATM	Easier to configure than many MAN/CAN/WAN technologies and has grown in popularity compared to frame relay and SONET
Relative expense	Higher expense	Expense depends on the type of ISDN, but generally medium expense	Expensive to implement and maintain	Lower expense	Higher expense	Medium expense	Lower expense
Strong options for telephone communications (excluding voice over IP)	Yes	Yes	No	Yes	No	No	Yes

Putting It All Together: Designing for WAN Communications

There are many types of WAN communications technologies, and at this point determining which is best may be confusing. Table 9-5 reviews the WAN technologies presented in this chapter.

When you design for connectivity to a WAN (or MAN or CAN), what you use is related to the following factors:

- The options available in your area
- How you plan to use the WAN
- The size of your organization
- The cost of WAN services
- Your particular needs for reliability and fault tolerance

Consider a small urban company of 15 people, all with computers and an occasional need to access the Internet. In this situation xDSL for the WAN connection is a good first choice in terms of lower cost, speed, compatibility with a wireless router, and availability through the local telecommunications company. If DSL is not available, alternatives can be ISDN, MPLS, frame relay, or Optical Ethernet, whichever is available.

In a metropolitan area, consider an urban college campus that needs to link LANs in different buildings. Some of the buildings are adjacent to one another, and other buildings are separated by noncampus buildings. In this context, Optical Ethernet or MPLS might be good choices. ATM is also possible. Some college campuses started with ATM several years ago, have the expertise to configure and maintain it, and use it for LAN and WAN implementations. A newer urban college WAN installation might use Optical Ethernet or MPLS, because it is simpler and less expensive to install and maintain. Another option, discussed earlier in this book, is to use wireless communications between buildings.

Finally, consider an international automobile manufacturer that has plants and offices in different countries. What this company uses depends on what is available in specific locations. In Europe, it might employ SDH. Another option is frame relay. In Asia, it might use frame relay, SDH, or Optical Ethernet. For its North American locations, it might use a combination of SONET, frame relay, Optical Ethernet, and MPLS.

Chapter Summary

- WAN technologies have come of age with choices today ranging from frame relay to MPLS.

- Frame relay has some design elements that are similar to its predecessor, X.25, but it is a true high-speed WAN technology that reaches speeds up to 45 Mbps. Frame relay has corporate customers that use it to connect remote business sites. Frame relay voice communications, called voice over frame relay (VoFR), offer a way for companies to save on long-distance telephone charges.

- ISDN is a voice, video, and data WAN technology that RBOCs in the United States have made available in many areas to provide versatile telephone and data services. N-ISDN is the most commonly installed version of ISDN and currently has a practical data transmission rate that is equal to a T-1 line.

- ATM is a high-speed LAN and WAN technology that offers speeds up to 40 Gbps. ATM uses virtual circuits and offers QoS capabilities.

- DSL comes in many versions and attracts interest because it can turn existing twisted-pair telephone wire into a high-speed WAN for communications up to 200 Mbps (upstream and downstream). ADSL is currently the most commonly available version of DSL.

■ SONET WAN service is available through many RBOCs and telcos because it offers extremely high-speed WAN networking at speeds greater than 39.813 Gbps and because it provides a good solution for linking high-speed LANs, including those based on ATM, without a reduction in bandwidth.

■ Optical Ethernet has become a strong contender for use in CANs, MANs, and WANs. It typically employs Gigabit or 10 Gigabit Ethernet on a fiber-optic backbone. Customers connect existing LANs to an Optical Ethernet CAN, MAN, or WAN by purchasing different classes of service.

■ MPLS is popular for WANs (and CANs/MANs) because it is efficient and cost effective. MPLS uses an MPLS label to eliminate router table lookup and the need for each router to make forwarding decisions.

Key Terms

adaptive differential pulse code modulation (ADPCM)   An audio file creation technique that converts an analog audio signal into an 8-bit digital signal, similar to regular pulse code modulation (PCM), but it transmits voice communications at less than half or one-quarter the speed of regular PCM communications.

Asymmetric Digital Subscriber Line (ADSL)   A high-speed digital subscriber line technology that can use ordinary telephone lines for downstream data transmission of up to 9 Mbps, and 1 Mbps for upstream transmissions.

Asynchronous Transfer Mode (ATM)   A transport method that uses cells, multiple channels, and switching to send voice, video, and data transmissions on the same network.

ATM permanent virtual circuit (ATM PVC)   A dedicated circuit that has a preassigned path and fixed allocated bandwidth between two designated endpoints.

ATM smart permanent virtual circuit (ATM SPVC)   Combines characteristics of PVCs and SVCs. Like a PVC, an SPVC must be manually configured, although only at the end devices; and similar to an SVC, each transmission has its own defined path to the switch or switches through which it must pass.

ATM switched virtual circuit (ATM SVC)   A circuit that is set up and used for a discrete communications session and is taken down when that session is finished.

Basic Rate Interface (BRI) ISDN   An ISDN interface that consists of three channels. Two are 64-Kbps channels for data, voice, and video transmissions. A third is a 16-Kbps channel used for communications signaling.

broadband ISDN (B-ISDN)   A version of ISDN that has not been pursued because of newer WAN technologies.

cell   As used in WAN technology, a fixed-size data unit formatted for high-speed transmission, such as in broadband and ATM.

cell switching   A switching method that uses TDM and virtual channels and that places a short indicator or virtual channel identifier at the beginning of each TDMA time slot.

circuit mode   On an ISDN network that uses T-carrier communications, this means the communications circuit lasts for the duration of the communications session and is used exclusively by the two connected devices until it is terminated.

digital subscriber line (DSL or xDSL)   A technology that uses advanced modulation technologies on existing telecommunications networks for high-speed networking between a subscriber and a telco and that has communication speeds up to 200 Mbps.

frame relay   A communications protocol that relies on packet switching and virtual connection technology to transmit data packets and that achieves higher transmission rates by leaving extensive error-checking functions to intermediate nodes.

frame relay assembler/disassembler (FRAD)   Also called a frame relay access device, FRAD is specialized equipment often found in the form of a module (card) in a switch or router that converts packets from the local network (LAN) into a format that can be transmitted over a frame relay network, and vice versa.

G.lite Asymmetric Digital Subscriber Line (G.lite ADSL) A Plug and Play–compatible version of ADSL that transmits at 500 Kbps upstream and 1.5 Mbps downstream.

hard QoS Providing a minimum level or guaranteed level of bandwidth. *See* **Quality of Service (QoS)**.

High Bit-Rate Digital Subscriber Line (HDSL) A form of high-speed digital subscriber line technology that has fixed upstream and downstream transmission rates of either 1.544 or 2.048 Mbps.

Integrated Services Digital Network (ISDN) A standard for delivering data services over telephone lines, with a current practical limit of 1.536 Mbps, and a theoretical limit of 1 Gbps.

Integrated Services Digital Network Digital Subscriber Line (IDSL) A DSL version that is compatible with a Digital Loop Carrier device that may be used on some telephone networks. IDSL provides upstream and downstream communications at 144 Kbps.

Link Access Protocol for Frame Mode Bearer Services (LAPF) The frame relay communications layer that corresponds to the OSI Data Link layer.

Metro Ethernet Forum An industry alliance to promote Carrier Ethernet, which is a form of Optical Ethernet. *See* **Optical Ethernet**.

Multiprotocol Label Switching (MPLS) A switching protocol for backbone or label edge routers to optimize IP packet exchange through creating labels that integrate the equivalent of Data Link and Network layer information.

Network Termination Unit (NTU) On an ISDN network this device provides a U interface for an incoming ISDN line and an S/T interface to connect to ISDN devices, such as computers, ISDN fax machines, and ISDN telephones.

Optical Ethernet High-speed Ethernet, such as Gigabit or 10 Gigabit Ethernet, carried on fiber-optic cable and used for CANs, MANs, and WANs.

packet mode On an ISDN network that uses T-carrier communications, packet mode means that several circuits can be used during a communications session, and each connected device is assigned an address and sequence number at the start of the session to ensure that data arrives at the correct destination.

packet switching exchange (PSE) A switch located at the vendor's site in a frame relay (or X.25) WAN network that connects with a DCE (data communications equipment).

permanent virtual circuit (PVC) Used in frame relay, a continuously available path between two nodes, even when the nodes are not communicating.

Point-to-Point Protocol over Ethernet (PPPoE) An addition to PPP that builds in the capability for virtual point-to-point connections (like virtual tunnels between two points) on an Ethernet network consisting of multiple end points. PPPoE is particularly well suited for communications through ISPs on DSL networks.

Primary Rate Interface (PRI) ISDN An ISDN interface that consists of switched communications in multiples of 1.536 Mbps.

pulse code modulation (PCM) An audio file creation technique that converts an analog audio signal into an 8-bit digital signal. PCM is used in frame relay audio communications and on the Internet.

Quality of Service (QoS) A measurement of the transmission, quality, throughput, and reliability of a network system.

Rate Adaptive Asymmetric Digital Subscriber Line (RADSL) A high-speed data transmission technology that offers upstream speeds of up to 1 Mbps and downstream speeds of up to 7 Mbps. RADSL uses ADSL technology (*see* **ADSL**), but enables the transmission rate to vary for different types of communications, such as data, multimedia, and voice.

silence suppression A voice communications method over data communications lines, such as over frame relay, in which voice transmissions are sent during moments of inactivity (silence) on the lines.

sub-band adaptive differential pulse code modulation (SB-ADPCM) A variety of ADPCM that is tailored to work over ISDN and frame relay.

switched virtual circuit (SVC)   Used in frame relay, a means of connecting for a transmission session by sending a special control signal between two nodes to establish communication. Once the communication is finished, the call control signal issues a command for each node to disconnect. This type of circuit enables the network or T-carrier provider to determine the data throughput rate.

Symmetric Digital Subscriber Line (SDSL)   A form of digital subscriber line technology that is often used for video conferencing or online learning. It offers a transmission speed of 1.544 or 2.048 Mbps for upstream and downstream communications.

Symmetric High Bit-Rate Digital Subscriber Line (SHDSL)   Also called G.shdsl, a DSL technology that can be transmitted over one or two wires and that can reach up to about four miles (over two wires). The upstream and downstream rates can vary in the range of 192 Kbps to 2.3 Mbps.

Synchronous Digital Hierarchy (SDH)   A standard that is similar to synchronous optical network (SONET) that is used in Europe.

synchronous optical network (SONET)   A fiber-optic communications technology that is capable of high-speed (up to 39.813 Gbps) data transmission. Networks based on SONET can deliver voice, data, and video communications.

Very High Bit-Rate Digital Subscriber Line (VDSL)   A digital subscriber line technology that works over coaxial and fiber-optic cables yielding up to 52 Mbps downstream and 2.3 Mbps upstream communications.

Very High Bit-Rate Digital Subscriber Line version 2 (VDSL2)   An enhancement to VDSL that can offer upstream and downstream speeds of up to 200 Mbps. *See* **Very High Bit-Rate Digital Subscriber Line (VDSL)**.

voice compression   A method for transmitting voice communications by converting them from an analog format to a digital format, thus creating digital audio files that are played back to the listener.

voice over frame relay (VoFR)   Using frame relay to transmit voice signals as a way to replace the need for regular telephone communications.

X.25   An older, very reliable packet-switching protocol for connecting remote networks at speeds up to 2.048 Mbps. The X.25 protocol defines communications between DTEs and DCEs.

Review Questions

1. You are consulting for a large investment company that wants to install frame relay to an off-location backup site so that it can perform continuous backups of databases and changing investment information. The information technology chief mentions that the frame relay capability must be 100 percent available at all times. Which type of virtual circuit should be used in this circumstance?

   a. open

   b. switched

   c. permanent

   d. total

2. You are working with a small furniture manufacturing company that is five miles from town. The company initially wanted to obtain DSL for Internet services, but DSL is not available that far out of town. What other telecommunications-based Internet access possibilities should you look into besides DSL that can combine data and voice communications? (Choose all that apply.)

   a. optical multiplexing

   b. hybrid frame relay for voice

   c. ISDN

   d. SSH

3. An MPLS label is placed on a packet by which of the following? (Choose all that apply.)

   a. label edge router

   b. synthesizing switch

   c. MPLS labeler

   d. backbone router

4. Your community college installed ATM LANs several years ago because of the high-speed capabilities and Quality of Service. What are the advantages of Quality of Service? (Choose all that apply.)

   a. All portions of the network must be fiber-optic, including to the desktop.

   b. The appropriate network resources are assigned for specific applications.

   c. Packet collisions are impossible.

   d. It reduces the likelihood that network resources are underutilized.

5. After talking with your telephone line installer, you discover that your newly created business/industrial park area has a Digital Loop Carrier installed. What kind of DSL should you request for the Internet connection to your small business?

   a. IDSL

   b. RADSL

   c. CS-1

   d. T-1 xDSL

6. The Link Access Protocol for Frame Mode Bearer Services (LAPF) communications layer in frame relay corresponds to which OSI layer?

   a. Application

   b. Network

   c. Data Link

   d. Physical

7. You are moving your small water resources consulting company to a city that has the complete range of DSL services. You need a DSL service that provides at least 20 Mbps upstream and downstream speeds for the types of files and applications you use through the Internet. Which of the following DSL services should you order from the local telephone company?

   a. SHDSL

   b. VDSL2

   c. RADSL

   d. IDSL

8. SONET can connect to interfaces for which of the following? (Choose all that apply.)

   a. routers

   b. analog modems

   c. ATM

   d. ISDN

9. Your company has an ATM WAN and uses it for live video conferencing. Which of the following enables you to configure the WAN for this purpose?

   a. video frequency duplexing

   b. video virtual circuit

   c. QoS service attribute for real-time video

   d. a PAX

10. What network topology is used in SONET?

    a. ring

    b. bus

    c. star

    d. star-bus hybrid

11. Your company has been looking for a fast, but relatively low-cost MAN communications method. Which of the following is most likely to match these two requirements?

    a. ISDN

    b. Optical Ethernet

    c. SONET

    d. frame relay

12. Your university has an extensive outreach program at over 10 locations in the inner city. There is a need for the main campus to have MAN access to each of the inner-city branch locations. Also, each branch location needs the ability to connect with every other branch location. Which of the following available options is the most effective MAN solution?

    a. frame relay

    b. X.25

    c. ISDN

    d. MPLS

13. Multilink PPP can be used for which of the following?

    a. connecting SONET to frame relay

    b. tripling the speed of Optical Ethernet

    c. bonding ISDN lines

    d. using frame relay over ISDN

14. Which of the following is used for communications over ATM channels?

    a. circuit switching

    b. compressed packaging

    c. circuit routing

    d. cell switching

15. Which of the following transmission media are used by SONET? (Choose all that apply.)

    a. T-carrier

    b. single-mode fiber-optic cable

    c. STP

    d. UTP

16. In checking with local MAN providers, you have learned that you can obtain Carrier Ethernet. This is a form of which of the following technologies?

    a. SONET

    b. ISDN

    c. Optical Ethernet

    d. MPLS

17. Your large corporation has decided to use frame relay for its WAN services. The next step is to negotiate for the type of frame relay service. Which of the following are frame relay services that can be in the negotiations? (Choose all that apply.)

    a. port

    b. committed information rate

    c. permanent virtual connection

    d. multidirectional information rate

18. What communications devices would you find on a network that uses frame relay? (Choose all that apply.)

    a. FRAD

    b. CHAD

    c. DTE

    d. DCE

19. When you configure a DSL adapter in Windows 7 or Windows Server 2008 R2, which of the following WAN protocols do you select?

    a. SLIP

    b. SLIPv2

    c. PRI

    d. PPPoE

20. What GNOME 3.x tool in Linux enables you to configure a DSL connection?

    a. System Networking tool

    b. Ethernet tool

    c. Network Connections tool

    d. WAN Networking tool

21. Your business uses Mac OS X Lion computers. Which of the following tools can you use to configure DSL through the operating system?

    a. DSL Utility

    b. Network option in System Preferences

    c. Configuration option from the Apple icon

    d. Hardware Utility in the Utilities window

Case Projects

Canyon College began strictly as a liberal arts college, but for the past five years it has begun developing programs for business and professional students, including outreach programs to new areas within the same region. The college hires you to provide help with emerging WAN needs as it is developing these new programs.

Case Project 9-1: Providing WAN Services to Remote Cities

Canyon College plans to offer night classes for business school students, paralegal students, and nurses, in five remote cities. Its plan is to have professors offer the classes from the main site and to use video conferencing and multimedia options at the remote sites. The main site has a TCP/IP Ethernet network. The remote sites, which are not yet set up, will also have TCP/IP Ethernet networks. The Canyon College director of information technology is asking you to recommend two WAN options to connect the remote sites to the main campus and to provide a rationale for the options you recommend. If you have the software available, prepare a sample network diagram along with your recommended options. (If you don't have access to network diagramming software, you might use Microsoft Paint and the network device figures available from your instructor.)

Case Project 9-2: European WAN Technologies

While you are on campus, a professor mentions that she is going on sabbatical in England and is curious about the types of WANs used in Europe. What WANs are likely to be available?

Case Project 9-3: Teaching Classes from Home

The Canyon College president enjoys participating in several classes once a week as a guest lecturer or tutor, but she wants to do this from home, so she can spend more time with her family instead of driving back to the college, which is about two miles away. Explain how the college president might be connected to the main college network through a particular WAN technology, and why you recommend that technology. One of the requirements is that she needs to be able to use the telephone in her home office at the same time that she is connected to the main college network.

Case Project 9-4: Saving Money on Telephone Communications

As you are working with Canyon College, you learn that it is interested in saving money on telephone communications between the main campus and the remote teaching sites. What WAN technology is a possible candidate to enable it to reduce long-distance telephone charges? How does that technology work?

Case Project 9-5: WAN Connectivity for a Business Incubator

The college is starting a business incubator on the main campus. The business incubator provides one year of resources for up to five new small businesses, including a business location and office resources, such as computers and Internet access. What WAN connectivity option is appropriate for these small businesses, so that it is consistent with what they can use when they leave the incubator facilities?

chapter 10

Basic Network Design

S ome networks work flawlessly from the start and quickly adapt to accommodate changes and new technologies. Others are plagued with technical or traffic problems and never reach their full potential. The design makes all the difference in how a network performs. By following simple but powerful design principles, you can create a network so successful that users are barely aware it exists.

After reading this chapter and completing the exercises, you will be able to:

- Determine factors that affect network design

- Implement guidelines for installing cable

- Use structured wiring and networking in your network designs

- Design a network for a home

- Design a network for an office or organization

This chapter shows you how to craft the topics you have mastered in this book into a smoothly running network. It introduces general network design principles, such as planning for growth and security, implementing the cable plant, and using structured wiring and structured networking techniques. The network design principles you learn in this chapter work in a home, an office, or an entire organization. You learn where to locate hosts and servers, how to design for cabled and wireless networks, and basic tips for maintaining and supporting a network. Toward the end of the chapter, practical network design approaches are presented in separate sections for home networks and for office and organization networks.

Factors that Affect a Network Design

When you decide to install a new network or upgrade an older one, it can be tempting to immediately buy and set up the new network devices. The attraction of getting your hands on new, flashy devices can be irresistible, particularly if the marketing information promises remarkable features. In all cases, though, it makes most sense to do some advance planning before reaching for your checkbook (or purchase order form). A little planning enables you to develop a blueprint for a successful network. There are several factors to consider as part of your advance planning, nine of which are listed here and discussed in the next sections:

- Purpose of the network
- Anticipated network traffic
- Redundancy requirements
- User movement
- Accommodating future growth
- Planning for security
- WAN connectivity considerations
- LAN and WAN costs
- Existing network topology and resources

Purpose of the Network

The number one task when designing a network is to match the network with the needs of users. A network in a small office of architects may require enough bandwidth to handle transmitting large files containing architectural drawings. An office of copywriters in a marketing company might not need as much bandwidth as the architects because the files they regularly transmit are tiny by comparison.

In another example, a group of geographers may rely on a single network large-format printer to print maps—making the network connection to the printer particularly important to their work. In still another example, a college computer lab might concentrate many computers in a relatively small area with two or three network printers. Above the college computer lab, there might be a floor of professors' offices, on which computers are more spread out. On the floor with offices, computer use is less when professors are teaching in the classroom or are in a research lab.

Some general considerations when assessing the purpose of a network are:

- What type of information is to be shared on the network?
- What software applications are used, and what network resources are required to run those applications?
- What devices are to be shared, such as printers, DVD/CD-ROM arrays, entertainment devices, storage, and backup devices?
- What are the business patterns in the organization, and how are those business patterns associated with network use?
- What role does the network play in the business or operational strategy of the organization?
- What types of computers are to be connected, and what is their function on the network?
- What mobile devices will connect to the network, such as laptops, tablet PCs, and smartphones?

- What types of printers will connect to the network and for what purpose(s)?
- What kinds of LANs and WANs are to interconnect with the network?
- Will cloud computing be used, and if so, in what way?

Anticipated Network Traffic

As you plan a network, factor in the anticipated traffic. On new networks, consider the number of users and the types of servers or hosts that will be on the network. For instance, on one home network without a server, the network traffic may be relatively low, with most of the traffic resulting from sharing files. On another home network that is used intensively for home entertainment and streaming video, the traffic is heavier. In an office with one server, there will be heavier traffic going into and out of the server than to other areas of the network. In an office that has multiple servers performing distributed tasks, the traffic to any one server location is likely to be lighter.

In a large organization that has a server farm in an operations or computer room, network traffic to and from that room can be very heavy. Traffic from a LAN to a WAN connection may also be heavy on a large organization's network.

When you upgrade a network, obtain benchmarks of current network use and consider the traffic from specific devices, including servers and host computers. A **benchmark** is a performance assessment of a network under varying loads or circumstances. Some types of benchmarks you might collect include the following:

- Slow, average, and peak network activity in relation to the work patterns at your organization
- Slow, average, and peak network activity at different points on your network, such as at servers or on different subnets
- Typical network activity that is related to certain software applications, such as voice and video applications or client/server software
- Network activity when only one workstation is running a traffic-intense application compared to the activity when many users are employing that application

Examples of tools to help benchmark a network include:

- Performance Monitor in Windows Server 2008/Server 2008 R2
- Microsoft Network Monitor (for Windows Server computers)
- The *netstat* utility in Windows 7, Windows Server 2008/Server 2008 R2, UNIX/Linux, and Mac OS X
- The *tracert/traceroute* utilities in Windows 7, Windows Server 2008/Server 2008 R2, UNIX/Linux, and Mac OS X

A protocol analyzer is another tool that is useful for benchmarks. All of these tools are discussed in Chapter 12, "Maintaining and Troubleshooting Your Network," and you learn how to use several of these tools in Chapter 12.

There are also third-party benchmarking and network management tools, such as OpManager from ManageEngine, InterMapper from InterMapper, and Spiceworks by Spiceworks.

For example, when a company's network houses a database server used for storing, updating, and reporting on customer information, obtain benchmarks to determine slow, average, and peak access times on the network at that server. In another situation, consider a server used to track meals in a dining hall on a college campus by communicating with devices that scan meal cards. Monitor traffic at mealtimes and at other times of day to plan an efficient network around the anticipated traffic.

E-mail can be another source of significant traffic, as in situations where all members in a particular workgroup frequently send large spreadsheets as e-mail attachments. This is particularly a concern where relatively untrained users may, for example, attach to one e-mail an entire workbook of Microsoft Excel spreadsheets, instead of a single spreadsheet within the workbook.

Real-Life Networking

A public library is planning to implement e-reader services for library members. The services enable members to download e-books to their readers for a period of weeks before the book is "returned" or automatically deleted from the e-reader. Members can download a book either from the library's Web site or through a Wi-Fi connection while in the library. The library will need to anticipate how much extra traffic the e-reader services will generate, both on its local Wi-Fi network and on the library Web site, which is managed on a Windows server at the library. The library has already been gathering benchmark data about current network activity, and it is testing e-reader distribution applications to determine sample wireless LAN and Web server WAN traffic to compare with its benchmarks. The benchmarks will enable the network administrator to plan effectively for the new e-reader services and for future growth.

Redundancy Requirements

Another factor is the need for redundant network paths. **Redundancy** involves providing extra cable and cabled and wireless equipment to ensure that computers and computer systems continue to function even when one or more network or computer elements fail.

In some cases, the LAN is important to users, but the nature of their business or activity allows them to tolerate short periods when a portion of the LAN is down because of a malfunctioning switch, for example. Other situations require redundant network paths so that traffic is rerouted and users never know when equipment is malfunctioning (see Figure 10-1).

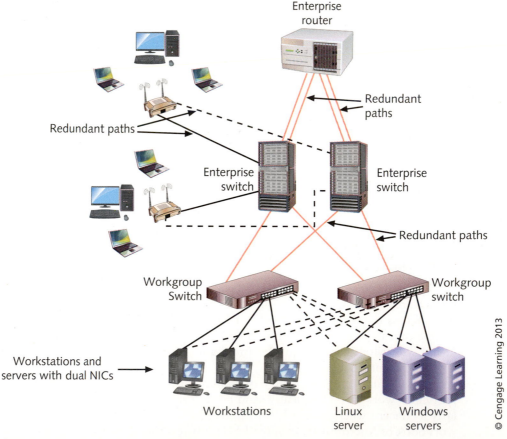

© Cengage Learning 2013

Figure 10-1   Designing for redundancy

Redundancy might be a requirement, for example, in an organization that loses thousands of dollars or wastes customer and employee time each minute that a portion of the network is down. This is the case in a business office in a university, in which a large number of users cannot complete their work if they cannot access financial programs on a server. It wastes both students' and employees' time. Another example is a business, such as a bank, that cannot process user and cash transactions if there is no access to shared database resources. A third example is a company whose business is performed over the Internet, but no business can be transacted if the company's Web server is down.

Real-Life Networking

A discount outdoor store lost customers and money during a holiday season because the WAN access to its Web server was down for over two hours, preventing customers from placing orders through the Internet. The cause was a broken router. The cost of having a redundant router would have been much less than the cost of the lost business.

In another instance, at a department store during Black Friday, clerks were using wireless barcode scanners to scan items in each customer's basket while the customer was standing in line at the cash registers. The scanned list of items to be purchased and price totals were stored on a plastic card that the customer presented to the person at the cash register for faster processing. The wireless access point with which the scanners communicated suddenly stopped working, and so the scanners were no longer effective in helping to quickly move the lines of customers through the cash registers. Problems could have been avoided by having a redundant or backup access point.

User Movement

Still another factor is the need to accommodate users who regularly move to different locations. Some businesses undergo frequent reorganizations to stay current with quickly changing market forces. Other organizations may be frequent candidates for mergers. In these situations, job functions at office locations change quickly and require a network that can do the same.

In other organizations, users need to be able to physically move around a building, such as in a warehouse or in a hospital, carrying a handheld computing device or a portable computer. This scenario also needs to be considered so that the right wireless network design is applied to give these users a full range of access to their networks.

Further, there is a need to consider users who travel or work remotely. For these users a VPN (virtual private network; see Chapter 7, "Sharing Resources on a Network") might be needed for secure remote access. Access to a network through mobile devices, such as smartphones and tablet PCs, is also a consideration.

Accommodating Future Growth

All successful networks must have growth potential and should be designed accordingly. The network investment is retained over a longer period of time when the original design accommodates growth. For example, it is easier to grow a cabled network that already has Category (Cat) 6a cable than one with Cat 5 cable (see Chapter 4, "Connecting Through a Cabled Network"). It is also easier to grow a cabled network when extra cable runs and cable lengths have been installed. Further, it is easier to grow a wireless network that has devices conforming to common Wi-Fi standards than one that uses devices that operate only with other devices from specific vendors. In addition, it is easier to accommodate growth on a network designed around modern routers and switches.

These scenarios suggest a few basic strategies for accommodating growth:

- Follow accepted networking standards, including using devices that conform to those standards and strictly adhering to distance requirements for cabled networks.
- Use modular design strategies to enable growth.
- Use modern cable and pull extra cable for cabled networks.
- Use wireless devices that are certified by the Wi-Fi Alliance.
- Use modern network equipment, including routers and switches.

Planning for Security

While most networks require some security, not all network traffic needs the same level of protection. For instance, a network used by an outsourcing company that processes payroll data and paychecks for other companies must have a high level of security, which can be attained by using routers and their associated tools and by securing the network cable plant. However, a company that provides a public database of health statistics will not require as high a level of security as the payroll-processing company.

It is important to remember, though, that security is nearly always vital. For many people, security on their home network that contains personal and financial information, and files for work, is as important as security in an office. You learn about designing for security in Chapter 11, "Securing Your Network."

WAN Connectivity Considerations

WAN connectivity is another important consideration in the design of a LAN. Some LANs require only basic WAN connectivity through DSL or cable modem lines that connect to the Internet. Other LANs employ a variety of WAN connectivity options for needs such as satellite communications for overseas connections, frame relay to join LANs in neighboring states, and T-3 lines for universal access to a Web site used to market products. When you design a network, consider both LAN and WAN needs and how one type of network will connect to another.

LAN and WAN Costs

Like it or not, cost is always a factor when you undertake any LAN or WAN project. For example, on a home network, the cost comes out of a family's budget. Fortunately there are many economical wireless options available to home users.

In most organizations, installing a new network or upgrading an existing network is governed by a budget or a specific amount of money that has been allocated for the project. When you design a network, you need to project the costs of elements such as the following:

- Communications cable (for a cabled network)
- Network devices
- Additional computers and printers required for the network
- Network management and analysis software and hardware
- Installation
- HVAC (heating, ventilation, and air condition) requirements, such as in a computer or machine room in an organization
- Electrical power costs and needs for computer and network equipment
- Training
- Vendor consulting
- WAN service or leasing fees

Existing Network Topology and Resources

On a network that is already in use, the LAN topology and resources need to be periodically analyzed. Your analysis might range from a simple cable plant inspection to compiling bandwidth utilization baseline data from a network analyzer to make sure the LAN is meeting existing demands and also has the ability to foster growth. In addition, resources should be audited to determine which are being used and which are not used, because there is no reason to leave switches or connections connected if they are no longer in use. The following questions can be considered as you analyze existing resources:

- What are the bandwidth requirements?
- Is there a significant increase in the number of network users?
- Is there a change in the types of user workstations and applications?
- Should servers be consolidated using virtual servers and blade- or rack-mounted servers?
- Are users demanding additional network services?
- Is the network to support multimedia or voice transmissions?
- Is the network relatively easy to manage?
- Are there new demands for greater network reliability and additional redundancy?
- Can existing network equipment be upgraded, or is it out of date?

The first four questions are traffic related and should be reviewed constantly. Some network administrators perform network capacity management, which is similar to the disk storage capacity management performed by host and server administrators. Network capacity management is a planning process that examines current and future needs—the number of users, the need for new software, the network servers' user load capacity, the ability of workstations to meet user and software demands, and the network bandwidth needed to accommodate the load on each network segment.

In Windows 7 and Windows Server 2008/Server 2008 R2, you can get a basic picture of bandwidth utilization through the Task Manager. Windows Server 2008/Server 2008 R2 also offers the Performance Monitor tool, which provides even more information. In UNIX/Linux systems, you can get a basic idea of network use through the *tcpdump* utility. Mac OS X offers Activity Monitor for a quick picture of network activity. In Activity 10-1, you use Task Manager to analyze network utilization. Activity 10-2 enables you to use *tcpdump* in UNIX/Linux, and Activity 10-3 enables you to use Activity Monitor in Mac OS X Snow Leopard or Lion.

In some Windows 7 or Server 2008/Server 2008 R2 projects, you may see the User Account Control (UAC) box, which is used for security to help thwart intruders. The UAC box asks for permission to continue with an action or asks for the administrator password. If you see this box, click **Continue**. Because computer setups may be different, the box is not mentioned in the actual project steps.

Activity 10-1: Using Task Manager in Windows to Assess Network Utilization

Time Required: 10 minutes

Objective: Use the Networking feature of Task Manager to watch network utilization.

Description: Task Manager offers a fast and easy way to glimpse network utilization. In this activity, you use Task Manager in Windows 7 or Windows Server 2008/Server 2008 R2. Also, your computer should have an active network connection.

1. In Windows 7 and Windows Server 2008 R2, right-click the **taskbar** and then click **Start Task Manager**. In Windows Server 2008, right-click the **taskbar** and then click **Task Manager**.

2. Click the **Networking** tab. There should be a window within the tab for monitoring utilization on each network connection. For example, if you have a local area connection and

a WAN connection, you should see a window for each one. These windows provide a graphical picture of the network utilization. At the bottom of the tab, you see a statistics summary box with column headings for Adapter Name, Network Utilization, Link Speed, and State.

3. Click the **View** menu and click **Select Columns**.

4. By configuring the Select Networking Page Columns dialog box (see Figure 10-2, which is for a computer that has a wireless network and local area connection), you can customize the columns of information displayed in the box at the bottom of the Networking tab. Remove (uncheck) **Link Speed** and **State**, if these are selected by default. Ensure that **Network Utilization** is selected. Also, select **Bytes Sent** and **Bytes Received**. Click **OK**. If necessary, resize or maximize the Windows Task Manager window and notice the columns you selected are now displayed at the bottom of the Networking tab.

5. Continue monitoring the network activity for a few minutes. When you are finished, close the Windows Task Manager window.

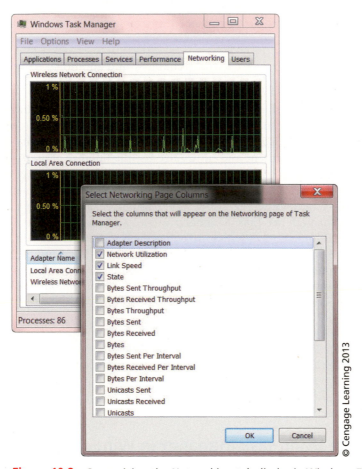

Figure 10-2   Customizing the Networking tab display in Windows 7

Activity 10-2: Using *tcpdump* in UNIX/Linux to Assess Network Traffic

Time Required: 10 minutes

Objective: Use the *tcpdump* command to monitor network traffic.

Description: UNIX/Linux systems come with a very basic tool called *tcpdump* that enables you to watch network communications on a network segment. In this activity you use *tcpdump* to track network activity. You need an active network connection and access to the root account. (You can make sure your wireless or cabled connection is set up by accessing the GNOME-based Network Connections tool that you have used in Chapter 3, "Using Network Communication Protocols," and Chapter 6, "Connecting Through a Wireless Network." For a wireless connection, you need to provide to the Network Connections tool the SSID and security code, such as for WPA/WPA2.)

1. Open a terminal window from which to enter commands.

2. Type **su root** and press **Enter**. (When you use Fedora 15 Live Media or higher, you do not need to enter a root password. For other Linux distributions, enter the root password and press **Enter** at this point.)

3. Notice the time on your watch. Type **tcpdump** and press **Enter**.

4. You see information about packets sent on your network segment, including the time a packet is sent; the type of communication, such as IP; the network address of the node transmitting the packet; and the network address of the node designated to receive the packet. Watch the network activity for five minutes (see Figure 10-3). This gives you a very rough understanding of the network traffic. Does new information fly by on your screen (a busy network), or is it displayed at a slow pace? Note that the information also enables you to identify which nodes transmit most frequently.

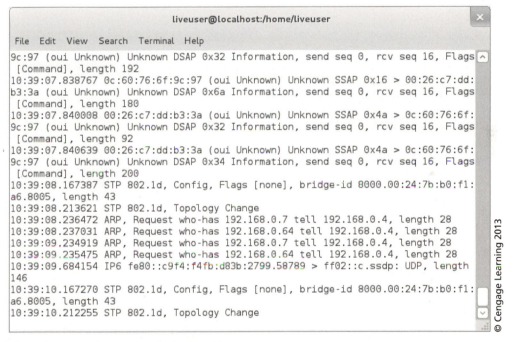

Figure 10-3   Using *tcpdump* in Fedora Linux

5. After five minutes, press **Ctrl+C** to stop the process. Record the number of packets captured, which is the information *tcpdump* displays when you stop the process. Divide the number of packets by 5 to determine the number of packets sent per minute.

6. Another way to monitor traffic is to determine the length of time it takes for *tcpdump* to capture a specific number of packets. To do this, notice the exact time in minutes and seconds, type **tcpdump -c 100**, and press **Enter**. This command causes *tcpdump* to capture 100 packets and then stop.

7. Record the time when *tcpdump* completes, which is the amount of time it took for 100 packets to be sent on the network segment.

Your version of UNIX/Linux, along with the GNOME desktop, may offer GUI tools for monitoring network activity. One such example is the System Monitor tool that comes with Fedora Live Media and that offers the Resources tab that can display Network History along with a simple graph on which to watch real-time network utilization. Another option is Wireshark (formerly Ethereal), which is a network protocol analyzer you can obtain at *www.wireshark.org*.

Activity 10-3: Using Activity Monitor in Mac OS X to Assess Network Traffic

Time Required: 10 minutes

Objective: Use the Mac OS X Activity Monitor to assess network traffic.

Description: In this activity, you use the Activity Monitor in Mac OS X Snow Leopard or Lion to monitor network traffic levels. Your computer should have an active network connection from which to monitor network traffic.

1. Click **Finder** in the Dock or click an open area on the desktop to access Finder.

2. Click **Go** in the menu bar and click **Utilities**.

3. Double-click **Activity Monitor** in the Utilities window.

4. Click the **Network** tab in the Activity Monitor window, if it is not already selected (see Figure 10-4). Notice the network monitoring information in the lower portion of the Activity Monitor window.

Figure 10-4   Using Activity Monitor in Mac OS X to monitor network traffic

5. Under the graph, click **Packets** to view the packet activity through the computer's WNIC or NIC.

6. Monitor the network traffic for a few minutes.

7. Click **Activity Monitor** in the menu bar and click **Quit Activity Monitor**.

8. Close any remaining open windows.

Guidelines for Installing Cable

The cable plant is the lifeline of the network for many organizations—all other components are dependent upon it. As a network designer, install the highest-quality cable possible. Also, install extra cable to anticipate future growth and the movement of users. In an organization that already has a cable installation, you may be called upon to perform an audit of existing cable runs. Plan to locate old cable and develop a cable upgrade plan that opens the way for network expansion, high-speed communications, and flexible WAN connectivity. In addition to being older, the cable also may not comply with current IEEE specifications or fire codes, which have changed over time.

Strategies for Upgrading Cable

As you plan to replace cable, take these factors into account:

- Replacement of legacy cable, such as old thinnet, and Cat 3 through Cat 5 cable
- Cable and connector costs
- Installation costs
- Environmental requirements, such as plenum areas and areas that have EMI/RFI
- Extra cable requirements, for example, in storerooms that might later be converted to offices, or in offices that might hold additional users in the future
- Wiring closet location(s)
- Using wireless networking where wireless can save money and still meet your organization's requirements for connectivity and security

In some circumstances, when you replace legacy cable with new cable, you can tie the new cable to the old cable so that as you pull out the old cable from its location, the new cable is pulled in.

In all cases, create a plan to replace older cable on a legacy network. Also, never assume that a building has no old cable segments, because they will become the weak links in your network if left in place. For example, inside a building replace older backbone copper cable with multimode fiber-optic cable and replace any old repeaters or bridges with switches or routers. Replace older copper cable to workstations with Cat 5e or better cable, but keep in mind that you may also have to upgrade NICs in existing computers to take advantage of the cable speed upgrades. For CAN/MAN cable runs between buildings, replace older copper cable with single-mode or multimode (depending on the distance) fiber-optic cable—or consider using WiMAX as a wireless solution (see Chapter 6).

In many instances, the cable and connector costs of modern cable are lower than those for old cable because of current high-volume demand. When you calculate the costs of replacing old cable, compare them to the savings in maintenance and support. Also, factor in the increased productivity of users who rely on fast and dependable communications.

Installing new cable can be expensive in terms of labor, depending on the degree of difficulty in removing old cable, and such complications as the need to remove or neutralize hazardous building materials. Cable costs may be higher if there is a need to purchase plenum cable or EMI/RFI-resistant shielded cable due to building code requirements and/or environmental factors.

As you learned in Chapter 6, if cable installation costs are high because of requirements to remove hazardous materials or because plenum cable is required, consider using wireless solutions.

In all cases, it is advisable to install 20 to 50 percent extra cable to make it easier and cheaper to connect future workstations, since the primary expense is the labor of pulling the cable rather than the cost of the cable itself. This means leaving extra cable in the wall, providing extra outlets, running extra cable paths, and so on (but check the cable length and other specifications mentioned in Chapter 4). It is always cheaper to install cable the first time than it is to go back later to install more. Organizations grow, and an office that today holds five people in cubicles may later be remodeled to hold eight. Another reason to put in extra cable is to build redundant transmission paths.

Strategies for Installing Cable

If you follow sound installation guidelines, the cable plant that you install is more likely to handle the anticipated network traffic now and into the future. Plus, no one wants to install a cable plant that does not work well from the start. There have been expensive cable plants that did not work from the start and have required expensive repairs or completely new installations, resulting in wasted time and expense.

When you install a cable plant, use the following guidelines to ensure a successful network:

- Use structured wiring and structured networking principles (described later in this chapter).
- Install wiring to meet or exceed the maximum bandwidth required for a particular area (based on the anticipated use of software applications, computers, and network resources).
- Install Cat 5e or better UTP cable to the desktop.
- Install multimode fiber-optic cable between floors.
- Make sure all cable run distances fit the appropriate IEEE specifications for the medium used.
- Install single-mode fiber-optic cable for long runs, such as for long distances between buildings, or use wireless options such as 802.11 and 802.16.
- Install 802.11 wireless options in areas where cable is too expensive to install or where the installation obstacles are too great. If you select this option, ensure that all available standards are followed and that you carefully select the vendor's equipment according to existing or developing standards.
- Install star-based cable plants.
- Install only high-quality cable.
- Follow all building codes, such as those for plenum cable.
- Ensure that the tension when pulling twisted-pair cable does not exceed 25 pounds of force.
- Follow exactly the rules for the cable bend radius, so that cable is not compromised from crimps or excessive bends.
- Leave plenty of extra cable at endpoints to provide flexibility for future changes, remodeling, and shifts in the locations of computers.
- If a contractor is selected to perform the installation, make sure that the contractor is a certified cable installer with the necessary qualifications, licenses, and insurance, and provides all of the cabling plant documentation and testing documents.

Real-Life Networking

A credit union that planned to move into a larger building hired an inexperienced (and inexpensive) cable installer. The cable installer did not follow IEEE specifications exactly, including creating cable runs that were too long. When the credit union tested the installation, many network locations did not work reliably. The cable installer was fired and could not refund most of the money already paid for the installation. A certified cable installer was hired to pull out the old cable and install new cable, causing opening day delays and much more expense.

- Make sure the cable and installation are certified for adherence to IEEE specifications.
- Label all cable following the EIA/TIA-606 (Administration and Labeling) standard, such as labeling at all ends and labeling terminations.
- Properly ground all cable plants, consulting the EIA/TIA-607 (Grounding and Bonding) standard.

You can obtain EIA/TIA standards at the Web site *www.tiaonline .org/standards*. Also, visit *www.ieee.org* for the IEEE standards and *www.ul.com/global/eng/pages/solutions/standards* for the UL standards.

When you address cable certification, keep in mind that it involves two steps. First, cable manufacturing companies certify cable to meet EIA/TIA, IEEE, and UL standards. Second, all cable installations are tested, using certified equipment, to ensure that they meet EIA/TIA and IEEE standards.

In general, remember that the maximum cable bend radius for four-pair twisted-pair cable is about four times the circumference of the cable, and for more than four-pair wire it is 10 times the circumference.

Using Structured Wiring and Structured Network Designs

Many networks are built using structured wiring and structured networking techniques, which are design themes emphasized in this book. In the sections that follow you learn design guidelines for implementing these techniques.

Using Structured Wiring

Structured wiring can mean different things to different cable installers and network designers. In the context of this book, it refers to installing cable that fans out in a horizontal star fashion from one or more centralized switches or routers, for example, located in telecommunications rooms or wiring closets (telecommunications rooms are defined by the EIA/TIA-569-B standard). Often the switches are housed in a wiring closet on the same floor as shown in Figure 10-5.

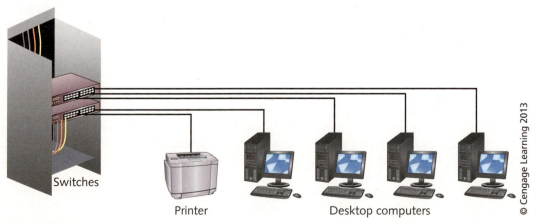

Figure 10-5 Structured wiring

Structured wiring requires the following:

- Flexible cabling, such as twisted pair
- Wiring nodes into a physical star
- Adherence to the EIA/TIA-568-B and EIA/TIA-568-C standards for horizontal wiring
- Centralizing the cable plant in switches or routers (which might be thought of as a series of cabling subunits that can be joined by backbone or vertical cabling)
- Intelligence built into the switches and routers to detect problems at the nodes
- Ability to isolate hosts and servers on their own cable segment
- Ability to provide high-speed links to hosts and servers and other network devices

Typically, **horizontal wiring** encompasses a single floor in a building, fanning out to various rooms and office areas. If the building is multilevel, then there are multiple levels of horizontal cabling joined by vertical wiring (see the next section) to form a structured network. One advantage of using the concept of horizontal cabling is that it divides the cable plant into discrete units for easier design, much like a programmer creates subroutines in programs and then links them together as a whole functioning unit. In a building, each floor represents a discrete unit of cabling or portion of a network.

Using Vertical Wiring and Structured Networking

Join the structured wiring on each floor in a multifloor building by following a careful vertical wiring scheme so that you have a structured network. The **vertical wiring** component of a **structured network** consists of cabling and network equipment that is used between the floors in a building and that often physically links the telecommunications room or rooms on one floor to adjoining floors. The vertical wiring, sometimes called **riser cable**, is used to tie the horizontal cable on each floor in a building into a logical backbone.

The vertical wiring on your network should follow these principles:

- Deploy an extended star topology between devices (or sometimes daisy-chained when you connect wiring closets between floors).
- Use high-speed cable, typically multimode fiber-optic cable, to reduce the congestion on the backbone and because it is not susceptible to EMI and RFI.
- Follow the EIA/TIA-568-B or EIA/TIA-568-C standards for vertical or backbone cabling.
- Use riser-rated cable (cable rated to go between floors) for cable runs through cable ports or vertical shafts, following Underwriters Laboratories (UL) and National Electrical Code (NEC) standards for fire and flame resistance.
- Install fire-stop material to cover cable throughway openings between floors, particularly when there are three or more floors (or as specified by UL and NEC standards and local building codes).

The first two points require some extra explanation. First, using the extended star topology between floors follows the EIA/TIA-568-B and EIA/TIA-568-C specifications and has the advantage that it is easier to manage the number of technical repeater connections that a signal must cross. The disadvantage is that it can create a single point of failure in a centralized switch or router. To avoid the single point of failure, you can purchase devices that have redundancy, such as redundant backplanes and power supplies. In addition, you can put such devices on an uninterruptible power source (UPS) that provides power when there is a general power failure, surge, or brownout.

Second, using fiber-optic cable for vertical wiring not only enables you to scale the speed of your backbone for high-speed communications, but has the advantage that it is not affected by EMI or RFI. This means that you can run the cable near power lines, electrical cables, lights, and elevators. In addition, fiber-optic cable is not subject to grounding issues as is true of copper cable.

Combining structured wiring with solid vertical wiring design enables you to develop a structured network. In a structured network, you centralize the network at strategic points, for example, by placing the switches in wiring closets, and then you connect each of those via high-speed links into a main chassis switch, for example, placed in a machine room or at a main cabling demarcation point in a building. A chassis switch is one in which you can install optional modules. Often servers are directly connected to a main or centralized switch using a high-speed link, such as a 1- or 10-Gbps link, as shown in Figure 10-6. This is accomplished by using chassis switches at the main points to centralize cable media, router modules, and switch modules. A chassis switch also provides one way to connect servers to a network so that traffic to and from the servers can be managed efficiently through the switch.

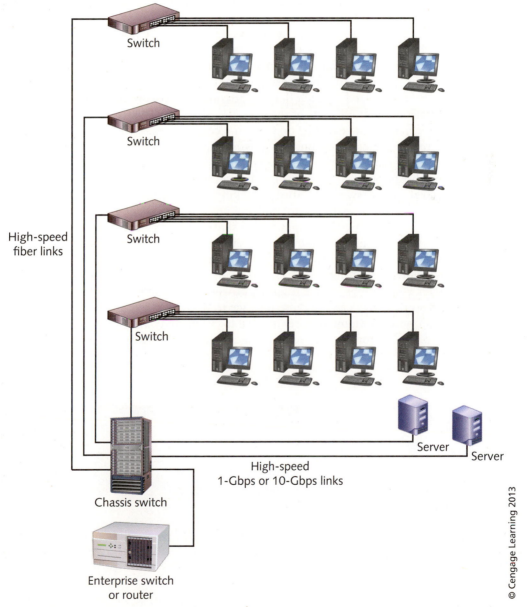

Figure 10-6 Structured network for centralized management

Structured networks enable the network administrator to do the following:

- Centralize or distribute network management
- Incorporate vertical and horizontal network design using high-speed communications on the backbone (fat pipes)
- Reconfigure the network physically and logically
- Segment the network according to workgroup patterns
- Add redundancy
- Quickly expand the network and introduce new high-speed network options
- Proactively monitor and diagnose problems for quick resolution

Besides centrally locating key network devices, another benefit of structured networking is that it enables centralized network management. In centralized network management, central points are established for critical network functions. For example, network monitoring can be performed at a network management station using SNMP (SNMP is used generically here to include SNMPv2 and SNMPv3) and connected to the intelligent chassis switch. Recall from Chapter 3, "Using Network Communication Protocols," that SNMP is a management and monitoring protocol. Also, a network management station uses SNMP on intelligent devices for network management and monitoring. SNMP-capable information-gathering switches (network agents) are dispersed on each floor to provide the network management station with continuous information about all parts of the network. With centralized network management, much of the network maintenance can be done from a central area. This is especially important on medium-sized and large networks, but it also works well on small networks.

Centralized network management also simplifies such activities as the maintenance of servers and hosts. Servers and hosts can be placed in areas where they are easy to maintain, such as at central chassis switch locations. Backups and software upgrades can be performed from one location instead of many, often reducing network traffic.

The server and host computers can share one UPS and conditioned power source, saving the cost of replicating these resources at several locations. A **conditioned power source** is a device, sometimes combined into a UPS device, that smoothes out small and large fluctuations in the power delivered by the power company, providing a known range of power. The advantage of a power conditioner is that frequent power level changes from the power company are conditioned so that they cannot cause damage to devices or extra wear to the components in devices. The computer equipment in centralized locations may also require that the area be environmentally controlled for heat, humidity, and dust levels. Try Activity 10-4 to create a network drawing of a sample structured network.

Real-Life Networking

Some organizations pay little attention to the quality of the room in which computer equipment is kept until problems occur. One extreme example is a community college that was undergoing construction and placed its servers and mainframe computer in a large trailer. During the first rainstorm the roof of the trailer leaked water onto the mainframe. In another example, a small four-year college had an inexperienced electrician rework the wiring to its computer room. After the job was completed, all of the power to the room went out each time the entry door was closed hard enough to shake the wall.

Activity 10-4: Creating a Structured Network Diagram

Time Required: 30 minutes or more
Objective: Create a diagram of a structured network.

Description: In this activity, you draw a basic structured network design covering three floors in a single building. You need network drawing software or Microsoft Paint. See Figure 10-7 for an example of this diagram.

 Some examples of network drawing programs include SmartDraw (by SmartDraw), Visio (by Microsoft), AutoCAD (by Autodesk), TurboCAD (by IMSI), and DiagramStudio (by Gadwin Systems). Some vendors, such as SmartDraw and Microsoft, enable you to try out their software using a free evaluation copy.

1. Start the network drawing software available to you or start Microsoft Paint.

2. If necessary, open a clear drawing area.

3. Select an intelligent chassis switch from a stencil in the drawing package or use the file chassisswitch.bmp (or in another format besides .bmp, such as .jpg), available from your instructor.

 Clipart files in various formats, such as .bmp, .jpg, .vss, .pcx, and .wmf, can be obtained from your instructor.

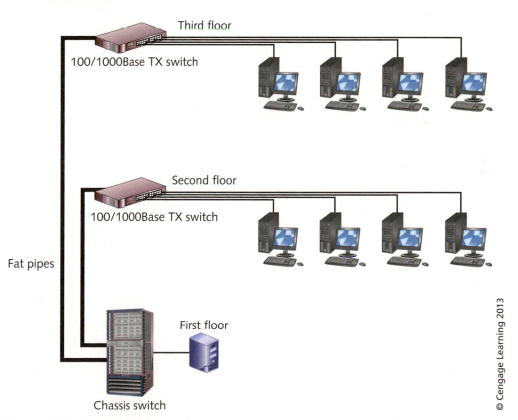

© Cengage Learning 2013

Figure 10-7 Structured network diagram

4. Place or drag the chassis switch to the bottom-left side of the drawing area.

5. Select a 100/1000BaseTX switch from a stencil in the drawing package or use the file 100/1000BaseTX.bmp, available from your instructor.

6. Place or drag the switch to the middle-left side of the drawing area, as though it were on the second floor of a building and directly above the chassis switch on the first floor.

7. Repeat Steps 5 and 6, but place the switch in the upper-left side of the drawing area (third floor), directly above the switch on the second floor.

8. Use the line-drawing capability to connect the second-floor switch to the chassis switch just below it. Next, create another line to connect the third-floor switch to the chassis switch. Make these lines heavier than others you will draw later. Activate the text tool and label these lines as fat pipes or fiber-optic links. Label the chassis switch and the 100/1000BaseTX switches.

9. Select a server from a stencil or use the server.bmp clip art, available from your instructor, and place it just to the right of the chassis switch. Use the line-drawing capability to connect the server to the chassis switch, using a thinner line than those used to connect the chassis switch to the 100/1000Base TX switches.

10. Select a PC from a stencil or use the pc.bmp clip art file, available from your instructor.

11. Place or drag the PC so it is just to the right of the second-floor switch.

12. Copy the PC or repeat Steps 10 and 11 and place the new PC just to the right of the first one.

13. Repeat Step 12 until there are four PCs to the right of the second-floor switch.

14. Copy one of the PCs again and place it to the right of the third-floor switch.

15. Repeat Step 14 until there are four PCs to the right of the third-floor switch.

16. Use the line-drawing tool to connect the first PC to the right of the second-floor switch to that switch, using a thinner line than those used to connect the chassis switch to the 100/1000Base TX switches.

17. Repeat Step 16 until all PCs on the second floor are individually connected to the second-floor switch.

18. Connect each of the third-floor PCs to the third-floor switch.

19. Use the text tool to label the first, second, and third floors.

20. Print the network drawing and save the drawing to a file before exiting the network drawing software.

Integrating Wireless Communications

A small network, as in a home or small office, may work well using one wireless access point, such as a wireless bridge, switch, or router. This is a simple network design, and many small networks use it. On a larger network, you can combine wireless communications into the structured networking concept. For instance, on a single floor that requires three or four access points, you can use cable to connect the access points to a router. For Internet access, a DSL or T-3 line might also link into the router as shown in Figure 10-8, creating a four-cell network (with each access point representing a cell).

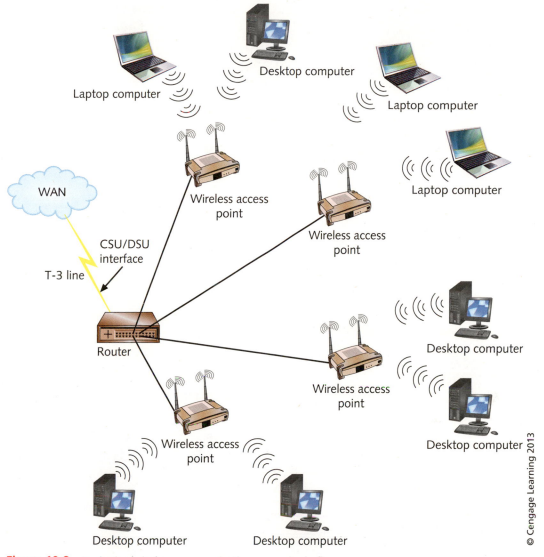

Figure 10-8 Designing wireless communications on a single floor

On a multiple-floor network, the vertical portion of the network might consist of switches on each floor connected to one another by high-speed fiber links, similar to the design shown in Figure 10-6. The vertical portion of the network might be access points connected to a switch. For example, Figure 10-9 illustrates how wireless communications might replace the design concept shown in Figure 10-6.

When you design a wireless structured network, ensure you take into account the practical maximum distance for the wireless technology you use. The practical distance determines how many access points are necessary and how far apart they can be spaced. The maximum practical distances for 802.11 devices, as explained in Chapter 6, are summarized in Table 10-1. Also, keep in mind that, if necessary, you can extend the reach of a wireless access point or router using a wireless repeater (see Chapter 5, "Devices for Connecting Networks").

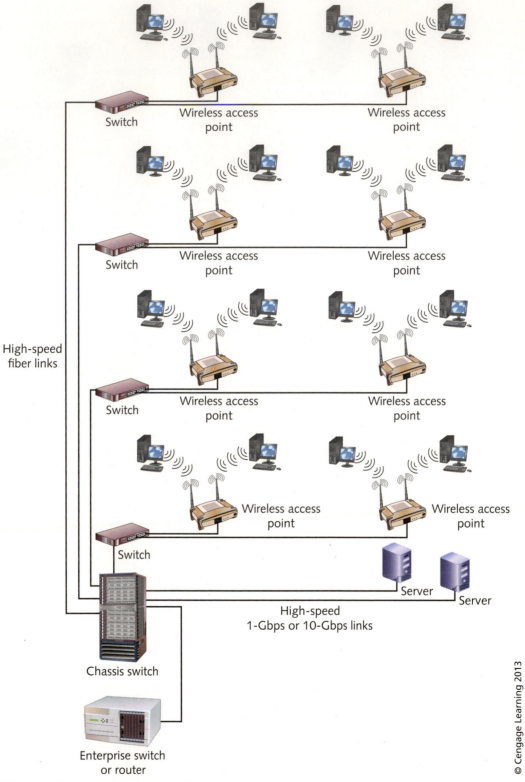

Figure 10-9   Designing a multiple-floor structured network with wireless communications

Table 10-1　Practical distances for 802.11 devices

802.11 Technology	Current Practical Maximum Distance
802.11a	About 18.18 meters (60 feet)
802.11b	About 91 meters (300 feet)
802.11g	A little less than 100 meters (approximately 330 feet), but some network devices actually work at only up to approximately 30 meters (about 98 feet)
802.11n	About 200 meters (approximately 650 feet)
802.11ac	Under development at this writing
802.11ad	Under development at this writing

© Cengage Learning 2013

For more information about creating wireless networks, see *Guide to Designing and Implementing Wireless LANs*, 3rd Edition, by Mark Ciampa (Cengage Learning 2013, ISBN-13: 9781133132172).

Using Full-Duplex Communications in a Network Design

As you learned in Chapter 2, "How LAN and WAN Communications Work," full duplex is the ability to send and receive simultaneously. When you design a network, keep in mind that full duplex should be used in areas of the network that have high-speed links, such as links between switches or between a switch and a router. Full duplex also improves network performance when it is used in connections between switches and workstations.

Full duplex eliminates collisions, because incoming and outgoing frames never meet on the wire. Network throughput is significantly increased because, in the absence of collisions, there is no dead time while stations wait to transmit after a collision. In addition, there is a reduction in the number of lost frames.

10

Full duplex is commonly available on network devices, NICs, and WNICs, but always make sure your devices are in full-duplex mode. On a network device, check the settings for the duplex mode; and on NICs or WNICs, check the setup properties for duplex mode (or be sure to purchase NICs and WNICs that automatically sense duplex mode).

10-Gbps and faster devices operate using full duplex only.

Another reason for using full duplex on high-speed links is that most switches employ one of two types of flow control: jamming or buffering. When a switch is communicating in half-duplex mode, it uses jamming to signal that it or one of its nodes is being overrun. **Jamming** is simply the process of amplifying the carrier signal to simulate a collision. The drawbacks to jamming are that it halts network traffic and that currently active frames can be lost. **Buffering** saves frames in memory until they can be sent on to their destination, and it is used in full-duplex mode (in full duplex there are no collisions, and thus jamming cannot be used). In full-duplex mode, a switch sends a special frame to initiate a slower rate of transmission. This provides adequate time for active frames to be buffered so no frames are lost, and transmissions continue without interruption (only more slowly).

When you purchase a switch, make sure that the buffer sizes are designed to be large enough to store data on each interface.

Designing a Network for a Home

Designing a network for a home is similar to designing a network in a business or organization, but on a smaller scale. As on a larger network, advance planning can help ensure a successful result. In this section you learn tips for locating computers, using cabled or wireless designs, and how to maintain a home network.

Locating Computers

A home network might be a combination of desktop and laptop computers and mobile devices. Locate desktop computers to be out of harm's way. This is likely to be in places such as a bedroom, home office, or in a corner of a living or dining room. Plug the computer and peripherals into a power strip with a surge protector (or combination surge protector and UPS) and connect it to a reliable, grounded outlet. If you use a DSL telephone cable connection, connect that through the surge protector. Also, connect a DSL or cable combination wireless digital modem and router to a power strip with a surge protector.

Laptop computers and mobile devices such as tablet PCs and smartphones, naturally, are made to travel. Still, when you use these devices at home, it is safer to keep them out of the reach of food, drinks, and very small children. Also, these devices will last longer if you avoid putting books and other heavy items on top of them. For a laptop, always place it so that heat can be properly vented from the computer.

If you are using wireless communications, avoid locating your computers and mobile devices too close to sources of interference, such as radios, cordless phones, and microwave ovens.

 If you are using wireless Internet TV access, such as for Netflix or Google Chrome, you may notice connection problems or buffering when you turn on a nearby microwave oven to make your popcorn.

Walking Through a Cabled Design

In a home, a wireless network is simpler than cable, but it is not for everyone. It is subject to interference from an array of home devices and is relatively less secure than cable. For these reasons, some people prefer to install cable. Cable installations in homes can follow structured wiring and networking principles. Here are several ideas for a cabled home network design:

- Plan where to locate a central switch, such as a 10/100BaseTX switch in a single-story home. Choose a protected area as in a home office or a den.

- Determine the farthest reach of all of the computers in the home so that no cable segment is over 100 meters (about 330 feet).

- If you have a multiple-story home and you need to have a switch on more than one floor, consider using 10/100/1000BaseTX switches and connect the switches using Cat 5e, 6, 6a, 7, and 7a cables and 1000BaseTX connections for high-speed communications between the switches.

Real-Life Networking

Not all power outlets are equal in a home (or office). Some may be grounded (with three prongs), and some may not be (two prongs). Some three-pronged outlets may not have a true ground. Also, some outlets, even in a new home, may be poorly wired. This author plugged a UPS into a three-pronged outlet in his home and plugged a computer into the UPS. He noticed that at various times the UPS repeatedly engaged and disengaged, and his computer made a buzzing sound at the same time. An electrician determined that the outlet was improperly wired and had a short.

- Install Cat 5e cable or better for switch connections to computers. Cat 6 and 6a cables are generally more expensive, but if your budget allows, they position your cabled network for new technologies in the future. Cat 7 and 7a are more expensive, but are fast and very resistant to EMI/RFI. Cat 7a has the advantage that it is likely to handle communications up to 100 Gbps. Also, purchase certified cable from a vendor who specializes in high-quality cable.

- Even though it costs more, use plenum cable in attics and crawl spaces. Do this even if your local building codes don't require it. If there is a fire, plenum cable doesn't give off noxious chemicals when it is exposed to flames. The safety of your family is worth the expense.

- Plan to run the cable through walls rather than to staple it on the outside of walls, on the ceilings, and through doorways. Cable doesn't work well when it is crimped too tight or smashed.

- Run cable away from sources of interference, such as fluorescent lights, motors, junction boxes, and so on.

Walking Through a Wireless Design

A wireless design makes sense for many homes, because of its simplicity and lower expense than cable. The prevalence of low-cost multifunction wireless access points, such as routers, along with 802.11g, 802.11n, or 802.11ac/ad communications, makes wireless an attractive alternative to cabled networks in a home. The following are some points to consider when you decide on a wireless design:

- For better access and more reliable communications (and around a $100), consider using an access point (or a DSL or cable modem/wireless router combination for Internet access and a wireless network) and an extended service set (ESS; refer to Chapter 6) topology instead of the independent basic service set (IBSS; also refer to Chapter 6) topology that does not use an access point.

- If you use an access point, try placing it in different parts of your house to determine the best reach to your computers (and with less interference from portable phones, microwaves, and other devices). However, the flexibility of where the access point is placed may be limited to a location near a cable modem or DSL telephone line for shared Internet access. (See the "802.11 Deployment Tips" section in Chapter 6.)

- Locate the access point in a protected area with stable power and consider a surge protector or combined surge protector and UPS (uninterruptible power supply).

- If you are in an apartment or townhouse where your neighbors use wireless communications, configure strong security, including configuring an SSID and using WPA/WPA2 Personal and 802.11i. Also, consider purchasing an access point that comes with firewall software or router capabilities. You most likely don't want your neighbors to share your files and Internet connection.

- Recognize that vendors might print on the box optimistic data showing the longest reach of a wireless device. The actual reach in your home might not reflect this optimism, not only because of devices that cause interference, but because of building materials and other factors. Metal studs in walls, refrigerators, metal doors, and large metal cabinets are examples of some other factors. Under 30 meters (100 feet) is more realistic for 802.11g communications, and under 200 meters (650 feet) is more realistic for 802.11n. Further, if you have an 802.11n access point, but several computers still have 802.11g WNICs, your wireless network will negotiate down to 802.11g specifications while those computers are communicating. The same is true when combining 802.11n and 802.11ac/ad devices on the same network.

Access points and modem/router combination devices come with configuration software, such as for configuring the SSID and security. The configuration software may also include a setting for signal strength. If your device's reach seems limited, check the configuration settings to make sure the signal strength is at the highest setting.

Some wireless network manufacturers offer intrusion prevention systems with their wireless network devices. For example, Cisco offers the Cisco Adaptive Wireless Intrusion Prevention system that can detect and defend against malicious attacks. Motorola offers AirDefense to help monitor and defend a wireless network. You can also obtain open source wireless intrusion detection software, such as Kismet, which works with Linux and Mac OS X systems, and Netstumbler, which works with Windows.

Maintenance and Support Issues

After your network is installed, plan to keep it maintained. Maintenance and support issues include the following tips, which apply to both home and office networks:

- When you remodel a house or rearrange appliances and furniture, you may need to relocate the wireless access point for better reception.

- Sometimes a link on a cabled or wireless switch or router stops functioning properly. If this happens, ensure that no one is using the network and press the reset button on the switch or router.

- Periodically inspect the visible cable and cable connections on a cabled network and replace damaged cable components.

- If you set up a network, but a computer has problems connecting or maintaining a connection, start by (1) checking the network connection configuration on the computer, and (2) checking the Web site of the NIC or WNIC manufacturer to ensure you have the most recent NIC/WNIC driver.

- Sometimes a NIC or WNIC malfunction floods the network with unnecessary traffic. Use tools such as Task Manager in Windows, *tcpdump* in UNIX/Linux, and Activity Monitor in Mac OS X to assess network traffic. *tcpdump* is particularly useful because it identifies IP addresses used on the network. Regularly monitoring network traffic enables you to realize when there is a problem, such as a malfunctioning NIC or WNIC, so that you can further track the problem and correct it.

- Some general tips about checking the connection configuration on a computer include: (1) ensure that TCP/IP is installed in the operating system, (2) check the IP address and netmask configuration, (3) ensure that all computers on your network have the same network ID, (4) make sure that no two computers have the same IP address, and (5) ensure the computers sharing information with one another are in the same homegroup, workgroup, or domain (for Windows-based networks).

- You can quickly determine if the physical connection on a computer is working by looking at the NIC/WNIC. Most have an LED on the outside of the computer, such as on the back of a desktop computer. If the connection is working, the LED will be blinking (or remain on) to indicate it is communicating. If it is not blinking on a cabled computer, suspect a problem with the NIC, the cable or connector, or a switch port. If the LED is not blinking on a WNIC, ensure that the computer is in range of the access point and that the access point is turned on. If these are not the problem, try a different WNIC in the computer. Activity 10-5 enables you to examine a NIC or WNIC to see if it is working.

- On a wireless network ensure that the same SSID and security configuration is used on all wireless devices.

- If network computers use leased IPv4/IPv6 addresses (refer to Chapter 3), make sure that the DHCP server is accessible on all portions of the network. If the network uses static (manually configured) IPv4/IPv6 addresses, plan to keep a spreadsheet of addresses in use and noting the computer to which each address is assigned, to help avoid assigning the same address to two or more computers.

- Assign static IPv4/IPv6 addresses to servers, network printers, and other network devices that need an address that does not change, so that client computers can easily find them on the network.

This section is only an introduction to support and maintenance. You learn more about supporting a network in Chapter 12, "Maintaining and Troubleshooting Your Network."

Activity 10-5: Verifying if a NIC or WNIC Is Working

Time Required: 5 minutes
Objective: Quickly determine if a NIC or WNIC is working.

Description: Many NICs and WNICs have visible LEDs for verifying that they are communicating on the network. This is a simple activity to have you check the NIC or WNIC on a computer. You need a computer that has a cable connection or a wireless computer connection that has an external antenna, a card with an LED exposed in the back, or a USB WNIC that has an LED.

1. Ensure that the computer is turned on and you are logged into an account.

2. Locate the NIC or WNIC outlet on your computer. On a cabled network, it is where the cable is connected to the computer. On a wireless network, it is where the antenna is connected—if there is an external antenna, it is on the outside of a card installed in the computer or it is on a USB WNIC.

3. Look for an LED, which is a small light, often green, red, or yellow. Verify that the LED is blinking (or it may be continuously on) to show it is communicating on the network.

In Chapter 12, "Maintaining and Troubleshooting Your Network," you learn other ways to verify that a NIC or WNIC is working.

Designing a Network for an Office or Organization

Modern network designs in offices and organizations combine routers and switches. Both of these devices enable you to deploy structured wiring and networking techniques. Another advantage is that they enable you to create a modular design, building a network segment by segment. Routers enable you to segment networks and control network traffic, and switches permit you to establish separate collision domains while ensuring faster flow of network traffic.

In many organizations the traffic between departments is likely to be less than that within departments. Consider an engineering network in a company that is on a very secure segment that connects to a router, which acts as a firewall. A different network segment in the same company, used by the Marketing Department, requires less security but has a high volume of traffic. In this case, the router can help reduce overall network traffic by keeping it on the segment for which it is intended and at the same time acting as a firewall to protect one or more networks.

Modern routers use fast RISC or other 64-bit processors or **application-specific integrated circuits (ASICs)** for enhanced throughput. An ASIC is a customized integrated circuit on a chip, containing logic for a specific application, such as fast routing logic.

Initially, switches were primarily multiport bridges, but today some types of switches provide Layer 3 routing functions, and some vendors offer Layer 4 functionality, as their switches check the order of packets received and even identify the type of application sending the packet by using port ID information. Most switches use circuit-based logic or an ASIC chip to provide fast algorithm-based processing. Switches generally do not have the same programming and setup flexibility as routers, but they are easier to set up and administer, reducing the training load on the network administrator. Layer 3 and Layer 4 switches perform the same functions as routers, but, because they don't have the same configuration flexibility, they must be carefully selected to match the networking application.

When you create or upgrade a network in an organization, implement the design in a modular fashion, making sure to:

- Replace older switches that do not offer SNMP/SNMPv2/SNMPv3 compatibility with newer ones that do have this compatibility

- Connect high-speed workstations to switches

- Connect servers to high-speed switched ports
- Connect integrated or workgroup area switches to high-speed switches, using high-speed links.
- Connect major department segments or high-speed switches to routers, using high-speed links where appropriate.

Locating Hosts and Servers

Hosts and servers can be located on the network in centralized farms or in different locations throughout the network. A host or server farm, where these high-network-bandwidth computer systems are kept in the same location, is usually installed in a controlled-environment machine room with power-conditioning equipment that prevents power fluctuations and temperature conditioning to keep operations in a consistent temperature range. In addition, this room contains UPS and system backup resources and is physically secured.

Host and server farms save money, because certain equipment, such as power conditioners, UPSs, and backup devices, can serve the entire location and need not be purchased for each host and server. Also, the use of virtual servers can significantly reduce energy expenses and server management headaches. The disadvantage is the high traffic into and out of the portion of the network in which the host or server farm resides.

Links to servers and hosts from network devices should be high speed, and they should be isolated from the segments that contain workstations. High-speed connectivity ensures that there is enough bandwidth for all of the users who access the host or server. Isolating the hosts and servers also provides redundancy options. One way to connect hosts is to connect them to their own full-duplex interface on a switch, as shown in Figure 10-10.

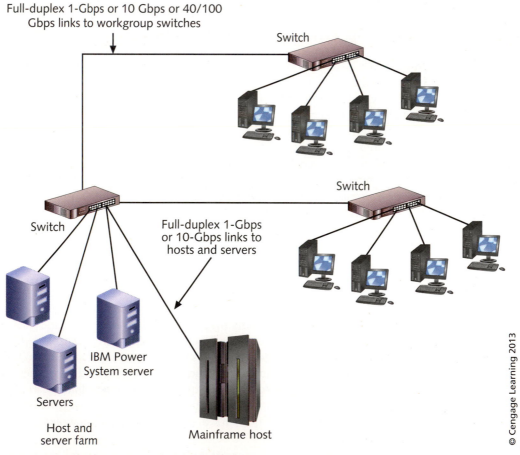

Figure 10-10   Connecting hosts and servers

© Cengage Learning 2013

Another way to ensure redundancy is to equip servers with at least two NICs so that if one NIC fails, the server remains connected through the other NIC. Consult the documentation for each server operating system to determine the best way to set up multiple NICs.

Some NICs come with two or more Ethernet ports, which provide some redundancy, but still represent a single point of failure.

Some organizations prefer to build in redundancy so that if one network device fails, network access is unimpeded. Using the example shown in Figure 10-10, you can build in redundancy by adding a second or backup switch between the host and server farm and the computers that need to access it, as shown in Figure 10-11. Should the main switch fail, the backup switch is activated by the network administrator or can be configured to come online without intervention by a network administrator.

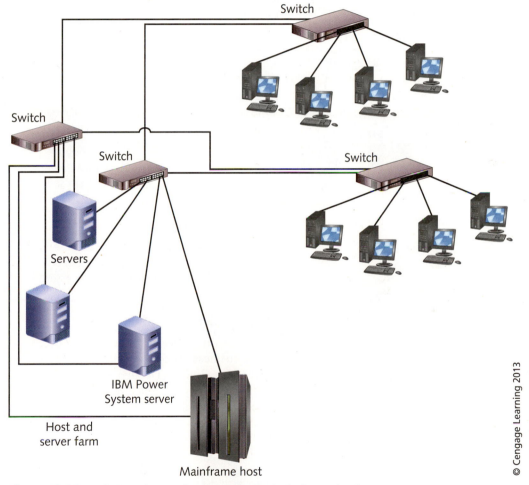

Figure 10-11　Isolating a host and server farm plus including redundancy

Hosts and servers that are interspersed throughout the network should also be attached directly to switches and provided with high-speed data links. The advantage of locating hosts and servers throughout the network is that traffic is less concentrated than it is with a host or server farm. Two other interrelated advantages of interspersing mission-critical hosts are (1) flexibility in the event that a disaster destroys one location and (2) the ability to have redundant hosts at different locations, in case one host malfunctions or cannot be reached because of network problems.

A disadvantage of locating hosts and servers throughout the network is that extra equipment may be required, such as UPSs, SANs, and DVD/CD-ROM or tape backup systems for each server or host location. In addition, interspersing makes centralized management of hosts and servers more difficult, although many operating systems come with remote management tools.

Figure 10-12 illustrates a network design for hosts and servers that are spread throughout a network.

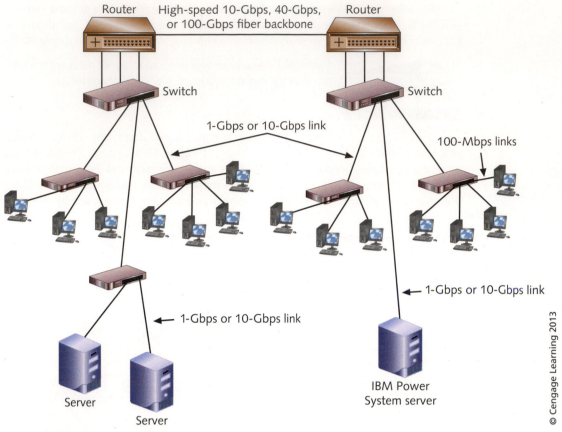

Figure 10-12   Connecting interspersed hosts and servers

Notice in Figure 10-12 that the IBM Power System server is connected directly to the intermediate switch using a high-speed link; because it is the only host, another switch in between is not necessary.

Walking Through a Cabled Design

Consider a secure workgroup segment for one office that needs to be connected to another segment that is not secure; for example, a business office segment and a payroll office segment on a college campus need to be connected to the Biology Department's segment in another building. In this instance, build the business office and payroll office segments first, as in Figure 10-13, by connecting the respective segments to two separate appropriate interfaces on the router using the appropriate rules and/or access lists.

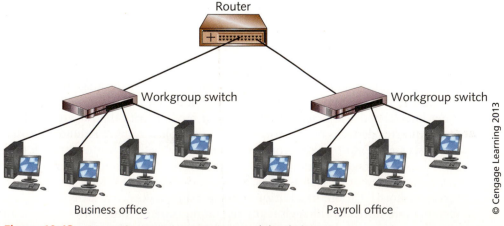

Figure 10-13   Connecting two segments in a modular design

Next, build the Biology Department segment, using one switch, and connect that switch to a separate interface on the router, as shown in Figure 10-14.

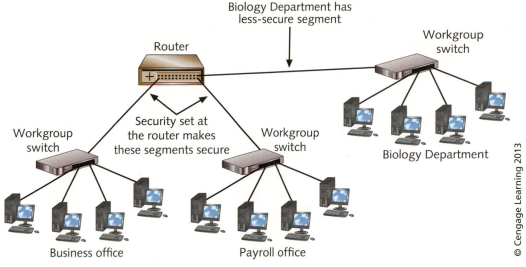

Figure 10-14   Building a new segment in a modular design

The advantage of this modular design is that additional segments can be added in several places. Segments can be attached to the router for expansion in a given building, for example, by adding a segment for the Physics Department in the same building as the Biology Department. If the Biology Department segment needs to be secured, the router can act as a firewall for it, while leaving the Physics Department segment open for anyone to access. In addition, the department head, administrative assistant, and professors in the Biology Department can have controlled access to the business office segment, but student labs connected to the router through additional switches and router interfaces can be locked out at the MAC address level. This network is an example of the advantages of designing around routers and switches, which give you many upgrade paths for future adjustments.

If very high-speed connections plus redundancy are needed between the router and the switches, one option is to use switches and a router that enable links to be aggregated or trunked. **Trunking** involves running duplicate links in an aggregate that is treated as one link that has the total speed of each link added together. For example, three trunked 1-Gbps links form an aggregated link with a speed of 3 Gbps. Another advantage of trunking is that one link can fail, but the remaining links continue to function, providing slower but uninterrupted service. Figure 10-15 illustrates how trunking can be used to connect the Biology Department with the business and payroll offices. Try Activity 10-6 to create a network diagram of trunking.

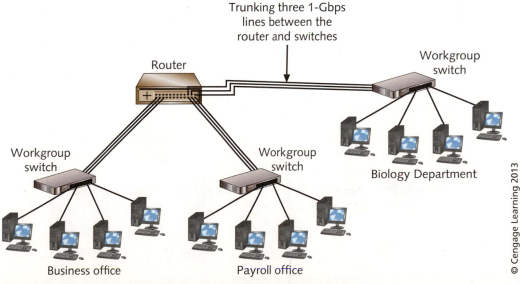

Figure 10-15   Using trunking for speed and redundancy between devices

Trunking, or aggregation, of bandwidth is often vendor-specific and must be designed with this limitation in mind. Make sure that vendor compatibility is ensured throughout the network design.

Activity 10-6: Creating a Network Diagram of Trunking

Time Required: 30 minutes

Objective: Create a network diagram to show trunking.

Description: In this activity you create a network diagram to show how to use trunking to connect a switch to a router. Use Figure 10-16 as an illustration of how to create the network diagram.

1. Start the network drawing software available to you or start Microsoft Paint.

2. If necessary, open a clear drawing area.

3. Select a router from a stencil in the drawing package or use the file router.bmp, available from your instructor.

4. Place or drag the router to the top center of the drawing area.

5. Select an enterprise or chassis switch in a stencil in the drawing package or use the file chassisswitch.bmp, available from your instructor.

6. Place or drag the switch to just below the router.

7. Use the line-drawing capability to draw three lines between the router and the enterprise or chassis switch.

8. Select a basic switch in a stencil in the drawing package or use the file 100BaseTX.bmp, available from your instructor.

9. Place or drag the 100/1000BaseTX switch so that it is under the enterprise or chassis switch and slightly to the left.

10. Use the line-drawing capability to connect the switch you just placed to the enterprise or chassis switch above it.

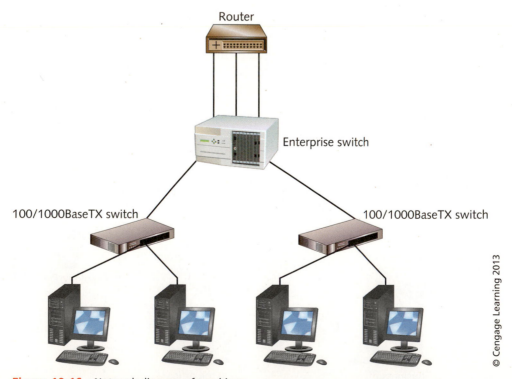

Figure 10-16 Network diagram of trunking

© Cengage Learning 2013

11. Repeat Steps 8 and 10, but place the second switch under the top switch and to the right.

12. Select a PC from a stencil or use the pc.bmp clip art file available from your instructor.

13. Place or drag the PC so that it is under the switch on the left.

14. Repeat Steps 12 and 13 so that there are two PCs under the switch.

15. Use the line-drawing capability to connect each PC to the switch.

16. Place two more PCs under the switch on the right and connect them to that switch.

17. Use the text tool to label the router and switches.

18. Print the network drawing and save the drawing to a file before exiting the network drawing software.

Walking Through a Wireless Design

In the context of one or more offices within an organization, wireless networks typically use the ESS (refer to Chapter 6) topology with communications directed by one or more access points. When there are two or more access points, the network can be configured in two general ways. One way is to configure all of the access points in the same way, so that users can move from cell to cell, with one cell formed around each access point. Another approach is to configure one or more access points and the computers that access them differently, forming different wireless networks (cells) without roaming. As you learned in Chapter 6, cells are configured to enable roaming through the same roaming protocol, such as Interaccess Point Protocol (IAPP).

Consider a small airline in which the administrative offices are in a single-story building. There are two network segments that each use a switch connected to a router. The Administrative Department and Human Resources Department are on one segment, and the Marketing and Reservations departments are on another. There are two office areas with dividers for employees that use cabled network communications. Also, there is a conference room in each office area that provides wireless communications, so employees can take their laptops to meetings. Each conference room is equipped with an access point, and both access points are configured the same way to represent cells that enable roaming. In this way, any group can use either of the conference rooms without reconfiguring laptop computers. Figure 10-17 illustrates the design used by the airline.

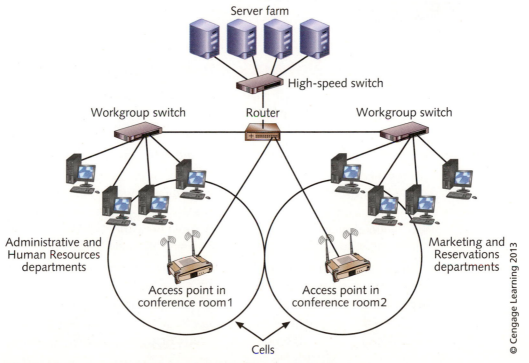

Figure 10-17 Designing a combined cable and wireless network

An alternative method for the airline would be to connect only access points to the router and create an entirely wireless network. This model is used in some organizations in which employees are enabled to work in alternate locations, such as moving between a desk and temporary work areas near windows and coffee dispensers.

Maintenance and Support Issues

Maintenance and support includes inspecting cable for problems and identifying sources of interference for wireless portions of a network. Also, make sure that network equipment is functioning properly and is periodically updated or replaced with newer devices. Vendors often establish an end-of-life (EOL) point for equipment, beyond which they cease to provide hardware upgrades or software enhancements. (Sometimes the EOL is extended on equipment that is deployed in critical federal government or military functions, until there is time or money in the budget to replace it.)

If the equipment is intelligent, such as through SNMP support, there can be special problems because there may no longer be software or firmware upgrades to keep that equipment compatible with new networking features (such as SNMPv2 and SNMPv3) or newer network equipment. In addition, the vendor may refuse to repair malfunctioning hardware beyond the EOL date and may not issue software patches/upgrades for known security vulnerabilities.

Relatively new network equipment has several advantages. The most obvious advantage is that the equipment is at the beginning of the EOL cycle, so that software, firmware, and other upgrades are available. In addition, newer equipment can be sent back to the manufacturer for repair. Some manufacturers offer technology upgrade programs that permit clients to trade in aging equipment for newer versions or better alternatives and at attractive trade-in prices. Major vendors have Web sites that allow clients to download software and firmware upgrades. On these sites, clients can report problems and find information about installation, configuration, and problem resolution. Another common option is to contact a vendor's technician for help on a perplexing problem and to find training programs for certain types of equipment, such as routers. Training programs are more likely to be available for relatively new equipment than for older equipment.

Before you purchase a device that is new to the market, wait for several months to let others discover the problems and enable the manufacturer to solve them.

Putting It All Together: Network Design Summary Tips

You have now learned a broad range of ideas for designing a network. As you put these ideas together, consider the following list of tips:

- Start by determining why the network is needed.

- Determine your budget for implementing and maintaining the network.

- For most networks, particularly networks in an organization, create a network diagram to serve as a blueprint and to have later for troubleshooting problems.

- If you decide on a cabled network, use cable appropriate to horizontal or vertical cabling needs. Follow structured wiring and structured networking design concepts. Learn the local building codes and follow them to ensure a safe and functional network.

- Install extra cable to accommodate user movement and expansion for the future.

- Cable installations should follow EIA/TIA-568-B and EIA/TIA-568-C standards and use certified cable. Also, have cable installers certify that your installation follows the standards.

- Consider wireless options for home networks and office networks, which can reduce the expense of installing cable and enable greater flexibility for users. Include strong security in your wireless network planning.

- Use modern switches and routers with fast circuit-logic, processor, or chip technologies.
- Employ full-duplex communications for faster throughput.
- Use redundant network devices and network paths in situations that require fault tolerance.
- Take the time to learn how to maintain your network.

Consider a homeowner who purchased a home in an historic downtown neighborhood and carefully restored it. In keeping with the historic nature of the home, the homeowner decided not to install cable for networking. Instead, she researched wireless options. She planned to make wireless networking available in the study she shares with her husband, to all of the bedrooms, to the kitchen and dining room, and on the patio. She also decided to have a DSL Internet connection. She purchased a wireless digital modem/router with this plan in mind and had several friends come over with their laptop computers equipped with WNICs. Each friend went to one of the locations in her network plan. She then tried the wireless router in different locations and settled on one location for the best coverage combined with DSL connectivity. Before bringing the network up for use, she configured the SSID, WPA2, and 802.11i for wireless security. Her home network continues to work without problems.

In another context, the president of a small lumber company contracted to expand the cable network in the main office building. His approach was to let the contractor decide where to run the cable, because he didn't have a well-defined plan other than to spend a modest amount on the cable installation. When the contractor finished, he submitted a bill to the company president and was paid. Cable runs weren't tested, and there was no guarantee about what cable was used. As the company connected computers to the new portion of the network, some cable runs didn't work consistently. Also, as more computers were connected, the entire network experienced slowdowns. If the company president had done some research in advance or gone to a network consultant, a more reliable contractor would have been hired. There would have been assurances to use certified cable, employ structured wiring and networking, and follow IEEE specifications. Also, extra cable would have been installed to provide options for further expansion without much extra cost.

10

Chapter Summary

- When you design a network, begin by learning the purpose of the network. Look at additional factors such as anticipated network traffic, redundancy requirements, user movement, future growth, security needs, WAN connectivity, and cost. On a cable-based network, the selection of the appropriate cable plant is crucial because it provides the infrastructure for the network.

- Sound cable implementations consist of flexible multipurpose horizontal cabling set up in a structured wiring format, such as twisted-pair cabling in a star topology connecting workstations to switches.

- Vertical wiring in a structured network is the high-speed cable between floors, such as multimode fiber-optic cable.

- In a structured network, there can be centralization at key points to enable expandability and network management.

- Another important design technique is the implementation of full-duplex communications, which eliminates collisions.

- Designing a network for a home involves similar basic considerations as those for an office network. If you plan to use cable, purchase high-quality cable that can be used for future advances in networking. However, for many homes, a wireless network might make the most sense in terms of the simplicity of the setup.

- Modern networks in organizations deploy switches and routers for design flexibility, high-speed networking options, and redundancy. Many network administrators design their networks for redundancy to provide virtually uninterrupted services, even when a portion of the network has failed.

- Network administrators design networks in an organization to isolate host and server traffic to reduce network traffic and provide security to the hosts and servers.

- As in a home, an organization might have an all-wireless network design. Many organizations, though, use a combination of cable and wireless designs to match user needs for stability and mobility.

- LAN maintenance is a constant process on networks, and one way to reduce maintenance is to develop schemes to replace aging devices before they become a maintenance problem.

Key Terms

application-specific integrated circuit (ASIC)   A customized integrated circuit on a chip that contains logic for a specific application, such as fast routing logic.

benchmark   A performance assessment of a network under varying loads or circumstances.

buffering   The capability of a device, such as a switch, to temporarily save information in memory.

conditioned power source   A device, sometimes combined into a UPS device, that smoothes out small and large fluctuations in the power delivered by the power company, providing a known range of power.

horizontal wiring (or horizontal cabling)   As defined by the EIA/TIA-568 standard, cabling that connects workstations and servers in the work area.

jamming   A flow control technique used by switches to indicate that they are being overrun by too much traffic. In jamming, the switch doubles the carrier signal to simulate a collision.

redundancy   Providing extra cable and cabled and wireless equipment to ensure that computers and computer systems can continue to function even when one or more network or computer elements fail.

riser cable   Another term for vertical cable; refers to cable that goes between floors in a building.

structured network   A network that uses a horizontal and vertical wiring design that enables centralizing a network at strategic points, such as placing switches in wiring closets and connecting them via high-speed links into a main chassis switch placed in a machine room or at a main cabling demarcation point in a building.

structured wiring   Installing cable that fans out in a horizontal star fashion from one or more centralized switches or routers located in telecommunications rooms or wiring closets.

trunking   Physically connecting two or more links between two network transmission devices to form an aggregate that is treated as one link that has the total speed of each link added together.

vertical wiring (or vertical cabling)   Cabling and network equipment used between the floors in a building and that often physically links the telecommunications room or rooms on one floor to adjoining floors.

Review Questions

1. Which of the following is the number one task in designing a network?

   a.   Install enough routers.

   b.   Use switches instead of routers to reduce costs.

   c.   Determine what information is to be shared over a network.

   d.   Match the network with the needs of its users.

2. When a network must be available at all times with no room for failure, you can address this need by building in which of the following?

   a.   redundancy

   b.   tracking

   c.   SNMP

   d.   quality of communications (QoC)

3. Which of the following represent costs that are important to consider when designing or upgrading a network? (Choose all that apply.)

   a. installation costs

   b. network management costs

   c. training costs

   d. network device costs

4. You are designing the network backbone in a multistory building. What kind of cable should you use for the backbone?

   a. STP

   b. hybrid coax

   c. fiber-optic

   d. thinnet

5. You have been hired to install cable in a three-story house near the downtown that has been converted into a small business building. As part of the installation, you will be running cable through the attic. What kind of cable should you use in the attic?

   a. fiber optic

   b. plenum

   c. Cat 10A

   d. broadband coax

10

6. As you are monitoring the progress of a contractor who is constructing your new office building, you are not convinced he is assuring the proper installation of grounding for the cable plant in the building. When you talk with him, what guidelines do you ask him to consult for proper grounding of the cable plant?

   a. county grounding guidelines

   b. IEEE 802.4 grounding standard

   c. EIA/TIA-607 standard

   d. RJ-45 ground wiring guideline

7. You are creating a wireless network for a small firm of graphic artists. Which of the following wireless technologies should you use for the most modern standards and longest reach?

   a. infrared

   b. Bluetooth

   c. 802.11b or 802.11g

   d. 802.11n or 802.11ac/ad

8. The electric company in your part of the city is continually replacing old transformers and other equipment that can no longer assure high-quality power. What extra equipment should you consider for the room containing your company's server farm? (Choose all that apply.)

   a. an ionizer for each server

   b. a discharge device for static electricity that is in the air

   c. a power conditioner

   d. a UPS

9. Full duplex is a better choice than half-duplex communications for which of the following reasons? (Choose all that apply.)

    a.   Full duplex uses buffering.

    b.   Full duplex uses jamming.

    c.   Full duplex has an automatic QoS configuration.

    d.   Full duplex enables simultaneous sending and receiving.

10. Which of the following are capabilities included in structured wiring techniques? (Choose all that apply.)

    a.   ability to isolate servers

    b.   exclusive use of fiber-optic cable

    c.   providing high-speed links to servers

    d.   wiring nodes into a physical star

11. You are having problems accessing the Internet from your desktop computer at work that is networked through a cabled connection. Which of the following can you do to check the network connection?

    a.   Type nettest as the URL in the Internet browser.

    b.   Right-click the taskbar and click Test connection.

    c.   Turn off the computer, turn it back on, and press F12.

    d.   Check the LED on the NIC near where the cable is attached.

12. Before you upgrade a network, you should consider obtaining which of the following?

    a.   the IEEE 802.9 upgrade standards

    b.   all new computers

    c.   an OSI 44–certified contractor

    d.   benchmarks on the current network performance

13. When you install new cable from a switch to network workstations, install which of the following?

    a.   single-mode fiber

    b.   Cat 5e or higher

    c.   Cat 3 or lower

    d.   STP 1.2

14. When you design a wireless network for your home, which of the following should you consider for your access point? (Choose all that apply.)

    a.   Place it on a stable source of power.

    b.   Locate it in a place that is out of reach, such as behind the refrigerator.

    c.   For best security, configure a unique SSID that is not used by the computers communicating with it.

    d.   Purchase an access point that is CICS compatible.

15. You are designing a cable-based network to replace an old one already installed in a large professional building. What factors should you consider? (Choose all that apply.)

    a.   wiring closet locations

    b.   environmental requirements

    c.   installation costs

    d.   cable costs

16. Which of the following are factors to consider when installing twisted-pair cable? (Choose all that apply.)

    a. Consider using aluminum/copper combination cable for lighter weight.

    b. Carefully follow the IEEE distance specifications.

    c. Ensure the tension when pulling cable does not exceed 25 pounds of force.

    d. Pay attention to the cable requirements for the bend radius.

17. Which of the following is one option for achieving a high-speed connection while also enabling communications even when a specific connection fails?

    a. connection matching

    b. VPN joining

    c. multitracking

    d. trunking

18. Your home office network seems to be slow, and you want to view the packet transmission activity through your Mac OS X Lion computer. Which of the following tools should you use?

    a. Packet Director

    b. Activity Monitor

    c. Network Monitor

    d. *netactivity* command in the Terminal window

19. What tool in Windows 7 enables you to get a quick picture of network utilization?

    a. Network Utility

    b. Network and Sharing Center Monitor tool

    c. System window

    d. Task Manager

20. You have to go to a meeting in about an hour to discuss upgrading your organization's network. Your computer runs Linux. What tool can you use to get a quick picture of network activity to prepare for the meeting?

    a. *netpeek*

    b. *free*

    c. *tcpdump*

    d. *ipchains*

Case Projects

The Marine Explorer is a new four-deck ship to be used by marine biologists for studying fish and plant life in the Atlantic Ocean. The ship is to be equipped with both cable and wireless network access on all decks. Several work areas of the ship have stationary desktop computers, printers, and large-format printers that will be connected by cable. The top two decks will each have 15 desktops, two laser printers, and a large-format printer. The lower decks will have about 10 desktops each. Also, many of the ship's scientists and technicians will use laptop computers, moving them to several different work locations on the ship. Windows 7, Linux, and Mac OS X Lion workstations will be used. The ship will have five servers for research and administrative use that will be housed in a server room on the top deck. You are retained through Network Design Consultants to work on the design of the network.

Case Project 10-1: Gathering Information

As you often do for a new network design, you decide to begin by collecting information about this project. The senior research scientist who is coordinating the project asks for a list of topics you plan to research so that she can connect you with the right people to provide information. Prepare a list of the information you will be gathering.

Case Project 10-2: Cable Installation Preparations

You are currently developing plans for cable installation and to hire a professional cable installation company. As you contact different cable installation companies, what types of issues do you discuss with them?

Case Project 10-3: Vertical Cabling

The ship will be filled with scientific devices on the top two decks. The bottom deck houses the engine room. How would you connect networks on each deck considering these factors?

Case Project 10-4: Creating a Preliminary Network Diagram

The scientist who is coordinating the network project would like you to create a general network diagram of the design ideas you have discussed to this point, showing the design principles for connecting cabled computers, printers, and plotters, on each deck in the ship. Include in your diagram how you would isolate the servers on the network.

Case Project 10-5: Implementing Wireless Communications

The next step in the project is to find a way to enable mobile laptop users to connect to the network on the top two decks. On the top deck, they need to have network communications in a work area that spans about 27 meters (about 90 feet) in diameter. On the same deck, there is an area within the dining hall that is about 12 meters (about 40 feet) in diameter where laptop users will occasionally work, such as during meetings. On the next deck below there is a work area about 21 meters (about 70 feet) in diameter in which mobile laptops will be used. How would you design wireless communications for these areas? Add your design ideas to the network drawing you created in Case Project 10-4.

chapter 11

Securing Your Network

Years ago many organizations approached network security like people in a small town who leave their doors unlocked because intrusions are rare. The Internet and global presence of networks have eliminated the small-town feel of networks so that open doorways must be closed and locked.

After reading this chapter and completing the exercises, you will be able to:

- Explain why security is important
- Discuss practical security preparations
- Explain how malicious attacks occur
- Use techniques to protect a network
- Design security into home and office networks

Implementing security is as important to networking as choosing the right switch, wireless standard, or cable medium. In this chapter you begin by learning why security is essential on a network. You learn to make practical security preparations, including using operating system and network security features. You learn about malicious attacks and how to protect your network from these attacks. Finally, you learn how to design secure home and office networks.

Why Security Is Essential

Security is necessary because computer systems and networks house a wide range of information and resources that need to be protected. When you use your credit card to make a purchase over the Internet, you rely on the Internet vendor to provide you with a secure connection while you are transacting business, and to ensure that the information you have provided is not compromised. With today's concerns about identity theft, an employee in an organization relies on the Human Resources Department to guard sensitive information, such as a Social Security number and family information. When a student enters a statistics lab, she depends on having access to a computer and to software that works time after time. These are just some of the reasons why network security is needed. These and other reasons can be grouped under the following:

- Protecting information and resources so that a business or an organization can keep doing business without problems or interruptions

- Ensuring privacy of personal information, such as medical records

- Protecting against identity and credit card theft

- Facilitating workflow so that the work and play of family members, students, and members in an organization is not delayed or brought to a halt

- Discouraging computer attackers from further malicious attacks

Practical Security Preparations

Practical defenses against an attack are steps in the process of hardening. Hardening involves taking specific actions to block or prevent attacks by means of operating system and network security methods. There are several general steps to keep in mind as you work to harden a system:

- Learn about as many of the operating system and network security features as possible and learn how to use them.

- Frequently consult the Web sites of security organizations to learn about new threats and how to handle them.

- Deploy only the services and processes absolutely necessary for the way you use an operating system and remove the ones that are not needed, because this reduces the number of open TCP/UDP ports and application or operating system processes exposed to attackers (known as reducing the attack surface).

- Deploy dedicated servers, firewalls, and routers, if possible. Computers and network devices that serve multiple functions can create more openings for attackers. For example, don't combine Internet, DNS, and routing functions on a single server. Dedicated servers and devices are simpler to manage and easier to defend.

- Learn about and use operating system features that are provided for security, including user accounts and passwords, security groups, permissions, security policies, account lockout, secure protocols, and encryption and authentication.

- Deploy as many obstructions as possible to discourage attackers.
- Regularly audit how security is set up, as a means to locate and address security holes.
- Train users to be security conscious.
- Regularly monitor operating systems and networks for evidence of attackers.
- Don't assume one operating system, such as Mac OS X, is less susceptible to attack than another, such as Windows 7. All operating systems have vulnerabilities, and attackers have written malicious software to attack all types of operating systems. Mobile operating systems such as Android and iOS are no exception. For example, within the first year of operation, attacks on mobile Android smartphones and tablet PCs increased by 400 percent, mostly introduced through downloading apps. Attacks on iOS mobile devices have not been as numerous as those on Android mobile devices, but nonetheless have been growing as well.

At this writing, the Weyland-Yutani BOT malware has been attacking Mac OS X systems in a manner similar to malware called Spyeye. This malware, which is on the user's computer, can request extra information from a user that is sent back to an attacker. For instance, when the user is performing online bank transactions, the malware may ask the user to provide the account name and password as a verification and send this information to an attacker. The malware can also process a debit card transaction, wait until the user logs off from an online banking session, and then the next time the user logs on to a banking session the malware disguises the transaction so it cannot be seen in the user's account.

Using Operating System Security Features

Operating systems provide many features for hardening a system. Examples of features that can be configured include the following:

- Require every user to log on to the network using an account protected by a strong password.
- Use the most advanced forms of authentication and encryption available in your operating systems when users log on to the network.
- Use digital certificate security for network communications. Digital certificates are used between network computers to verify the authenticity of the communication—to ensure that the communicating parties are who they say they are.
- Configure permissions for file and folder security.
- Employ shared resource security, such as share permissions.
- Set up security policies, such as requiring "strong" passwords for accounts and locking out accounts after a specific number of unsuccessful logon attempts.
- Configure the strongest wireless networking security available on your systems.
- Set up virtual private networks (VPNs) for secure remote communications, particularly for wireless networks.
- Use disaster recovery techniques, such as regular backups.

Real-Life Networking

Even people who should know better sometimes bring home sensitive information from work and fail to use operating system security measures. One example is a high-ranking national intelligence officer who downloaded secret files and brought them home to work on them. The files were not adequately protected and could have been accessed by anyone, including an attacker over the Internet or an intruder from a foreign intelligence agency.

In another example, a server administrator for a company remotely accessed a server from his home computer to perform some maintenance. Unfortunately, his home computer was infected with a virus because its virus-checking software updating service had expired. The virus spread to the server.

Using Network Security Features

There are several hardening techniques you can use with networks. Some of these techniques involve using specialized network devices, and others include using software. A sampling of network-hardening techniques includes:

- Design networks around switches and routers to control who accesses specific portions of a network.
- Employ network firewalls and firewalls in operating systems.
- Use a star-based network topology for more secure cabled network designs.
- Regularly monitor network activity.

Learning More About Security

There are several public organizations that provide information, assistance, and training in the types of attacks and how to prevent them. The following is a partial listing of the security organizations, along with their Web sites:

- *American Society for Industrial Security (ASIS)*: Offers training in security needs and hosts the Certified Protection Professional certification. Its Web site with information about members and chapters is *www.securitymanagement.com/library/000077.html*.
- *Computer Emergency Response Team Coordination Center (CERT/CC)*: Started by the U.S. Department of Defense's Defense Advanced Research Projects Agency to research computer and network attacks, find ways to protect systems, and provide general information about attacks—and now located in the Software Engineering Institute at Carnegie Mellon University. You can visit its Web site at *www.cert.org*.
- *Forum of Incident Response and Security Teams (FIRST)*: An international security organization composed of over 100 members from educational institutions, governments, and business. FIRST was established to help prevent and quickly respond to local and international security incidents. Its Web site is *www.first.org*.
- *InfraGard*: A consortium of private industry and the U.S. federal government, coordinated through the FBI, that exchanges information as a means to protect the U.S. infrastructure of critical information systems. To learn more about InfraGard, go to *www.infragard.net*.

- *Information Security Forum (ISF)*: Started by Coopers and Lybrand as the European Security Forum, this organization expanded its international scope and became the ISF in 1992. The ISF focuses on providing "practical research" through publications and hosting regional summits. You can find out more about this organization at *www.securityforum.org*.

- *Information Systems Security Association (ISSA)*: Also an international organization that provides education and research about computer security. The ISSA helps to sponsor many certification programs, including the Certified Information Systems Security Professional (CISSP), Systems Security Certified Practitioner (SSCP), and Certified Information Systems Auditor (CISA) programs. To learn more about ISSA, visit its Web site at *www.issa.org*.

- *National Security Institute (NSI)*: Provides information about all kinds of security threats. The computer security portion of this organization includes alerts, research papers, publications for managers, and information about security legislation and government security standards. Its Web site is *nsi.org*.

- *SysAdmin, Audit, Network, Security (SANS) Institute*: Provides information, training, research, and other resources for security professionals. SANS Institute started the Global Information Assurance Certification (GIAC) program. The organization offers a full training schedule in the United States and internationally, and it provides online security training along with mentoring programs. SANS Institute is a founder of the Internet Storm Center (isc.incidents.org) for investigating the level of seriousness of particular Internet attacks. The SANS Institute Web site is *www.sans.org*.

NOTE Many public and private schools offer a certification in homeland security. To learn more about these programs, search the Web for "homeland security certification." Note that the U.S. Department of Homeland Security (visit *www.dhs.gov*) recommends CERT/CC and the SANS Institute as examples of organizations that provide information about best practices for information systems protection.

Anatomy of Malicious Attacks

There are many kinds of attacks on computers, some targeted at operating systems, some at networks, and some at both. This section is a basic introduction to the types of attacks, not an attempt to describe all known attacks. Some typical attacks include:

- Stand-alone workstation or server attacks
- Attacks enabled by access to passwords
- Viruses, worms, and Trojan horses
- Buffer attacks
- Denial-of-service attacks
- Man-in-the-middle attacks
- Source routing attacks
- Application-layer attacks
- Spoofing
- Programmable logic controller attacks
- Sniffer attacks
- E-mail attacks
- Port-scanning attacks
- Wireless attacks
- Spam

- Spyware
- Inside attacks
- Social engineering attacks

Each of these types of attacks is introduced in the sections that follow.

Stand-Alone Workstation or Server Attacks

One of the simplest ways to attack an operating system is to take advantage of someone's logged-on computer when that person is not present. Some computer users do not log off when they go away from their desks or do not configure a screen saver with a password. Many operating systems enable you to configure a screen saver that starts after a specified time of inactivity. The screen saver can be set up to require the user to enter a password before resuming operations.

When you configure a screen saver that can lock people out, plan to set a time interval so that the screensaver waits for an appropriate amount of time before it turns on, such as 10 to 20 minutes. Otherwise, it can be inconvenient to continually have to enter your password to get back to your session after turning away from the computer for a few minutes.

A workstation or server left unprotected in this way is an easy target when no one is around. Such an attack may not be localized at the workstation or server, but can be spread throughout a network, such as through a virus or worm. For example, in some organizations all of the members of a particular unit go on coffee break together, leaving their area unattended. In this situation, a logged-on computer is an invitation to an intruder. Sometimes even servers are targets, because a server administrator or operator may step away, leaving an account with administrator permissions logged on for anyone to use. Even if a server is in a locked computer room, the server may become a target of anyone who has access to that room, including programmers, managers, electricians, maintenance people, and others. As Activities 11-1, 11-2, and 11-3 illustrate, configuring a screen saver with a password is a simple way to protect a computer and the network to which it is attached.

In some Windows 7 or Server 2008/Server 2008 R2 projects, you may see the User Account Control (UAC) box, which is used for security to help thwart intruders. The UAC box asks for permission to continue with an action or asks for the administrator password. If you see this box, click **Continue**. Because computer setups may be different, the box is not mentioned in the actual project steps.

Real-Life Networking

Even a locked computer room can have vulnerable computers. At one university, a system programmer for a large UNIX system left its management console unattended while logged on to root when he went to lunch. A different system programmer came in to the machine room to check a Windows Server system. When he noticed the UNIX console, he decided to play a prank and reset the root password and the password to the UNIX system programmer's account. He then logged off the root account. The prankster was later called away to an emergency at home. When the UNIX system programmer returned, he couldn't access the UNIX system to complete his work.

Activity 11-1: Configuring a Screen Saver with Security in Windows 7 and Windows Server 2008/Server 2008 R2

Time Required: 5 minutes

Objective: Configure a screen saver to have a password in Windows 7 and Windows Server 2008/Server 2008 R2.

Description: Screen savers can be configured to require a password for reentering a system. In this activity, you learn how to configure a screen saver for Windows 7 and Windows Server 2008/Server 2008 R2.

1. Click **Start** and click **Control Panel**. In Windows 7 and Server 2008 R2, set **View by** to **Category**. In Windows Server 2008, select **Control Panel Home**.

2. In Windows 7 and Server 2008 R2, click **Appearance and Personalization**. Or in Windows Server 2008, click **Appearance**.

3. Click **Change screen saver** under Personalization in Windows 7 and Server 2008. In Windows Server 2008 R2, click **Change screen saver** under Display.

4. Select a screen saver in the Screen saver box, such as **Mystify**. (Your version of Windows Server 2008/Server 2008 R2 may not have a screen saver figure from which to choose, in which case you can use **None**. Using None, the screen will go blank when it locks rather than to show a screen saver figure.)

5. In the Wait box, enter **10** minutes.

6. Ensure that **On resume, display logon screen** is selected (see Figure 11-1).

7. Click **OK**.

8. Close the Appearance and Personalization or Appearance window.

Figure 11-1   Configuring a screen saver with password protection in Windows 7

If you need to leave your desk and want to secure your computer without waiting for the screen saver to activate, press **Ctrl+Alt+Del** and click **Lock this computer**.

Activity 11-2: Configuring Screen Locking for Security in the UNIX/Linux GNOME Desktop

Time Required: 5 minutes
Objective: Configure screen locking in the GNOME 3.x desktop.

Description: In this activity you configure screen locking in GNOME 3.x in Fedora. Once screen locking is turned on, it is necessary to enter a password to re-access an account (unless that account has no password). Log on to the Live System User account in Fedora Live Media or your own Linux account for this activity.

1. Click **Activities** and click **Applications**.

2. Click **System Settings**.

3. Click **Screen**.

4. Ensure that **Turn off after** is set at **10** minutes. Also, the screen **Lock** should be set to **On** (the default) and **Lock screen after** should be set to **Screen turns off** (see Figure 11-2; in Fedora Live Media the *Lock* and *Lock screen after* parameters may be set to the defaults and deactivated so they cannot be changed). The Lock screen after parameter setting locks the screen as soon as the screen turns off after sitting idle.

5. Close the Screen window.

Figure 11-2 Configuring screen locking in Linux with the GNOME 3.x desktop

Activity 11-3: Configuring a Screen Saver with Security in Mac OS X Snow Leopard and Lion

Time Required: 5 minutes
Objective: Configure a screen saver to have a password in Mac OS X.

Description: In this activity you configure a screensaver to have a password in Mac OS X Snow Leopard or Lion. Log on to your own account for this activity. Also for your user account, automatic login should be disabled in the account configuration.

1. Click the **System Preferences** icon in the Dock, or click the **Apple** icon in the menu bar and click **System Preferences**.

2. In the System Preferences window under Personal, click **Desktop & Screen Saver**.

3. Make sure the **Screen Saver** tab is selected.

4. Select a screen saver picture or a theme of pictures (under Pictures), such as **Beach** in the Screen Savers list.

5. Move the pointer for **Start screen saver** to **10 minutes** (see Figure 11-3). (After you set this parameter, and once the computer is idle for over 10 minutes, the screen saver turns on and you must enter your account name and password to go back to the desktop. If you do not have to enter your account name and password, then check the user account setup for your account via System Preferences and make sure automatic login is disabled.)

6. Click **System Preferences** in the menu bar and click **Quit System Preferences**.

Figure 11-3   Configuring a screen saver in Mac OS X

Attacks Enabled by Access to Passwords

Access to operating systems can be guarded by a user account name and a password. Sometimes account users defeat the purpose of this protection by sharing their passwords with others. Another way that users defeat password protection is by writing down passwords and displaying them or leaving them where they can be found in the work area.

Attackers have other more sophisticated ways of gaining password access. Knowledgeable attackers know that there are key administrative user accounts, such as the Administrator account in Windows-based systems, the root account in UNIX and Linux systems, and administrative user accounts in Mac OS X. Attackers can attempt to log on to these types of accounts either locally or through a network, using an open TCP/UDP port, for example (see Chapter 3, "Using Network Communication Protocols").

If an attacker is searching for an account to access, she or he might use the Domain Name System (DNS, see Chapter 3) on a network connected to the Internet to find possible user account names. After finding a user account name, the attacker can use password cracker software that repeatedly tries different possible passwords. This software composes password possibilities by using and combining names, words in the dictionary, and even numbers.

One way to help protect a network is to use an internal DNS server on a private network that cannot be accessed through the Internet.

Viruses, Worms, and Trojan Horses

Most people have heard of or experienced a virus, a worm, or a Trojan horse. A **virus** is a program that is relayed by a disk or a file and has the ability to replicate throughout a system. Some viruses can damage files or disks, and others replicate without causing permanent damage. For instance, the DasBoot virus, which was first introduced in 2000 and periodically has been distributed in much later years, infects the Master Boot Record (MBR; the beginning of a disk that stores partition information and is the starting location for accessing the disk) on hard drives. This virus replicates each time a file is executed on the computer, reducing the efficiency of the computer and occupying disk space.

A **virus hoax** is not a virus, but an e-mail falsely warning of a virus. Sometimes the virus hoax e-mail contains instructions on how to delete a file that is supposedly a dangerous virus—but is actually an important system file. Those who heed the "warning" may experience system problems or may simply need to reinstall the file. Virus hoaxes are intended to stir people up so they forward the warning to others, resulting in a high number of e-mails that cause even more needless worry and network traffic. For example, the Baby New Year Virus hoax sends a warning that the user's computer is probably infected with a virus and that the virus has spread to the computers of family, friends, and coworkers through e-mail. This virus hoax warns that 42 million computers have already been infected, and the only way to remove the virus is to download an antidote. The Web site it provides for the antidote is bogus. A **worm** is a program that endlessly replicates on the same computer or sends itself to many other computers on a network. The difference between a worm and a virus is that a worm continues to create new files, while a virus infects a disk or file and then that disk or file infects other disks or files with the virus. Another difference between a worm and a virus is that a worm can continue to replicate and travel to other computers without human involvement, such as a human running an executable file or sending an e-mail. In contrast, a virus attaches to a file and replicates when the file is opened, a program is run, or an e-mail is sent by the user. A worm does not depend on such an attachment to a file or program, because it replicates on its own.

One example of a worm is the SB.BadBunny worm that attacks Windows computers and the mobile devices with which they communicate. This worm replicates without human intervention to all mobile devices that connect to the infected computer. The Code Red and Code Red II worms replicate and replicate on the same computer and can be sent to other computers on a network or through the Internet via Web services and router management software. TCP/UDP port 80, which is used for HTTP Web browsing services (see Chapter 3), is a port that is particularly susceptible to spreading this worm.

A **Trojan horse** is a program that appears useful and harmless, but instead does harm to the user's computer. Often a Trojan horse is designed to provide an attacker with access to the computer on which it is running, or it may enable the attacker to control the computer. Backdoor.IRC.Yoink, Trojan.Idly, B02K, NetBus, Flashback Trojan Horse, Spy, and Mac Defender are examples of Trojan horses designed to provide malicious access and control of an operating system. For example, Trojan.Idly is designed to give the attacker the target's user account and password.

The widespread presence of viruses, worms, and Trojan horses speaks to the need for all network users to have full-service virus-checking software that can find and remove all three of these types of threats, plus other threats such as spyware, which is discussed in the "Spyware" section of this chapter.

Buffer Attacks

Many systems use **buffers** to store data until it is ready to be used. Suppose that a server with a high-speed connection is transmitting multimedia data to a workstation over a network, and the server is transmitting faster than the workstation can receive. The workstation's network interface card employs software that can buffer information until the workstation is ready to process it. As you have learned, network devices such as switches also use buffers, so that when there is heavy network traffic, they have a means to store data until it can be forwarded to the right destination. A **buffer attack** is one in which the attacker tricks the buffer software into storing more information than the buffer is sized to hold (a situation called **buffer overflow**). That extra information can be malicious software that then has access to the host computer.

Denial-of-Service Attacks

A **denial-of-service (DoS) attack** is used to interfere with normal access to a network host, Web site, or service, by flooding a network with useless information or with frames or packets containing errors that are not identified by a particular network service. For example, a denial-of-service attack might target HTTP (Hypertext Transfer Protocol) or FTP (File Transfer Protocol) communications services on a Web site. A DoS attack is typically intended to shut down a site or service, but normally does not permanently damage information or systems. The actual damage is that a site or host computer cannot be reached for a period of time, resulting in the loss of business functions or commerce. Many e-commerce Web sites have experienced DoS attacks, including Amazon.com, Buy.com, and eBay.com.

Sometimes a DoS attack takes place on a particular operating system when the attacker works from the local network, for instance, by gaining access to the Administrator account in Windows Server and simply stopping the Workstation and Server services, which prevents users from having network access to that server. In more extreme cases, the attacker may remove or reconfigure a service to disable it. Another method is to overrun the disk capacity on a system that does not have disk quotas set up, causing one or more drives to completely fill up with files. This was particularly a problem on early server systems that did not come with disk quota management options. But it is still a problem because some server administrators do not configure disk quotas. A **disk quota** involves allocating a specific amount of disk space to a user or application with the ability to ensure that the user or application cannot use more disk space than is specified in the allocation.

A remote attack (an attack that does not originate from the local network) might take the form of simply flooding a system with more packets than it can handle. For instance, the Ping of Death uses the *ping* utility available in Windows, UNIX/Linux, and Mac OS X systems to flood a system with oversized packets, blocking access to the target system while it labors to handle the traffic. *ping* is a utility that network users and administrators frequently use to test a network connection. A different type of remote attack is the use of improperly formed packets or packets with errors. The Jolt2 DoS, for example, sends packet fragment after packet fragment in such a way that the fragments cannot be reconstructed. The target computer's resources are fully consumed by trying to reconstruct the packets. Another example is Winnuke, which sends improperly formatted TCP frames, eventually causing a system to hang or crash.

In some attacks, the computer originating the attack causes several other computers to send attack packets. The attack packets may target one site or host, or multiple computers may attack multiple hosts. This type of attack is called a **distributed denial-of-service (DDoS) attack**. Recent DDoS attacks have been by computers taken over and remotely controlled by attackers. These compromised computers are called *zombies* or *botnets*. Once an attacker has enough zombies, the attacker can generate excessive traffic on a network to cause a DDoS attack. Attackers sometimes auction or share zombies with other attackers so that a single computer may be remotely controlled by more than one attacker.

Man-in-the-Middle Attacks

As the name suggests a **man-in-the-middle attack** occurs when the attacker is able to intercept or monitor transmissions meant for a different computer. You might think of this as similar to when someone impersonates another person. In the case of a man-in-the-middle attack, the attacker is literally operating between two communicating computers and has the opportunity to:

- Listen in on communications
- Modify communications

Wireless networks are particularly susceptible to man-in-the-middle attacks. For example, on some wireless networks, the communicating devices may be set to wait several minutes between the time one device initiates a communication and the time the other device synchronizes with that communication. When the wait time is set between several minutes to up to 30 minutes, this provides an ideal opening for an attacker to synchronize with the communications initiator and to pretend to be the computer that the initiating computer is contacting.

Source Routing Attacks

In **source routing**, the sender of a packet specifies the precise path that the packet will take to reach its destination. Source routing is not typically used in regular network communications, because token ring networks which use source routing are rare. However, source routing is used for other purposes, such as for network troubleshooting. For example, the Windows, UNIX/Linux, and Mac OS X troubleshooting utility, *traceroute*, uses source routing to map the route a packet takes from one point to another on a network.

In a source routing attack, the attacker modifies the source address and routing information to make a packet appear to come from a different source, such as one that is already trusted for communications on a network (refer to Chapter 3 for information about public and private IP addressing in relation to trusted communications). Besides appearing as a trusted user on a network, the attacker also can use source routing to breach a privately configured network, such as one protected by a network device that uses Network Address Translation. **Network Address Translation (NAT)** can translate an IP address from a private network to a different address used on a public network or the Internet—a technique used to protect the identity of a computer on the private network from attackers, as well as to bypass the requirement to employ universally unique IP addresses on the private network.

Attackers may get through a specific NAT device by using a form of source routing called loose source record route (LSRR), which does not specify the complete route for the packet, but only one portion—one or two hops or specific network devices, for example—in the route, which is through the NAT device.

Application-Layer Attacks

An **application-layer attack** can be used to attack any type of application, including an operating system or an application used over a network. An application-layer attack can take control of an application or a computer through issuing commands. This type of control can be used to alter data, enable an attacker to monitor network activity, stop or alter applications including operating systems, and basically do anything someone in control of a computer or application can accomplish.

An application-layer attack is a particular threat to cloud services because once in the cloud it can halt the use of programs, modify data, and even make data from the cloud available to an attacker. An application-layer attack can also be used to launch a denial-of-service attack in the cloud. All of these scenarios can affect thousands of cloud users.

Spoofing

In **spoofing**, the address of the source computer is changed to make a packet appear to come from a different computer. Using spoofing, an attacker can initiate access to a computer or can appear as just another transmission to a computer from a legitimate source that is already connected. A source routing attack can be considered a form of spoofing. Also, a DoS attack that floods a host with packets from many bogus source addresses is a form of spoofing.

Programmable Logic Controller Attacks

A programmable logic controller is a computer that is used in industrial manufacturing and other similar environments to control or automate specific manufacturing or mechanical processes. Computer worms and malware have been written that interfere with programmable logic controllers and consequently interfere with the manufacturing or mechanical processes they manage. Such worms and malware constitute a **programmable logic controller attack**. The Stuxnet worm is an example. It is believed that Stuxnet was created to target industrial software and equipment involved with uranium enrichment in Iran and other countries.

Sniffer Attacks

A **sniffer attack** refers to when an attacker uses software to intercept and read packet traffic. Sniffer software has traditionally been used (and is named after an early network analysis device) to enable network administrators to monitor network traffic and diagnose problems. However, attackers can also obtain such software, which is openly available to download from Web sites that provide popular attack software.

Sniffer software enables the user to view the contents of packets. It also can be used to obtain information that is used by attackers to interfere with network communications. An important way to help thwart a sniffer attack is to make sure network communications and user account passwords are encrypted.

E-Mail Attacks

Most people who use e-mail realize they may be targets of an e-mail attack. An e-mail attack may appear to come from a friendly or even trusted source—a familiar company, a family member, or a coworker. The sender may simply forge the source address or use a newly started e-mail account to temporarily send damaging e-mail. Sometimes an e-mail is sent with an appealing subject head, such as "Congratulations you've just won free software." The e-mail that is received may have an attached file containing a virus, worm, or Trojan horse. A word-processing or spreadsheet attachment may house a macro (a simple program or set of instructions) that contains malicious code. Or, the e-mail may contain a Web link to a rogue Web site. A **rogue Web site** is one that performs unlawful activity or that puts the user who accesses it at risk, such as by downloading malicious software to the user's computer, gaining unauthorized access, or stealing account password or other personal information.

Another example is a bogus e-mail that is sent to users of a popular Internet company that registers Web sites, requesting each recipient to supply name, address, and credit card information for the alleged purpose of updating company records. The real purpose is to surreptitiously gather credit card data for identity theft.

Port-Scanning Attacks

As you learned in Chapter 3, communications through TCP/IP use TCP ports or UDP ports when User Datagram Protocol (UDP) is used with IP. A port, sometimes called a socket, is a way to access a specific service, process, or function. A port is like a virtual circuit between two services or processes communicating between two different computers or network devices. The services might be FTP, e-mail services, or many others. There are 65,535 ports in TCP and UDP. For example, DNS runs over port 53, and FTP uses ports 20 and 21 (see Chapter 3 to review TCP/UDP ports). Table 11-1 lists a sampling of common TCP/UDP ports.

Of the 65,535 TCP/UDP ports, ports 0–1023 are ports commonly used by operating systems and networking communications. Because of their common use, these ports are called **well-known ports**.

Table 11-1   Examples of well-known TCP/UDP source and destination ports

Port Number	Purpose	Port Number	Purpose
1	Multiplexing	80	HTTP Web browsing
5	RJE applications	93	Device controls
9	Transmission discard	102	Service access point (SAP)
11	Active users	113	Authentication service
20	FTP data	118	SQL database services
21	FTP commands	119	Usenet news transfers
22	Secure Shell (SSH)	139	NetBIOS applications
23	Telnet applications	143	Internet Message Access Protocol (IMAP)
25	SMTP e-mail applications	161	Simple Network Management Protocol
37	Time transactions	443	Transport Layer Security (TLS) or Secure Sockets Layer (SSL)
53	DNS server applications	531	Chat
79	Find active user application	537	Networked Media Streaming Protocol

© Cengage Learning 2013

After an attacker determines one or more IP addresses of systems that are live on a network, that attacker may then run port-scanning software to find a system on which a key port is open or not in use. The attacker may access and attack DNS services, for example, on port 53 of a DNS server. Telnet on port 23 provides another port that is attractive to attackers for gaining remote access to a computer, if Telnet is not blocked or required to use a password (or both). Two popular port-scanning programs are Nmap and Strobe. Nmap is used against Windows, UNIX/Linux, and Mac OS X computers, and a version has been adapted for Windows server systems. Besides attackers, some security professionals use Nmap to identify security risks through open ports. Strobe is also used to scan for open ports, but is designed to attack UNIX/Linux systems. Some organizations combat port-scanning attacks by purchasing software that enables them to continuously monitor all of their network computers for open port vulnerabilities. Two examples of such software are Nessus by Tenable Network Security and LanGuard by GFI. In addition, some virus-checking software companies such as McAfee offer software that can scan for open ports and other network vulnerabilities on individual computers.

You can download Nmap at *nmap.org/download.html* to test your network's security. In addition, you can obtain the GUI-based SuperScan TCP port scanner and the command-line ScanLine port scanner from McAfee at *www.mcafee.com/us/downloads/free-tools/index.aspx* (look under Scanning Tools).

One way to block access through an open port is to stop operating system services or processes that are not in use, such as instant messaging, or to configure a service only to start manually with your knowledge. Consider reviewing Activities 3-1 and 3-2 in Chapter 3, which demonstrate how to stop services, such as Remote Desktop and SSH, in Windows-based and UNIX/Linux systems.

Wireless Attacks

Wireless networks are particularly vulnerable to attacks, because it can be hard to determine when someone has compromised a wireless network. Attacks on wireless networks are sometimes called war drives, because the attacker may drive around an area in a car, using a portable computer to attempt to pick up a wireless signal (see Chapter 6, "Connecting Through a Wireless Network"). However, attackers may walk through hallways or in parking lots with their portable computers.

As you learned in Chapter 6, two key elements used in wireless attacks are a wireless network interface card and an omnidirectional antenna. Another element is war-driving software that is used to capture and interpret the signals brought in by the antenna through the network interface card. Wireless attacks generally involve scanning multiple channels that are used for wireless communications, which is similar to using a scanner to listen to police and fire department channels.

The term "war driving" evolved in part from "war dialing." War dialing was the practice of dialing a large number of telephone numbers in an effort to find a telephone associated with a computer modem. War dialing was showcased in the 1983 movie *WarGames*. The term "firewall" was also introduced by the movie.

If you manage a wireless network that has multiple access points, there are several free security tools available. For example, Xirrus Wi-Fi Inspector (visit *www.xirrus.com/Products/Wi-Fi-Inspector*) is a Windows-based tool that shows information about all surrounding access points, a signal history, and the addresses of those connected to access points. KisMAC (found at *kismac-ng.org*) is for Mac OS X networks and shows information about access points, noise levels, and access point clients. Kismet (visit *www.kismetwireless.net*) offers wireless intrusion detection for Windows, Linux, and Mac OS X wireless networks. Kismet is additionally helpful for identifying war drivers who may be using one of these tools.

Spam

Spam is unrequested e-mail that is sent to hundreds, thousands, or even millions of users. As an Internet user, you may have come to think of spam as similar to the junk mail solicitations and advertisements that you receive through your ground-based postal service. For this reason, spam is sometimes additionally called unsolicited bulk e-mail (UBE) or unsolicited commercial e-mail (UCE). Spam is relatively inexpensive for the sender, but it is very expensive for organizations whose network resources are diminished because of spam traffic. It is also expensive in terms of the time wasted by employees and organizations that have to employ methods to control or delete spam. Home users also find spam time consuming. Although the actual amount of spam is not fully documented, operating system vendors estimate it occupies about 80 percent of all Internet e-mail traffic.

An option for a home user or members of an office is to set up filters in particular e-mail systems to block unwanted e-mail. A way to help control spam in an organization is to ensure that its e-mail servers are not configured as open SMTP relay servers (see Chapter 3 to review SMTP). An **open SMTP relay server** is one that not only accepts e-mail, but also resends the e-mail to other servers without restrictions. An open SMTP relay server is vulnerable in two ways. One is that it can generate unneeded network traffic, which slows the response of the network and the server. Another vulnerability is that an e-mail queue on an SMTP relay server can get clogged when there is lots of spam going through, and it may be necessary for the server's administrator to delete e-mail to help unclog the queue.

The best way to block spam is to turn off the relay capability if it is not needed in an SMTP server. If it is necessary to relay specific e-mail, one solution is to configure an SMTP server to have restrictions. For instance, in Microsoft Exchange, the administrator may specify which computers can relay or route through it—on the basis of the computer's IP address or computer name and domain, for example. Another option is to require a computer to authenticate to Microsoft Exchange before its e-mail is relayed.

Spyware

Spyware is software that is placed on a computer, typically without the user's knowledge, and then reports back information—to an attacker or an advertiser, for example—about that computer user's activities. Spyware also may operate without being installed on a user's computer, by capturing information related to the user's Internet activities. One way in which spyware is installed is through a computer virus or Trojan horse. Alternately, advertising and marketing firms may offer appealing "freeware" programs that, besides installing the legitimate program, also install spyware to monitor your computer use. On the Internet, some forms of spyware operate through monitoring cookies. A cookie is information that a Web server stores on a client computer, such as the client's preferences when accessing a particular Web site, or where the client has been on the Web site.

Often commercial virus-checking software includes the ability to check for spyware. You can also obtain free spyware-checking software. Spybot is free spyware-checking software available at *www.safer-networking .org*. Ad-Aware is also free spyware-checking software that you can find at *www.lavasoft.com*.

Some types of spyware used by attackers can capture cookies or information written to cookies, so that the spyware operator can reconstruct a user's every move on the Internet. This type of attack is also called "cookie snarfing," and some notorious tools enabling cookie snarfing are SpyNet and PeepNet, which are often used together. SpyNet captures the network traffic related to cookies during a user's Internet session, and PeepNet is used to fully decode the cookie information so that the attacker can unravel a step-by-step sequence of all of the activity performed by the Internet user.

One way to discourage cookie snarfing spyware is to disable the creation of cookies through your Internet browser. Activities 11-4, 11-5, and 11-6 enable you to configure cookie handling in Internet Explorer (for Windows), in Firefox (for Linux), and Safari (for Mac OS X).

Activity 11-4: Configuring Cookie Handling in Internet Explorer

Time Required: 10 minutes
Objective: Configure to block cookies in Internet Explorer in Windows 7 or Server 2008/ Server 2008 R2.

Description: In this activity, you configure to block cookies in Internet Explorer in Windows 7 or Windows Server 2008/Server 2008 R2. Log on using your own account. These steps work for Internet Explorer 7 and higher.

1. Click **Internet Explorer** in the Taskbar near the Start button or click **Start,** point to **All Programs,** and click **Internet Explorer** or **Internet Explorer (64-bit).**

2. Click the **Tools** menu (the gear icon in Internet Explorer 9 and higher) and click **Internet Options.**

3. Click the **Privacy** tab.

4. Click the **Advanced** button (see Figure 11-4). If you see an information box that the Enhanced Security Configuration option is enabled, click **OK.**

5. Ensure that **Override automatic cookie handling** is selected. What options do you see under First-party Cookies and Third-party Cookies? What option would you select to prompt the user before writing a cookie?

6. Click the **Block** option for First-party Cookies and Third-party Cookies.

7. Click **OK.**

8. Click **OK** in the Internet Options dialog box and close Internet Explorer.

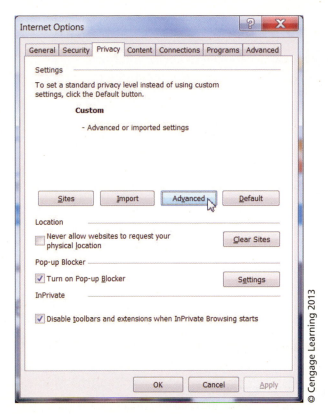

Figure 11-4 Configuring cookie security in Internet Explorer

Activity 11-5: Configuring Cookie Handling in Firefox

Time Required: 10 minutes
Objective: Configure to block cookies in Firefox.

Description: In this activity, you set up Firefox in GNOME 3.x in Linux to block cookies. Log on using your own account. Also, you need an Internet connection so that you can connect Firefox to a Web page.

 Depending on your version of Firefox, specific steps may vary. For example, Preferences (as in Step 7) might be under a Tools>Options menu rather than an Edit menu.

1. Click **Activities**.

2. Click the **Firefox** icon in the left portion of the desktop.

3. Open a Web site of your choice or use the default Web site. You can block cookies from a specific Web site, such as the one you have open now. Right-click within the Web site window and then click **View Page Info** in the shortcut menu.

4. Click **Permissions** at the top of the Page Info window (see Figure 11-5).

5. Under Set Cookies, remove the **checkmark** from the box in front of **Use Default** and then click to place a **checkmark** in the box in front of **Block** for Set Cookies. Access to the current Web page is now blocked.

6. Close the Page Info window.

7. Next, to block cookies from all Web sites, click the **Edit** menu and click **Preferences**.

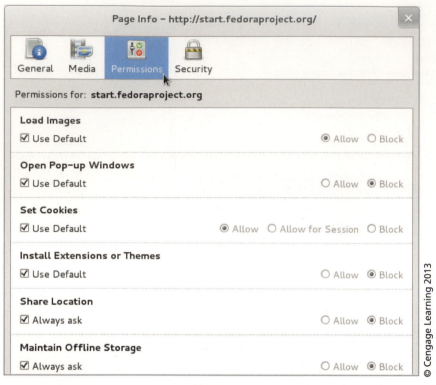

Figure 11-5   Selecting the Permissions button in the Page Info window in Firefox

8. Click **Privacy** at the top of the Firefox Preferences window.

9. In the Firefox will box, click the **up/down** arrows to list the options and click **Use custom settings for history** (see Figure 11-6).

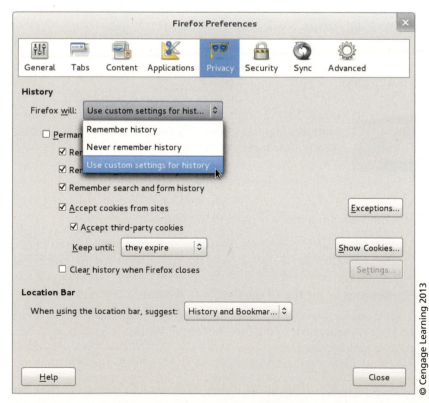

Figure 11-6   Selecting Use custom settings for history

10. Remove the **checkmark** from the box in front of **Accept cookies from sites**. Also, what button can you use to set up exceptions so that specific Web sites can write cookies?

11. Click **Close** in the Firefox Preferences window.

12. Close Firefox.

Activity 11-6: Configuring Cookie Handling in Safari

Time Required: 10 minutes

Objective: Configure to block cookies in Safari.

Description: In this activity, you configure Safari in Mac OS X Snow Leopard or Lion to block cookies. Log on using your own account. Also, you need an Internet connection so that you can connect to a Web page.

1. Click **Safari** in the Dock.

2. In the menu bar at the top of the desktop, click **Safari** and then click **Preferences** in the Safari menu.

3. In the dialog box, click **Privacy** at the top of the box.

4. For Block cookies, click the **Always** option button (see Figure 11-7). (But notice there is also an option to just block third parties and advertisers.)

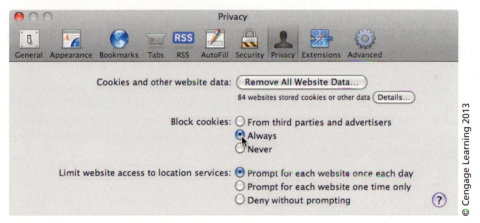

Figure 11-7   Blocking cookies in Safari

5. Click **Safari** in the menu bar and click **Quit Safari**.

Inside Attacks

Attacks on networks and computers from the inside are a common threat to businesses and organizations. Their computer systems are often loaded with information and resources to protect. In a business these may include accounting, human resource, management, sales, research, inventory, distribution, factory, and research system information. For many businesses, the heart of their work is contained in databases and the programs that retrieve information from them. System attacks on that information may come from insiders, such as dissatisfied or temporary employees, disgruntled past employees, consultants, vendor representatives, industrial spies, and others.

Social Engineering Attacks

A **social engineering attack**, in relation to computer system attacks, refers to the use of human interaction to gain access to a system or to do damage. These interactions may be as simple as providing an enticing subject head on an e-mail or sending an e-mail message that makes opening an attachment look attractive. In another example, the user may receive a bogus e-mail from an attacker claiming to be a vendor asking for name, address, and credit card information to update its records.

The interactions may also involve a deceptive telephone call—to obtain information that would enable the caller to access a user's account, for example. The caller might claim to be a representative of an ISP and ask for a person's account number and password to "verify" the ISP's records. Organizations can defend themselves against social engineering attacks by training users so they are informed and alert to these attacks.

How to Protect Your Network

There are many ways to attack a network, but fortunately there are many ways to defend against attacks. You have already learned some ways to thwart attacks, but there are others that include:

- Updating operating systems
- Using IP Security
- Establishing border and firewall security

In the following sections you learn the tools that are available for each of these approaches.

Real-Life Networking

The Slammer worm, only 376 bits in size, overloaded servers and routers throughout the Internet, and when it hit, it was one of the fastest moving worms on record. About 75,000 servers were infected over the Internet in only 10 minutes. The irony in the spread of this worm was that Microsoft had issued preventive security patches well in advance of the Slammer's attack, but the patches were not widely installed by SQL Server administrators.

Installing Updates

Installing updates and patches is an effective way to prevent attacks on networks via the computers attached to them. For example, one reason that the Slammer worm was successful against SQL Server database servers in early 2003 was that many administrators had not installed new patches designed to block this attack. Now that the Slammer controversy has largely been forgotten, it is once again common for SQL Server and other server and network administrators to be behind on installing new patches. Windows 7, Windows Server, Linux distributions like Fedora and Red Hat Enterprise Linux, and Mac OS X Snow Leopard and Lion all provide ways to install updates and patches.

Installing Updates in Windows 7 and Windows Server   The two main ways to install updates for Windows 7 and Windows Server are Windows Update and service packs. Windows Update is used to provide access to patches that are regularly issued, particularly security patches. When you use Windows Update, the program connects to the Web update page that is appropriate for the operating system, such as the Windows 7 update Web page. After the connection is made, the user can select options to have the operating system scanned to determine which updates have not been made and then to load any or all of the updates recommended after the scan is completed.

For Windows 7 and Windows Server, there are two ways to launch Windows Update. One way is to click Start, point to All Programs, and click Windows Update. A second method is to start Windows Update from Control Panel (see Figure 11-8).

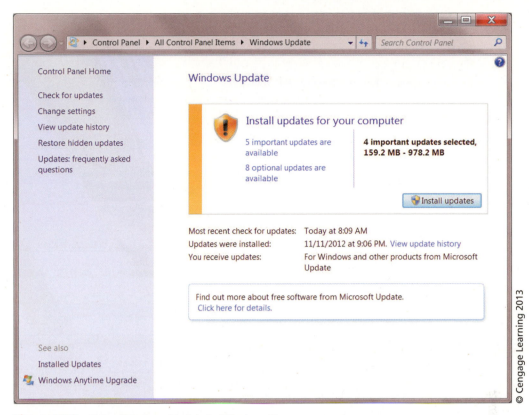

Figure 11-8   Using Windows Update in Windows 7

In Windows 7 and Windows Server 2008/Server 2008 R2, you can (try Activity 11-7):

- Enable automatic updating
- Have the operating system automatically download updates, but let you choose whether to install them
- Automatically check for updates, but let you determine whether to download or install the updates
- Automatically download new updates and install them according to a specific schedule, such as every Tuesday night at 12:00 PM (or at noon)

Activity 11-7: Configuring Automatic Updating in Windows 7 and Windows Server 2008/Server 2008 R2

Time Required: 10 minutes
Objective: Configure Automatic Updating to keep Windows 7 and Windows Server 2008/Server 2008 R2 up to date on security and other patches.

Description: In this activity, you configure automatic updating in Windows 7 or Windows Server 2008/Server 2008 R2. Log on using an account that has Administrator privileges.

1. Click **Start,** point to **All Programs,** and click **Windows Update.**
2. In the Windows Update window, click **Change Settings.**
3. Under Important Updates, ensure that **Install updates automatically (recommended)** is selected.
4. Set Install new updates to **Every Tuesday** at **12:00 PM** and click **OK** (see Figure 11-9).
5. Close the Windows Update window.

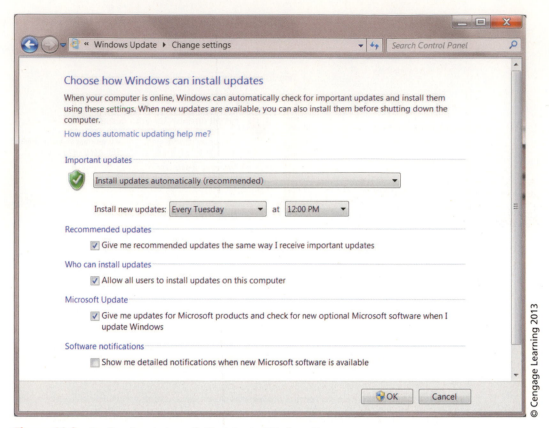

Figure 11-9   Configuring Automatic Updates in Windows 7

Service packs are designed to address security issues as well as problems affecting stability, performance, or the operation of features included with the operating system. Service packs come out less frequently than the patches you obtain from Windows Update, but they generally include, in one place, patches that can be obtained from Windows Update, major fixes, new operating system features, and any previous service packs. Once you have installed any Windows operating system or Microsoft software, such as Microsoft Office, it is always good practice to download and apply the latest service pack to fix any known problems and patch known security holes. The latest service packs for different Microsoft operating systems and software can be found at *www.microsoft.com/downloads*.

Installing a service pack is considered a major update; it should be given serious consideration, since some of the operating system files will be replaced. There is always a chance that the update will fail or that new problems will be caused by installing the service pack. This is more of an issue for those workstations and servers that are already running on the network and being used by clients than for newly installed workstations and servers that are still in a development phase prior to being brought online for full production.

Use the following guidelines when installing the latest service packs for Windows 7 and Windows Server:

- Download the latest service pack from the Microsoft download site. The service pack is also usually available for order on a DVD/CD-ROM or is included either as a download or on DVD with TechNet subscriptions.

- Review the documentation that comes with the service pack. This details the installation procedures and alerts you to any problems associated with installing the service pack.

- If the workstation or server is in the production environment, be sure to perform a full backup before you do the installation.
- For development and production servers available to clients, schedule a time for the service pack to be installed, as the server will need to be rebooted during the installation. This will alert clients to any downtime.
- Once the service pack is installed, document any problems that occurred and how you fixed them, for future reference.

UNIX/Linux   Fedora, Red Hat, and other UNIX/Linux distributors issue updates that can be downloaded. In the case of Fedora, the GNOME 3.x desktop offers a tool for configuring updates and another tool to immediately launch updates. Activity 11-8 enables you to learn where to immediately obtain the latest updates and where to configure updates.

Activity 11-8: Configuring Automatic Updating in Linux

Time Required: 15 minutes

Objective: Configure automatic updating in Linux with the GNOME 3.x desktop.

Description: In this activity, you learn from where to launch an update for the Fedora Linux operating system with the GNOME 3.x desktop and how to configure automatic updating. Log on to an account that has root privileges or use the Live System User account in Fedora Live Media. An Internet connection is helpful, but not required.

1. Click **Activities** and click **Applications**.
2. Click the **Software Update** application (make sure you click "Software Update" and not "Software Updates").
3. The Software Update window shows that the application is checking for updates (see Figure 11-10). If there are no updates, click **OK** in the message box. If there are updates, you see them listed as shown in Figure 11-11. For this activity, click **Quit** to exit (or if your instructor wants you to install the updates, click **Install Updates** and follow any instructions for the updates, but first be sure you have 2 GB or more memory in your computer if you are using Fedora Live Media).
4. Click **Activities** and click **Applications**.
5. Click **Software Updates**.
6. In the Software Update Preferences window, ensure that the **Update Settings** tab is selected.
7. Set Check for updates to **Daily**, if Daily is not already selected.

Real-Life Networking

A few years ago an operating system vendor issued a major update for its server systems. The update inadvertently removed the password from the Guest account, creating a backdoor into the server. Whenever you install an operating system update, consider checking the security on default accounts, such as the Guest account.

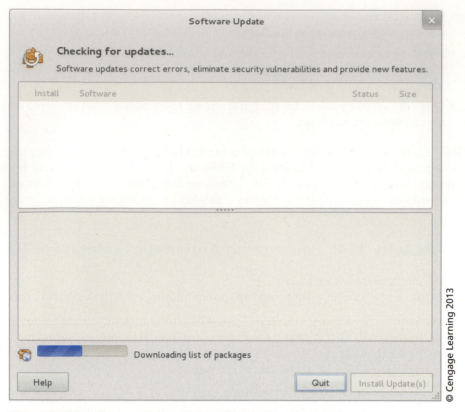

Figure 11-10   Software Update window checking for updates in Linux

Figure 11-11   Software Update window with the list of updates in Linux

8. Set Automatically install to **All updates**, if All updates is not already selected. (If All updates is not shown as an option, select **Only security updates**.) Notice that there is also a box that enables you to check for updates when you are connected through mobile broadband, such as through a 4G network (see Figure 11-12). Also, notice that you can check for updates at this point by clicking *Check Now*.

Figure 11-12   Configuring update preferences in Linux

9. Click **Close**.

Mac OS X

Mac OS X   As is true for other operating systems, Mac OS X Snow Leopard and Lion offer software updates, many of which are security updates. It is common for some Mac OS X users to believe that attacks on Mac OS X systems are rare. However, there is malware designed to attack these systems like any other operating system. The Blackhole Remote Access Trojan (RAT) is one example. This malware can display a fake password window so that its originator can obtain a user's password, if the user enters it in the window. RAT can also direct a user to URLs for malicious Web sites. Still another element of RAT is to display a screen that only lets the user reboot. Another example of malware is MAC Defender that takes the user to a Web site that can download malicious software from a harmless appearing Java script. Further, the Tsunami Trojan has been adapted so that it can attack Mac OS X systems as well as Linux systems. Tsunami Trojan is used to start a denial-of-service attack from Linux or Mac OS X.

To protect Mac OS X and the network it uses, Mac OS X users can use the Software Update tool, which is illustrated in Activity 11-9.

Activity 11-9: Using Software Update in Mac OS X

Time Required: 15 minutes
Objective: Configure automatic updating in Mac OS X Snow Leopard or Lion.

Description: In this activity, you learn how to configure automatic software updating in Mac OS X Snow Leopard or Lion. You need to be logged onto an account that has Administrator privileges. Also, it is helpful but not required to have an Internet connection.

1. Click **System Preferences** in the Dock, or click the **Apple** icon in the menu bar and click **System Preferences**.

2. In the System Preferences window under System, click **Software Update**.

3. Make sure that the **Scheduled Check** tab is selected in the Software Update window.

4. In the Software Update window, click **Check Now** to check for updates. (It might take a few minutes to check for the updates. Also, if you do not have an Internet connection, the update will fail and skip to Step 6.)

5. When there are software updates to install, you see a message box as shown in Figure 11-13. For this activity, click **Not Now**. If there are no software updates to install, click **Quit** in the message dialog box.

© Cengage Learning 2013

Figure 11-13   Message dialog box showing there are updates to install in Mac OS X

6. In the Software Update window, ensure that there is a **checkmark** in the box for **Check for updates** and that it is set to **Daily**. (Click the lock to open it, if necessary, and provide the account name and password and click OK before you make changes.)

7. Also, make sure there is a **checkmark** in the box for **Download updates automatically** (see Figure 11-14).

8. Click **System Preferences** in the menu bar and click **Quit System Preferences**.

© Cengage Learning 2013

Figure 11-14   Configuring automatic updates in Mac OS X Lion

Using IP Security

One of the best ways to secure communications on a network is to use **IP Security (IPSec)**. IPSec is a set of IP-based secure communications and encryption standards created by the IETF and was developed to provide secure network communications. IPSec goes to the source of the TCP/IP communications by securing IP in its Network layer, or Layer 3, communications, which are at the heart of IP. As you learned in Chapter 3, the Network layer reads IP packet protocol address information and forwards each packet along the most expedient route for efficient network communications. The Network layer also permits packets to be sent from one network to another through routers. Another function of the Network layer is to use session authentication to check the sequence of packets and to correct any sequencing errors.

Attackers use knowledge of the Network layer to exploit packet addressing and the sequencing of packets. Without protection, operations at the Network layer can be exploited in many ways by attackers, such as by intercepting packets destined for a specific IP address and substituting their own packets. They are also vulnerable to sniffer software, which may be able to associate IP address information with account and password communications.

When an IPSec communication begins between two computers, the computers first exchange certificates to authenticate the receiver and sender. Next, data is encrypted at the sending computer as it is formatted into an IP packet, which consists of a header containing transmission control information, the actual data, and a footer with error-correction information. On the sending computer the data is encrypted at the Presentation layer, or Layer 6. This is the layer of communications in which data is formatted for its "look"; for example, data is translated from binary ones and zeros into recognizable letters of the alphabet at the Presentation layer. Also at the Presentation layer, a string of data can be scrambled or encrypted to keep it safe from prying eyes. IPSec can provide security for all TCP/IP-based application and communications protocols, including FTP and HTTP.

An effective way to understand IPSec is to look at how it is configured in the security policies in Windows Server. In Windows Server, IPSec security policies can be managed from the IP Security Policy Management snap-in in the Microsoft Management Console (MMC)—you learned how to install an MMC snap-in in Activities 8-2 and 8-3 in Chapter 8, "Using a Server." A computer that is configured to use IPSec communication can function in any of three roles (see Figure 11-15):

- *Client (Respond Only)*: When Windows Server is contacted by a client using IPSec, it responds by using IPSec communication.

- *Secure Server (Require Security)*: Windows Server responds only using IPSec communication, which means that communication via any account and with any client is secured through strict IPSec enforcement.

- *Server (Request Security)*: When Windows Server is first contacted, or when it initiates a communication, it uses IPSec by default. If the responding client does not support IPSec, Windows Server switches to the clear mode, which does not employ IPSec.

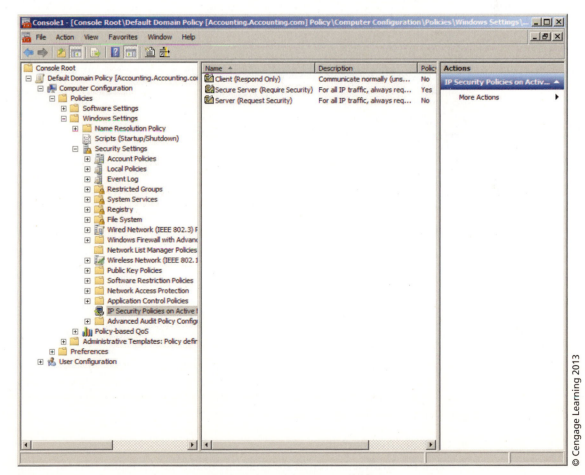

Figure 11-15   IPSec security roles in Windows Server 2008/Server 2008 R2

IPSec security policies can be established through the Group Policy Management snap-in so that specific security standards apply to only a local computer or to all computers that log on to a domain configured through Active Directory. Activity 11-10 is an optional activity that enables you to configure IPSec in Windows Server.

Activity 11-10: Configuring IPSec as a Security Policy in Windows Server

Time Required: 15–20 minutes

Objective: Configure Windows Server 2008/Server 2008 R2 network communications to use IPSec.

Description: A Windows server can be configured to communicate with clients using IPSec. In this activity, you learn how to configure IPSec in the default domain security policy for Windows Server 2008/Server 2008 R2. Although this activity is relatively complex, it is a procedure well worth knowing to protect any Windows server–based network. You need access using an account that has Administrator privileges. Also, the server you use should be in a Windows domain as a domain controller (a server that has Active Directory installed).

1. Click **Start**. In Windows Server 2008 type **mmc** in the Start Search box at the bottom of the start menu, or in Windows Server 2008 R2 type **mmc** in the Search programs and files box.

2. Click **mmc** under Programs.

3. In the Console1 - [Console Root] window, click **File** and click **Add/Remove Snap-in** in the File menu.

4. Under Available Snap-ins click the second **Group Policy Management** snap-in option (see Figure 11-16).

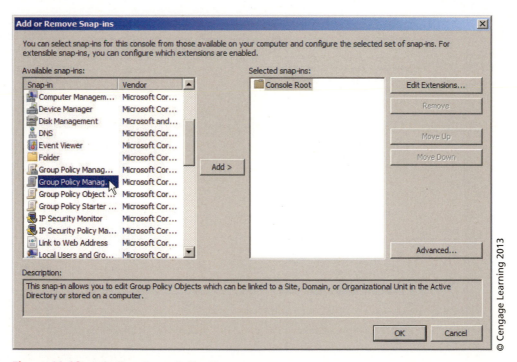

Figure 11-16   Selecting Group Policy Management

5. Click the **Add** button.

6. Click the **Browse** button in the Welcome to the Group Policy Wizard dialog box.

7. Click **Default Domain Policy** in the Browse for a Group Policy Object dialog box (see Figure 11-17). Click **OK**.

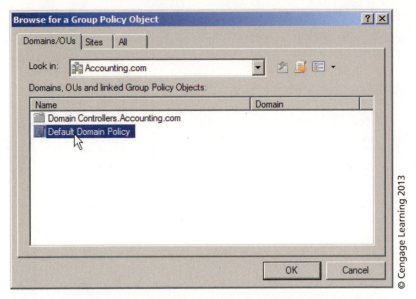

Figure 11-17   Browse for a Group Policy Object dialog box

8. Click **Finish** in the Welcome to the Group Policy Wizard dialog box.

9. Click **OK** in the Add or Remove Snap-ins dialog box.

10. In the tree in the left pane, click the **+ plus sign** in front of **Default Domain Policy [***serversname* *.domainname***] Policy**. In the tree, click the **+ plus sign** in front of **Computer Configuration** (see Figure 11-18).

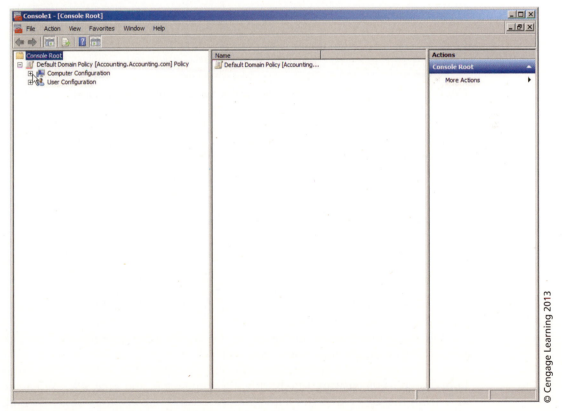

Figure 11-18   Clicking the + (plus sign) in front of Computer Configuration

11. In the tree, click the **+ plus sign** in front of **Policies**.

12. In the tree, click the **+ plus sign** in front of **Windows Settings**.

13. In the tree, click the **+ plus sign** in front of **Security Settings**.

14. In the tree, double-click **IP Security Policies on Active Directory (*domainname*)** as shown in Figure 11-19.

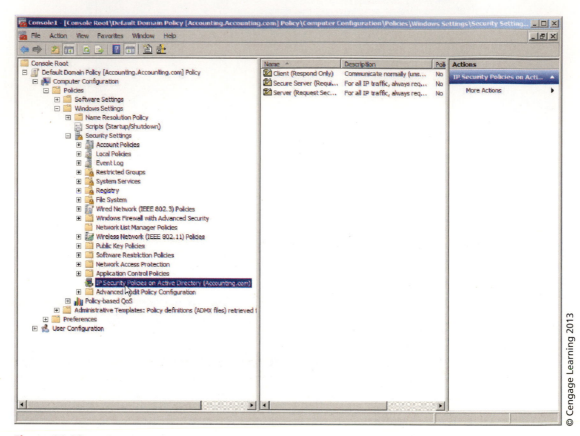

Figure 11-19 Selecting IP Security Policies on Active Directory (*domainname*)

15. In the middle pane, right-click **Secure Server (Require Security)**—which is the middle option listed. Click **Assign** (see Figure 11-20). (Note that you can expand the Name column by dragging the right-side boundary line to view more of its contents.)

16. The Policy column should now show *Yes* for Secure Server (Require Security).

17. Close the Console1 window.

18. Click **No** so that you do not save the console settings.

Data is encrypted in IPSec using the **Encapsulating Security Payload (ESP)**. ESP is designed to "provide confidentiality, data origin authentication, connectionless integrity, an anti-replay service (a form of partial sequence integrity), and limited traffic flow confidentiality" (as defined in the network standards document, Request for Comment 2406). Many applications take particular advantage of the ability to provide data confidentiality through ESP's use of data encryption.

On a UNIX/Linux system and in Mac OS X, IPSec can be configured using the *setkey()* function with the *spdadd* instruction in a shell script, such as one that you create to execute each time you log into your account. You can also find free open systems IPSec software for UNIX/Linux, such as Openswan, VPNbc (for VPN tunneling), and Free S/WAN. This software is available from the GNU Web site *www.gnu.org*. Also, some versions of UNIX/Linux, such as Red Hat Enterprise Linux, using the GNOME 3.x desktop have incorporated IPSec communications in the Network Connections tool.

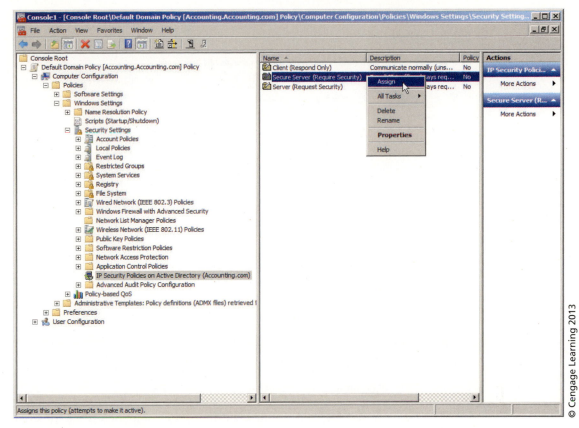

Figure 11-20 Assigning Secure Server (Require Security) for IPSec

In Mac OS X, L2TP over IPSec or Cisco IPSec can be used when creating a VPN (virtual private network; see Chapter 7, "Sharing Resources on a Network"). When you use L2TP (Layer Two Tunneling Protocol; see Chapter 7) over IPSec, this means the protocol (L2TP) used to establish secure communication tunnels is transported over IPSec, thus creating an extra level of security. Cisco IPSec is used if you are connecting through a Cisco VPN, which is one that uses Cisco network devices that employ Cisco VPN technology. For example, if you connect to your workplace over a VPN, the workplace network may employ a Cisco VPN and Cisco IPSec. Cisco is a popular network device vendor.

If you are using Mac OS X Snow Leopard or Lion, you can view the IPSec options when creating a VPN by using the following general steps:

1. Click System Preferences in the Dock, or click the Apple icon in the menu bar and click System Preferences.

2. Click Network.

3. If necessary, click the lock to unlock it, provide your account name and password, and click OK.

4. In the Network window, click the + plus sign just above the lock.

5. Configure the Interface text box to VPN.

6. Click the up/down arrows for the VPN Type text box to view the options, which include two options for IPSec: L2TP over IPSec and Cisco IPSec (see Figure 11-21).

7. Click Create to finish creating a VPN or click Cancel.

8. Click System Preferences in the menu bar and click Quit System Preferences.

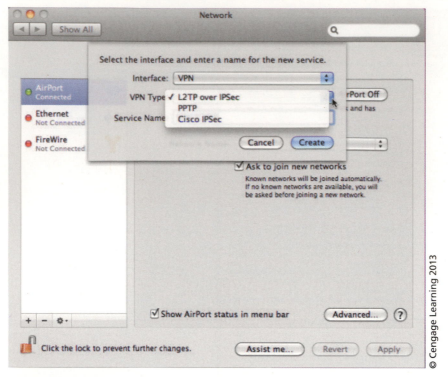

Figure 11-21   IPSec options when creating a VPN in Mac OS X

The Linux-based Android mobile operating system supports IPSec for smartphones and tablet PCs. Although there is not native support for Cisco IPSec, apps can be downloaded to enable you to use Cisco IPSec on Android devices. These apps include Cisco VPN Client and Cisco Any-Connect Client (SSL).

Both the Apple iPad and iPhone, which use the iOS operating system, also support the use of IPSec for secure network communications.

It is possible to run Linux on the iPad, but so far there has been little interest in doing so.

Establishing Border and Firewall Security

Each country has borders between it and neighboring countries, and border crossings are usually controlled to monitor traffic into and out of a country. As the Internet and other networks have grown in past years, borders and border patrol devices are needed to protect internal networks from attackers, viruses, worms, and other threats. One difference between countries and the web of networks formed by the Internet is that countries often use different languages, whereas networks connected by the Internet use the same universal language, TCP/IP.

Borders are typically established between a private network—one used by a company, for example—and a public network, in particular the Internet. Other examples of borders are the boundaries between the networks of two different organizations. For example, state universities often have links to state government networks, to transmit information about enrollment numbers, accounting and payroll data, and retirement information. On each end there are enterprise networks of multiple LANs and one or more WANs that link the university networks to the state government's network. The WAN connections at each end might be considered the borders. The same relationship might exist in a large company that has four subsidiaries. In this case there is a border at the company's enterprise network and a border at the entrance to each subsidiary's network.

For security, organizations establish border gateways at each border crossing. The **border gateway** is a firewall that is configured with security policies to control the traffic that is permitted to cross a border in either direction. For example, if an organization has experienced hacking problems from a particular set of IP addresses, the security policies configured on its firewalls might block communications from those IP addresses. Another policy might be to block all access from the Internet to the private network, unless access is first initiated from someone inside the private network. For example, a computer outside the private network might be blocked from crossing the border gateway unless someone inside the private network initiates a Web-based or Telnet session with that computer. Communications from the outside computer are allowed only for the duration of the communication session initiated by the private network user.

The strongest border security design is to protect every border point, including:

- Connection points between LANs and public or private WANs, such as DSL, T-carrier, ISDN, frame relay, SONET, MPLS, Optical Ethernet, and others
- Dial-up and cable modem access
- Virtual private network (VPN) access
- Short-range wireless access, including 802.11, Bluetooth, and HiperLAN
- Long-range wireless access, including satellite and microwave

For example, consider a large company that has four subsidiaries. The headquarters is located in Chicago, and subsidiaries are in St. Louis, Nashville, Cleveland, and Kansas City. Assume that the headquarters and its subsidiaries are connected to one another by means of a public telecommunications network. Also, telecommuters use a VPN over the Internet to access the headquarters through dial-up modems. The network designer might place firewalls at each border point, as illustrated in Figure 11-22.

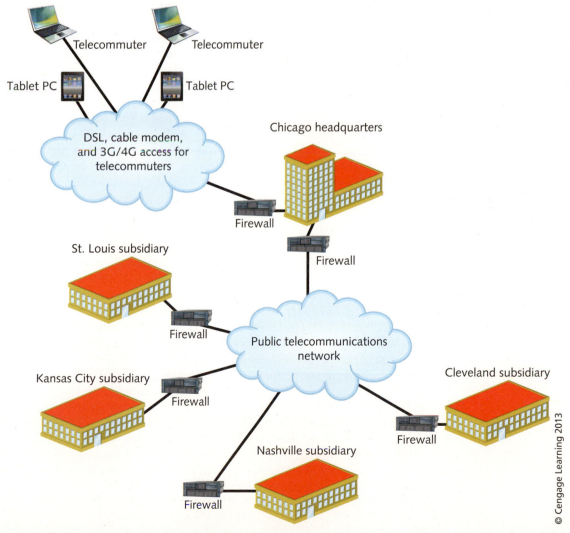

© Cengage Learning 2013

Figure 11-22   Implementing border security

Another element in border security is to configure security policies on each firewall so that access is automatically denied, except for those who are manually configured to have access through the firewall. This approach helps to ensure stronger security than the opposite configuration, which automatically lets everyone through except those who are specifically denied access. Further, every firewall on the border of a particular network should be configured to enable the same security. If one firewall provides more access than the others on that network, you can count on an attacker to find the opening in that firewall and take advantage of it.

The following are examples of commonly used border and firewall techniques:

- Packet filtering
- Network Address Translation
- Proxies
- Routers
- Demilitarized zones
- Operating system firewalls

Each of these methods is discussed in the next sections.

Using Packet Filtering
Packet filtering typically involves using characteristics of TCP (or UDP) and IP to establish filters between two connected networks. Another type of packet filtering is to allow or block packets from specific protocols.

When you create a filter for TCP/IP, two important characteristics are the IP address information in a packet and the TCP or UDP port information. As you learned in Chapter 3, the IP portion of a packet contains the source and destination IP addresses of a communication. On a firewall, you can set up a database that specifies which IP addresses or address characteristics are allowed to pass from a public network into your private network. For example, consider a university's network that has been attacked by individuals using different IP addresses all beginning with the network ID 182.100. A network firewall administrator from that university might configure each firewall to prohibit access to all incoming packets with the network ID 182.100 in the source address. At the same university, there might be a subnet consisting of a block of addresses from 172.16.128.1 to 172.16.159.254 (with a network ID of 172.16.0.0 and a customized subnet mask of 255.255.224.0) that is devoted to the accounting and payroll offices and that needs to be protected using packet filtering. A firewall can be set up to guard the subnet, preventing any address from crossing the firewall except ones using the range of addresses for the subnet identification. As these examples suggest, a firewall's database can contain specific IP addresses to prohibit, a range of addresses to block, or address characteristics to filter (for example, the network ID).

Another way to use a firewall is to control access across the firewall by TCP and UDP port number. This can be an effective technique to discourage port sniffing. For example, if you want to block access to Telnet, then consider blocking TCP/UDP port 23; to control Secure Shell (SSH) access, block TCP/UDP port 22. Also, you can control Internet and file transfer access by blocking port 21 for FTP, port 80 for HTTP, port 119 for network news (NNTP), and port 443 for secure HTTP or HTTPS (refer to Table 11-1). Using the example of the accounting and payroll offices at a university, the university's financial auditors might recommend that the accounting and payroll office personnel have no access to Internet Web sites and FTP sites. This can be enforced by blocking all traffic for ports 21, 80, 119, and 443.

Packet filtering is accomplished using one of two techniques: stateless filtering and stateful filtering. In stateless packet filtering the firewall examines every individual packet and decides whether to pass or block the packet, depending on that packet's contents. Stateless filtering does not filter on the basis of the context of the communication, and so it has limited value in a firewall. Stateful packet filtering tracks information about a communication session, such as which ports are in use, drawing from the contents of multiple packets. It enables the firewall to build a more complete picture of a communication session in order to determine which traffic to allow through and which traffic to deny.

Using Network Address Translation (NAT)

One way to protect a network is by reducing what is revealed about that network to those on networks outside of it, such as to those on the Internet. A firewall configured to provide NAT does exactly that. When NAT is used, all network addresses on the network protected by NAT are seen by outsiders as a single address, the address of the device configured for NAT, or an address from a pool of decoy or dummy addresses. For example, the IP address of the NAT device might be 129.81.1.1. On the internal network behind the NAT, the network administrator can use a range of addresses for each of that network's clients, such as 192.168.18.1, 192.168.18.2, 192.168.18.3, and so on. When the computer on the internal network, such as one that has the address 192.168.18.22, communicates with a computer on the other side of the NAT device, its address is translated to 129.81.1.1, for example.

Using NAT discourages attackers, because they cannot identify a specific computer to attack behind the NAT device on the internal network. Instead, the attacker sees only the address of the NAT device or an address in the range of decoy addresses used by the NAT device. Another advantage of NAT is that it enables a network to use IP addresses on the internal network that are not formally registered for Internet use.

Although it is possible to use any range of addresses on the network protected by the NAT device, the best approach is to use addresses in the following ranges:

- *For class A networks*: 10.0.0.0 to 10.255.255.255
- *For class B networks*: 172.16.0.0 to 172.31.255.255
- *For class C networks*: 192.168.0.0 to 192.168.255.255

Using these address ranges helps to prevent unexpected problems when addresses are translated for use on an external network and a host is accessed that has an IP address identical to the address used by a computer on the internal network protected by NAT.

NAT is an important security tool for protecting a network, but dedicated attackers can still find ways to lessen its effectiveness by intercepting the legitimate communications on the external network that are allowed through NAT. Attackers do this, for example, by using network-monitoring software to watch the traffic going into and out of the NAT device, and then using spoofing to appear as though they are a legitimate computer on the external network with which the NAT device is communicating. For this reason, NAT is often used with a proxy.

Configuring NAT in Windows Server

Windows Server can be configured to provide NAT firewall services for connections that go over the Internet, for example. NAT is just one of several services that can be set up in Windows Server through Microsoft Routing and Remote Access Services. Microsoft Routing and Remote Access Services provide a set of services that enable or manage remote access to Windows Server 2008/Server 2008 R2, for instance, through telecommunications lines. Routing and Remote Access Services include services such as:

- Remote access server (dial-up or VPN)
- Network Address Translation (NAT)
- Virtual private network (VPN) access and NAT
- Secure connection between two private networks
- Custom configuration

If you use DSL or cable modem services on a home, home office, or small office network, the telecommunications or cable provider is likely to offer a wireless modem/router that can be manually or automatically configured to provide NAT when you run its installation program or when you access its setup parameters.

When you configure NAT in Windows Server, you can configure it to work via one or more network interface cards attached to the local network, through a WAN connection to the server, or both. For instance, consider a small business that uses Windows Server for border security between a DSL connection to the Internet and the connection to the local network. The server has a DSL adapter installed in one of its expansion slots that is connected to a telephone line, and it also has a network interface card that connects it to the local network. When the server is set up for NAT, it performs address translation between the local network clients (including the server as an Internet user) and the Internet, as shown in Figure 11-23. Configuring NAT also provides Internet connection sharing services for the small office in this example.

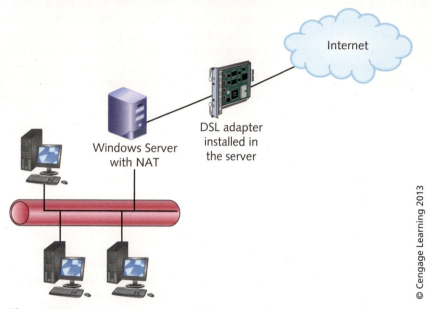

Figure 11-23   Using NAT on a small office network

After Windows Server NAT is installed, you can choose to enable the computers on the private network to keep the IP addresses they are using already, or you can assign a range of addresses for the computers. If you assign a range of addresses, the NAT setup offers addresses in the 192.168.0.0 range as the default option. Activity 11-11 is an optional advanced activity that enables you to install NAT in Windows Server 2008/Server 2008 R2 by using the Routing and Remote Access Server Setup Wizard, which guides you through the steps.

If you use an ISP, consult with the ISP staff about what address range to use, because they may have some guidelines for you to follow.

Activity 11-11: Configuring NAT in Windows Server

Time Required: 15 minutes
Objective: Configure NAT to secure a Windows Server Network.

Description: In this activity, you configure Windows Server 2008/Server 2008 R2 as a NAT firewall for clients who connect to the Internet. The server that you use should not already be configured for routing and remote access services. Note that to configure Microsoft Routing and Remote Access Services, NAT and ICF should not be enabled already. You need to use an account that has Administrator privileges.

1. Click **Start,** point to **Administrative Tools,** and click **Routing and Remote Access.**

2. Right-click the server in the tree that you want to configure for NAT and click **Configure and Enable Routing and Remote Access.**

3. Click **Next** when the Routing and Remote Access Server Setup Wizard starts.

4. In the Configuration dialog box, click **Network address translation (NAT)** as shown in Figure 11-24. Click **Next.**

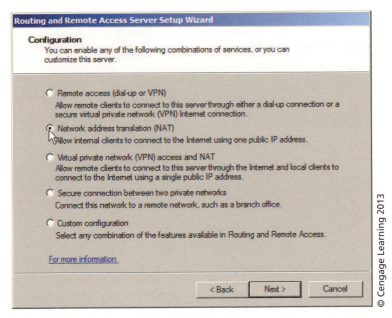

Figure 11-24   Configuration dialog box

5. The NAT Internet Connection dialog box (see Figure 11-25) enables you to configure which network interface to use, if there is more than one in the computer. If there is only one, it is selected by default, and the Use this public interface to connect to the Internet option is deactivated (forcing you to select this interface). Also, make sure that **Create a new demand-dial interface to the Internet** is selected. This option is used when the server uses the Point-to-Point Protocol for remote communications, and it is used when there is a 56-Kbps asynchronous modem (the typical modem installed), a cable modem, an ISDN terminal adapter, or a DSL adapter installed in the computer. Click **Next**.

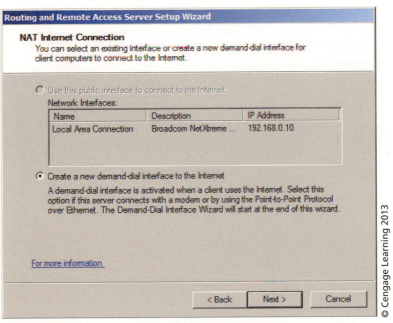

Figure 11-25   NAT Internet Connection dialog box

6. Click **Next** in the Ready to Apply selections dialog box.

7. Click **Next** to use the Demand Dial Interface Wizard.

8. Click **Next** in the Interface Name dialog box.

9. The Connection Type dialog box offers two choices: Connect using virtual private networking (VPN) or Connect using PPP over Ethernet (PPPoE). For this activity, click **Connect using PPP over Ethernet (PPPoE)** as shown in Figure 11-26). Click **Next**.

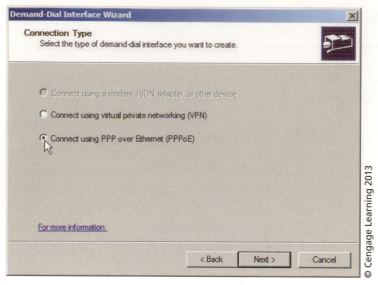

Figure 11-26   Connection Type dialog box

10. In the Service Name dialog box, leave the Service name box blank for this activity and click **Next**.

11. In the Protocols and Security dialog box, ensure that only **Route IP packets on this interface** is selected and click **Next**.

12. Enter your username, the name of your domain, and the password for your account, and then confirm the password. Click **Next**.

13. Click **Finish**.

14. Click **Finish** again.

15. In the Routing and Remote Access window, expand the tree to view the elements under the computer on which you configured NAT, if necessary.

16. Click IPv4 in the tree in the left pane. Right-click **NAT** and click **Properties**. You should see the NAT Properties dialog box, as shown in Figure 11-27.

17. Click each tab to view the options you can configure, and record your observations. Which tab enables you to assign IP addresses for the clients on the internal network?

18. Click **Cancel** and close the Routing and Remote Access window.

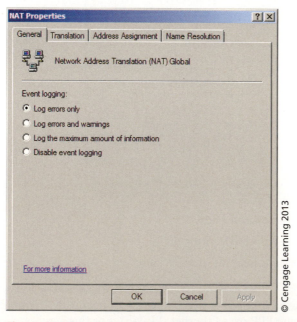

Figure 11-27   NAT Properties dialog box in Windows Server 2008 R2

Configuring NAT and a Firewall Using IPTables in UNIX/Linux

UNIX and Linux systems offer the IPTables interface for configuring NAT and complex firewall security from the command line in a terminal window. If you are configuring a server or you want to fine-tune your firewall security on a workstation, configure the firewall using IPTables. IPTables is a powerful tool that can be used to implement network security in many ways; it is configured through a terminal window using the *iptables* command.

IPTables enables you to configure packet filter rules through the use of tables. A set of rules is called a chain, and it is applied to packets containing specific information. For example, you might configure a rule to drop incoming packets containing a source address from network ID 201.199 or to only drop packets from the IP address 168.52.15.184. Or there might be a rule to only accept packets from the local network (on the basis of its network ID). You can also accept or drop packets containing specific active TCP ports, UDP ports, or both. Table 11-2 shows a sampling of the parameters that you can use with the *iptables* command.

Table 11-2 Sample *iptables* parameters

Parameter	Description
filter	Used by default, a table that specifies chains that typically help to enforce strong security
nat	Used in association with NAT functions
-A	Adds new rules to a particular chain
-L	Lists the rules for a particular chain
-N	Configures a new chain
-P	Configures policies, including default chains
-X	Deletes a chain
-p	Specifies the protocol to examine TCP, IP, or ICMP
-s	Specifies the source address information to filter
-d	Specifies the destination address information to filter
-i	Designates the input network interface (where the packet is received) on which to filter packets
-o	Designates the output network interface (where the packet is sent) on which to filter
-- source-port	Specifies a specific source port or a range of ports to examine and is used with either the *tcp* or *udp* command preceding it
-- destination-port	Designates the particular destination port or a range of ports to examine and is used with either the *tcp* or *udp* command preceding it

© Cengage Learning 2013

To use IPTables in Fedora and Red Hat Enterprise Linux, you must first make sure that IPChains, the firewall service designed for earlier Red Hat Linux versions, is turned off. To make sure, use the following commands:

```
service ipchains stop
chkconfig ipchains off
```

Next, use the following two commands to start the IPTables service and to ensure that the IPTables service starts automatically each time you boot the operating system (the second command sets the runlevel status to start it automatically):

```
service iptables start
chkconfig --level 345 iptables on
```

One approach to setting up a firewall is to block incoming, outgoing, and forwarded packets and then to make specific exceptions to these global rules on a case-by-case basis. For example, consider a network used by the Payroll Department of an organization. On this network, you want to allow only the payroll supervisor to use the Internet to upload payroll data to a national check deposit clearinghouse. In this case, you deny all incoming, outgoing, and forwarded packets. Next, you make an exception for the payroll supervisor's IP address so that the payroll supervisor can send outbound (output) traffic.

To configure the firewall to deny incoming, outgoing, and forwarded packets, enter the following commands:

```
iptables -P OUTPUT REJECT
iptables -P INPUT DENY
iptables -P FORWARD REJECT
```

Finally, to make sure that all of the options you have configured are saved and reused each time the computer is booted, use the following command:

```
/sbin/service iptables save
```

Using NAT on a MAC OS X Server
When you have a MAC OS X Snow Leopard or Lion Server network, NAT is automatically configured for internal network addresses and works with one or more local routers. However, for NAT to work, the firewall service must be enabled. If NAT is deactivated use the following general steps to activate it:

1. Open the Server Admin tool.

2. Connect to the Mac OS X server.

3. In the Computers & Services list, select NAT.

4. Click Start NAT.

5. Click Save.

Also, to start the firewall service use these general steps:

1. Open the Server Admin tool.

2. Connect to the Mac OS X server.

3. In the Computers & Services list, select Firewall.

4. Click the Start Firewall button.

Deploying Proxies
A proxy is a computer that is located between a computer on an internal network and a computer on an external network with which the internal computer is communicating. As a "middleman," a proxy can fulfill one or a combination of tasks:

- Act as an application-level gateway

- Filter communications

- Create secure tunnels for communications

- Enhance application request performance through caching

One function of a proxy is to screen application requests that go across a firewall placed between an internal network and an external or public network. In this sense, you might think of a proxy as similar to an administrative assistant who works for a busy department head. The administrative assistant screens all mail, e-mail, and calls to the department head, so that the department head receives only the communications she has instructed the administrative assistant to allow through. All other communications are discarded and never reach the department head, which helps to protect the department head's valuable time. A proxy is often combined on a firewall with NAT, so that while NAT is disguising the addresses of computers on the internal network, the proxy is operating to screen the application requests that go through the network. In this capacity, the proxy is working at the Application layer or Layer 7.

Proxies that are configured as application-level gateways can have different levels of ability. For example, a simple application-level proxy might be configured as a filter to allow only

HTTP and FTP through to the internal network—for instance, from an Internet connection. Or the application-level proxy might allow only Simple Mail Transfer Protocol (SMTP) communications for e-mail exchanges to go through (see Figure 11-28). A more advanced application-level proxy might direct all HTTP and FTP communications to a specific Web server on an internal network, so the communications cannot be seen by any other computers on that internal network, protecting the other computers. An even more advanced application-level proxy might allow only HTTP communications through on TCP port 80 and strip out other information in a packet, such as IP address information. Yet another application-level proxy might allow HTTP communications through, but examine each packet for ActiveX information and block any ActiveX information from going through, thus preventing a worm from finding its way into the internal network. Some proxies enable the installation of specialized modules for specific application-level communications, for example, a special security module for FTP communications and a different module for SSH or Telnet communications. All of these examples show that proxies can engage in very complex filtering of communications to increase the security of a network.

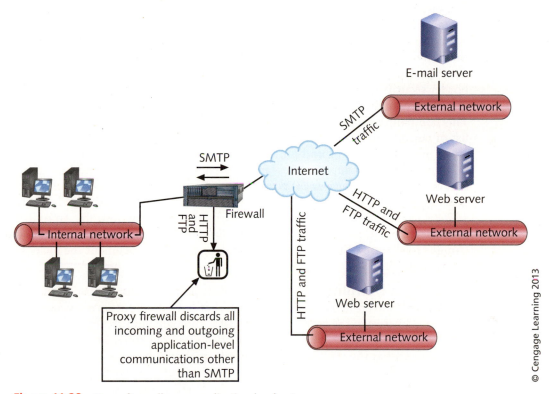

Figure 11-28   Proxy firewall as an application-level gateway

Some proxies function as **circuit-level gateways**, creating a virtual tunnel between the proxy and an external computer, such as a Web server. This process works, for example, when a computer on the internal network requests a Web page on a server on an external network. The internal network client sends the request to the proxy server over a virtual circuit that goes only to the proxy server, like a secret or private tunnel over the internal network. The proxy server next disguises the address of the client using NAT and then communicates over the Internet with the external Web server. When the Web server replies to the proxy server, it converts the IP address to the actual address of the client on the internal network and sends the reply back over the virtual circuit through the internal network.

Some proxies are able to provide caching services as a way to reduce the load on servers within the internal network. **Cache** is storage used by a computer system to house frequently used data in quickly accessed storage, such as memory. Proxies cache recently made service requests, which allows them to fulfill an individual client's request from the cache, without needing to contact the server on the internal network. Consider, for example, a busy database server that is located in the internal network. The database server is used by research scientists all over the world who access the server from external networks. The research scientists often make nearly identical requests for information, because they run data queries from a series of preconfigured reporting tools. When one scientist in Montreal requests a report by going through the proxy, that proxy caches the report sent from the database server. Within a few minutes another scientist from Montreal requests the same report. Instead of contacting the database server, the proxy extracts the report from its cache and sends it to the second scientist in Montreal.

Using Routers for Border Security
A router performs packet filtering and is often used as a firewall on a network, in addition to the other functions it performs. Routers have built-in intelligence and can be customized through configuration to direct packets to specific networks, study network traffic, quickly adapt to changes detected in the network, and protect networks by determining which packets are to be blocked.

Routers can filter packets on the basis of information associated with each port (inbound and outbound connections), to control network traffic, for example. The ability to filter packets can also be applied for security in the role of a firewall. As you learned in Chapter 5, "Devices for Connecting Networks," a router can be configured to allow or deny packets on the basis of the individual IP address, network ID, or subnet. Also, a router can be configured to allow or deny specific protocols. Because of these capabilities, routers have long been used as firewalls for border security on networks.

Cisco Systems routers are one example of the flexibility that routers have to filter packets. This company's routers use access control lists to enable packet filtering. In this case an ACL is a list of permit and deny conditions that can be associated with a particular router interface, such as an inbound or outbound port. The permit or deny condition is in the form of a statement and may specify a source address in an IP packet, a destination address, a particular protocol, and other conditions (over 50 possibilities). For instance, the router administrator might use a deny statement (an action statement) to prevent a packet containing the destination IP address 122.88.11.5 from leaving the network through an outbound port. An ACL consists of one or more deny or permit action statements. Remark statements also can be included in an ACL (similar to the use of remarks in program languages) to document the purpose of a grouping of action statements, to avoid confusion later.

Creating a Demilitarized Zone
A demilitarized zone (DMZ) is a portion of a network that exists between two or more networks that have different security measures in place, such as the "zone" between the private network of a company and the Internet. An organization might place publicly accessed Web servers in its demilitarized zone, such as the Web servers of a state government that the public accesses for informational brochures and state tax forms. These are servers that do not require the same security as servers and workstations on the private network. Also, the advantage of placing servers in the DMZ is that the less secure network communications required for access to the servers do not have to cross the border security into the private network—thus keeping the private network more secure.

Configuring Operating System Firewalls
Some operating systems allow you to configure firewall services for border security. This capability is particularly important when the computer on which the operating system is running is directly connected to the Internet—through a cable modem or DSL connection, for example—and when the computer is in a demilitarized zone.

When a computer running Windows 7 or Windows Server 2008/Server 2008 R2 is directly connected to the Internet, for example, through a cable modem or DSL connection, then Windows Firewall should be enabled, as shown in Figure 11-29. Windows Firewall is provided in modern Windows operating systems and is enabled by default. Activity 11-12 shows you how to ensure that Windows Firewall is enabled in Windows 7 and Windows Server 2008/Server 2008 R2.

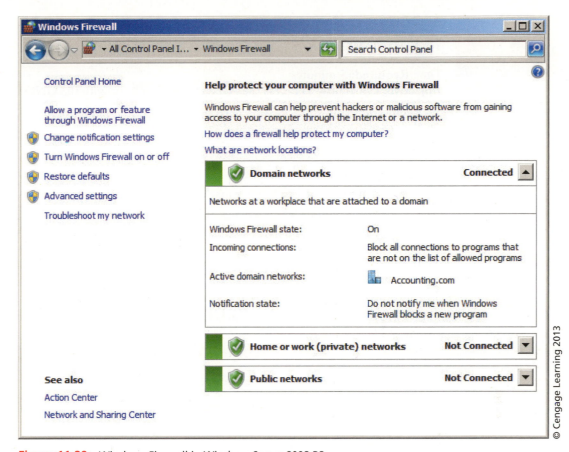

Figure 11-29   Windows Firewall in Windows Server 2008 R2

Activity 11-12: Configure Windows Firewall

Time Required: 5 minutes

Objective: Ensure that Windows Firewall in Windows 7 or Server 2008/Server 2008 R2 is turned on or that your system's firewall functions are managed by a vendor application, such as virus-checking and security software from a third party.

Description: In this activity, you verify that Windows Firewall is turned on or that your system's firewall functions are managed by a vendor application.

1. Click **Start** and click **Control Panel**. In Windows 7 and Server 2008 R2, make sure **View by** is set to **Large icons** or **Small icons**. In Windows Server 2008, use the **Classic View**.

2. Click (in Windows 7 or Server 2008 R2) or double-click (in Windows Server 2008) **Windows Firewall**.

3. In the Windows Firewall window, make sure that the firewall is on or that there is a message that these settings are managed by a vendor application. Note that in Windows 7 and Server 2008 R2, the firewall should be turned on for the type of network, such as a domain, home or work, or public network. In the left pane of the Windows Firewall window notice there are options to manage the firewall, including the ability to turn it on or off (refer to Figure 11-29).

4. Close the Windows Firewall window and any other open windows.

As you learned earlier, UNIX/Linux systems offer the IPTables tool for configuring a firewall. In the GNOME 3.x desktop there is also the Firewall tool that you can use to configure a firewall. Activity 11-13 enables you to learn how to access the Firewall tool in GNOME.

Activity 11-13: Configure a Firewall Using the GNOME Firewall Tool in Linux

Time Required: 5 minutes
Objective: Learn how to access the Firewall tool in Linux with the GNOME 3.x desktop.

Description: In this activity, you learn how to access the Firewall tool in Linux with the GNOME 3.x desktop.

1. Click **Activities** and click **Applications**.

2. Click **Firewall**.

3. If you see an information box, click **Close** in the box.

4. Notice that there should be a message at the bottom of the Firewall Configuration window that the firewall is enabled, which is the default. If the firewall is disabled, click the **Enable** button to enable the firewall (the Enable button is deactivated when the firewall is enabled).

5. In the left pane, ensure that **Trusted Services** is selected. In the right pane, scroll through the list of services that can be selected as trusted services, including such services as DNS, FTP, and others (see Figure 11-30). You can select a service to be trusted by placing a checkmark in its checkbox.

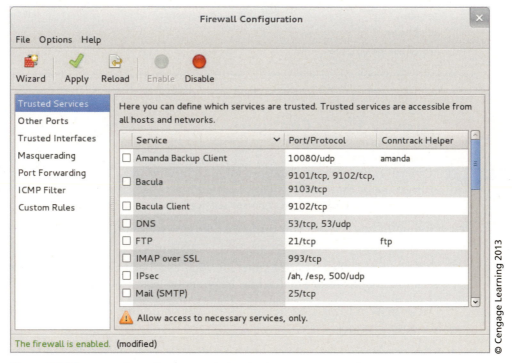

Figure 11-30   Firewall Configuration window in Linux

6. Also, notice in the button bar at the top of the window that you can start a wizard to guide you through setting up a firewall.

7. Close the Firewall Configuration window.

Mac OS X Snow Leopard and Lion offer a firewall that you can configure through System Preferences. Try Activity 11-14 to learn where to configure the Mac OS X firewall.

Activity 11-14: Ensure that the Mac OS X Firewall Is Enabled

Time Required: 5 minutes

Objective: Check the Mac OS X Snow Leopard or Lion firewall to ensure it is enabled.

Description: In this activity, you learn how to verify that the Mac OS X Snow Leopard or Lion firewall is enabled.

1. Click **System Preferences** in the Dock, or click the **Apple** icon in the menu bar and click **System Preferences.**

2. In the System Preferences window, click **Security** (Snow Leopard) or **Security & Privacy** (Lion) under Personal.

3. If the lock at the bottom of the Security window is locked, click the **lock**. Provide your account name (if necessary) and password and click **OK.**

4. In the Security (Snow Leopard) or Security & Privacy (Lion) window, ensure that the **Firewall** tab is selected (see Figure 11-31; note that Snow Leopard does not have the Privacy tab as is in Lion).

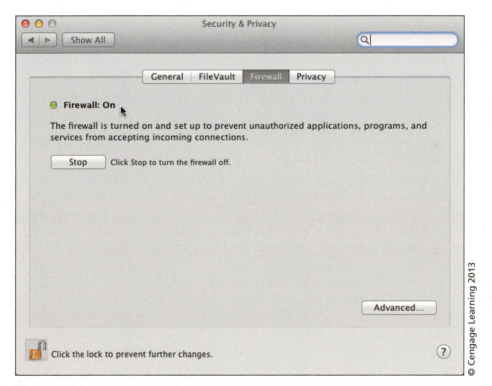

Figure 11-31   Security & Privacy window in Mac OS X Lion

5. If the firewall is not turned on (and your firewall settings are not managed by third-party virus software), click the **Start** button to turn on the firewall. Also, click the **lock**, if necessary to relock it.

6. Click **System Preferences** in the menu bar and click **Quit System Preferences.**

Putting It All Together: Designing Security for Home and Office Networks

As you have learned in this chapter, there are many steps you can take to secure networks in different circumstances. This section summarizes pointers for making your home or office network as secure as possible.

Designing a Secure Home Network

Security on a home network is important because computers are likely to house personal information, such as expense records, investments, bank account records, and private correspondence, as well as music and photo collections that would be hard if not impossible to replace. Some computers may also have confidential work records. If a home network is not properly secured, your personal information may fall into the hands of someone else. An Internet attacker may gain access to your computer and access those records, or someone may break into your home and obtain credit card and bank account information from a computer.

The basic steps you can take in designing security on computers connected to a home network include:

- Set up accounts with passwords on home computers.

- Ensure that the Guest account is disabled or has a password, if your operating system has a default Guest account.

- Configure permissions for file and folder security, particularly to protect folders and files containing personal or work information.

- Protect shared folders that contain personal or work information by using share permissions.

- Purchase virus-, spyware-, and spam-checking software and schedule the software to run on a regular basis.

- Configure security, such as WPA2 Personal, on wireless systems.

- Turn off services you don't use, such as Telnet.

- Configure all computers on the network to automatically obtain operating system and application software updates.

- Have virus-checking software on all network computers and configure a firewall if firewall services are not provided through the virus-checking software.

- If you have a home server, consider using NAT or find an ISP that offers NAT protection. Or, if you use DSL or cable modem WAN access, consider purchasing a wireless modem/router that provides NAT protection for computers on the internal home network.

Designing a Secure Office Network

Organizations also have a responsibility to ensure their networked resources are protected. Consider a small office of physicians whose networked computers contain all types of personal information about patients including Social Security numbers, medical histories, medical insurance information, and many other forms of information. Also, one computer in the physicians' office is connected to a DSL connection sharing Internet connectivity. The security on each computer in this office should include file and folder permissions. Each computer should have a firewall configured (if not provided by virus-checking software), particularly the computer with the DSL connection. Furthermore, updates to the computer operating systems should be installed regularly and all computers should have a password-protected screensaver.

On a larger scale, a company that produces breakfast cereal might use several security techniques beyond those mentioned for a home and for the physicians' office. These techniques include:

- Using NAT between the internal network and the Internet so that outsiders cannot view the IP addresses on their internal network.

- Configuring servers to use IPSec to discourage attackers from intercepting packets.

- Using packet filtering, such as through routers, to protect areas of the network that must be kept particularly secure. This might include areas such as those that contain servers with files about cereal recipes and production methods.

- Installing a proxy for e-mail (SMTP) communications through the Internet.
- Placing the Web server that provides general information about cereal products in a DMZ between the internal company network and the Internet. Also, a firewall can be configured via the operating system on the server's connection to the Internet.

Chapter Summary

- You can take several practical steps to harden a network. These include using security features of operating systems, using the Web to research new security developments, deploying firewalls and other security precautions, auditing your security, training users, and monitoring for attacks.

- Attackers use many methods to gain access to a network and its resources. One of the simplest attacks is when an unauthorized person has access to an unprotected, unattended computer. Other attacks focus on determining account names and passwords and remotely accessing a computer from an open service, such as Telnet.

- Viruses, virus hoaxes, worms, and Trojan horses are common attack methods, and many computer systems have succumbed to these. Buffer attacks are another way to introduce malicious software in a computer. Denial-of-service attacks can flood a network so that communications are slowed or even halted. Man-in-the-middle attacks enable an attacker to operate between the sending computer and the receiving computer as a way to intercept transmissions.

- An application-layer attack can be used to control applications, alter data, monitor a network, or take over a computer. A source routing attack and spoofing can make the attacker look like a trusted computer on a network. A programmable logic controller attack takes over a control computer that manages automated manufacturing or mechanical processes. Sniffer attacks use software to intercept and read network packet contents. An e-mail attack may contain a virus or worm. Port scanning takes advantage of an open TCP or UDP port to gain entry into a system on a network. Wireless attacks use war-driving software and devices such as an omnidirectional antenna.

- Spam is a common headache for e-mail users, and spyware is commonplace for tracking a computer user's activity.

- Installing updates on computers can be an effective way to ensure security and block some forms of attacks. Using IP Security (IPSec) enables secure communications through authentication and encryption.

- Border and firewall security provide increased levels of security. For example, packet filtering can be used to control traffic that goes into and out of a network. Network Address Translation (NAT) helps to protect the IP addresses on an internal network from view by those on an external network.

- Proxies are computers that act as middlemen to screen communications between an internal network and an external network. Routers are used for border security and can filter packets. A demilitarized zone may be implemented with different security than is used on the internal network, such as for public access servers.

- Windows 7, Windows Server, UNIX/Linux, and Mac OS X systems can help offer border and internal network security through firewalls incorporated into the operating system.

Key Terms

application-layer attack A malicious attack on any type of application, including an operating system, so that an attacker can control the application or prevent it from working. Application-layer attacks are of particular concern to cloud computing providers.

application-level gateway A proxy that filters application-level protocols and requests between an internal network and an external network. *See* **proxy**.

border gateway   A firewall that is configured with security policies to control the traffic that is permitted across a border (in either direction) between a public and private network.

buffer   A storage area in a device (for example, in a network interface card, a computer system, or a network device such as a switch) that temporarily saves information in memory.

buffer attack   An attack in which the attacker tricks the buffer software into attempting to store more information in a buffer than the buffer is able to contain. The extra information can be malicious software.

buffer overflow   A situation in which there is more information to store in a buffer than the buffer is sized to hold.

cache   Storage used by a computer system to house frequently used data in quickly accessed storage, such as memory.

circuit-level gateway   A proxy that creates a secure virtual circuit through an internal network to a client computer that is communicating with a computer on an external network via the proxy. *See* proxy.

cookie   Information that a Web server stores on a client computer, such as the client's preferences when accessing a particular Web site, or where the client has been on the Web site.

demilitarized zone (DMZ)   A portion of a network that exists between two or more networks that have different security measures in place, such as the "zone" between the private network of a company and the Internet.

denial-of-service (DoS) attack   An attack that interferes with normal access to a network host, Web site, or service, for example, by flooding a network with useless information or with frames or packets containing errors that are not identified by a particular network service.

disk quota   Allocating a specific amount of disk space to a user or application with the ability to ensure that the user or application cannot use more disk space than is specified in the allocation.

distributed denial-of-service (DDoS) attack   A denial-of-service attack in which one computer causes other computers to launch attacks directed at one or more targets.

Encapsulating Security Payload (ESP)   Used in IPSec communications for encrypting packet-based data, authenticating data, and generally ensuring the security and confidentiality of Network layer information and data within a packet.

hardening   Taking specific actions to block or prevent attacks by means of operating system and network security methods.

IP Security (IPSec)   A set of IP-based secure communications and encryption standards developed by the Internet Engineering Task Force (IETF) and used to protect network communications through IP.

man-in-the-middle attack   The interception of a message or transmission meant for a different computer, by an attacker who is literally operating between two communicating computers.

Network Address Translation (NAT)   A technique used in network communications that translates an IP address from a private network to a different address used on a public network or the Internet, and vice versa. NAT is used to protect the identity of a computer on the private network from attackers, as well as bypass the requirement to employ universally unique IP addresses on the private network.

open SMTP relay server   An e-mail server that not only accepts e-mail, but also resends the e-mail to other servers without restrictions.

packet filtering   Using characteristics of a packet—such as an IP address, network ID, or TCP/UDP port use—to determine whether a packet should be forwarded or blocked in its transport between two networks or across a packet-filtering device (for example, a firewall).

programmable logic controller attack   An attack on a programmable logic controller that interferes with manufacturing or mechanical processes. A programmable logic controller is a computer that is used in industrial manufacturing and other similar environments to control or automate specific manufacturing or mechanical processes.

proxy   A computer that is located between a computer on an internal network and a computer on an external network, with which the internal computer is communicating. The proxy acts as a "middleman" to filter application-level communications, perform caching, and create virtual circuits with clients for safer communications.

rogue Web site   A Web site that performs unlawful activity or that puts the user who accesses it at risk, such as by downloading malicious software to the user's computer, gaining unauthorized access, or stealing account password or other personal information.

service pack   An operating system update that provides fixes for known problems and offers product enhancements.

sniffer attack   When an attacker uses software that can intercept and read packet traffic.

social engineering attack   In relation to a computer attack, refers to the use of human interaction to gain access to an individual's personal information or to a computer system to do damage or acquire access or information—for example, through a bogus e-mail or telephone call.

source routing   A routing technique in which the sender of a packet specifies the precise path (through hops) that a packet will take to reach its destination.

spam   Unrequested commercial e-mail that is sent to hundreds, thousands, or even millions of users in bulk.

spoofing   When the address of the source computer is changed to make a packet appear as though it originated from a different computer.

spyware   Software that is placed on a computer, typically without the user's knowledge, and then reports back information—to an attacker or an advertiser, for example—about that computer user's activities. Some spyware also works by simply capturing information about cookies sent between a Web server and a client.

stateful packet filtering   Tracks information about a communication session, such as which ports are in use, by drawing from the contents of multiple packets.

stateless packet filtering   A packet-filtering technique in which the firewall examines every individual packet and decides whether to pass or block the packet on the basis of information drawn from single packets.

Trojan horse   A program that appears useful and harmless, but instead does harm to the user's computer. Often a Trojan horse provides an attacker with access to the computer on which it is running or enables the attacker to control the computer.

virus   A program that is borne by a disk or a file and has the ability to replicate throughout a system. Some viruses cause damage to systems, and others replicate without causing permanent damage.

virus hoax   An e-mail falsely warning of a virus.

well-known ports   TCP/UDP network ports 0–1023 that are most commonly used by applications (technically called application end points) that use TCP or UDP for communications. The well-known port designation is included in the TCP or UDP header within a packet or frame. Ports 1024–49151 are registered by IANA (Internet Assigned Numbers Authority) to ensure they remain in the public domain for current or future use. Ports 49152–65535 are ports reserved for private use.

Windows Firewall   A software firewall provided by Microsoft that controls information exchanged between a Microsoft operating system or shared network connection and an external network connection, such as the Internet.

worm   A program that replicates and replicates on the same computer or sends itself to many other computers on a network, but does not infect existing files.

Review Questions

1. You and your business partner are planning to set up a small downtown office that will have six employees, all of whom need Internet access. You intend to use DSL and a wireless modem/router. As a way to shield the actual IP addresses on your business network from Internet outsiders, what capability should be a feature of the wireless modem/router?

   a.   clear text security (cts)

   b.   Secure Shell Addressing (SSA)

   c.   Remote Access Tracking (RAT)

   d.   Network Address Translation (NAT)

2. Your specialized firewall software on a router enables you to close specific TCP and UDP ports. The company security policy states that employees are not to download files using FTP. What port or ports should you close via the firewall? (Choose all that apply.)

   a. 12

   b. 20

   c. 21

   d. 51

   e. 53

3. Your friend has sent you a CD containing a fun free game he downloaded from the Internet. However, you have seen an alert that this game, although lots of fun, also contains malicious software. Which of the following best describes this gaming software?

   a. It is a worm.

   b. It is a man-in-the-middle attack.

   c. It is a Trojan horse.

   d. It is an example of spoofing.

4. Which of the following are operating system features that can be used to help protect a network? (Choose all that apply.)

   a. ability to use digital certificates

   b. ability to use encryption features for network communications

   c. ability to set permissions on files

   d. ability to use VPN capabilities

5. Some of the staff in the warehouse building of a company like to end the day playing games over the Internet. However, none of their job duties necessitates access to the Internet, and playing the games exposes the computers in their building to unnecessary security risks. Which of the following offers the best solution?

   a. Restrict the staff to only communications via TCP, and not IP.

   b. Close off their network from having access to the main business network, even though they need this access.

   c. Place a proxy that filters out HTTP and FTP traffic between their building and the Internet connection.

   d. Convert the entire business network to strictly use SMTP for communications.

6. Your company has been the target of industrial spying, which is often performed by a company insider. What is a simple way to help discourage industrial spying to make it harder for an insider to access someone's computer when he or she is away from his or her desk?

   a. Purchase SpyGuard software for each computer.

   b. Use file encryption.

   c. Set all computers to automatically shut down after 10 minutes of no keyboard activity.

   d. Use a timed, password-protected screen saver.

7. As you monitor switches on your network, what should you be aware of in terms of a potential attack?

   a. buffer attack

   b. MAC attack

   c. NAT overflow

   d. relay switching

8. Spyware often works through which of the following?

    a. cookies

    b. disk buffers

    c. capture filter

    d. access timer

9. Your network design team is currently focusing on security issues. Which of the following are "borders" the team should consider for border security? (Choose all that apply.)

    a. a frame relay link for WAN communications

    b. a VPN

    c. a microwave link to a subsidiary

    d. a DSL link used by the payroll office to upload automatic deposit information

10. In IPSec, computers start a network communication through which of the following means?

    a. encoded verifier packets

    b. hacker testing

    c. exchanging certificates for authentication

    d. MAC identification

11. Your colleague is configuring packet filtering on a router. Which of the following is the best method to use for firewall purposes?

    a. state transition packet filtering

    b. stateful packet filtering

    c. static packet filtering

    d. stateless packet filtering

12. You are setting up a proxy to create a secure tunnel for communications between the proxy, which is on the internal network, and another company's external Web server that is accessed every day by company employees to order raw materials for manufacturing. In this case the proxy is used as which of the following?

    a. caching proxy

    b. public filter

    c. application manager

    d. circuit-level gateway

13. Your university maintains a public affairs Web server to provide general information about the university, university programs, outreach schools, and college sports events. This Web server is on a part of the university's network that is less secure than the internal network used for academics and administrative functions. Which of the following terms describes the Web server's portion of the network?

    a. protected region

    b. demilitarized zone

    c. buffer unit

    d. minimum security subnet

14. Which of the following are ways to help control problems caused by unwanted e-mail in a business? (Choose all that apply.)

    a. Ensure e-mail servers are not configured as open SMTP relay servers.

    b. Create a managed e-mail server.

    c. Set up a spam charge-back system.

    d. Use the blocking feature in *traceroute*.

15. When you configure IPSec on a Windows Server system, which IPSec setting ensures that communication through any server account or client must use IPSec?

   a. Server

   b. Client

   c. Secure Server

   d. IPSec Client

16. Your company requires that employees regularly update their Windows 7 computers to be sure each computer is current on security patches. Which of the following provides an easy way to do the updating?

   a. Each month, the company routes to each employee the latest Microsoft Windows Patch DVD.

   b. Have employees regularly access the Windows Service Pack Automator.

   c. Use the Patches application from the Start menu.

   d. Configure Windows Update to obtain and install updates automatically.

17. One way to configure NAT in Linux is to use which of the following?

   a. Network Connections tool in the GNOME 3.x desktop

   b. the IPTables interface

   c. *nat* command-line command in a terminal window

   d. *ipsec* command-line command in a terminal window

18. Your engineering firm uses Linux on desktop computers and the Firefox Web browser in Linux. Is there a way to manage cookies for specific Web sites in this environment?

   a. Configure cookie management through the Permissions button in the Page Info window in Firefox.

   b. Use the Tools menu in Firefox.

   c. Use the Cookies app in the GNOME 3.x desktop.

   d. Use the System Setting app in the GNOME 3.x desktop.

   e. There is no way to manage cookies in Linux.

19. In your small office all networked computers are running Mac OS X Lion. To help protect all of the networked computers, office members have decided to make sure their operating systems are regularly updated. From where can they set up automatic updating?

   a. Update application in the Applications window

   b. Finder File menu

   c. Finder Updates menu

   d. System Preferences Software Update selection

20. In Mac OS X Lion, you see a warning message that the firewall is disabled. From where can you enable the firewall?

   a. Network window opened through System Preferences

   b. Firewall application in the Utility window

   c. Security& Privacy window opened through System Preferences

   d. Firewall icon in the Macintosh HD window

Case Projects

The Maple County court is redesigning its network to ensure more security. The court has four Linux servers and three Windows Server systems. One of the Windows Server systems is connected to a DSL line and shares network connectivity with other computers on the court's network. The same server also has e-mail and SMTP services for handling e-mail. All of the users on the court's network have computers running Windows 7 or Mac OS X Snow Leopard and Lion.

The court has an Optical Ethernet WAN connection to the Sheriff's Department and to the Maple City Police Department. There is also an Optical Ethernet WAN connection to the Maple City and County Building. The county judges are concerned about security on the Maple County court network and hire you via Network Design Consultants to assess their security needs.

Case Project 11-1: Border Locations

Create a document that explains network borders to the judges and the border points you plan to examine for security.

Case Project 11-2: Preparing a Seminar About Attacks

The judges ask you to give all court employees a short seminar about malicious attacks on computers and networks. Prepare some notes you can use in your presentation.

Case Project 11-3: Security for a Server

When you examine the DSL connection to the Windows server you realize there is no particular security on the server other than file and folder permissions. What security improvements do you recommend to the judges?

Case Project 11-4: Locating a New Web server

The clerk of the court wants to add a Web server to the network for public access to general information about the court system and its judges. Where would you place the Web server?

Case Project 11-5: Spam Problem

The court has always had an annoying and time-wasting problem with spam. What steps do you recommend for the court to address this problem?

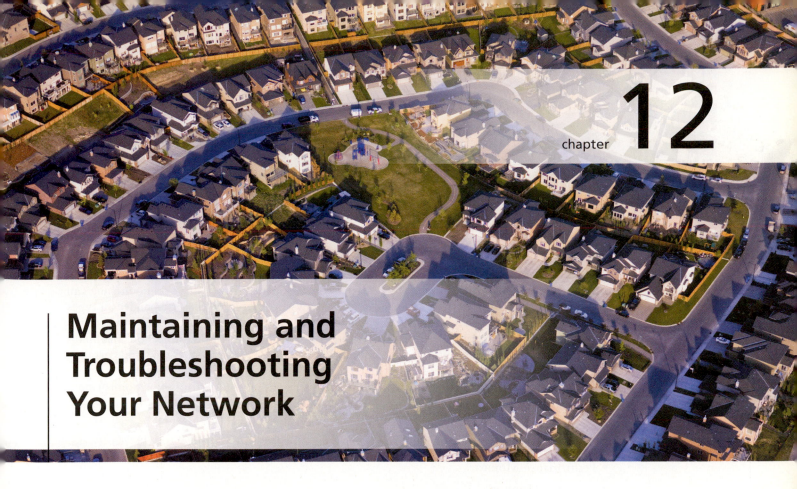

Maintaining and Troubleshooting Your Network

No matter how well you design and secure your network, problems happen. The difference between spending hours of misery troubleshooting a problem and solving the problem right away equates to preparation. If you know your network and your troubleshooting tools and have a solutions strategy, you can take care of problems with less stress and without going into overtime.

After reading this chapter and completing the exercises, you will be able to:

- Use hardware and software methods to monitor a network
- Perform backups over a network
- Solve a broad range of network problems
- Design a solutions strategy for network troubleshooting

Understanding how to monitor and troubleshoot your network is simply part of the networking process. In this chapter, you learn about devices and software for monitoring a network. You learn how to protect network data by using backups. You also learn how to solve network problems such as connectivity, NIC and WNIC, cable, wireless, and network printing problems. Finally, you bring all of the pieces of network monitoring and troubleshooting together into a solutions strategy for quickly handling network problems.

How to Monitor Your Network

After your network is installed, plan to regularly monitor the network. Network monitoring can serve two purposes. One purpose is to get to know how your network performs under all types of conditions. This enables you to become familiar with your network, so you know when it is healthy and when it is not. A second purpose is to quickly locate and troubleshoot problems as they come along. Dealing with a problem quickly often keeps it from growing and certainly keeps network users happy.

In the following sections you learn about hardware and software tools for monitoring a network, which include:

- Network-monitoring devices
- Basic network-monitoring tools in operating systems
- Performance Monitor
- Network Monitor
- SNMP service

Network-Monitoring Devices

Network-monitoring devices range from simple voltage testers to very complex protocol analyzers. Prices go up for devices that have more network-monitoring functions. If you have a small network of 10 to 20 workstations, you probably need only simple equipment, such as a voltmeter or multimeter. If you manage a large enterprise network with hundreds of nodes, you may need several types of equipment, such as a time domain reflectometer and a protocol analyzer. Some examples of test and monitoring devices are:

- Voltmeter, multimeter, and optical power meter
- Cable continuity tester
- Cable scanner
- Time domain reflectometer
- Wireless testing tool
- Protocol analyzer

Voltmeter, Multimeter, and Optical Power Meter   A voltmeter is used to test the voltage on a network cable and to test signal strength on any network device. For a few dollars more you can purchase a multimeter (see Figure 12-1), which combines the functions of a voltmeter and an ohm meter. The ohm meter enables you to test the cable resistance, such as 100 ohms for UTP, to make sure it meets IEEE specifications.

© Sergii Korolko/www.Shutterstock.com

Figure 12-1   A multimeter tests voltage and resistance

To measure the light signal strength on fiber-optic cable, you need an optical power meter (refer to Figure 4-12 in Chapter 4, "Connecting Through a Cabled Network"). For small to medium-sized networks, the best course is to retain the services of an optical cable expert to measure the signal strength and to troubleshoot other optical cable problems.

Cable Continuity Tester   A cable continuity tester enables you to check for opens or breaks in a cable by determining if the signal sent from one end reaches the other end of the cable. Some cable continuity testers also test the integrity of cable pairs, such as testing for shorted or crossed pairs. A cable continuity tester for fiber-optic cable tests if the light impulse reaches from end to end.

Cable Scanner   Cable scanners, also called cable testers (refer to Figure 4-8 in Chapter 4) or cable performance testers, are used to test the length and other characteristics of co-axial (such as short coaxial runs to connect devices in a computer room on high-speed links), twisted-pair, or fiber-optic cable. To test the cable, a connector on a section of cable is attached to the scanner. The scanner measures the cable by transmitting an electrical signal. It times the signal to determine where it stops. This information is used to determine the cable length, which is shown on an LCD display, is printed out, or both. Scanners are made to test cables at various speeds.

If the signal transmission is interrupted, the scanner determines if an open or short circuit exists. An open circuit is one where the connection is severed, such as a cable that is inadvertently cut in two. A short circuit is an incomplete or damaged connection, such as when the two conductors in a twisted-pair set come in contact in a poorly built connector. The scanner reports the distance to the problem so it can be located and repaired. Many scanners also can indicate if a cable segment has RFI or EMI.

Some scanners can monitor for cable problems continuously, producing a report of the information they have collected. This feature is useful when you are working to locate an intermittent problem, such as an occasional short or a defective connector. Activity 12-1 enables you to learn to use a cable scanner.

You may have a continuous or intermittent short circuit in a network connection or connector. Electrically, a short is a situation in which a circuit has low impedance (resistance), which results in too much current. On the physical level, any kind of short can cause a circuit to overheat and damage electrical components or cause a fire, if there is enough current. On a network, a short can cause a broadcast storm or excessive packet collisions. If the short is intermittent, when you test the network you will see intermittent periods of excessive packet collisions or an intermittent broadcast storm, or intermittent periods of no network traffic. For a continuous short, there can be continuous excessive packet collisions or a continuous broadcast storm. When there is an open in a network connector or connection, this means current does not flow (even though you may measure a voltage on the circuit), and so network communications cease at that point. Many people confuse opens with shorts. If you trace the problem to a cable, replace the cable or connector. If you trace the problem to a NIC, replace the NIC (remember that a NIC contains a built-in terminator that provides resistance and that if the terminator is defective you can have a short as expressed through a broadcast storm). If you trace the problem to a router or switch connection, check the cabling and connectors to the router or switch.

Activity 12-1: Using a Cable Scanner

Time Required: 10 minutes

Objective: Learn to use a cable scanner.

Description: If a cable scanner for twisted-pair cable is available to you, try this activity to measure the cable distance on a small network. You need access to a network that is not in use by others, or you need to make your own network. If you make your own, connect two workstations to a switch using UTP cable and make sure the switch is connected to power. Use the following steps to measure a cable segment:

1. First review the instructions for using the scanner.

2. Unplug the connector and cable to one of the workstations.

3. Attach the cable scanner to that connector and cable (see Figure 12-2).

4. Follow the scanner directions to measure the cable distance.

5. Try measuring the cable length from another workstation connected to the network.

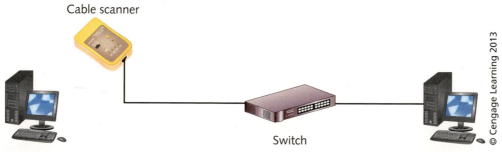

Figure 12-2 Using a cable scanner

Time Domain Reflectometer

The **time domain reflectometer (TDR)** has more options than a cable scanner and is more expensive (see Figure 12-3). It monitors line impedance (the total amount of opposition to the flow of current), opens, shorts, RFI/EMI, cable distances, and connector and terminator problems. A TDR works by transmitting a signal and gathering information on the signal reflection that is returned. TDRs can duplicate the wave pattern of the signal to show impedance, signal strength, signal interference, distance, and other information. Some TDRs have a memory feature to capture several snapshots at different times and to record the information in a printed report. This feature is used in tracking intermittent cable problems or problems due to occasional electrical interference.

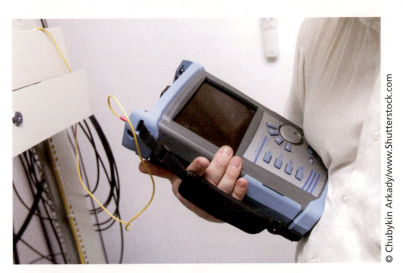

Figure 12-3   Time domain reflectometer

Optical time domain reflectometers (OTDRs) are available for testing fiber-optic cable. These devices transmit a light wave instead of an electrical impulse. The reflected signal is measured for distance and strength. An OTDR can also test for bad splices, connector problems, and problems with the bending radius.

If you purchase a device with relatively complex features, consider training on that device. This is particularly true for TDRs, OTDRs, and protocol analyzers (discussed later). Many vendors offer training classes for their equipment.

Wireless Testing Tool   Wireless testing tools are available that enable you to determine performance characteristics of a wireless network. For example, a wireless testing tool can be used to determine if an access point is working properly and the strength of the signal sent from the access point. The tool can also determine noise and signal loss problems and move through cells to test for problems from cell to cell.

If you are setting up a wireless network, you can use a wireless network testing tool to determine the range of access points, the placement of cells, and the placement of computers with WNICs. If your budget does not allow for a wireless testing tool, you can use a laptop computer, WNIC, and the Currently connected to window in Windows 7 or the Windows Wireless Network Connection Status dialog box to test access, signal strength, and the ability to move from cell to cell (see "Using the Windows Network Connection Status Dialog Box" later in this chapter).

Protocol Analyzer   The most full-functioned network-monitoring device is the **protocol analyzer** or **packet analyzer**. Often on a device that looks like a portable computer (or actual software on a portable computer), this device works in promiscuous mode to capture detailed information about the traffic moving across a network, including protocol and OSI layer information. The promiscuous mode means a device can pick up frames and packets on the network segment regardless of the destination address and read the frame or packet contents (see Chapter 5, "Devices for Connecting Networks"). Some protocol analyzers provide information derived from the OSI Physical, Data Link, and Network layers. Others can analyze the upper OSI layers also.

Protocol analyzers are sometimes called "sniffers." Over time, this has become a generic term, like "Kleenex" is for facial tissue. The Sniffer is a protocol and network analysis device originally developed by a company with the same name. Today NetScout Systems offers Sniffer products. Several other companies, such as Agilent Technologies, Fluke, Hewlett-Packard, and Tektronix, offer protocol analyzers.

At the Physical layer, a protocol analyzer detects problems such as opens, shorts, and electrical interference. The analyzer may be attached to the network backbone or to a particular segment of the network. The Data Link layer analysis produces information on data errors, including packet collisions, incomplete packets, corrupted packets, CRC errors, network bottlenecks, and broadcast storms.

At the Network layer, a protocol analyzer monitors routing information contained in data packets. By viewing this information, you can analyze distances traveled by packets. For example, it may show that a packet takes an unusually long route from a workstation in one building to a server in another, perhaps indicating the need to adjust a router's setup.

Some protocol analyzers can examine the Transport, Session, Presentation, and Application OSI layers.

For a security-minded network administrator, a protocol analyzer can be used to help determine where to place firewalls or use intrusion detection software. It also can be used to test firewalls and intrusion detection methods.

A protocol analyzer may come in the form of a dedicated hardware device or a software program for a computer, such as for a laptop that can move to different points on a network. Try Activity 12-2 to learn more about protocol analyzers from different vendors.

Activity 12-2: Protocol Analyzers

Time Required: 15 minutes
Objective: Learn about protocol analyzers from different vendors.

Description: In this activity you use the Internet to find out about protocol analyzers available from two different vendors.

1. Open a Web browser such as Internet Explorer, Firefox, or Safari.

2. Use the Internet to find information about two different manufacturer's protocol analyzers, either software or hardware. (*Hint:* Consider visiting Web sites such as *www.ethereal.com*, *www.agilent.com*, *www.netscout.com*, or *www.tek.com*.)

3. Create a small table you can use for a side-by-side comparison of features, such as protocols that can be analyzed, GUI features, and error conditions that can be monitored.

4. Close the Web browser when you are finished.

Using Basic Network-Monitoring Tools in Your Operating System

For many common problems you don't need a cable-testing device to tell you if a connection is working. Your computer operating system offers tools that provide basic information about a network connection and that can provide statistics about network performance. In the following sections you learn to use some of these basic but invaluable tools.

Using the Windows Network Connection Status Dialog Box   Windows 7 and Windows Server 2008/Server 2008 R2 offer the Network Connection Status dialog box to provide a simple way to monitor and test a computer's connection. From the Network Connection Status dialog box, you can:

- Verify that a computer and its network segment are connected and communicating
- Determine the duration of the computer's connection
- View the connection speed
- Determine the number of bytes sent and received
- Determine the SSID for wireless networks
- View the signal quality of a wireless connection
- Diagnose connection problems

You can use the Network Connection Status box on any network connection, including a local area connection (cabled), a wireless connection, and a DSL or cable modem connection. For example, if you are having trouble with a wireless connection, use the Wireless Network Connection Status dialog box to determine if you are connected and the speed of transmission. Figure 12-4 shows the Wireless Network Connection Status dialog box for a wireless connection in Windows 7. In Activity 12-3 you use the Network Connection Status dialog box to verify a connection on a computer running Windows 7 or Windows Server 2008/Server 2008 R2.

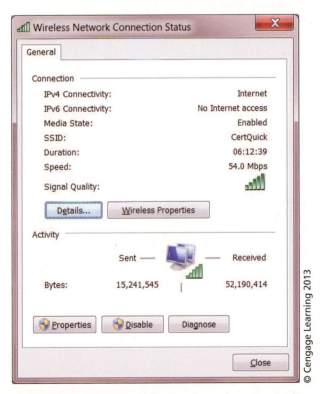

Figure 12-4   Windows 7 Wireless Network Connection Status dialog box

In some Windows 7 or Server 2008/Server 2008 R2 projects, you may see the User Account Control (UAC) box, which is used for security to help thwart intruders. The UAC box asks for permission to continue with an action or asks for the administrator password. If you see this box, click **Continue**. Because computer setups may be different, the box is not mentioned in the actual project steps.

Activity 12-3: Using the Network Connection Status Dialog Box

Time Required: 10 minutes

Objective: Use the Network Connection Status or Wireless Network Connection Status dialog box to verify the network connection in Windows 7 and Windows Server 2008/ Server 2008 R2.

Description: Sometimes you need a fast way to verify a computer's connection and the segment it is attached to. In this activity you use the Network Connection Status dialog box or the Wireless Network Connection Status dialog box in Windows 7 or Windows Server 2008/ Server 2008 R2 to verify a connection. Log on to an account with Administrator privileges for this activity.

1. Click **Start** and click **Control Panel.** In Windows 7 and Windows Server 2008 R2, ensure that **View by** is set to **Large icons** or **Small icons** and click **Network and Sharing Center.** In Windows Server 2008, make sure you are in **Classic View** and double-click **Network and Sharing Center.**

2. In Windows 7 and Windows Server 2008 R2, click **Change adapter settings** in the left pane. In Windows Server 2008, click **Manage Network Connections.**

3. Double-click a live (no red x displayed) network connection, such as **Local Area Connection** or **Wireless Network Connection** (refer to Figure 12-4).

4. What is the media state of the connection, and what is its speed? How many bytes have been sent and received?

5. Click the **Details** button and notice the information that is available for your connection in the Network Connection Details dialog box (see Figure 12-5).

6. Click **Close** to close the Network Connection Details box.

Figure 12-5   Network Connection Details dialog box in Windows 7

7. Notice the Diagnose button that gives you one way to troubleshoot a network connection.

8. Click **Close** to close the Network Connection Status or Wireless Network Connection Status dialog box.

Using *ping* to Test a Network Connection

In Chapter 2, "How LAN and WAN Communications Work," you briefly learned about the *ping* command-line utility as an example of a network program that uses the OSI Application layer. This utility is widely used by network administrators and users to perform a fast test of a network connection.

For example, consider a situation in which the chief financial officer (CFO) in a company needs to access a shared folder on the computer of the marketing director. Their computers are on different network segments, and the CFO is unable to connect to the marketing director's computer. The CFO believes that the network is not working. A network administrator can use *ping* to test the network path from the CFO's computer to the marketing director's computer. If the marketing director's IP address is 184.92.15.70, then the network administrator enters *ping 184.92.15.70* from the CFO's computer to test the connection. A successful *ping* shows that both computers are connected and the network is working between their computers. The problem is not a network problem, but is related to something else, such as the permission settings.

Some typical uses of *ping* include:

- Testing the connection at the host computer

- Testing the connection of a target computer

- Testing connectivity from one segment or network to another

- Testing access over a WAN connection, such as the Internet

- Testing to determine if a particular server is up and working on a local network or over a WAN connection, such as a Web server on the Internet

- Testing the time it takes for the *ping* communication to make a round trip from the source node to the destination and back

When you use the *ping* utility, besides reporting if the ping reached the target node, the command also gives you two valuable statistics to take a snapshot of the network performance. One statistic is the number of packets lost, which normally should be zero for a series of four or five pings.

Another statistic is the round-trip time for each ping, which is given in milliseconds (ms; millionth of a second). The *ping* utility also presents a summary of the round-trip times for several pings, providing the minimum time, the average time, and the maximum time, and for the Linux and Mac OS X operating systems, the standard deviation is given. The standard deviation is a numerical statistic that shows how spread out the overall round-trip time results are—a low number means each result in a series is very close to the other results in that series, whereas a high standard deviation means that each result is relatively spread out from other results. A high standard deviation can mean you should look into the network performance further to determine if there are problems causing such wide differences in round-trip times to the same destination. In Windows, the round-trip times are clearly presented and easy to understand. In Linux and Mac OS X they are presented in a shorthand manner, such as:

```
min/avg/max/mdev = 2.179/2.458/2.781/0.244 ms
```

where *mdev* is the standard deviation. In Activity 12-4 you use *ping* in Windows 7 or Windows Server 2008/Server 2008 R2. In Activity 12-5 you use *ping* in UNIX/Linux, and in Activity 12-6 you use *ping* in Mac OS X. Notice in these activities that information is displayed showing the time to make a round trip from your computer to the destination and back in milliseconds. This information provides one way to test the efficiency of a network.

Activity 12-4: Using *ping* in Windows 7 and Windows Server 2008/Server 2008 R2

Time Required: 5 minutes

Objective: Test a Windows 7 or Windows Server 2008/Server 2008 R2 connection using *ping*.

Description: In this activity you use the *ping* utility to test a network connection through Windows 7 or Windows Server 2008/Server2008 R2. Log on using your own account. You need a computer that is connected to a LAN or to the Internet. Obtain the IP address of another computer on the LAN or use your own IP address (see Activity 12-3 to obtain your IPv4 or IPv6 address from the Network Connection Details dialog box). You need a live network connection. If you have an Internet connection, you can choose to *ping* a Web site.

1. Click **Start**. Type **cmd** in the Search programs and files box (in Windows 7 or Server 2008 R2) or in the Start Search box in Windows Server 2008.

2. Click **cmd** under Programs to open the Command Prompt window.

3. Type **ping** and the IP address, such as ***ping 192.168.0.4*** and press **Enter** (see Figure 12-6). Also, if you know the name of the computer you are pinging try using the *ping* command plus the computer's name, such as ***ping ACCOUNTS***, and press **Enter**. Notice that there are four *pings* by default.

If you are unsure of an IP address to use, try using the loopback test address, 127.0.0.1, or use 10.0.2.1 (for *www.example.com*). Also note that instead of an IP address you can use a Web site, such as by entering *ping www.example.com*. However, some Web sites block *ping*.

4. Type **cls** and press **Enter** to clear the screen.

5. Leave the Command Prompt window open for the next Windows activity.

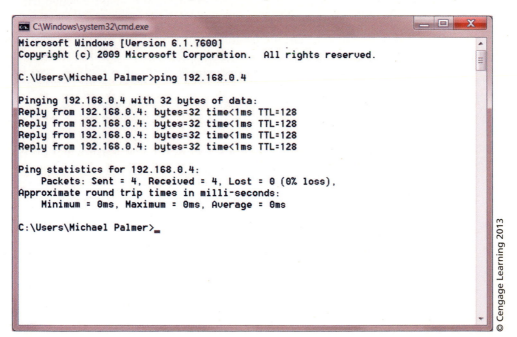

Figure 12-6   Using *ping* in Windows 7

Windows operating systems also include a command-line tool called *pathping*. This utility tests a connection for 25 seconds per hop and then prints statistics showing the round-trip time, number of lost packets, and the number of hops (each time a packet goes through a switch or router on its way to its destination is called a "hop"). If the path includes many hops, you may have to wait several minutes for the utility to finish.

Activity 12-5: Using *ping* in UNIX/Linux

Time Required: 5 minutes

Objective: Test a UNIX/Linux connection using *ping*.

Description: In this activity you use the *ping* utility to test a network connection on a computer running Linux. Log into your own account. You need a live network connection.

If you are using Fedora Live Media, be sure a network connection is configured via the Network Connections tool. Click **Activities**, click **Applications**, and click **Network Connections**. For a cabled connection, click **Wired** and use the **Add** or **Edit** (highlight the connection name) buttons to configure your connection. For a wireless connection, click **Wireless** and use the **Add** or **Edit** buttons to configure a connection (be sure to input the SSID on the Wireless tab and the security information, such as WPA & WPA2 Personal on the Wireless Security tab).

1. Open a terminal window from which to enter commands (in GNOME 3.x, click **Activities**, click **Applications**, and click **Terminal**).

2. Type **ping**, the IP address, and **-c5**, such as *ping 192.168.0.4 -c5*, and press **Enter** (see Figure 12-7). The reason for entering -c5 is to limit the number of pings to five. Otherwise in some UNIX/Linux systems, such as Fedora, the default is to keep pinging the node until you manually stop it or close the terminal window. Another way to use the *ping* command is to enter a domain name with it. If you have an Internet connection, type **ping www.redhat.com -c5** or **ping redhat.com -c5** to test your connection to the Red Hat Web site.

If you are unsure of an IP address to use, try using the loopback test address, 127.0.0.1, or use 10.0.2.1 (for *www.example.com*). Also, note that you can enter *ping www.example.com*. However, some Web sites now block *ping*.

3. Type **clear** and press **Enter** to clear the screen.

4. Leave the terminal window open for the next Linux activity.

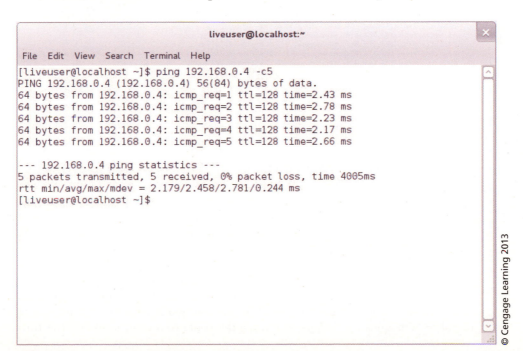

```
                            liveuser@localhost:~                          ×

File  Edit  View  Search  Terminal  Help
[liveuser@localhost ~]$ ping 192.168.0.4 -c5
PING 192.168.0.4 (192.168.0.4) 56(84) bytes of data.
64 bytes from 192.168.0.4: icmp_req=1 ttl=128 time=2.43 ms
64 bytes from 192.168.0.4: icmp_req=2 ttl=128 time=2.78 ms
64 bytes from 192.168.0.4: icmp_req=3 ttl=128 time=2.23 ms
64 bytes from 192.168.0.4: icmp_req=4 ttl=128 time=2.17 ms
64 bytes from 192.168.0.4: icmp_req=5 ttl=128 time=2.66 ms

--- 192.168.0.4 ping statistics ---
5 packets transmitted, 5 received, 0% packet loss, time 4005ms
rtt min/avg/max/mdev = 2.179/2.458/2.781/0.244 ms
[liveuser@localhost ~]$
```

Figure 12-7   Using *ping* in Fedora

Activity 12-6: Using *ping* in Mac OS X

Time Required: 5 minutes

Objective: Test a Mac OS X Snow Leopard or Lion connection using *ping*.

Description: In this activity you use the *ping* utility to test a network connection on a computer running Mac OS X Snow Leopard or Lion. The *ping* utility is used through the Network Utility. Log in to your own account. You need a live network connection.

1. If Finder is not open, click **Finder** in the Dock or click an open area on the desktop.

2. Click **Go** in the menu bar and click **Utilities**.

3. In the Utilities window, double-click **Network Utility**.

4. In the Network Utility window, click the **Ping** tab.

5. In the Enter the network address to ping text box, enter an IP address to ping, such as **192.168.0.4**. In the Send only ____ pings box, enter **5**. Click the **Ping** button (see Figure 12-8).

 If you are unsure of an IP address to use, try using the loopback test address, 127.0.0.1, or use 10.0.2.1 (for *www.example.com*). Also note that instead of an IP address you can use a Web site, such as by entering *www.example.com*. However, some Web sites now block *ping*.

6. Leave the Network Utility window open for the next Mac OS X activity.

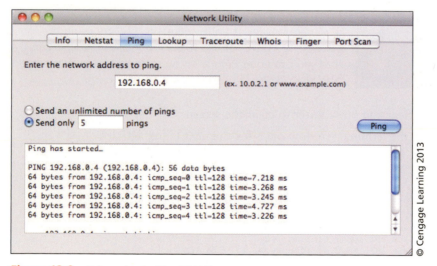

Figure 12-8   Using *ping* in Mac OS X Lion

Using *tracert* or *traceroute* to Test a Network Connection

Windows 7, Windows Server 2008/Server 2008 R2, UNIX/Linux systems, and Mac OS X Snow Leopard and Lion all support the use of the *tracert* or *traceroute* command-line utility to trace a network connection. In Windows systems this is entered at the command line as *tracert*, and in UNIX/Linux it is *traceroute*. In Mac OS X, you can use the *traceroute* command from a GUI window in the Network Utility.

The results of the *tracert/traceroute* utility show the number of hops between two nodes and the nodes through which the communication goes to reach the destination. This utility also shows the time it takes to reach the destination, so you can monitor the speed of communications between different points on one or more networks. Figure 12-9 illustrates the *tracert* command in Windows 7 when used to trace the route to a destination on the Internet. The *tracert/*

traceroute utility employs UDP instead of TCP and **Internet Control Message Protocol (ICMP)**. ICMP is used for network error reporting particularly through routers, showing whether or not a packet successfully reaches its destination.

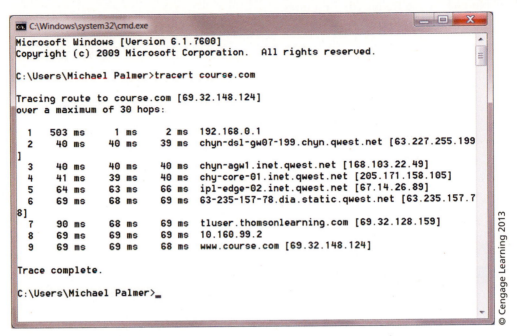

```
C:\Windows\system32\cmd.exe                                          ☐  ☐  ✕

Microsoft Windows [Version 6.1.7600]
Copyright (c) 2009 Microsoft Corporation.  All rights reserved.

C:\Users\Michael Palmer>tracert course.com

Tracing route to course.com [69.32.148.124]
over a maximum of 30 hops:

  1    503 ms      1 ms      2 ms  192.168.0.1
  2     40 ms     40 ms     39 ms  chyn-dsl-gw07-199.chyn.qwest.net [63.227.255.199
]
  3     40 ms     40 ms     40 ms  chyn-agw1.inet.qwest.net [168.103.22.49]
  4     41 ms     39 ms     40 ms  chy-core-01.inet.qwest.net [205.171.158.105]
  5     64 ms     63 ms     66 ms  ipl-edge-02.inet.qwest.net [67.14.26.89]
  6     69 ms     68 ms     69 ms  63-235-157-78.dia.static.qwest.net [63.235.157.7
8]
  7     90 ms     68 ms     69 ms  tluser.thomsonlearning.com [69.32.128.159]
  8     69 ms     69 ms     69 ms  10.160.99.2
  9     69 ms     69 ms     68 ms  www.course.com [69.32.148.124]

Trace complete.

C:\Users\Michael Palmer>_
```

Figure 12-9   Using *tracert* in Windows 7

The *tracert/traceroute* utility is useful for determining the number of hops designed into a network from one point to another, indicating the efficiency of communications. It can also signal problem areas, such as points of congestion between one router and another. Of course, if a network path is down, it provides an indication of this problem. *tracert/traceroute* typically stops at a firewall, if one exists on the path between the source and the destination. This makes *tracert/traceroute* one way to test the security of a firewall. Activity 12-7 enables you to use *tracert* in Windows 7 or Windows Server 2008/Server 2008 R2. Activities 12-8 and 12-9 employ *traceroute* in UNIX/Linux and Mac OS X Snow Leopard or Lion, respectively.

Real-Life Networking

Utilities such as *ping* and *tracert/traceroute* have a useful place in your toolbox, but be careful about overusing them. In one business a network analyst showed the IT director, who was not experienced in networking, how to use the tools. The IT director ran both utilities very often while in his office and would frequently call the network analyst to discuss the results. The IT director's actions often kept the network analyst from his work, added traffic to the network, and were not productive in terms of spotting problems.

Activity 12-7: Using *tracert* in Windows 7 and Windows Server 2008/Server 2008 R2

Time Required: 5 minutes
Objective: Determine the number of hops between two nodes using *tracert*.

Description: In this activity you use the Windows *tracert* utility to test a network connection and determine the number of hops between two computers.

1. Open the Command Prompt window if it is not already open.

2. Type **tracert** along with an IP address (or you can use a host or domain name), such as **tracert 192.168.0.1**, and press **Enter**.

3. How many hops were needed to reach the destination?

4. Type **cls** and press **Enter**.

5. Leave the Command Prompt window open for the next Windows activity.

Activity 12-8: Using *traceroute* in UNIX/Linux

Time Required: 5 minutes
Objective: Determine the number of hops between two nodes using *traceroute*.

Description: In this activity you use the UNIX/Linux *traceroute* command to test a network connection and determine the number of hops between two nodes.

1. Access the command line or open a terminal window, if one is not already open.

2. Type **traceroute** with an IP address or host or domain name, such as **traceroute 192.168.0.1**, and press **Enter** (see Figure 12-10).

3. How many hops are between the source and the destination?

4. Type **clear** and press **Enter**.

5. Leave the terminal window open for the next Linux activity.

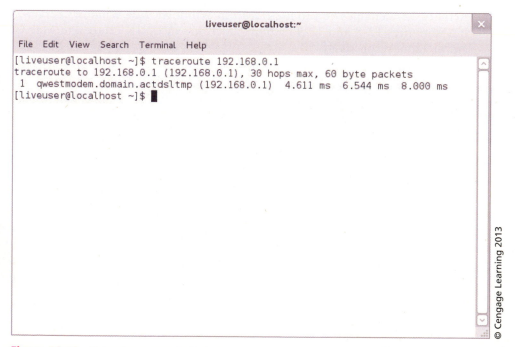

Figure 12-10 Using *traceroute* in Fedora

Activity 12-9: Using *traceroute* in Mac OS X Snow Leopard or Lion

Time Required: 5 minutes

Objective: Determine the number of hops between two nodes using *traceroute* in Mac OS X Snow Leopard or Lion.

Description: In this activity you use the Mac OS X *traceroute* capability to test a network connection and determine the number of hops between two nodes.

1. Open the Network Utility window if it is not already open (refer to Activity 12-6).

2. Click the **Traceroute** tab in the Network Utility window.

3. In the text box for Enter the network address to trace an Internet route to, type a network address, such as **192.168.0.1**. Click the **Trace** button to view the results as shown in Figure 12-11.

To trace a Web site with many hops, try entering *www.apple.com*, if you have an Internet connection.

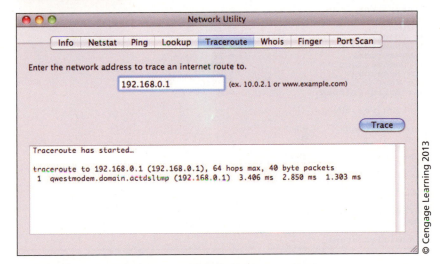

Figure 12-11 Using *traceroute* in Mac OS X Lion

4. How many hops are between the source and the destination?

5. Leave the Network Utility window open for the next Mac OS X activity.

Using *netstat*

netstat is a command-line utility available in Windows 7, Windows Server 2008/Server 2008 R2, UNIX/Linux, and Mac OS X Snow Leopard and Lion for use in gathering statistics and information about TCP/IP communications on a computer. The network communications information you can view through *netstat* includes:

- Protocol communications through TCP and UDP
- Network connections established by the host computer
- TCP and UDP ports in use
- Routing table information
- Information about computers remotely logged onto the host computer
- Multicast participation
- Data and communication errors

A user or server administrator might use *netstat* to monitor ports by listening for activity, because activity represents open ports. In another example, consider a business that has four servers used for distributing file access. One of the servers seems to operate more slowly than the others. The server administrator can use *netstat* to monitor incoming and outgoing traffic handled by that server. If the traffic is slower than the other servers and is experiencing more errors, this might be an indication that the server's NIC is malfunctioning or that there is a problem with the server's network segment. In another example, a server administrator might regularly use *netstat* with the *-s* option to monitor a server during busy and light traffic times to get an idea of the typical number of packets sent at those times (see Figure 12-12).

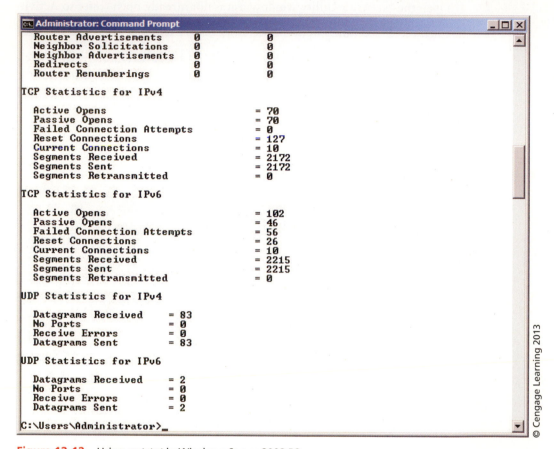

Figure 12-12 Using *netstat* in Windows Server 2008 R2

In both Windows and UNIX/Linux, *netstat* is used with switches that enable you to view specific network data. Table 12-1 presents commonly used *netstat* switches.

Table 12-1 Commonly used *netstat* switches for Windows and UNIX/Linux

netstat Switch	Description for Windows	Description for UNIX/Linux
-a	Displays statistics for all ports, including those that are listening or not listening	Displays statistics for all ports, including those that are listening or not listening
-c	N/A	Displays statistics every second
-e	Displays statistics for Ethernet communications	Displays extended detail and in most UNIX/Linux distributions is the same as using *netstat* without a switch
-p	Is used with a protocol name to display connection information about that protocol, such as *netstat -p TCP*	Shows programs related to ports (sockets)
-l	N/A	Displays all ports (sockets) that are listening
-n	Displays communications via IP addresses and port numbers	Displays communications via IP addresses and port numbers

Table 12-1 Commonly used *netstat* switches for Windows and UNIX/Linux (*continued*)

netstat Switch	Description for Windows	Description for UNIX/Linux
-r	Shows the routing table	Shows the routing table
-s	Shows all kinds of communications statistics including errors	Shows all kinds of communications statistics including errors
/?	Displays *netstat* online documentation	N/A (for *netstat* online documentation enter *man netstat* at the command line)

© Cengage Learning 2013

Instead of switches, Mac OS X Snow Leopard and Lion offer *netstat* options through the Network Utility window. These options include:

- Display routing table information (similar to *netstat -r*)
- Display comprehensive network statistics for each protocol (similar to *netstat -s*)
- Display multicast information (does not have an exact *netstat* switch equivalent)
- Display the state of all current socket connections (similar to *netstat -a*)

Try Activity 12-10 to use *netstat* in Windows 7 and Windows Server 2008/Server 2008 R2. In Activities 12-11 and 12-12, you use *netstat* in UNIX/Linux and in Mac OS X Snow Leopard or Lion.

Activity 12-10: Using *netstat* in Windows 7 and Windows Server 2008/Server 2008 R2

Time Required: 10 minutes

Objective: Use *netstat* to gather network performance statistics in Windows 7 and Windows Server 2008/Server 2008 R2.

Description: Through a range of switches, *netstat* offers many ways to view network performance statistics. In this activity you use *netstat* to monitor a network through Windows 7 or Windows Server 2008/Server 2008 R2.

1. Open the Command Prompt window if it is not already open.

2. Type **netstat** -a and press **Enter** to display information about all ports. For what protocols is information displayed?

3. Type **netstat** -s and press **Enter** (refer to Figure 12-12). What categories of statistics do you see? Are any communications errors reported?

4. Close the Command Prompt window.

Activity 12-11: Using *netstat* in UNIX/Linux

Time Required: 10 minutes

Objective: Use *netstat* to gather network performance statistics in UNIX/Linux.

Description: The way in which *netstat* statistics are displayed varies a little between Windows and UNIX/Linux systems. In this activity, you use *netstat* in Fedora Linux.

1. Access the command line or open a terminal window, if one is not already open.

2. Type **netstat** -a and press **Enter**. This display is somewhat different from the one for the same command in Windows 7 and Windows Server 2008/Server 2008 R2, but both provide information related to protocols in use and show the state, such as LISTENING or CONNECTED, in UNIX/Linux (see Figure 12-13).

3. Type **netstat** -s and press **Enter**. What categories of statistics do you see in the display? Do you see any communications errors?

4. Close the terminal window.

```
                        liveuser@localhost:~                                    x

 File   Edit   View   Search   Terminal   Help
unix   3        [ ]           STREAM      CONNECTED      13663
unix   2        [ ]           DGRAM                      13661
unix   3        [ ]           STREAM      CONNECTED      13674    /var/run/dbus/system_bu
s_socket
unix   3        [ ]           STREAM      CONNECTED      13654
unix   2        [ ]           DGRAM                      13651
unix   3        [ ]           STREAM      CONNECTED      13671    /var/run/dbus/system_bu
s_socket
unix   3        [ ]           STREAM      CONNECTED      13625
unix   3        [ ]           STREAM      CONNECTED      13597
unix   3        [ ]           STREAM      CONNECTED      13596
unix   2        [ ]           DGRAM                      13593
unix   2        [ ]           DGRAM                      13586
unix   3        [ ]           STREAM      CONNECTED      13668    /var/run/dbus/system_bu
s_socket
unix   3        [ ]           STREAM      CONNECTED      13123
unix   3        [ ]           STREAM      CONNECTED      13665    /var/run/dbus/system_bu
s_socket
unix   3        [ ]           STREAM      CONNECTED      13366
unix   3        [ ]           DGRAM                      9186
unix   3        [ ]           DGRAM                      9185
unix   2        [ ]           DGRAM                      8185
unix   2        [ ]           DGRAM                      8184
[liveuser@localhost ~]$ ▮
```

© Cengage Learning 2013

Figure 12-13   Using *netstat -a* in Fedora

Activity 12-12: Using *netstat* in Mac OS X Snow Leopard or Lion

Time Required: 5 minutes

Objective: Use *netstat* to gather network performance statistics in Mac OS X Snow Leopard or Lion.

Description: In this activity you use the Mac OS X *netstat* capability to display network performance statistics in Mac OS X Snow Leopard or Lion.

1. Open the Network Utility window if it is not already open (refer to Activity 12-6).

2. Click the **Netstat** tab in the Network Utility window.

3. Select **Display comprehensive network statistics for each protocol,** if it is not already selected. Click the **Netstat** button to view the network performance statistics as shown in Figure 12-14. For what protocols is information displayed?

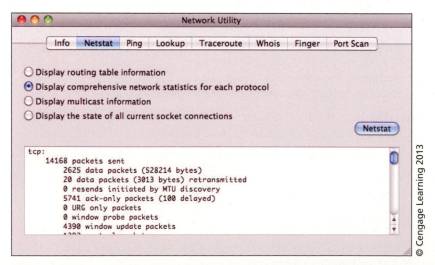

Figure 12-14   Viewing network performance statistics via *netstat* in Mac OS X Lion

4. On the Netstat tab, select **Display the state of all current socket connections** and click the **Netstat** button. For what protocols is information displayed? Also, notice the state information, such as ESTABLISHED or LISTEN.

5. Click **Network Utility** in the menu bar and click **Quit Network Utility**.

6. Close any remaining open windows.

Using *nslookup*   Some types of Domain Name System (DNS) questions can be answered by using the *nslookup* command-line utility. You learned about DNS in Chapter 3, "Using Network Communication Protocols." DNS is a TCP/IP service that converts a computer or domain name to an IP address or that converts an IP address to a computer or domain name.

The *nslookup* utility is available in Windows 7, Windows Server 2008/Server 2008 R2, and UNIX/Linux. Mac OS X Snow Leopard and Lion offer a similar tool in the Network Utility window through the Lookup tab. Actions you can perform using *nslookup* include:

- Verifying that a DNS server is online and working

- Determining the host name of a device if you know the IP address or determining the IP address if you know the host name

- Determining the primary DNS server on a network

- Querying the DNS database for information, such as a list of host names and IP addresses (not available in Mac OS X)

In Windows and UNIX/Linux systems, for example (including from the Mac OS X Darwin terminal window), you might use the command *nslookup ftp.gnu.org* to determine if the ftp.gnu .org FTP site is working and to view its IP address, or you can use the command to test your own network. In another example, you can use *nslookup* in an interactive mode by simply entering *nslookup*. Alternatively, you see an *nslookup* command-line prompt (>) at which you can issue commands. In Windows 7 or Windows Server 2008/Server 2008 R2, type "?" (don't include the quotation marks) at the *nslookup* command-line prompt and press Enter to view the commands you can use to query the contents of a DNS server. In UNIX/Linux, you can find out about interactive commands by entering *man nslookup* (before you use *nslookup*) at the regular command line to see the manual pages for the *nslookup* command. For example, some versions of *nslookup* support a *finger* interactive command to view information about a user. Other versions enable you to enter a host name to find out more about that host.

In Mac OS X Snow Leopard and Lion, the Lookup tab in the Network Utility window includes options to select. For example, when you enter the host name of a node, you can select to view the Internet address of a Web site or node or the CPU/OS type. You can also look up default information about a DNS server by entering its Web site or domain name.

Using Performance Monitor in Windows Server

One of the most versatile tools used to help detect and troubleshoot network and performance issues via Windows Server is Performance Monitor. **Performance Monitor** can be used to monitor server components such as hard disks, memory, and the processor. It can also be used to monitor network performance and network protocols, such as IP and ICMP. For example, you might monitor the network interface on a server to track the number of bytes or packets received. Another option is to monitor IPv4 traffic to assess the number of datagrams or fragmented packets. Both monitoring options enable you to determine if there are problems with the server, other computers, or network devices on the same segment as the server.

Capturing Data Using Performance Monitor   Performance Monitor is opened from the Administrative Tools menu by clicking Performance Monitor (in Windows Server 2008 R2) or Reliability and Performance Monitor (in Windows Server 2008) to view the console screen, which enables you to open Performance Monitor from the tree under Performance in the left pane of the Performance Monitor window (see Figure 12-15). The default view is in the line mode, showing a grid that you use for graphing activities on a server. To begin gathering data for your analysis, select one or more objects to monitor. A Performance Monitor object may be memory, the processor, the network interface, or IPv4, for example. You can monitor one or several objects at the same time. Table 12-2 presents examples of network objects to monitor.

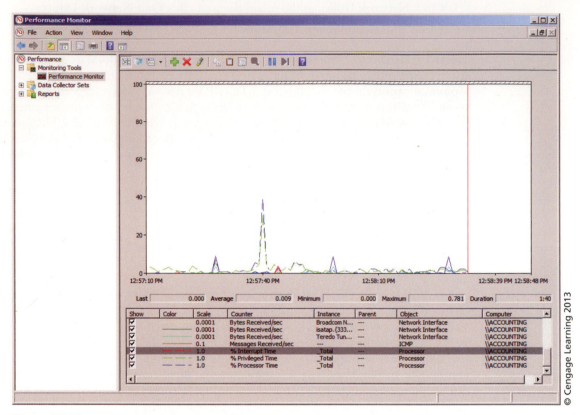

Figure 12-15   Performance Monitor in Windows Server 2008/Server 2008 R2

Table 12-2   Performance Monitor performance objects

Performance Object	Description
Network Interface	Monitors bytes sent and received, bandwidth, output queue length, and packet traffic
ICMP	Monitors ICMPv4 message traffic
ICMPv6	Monitors ICMPv6 message traffic
IPv4	Monitors IPv4 datagrams and fragmented communications
IPv6	Monitors IPv6 datagrams and fragmented communications
IPSec Driver	Monitors IPSec traffic, security associations, key exchange operations, and other IPSec activities
IPSec IKEv1 IPv4	Monitors IPSec security association list information, authentication failures, negotiation failures, and other information associated with IPv4 communications
IPSec IKEv1 IPv6	Monitors IPSec security association list information, authentication failures, negotiation failures, and other information associated with IPv6 communications
TCPv4	Monitors TCPv4 connection resets and segment traffic
TCPv6	Monitors TCPv6 connection resets and segment traffic
UDPv4	Monitors UDPv4 datagram traffic
UDPv6	Monitors UDPv6 datagram traffic

© Cengage Learning 2013

For each object, there are one or more counters that can be monitored. A **counter** is an indicator of a quantity of the object that can be measured in some unit, such as percent, bytes sent per second, or number of reset connections, depending on what is appropriate to the object. For example, the TCPv4 counter tracks the following:

- Connections Active
- Connections Reset
- Segments Received/sec
- Segments Retransmitted/sec
- Segments Sent/sec
- Segments/sec

 A TCPv4 segment is essentially a TCPv4 frame consisting of the frame header and data payload. Refer to Figure 3-2 in Chapter 3.

If you monitor using Connections Reset and Segments Retransmitted/sec, this can give you information about whether there is a network problem, such as a defective switch. In another situation, you might be gathering benchmarks about typical network traffic and monitor Segments Received/sec and Segments Sent/sec.

Sometimes there are instances associated with a counter. An **instance** exists when there are different elements to monitor, such as individual processes when you use the process object, or when a process contains multiple threads or runs subprocesses under it for the thread object. Other examples are when there are two or more NICs or WNICs, multiple disks, or multiple processors to monitor. In many cases, each instance is identified by a unique number for the ease of monitoring.

Performance Monitor offers several buttons to use its features and to set up the display options. After the tool is opened, click the Add button (represented by a plus sign) on the button bar just above the tracking window (refer to Figure 12-15). This opens the Add Counters dialog box (see Figure 12-16) from which to select objects to monitor, counters, and instances.

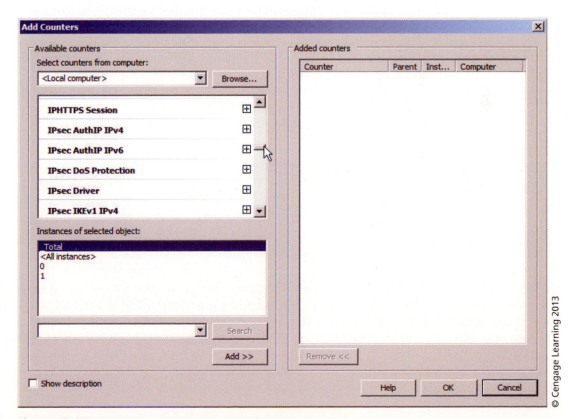

Figure 12-16   Add Counters dialog box in Performance Monitor

You can monitor one or more objects at a time as a way to get a better understanding of how particular objects interact, for example, by monitoring both TCPv4 and IPv4. Also, you can monitor the same object using different combinations of counters. You stop monitoring by clicking the Delete button (represented by an X) on the button bar.

There are three views you can use when monitoring objects: line, histogram bar, and report.

- The line mode is a running line chart of the object that shows distinct peaks and valleys. For example, when you use the line mode and monitor for different objects, a line with a unique color, such as red or green, represents each object.

- The histogram bar mode is a running bar chart that shows each object as a bar in a different color.

- The report mode simply provides numbers on a screen, which you can capture to put in a report.

Each of these options is set from the *Change graph type* button in the button bar just above the tracking window. You can change the view mode at any time by clicking the appropriate selection.

Each object and counter combination is displayed using a different color, so they are easily identified. In Figure 12-15 the graph is monitoring Bytes Received/Sec on three different network interfaces—distinguished by instances for three different network interfaces in the computer. One network interface counter is tracked using a yellow line graph, one is in blue, and the third is tracked in a green line graph. The counters are shown at the bottom of the screen with a key to indicate the graphing color for each one. When you click one of these counters, the status information just above the counters shows the following for that counter:

- *Last*: The current value of the monitored activity

- *Average*: The average value of the monitored activity for the elapsed time

- *Maximum*: The maximum value of the activity over the elapsed time

- *Minimum*: The minimum value of the activity over the elapsed time

- *Duration*: The amount of time to complete a full graph of the activity

Performance Monitor is a particularly valuable tool for a network that uses Windows servers. Because you can monitor several things at once, you have a better chance for pinpointing a particular problem. For example, a common problem is to assume that if access to a server is slow, this is caused by a slow network. You might spend hours looking for a network problem, such as a bad NIC, WNIC, switch, or cable. In reality the problem might be that the server's processor is overloaded for the type of work expected. Slow response by the server often looks like slow response by the network. Try Activity 12-13 to become familiar with Performance Monitor and then Activity 12-14 to learn how to monitor for a processor and network problem at the same time.

Real-Life Networking

Payroll clerks in a university experienced frequent wait times when accessing a server to answer paycheck questions. Out of frustration, the payroll supervisor called a network analyst to report that the network was extremely slow. The network analyst spent several days in the payroll office testing workstations and in other parts of the building tracing through network cable and devices looking for problems. After finding no network problems, he finally checked the server and found that its processor was frequently overburdened. The problem was fixed by implementing a server with a faster processor.

Activity 12-13: Exploring Performance Monitor in Windows Server 2008/Server 2008 R2

Time Required: 15 minutes

Objective: Use Performance Monitor to gather network performance statistics in Windows Server 2008/Server 2008 R2.

Description: This activity gives you an opportunity to practice viewing objects and counters in Performance Monitor in Windows Server 2008/Server 2008 R2. Log on using an account with Administrator privileges.

1. Click **Start,** point to **Administrative Tools,** and click **Performance Monitor** (in Windows Server 2008 R2) or **Reliability and Performance Monitor** (in Windows Server 2008).

2. In the tree in the left pane under Monitoring Tools (click the **+ plus sign** in front of Monitoring Tools, if necessary to view the items under it), click **Performance Monitor** (see Figure 12-17).

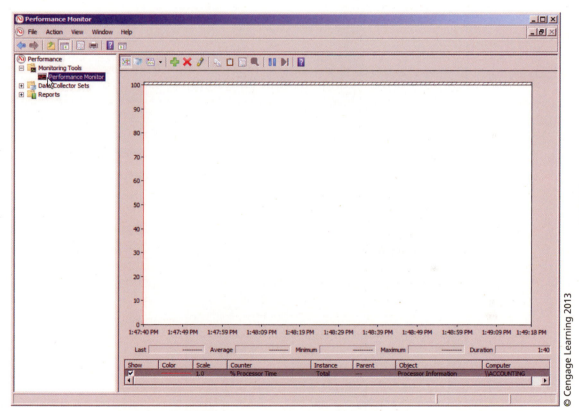

Figure 12-17   Opening Performance Monitor in Windows Server 2008 R2

3. Move your pointer over each of the buttons on the button bar to view its description.

4. If there currently are performance objects started by default, select each one at the bottom of the right pane in the Performance Monitor window and click the **X** in the button bar (see Figure 12-18) to turn off the objects.

5. Click the **Add** button (a **+ plus sign**) in the button bar in the right pane. What computer is selected by default for monitoring? How would you monitor activity on a different computer? Record your observations.

6. Click the down arrow in the box listing the objects. Scroll through the options.

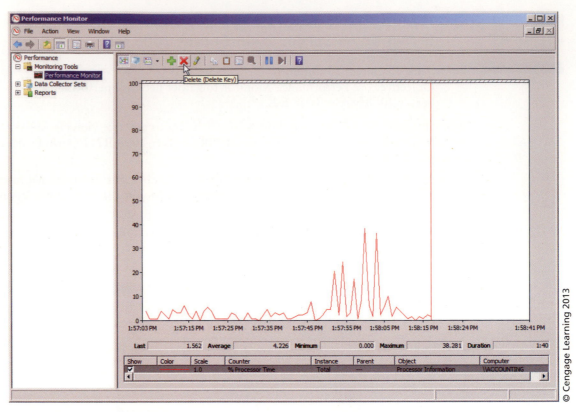

Figure 12-18   Deleting a performance object in Performance Monitor

7. Click the **+ plus sign** for **IPv4**. Scroll to view the counters associated with the IPv4 object.

8. Next, select **Datagrams/sec** as the counter.

9. Click **Add** (see Figure 12-19).

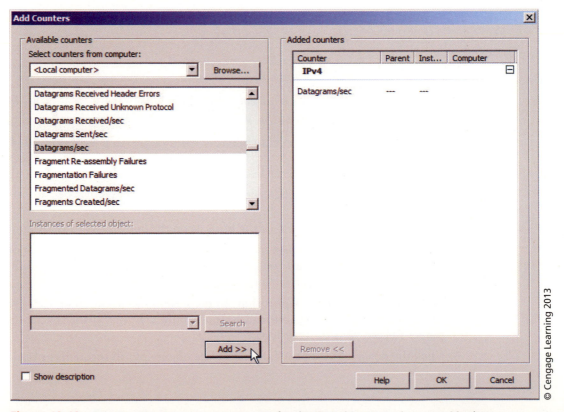

Figure 12-19   Selecting the Datagrams/sec counter for the IPv4 object in Performance Monitor

10. Scroll to the TCPv4 object. Click the **+ plus sign** for **TCPv4**. Click the **Segments/sec** counter. Click the checkbox in front of **Show description** near the bottom of the Add Counters dialog box and notice the description of this counter.

11. Click **Add**.

12. Click **OK** in the Add Counters dialog box.

13. Monitor the IPv4 and TCPv4 activity for several minutes.

14. Click each object at the bottom of the right pane and use the **X** (**Delete**) button in the button bar to remove both performance objects.

15. Leave the Performance Monitor window open for the next activity.

Activity 12-14: Monitoring for Network and Processor Problems

Time Required: 15 minutes or more
Objective: Learn how to monitor for network and processor bottlenecks.

Description: In this activity you use Performance Monitor in Windows Server 2008/Server 2008 R2 to monitor for a network or processor bottleneck.

1. Make sure that Performance Monitor is already open, and if not, open it to display Performance Monitor (refer to Activity 12-13).

2. If any object/counter combinations are currently running, stop each one by clicking the object/counter combination in the lower-right part of the window and then clicking the **X** (**Delete**) button in the button bar at the top of the right pane in the Performance Monitor window.

3. In the Performance Monitor window, click the **+ plus sign** (**Add**) button in the button bar to add counters.

4. In the Add Counters dialog box, click the **+ plus sign** for **Processor**.

5. Click **% Processor Time**. Leave **_Total** as the default for instances. What information does this counter provide for the Processor object? How would you find out, if you didn't know? Record your observations. Note that when you monitor % Processor Time, sustained values of 80–85% or higher indicate a heavily loaded machine; consistent readings of 95% or higher may indicate a machine that needs to have its load reduced or its capabilities increased (with a new machine, a motherboard upgrade, or an additional or faster CPU).

6. Click **Add**.

7. For the Processor object, click **% Interrupt Time** as the counter and leave **_Total** as the instance. Click **Add**. Note that the % Interrupt Time is useful to monitor because it measures the amount of the processor's time that is used to service hardware requests from devices such as the NIC or WNIC, disk, DVD/CD-ROM drives, and USB peripherals. A high rate of interrupts when compared to your baseline statistics indicates a possible hardware problem, such as a malfunctioning NIC—which is another reason why a server's response over a network might be slow.

8. Under the Processor object, click **Interrupts/sec**. Leave **_Total** as the instance and click **Add**. This counter measures the average number of times per second that the CPU is interrupted by devices requesting immediate processing. Network traffic and system clock activity establish a kind of background count against which this number should be compared. Problem levels occur when a malfunctioning device begins to generate spurious

interrupts or when excessive network traffic overwhelms a network adapter. In both cases, this usually creates a count that is five times or more greater than a lightly loaded baseline situation.

9. Scroll to the **System** object and click its **+ plus sign**.

10. Under the System object click **Processor Queue Length**. Click **Add**. This counter for the system object measures the number of execution threads waiting for access to a CPU. If this value is frequently over 4 on a single CPU, it indicates a need to distribute this machine's load across other machines or the need to increase its capabilities, usually by adding an additional CPU or by upgrading the machine or the motherboard. When the value is over 2 per each CPU on multiple-processor systems, you should consider adding processors or increasing the processor speed.

11. Scroll to the **Network Interface** object and click its **+ plus sign**.

12. Under the Network Interface object, click **Output Queue Length**. Notice the items listed in the *Instances of selected object* box. If your computer has more than one NIC/WNIC, two or more instances may be listed. Click an instance that represents an active NIC/WNIC in the computer, such as ***Broadcom NetXtreme Gigabit Ethernet*** (check with your instructor if you are unsure what to select, or choose the first one listed after <All instances>). Click **Add**. This counter shows the number of packets waiting to be sent as output to the network. If this number is frequently over 2, there is a bottleneck, and it may suggest there is a problem with the NIC/WNIC.

13. Scroll to find the **IPv4** object and click its **+ plus sign**.

14. Under IPv4, select **Datagrams/sec**. Click **Add**. This counter enables you to view the frequency of IPv4 traffic into and out of the computer's NIC/WNIC. The Add Counters dialog box should now look similar to that shown in Figure 12-20.

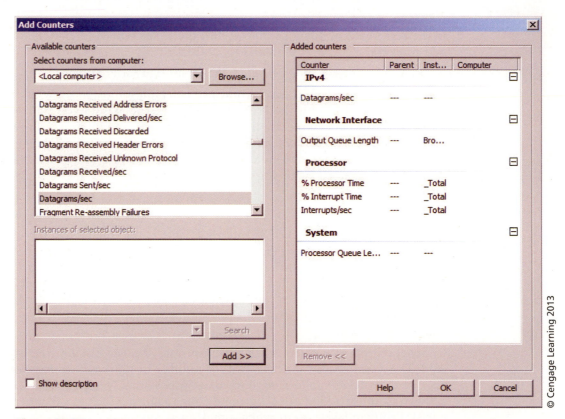

Figure 12-20   Add Counters dialog box with counters selected

15. Click **OK** in the Add Counters dialog box.

16. Monitor the system for several minutes to determine if there are any processor problems, signs of a NIC/WNIC problem, or very busy network traffic.

17. In the button bar, click the down arrow for the **Change graph type** button and click **Histogram bar** (see Figure 12-21) in the shortcut menu.

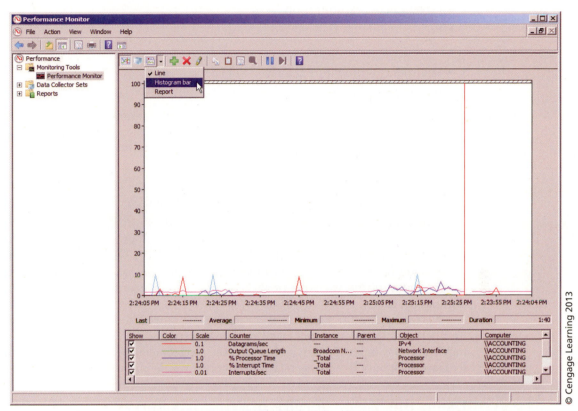

© Cengage Learning 2013

Figure 12-21   Selecting to view a histogram bar display while in the line mode in Performance Monitor

18. Click the down arrow for the **Change graph type** button and click **Report** in the shortcut menu.

19. Close the Performance Monitor window when you are finished.

Real-Life Networking

Avoid leaving Performance Monitor on for too long, or monitoring from multiple servers, because your monitoring creates network traffic and may be the cause of a slow server or network. One company introduced a new server and decided to benchmark its response capabilities. Four different network and server analysts used Performance Monitor at the same time from different servers to monitor the new server. Not surprisingly, the new server's actual response capabilities were not measured because the server was burdened by the intense monitoring.

Using Network Monitor

Besides Performance Monitor, Windows Server computers can run **Network Monitor**, which is not included on the Windows Server 2008/Server 2008 R2 installation DVD, but can be downloaded from Microsoft's Download Center (found at *www.microsoft.com/download/en/default.aspx* at this writing). Network Monitor is a basic network analyzer that can provide the following information:

- Percent network utilization
- Frames and bytes transported per second
- Network station statistics
- Statistics captured during a given time period
- Information concerning transmissions per second
- Information about broadcast, unicast, and multicast transmissions
- NIC statistics
- Error data
- Addresses of network stations
- Network computers running Network Monitor and Network Monitor Driver

When you run Network Monitor to monitor traffic across a network, it detects many forms of network traffic and captures packets and frames for analysis and reporting by Network Monitor. All packets and frames that pass through the server's NIC or WNIC are monitored (although not all contents are viewed) so that it is possible to determine basic information about the network, such as the amount of traffic, the types of packets, and the source and destination addresses of computers transmitting data.

Network Monitor supports event management, which enables a server administrator to set up filters to capture a certain event or type of network activity. For example, the administrator may want to watch only activity between the server and a specific workstation. Another possibility is to track only IP activity related to Internet traffic into the server.

Using the SNMP Service in Windows Server

As you learned in Chapter 3, the Simple Network Management Protocol (SNMP) is used for network management on TCP/IP-based networks. It provides administrators with a way of centrally managing workstations, servers, hubs, and routers from a single computer running management software. SNMP can be used for the following:

- Configuring network devices
- Monitoring the performance of a network
- Locating network problems
- Monitoring network usage

 Refer to Chapter 3 to review SNMPv1, SNMPv2, and SNMPv3 so that you are familiar with the differences between all of these versions.

SNMP provides network management services through agents and management systems. The SNMP management system (a computer running management software) sends and requests information from an SNMP agent. The SNMP agent (any computer or network device running SNMP agent software) responds to the management system's request for information.

(In Activity 3-9 in Chapter 3, you configured Windows 7 as an SNMP agent.) The management systems and agents can be grouped into communities for administrative and security purposes. Only those management systems and agents in the same community can communicate with each other.

When there is a network management station set up on a network, the following Microsoft operating systems and components are compatible with SNMP:

- Windows Server 2008/Server 2008 R2 servers
- Windows Server 2003 and Windows 2000 Server servers
- Windows 7 and Vista workstations
- Windows XP and 2000 workstations
- WINS (Windows Internet Naming) servers
- DHCP servers
- Internet Information Services (IIS) servers (providing Web services)
- Microsoft RAS (Remote Access Services) and VPN servers

If you use a network management system to monitor network and SNMP-compliant devices, consider installing the SNMP service. Another reason to install the SNMP service is if you have obtained and are running Network Monitor on a Windows Server, because Network Monitor can use SNMP to help monitor a network. Activities 12-15 and 12-16 are optional activities that show you how to install and configure the SNMP service in Windows Server 2008/Server 2008 R2.

 At this writing, Windows Server 2008/Server 2008 R2 do not come with a full-fledged SNMP network management system application. However, the Windows Management Instrumentation (WMI) Software Development Kit (SDK) enables SNMP applications to access SNMP data.

 12

 ### Activity 12-15: Installing the SNMP Service in Windows Server 2008/Server 2008 R2

Time Required: 10 minutes
Objective: Install SNMP in Windows Server 2008/Server 2008 R2.

Description: In this optional activity, you use Server Manager to install the SNMP Services feature in Windows Server 2008/Server 2008 R2. You need to log on using an account that has Administrator privileges.

 TCP/IP must be installed in an operating system, such as Windows Server 2008/Server 2008 R2 before you can install SNMP services.

1. If Server Manager is not already open by default, click **Start,** point to **Administrative Tools,** and click **Server Manager.**
2. Scroll to the **Features Summary** section and click **Add Features** (see Figure 12-22).

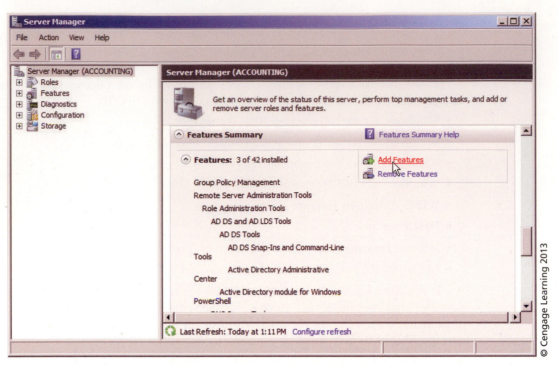

Figure 12-22   Selecting Add Features in Server Manager in Windows Server 2008 R2

3. Click the checkbox for **SNMP Services**. Click **Next** (see Figure 12-23).

4. Click **Install**.

5. Click **Close**.

6. Leave Server Manager open for the next activity.

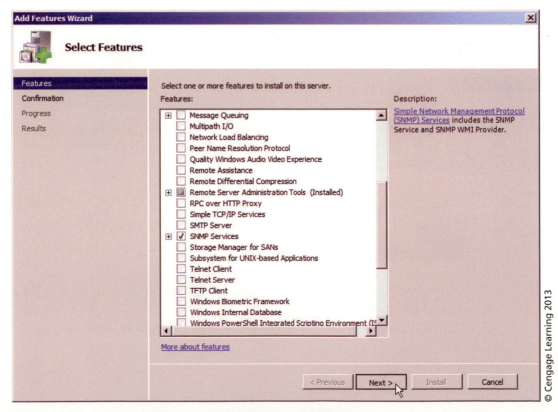

Figure 12-23   Selecting SNMP Services in Windows Server 2008 R2

After you install the SNMP service, make sure that it is started, it is set to start automatically, and it is set up to have a community of hosts that share use of the service and a community name, which is similar to having a rudimentary password used among the hosts. The default community name is "public." Try Activity 12-16 to configure the SNMP service in Windows Server 2008/Server 2008 R2.

Activity 12-16: Configuring the SNMP Service in Windows Server

Time Required: 10 minutes

Objective: Learn how to configure the SNMP service in Windows Server 2008/Server 2008 R2.

Description: In this optional activity, you learn how to configure the SNMP service and the SNMP Trap service in Windows Server 2008/Server 2008 R2. Log on using an account with Administrator privileges.

After you configure the SNMP and SNMP Trap services, the server can be an SNMP agent for network management services and can be used in Network Monitor on a Windows Server.

1. Open Server Manager, if it is not already open (refer to Activity 12-15).
2. In the tree in the left pane, click the **+ plus sign** for **Configuration** to expand it.
3. Click **Services** in the tree under Configuration (see Figure 12-24).

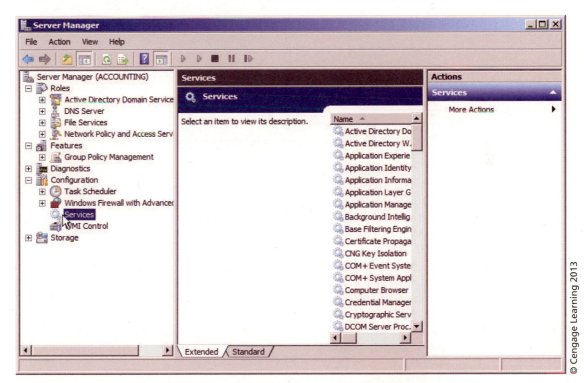

Figure 12-24   Selecting Services in the tree in Server Manager in Windows Server 2008 R2

4. In the middle pane, double-click **SNMP Service**.
5. Ensure the **General** tab is selected in the SNMP Service Properties dialog box. On the General tab, make sure the Startup type is set to **Automatic** and that the service is started.

6. Click the **Security** tab in the SNMP Service Properties dialog box (see Figure 12-25). From here you can configure the accepted communities for the agent. For example, Public is a community name that is often accepted by SNMP implementations. You would click the Add button in the upper half of the dialog box to configure community names. Also, by default, the SNMP agent is configured to accept SNMP packets from localhost. You can configure the SNMP agent to accept SNMP packets from additional hosts by clicking the Add button in the lower half of the dialog box. Additional hosts are specified by host name or by the IP address of the host from which the agent can accept SNMP packets.

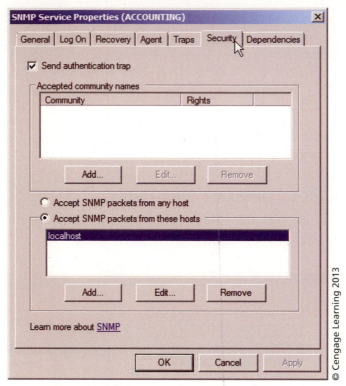

© Cengage Learning 2013

Figure 12-25 SNMP security parameters in Windows Server 2008 R2

7. Click the **Traps** tab in the SNMP Service Properties dialog box (see Figure 12-26). When a certain type of event occurs on an SNMP agent (such as the system being restarted), the agent can send a message known as a **trap** to a management system. A trap is a specific situation or event detected by SNMP that a network administrator may want to be warned about or to track via network management software, for example, when a network device is unexpectedly down or offline. The management system that receives the trap is known as the trap destination. To configure a trap, you would type in the name of the community to which the SNMP agent should send trap messages and click **Add to list**. Next, you would click **Add** in the Trap destinations and type in the host name or the IP address of the management system that will receive the trap messages. (Although shown in the dialog box, it would be rare to have to enter an IPX address, because IPX is not used in modern Novell servers.)

8. Click **Cancel** in the SNMP Service Properties dialog box.

9. Double-click the **SNMP Trap** service in the Server Manager window (see Figure 12-27). If you plan to create traps, you need to configure this service, which is set to start manually by default. Set the *Startup type* to **Automatic,** so that you do not have to remember to start the service after every reboot of the system. Click **Apply**. Click the **Start** button in the SNMP Trap Properties dialog box.

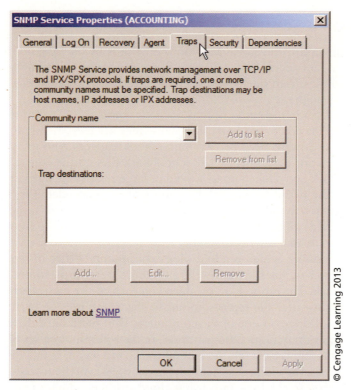

Figure 12-26   SNMP trap parameters in Windows Server 2008 R2

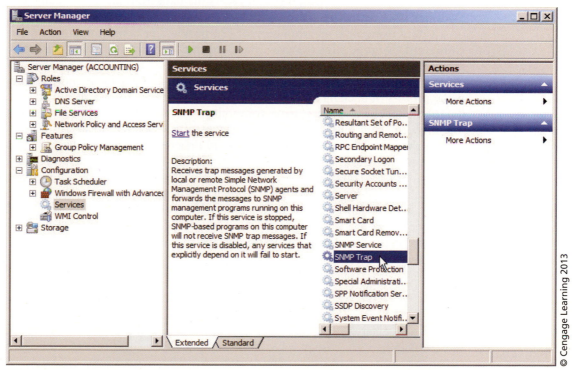

Figure 12-27   Selecting to configure the SNMP Trap service in Windows Server 2008 R2

10. In the SNMP Trap Properties dialog box, click **OK**.

11. Close the Server Manager window.

Using Your Network for Backups

An important way to maintain and safeguard your network is by backing up the computers on the network. You can use a backup device directly connected to the computer you want to back up, or you can back up files from one computer to a hard disk or to a backup storage medium on another computer through the network connection.

For example, consider a home network that has four computers. Two of the computers are desktops that have files that don't change much because they are used mainly for Internet access. Two other computers are laptops used by two high school students who use them to write papers and complete homework assignments. The schoolwork files on the laptop computers might be shared over the network and backed up to a fixed or large removable hard drive on one of the desktop computers via the network each week or more often, as needed. Or these schoolwork files might be backed up to a thumb drive, a CD, or a DVD once a week or more. Once every few months or more (as needed) all of the computers might be fully backed up to one or more fixed or removable hard drives or to a rewriteable tape.

Consider another example, which is a hydrology consultants' office of five hydrologists. In this office, reports on water samples, water levels, and future water projections are compiled and sent to clients once a week. The reports are produced on each of the hydrologist's computers on shared drives. Every Friday after the reports go out to clients, all files on each shared drive are saved onto one fixed hard drive on one of the computers. That fixed hard drive is backed up to a series of DVD±RW discs that are in a disc rotation. In the rotation, one set of DVD±RW discs is used the first week, another set is used the second week, and so on. If one or more DVD±RW discs is damaged in one set, the maximum data loss is one week. As their need for higher capacity grows, the hydrologists might look into using cloud storage, which satisfies several goals. Cloud storage enables them to have offsite backups so that if there is a fire or flood, their data is still saved in the cloud. Also, they can access the data from the cloud while working at customer locations or at the home office.

A third example is a corporation of 721 people. The corporation has 25 servers in a machine room and five tape silos (devices that hold multiple tapes) for performing backups. Backups are performed over the network to the tape silos, so that up to five servers can be backed up at the same time. Monday through Friday the company performs incremental backups, which is the process of backing up files that are new or changed for the specific day. Each Saturday the company backs up all files, for a comprehensive backup. For instance, assume that the server loses information on its hard drives because of a virus that strikes on Thursday morning. To restore the information, the company would first restore the tapes from Saturday's full backup. Next, it would restore the incremental tapes from Monday, Tuesday, and Wednesday.

Besides using tapes for backups, the corporation is also using cloud storage for some files that are accessed by employees who travel on company business. The files stored in the cloud are easy to access while on the road and have the advantage that they are stored off the traveling employee's laptop. If a laptop is stolen or left in a motel, the files are still protected because they are stored in the cloud rather than on the laptop.

Table 12-3 summarizes devices typically used for backing up computers.

Table 12-3 Backup devices

Backup Device	Description
Fixed hard drive	Another hard drive on the same computer or a hard drive on another computer on the same network that can hold many gigabytes or several terabytes of data (depending on the size of the hard drive)
Large-capacity removable hard drive	An externally connected hard drive that can be removed and ported to another computer. USB is currently the most common connection, but other options are external Serial Advanced Technology Attachment (e-SATA) drives, Serial Attached Small Computer System Interface (SAS) drives, and the rapidly emerging solid-state drives (SSDs), which use a storage technology similar to a thumb drive, but that hold 60 to over 250 GB at this writing

Table 12-3 Backup devices (*continued*)

Backup Device	Description
CD-R or CD-RW	A CD disc that holds about 737 MB
DVD-R, DVD+R, DVD-RAM, DVD-RW/DVD-ER, DVD+RW, DVD-RW	A DVD disc that typically holds about 4.7 GB, but some types (double layer, double sided) can hold up to 17.08 GB
Blu-Ray disc	A disc that uses a wireless Blu-Ray drive and that can hold up to 50 GB at this writing, but the technology has the potential to hold up to 500 GB per disc.
Solid state drive (SSD)	A fixed or removable hard drive that uses semiconductors for storage, similar to the technology in a thumb or flash drive, and at this writing stores 60 to over 250 GB
Mini or thumb drive	A device just larger than the size of a thumb, that connects through a USB port, and that typically holds 4, 8, 16, 32, 64 GB (and growing)
Tape drive	A tape, some of which are similar in appearance to an audio tape, that is used for large data backups and that can hold 2 GB to 2.4 TB depending on the tape technology (tapes have an archival lifespan of about 15 to 30 years depending on the tape technology, which makes tapes a good choice for archiving important data, such as financial data)
Cloud storage	Storage in a public or private cloud that offers the advantage of off-site storage, storage redundancy (storage backup in case one site fails), anytime access to data through a network or the Internet, ease of use without complicated software, and large capacity

© Cengage Learning 2013

Backup Services in Windows 7 and Windows Server 2008/ Server 2008 R2

Windows 7 offers the Backup and Restore utility for backups, and Windows Server 2008/2008 R2 have the Windows Server Backup utility. Both utilities allow different combinations of backups, along with the ability to restore backed up information. The options in the Backup and Restore and the Windows Server Backup utilities are as follows:

- *Full backup*: A file-by-file backup of an entire system, including all operating system files, programs, and data files. The full backup changes each file's archive attribute to show that it has been backed up. The **archive attribute** is a file or folder property that shows whether or not a file or folder has been backed up since it was last modified. A full backup is performed the first time you back up a server, and afterward once a night, once a week, or at regular intervals depending on the number of files on your computer and your or your organization's particular needs.

- *Incremental backup*: Backs up all files that are new or have been updated, which comprises files marked with the archive attribute (which shows the file needs to be backed up) and removes the archive attribute from each file after the incremental backup. Using incremental backups can save time backing up a computer when there are large numbers of files to back up. Many files, such as system and many user files, don't change on a regular basis and so don't have to be backed up every time you perform a backup.

- *Custom backup*: Enables you to configure backups differently for each disk volume, such as doing an incremental backup every time you back up the C: drive containing the operating system and program files and a full backup each time you back up the D: drive containing data files, such as documents, spreadsheets, and database files.

In addition to these options, you can also perform an *image backup* using the Backup and Restore utility or Windows Server Backup utility. An image backup creates an image of all of the files on a disk volume in binary format. The practical difference between an image backup and a full backup is that in order to restore files from an image backup you must restore all files you backed up, creating a disk image exactly like the one you backed up. Thus, you must have a disk the same size as or larger than the disk from which you made the image backup. From a full backup, you can select to restore one file, several files, a folder, or all files, as needed. The full backup enables this type of restore because it backs up in a file-by-file manner. If you want to port the operating system and all files to another computer, the image backup is usually the best option. If you want flexibility to restore individual files and folders or all files and folders, the full backup is the best option.

For many backup situations, a combination of the full backup and incremental backups is a popular solution. For example, you might perform a full backup once a week, such as on Fridays, and then perform incremental backups all other days. On your backup medium, you will see backup files with the date in the file name. The largest backup files will be full backups, and smaller backup files will be incremental backups.

The general steps to start a backup in Windows 7 are as follows:

1. Click Start and click Control Panel.

2. Set View by to Large or Small icons.

3. Click Backup and Restore. The first time you open the Backup and Restore utility, you follow steps to configure the backup and then perform a full backup. For subsequent backups, you can open the Backup and Restore utility and click *Back up now* to start a backup.

The general steps for starting a backup in Windows Server 2008/Server 2008 R2 are as follows (the Windows Server Backup Features option must first be installed as a feature through Server Manager):

1. Click Start, point to Administrative Tools, and click Server Manager.

2. In the tree in the left pane, click the + plus sign in front of Storage.

3. Click Windows Server Backup in the tree under Storage.

4. Click Action in the menu bar and click Backup Schedule (see Figure 12-28) to start the Backup Schedule Wizard to configure a backup schedule or to run a one-time backup.

Figure 12-28   Starting the Backup Schedule Wizard in Windows Server 2008 R2

© Cengage Learning 2013

Several third-party backup systems are available for Windows 7 and Windows Server systems. Some examples of these systems are NovaBackup by NovaStor (*www.novastor.com*), Genie Backup Manager by Genie-Soft (*www.genie9.com*), BackupNow from New TechInfosystems (*www.nticorp.com*), and Double Image by Host Interface International (*www.hostinterface.com*). Further, some external hard drive manufacturers provide free backup software when you purchase the drive.

Windows Sync Center

Windows 7 offers Sync Center, which enables you to synchronize files including documents, photos, and music, when the files are stored or backed up in more than one place. For example, you might store photos and music on a workstation and on a tablet PC. Each time you download a photo to your workstation from your camera, with Sync Center you can also automatically copy the photo file to your tablet PC when it is connected to the workstation, such as through a USB connection. Similarly, if you store the same Microsoft Word documents on two different workstations in your home, you can use Sync Center to keep the documents synchronized on the two workstations. If you update a document on one workstation, Sync Center automatically updates the same document on the other workstation via the home network. New documents also are automatically copied to the other workstation—which is functionally an automatic backup via a network. If you use a portable music player, Sync Center can keep music files synchronized between your computer and the music player.

Whenever Sync Center cannot tell which file version to use for synchronization, it checks with you before taking action, so that it does not overwrite a version you want to keep.

Sync Center works through partnerships. There are two types of partnerships that can be configured:

- *One-way sync*: In which files are only copied from one device to another device, such as copying photos only from a workstation computer to a tablet PC or copying music only from a workstation computer to a portable music player (only one device/computer can update the other)

- *Two-way sync*: In which files are synchronized both ways between devices, for example, if a file on one computer in a partnership is changed, the file is automatically updated on the other computer (any one of the two devices/computers can update the other)

To access Sync Center and configure a partnership, use these general steps in Windows 7:

1. Click Start.
2. Point to All Programs.
3. Click the Accessories folder.
4. Click Sync Center.
5. Click Set up new sync partnerships.

Backup Services in UNIX/Linux

The *dump* utility is used in UNIX/Linux systems for full or partial file-by-file backups. (These backups are often called "dumps.") The *dump* utility backs up all files, files that have changed by date, or files that have changed after the previous backup. Files can be backed up using a dump level that correlates a dump to a given point in time. For example, a Monday dump might be assigned level 1, Tuesday's dump level 2, and so on. Up to nine dump levels can be assigned (see Figure 12-29). A dump is restored via one of three commands, depending on the flavor of UNIX or Linux: *restore* (in Fedora and Red Hat Enterprise Linux), *ufsrestore*, and *restor*.

In Figure 12-29, the *dump* command is used to back up user account smartinez's documents directory to the user backup dump file. The *-0* dump-level option is used for a full backup of all the directory's contents, the *u* option is to update the dumpdats file to keep a log of the backup, and the *f* option signifies to make a backup of the specified directory, which is /home/smartinez/documents.

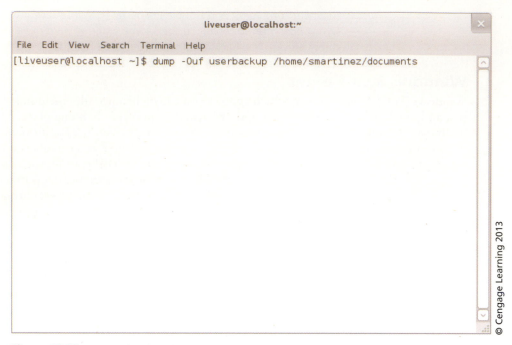

Figure 12-29 Using the *dump* command to back up the /home/smartinez/documents directory

Another utility, called *tar*, is available in most versions of UNIX and Linux, including Fedora and Red Hat Enterprise Linux, and is sometimes used in addition to *dump*. The *tar* utility is designed for archiving data to tapes and includes file information, as well as the archived files, such as security information and dates when files were modified. UNIX/Linux system users may retrieve drivers and other software in a *tar* format. *tar* files can be used as archives that group multiple files into a single distribution file, for a restore later or to distribute to another user, such as an archive of hardware drivers. *tar* doesn't compress the files; it merely groups files to make it easier to copy and distribute multiple files together.

 A third backup utility is *volcopy*, which is not available in Fedora and Red Hat Enterprise Linux, but is used by some UNIX systems. *volcopy* is a binary backup that creates a mirror image of a disk onto the backup medium, such as an external hard drive, tape, or DVD. The *volcopy* utility requires that you provide specifics about the length and density of the information to be backed up. It can write to one or multiple tapes, calling for additional tapes if the information does not fit on the first one. The utility also can back up to multiple tape drives. It is sometimes used with the *labelit* utility, which can label file systems or unmounted volumes to provide unique identification for each one copied in the backup.

 Some third-party backup systems for UNIX/Linux include Bacula open source software found at *www.bacula.org*; fwbackups, which is open source software by Diffingo Solutions, Inc. (*www.diffingo.com*); CA ARCserve from Computer Associates (*www.ca.com*); and EMC NetWorker by EMC[2] (*www.emc.com*).

Backup Utility in Mac OS X

Mac OS X Snow Leopard and Lion offer Time Machine as the backup software (see Figure 12-30). Time Machine constantly keeps a current copy of all files on the hard drive through the following means:

- Hourly backups for any changes within the last 24 hours
- Daily backups over the current month
- Weekly backups for all months to date

Figure 12-30   Time Machine in Mac OS X

Through this comprehensive series of backups, you can restore to nearly any point in time. Time Machine can back up files and folders to a removable hard drive attached to the computer or over a network to a network backup drive.

The general steps to initially configure Time Machine in Mac OS X Snow Leopard or Lion are:

1. Ensure that a removable hard disk is attached to the computer or that you can access a network drive to use as a backup drive.

2. Click the Apple icon in the menu bar and click System Preferences, or click System Preferences in the Dock.

3. Click Time Machine in the System Preferences window.

4. Click the Select Backup Disk button.

5. Select the backup disk in the list of available backup disks.

6. If it is not set to On, click and move the slider control to the ON position.

7. Click System Preferences in the menu bar and click Quit System Preferences.

How to Solve Network Problems

There are many types of network problems that you may encounter. Fortunately, there are also many effective ways to solve network problems. The next sections discuss examples of network problems and give you tools and concrete approaches for solving them.

Solving Client, Server, and Network Connectivity Problems

A server or workstation may have problems connecting to the network or to other computers on the network for several reasons. When you experience a connection problem, try the following:

- Check to see if only one station, several stations, or all stations are having problems.

- Check that the workstation's or server's NIC/WNIC driver is properly installed and is a current version.

- Use the NIC/WNIC test software to determine that the NIC/WNIC is functioning and reseat or replace the NIC/WNIC if it fails the test.

- Verify the protocol setup, particularly the IP addressing. Two of the most common problems on networks that do not use DHCP or automatic private addressing are that the IP address or subnet mask are inappropriately configured.

- Make sure that the NIC/WNIC properties are configured correctly. For example, a cabled NIC configured for half duplex does not communicate properly on a network in which switches are configured for full duplex. Also, for a cabled NIC that does not automatically detect the media type (cable setting), make sure that the media type is configured to match the type of cable connected to the NIC, such as a 100 Mbps or 1 Gbps connection.

- Ensure the correct protocols are installed for network communications.

- Ensure that all server or workstation clients are configured to use the correct domain or workgroup to access the server or workstation. Also, ensure that computers are identified by a unique computer name and a unique IP address. (If there are two stations using the same IP address, one or both of the stations will display an error message warning there is another station using the same IP address.)

- On a cabled network, check the cable connection into the NIC or reconnect the cable. Also, examine the network cable and connector to the NIC for damage.

- For wireless communications, ensure that all nodes are configured for the same security, including the SSID.

- Ensure that a WNIC is properly installed or seated in a slot and that the antenna is not damaged or near a source of interference, such as a cordless phone using the same frequency.

For example, if you are using an out-of-date NIC or WNIC driver, the server or workstation may have difficulty connecting to the network or it may periodically lose connection.

If a computer is unable to communicate because TCP/IP addressing is not configured correctly, fix the problem by checking the TCP/IP properties for the network connections having trouble. Ensure that the IP address and the subnet mask are configured correctly, if you are not using automatic IP addressing. Remember that it is important for each computer to have a unique IP address that is consistent with other IP addresses used on the network. If DHCP is in use, make certain that Obtain an IP address automatically is selected and that the DHCP server is working properly and can be reached through the network.

When multiple users have trouble accessing a server that is on a network cable, check to ensure that the server is on and completely booted and it has a good network connection in terms of the NIC, connector, and cable; or that the WNIC is not close to a source of interference and does not have damage to an external antenna. Always ensure that servers have the latest NIC/WNIC drivers. Sometimes users cannot connect to a server because one or more disk drives have failed or a SCSI adapter is malfunctioning. Also, check the network equipment that the user must pass through to reach the server. Table 12-4 lists a variety of network connectivity problems and their solutions.

Table 12-4   Solving network connectivity problems

Connectivity Problem	Solutions
The NIC will not connect to the network (no computers are visible in the Network window).	• For a cable connection, check the cable and cable connection to the NIC for damage or for a loose connection. Do the same for the connection into the wall or switch. Also, check to ensure intermediate network equipment (such as switches and routers) is working. • For a cable connection, check that the media type (cable type) set for the NIC is the same as is used on the network. • Check to ensure the NIC or WNIC driver is installed and is current. • For a WNIC, check the SSID and security parameters and check the antenna. Also, ensure you are in range of other wireless devices, such as an access point. • For a WNIC, check for sources of interference, such as a cell or cordless phone. • Check to make sure the correct protocol is installed and that all protocol parameters are correct. • Run the NIC or WNIC manufacturer's diagnostics program to locate problems. • Replace the NIC or WNIC with one you know is working.

Table 12-4 Solving network connectivity problems (*continued*)

Connectivity Problem	Solutions
A server or workstation periodically disconnects from the network, or it experiences a connectivity problem when a particular client is logged on.	• For a cabled network, check the cable segment to ensure it is within IEEE specs for distance and cable type. Also, check for electrical interference on the cable segment, check the cable and connector for damage, check for a problem with that port on the network switch or router, and check for a problem with the workstation NIC. • For wireless communication ensure that you are in range, and if you are moving from cell to cell, ensure that the cells are configured to use the same roaming protocol. • Ensure no other station on the network has the same computer name. • If using TCP/IP, make sure no other station is using the same IP address (use *ipconfig* in Windows, *ifconfig* in UNIX/Linux, or the Network Utility Info tab in Mac OS X to quickly determine a computer's IP address information).
Clients cannot run logon scripts when connecting to a Windows server.	Ensure the location of logon scripts matches the location specified via the Local Users and Groups or Active Directory Users and Computers tool for each account.
Clients cannot access a login script when connecting to a UNIX/Linux server (Windows systems use the terminology "logon" while UNIX/Linux systems use "login").	Ensure that clients have the right permissions to run login scripts used from a general location.
Clients cannot access a shared directory or printer.	Check the group memberships, share permissions, and regular permissions associated with the shared resource.
Clients cannot log onto a Windows, UNIX/Linux, or Mac OS X server.	• Make sure the server is powered on and properly connected to the network. • Ensure that the clients are using the correct network ID in their IP address. • In Windows Server ensure that the Server, Workstation, and Computer Browser services are started (use the Computer Management tool).
Windows 7 or Windows Server is not responding as an SNMP agent.	• Ensure that the SNMP service is installed and is set to automatically start when the computer is booted. • Make sure that the SNMP and SNMP Trap services are started (use the Computer Management tool to check). • Ensure that the community names are set correctly.
TCP/IP packets sent from Windows Server are not routed.	Enable IP routing by clicking Start, pointing to Administrative Tools, clicking Routing and Remote Access, right-clicking the computer under the tree, clicking Properties, clicking the General tab, and configuring the appropriate IP routing parameters.

© Cengage Learning 2013

Solving NIC and WNIC Broadcast Problems

Sometimes a NIC or WNIC malfunctions and broadcasts continuously, creating a broadcast storm that causes the entire network to slow down. A broadcast storm is a condition in which so many broadcasts are sent at the same time that the network bandwidth is saturated and the network slows significantly or times out. Use Performance Monitor as you learned earlier in this chapter to trace a malfunctioning NIC or WNIC. Another option is to use a protocol analyzer.

Solving Cable Problems

Network cabling is one of the most common sources of network problems. Cabling problems have many symptoms, such as disconnecting workstations, slow network services, a high level of packet errors, and unreliable data transmission. If you have reports of any of those problems, one place to start is by investigating the network cabling. There are several things to check related to cabling problems, such as cable length, cable type, cable impedance, connectors, and open or short circuits.

Network problems may show up in Performance Monitor as dropped frames, CRC errors, or other error conditions. As you learned in Chapter 2, a CRC is an error-checking technique used in network protocols to signal a communication problem. Dropped frames are those that are discarded because they are improperly formed, such as failing to meet the appropriate packet size.

On a small network it is good practice for the server or network administrator to periodically inspect the visible cabling for damage. Cable may be pinned under a table leg, excessively bent or knotted, or damaged from exposure to a portable heater. Also, cable connectors may be broken or have an exposed wire. The best solution for damaged cable is to replace it immediately. On large networks, cable problems can be traced through the use of network test equipment or by means of enterprise-wide network-monitoring software.

An economical solution for a small network is to use Performance Monitor along with inexpensive test equipment such as a cable scanner, which tests the length of cable and looks for electrical problems. For a small to medium-sized network, if a network problem cannot be found immediately, it may be most cost effective to hire a network professional rather than to purchase equipment and spend many personnel hours locating a problem. The network professional will likely have equipment to help quickly locate and solve a problem, including problems with fiber-optic cable. Table 12-5 lists common cable problems that you should look for and how to troubleshoot them.

Table 12-5 Solving cable problems

Cable Problem	Solutions
A cable segment is too long.	If a network segment is extended beyond the IEEE specifications, there will be communication problems affecting all nodes on that segment. Use a cable scanner or TDR to measure the distance of the cable.
Mismatched or improper cabling	Check the labeling on the cable jacket to make sure it is right for your network.
Improper grounding	Proper grounding is critical to packet transmission on the cable. Without it, the network packet transmissions will have many CRC errors. Ethernet frames include this check to ensure the reliability of data transfer from the source node to the recipient node. Performance Monitor reports information about CRC errors.
Open or short circuits	Use a cable scanner or TDR to find opens and shorts. Also, use Performance Monitor to look for CRC errors and dropped frames.
Electrical and magnetic interference	Electrical and magnetic interference result in excessive noise or jabber on the cable. This happens when the cable is run too close to an electrical field, such as over fluorescent lights in the ceiling or through a machine shop with heavy electrical equipment. Check the cable for these possibilities.
Defective connector	A faulty connector can cause a short or open on the cable. If several workstations on a segment are experiencing problems, or a segment is automatically shut down by network equipment, this may be caused by a cable connector on a workstation or server. Use a cable scanner to identify shorts and opens due to a faulty connector. Also, Performance Monitor can help by identifying a high rate of CRC errors and dropped frames.

© Cengage Learning 2013

Solving Wireless Problems

You have already learned several ways to solve wireless networking problems earlier in this book, which include:

- Observe the distance requirements for the wireless technology you use.
- Configure security in the same way on all devices so that wireless devices can communicate with one another.
- Use the same roaming protocol in each cell intended to support roaming.
- For best throughput, use WNICs and access points that employ the same technology, such as 802.11n.

Table 12-6 lists solutions for some wireless networking problems experienced by computers running Windows 7, Windows Server 2008/Server 2008 R2, UNIX/Linux, and Mac OS X Snow Leopard and Lion. Table 12-7 presents solutions for Wi-Fi connection problems experienced by mobile devices, such as tablet PCs, smartphones, cell phones, and e-readers.

Table 12-6 Solving wireless networking problems in Windows, UNIX/Linux, and Mac OS X

Wireless Problem	Solutions
Network access is denied to a specific workstation.	• Ensure the WNIC is configured to have the same SSID, WEP (not recommended), WPA/WPA2 (recommended), and 802.1x/802.11i security as the access point and other wireless devices. • If accessing a secure VPN, ensure you have the right account and password and all necessary VPN services installed.
The network cannot be accessed.	• Use the *Currently connected to* window to determine if you have a viable network connection in Windows. *ipconfig* is another tool for verifying a connection in Windows. • Use the Network Connections tool in the GNOME 3.x desktop to verify a connection in UNIX/Linux. *ifconfig* is another tool for verifying a network connection in UNIX/Linux. • Use the Network Utility Info tab in Mac OS X to verify a connection and watch packet transfer statistics. • Ensure that the WNIC in the workstation is fully seated in its slot. • Ensure that the workstation is in range of the access point or other wireless devices.
An access point cannot be reached by any workstation.	• Ensure the access point's communications are not blocked by a competing wireless device or by a natural or human-made source of interference. • Ensure the access point is plugged in and turned on. • Reset the access point.
An 802.11g, 802.11n, or 802.11ac WNIC does not communicate with some access points, even though all are configured with the same security.	• Ensure the WNIC and the access points are all Wi-Fi certified. • Ensure the WNIC is configured for 802.11g, 802.11n, or 802.11ac, if it supports multiple technologies. • If this is a multiple-cell wireless LAN, ensure that all devices are configured to use the same roaming protocol.

© Cengage Learning 2013

Table 12-7 Solving Wi-Fi networking problems for tablets, smartphones, cell phones, and e-readers

Wireless Problem	Solutions
Network access is denied to a specific mobile device.	• In the mobile device's settings function, ensure the WNIC is configured to have the same SSID and security, such as WPA/WPA2 Personal, as the access point and other wireless devices. • Make sure that you have specified the correct wireless network as the preferred network to try to connect to first.
The network connection periodically disconnects.	• Check the signal strength in the device's settings for your Wi-Fi network and use it to gauge how to move to a location or position that has better signal strength. • Notice if there are nearby sources of interference, such as periodic use of a nearby microwave oven or portable phone.
Your mobile device was connecting, but now no longer connects to the Wi-Fi network.	• Ensure that the Wi-Fi settings on the mobile device have not been inadvertently changed. • Make sure that the access point you use is still on the eligible network list. • Physically check the Wi-Fi network's access point in case it needs to be rebooted, reset, or turned on (look for green lights showing a functioning network and/or Internet connection on the access point and press the reset button if a light is out or red). • Determine if the Wi-Fi network's access point has been automatically updated and if there are parallel updates you need to obtain for the mobile device (it is always good to regularly obtain and install mobile device updates, such as for the iOS or Android operating systems).

© Cengage Learning 2013

Solving Network Printing Problems

Network printing problems are common. The best advice is to check out the simplest solutions first. These include the following:

- Make sure the printer has power.
- If the printer is physically connected to a workstation or server, ensure that the computer is turned on and working.
- Be certain the printer is online (that is, the online light or button is active).
- Press the printer reset button, in case the printer has not fully reset after the last print job.
- Make certain all printer trays have paper.
- If the printer uses ink or toner cartridges, ensure it is not out of ink or toner.
- For a cabled printer, check that the printer data cable is properly connected between the computer and the printer. Also, check that the network cable is properly connected when a print server card is used in the printer.
- For a wireless printer, check for sources of wireless interference near the printer.
- Make sure that the printer has a static IP address rather than an IP address leased through DHCP that can change from time to time (because if the address changes, clients won't be able to find the printer until each client's printer connection is reconfigured for the newly leased IP address).

These are obvious solutions but are not always checked first. Perhaps the most overlooked solution is to press the reset button on the printer (if it has one) or to simply turn it off and back on again. When several people share one printer, it may be printing documents with different fonts and formats. A slight miscue at the printer or in a printer connection may cause it to miss the software reset instruction sent at the beginning of each document.

If the problem is related to the server or workstation, the most likely areas to check are the following:

- The printer driver is improperly installed and selected for the print job.
- Printer sharing is not enabled.
- The printer share permissions are set incorrectly.
- The software used to produce the print job is incorrectly installed at the workstation.

Table 12-8 provides a series of steps you can take to resolve different types of network printing problems.

Table 12-8   Solving network printing problems

Network Printing Problem	Solutions
Only one character prints per page.	• If only one workstation experiences this problem, reinstall the printer driver on that workstation (use the most recent printer driver from the printer manufacturer). • If all workstations are experiencing the problem, reinstall the printer and printer driver at the computer or print server offering the printer share.
Some users get a no-access message when trying to access the shared printer.	Check the share permissions. Make certain the clients belong to a group for which at least Print permission has been granted and that none of the groups to which these users belong are denied Print permission.
Printer control codes are on the printout.	• If only one workstation experiences the problem, reinstall the printer driver on that workstation. Also, ensure the software generating the printout is installed correctly. • If all workstations are experiencing the problem, reinstall the printer and printer driver at the computer or print server offering the printer share. • In Windows, ensure the printer share is set up for all operating systems that access it, that the right print monitor is installed, and that the right data type is used. • Reset or restart the printer.

Table 12-8   Solving network printing problems (*continued*)

Network Printing Problem	Solutions
A print server card is used in the printer and shows an amber or red data error light.	Power off the printer. Disconnect the network cable to the printer. Reconnect the network cable and turn on the printer.
A print job shows it is printing in Windows, the printer looks fine, but nothing is printing.	Double-click the printer in the Control Panel Devices and Printers window. Check for a problem with the print job at the top of the print queue. If it shows the job is printing but nothing is happening, delete the print job because it may be hung (and resubmit the print job).
The wrong print form is used.	Check the setup of the document in the software at the client.
A workstation cannot view the shared printer via network printer access software, such as in the Network window in Windows operating systems.	• Check the network connection to that workstation, including connectors, cable, network hub, and the workstation's NIC or WNIC. • Also, check the protocol setup at the workstation. In Windows, ensure the workstation is a member of the domain, if Active Directory is implemented, or a member of the appropriate workgroup.
Some clients find that the ending pages are not printed for large print jobs.	Check the disk space on the server or workstation from which the job is printed. It may not have enough space to fully store (spool) print jobs before they are printed.

© Cengage Learning 2013

Putting It All Together: Designing a Solutions Strategy

Whether you have a home, small office, or large enterprise network, you will encounter occasional network problems. In this chapter you have learned about devices and software for monitoring and detecting problems. Also, you have learned solutions to many common problems. The next step is to put what you have learned into designing a solutions strategy that you can use whenever a problem arises. Designing a strategy can save you lots of time and keep your network users pleased with your quick solutions to problems.

An effective solutions strategy can be built around three combined approaches: steps to prepare for solving problems, steps to take when a problem surfaces, and steps to take after you have solved a problem.

The first approach consists of taking several general steps from the beginning:

- Continue to build on your understanding of how the network and network devices interact with the workstations, servers, printers, mobile devices, and other devices connected to the network. For example, as you have learned in this chapter, what initially seems like a slow network might really be a slow server.

- Regularly use tools such as *ping*, *netstat*, *tracert/traceroute*, *nslookup*, Performance Monitor, Network Monitor, and other network-monitoring software to get to know well your network's normal daily workings. You can more quickly spot and decide how to deal with a network problem when you first know what is normal for your network.

- Train your network users to help. Users can help by fully recording error messages, reporting their experience of the problem, and reporting what they were doing at the time of the problem. Also, train users to promptly save their work and to report problems right away.

- If your network is used in an organization, work to understand the business, academic, and research processes that rely on the network, so you can solve problems in the context of the purpose of the network.

When a problem occurs, develop a consistent set of steps to follow. Here are some examples to give you a start:

- *Get as much information as possible about the problem—before you start working on it*: If the problem is reported by a network user, listen carefully to his or her description. Even if he or she does not use the right terminology, the information is still valuable. Part of your challenge is to ask the right questions to get as much information as possible. Patience and social skills in working with other people are helpful for effective communications with network users about technical issues.

- *Record the error message at the time it appears or when a user reports it to you*: This is an obvious but sometimes overlooked step. If you try to recall the message from memory, you may lose some important information. For example, the error "Network not responding" can lead you to a different set of troubleshooting steps than the message "Network timeout error." The first message might signal a damaged NIC, whereas the second message could mean that a database server is overloaded, and the application is waiting to obtain data.

- *Start with simple solutions*: Often the solution to a problem is as simple as connecting a cable or power cord or moving a wireless laptop closer to an access point.

- *Determine if anyone else is experiencing the problem*: For example, several people may report they cannot run reports on a database. This may be caused by a problem at the server they use to access the data. If only one person is experiencing this problem, it may point to trouble with the report-generating software on her or his workstation.

- *Check to see if any recent alerts have been sent to your account*: If your network-monitoring software supports sending alerts, check to determine if any have been sent warning you of a problem. For example, Fedora and Red Hat Enterprise Linux systems send problem alerts to the root account via e-mail. Also, as you gain more experience with Performance Monitor in Windows, you can set up alerts about specific problems.

- *Check the event logs*: Windows, UNIX/Linux, and Mac OS X systems track some types of errors in their event logs. In Windows you can use the Computer Management tool to access the Event Viewer to display logs. In Linux, the logs are in the /var/logs or /var/log directory. In Mac OS X Snow Leopard and Lion, open the Console application in the Utilities folder (in Finder click Go, click Utilities, and double-click Console).

- *Check for power interruptions*: Power problems are a common source of server and network difficulties. Even though the server is on a UPS, its cabled network connection can still be a source of problems because the network cable can carry current to the server's NIC during a lightning storm or because of a major power-related problem. Also, keep in mind that even if a power interruption is over, an affected server, switch, router, or access point may need your attention if it was affected and did not reboot correctly.

- *Call the vendor*: Sometimes a problem is related to a bug or defect already known by a software or hardware vendor. You might save time by calling the vendor to see if they know about the problem and its solution.

After you solve a problem, keep a written record that describes the problem and how you solved it. Some network professionals log problems in a database created for that purpose. Others build problem logging into help desk systems maintained by their organization. A help desk system is application software designed to maintain information on computer systems, user questions, problem solutions, and other information that members of the organization can reference.

The advantage of tracking problems is that you soon accumulate a wealth of information on solutions. For example, to jog your memory about a solution, you can look up how you handled a similar problem six months ago. The log of problems also can be used as a teaching tool and reference for other computer support staff. Problems that show up repeatedly in the log may indicate that special attention is needed, such as replacing a server that experiences frequent hardware problems.

Chapter Summary

- Regular network monitoring helps you learn about the normal activities of your network and to identify problems.

- Examples of hardware devices used for network monitoring are voltmeters, multimeters, optical power meters, cable continuity testers, cable scanners, time domain reflectometers, wireless testing tools, and protocol analyzers.

- Computer operating systems offer network-monitoring tools. One example is the Windows Network Connection Status dialog box. Other tools available in Windows systems, UNIX/Linux, and Mac OS X are *ping*, *traceroute/tracert*, *netstat*, and *nslookup*.

- Microsoft Performance Monitor is a multifeature tool for monitoring operating system, computer, and network performance.

- Microsoft Network Monitor is software you can obtain from Microsoft that is used to monitor network performance, network connections, and compile network performance and error statistics.

- The SNMP service in Windows enables you to employ SNMP for monitoring network activity through a network management station and through Microsoft Network Monitor.

- Regularly backing up computers on your network gives you a fail-safe option in case there is a problem that causes data loss, such as a failed disk. Windows, UNIX/Linux, and Mac OS X systems offer tools for performing backups locally or over a network. Windows 7 has the Backup and Restore utility, while Windows Server 2008/Server 2008 R2 offers the Windows Server Backup utility. UNIX/Linux systems offer *dump*, *tar*, and *volcopy* for backups. Mac OS X Snow Leopard and Lion have Time Machine for backups.

- Examples of network problems you might encounter include connectivity problems, NIC/WNIC broadcast problems, cable problems, wireless network problems, and network printing problems.

- A network solutions strategy can help you solve problems faster. Plan to develop a strategy that includes preparatory steps, actual solution steps, and steps to document how you solved specific problems.

Key Terms

archive attribute   A file property that shows whether or not a file or folder has been backed up since it was created or last modified.

cable continuity tester   A device that enables you to check for opens or breaks in a cable by determining if the signal sent from one end reaches the other end of the cable.

cable scanner   A device used to test the length and other characteristics of a cable.

community   A group of hosts that share the same SNMP services.

community name   In SNMP communications, a rudimentary password (name) used by network agents and the network management station (or software) in the same community so that their communications cannot be easily intercepted by an unauthorized workstation or device.

counter   Used by Performance Monitor, this is a measurement technique for an object, as when measuring the processor performance by percentage in use. *See* **Performance Monitor**.

instance   Used by Performance Monitor, when there are two or more types of elements to monitor, such as two or more NICs/WNICs or disk drives. *See* **Performance Monitor**.

Internet Control Message Protocol (ICMP)   A protocol used for network error reporting particularly through routers, showing whether or not a packet successfully reaches its destination.

multimeter   A device that tests voltage and resistance, combining the functions of a voltmeter and an ohm meter.

Network Monitor   A Windows Server network-monitoring tool that can capture and display network performance data.

open circuit   A circuit in which the connection is severed, such as a cable that is inadvertently cut in two.

optical time domain reflectometer (OTDR)   A device for testing fiber-optic cable distance, bad splices, connector problems, and bending radius problems.

packet analyzer   *See* protocol analyzer.

Performance Monitor   The Windows Server utility used to track network, system, or application objects. For each object type there are one or more counters that can be logged for later analysis or tracked in real time for immediate system monitoring. *See* **counter** and **instance**.

protocol analyzer   A network testing device that works in promiscuous mode to capture detailed information about the traffic moving across a network, including protocol and OSI layer information.

short circuit   An incomplete or damaged connection, such as when the two conductors in a twisted-pair set come in contact in a poorly built connector.

time domain reflectometer (TDR)   A device for cable testing that can monitor line impedance, opens, shorts, RFI/EMI, and cable distances, and detect connector and terminator problems, as well as other problems.

trap   A specific situation or event detected by SNMP that a network administrator may want to be warned about or to track via network management software, for example, when a network device is unexpectedly down or offline.

voltmeter   A device that tests voltage.

Review Questions

1. Which of the following can a time domain reflectometer monitor? (Choose all that apply.)

   a.   RFI/EMI

   b.   cable distances

   c.   opens and shorts

   d.   cable connector problems

2. In an office at your company, a printer shared from a workstation does not print the last several pages of large print jobs. Which of the following might be the problem?

   a.   The printer share permissions are incorrectly configured.

   b.   The USB cable connecting the printer to the workstation is only four feet long and must be at least six feet in length.

   c.   The workstation to which the printer is connected is running low on disk space for storing print jobs.

   d.   The printer is connected via an older serial cable instead of a modern USB cable.

3. Your investment company is required to archive fiscal year end files for at least 10 years. Which of the following is a sound choice as an archival medium in this situation, which requires 1.4 TB of storage capacity?

   a.   DVD+R

   b.   tape

   c.   Blu-Ray disc

   d.   SSD

4. A protocol analyzer works in which of the following?

   a.   promiscuous mode

   b.   Data Link layer mode only

   c.   Network layer mode only

   d.   NIC detection mode

5. You are considering the use of SNMP on your network. What elements should you be prepared to implement to effectively use SNMP? (Choose all that apply.)

   a.   a cable meter

   b.   network agents

   c.   an SNMP level monitor

   d.   an SNMP management system

6. You have employed a cable installation company to install fiber-optic cable for your network backbone. After the cable is installed, you require that the company test and certify the fiber-optic cable installation. What device will the cable installation company use to do the testing?

   a. OTDR

   b. amp meter

   c. sniffer

   d. multimeter

7. Network access to a database server is particularly slow. In a meeting, several high-level network users have asked you to upgrade the network to make it faster to the server. What is your response?

   a. You encourage the users to purchase faster workstations instead.

   b. You recommend an immediate conversion to a wireless network.

   c. You order a new switch to replace the one that connects these users.

   d. You monitor access to that server to study the speed of the network at that point and the ability of the server to handle the load from the network.

8. A cable scanner for UTP cable tests for which of the following? (Choose all that apply.)

   a. TCP header information

   b. routing table data

   c. cable length

   d. an open circuit

9. A contractor has installed UTP cable in a new wing of your company's manufacturing plant. The cable is unmarked, and so to gain information about its fitness for network communications you decide to test the cable resistance. What tool do you use to test the resistance?

   a. amp meter

   b. multimeter

   c. optical meter

   d. net meter

10. In Question 9, what should be the resistance of the cable?

    a. 45 volts

    b. 150 volts

    c. 75 ohms

    d. 100 ohms

11. Which of the following can *netstat* help you monitor? (Choose all that apply.)

    a. routing table information

    b. data errors

    c. TCP ports that are active

    d. UDP communications

12. Your tool and parts company sells specialized products used in manufacturing. The company has 78 sales representatives who constantly travel to visit manufacturers and who need instant access to tool and parts data as well as the ability to place orders. Which of the

following network storage options gives them the most flexibility to demonstrate the latest specs of the company products, to place orders, and to regularly file sales reports?

a. portable thumb drives

b. cloud storage in a cloud computing environment

c. Blu-Ray discs

d. tape drives located at company headquarters

13. A user calls to say his workstation has lost its connection to the network. How can you quickly test the workstation's network connection from your office when you already know the host name of the computer?

a. Use *ping* to test the workstation's connection.

b. Use a TDR to remotely measure the temperature of the user's NIC.

c. Use Network Monitor to determine if socket 110 is live at the workstation.

d. Use a protocol analyzer to determine if the workstation is sending Time to Live (TTL) packets to signal its presence.

14. What command enables you to determine the host name of a computer when you already know its IP address?

a. *nethost*

b. *whosit*

c. *dnsquery*

d. *nslookup*

15. A user is complaining about a slow wireless network connection on her Windows 7 computer. Which of the following enables you to quickly determine the speed of the WNIC in the computer?

a. Connection test window

b. *ipconfig /w* command

c. Wireless Network Connection Status box

d. *nettest /wnic* command

16. Your network uses IPv4 and IPv6. Which of the following Windows Server Performance Monitor objects enable(s) you to monitor IPSec authentication failures for IPv4 or IPv6? (Choose all that apply.)

a. TCPv4 and TCPv6

b. IPSec/MCSec

c. IPSec IKEv1 IPv4 and IPSec IKEv1 IPv6

d. UDPv4/UDPv6

17. You have a specialized array of hard disks connected to a Linux server, and the drivers for those disks were particularly hard to obtain from the manufacturer. What utility can you use to ensure the hard disk drivers are backed up together in case there is a disk failure and you need to reinstall the drivers?

a. *tar*

b. *volcopy*

c. *ufsrestore*

d. *saveit*

18. When you use *ping* in Linux, what *ping* option should you also include to limit the number of *pings*?

    a. *-l*

    b. *-c*

    c. *-short*

    d. *-limit*

19. You are using a client's Mac OS X Lion workstation to troubleshoot a network problem, and you want to use the *traceroute* utility. From where do you access this utility in Mac OS X Lion?

    a. from the Apple icon Network Info option

    b. from the System Preferences Network Troubleshooting option

    c. from the Test Applications option opened through the Applications window

    d. from the Network Utility option opened through the Utilities window

20. When you use the Lookup network utility in Mac OS X Lion, which of the following information can you obtain? (Choose all that apply.)

    a. host name of a node on the network

    b. Internet address of a Web site or node

    c. CPU/OS type of a node

    d. default information about a DNS server

Case Projects

CASE PROJECTS

12

Two clients are sharing your consulting help this week. One client is a small business called Unforgettable Adventures that organizes exotic tours to Belize, Cambodia, Thailand, Antarctica, Greenland, Peru, and Chile. This business consists of 18 people who each use Windows 7 and four people who use Mac OS X Lion in a wireless network that also has five wireless network printers and one Windows Server 2008 R2 computer. Wireless communications are coordinated through two wireless routers. Although the server is used for centralized storage of files, all of the 22 workstations also have specialized files with information about clients and particular tours.

The other client organization is the International School of Chefs (ISC) that has 500 students and 32 full-time and part-time faculty. There are two computer specialists who maintain the servers, workstations, and network. The school has five Linux servers and two servers running Windows Server 2008 R2. One of the Linux servers is used for the school's Web site. There are eight kitchens used for teaching, 15 classrooms, and two computer labs containing Windows 7 and Mac OS X Lion computers. Only the computer labs use wireless networking. ISC offers a two-year program that includes a full range of cooking courses plus courses in nutrition, health, and restaurant management.

Case Project 12-1: Developing a Backup Plan

Unforgettable Adventures has never had a cohesive backup plan for its server and client workstations. Create a report that describes a backup plan for this small business. In the report recommend the backup media, backup software, and how often to perform backups.

Case Project 12-2: Solving a Printer Problem

Unforgettable Adventures has an expensive wireless color laser printer that was set up by a member of the staff and has never worked. When the printer is turned on, its lights show that it is active and not in an error condition. The printer's print server software was preconfigured for Unforgettable Adventures by the vendor. A new member of the

Unforgettable Adventures staff calls you for help in getting this printer to work. What actions do you recommend?

Case Project 12-3: Network-Monitoring Hardware Recommendations

The computer specialists at the International School of Chefs have received funding to purchase network-monitoring hardware. Up to this point when there has been a problem with a network segment, they have called a local company that support networks. Now they plan to do much of this troubleshooting by using their own equipment. They plan to troubleshoot only those portions of the network that have UTP cable and wireless communications. What network-monitoring devices do you recommend they purchase, and why do you recommend them?

Case Project 12-4: Diagnosing a Broadcast Storm

One of the computer specialists at International School of Chefs believes there is a NIC in a faculty member's office that is creating a broadcast storm. He has noticed that when faculty members arrive to work on one floor of offices, access on their network segment slows down significantly. This is a problem because one of the Windows servers is on that segment. He asks you to recommend a way to monitor for a broadcast storm using software already available in the operating systems they use.

Case Project 12-5: Testing the Web Server and a Tablet Connection Problem

While the computer specialist is talking with you on the telephone to solve the broadcast storm problem, the school's vice president stops by the specialist's office to report she cannot access the school's Web server. The specialist asks you if there is a quick way he can test the Web server's connectivity from his Windows 7 workstation while the vice president is in his office. What test method do you recommend?

Also, while he has you on the telephone, the computer specialist mentions that he cannot connect his new Android tablet computer to the school's wireless network in the labs. What do you recommend?

A Short History of Networking

The history and development of networking technologies reflects the needs of a society that values rapid business, educational, recreational, and interpersonal communications. Even as more and more incredible ways to communicate emerge, the basic requirements remain the same: to reach more people in more places with ease and speed.

An effective way to understand how LANs, CANs, MANs, and WANs have evolved is to view their progression as a series of steps—both small and large. The following is a timeline of important steps. Some of this information is based on Robert Hobbes Zakon's *Hobbes' Internet Timeline*—Hobbes' Internet Timeline © 1993–2012 by Robert H. Zakon—which is located on the Internet at *www.zakon.org/robert/internet/timeline*. The timeline also can be read as RFC 2235.

1965

The first WAN is set up between MIT and the System Development Corporation (SDC) by Thomas Merrill and Lawrence Roberts. Also, the term "hypertext" is first used by Ted Nelson.

1966

Researchers use fiber optics for the first time to transmit telephone signals. Also, Donald Davies coins the terms "packets" and "packet switching," a method of using several paths to transmit packets. ARPA's Bob Taylor is funded to create an experimental network between several U.S. universities, a project that three years later evolves into the Advanced Research Projects Agency Network (ARPANET).

1967

While at a meeting of ARPA researchers, Wes Clark hatches the idea of using dedicated hardware for network functions. The devices later are called Interface Message Processors (IMPs). Also, Lawrence Roberts publishes the first ARPANET design paper, "Multiple Computer Networks and Intercomputer Communication."

1968

The National Research Laboratory (NRL) in Great Britain tests the first WAN to use packet switching. In August, ARPA distributes among vendors bid requests for the ARPANET. IBM and other large companies decline to submit bids because they do not believe this type of network is possible. In December, the small consulting company Bolt Beranek and Newman (BBN), located in Cambridge, Massachusetts, wins the contract. BBN has under a year and $1 million dollars to create a working network. Ken Thompson and Dennis Ritchie of AT&T's Bell Labs develop the UNIX operating system, which later becomes one of the main server operating systems used on information networks.

1969

Telephone equipment manufacturers challenge AT&T to allow devices not created by AT&T to be attached to its telephone system. The Federal Communications Commission (FCC) decides that independent telecommunications devices can be used as long as they cause no harm to the telephone network. The FCC's decision opens the way for modem manufacturers and data communications companies to enter the telecommunication equipment market.

The first IMP prototype, a modification of Honeywell's 516 computer, is produced by Honeywell and delivered to BBN. Called the IMP 0, the prototype does not properly function and it takes several weeks to rewire by hand. Also in the same year, the first Request for Comment (RFC) document, entitled "Host Software," is written by Steve Crocker. RFC 1 explains the interface between the IMP devices and host computers.

At this point, hosts are minicomputers that are accessed through the network. (In the context of a network, a host is a network node: a computer or network device that has a unique identifying address.) Each site participating in the ARPANET is responsible for creating the host software to connect its computers to the ARPANET's IMPs.

In September, the BBN's "IMP Guys" install the first ARPANET IMP node at UCLA, which flawlessly attaches to UCLA's Sigma-7 computer. In October, Stanford Research Institute (SRI) sets up a second node that attaches to its SDS 940 computer. Some adjustments are made to both early ARPANET nodes, which were connected over a 50 kilobits per second (Kbps) circuit. In November, the University of California at Santa Barbara becomes the third node, and in December, the University of Utah becomes the fourth node.

1970

Funded by ARPA, the ALOHAnet is created by Norman Abrahamson at the University of Hawaii. It transmits data at a slow 4.8 Kbps, but sets the stage for the popular network transport protocol, Ethernet. Also, BBN's headquarters become the fifth ARPANET node. The protocol used by host computers connected to ARPANET is called Network Control Protocol (NCP). It should not be confused with NetWare Control Protocol, which is a different protocol that also is abbreviated as NCP.

1971

The ARPANET has 15 sites with a total of 23 host computers in the following locations: UCLA, SRI, University of Utah, UCSB, MIT, BBN, RAND, SDC, Lincoln Lab, Stanford, Harvard, University of Illinois, NASA at Ames, Case Western Reserve University, and Central Michigan University. Daily network traffic equals 700,000 packets. Also, the File Transfer Protocol (FTP) is outlined in RFC 172.

1972

E-mail is created by Ray Tomlinson of BBN, and soon it is the ARPANET's most popular software. Also, network-based terminal emulation through the Telnet application protocol is proposed by Jon Postel in RFC 318. Later this year, Bob Kahn shows off the ARPANET network communications between 40 computers at the International Conference on Computer Communications, and the Inter-Networking Group (INWG) is established to create the ARPANET and networking standards.

1973

The University College of London, England, and the Royal Radar Establishment in Norway establish the first international connections to the ARPANET. By now, the ARPANET transmits more than 3 million packets per day. In March, Vinton Cerf creates a preliminary design for gateway architecture, and in May, Robert M. Metcalfe proposes Ethernet communications in his Harvard PhD thesis. Metcalfe and David Boggs later create the first Ethernet network operating system at nearly 3 million bits per second (Mbps). The experimental computers on their network are called Michelson and Morley after the 19th century scientists who proved that ether does not exist. Six years later, Metcalfe founds the 3Com Corporation that provides networking devices.

1974

The commercial digital transmission facilities and devices created by Dataphone Digital Service (DDS) play a role in pushing the Bell system to convert from analog to digital telecommunications networking systems. Also, Vinton Cerf and Bob Kahn propose the Transmission Control Protocol (TCP) in their paper, "A Protocol for Packet Network Internetworking," which introduces the term "Internet."

1975

Responsibility for the ARPANET's daily operations is placed under the Defense Communications Agency, which is now called the Defense Information Systems Agency. Also, the first digital telephone switch, called the SL-1, is made available by Northern Telecom.

1976

Switching achieves acceptance among computer network professionals based on Leonard Kleinrock's paper, "Queuing Systems Volume II—Computer Applications." Also, a new protocol for public packet switched networks, called X.25, is established and achieves widespread use by the end of the 1970s on the Tymnet and Telenet public networks.

1977

The Tymnet public network is started by Tymshare. Later this year, the first wireless gateway is connected to the ARPANET. This system transmits packets over radio waves using a technique called packet radio that is still employed today and sets the foundation for modern wireless networking technologies.

A

1978

Plans for the Internet Protocol (IP) are launched by Vinton Cerf, Steve Crocker, and Danny Cohen. IP is proposed as a routing function that is separate from TCP. TCP and IP become vital components of Internet communications in the years ahead. In the same year, the first hypermedia video disk is demonstrated at the Massachusetts Institute of Technology (MIT).

1979

The Internet Configuration Control Board (ICCB) is started and focuses on network gateway issues. Tom Truscott, Steve Bellovin, and Jim Ellis create the USENET network between Duke University and the University of North Carolina. Also, as the 1970s come to a close, integrated circuits (ICs) on chips are used in all types of electronic devices, including the sophisticated chips sporting large-scale integration (LSI) and very large-scale integration (VLSI). LSI and VLSI chips pave the way for faster and cheaper digital devices, such as computers and computer terminals, and the door is now open for the development of personal computers. Further, in 1979 Nippon Telegraph and Telephone in Japan initiates the first-generation (1G) cellular network for wireless telephone communications.

1981

The academic-based, Because It's Time NETwork (BITNET) is created by Ira Fuchs and Greydon Freeman between the City University of New York and Yale University. By the end of 1989, BITNET is a vast and successful cooperative of colleges and universities in all parts of the United States. Also this year, IBM's Personal Computer (PC) hits the market costing $4500, and it becomes an overnight success. Microsoft develops a version of MS-DOS called PC DOS that is the operating system used by the IBM PC. Further, 1981 marks the beginning of rapid developments in dial-up modem technology.

1982

Transmission Control Protocol (TCP) and Internet Protocol (IP) are adopted as the main protocol suite for the ARPANET. Also, the Defense Data Network is started for U.S. military use, which is later called Milnet (Military Network). At the National Computer Conference in June, Drew Major, Kyle Powell, and Dale Neibaur present the first PC LAN, using software that lays the foundation for Novell's NetWare network operating system.

1983

The ARPANET becomes a truly civilian-based network as Milnet goes its own way to focus on military applications. Their separation marks the arrival of the Internet. The ARPANET switches protocols from NCP to TCP/IP, and Berkeley UNIX is modified to include TCP/IP. The number of host computers connected to ARPANET reaches 500.

1984

Over 1000 hosts are connected to the Internet, and William Gibson's novel, *Neuromancer*, introduces the term "cyberspace." The divestiture of AT&T's Bell Systems causes the new telecommunications companies to accelerate competition in business communications. The competition is particularly intense in high-speed communications technologies, giving birth to T-carrier services at 1.544 Mbps.

1986

The Internet grows to over 5000 hosts. The National Science Foundation sponsors five supercomputing centers at universities throughout the United States, which are joined at 56 Kbps over the newly created NSFNET. The supercomputers and NSFNET open the way to conduct large-scale research projects from an array of U.S. colleges and universities already connected to networks such as BITNET and the Internet.

1987

The Internet connects over 10,000 host computers. The first hypermedia authoring system is marketed by Apple Computer, signaling the start of the age of desktop computer authoring and multimedia productions. Network management is a developing concern that is addressed by Jeff Case, Mark Fedor, Martin Schoffstall, and James Davin who create Simple Gateway Monitoring Protocol (SGMP), which is later integrated with TCP/IP and called the Simple Network Management Protocol (SNMP). Coincidentally, the first demonstration of SGMP is hindered by a widespread Internet outage that underscores the importance of network management.

1988

The Internet has over 60,000 host computers, and the NSFNET now operates at 1.544 Mbps, which increases the NSFNET traffic volume to over 75 million packets a day. In the same year, Europe and North America are linked by the first transatlantic fiber-optic cable that is capable of transmitting 40,000 telephone calls at one time. Robert Morris Jr.'s Internet Worm, the first virus targeted at the Internet, impacts nearly 10 percent of Internet host computers.

1989

Another 40,000 hosts are added to the Internet for a total of 100,000. Tim Berners-Lee distributes the first World Wide Web Project proposal to the Internet community. At the close of the 1980s, LAN deployment is everywhere, providing data communications networking in small offices and throughout buildings. Computer users are discovering that they can access anything from anywhere—computers, printers, and WANs such as the Internet—and they are the recipients of phenomenal technological and software advances. New network equipment is more and more able to expand LAN service areas and increase the speed of data transmissions. Internet and network hosts are migrating from mainframe platforms to smaller workstation and PC computers because of the popularity of UNIX and NetWare as network operating systems.

1990

The ARPANET, supplanted by the Internet, is officially retired. Signaling System 7 (SS7) is gaining in use as the digital switch protocol for public telephone networks. SS7 enables a range of customer services and makes it possible to locate telephone network problems quickly and to reconfigure network paths. The United States and Sweden are among the first countries to implement SS7 in telecommunications using a new technology called common channel signaling, which makes the following services available in conjunction with telecommunications servers:

- Call forwarding, conferencing, and call waiting
- Automated recall and callback
- Multiple telephone numbers through one residential telephone line
- Voice mail
- Caller ID
- Voice-activated dialing features
- Redirection of 800 number calls when needed because of excessive traffic

1990 marks the beginning of the decade of developing fast LAN and WAN communications technologies. Eleven countries become the newest members of NSFNET.

1991

Internet host computers exceed 600,000, with thousands coming online each month. The NSFNET is opened to commercial use, a landmark move that changes the nature of its use. Also, the NSFNET now operates at 44.736 Mbps, fostering transmission of 10 billion packets per month. Gopher and the World Wide Web technologies are available to be deployed by individual Internet hosts, launching a race to determine which will be most popular. In Finland, the first commercial second-generation (2G) wireless network is started. 2G mobile telephone networks have launched a new era of mobile wireless communications using modern digital signals broadcast from radio transmission antennas instead of analog signals.

1992

There are over 1 million Internet hosts and 13 new countries—from chilly Antarctica to warm Ecuador—that join the Internet. Also, people are now "surfing the Net," courtesy of Jean Armour Polly's new phrase.

1993

Internet host computers surpass 2 million, and 17 countries in Africa, Asia, Central America, and Europe are new NSFNET participants. The U.S. president and vice president acquire Internet access and e-mail addresses. At the start of the year, there are 50 Web-based servers, and by its end there are 500. Also, the Mosaic Web browser is released.

1994

There are over 3 million Internet hosts, and 20 new countries go online, from Armenia to Uzbekistan. The NSFNET transmission capability is expanded to 155 Mbps, resulting in over 10 trillion bytes sent each month. The first cyberbank, "First Virtual," opens for business, as does Mosaic Communications Corporation, the predecessor of Netscape Communications.

1995

There are 4 million Internet hosts, and the largest volume of Internet traffic is from Web-based communications. The NSFNET ceases operations and is transformed by the National Science Foundation into the dedicated research network called the very high-speed Backbone Network Service (vBNS). National and international network traffic is largely composed of diverse providers, called Internet service providers (ISPs), and the community of providers, users, and hosts is regarded as the Internet.

1996

There are 9 million Internet host computers and 30 new countries on the Internet, and the MCI telecommunications company establishes 622 Mbps communications. The Telecommunications Act of 1996 encourages the development of new interactive communications options, including networking options over TV cable and telecommunications lines.

1997

There are over 16 million Internet hosts and 20 new member countries.

1998

Traffic on the Internet doubles every 100 days, and business use of the Internet represents the largest area of growth. Over 10 million people in the United States and Canada are doing business on the Internet, purchasing airline tickets, books, appliances, computers, and cars. Also in 1998, 1 Gbps communications devices are widely offered by network equipment vendors.

Google is started, providing popular search engine capabilities on the Web.

1999

The Internet2 academic and research network begins to take hold, connecting university networks in Europe and the United States. Based in Indiana, the first full-service bank is established on the Internet. To accomplish faster networking, portions of the United States Internet backbone begin transmitting at 2.5 gigabits per second (Gbps). A backbone consists of high-capacity communications media that join networks in the same building, throughout a campus, or across long distances.

Also, U.S. law establishes domain names as property.

2000

The new version of IP, IPv6, is used for Internet2 backbone communications. Europe sets the stage to implement a new multicountry gigabit network to be called Géant. In addition, many news networks enable video clips to be viewed over the Internet and many radio stations can be played via the Internet.

2001

Vendors offer 10-Gbps communications devices for networks. In addition, the push to implement wireless communications is on. Some companies, such as Microsoft, implement widespread wireless network communications on their business campuses. Many radio stations stop using the Internet for broadcasts because of legal concerns about the distribution of royalties for intellectual property such as music. High schools in the United States gain access to the Internet2 research and education network.

2002

The 10-Gbps standard for Ethernet communications is ratified after some testing delays. Also, the prices of 1-Gbps devices fall dramatically because so many vendors, including new vendors, have entered the market. With advances in copper-wire, 1-Gbps communications also mean that this form of network transport can be installed on many existing networks. In addition, a major credit card company expands network and data center operations to locations in Europe, the Far East, and Latin America, causing networks in these regions to more broadly adopt TCP/IP. The first live commercial third-generation (3G) mobile wireless communications networks are launched, initially in South Korea and later the same year in the United States. 3G mobile telecommunications services enable users to access the Internet and transmit data through a 3G equipped device, such as a cell phone (initially) or by 2010 the small tablet computer, including the Apple iPad (introduced by Apple in January 2010).

2003

Switzerland holds an election in which voters can use the Internet. In the same year, several malicious attacks seriously affect the Internet, beginning with the SQL Slammer worm that rapidly spreads worldwide affecting transportation control systems, ATM machines, and emergency communications. The Blaster worm and the Sobig.F virus are two other malicious attacks on the Internet. In other Internet security developments, the number of computers "hijacked" by attackers averages 2000 per day.

There are about 131,000 residential subscribers using Internet telephony for personal telephone conversations.

2004

It is projected that the number of Internet telephony users will grow to over 17 million residential subscribers by 2008. Further, preparations are under way to handle spam over Internet telephony (spit), which can fill up voice-mail boxes with unwanted messages.

Wireless access to the Internet is introduced by Lufthansa Airlines on a flight from Munich, Germany, to Los Angeles. The wireless Internet communications are made possible by geostationary satellites (satellites in orbit at 36,000 kilometers). The average number of computers hijacked over the Internet by attackers each day rises to 30,000. In terms of advances in network security to combat attackers, the first network using quantum cryptography is tested at BBN Technologies in Cambridge, Massachusetts. This technology uses quantum quirks of photons for providing the most secure communications currently developed. Further, with quantum cryptography an alarm goes off if someone tries to intercept a message.

Facebook is started as a leap forward in social networking.

2005

Computer chip manufacturers, including Intel and Advanced Micro Devices (AMD), are creating a new generation of chips to stop some forms of malicious attacks, such as buffer overflows. A buffer overflow occurs when a memory storage area (a buffer) is sent more information than it can handle, and so the extra information overflows into another buffer.

Researchers at MIT make important progress in the development of data-switching techniques that are entirely optical. Fully optical data switching holds the promise of handling data at 100 terabits per second.

YouTube is started so that people can publish online videos, and later the same year YouTube is purchased by Google.

2006

The number of Web sites surpasses 100 million. Twitter goes online for people-to-people communications. Southeastern Asia Internet connectivity is significantly reduced because critical fiber-optic lines are damaged by an earthquake in Taiwan and resulting underwater mudslides.

Cloud computing interest is rising, and Amazon.com launches important public cloud computing development efforts beginning with Amazon Web Service.

The number of iTunes downloads through the Apple iTunes store exceeds 1 billion. In this year, the iTunes store becomes the largest music retailer.

2007

UC Berkeley Economist Hal Varian reports that with help from networks and the Internet, information (when considered as a product, such as cars or computers) is progressing 10 times faster than any other products in the world.

The number of users who blog reaches 12 million. Communication is further advanced through Apple's introduction of the iPhone, which spurs the use of smartphones and virtual keyboards.

The English edition of Wikipedia exceeds 2 million articles. Also, Amazon.com makes the Kindle e-reader available for downloading and storing e-books.

2008

The number of mobile Internet users reaches 95 million in the United States. In the same year, the first open-source private cloud platform is deployed via Eucalyptus.

Ninety percent of residences in the United States have broadband connections to the Internet, according to a Nielson study. Also, a study shows that 22 percent of people worldwide use the Internet.

The first cell phone using the Android operating system (developed by the Open Handset Alliance with Google as a major contributor) is introduced by T-Mobile. Also, in this year, 2.5 trillion text messages are sent throughout the world.

2009

The Scandinavian telecommunications company, TeliaSonera, brings online the world's first fourth-generation (4G) network in Stockholm, Sweden, and later in Norway. Wireless 4G telecommunications and data networks offer faster data transfer rates at up to 100 Mbps.

Over 100 million people have viewed at least one YouTube video. In the same year, China becomes the number one user of the Internet, with over 90 percent of Chinese Internet users having access to a broadband connection.

Australia announces plans for a 100 Mbps national broadband network. Also, UNESCO starts a worldwide digital library with holdings in Arabic, Chinese, English, French, Portuguese, Russian, and Spanish.

Amazon.com reports e-book sales exceed sales of physical books in its sales figures. Further, sales through Apple's App Store for iPhone and iPad apps exceed 2 billion downloads.

2010

Facebook is up to 400 million active subscribers, and Twitter has 175 million. Facebook is the most visited Web site in the United States in 2010. Steve Jobs introduces Apple's iPad tablet PC, while users have downloaded over 3 billion apps for iPhones and iPods over the past 18 months.

Google's presence in China is under review after its computers there come under attack. Besides Google, over 20 other foreign company's computers have experienced attacks in China.

Guber technologies of Germany introduces the first brain–computer interface that enables a computer to type out a user's thoughts.

2011

The number of Facebook subscribers doubles to 800 million; over 42 percent of the population in the United States uses Facebook.

By February, over 2 billion people use the Internet. Also, since one year ago Apple's iBookstore has sold 100 million downloaded iBooks. And Google is processing 1 trillion searches per day.

In May, the streaming and by-mail movie service Netflix is the largest upstream and downstream source of traffic on the Internet.

The British newspaper *News of the World* is shut down because of allegations that it uses information obtained through cell phone hacking and that it bribed London Metropolitan Police to ignore reports of cell phone hacking.

The Stanford University School of Engineering offers a free online course, *An Introduction to Artificial Intelligence*, that has over 58,000 students worldwide.

2012

A group launches a project to build a satellite network on which information cannot be censored.

Computer vendors begin launching a new category of computer called Ultrabooks, which are much thinner (about 21 mm or 0.8 inches wide) than notebooks and use second-generation Intel Core processors.

Minitube offers a desktop interface for Linux computers for delivering an enhanced experience of YouTube videos.

Computer industry observers note that mobile computing is significantly blurring the boundaries between personal and work life for many users.

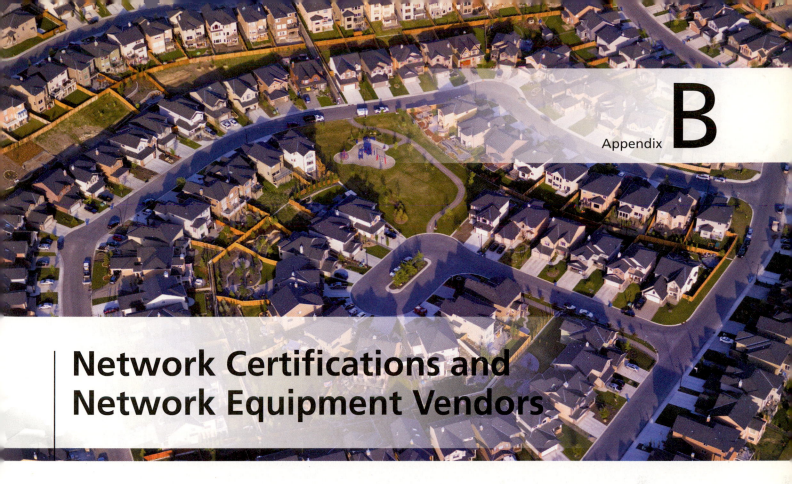

Network Certifications and Network Equipment Vendors

Many network professionals decide to seek certification to show their mastery of networking technologies and to advance their careers. This appendix presents several types of network certifications that some readers may choose to seek through additional preparation. In addition, it is valuable to know about the range of network equipment vendors. This appendix also provides information about vendors and the kinds of products they offer.

Network Certifications

A certification in networking offers one way to show employers or clients your mastery of networking theory and practice. Some people obtain certification for a salary increase, job advancement, and to have validation of their technical knowledge. Network certifications involve passing written and sometimes laboratory examinations. Table B-1 lists examples of network certifications.

Table B-1 Network certifications

Certification	Sponsoring Organization and Web Site	Description
CompTIA Network+	Computing Technology Industry Association *www.comptia.org*	A popular vendor-neutral certification for individuals with basic (about a year or more) network experience, training, or both. Areas of focus include topologies, network standards, network media, protocols, setup and support, and troubleshooting.
CompTIA Digital Home Technology Integrator (DHTI+)	Computing Technology Industry Association *www.comptia.org* and Consumer Electronics Association *www.ce.org*	A certification targeted at integrating home subsystems including networks, home security systems, entertainment equipment, telecommunications devices, Internet access, and electrical wiring.

(continues)

Table B-1   Network certifications (*continued*)

Certification	Sponsoring Organization and Web Site	Description
Cisco Certified Network Associate (CCNA)	Cisco Systems *www.cisco.com*	A beginning-level certification for those who work with small to medium-sized networks using Cisco network equipment.
Cisco Certified Design Associate (CCDA)	Cisco Systems *www.cisco.com*	A beginning-level certification for designing Cisco networks involving switching and routing.
Cisco Certified Design Professional (CCDP)	Cisco Systems *www.cisco.com*	An advanced-level certification for designing Cisco networks involving switching and routing.
Cisco Certified Internetwork Professional (CCIP)	Cisco Systems *www.cisco.com*	An advanced-level certification for service providers involving IP technologies and Cisco equipment.
Cisco Certified Network Professional (CCNP)	Cisco Systems *www.cisco.com*	An advanced-level certification for those who support medium-sized or enterprise-level Cisco networks of about 100 to over 500 nodes.
Cisco Wireless Certification (a CCNP specialization)	Cisco Systems *www.cisco.com*	A certification for wireless network professionals that focuses on wireless theory and practice, site survey, voice and mobility services, and wireless security involving Cisco equipment.
Cisco Security Certification (a CCNP specialization)	Cisco Systems *www.cisco.com*	An advanced-level certification for Cisco network security professionals focusing on security in network devices such as routers and switches.
Cisco Voice Certification (a CCNP specialization)	Cisco Systems *www.cisco.com*	An advanced-level certification for integrating voice communications on Cisco-based networks, particularly focusing on Voice over IP (VoIP).
Cisco Advanced Wireless LAN Design Specialist	Cisco Systems *www.cisco.com*	A certification for designing, setting up, and managing wireless networks by using advanced Cisco wireless networking features.
Cisco Certified Internetwork Expert (CCIE)	Cisco Systems *www.cisco.com*	The highest-level certification for Cisco networking professionals that involves "tracks" or specializations such as Security, Routing and Switching, Service Provider, Storage Networking, Wireless, and Voice.
Certified Wireless Network Administrator (CWNA)	Certified Wireless Networking Professional Alliance *www.cwnp.com*	A vendor-neutral certification for managing wireless networks.
Certified Wireless Security Professional (CWSP)	Certified Wireless Networking Professional Alliance *www.cwnp.com*	A vendor-neutral certification for securing enterprise wireless networks.
Certified Wireless Design Professional (CWDP)	Certified Wireless Networking Professional Alliance *www.cwnp.com*	A vendor-neutral certification for designing enterprise wireless networks and requires the CWNA certification first.
Certified Wireless Analysis Professional (CWAP)	Certified Wireless Networking Professional Alliance *www.cwnp.com*	A vendor-neutral certification for analyzing wireless networks to improve performance and reliability.
Certified Wireless Network Expert (CWNE)	Certified Wireless Networking Professional Alliance *www.cwnp.com*	A vendor-neutral certification to demonstrate the most advanced level of wireless networking expertise.
Microsoft Certified IT Professional (MCITP): Enterprise Administrator in Windows Server 2008	Microsoft *www.microsoft.com*	A certification for administering Microsoft Windows Server 2008 in an enterprise network that includes enterprise network applications and also includes basic networking expertise.
Microsoft Certified IT Professional (MCITP): Server Administrator in Windows Server 2008	Microsoft *www.microsoft.com*	A certification for administering Microsoft Windows Server 2008 in different environments and includes basic networking expertise.

Table B-1 Network certifications (*continued*)

Certification	Sponsoring Organization and Web Site	Description
Microsoft Certified Solutions Associate (MCSA)	Microsoft *www.microsoft.com*	Microsoft's new entry-level certification with emphasis on cloud computing; a prerequisite for the next level certification, the MCSE.
Microsoft Certified Solutions Expert (MCSE)	Microsoft *www.microsoft.com*	Microsoft's new expert-oriented level of certification for those who play a key role in migrating to and implementing cloud computing.
Microsoft Certified Solutions Master (MCSM)	Microsoft *www.microsoft.com*	Microsoft's new highest-level certification with emphasis on cloud computing technologies.
Red Hat Certified Engineer (RHCE)	Red Hat *www.redhat.com*	A certification that combines expertise in Red Hat Enterprise Linux systems and networking.
Red Hat Certified Architect (RHCA)	Red Hat *www.redhat.com*	An advanced certification for designing, implementing, and managing Red Hat Enterprise Linux networks with emphasis on security, advanced network skills, monitoring, directory services, and other skills.
Wireshark Certified Network Analyst	Wireshark University *www. wiresharktraining.com*	A certification specific to the Wireshark network analyzer, focusing on securing, troubleshooting, and optimizing a network through assessing network traffic data.

© Cengage Learning 2013

Network Equipment Vendors

There are many network equipment vendors. Some vendors provide a large range of network devices, and others emphasize particular niches, such as DSL and cable modem devices (broadband network devices). The following is a list of vendors, their Web sites, and a sampling of the products they offer. The list is not exhaustive, but it is provided to give you a starting point in locating the appropriate vendor for your interests.

B

Company: Adtran

Web site: *www.adtran.com*

Products:

- ATM devices
- Cables
- CSUs/DSUs
- DSL devices
- Frame relay devices
- ISDN devices
- Multiplexers
- Optical access devices
- Repeaters
- Routers
- SONET devices
- Switches
- T-carrier devices
- VoIP/IP telephony
- VPN gateways
- Wireless WAN devices

Company: Alcatel-Lucent

Web site: *www.alcatel-lucent.com*

Products:

- ATM devices
- DSL devices
- Frame relay devices
- Gateways
- Gigabit, 10 Gigabit, and 40/100 Gigabit Ethernet devices
- ISDN devices
- Microwave and satellite devices
- Optical network devices
- Remote access devices
- Routers
- Routing switches
- SONET multiplexers
- Switches
- Telecommunications devices
- Voice over IP devices

Company: Allied Telesis

Web site: *www.alliedtelesis.com*

Products:

- Chassis-based switches
- Stackable edge switches
- Gateways
- LAN switches
- Media conversion devices
- Multiservice access devices
- Network adapters for fiber and copper cables
- Network management software
- Optical and copper NICs
- Optical networking devices
- Optical transport devices
- Routers
- Transceivers
- Voice over IP devices
- Wireless networking devices

Company: Apple

Web site: *www.apple.com*

Products:

- Mobile devices, such as smartphones and tablet PCs
- Mobile device services
- Wireless devices

Company: Asante

Web site: *www.asante.com*

Products:

- Routers
- Transceivers
- Uplink connectors
- Wireless and cable NICs
- Wireless, cable, and DSL routers
- Workgroup and enterprise switches

Company: AT&T

Web site: *www.att.com*

Products:

- DSL access services and devices
- Mobile communications access services and devices
- Wireless network devices

Company: Aztech

Web site: *www.aztech.com*

Products:

- Analog modems
- Digital modem/routers
- DSL devices
- Voice over IP devices
- Wireless devices

Company: Belkin

Web site: *www.belkin.com*

Products:

- Cables and connectors
- Wireless devices including wireless routers

Company: Cisco Systems

Web site: *www.cisco.com*

Products:

- Access servers
- Cable products
- Digital voice and video devices
- DSL products
- Firewalls
- Internetworking devices
- IP TV devices
- Modules for chassis devices
- Network interfaces and modules
- Network security devices
- Optical networking devices
- Routers
- Switches
- Telephony devices
- Voice over IP devices
- Wireless networking devices

Company: Comcast

Web site: *www.comcast.com*

Products:

- Cable devices
- Cable TV, data, and voice telecommunications services
- Wireless devices

Company: Dell

Web site: *www.dell.com*

Products:

- Managed and unmanaged switches mostly from third-party vendors
- Wireless devices, such as wireless routers

Company: D-Link

Web site: *www.dlink.com*

Products:

- Cable modems and routers
- Cables
- DSL devices
- NICs
- Routers
- Switches
- Voice over IP devices
- VPNs and firewalls
- Wireless networking devices

Company: Enterasys

Web site: *www.enterasys.com*

Products:

- Cabling products
- Network management software
- Routers
- Switches
- VPN products
- Wireless networking devices
- Wiring closet products

Company: Extreme Networks

Web site: *www.extremenetworks.com*

Products:

- Ethernet switches and switch software for all types of applications
- Network management software
- Port extenders
- Wireless devices such as access points and controllers

Company: Fiberdyne Labs

Web site: *www.fiberdyne.com*

Products:

- Cables and cabling equipment
- Cable TV equipment
- Media converters
- Multiplexing devices
- NICs
- Routers
- Switches
- Transceivers
- Wireless devices

Company: Hewlett Packard

Web site: *www.hp.com*

Products:

- Modems
- Network access servers
- Network-monitoring devices
- Network storage equipment
- NICs
- Routers
- Switches
- Wireless networking devices

Company: IBM

Web site: *www.ibm.com*

Products:

- Cloud computing network devices
- Ethernet networking devices
- NICs
- SNA devices for networks
- Ethernet switches
- Partner vendor switches and routers
- Storage area network equipment
- System networking software

Company: Intel

Web site: *www.intel.com*

Products:

- Cable modems
- Ethernet expansion modules
- Ethernet transceivers
- Mobile communications equipment
- NICs and WNICs
- Optical networking components
- Repeaters
- Switching components
- Telecommunications devices
- Wireless networking devices

Company: Juniper Networks

Web site: *www.juniper.net*

Products:

- Cable modem termination systems
- Gateways
- Network management devices
- Routers
- Security and intrusion detection systems
- Switches
- Wireless networking devices

Company: Kentrox

Web site: *www.kentrox.com*

Products:

- Access servers/concentrators
- CSUs/DSUs
- Firewall devices
- Intrusion prevention devices
- IPSec VPN devices
- ISDN devices
- Network management systems

Company: Motorola

Web site: *www.motorola.com*

Products:

- Bluetooth devices
- Cable modems
- Headend products
- Mobile devices, including cell phones, smartphones, and tablet PCs
- Network management products
- Routers
- Satellite networking products
- SONET devices
- Switches
- Voice over IP devices
- Wireless networking devices

B

Company: Netgear

Web site: *www.netgear.com*

Products:

- Cables
- DSL devices
- Firewall and VPN devices
- Gateways
- NICs
- Printer servers
- Routers
- Switches
- Wireless networking devices

Company: Nortel Networks

Web site: *www.nortelnetworks.com*

Products:

- DSL devices
- Firewalls
- Optical networking devices
- PBXs
- Routers
- Switches
- Voice over IP devices
- Wireless networking devices

Company: Optimum (formerly Bresnan)

Web site: *www.optimum.com*

Products:

- Cable devices
- Cable TV, data, and voice telecommunications services
- Wireless devices

Company: Panduit

Web site: *www.panduit.com*

Products:

- Cable identification systems
- Cable installation tools
- Cable ties
- Copper and fiber-optic cable products
- Fiber-optic systems
- Grounding systems
- Power connectors
- Rack systems
- Surface raceway systems
- Wireless systems, including access points and controllers

Company: SMC Networks

Web site: *na.smc.com*

Products:

- Cable modems
- DSL devices
- NICs and WNICs
- Voice gateways
- Wireless networking devices
- Workgroup and managed switches
- Wireless touch-screen and keypad devices

Company: Sprint

Web site: *www.sprint.com*

Products:

- Mobile networking devices
- Mobile networking voice and data services

Company: Time Warner Cable

Web site: *www.timewarnercable.com*

Products:

- Cable devices
- Cable TV, data, and voice telecommunications services
- Wireless devices

Company: T-Mobile

Web site: *www.t-mobile.com*

Products:

- Mobile networking devices
- Mobile networking voice and data services

Company: Transition Networks

Web site: *www.transition.com/TransitionNetworks*

Products:

- Cabling connectors
- Device servers
- Fiber-optic NICs
- Managed and unmanaged switches
- Media conversion devices (to fiber optics)
- Multiplexers
- Network interface cards
- Network interface devices
- Optical transceivers

Company: Verilink

Web site: *www.verilink.com*

Products:

- Access routers
- ATM services and voice over ATM
- Bandwidth aggregation devices
- Chassis modules for network devices
- DSL networking products
- Frame relay services and equipment
- Integrated access devices
- Optical access devices
- T-carrier services and T-carrier equipment

Company: Verizon

Web site: *www.verizon.com*

Products:

- Mobile networking devices
- Mobile networking voice and data services

Company: ZyXEL

Web site: *www.zyxel.com*

Products:

- Analog modems
- Cable modems
- DSL devices
- Firewalls for VPNs
- Gateway security
- ISDN TAs
- Media converters
- Network-attached storage
- Routers
- Transceivers
- WAN gateways
- Wireless networking devices, including adapters, gateways, and antennas

List of Acronyms

2G: 2nd generation

3G: 3rd generation

4G: 4th generation

A

AAAA resource record: IPv6 host address (AAAA) resource record

AAL: ATM adaptation layer

ABR: available bit-rate service

ACK: acknowledge

ADPCM: adaptive differential pulse code modulation

ADSL: Asymmetrical Digital Subscriber Line

AES: Advanced Encryption Standard

AIFF: Audio Interchange File Format

ANSI: American National Standards Institute

API: application programming interface

APIPA: Automatic Private IP Addressing

ARP: Address Resolution Protocol

ARPA: Advanced Research Projects Agency

ARPANET: Advanced Research Projects Agency Network

ARQ: automatic repeat-request

ASCII: American Standard Code for Information Interchange

ASIC: application specific integrated circuit

ATDM: Asynchronous Time Division Multiplexing

ATIS: Alliance for Telecommunications Industry Solutions

ATM: Asynchronous Transfer Mode

ATM PVC: Asynchronous Transfer Mode permanent virtual circuit

ATM SPVC: Asynchronous Transfer Mode smart permanent virtual circuit

ATM SVC: Asynchronous Transfer Mode switched virtual circuit

AUI: attachment unit interface

B

B-ICI: broadband-intercarrier interface

B-ISDN: Broadband Integrated Services Digital Network

BIOS: basic input/output system

BNC: bayonet navy connector

BOOTP: Bootstrap Protocol

BPDU: bridge protocol data unit

bps: bits per second

Bps: bytes per second

BRI-ISDN: basic rate interface Integrated Services Digital Network

BUS: broadcast and unknown server

C

CaaS: Communication as a Service

CAN: campus area network

CAU: controlled access unit

CBDS: Connectionless Broadband Data Service

CBR: constant bit-rate

CCITT: Consultative Committee on International Telegraph and Telephone

CHAP: Challenge Handshake Authentication Protocol

CIDR: Classless Interdomain Routing

CIR: committed information rate

CLP: cell loss priority

CMIP: Common Management Interface Protocol

CPE: customer premise equipment

CRC: cyclic redundancy check

CSMA/CA: Carrier Sense Multiple Access with Collision Avoidance

CSMA/CD: Carrier Sense Multiple Access with Collision Detection

CSLIP: Compressed Serial Line Internet Protocol

CSU: channel service unit

CTS: clear to send

D

DaaS: Desktop as a Service

DACS: digital access cross-connect switch or digital access cross-connect system

dB: decibel

DCE: data communications equipment or data circuit equipment

DCT: Digital Carrier Trunk

DDoS: distributed denial of service

DEP: Data Execution Prevention

DES: Data Encryption Standard

DHCP: Dynamic Host Configuration Protocol

DHCPv6: Dynamic Host Configuration Protocol for IP version 6

DLC: Data Link Control protocol

DLCI: Data Link Connection Identifier

DMZ: demilitarized zone

DNA: Digital Network Architecture

DNS: Domain Name System

DOCSIS: Data Over Cable Service Interface Specification

DoS: denial of service

DQDB: Distributed Queue Dual Bus

DS: digital signal

DSAP: destination service access point

DSL: digital subscriber line

DSSS: Direct Sequence Spread Spectrum Modulation

DSU: data service unit

DTE: data terminal equipment

DVMRP: Distance Vector Multicast Routing Protocol

DWDM: dense wavelength division multiplexing

DXI: data exchange interface

E

EISA: extended industry standard architecture

EBCDIC: Extended Binary Coded Decimal Interchange Code

EDI: electronic data interchange

EIA: Electronic Industries Alliance

EOF: end-of-file delimiter

EOL: end of life

ELAP: EtherTalk Link Access Protocol

EMI: electromagnetic interference

ESP: Encapsulating Security Payload

ESS topology: extended service set topology

ETSI: European Telecommunications Standards Institute

F

FCC: Federal Communications Commission

FCS: frame check sequence

FDDI: Fiber Distributed Data Interface

FDMA: frequency-division multiple access

FHSS: Frequency Hopping Spread Spectrum

FRAD: frame relay access device

FTP: File Transfer Protocol

G

Gbps: gigabits per second

GBps: gigabytes per second

GFC: generic flow control

GFI: general format identifier

GID: group identification number

GIF: Graphics Interchange Format

G.lite ADSL: G.lite asymmetric digital subscriber line

GHz: gigahertz

GSM: Global System for Mobile Communication

H

HDLC: High-level Data Link Control

HDSL: High bit-rate Digital Subscriber Line

HDTV: high-definition digital TV

HEC: header error control

HFC: hybrid fiber/coax cable

host ID: host identifier

HTTP: Hypertext Transfer Protocol

HTTPS: Hypertext Transfer Protocol Secure

Hz: hertz

I

IaaS: Infrastructure as a Service

IAHC: International Ad Hoc Committee

IANA: Internet Assigned Numbers Authority

IAPP: Interaccess Point Protocol

IBSS topology: independent basic service set topology

IC: integrated circuit

ICANN: Internet Corporation for Assigned Names and Numbers

ICCB: Internet Configuration Control Board

ICMP: Internet Control Message Protocol

ICS: Internet Connection Sharing

IDSL: Integrated Services Digital Network Digital Subscriber Line

IEEE: Institute of Electrical and Electronics Engineers

IETF: Internet Engineering Task Force

IFF: Interchange File Format

IGMP: Internet Group Management Protocol

IHL: IP Header Length

IMT-2000: International Mobile Telecommunications-2000

IMT Advanced: International Mobile Telecommunications-Advanced

IP: Internet Protocol

IPng: Internet Protocol Next Generation

IPv4: Internet Protocol version 4

IPv6: Internet Protocol version 6

IPX: Internetwork Packet Exchange protocol

ISA: industry standard architecture

iSCSI: Internet Small Computer System Interface

ISDN: Integrated Services Digital Network

ISO: International Organization for Standardization

ISOC: Internet Society

ISP: Internet service provider

ITU: International Telecommunications Union

IWF: interworking function

IXC: interexchange carrier

K

kHz: kilohertz

L

L2TP: Layer Two Tunneling Protocol

LAN: local area network

LANE: LAN Emulation

LAPB: Link Access Procedure-Balanced

LAPD: Link Access Procedure D

LAPF: Link Access Protocol for Frame

LATA: local access and transport area

LCI: logical channel identifier

LDAP: Lightweight Directory Access Protocol

LEC: LAN Emulation Client

LECS: LAN Emulation Configuration Server

LED: light-emitting diode

LEO: low Earth orbiting satellite

LES: LAN Emulation Server

LLAP: LocalTalk Link Access Protocol

LLC: logical length control

LMI: local management interface extension

LSI: large-scale integration

M

MaaS: Monitoring as a Service

MAC: media access control

MAN: metropolitan area network

MAU: media access unit or multistation access unit

MSAU: multistation access unit

Mbps: megabits per second

MBps: megabytes per second

MCA: microchannel architecture

MIB: Management Information Base

MIB-I: Management Information Base version I

MIB-II: Management Information Base version II

MIMO: multiple-input multiple-output

MMC: Microsoft Management Console

MNP: Microcom Network Protocol

MOSPF: Multicast Open Shortest Path First protocol

MPEG: Moving Pictures Experts Group compression

MPLS: Multiprotocol Label Switching

MPOA: multiprotocol encapsulation over ATM

MSAU: multistation access unit

MSO: multiple system operator

MTTR: mean time to repair

MTU: maximum transmission unit

MUX: multiplexer

MVS: Multiple Virtual Storage

N

N-ISDN: Narrowband Integrated Services Digital Network

NaaS: Network as a Service

NAT: Network Address Translation

ND: Network Discovery protocol

NDIS: Network Driver Interface Specification

NetBEUI: NetBIOS Extended User Interface

NetBIOS: Network Basic Input/Output System

NET_ID: network identifier

NFS: Network File System protocol

NHRP: Next Hop Resolution Protocol

NHS: Next Hop Server

NI-1: National ISDN-1 protocol

NI-2: National ISDN-2 protocol

NIC: network interface card

nm: nanometer

NMS: network management station

NNI: network-to-network interface

NSF: National Science Foundation

NT: network terminal

NTA: network terminal adapter

NTSC: National Television Standards Committee

NTU: Network Termination Unit

NVRAM: nonvolatile random access memory

O

OC: optical carrier

ODA: Open Document Architecture

ODBC: Open Database Connectivity

ODI: Open Datalink Interface

OFDM: Orthogonal Frequency Division Multiplexing

OHA: Open Handset Alliance

OSI: Open Systems Interconnect

OSPF: Open Shortest Path First protocol

OTDR: optical time domain reflectometer

P

PaaS: Platform as a Service

PABX: private automatic branch exchange

PAD: packet assembler/disassembler

PAL: phase alternation line

PAP: Password Authentication Protocol

PAX: private automatic exchange

PBX: private branch exchange

PCI: peripheral computer interface

PCM: pulse code modulation

PDN: public data network

PDU: protocol data unit

PIM: Protocol Independent Multicast

PMD: physical medium-dependent ATM sublayer

PNNI: private network-to-network interface

PnP: Plug and Play

POP: point of presence

POTS: plain old telephone service

PPM: pulse position modulation

PPP: Point-to-Point Protocol

PPPoE: Point-to-Point Protocol over Ethernet

PPTP: Point-to-Point Tunneling Protocol

PRI-ISDN: primary rate interface Integrated Services Digital Network

PROM: programmable read-only memory chip

PSE: packet-switching exchange

PSK: preshared key

PSTN: public switched telephone network

PTI: packet type identifier

PTI: payload type indicator

PTR resource record: pointer resource record

PVC: permanent virtual circuit

PVC: polyvinyl chloride

Q

QoS: Quality of Service

R

RAD: rapid application development tool

RADIUS: Remote Authentication Dial-In User Service

RADSL: Rate Adaptive Asymmetric Digital Subscriber Line

RARP: Reverse Address Resolution Protocol

RBOC: regional Bell operating company

RF: radio frequency

RFC: Request for Comment

RFI: radio frequency interference

RG: radio grade

RIP: Routing Information Protocol

RMON: Remote Network Monitoring

RPC: remote procedure call

RSN: Robust Secure Network

RSVP: Resource Reservation Protocol

RTCP: Real-Time Transport Control Protocol

RTP: Real-Time Protocol

RTS: request to send

S

S-HTTP: Secure Hypertext Transfer Protocol

SaaS: Software as a Service

SAN: Storage Area Network

SAP: service access point

SAR: segmentation and reassembly ATM sublayer

SB-ADPCM: subband adaptive differential pulse code modulation

SBUS: SPARC Bus

SCP: service control point

SCSI: Small Computer System Interface

SDH: Synchronous Digital Hierarchy

SDSL: Symmetric Digital Subscriber Line

SDU: service data unit

SECAM: System Electronique Couleur Avec Memoire

SIG: SMDS Interest Group

SIP: SMDS Interface Protocol

SHDSL: Symmetric High bit-rate Digital Subscriber Line

SLA: service-level agreement

SLIP: Serial Line Internet Protocol

SMAU: smart multistation access unit

SMB: Server Message Block

SMDS: switched megabit data service

SMDS-DXI: SMDS Data Exchange Interface

SMTP: Simple Mail Transfer Protocol

SNA: Systems Network Architecture

SNAP: SubNetwork Access Protocol

SNMP: Simple Network Management Protocol

SNMPv2: Simple Network Management Protocol version 2

SNMPv3: Simple Network Management Protocol version 3

SOA resource record: start of authority resource record

SOF: start of frame

SONET: synchronous optical network

SPE: synchronous payload envelope

SPVC: smart permanent virtual circuit

SPX: Sequence Packet Exchange

SS7: Signaling System 7 protocol

SSAP: source service access point

SSH: Secure Shell

SSID: service set identifier

SSL: Secure Sockets Layer

SSP: service switching point

STM: Synchronous Transport Model level

STS: synchronous transport signal

STP: shielded twisted-pair cable

SVC: switched virtual circuit

SVR RR: service resource record

SWAP: Shared Wireless Access Protocol

T

TA: terminal adapter

TC: transmission convergence ATM sublayer

TCM: time compression multiplexing

TCP: Transmission Control Protocol

TDD: time division duplexing

TDM: time division multiplexing

TDMA: Time Division Multiple Access multiplexing

TDR: time domain reflectometer

TE: terminal equipment

TFTP: Trivial File Transfer Protocol

THz: terahertz

TIA: Telecommunications Industry Association

TKIP: Temporal Key Integrity Protocol

TLD: top-level domain

TOS: type of service

Tracert: Traceroute

TTL: Time to Live

TTRT: target token rotation time

U

UBR: unspecified bit-rate service

UCE: unsolicited commercial e-mail

UDP: User Datagram Protocol

UID: user identification number

UNI: user-to-network interface

UPS: uninterruptible power source

USB: universal serial bus

UTP: unshielded twisted-pair cable

V

vBNS: very high-speed Backbone Network Service

VBR: variable bit-rate

VC: virtual channel

VDSL: Very High bit-rate Digital Subscriber Line

VDSL2: Very High bit-rate Digital Subscriber Line version 2

VL-bus: VESA local bus

VLAN: virtual LAN

VLAN ID: virtual LAN identification number

VLSI: very large-scale integration

VMS: Virtual Memory System

VoFR: voice over frame relay

VoIP: voice over IP

VP: virtual path

VPI/VCI: Virtual Path Identifier/Virtual Channel Identifier

VPN: virtual private network

VT: virtual tributary

W

WAN: wide area network

WDM: wavelength division multiplexing

WECA: Wireless Ethernet Compatibility Alliance

WEP: Wired Equivalent Privacy

Wi-Fi: wireless fidelity

WLANA: Wireless LAN Association

WNIC: wireless network interface card

WPA: Wi-Fi Protected Access

WPA2: Wi-Fi Protected Access version 2

X

XaaS: Anything or Everything as a Service

xDSL: digital subscriber line (refers to all types of DSL)

XNS: Xerox Network System

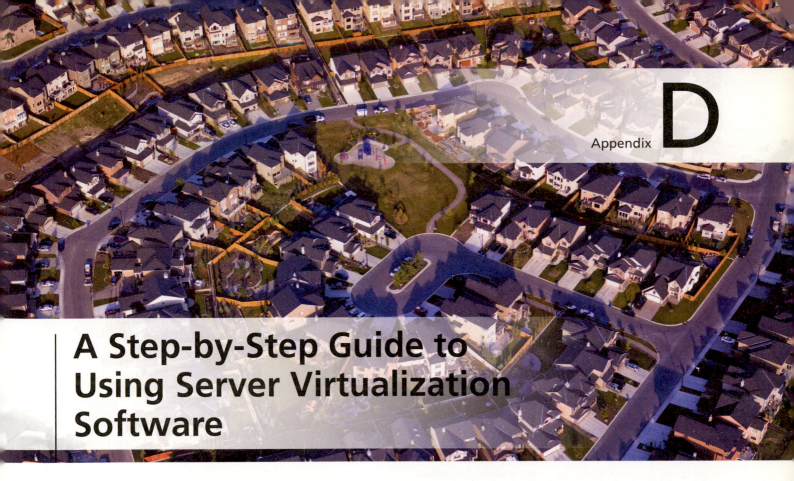

Appendix **D**

A Step-by-Step Guide to Using Server Virtualization Software

Virtualization enables a school or an individual student to get the most out of computer resources. Schools can use virtualization to turn a single server computer into a virtual server that can host two, three, or more operating systems. For example, one computer can house three virtual servers running Windows Server 2008/Server 2008 R2. This capability saves the school money on servers and enables more students to be able to work on their own operating systems.

Virtualization also allows a school or an individual student to turn a single PC into a virtual system on which to run another operating system—without having to alter the current operating system running on the PC. A single computer lab PC or a student's home PC can be turned into a host for multiple operating systems, such as hosting Windows 7 and Windows Server 2008 R2 or hosting Windows 7 and Red Hat Linux. You can install virtualization software, such as in a host computer running Windows XP, Windows Vista, or Windows 7—and then install Windows Server 2008 R2, for instance, to run as a guest in a virtual window (and called a virtual machine). Virtualization enables you to complete the hands-on activities in this book using different operating systems running from your home PC, for example. When you are finished learning with a guest operating system, such as Windows Server 2008 R2, you simply remove the virtualization software or the virtual operating system and you are back where you started with your original operating system.

You can download free evaluation versions of Windows 7 and Windows Server 2008 R2 at *www.microsoft.com/downloads*. You can download Fedora Linux for free at *fedoraproject.org*. Also in most cases, if virtualization software supports Red Hat Enterprise Linux, it will likely also support Fedora Linux, which is sponsored by Red Hat.

This appendix is a step-by-step guide for turning a single computer into a virtual system housing one or more virtual machines. (As a user, you might think of a virtual machine as simply a window within virtualization software that runs a guest operating system.) The main focus is on three popular virtualization systems that are available for free:

- *Microsoft Virtual PC 2007*: Intended for a Windows XP or Vista workstation-grade PC to host another operating system, such as a Windows Server 2008 or Windows Server 2008 R2 virtual machine
- *Microsoft Virtual Server*: Intended for a server-grade computer to host multiple virtual machines, including Windows Server 2008/Server 2008 R2 and other operating systems and can be downloaded for free
- *VMware Player*: Available as a free download and can host a variety of server and workstation operating systems

Microsoft Virtual PC is the newest version of this software (rather than the 2007 version), which works only on Windows 7 computers and higher. However, this new version does not support Windows Server 2008/Server 2008 R2 as guest operating systems, and so is not discussed in this appendix.

For each of these virtualization systems, you learn:

- How to obtain a free download version
- How to install it
- How to create a virtual machine
- How to install a guest operating system, such as Windows Server 2008 R2, as a virtual machine, and then how to access that virtual machine's operating system
- How to configure virtual networking
- How to configure hardware components

Microsoft Virtual PC 2007

Microsoft Virtual PC 2007 can be installed in Microsoft Windows XP, Vista, and Windows Server 2003 operating systems. Although Microsoft Virtual PC 2007 is intended to host workstation operating systems as virtual machines, you can also use it to create a Windows Server 2008/Server 2008 R2 Standard Edition virtual machine.

Microsoft Virtual PC 2007 is available from Microsoft as a free download. From the individual reader's or student's perspective, this is ideal for running the Windows Server 2008/ Windows Server 2008 R2 Standard Edition evaluation DVD on a Windows XP or Windows Vista computer. It works equally well on Windows XP or Windows Vista computers in a student computer lab.

Requirements for Microsoft Virtual PC 2007

Microsoft Virtual PC 2007 with Service Pack 1 (SP1) is the most recently available 2007 version. It can be loaded on the following operating system hosts:

- Windows XP Professional with SP2 or SP3
- Windows Server 2003 Editions SP2 (x86 or x64)
- Windows Vista Business Edition (x86 or x64 versions with or without SP1)
- Windows Vista Enterprise Edition (x86 or x64 versions with or without SP1)
- Windows Vista Ultimate Edition (x86 or x64 versions with or without SP1)

It is also possible to load Microsoft Virtual PC 2007 SP1 on Windows Server 2008/Windows Server 2008 R2.

The hardware requirements for Microsoft Virtual PC 2007 SP1 are as follows:

- *CPU*: Intel Celeron, Pentium II, Pentium III, Pentium 4, Core Duo, Core2 Duo CPU, or faster Intel CPU; or AMD Athlon or Duron CPU (400 MHz or faster; x86 or x64).

- *RAM*: Enough RAM for at least the minimum requirements of the total number of operating systems you will be running. For example, if you are running Windows XP Professional (128 MB minimum) and want to load Windows Server 2008 (512 MB minimum) as a virtual machine, you will need a minimum of 640 MB to 1 GB of RAM. If Windows Vista is the host and you want to run a Windows Server 2008 Standard Edition virtual machine, then you will need a minimum of 1 GB of RAM. Note that to run Windows Server 2008 R2 as a guest operating system, you will need a 64-bit computer with well over 1 GB of RAM.

- *Disk space*: Enough disk storage for the operating systems you plan to run. For example, Windows XP requires at least 1.5 GB, Window Vista requires at least 15 GB, and Windows Server 2008 requires at least 10 GB (but 15 to 20 GB is better for using different roles and services).

Virtual Machine Operating Systems Supported

After Virtual PC 2007 SP1 is loaded, you can run any of the following operating systems as virtual machines (guests) within Virtual PC 2007 SP1:

- Windows XP Home or Professional with SP1, SP2, or SP3 (or no service pack)
- Windows Vista Business Edition (x86 or x64 versions with or without SP1)
- Windows Vista Enterprise Edition (x86 or x64 versions with or without SP1)
- Windows Vista Ultimate Edition (x86 or x64 versions with or without SP1)
- Windows Server 2008/Server 2008 R2 Standard Edition

Windows 7 can also be loaded as a guest in Microsoft Virtual PC 2007 SP1, but is not formally listed as a guest operating system.

How to Download Microsoft Virtual PC 2007 SP1

Microsoft Virtual PC 2007 SP1 can be downloaded from Microsoft's Web site for no cost. The steps to download Microsoft Virtual PC 2007 SP1 are as follows (what you click is presented in bold):

In some Windows 7 or Server 2008/Server 2008 R2 steps in this appendix, you may see the User Account Control (UAC) dialog box, which is used for security to help thwart intruders. The UAC box asks for permission to continue with an action or asks for the administrator password. If you see this box, click **Continue**. Because computer setups may be different, the dialog box is not mentioned in the actual steps.

1. Log onto your computer.
2. Create a folder in which to download the setup.exe file for Microsoft Virtual PC (such as a temporary folder or a folder under your Program Files folder).

3. Open a Web browser, such as Internet Explorer.

4. Go to the URL **www.microsoft.com/downloads** or **www.microsoft.com/download/en/ default.aspx**.

Web links and specific instructions change periodically. You may need to search *www.microsoft.com* for the most current link if these links do not work.

5. In the Search Download Center box, enter **Microsoft Virtual PC 2007** and make sure **Search Download Center** is selected and click the **magnifying glass** to start the search.

6. Click the link for **Microsoft Virtual PC 2007 SP1**.

To use Microsoft Virtual PC 2007 with Windows Server 2008/Server 2008 R2 or Windows Vista as the virtual machine (guest) operating system, you must use the download containing SP1.

7. Click the **Download** button for the setup.exe file that is appropriate for your computer, which is 32 BIT/setup.exe for an x86 computer or 64 BIT/setup.exe for an x64 computer.

8. Click the **Save** button.

9. Select the folder you created for saving the setup.exe file.

10. Click **Save**.

11. Click **Close** in the Download complete box.

12. Close your Web browser.

How to Install Microsoft Virtual PC 2007 SP1

Microsoft Virtual PC 2007 SP1 is easy to install. The installation steps are as follows:

1. Browse to the folder where you saved the setup.exe file for Microsoft Virtual PC 2007 SP1.

2. Double-click **setup.exe**.

3. If you see the Open File – Security Warning dialog box, click **Run**.

4. Click **Next** after the Microsoft Virtual PC 2007 SP1 Wizard starts (see Figure D-1).

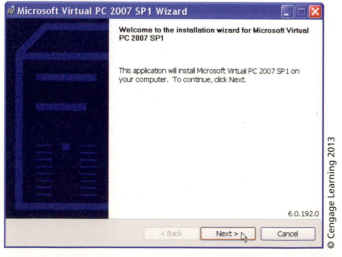

© Cengage Learning 2013

Figure D-1   Microsoft Virtual PC 2007 SP1 Wizard

5. Click the option button for **I accept the terms in the license agreement**. Click **Next**.

6. Enter your user name and name of your organization (if an organization name is appropriate). Notice that the product key should already be provided. Also, if you see this option, leave **Anyone who uses this computer (All Users)** selected. Click **Next**.

7. Click **Install**. The installation process will take a few minutes to complete.

8. Click **Finish**.

Creating a Virtual Machine and Installing a Guest OS

After Microsoft Virtual PC 2007 SP1 is installed, the next step is to create a virtual machine in which to install a guest operating system.

The following are example steps for setting up the virtual machine with Windows Server 2008 Standard Edition as the guest operating system:

 Microsoft Virtual PC 2007 SP1 may not be compatible with hardware virtualization on some CPUs. If you experience a crash dump when configuring the virtual machine or loading the guest OS, first make sure you have enabled hardware virtualization in Step 12. If this does not work, try disabling hardware virtualization in the BIOS and restart these steps from the beginning.

1. From the host operating system, such as Windows XP or Windows Vista, click **Start**.

2. Point to **All Programs** and click **Microsoft Virtual PC**.

3. The New Virtual Machine Wizard opens (see Figure D-2). Click **Next**.

© Cengage Learning 2013

Figure D-2   New Virtual Machine Wizard

4. Ensure that **Create a virtual machine** is selected and click **Next**.

5. Provide a name for the virtual machine, such as **Windows Server 2008** or **Windows Server 2008 R2**. Click **Next**.

6. Ensure Windows Server 2008 or Windows Server 2008 R2 is selected as the operating system to install and click **Next**.

7. Ensure that at least 512 MB to 1 GB of memory (use at least 1 GB for Windows Server 2008 R2) is allocated for the virtual machine. If necessary, click **Adjusting the RAM** and use the slider bar to allocate enough memory. Click **Next**.

8. Ensure that **A new virtual hard disk** is selected and click **Next**.

9. Make sure that the virtual hard disk is sized to meet your needs or leave the default size (you will need 15 GB for Windows Server 2008 and might use at least 20–40 GB, for example). Click **Next**.

10. Click **Finish**.

11. You should see the Virtual PC Console open in the desktop. If it is not open click **Start,** point to **All Programs,** and click **Microsoft Virtual PC.**

12. You can configure options at this point by clicking the **File** menu and clicking **Options** on the shortcut menu. Click each option to see what it does and configure any options as necessary. When you are finished, click **OK**. The options are as follows:

    - *Restore at Start*: Pauses a running virtual machine when you exit the console and restores the virtual machine when you reopen the console.

    - *Performance*: Specifies how the CPU time is allocated to virtual machines and specifies what happens when a Virtual PC is a process running in the background.

    - *Hardware virtualization*: Used to enable hardware virtualization, if your CPU has this capability.

    - *Full-Screen Mode*: Enables the screen resolution to be adjusted so it is the same for the host and guest OSs (note the caution if this is enabled).

    - *Sound*: Sound for virtual machines is muted by default. If you enable it, the sounds from the host and guest OS can be difficult to differentiate.

    - *Messages*: Used to turn off error and informational messages from Virtual PC.

    - *Keyboard*: Used to choose the host key for the guest operating system. The default host key is the right ALT key. When you press this key you can switch the mouse between the guest and host windows and you can execute guest key combinations, such as pressing ALT+DEL to send the CTRL+ALT+DEL key combination to the guest OS for logging on.

    - *Mouse*: Specifies how the pointer is captured for use in the virtual machine window.

    - *Security*: Determines how to control access to Virtual PC functions.

    - *Language*: Specifies the language to use for Virtual PC.

13. Insert the Windows Server 2008 or Windows Server 2008 R2 Standard Edition installation DVD.

At this point you could install any of the supported guest operating systems. If you are installing a different operating system, you would insert the CD/DVD now and complete Step 14, and then Steps 15 through 30 (or whatever steps are required) would be unique to the operating system you are installing.

14. Click the **Start** button in the Virtual PC Console window. This opens a second larger window, which is the Microsoft Virtual PC 2007 console window. Wait for a few minutes for the DVD to start loading. Click in the console window to enable the mouse to be operative within the console. (If necessary, you can switch the mouse movement back so that it can go all over the screen by pressing the right ALT key, which is the "host" key).

Occasionally the mouse may seem stuck, move slowly, or stop functioning in the active portion of the console window. If this happens, close all console windows and go to Step 11 to start again. Also, some installation processes take longer to install in a virtual machine. Don't close the window or stop the installation prematurely, even if you seem to be stuck on a black screen for several minutes.

15. Select the language to install, such as **English**, in the Language to install drop-down box. In the Time and currency format box, make your selection, such as **English (United States)**. In the Keyboard or input method box, make your selection, such as **US**. Click **Next**.

In any of the following steps while you are working in the Virtual PC Console window, you may have to click inside the active portion of the console window first to have the mouse function within it.

16. Click **Install now**. If you see a window prompting for the product key, provide the product key and click **Next**.

17. Select **Windows Server 2008 Standard (Full Installation)** or **Windows Server 2008 R2 Standard (Full Installation)** and click **Next**.

18. Read the license terms, click the box for **I accept the license terms**, and click **Next**.

19. Click **Custom (advanced)**.

20. You will see the amount of unallocated disk space highlighted, which is the disk space you specified when you configured the virtual machine. Ensure it is highlighted and click **Next**.

21. The installation program begins installing Windows Server 2008 or Windows Server 2008 R2. You will see progress information about Copying files, Expanding files, Installing features, Installing updates, and Completing installation. This part of the installation can take 30 minutes or longer.

22. The installation program restarts the operating system.

23. You see the message: *Please wait while Windows sets up your computer*.

24. Next you see the Install Windows window in the Completing installation phase (this step is not in the installation of Windows Server 2008 R2).

25. The system reboots again (this step is not in the installation of Windows Server 2008 R2).

26. You will see the message (a red circle with a white x in it): *The user's password must be changed before logging on the first time*. Click the **OK** button (remember you may have to click inside the active portion of the console window first to have the mouse function within it).

27. Enter a new password for the Administrator account and then enter the same password again to confirm it. Click the **blue circle** with the white right-pointing arrow inside.

If you enter a password that is not a strong password, you will see the message (with a white x in a red circle): *Unable to update the password*. This means that the value provided for the new password does not meet the length, complexity, or history requirements of the domain. Click **OK** and enter a different password that is over seven characters and uses letters, numbers, and characters such as &.

28. When you see the message *Your password has been changed*, click **OK**.

29. At this point, the Windows desktop is opened and the Initial Configuration Tasks window is displayed.

30. You can configure Windows Server 2008/Server 2008 R2 as you would in a nonvirtual environment.

31. When you close the Microsoft Virtual PC 2007 console window, you can either turn off the virtual machine or save its current state. Unless you want to save its state, a good practice is to shut down the server prior to closing the window. (Saving the state means to keep the server in its current state, without shutting it down.) When you shut down the server in this way, the Microsoft Virtual PC 2007 console window closes, but leaves the Virtual PC console window still open. Also, to restart the virtual machine, open the Virtual PC console window, click **Start**, and wait for the system to boot in the Microsoft Virtual PC 2007 console window.

When you log into Windows Server 2008/Server 2008 R2 from the console window, the normal CTRL+ALT+DEL key sequence does not work. Instead, click the **Action** menu and press **CTRL+ALT+DEL**. Another alternative is to press and hold the **right ALT** key and press the **DEL** key.

Installing an OS from an ISO Image

An ISO file is an optical disk (CD/DVD) image file that ends with the .iso file extension. An ISO file can be accessed in several ways, such as from a CD/DVD, a hard drive, or as a shared network file. Typically when you download an operating system, such as an evaluation copy of a Windows operating system, you download an ISO file. One advantage of using an ISO file for installing a guest operating system into a virtual machine is that the installation process can go faster. Microsoft Virtual PC 2007 SP1 enables you to install from an ISO file by using the following general steps:

1. Follow Steps 1 through 13 in the previous section, "Creating a Virtual Machine and Installing a Guest OS."

2. Click the **Start** button in the Virtual PC Console window.

3. After the Microsoft Virtual PC 2007 window opens, press the **right ALT key** if necessary to access the menu at the top of the window.

4. Click the **CD** menu and click **Capture ISO Image**.

5. Navigate to the ISO file, click the file, and click the **Open** button.

6. You return to the Microsoft Virtual PC 2007 window from which you should restart the virtual machine.

Configuring Networking and Hardware Options

You can configure a range of networking and hardware options in Microsoft Virtual PC 2007 SP1. For example, if the host computer has two or more NICs, you can specify which NIC to use for a virtual machine. In another example, you might need to create one or more additional virtual hard disks for a virtual machine.

Use these steps to configure networking and hardware options:

1. Open the Virtual PC Console, if it is not open.

2. Click the **Settings** button, or click the **Action** menu and click **Settings** (see Figure D-3).

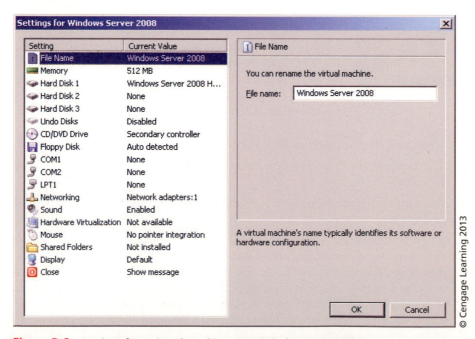

Figure D-3   Settings for a virtual machine using Window Server 2008

3. Click **Networking** in the left pane. If your computer has multiple adapters, you can select the specific adapter (or multiple adapters) to associate with a virtual machine.

4. In the right pane, click the down arrow for the adapter that is selected by default. The following options are available:

- *Not connected*: Used if you do not intend to enable the virtual machine to access a network (including the Internet) and so that it cannot be accessed from a network.

- *Local*: If two or more virtual machines are set up, they can access each other; however, virtual machines cannot access the network.

- *Network Interface Name*: The actual name of a NIC model, such as an Intel or Broadcom NIC, that the virtual machine is directly connected to for regular network and Internet access. With this selection, network configuration tasks that apply to other network computers also apply to the virtual machine. If a DHCP server is on the network or if the network uses a router with Network Address Translation (NAT), the virtual machine's network connection can be configured to use these. The same applies if a DNS server is set up.

- *Shared Networking (NAT)*: Used to create a private Virtual PC network, which has a virtual DHCP server and a virtual NAT-enabled router or firewall. Typically the first virtual computer created acts as the DHCP server and provides NAT services. In this arrangement Microsoft Virtual PC 2007 SP1 performs as a virtual DHCP server, leasing IP addresses for virtual machines in the range of 192.168.131.1 to 192.168.1.253. Further, the virtual machines appear as computers within a private NAT-protected network. A connection to the Internet is shared among the virtual machines and is protected in a way similar to a NAT-enabled router or firewall.

- *Loopback Adapter*: You will see this option if the operating system is configured to have a Microsoft loopback adapter (configured as a network adapter, such as through the Add Hardware option in Control Panel). This option is used in two contexts. One context is when no physical network connection is present, but you want to simulate network connectivity between the host and all virtual machines. A second context is when you are creating a network with many routers and firewalls as well as many virtual machines.

5. Make the networking selections that are appropriate to your situation and then click **OK**.

6. If necessary to go back to the Settings window, click **Settings** in the Virtual PC Console.

7. Click **Memory** in the left pane. Notice that you can increase the memory allocation for the virtual machine by using the slider bar in the right pane.

8. In the left pane, click **Hard Disk 1** and notice that the right pane shows the path to the virtual hard disk file. Also, notice you can configure the Hard Disk 2 and Hard Disk 3 options for additional virtual hard disks. To do this click Hard Disk 2 in the left pane, for example, and click the Virtual Disk Wizard button in the right pane. (A virtual machine can have up to three hard disks.)

9. Click **CD/DVD Drive** in the left pane and notice you can attach a CD or DVD drive via the right pane.

10. Click **Hardware Virtualization** in the left pane and notice in the right pane that you can configure to enable hardware virtualization, if your computer supports it.

11. Notice you can configure additional hardware, such as communication (COM) ports, a floppy disk, printer (LPT) ports, sound, the mouse, the display, and others.

12. When you are finished with the configurations, click **OK**.

Host Key Options

Because a virtual machine represents an operating system running inside an operating system, it is necessary to have a way to use the keyboard so that the keys you press communicate directly with the guest operating system. For example, you will notice that pressing CTRL+ALT+DEL brings up the Windows Security box or a menu of options, depending on which version of Windows is the host operating system. It does not take you to a log on screen in the guest operating system.

Microsoft Virtual PC enables you to communicate with the guest operating system by using the host key, which is the right ALT key by default. Table D-1 lists important host key combinations you can use while you are accessing a virtual machine.

Table D-1　Host key options for Microsoft Virtual PC 2007 SP1

Keyboard Combination	Result
HostKey	Enables you to move the mouse outside of the window area used by the guest OS (move the mouse back into the guest OS display and click when you want to work in the guest OS)
HostKey+DEL	The virtual machine OS responds to this as CTRL+ALT+DEL
HostKey+P	Toggles the virtual machine between pause and resume
HostKey+R	Causes the virtual machine to reset
HostKey+A	Selects all items in the active window in the guest OS
HostKey+C	Copies selected text and items in the active window in the guest OS
HostKey+V	Pastes text and items in the active window in the guest OS
HostKey+Enter	Switches between full screen and window modes
HostKey+DownArrow	Causes the virtual machine to minimize
HostKey+I	Enables you to install virtual machine additions

© Cengage Learning 2013

Microsoft Virtual Server

Microsoft Virtual Server 2005 is intended to host server operating systems as virtual machines. At this writing, Microsoft Virtual Server 2005 R2 SP1 is the most recent version, but you can also choose to download additional updates to fix mounting VHD files and to implement recent security updates. This version supports hardware (integrated in the CPU) virtualization, such as AMD CPUs equipped with AMD-V and Intel CPUs with Intel VT. Other features include:

- Can be installed in x64 operating systems
- Provides support for Internet Small Computer System Interface (iSCSI), which is a technology used in Storage Area Networks (SANs)
- Has the ability to cluster the virtual servers on a single computer
- Provides enhanced Active Directory support by publishing Virtual Server binding data through service connection points
- Virtual disks can expand dynamically
- Supports most popular x86 operating systems
- Can mount a virtual disk on a different operating system
- Enables the use of Volume Shadow Copy Service (VSS) for backups (used in newer versions of Windows operating systems, such as Windows Server 2008/Server 2008 R2, Windows 7, and Windows Vista)
- Offers virtual server management through Virtual Server Web console
- Can use scripting to control virtual machine setups
- Memory access can be resized

Microsoft Virtual Server Guest Operating Systems Supported

Microsoft Virtual Server can house virtual machines for popular Windows and Linux server and workstation operating systems. The following operating systems can be guests:

- Windows Server 2008 R2 Standard, Enterprise, Datacenter, and Web Server (comes in x64 versions only)
- Windows Server 2008 Standard, Enterprise, Datacenter, and Web Server (x86 and x64)
- Windows Server 2003 Standard, Enterprise, Datacenter, and Web Server SP1 or SP2 (x86 or x64)
- Windows Server 2003 Standard, Enterprise, Datacenter, and Web Server R2 (x86 or x64)
- Windows Small Business Server 2003 (Standard and Premium Editions)
- Windows 2000 Server
- Windows XP Professional SP2
- Windows Vista Business, Ultimate, and Enterprise
- Red Hat Enterprise Linux and Fedora
- SUSE Linux Enterprise Server
- SUSE Linux versions

Other operating systems can also run experimentally in Microsoft Virtual Server, such as Windows 7.

Microsoft Virtual Server Host Operating Systems Supported

Microsoft Virtual Server can be installed into the following Windows host operating systems:

- Windows Server 2008 R2 Standard and Enterprise (x64)
- Windows Server 2008 Standard and Enterprise (x86 or x64)
- Windows Server 2003 Standard, Enterprise, and Web Server with SP1 or SP2 (x86 or x64)
- Windows Server 2003 Standard, Enterprise, and Web Server R2 (x86 or x64)
- Windows Small Business Server 2003 (Standard and Premium Editions, also R2 versions)
- Windows 2000 Server with SP3 or SP4
- Windows XP Professional (x86 and x64)
- Windows Vista Business, Ultimate, and Enterprise Editions
- Windows 7 Professional, Business, and Enterprise Editions, with special technical modifications that are described on Microsoft forums for Windows 7 (for example, visit *social .technet.microsoft.com/Forums/en-US/w7itprovirt/thread/a98e77b7-95d4-444f-8dbc-630c98074436*, or to see another approach that demonstrates the whole installation on YouTube, visit *www.youtube.com/watch?v=Rm1yLII5-ZM*)

Requirements for Microsoft Virtual Server

The hardware requirements for Microsoft Virtual Server 2005 R2 with SP1 are as follows:

- *CPU*: Intel Celeron, Pentium III, Pentium 4, Xeon, or faster Intel processor; or AMD Opteron, Athlon, Athlon 64, Althon X2, Duron, or Sempron (550 MHz or faster; x86 or x64).
- *RAM*: Enough RAM to match at least the minimum requirements of the total number of operating systems you will be running. For example, if you are running Windows Vista

(1 GB minimum required for the Vista host) and want to load Windows Server 2008 (512 MB minimum) as a virtual machine, you will need a minimum of 1.512 to 2 GB of RAM. If Windows Server 2008 R2 Standard Edition is the host and you want to run a Windows Server 2008 R2 Standard Edition virtual machine, then you will need at least 2 GB of RAM.

- *Disk space*: Enough disk storage for the operating systems you plan to run. For example, Windows Server 2008 R2 Standard Edition requires at least 10 GB (but 40+ GB enables you to load more roles and services).

How to Download Microsoft Virtual Server

You can download Microsoft Virtual Server from Microsoft's Web site for free. To download Microsoft Virtual Server:

1. Log onto your computer.
2. Establish a folder in which to store the download (such as a temporary folder or a folder under your Program Files folder).
3. Start your Web browser, such as Internet Explorer.
4. Go to the URL **www.microsoft.com/downloads** or **www.microsoft.com/download/en/ default.aspx** (for English).

Web links and specific instructions change periodically. You may need to search *www.microsoft.com* for the most current link if these links do not work.

5. In the Search Download Center box, enter **Microsoft Virtual Server 2005**, make sure **Search Download Center** is selected, and click the **magnifying glass** to start the search.
6. Click **Microsoft Virtual Server 2005 R2 SP1 – Enterprise Edition**.
7. Click the **Download** button for the setup.exe file that is appropriate for your computer, which is 32 BIT/setup.exe for an x86 computer or 64 BIT/setup.exe for an x64 computer.
8. Click the **Save** button.
9. Select the folder you created for saving the setup.exe file.
10. Click **Save**.
11. Click **Close** in the Download complete box.
12. Close your Web browser.

How to Install Microsoft Virtual Server

The general steps used to install Microsoft Virtual Server into the host operating system are as follows:

1. Browse to the folder in which you saved the setup.exe file for Microsoft Virtual Server.
2. Double-click **setup.exe**.
3. If you see the Open File – Security Warning dialog box, click **Run**.
4. Click **Install Microsoft Virtual Server 2005 R2 SP1** (see Figure D-4).
5. Click **I accept the terms in the license agreement**. Click **Next**.
6. Enter your user name and the name of your organization (if you represent an organization). Notice that the Product Key information is provided by default. Click **Next**.

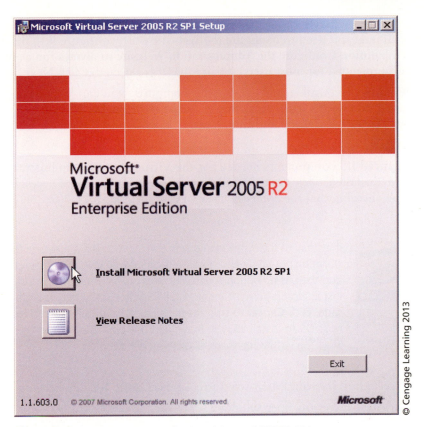

Figure D-4   Installing Microsoft Virtual Server 2005 R2 SP1

 After you click **Next,** you may see the informational message: *The installed version of Internet Information Services (IIS) does not allow multiple Web sites.* The Virtual Server Administration Web site will be added as a virtual directory under the default site.

7. Ensure that **Complete** is selected for the Setup Type, as shown in Figure D-5, and click **Next.**

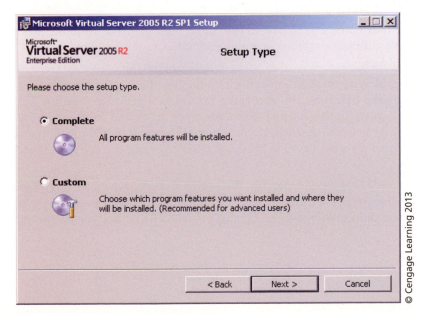

Figure D-5   Selecting the setup type

8. Notice that the Virtual Server Administration Web site will be added to Internet Information Services (IIS). If you need to configure the Web site port, configure it to be 1024. Further, if you see the option **Configure the Administration Web site to always run as the authenticated user (Recommended for most users)**, ensure that it is selected. Click **Next**.

9. If the Windows Firewall is enabled on your computer, you can have the setup process create firewall exceptions for Virtual Server. Make sure **Enable Virtual Server exceptions in Windows Firewall** is selected and click **Next**.

10. Click **Install**.

11. If the required IIS components needed for the Virtual Server Administration Web site are not already installed, click **Yes** to install them. Click **Install** again, if necessary. You will see a dialog box showing that the components are being installed.

If instead of the installation box in Step 10 you see a message that the installation program needs to have the IIS World Wide Web service installed and there is no option to install it, this typically means the Virtual Server installation program cannot install IIS. Click **OK** when you see the message, click **Cancel** to stop the installation, and follow the steps for your host OS to install IIS (you may need the host OS installation CD/DVD). Start the Virtual Server installation again from Step 1.

12. You will see a box showing Microsoft Virtual Server 2005 R2 SP1 is being installed.

13. Click **Finish** and close any open windows.

Creating a Virtual Machine and Installing a Guest OS

After Microsoft Virtual Server is installed, you can use the Virtual Server Administration Web site tool to configure Microsoft Virtual Server, configure a virtual machine, and install a guest operating system.

Here are the steps for creating a virtual machine and installing a guest operating system (using Windows Server 2008/Server 2008 R2 as the guest operating system):

1. Click **Start**, point to **All Programs**, and click **Microsoft Virtual Server**.

2. Click **Virtual Server Administration Web site**.

3. Provide a user name and password (for an account that has Administrator privileges), when you see the Connect to dialog box and click **OK**.

4. If you are using a recent version of the Windows Firewall, you may see the Internet Explorer box to enable you to add this Web site to the list of trusted sites. (You are likely to see this dialog box the first time you access the Virtual Server Administration Web site tool.) Click the **Add** button. In the Trusted sites dialog box, click the **Add** button for the site you are adding and click **Close**. Also, if you see the Microsoft Phishing Filter dialog box, select whether or not to turn on the Phishing Filter (turning the filter on is recommended) and click **OK**.

5. The Virtual Server Administration Web site tool is displayed through Internet Explorer as shown in Figure D-6. Notice that the left pane contains options to navigate, create, and add virtual machines; manage virtual disks; manage virtual networks; and manage the virtual server.

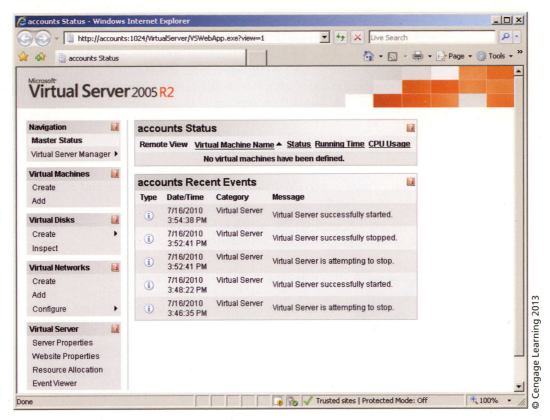

Figure D-6   Virtual Server Administration Website tool

6. In the left pane under Virtual Machines, click **Create**.

7. Enter the name for the virtual machine. Also, set the virtual machine memory. For Windows Server 2008 you should set this for at least 512 MB to 1024 MB or for Windows Server 2008 R2 set it for at least 1024 MB. Also, select to **Create a new virtual hard disk** with at least 40 GB (more is better) for Windows Server 2008/Server 2008 R2. Finally, specify the virtual network adapter, such as an external network interface. Click **Create**.

The virtual network adapter options are: Not connected, External Network, and Internal Network. Not connected (the default) does not provide any type of connection, so you can access the virtual machine only directly from the server. External Network means users can connect to the virtual machine through the computer's network interface card. Internal Network means that there can be a connection between the virtual machines on the same computer.

8. If you see a box to turn AutoComplete on (to remember your entries used in Web forms), select whether or not to use this feature by clicking **Yes** or **No**.

9. In the right pane, review the configuration information for your test server. Notice that you can use this pane to make changes to the configuration. (See the section that follows, "Configuring Networking and Hardware Options," for more information about configuring these options.)

10. So that you can access a window in which to use the virtual server, click **Server Properties** under Virtual Server in the left pane.

11. In the right pane, click **Virtual Machine Remote Control (VMRC) Server**.

12. Ensure that **VMRC server** is checked for **Enable** and that the TCP/IP address of the host server is entered. Also, ensure that Authentication is set to **Automatic**. Remove the check mark from the **Enable** box for **Disconnect idle connections** (so you are not disconnected during the OS installation). Check the **Enable** box for **Multiple VMRC connections** and check **Enable** for **SSL 3.0/TLS 1.0 encryption**. If necessary, set the SSL 3.0/TLS 1.0 certificate to **Keep** or **Request** (if Keep is disabled). Make sure that the host name is the same as the name of the computer you are using. Click **OK** in the bottom-right corner of the window. (If you have any problems using VMRC Server, remember that you can come back to this screen to adjust any parameters.)

13. In the left pane, point to **Configure** under Virtual Machines and click the name of the virtual machine you created.

14. Next you need to turn on the virtual machine. In the right pane, click the screen thumbnail for the virtual machine to turn on the virtual machine.

You may see a message that you need to configure Internet Explorer security to proceed. Make the necessary security configurations. Also, if you see a message from Internet Explorer to install an add-on, click the message and click **Install ActiveX Control** and follow the directions to continue.

15. Insert the Windows Server 2008 or Windows Server 2008 R2 installation DVD.

16. If necessary, click the thumbnail again for the virtual machine. If you see a security message, click **Yes** to proceed.

17. Enter your user name and password (using an account with administrator privileges). Click **OK**.

18. If you see another security message, such as for NTLM Authentication, click **Yes** to proceed.

19. If necessary, scroll down to view the information for working in the Remote Control window. Notice the options to Pause, Save State, Turn Off, and Reset the virtual machine.

20. Scroll back to the top of the Remote Control window.

21. You should see a beginning installation screen for Windows Server 2008/Server 2008 R2. Move the mouse pointer into that screen area (the mouse becomes a small black dot). Click in the area until you see the normal arrow for your mouse. Notice that you can work only within the console for the virtual machine. Press the **right ALT** key (the default host key) to be able to use the mouse throughout the Remote Control window. Remember that you can always use the right ALT key to leave the console area as needed. (Also, to work back inside the console, click the mouse pointer inside the console.) In the upper-right corner of the Remote Control portion of the window, click the down arrow for **Remote Control**. Review the options on the menu, such as Special Keys, Connect To Server, and the other options.

When you point to Special Keys, note that pressing the host key (the right ALT key) with the DEL key can be used to send the CTRL+ALT+DEL key sequence to the virtual machine (this is important to know later for logging in after you have installed Windows Server 2008/Server 2008 R2).

22. Move the mouse pointer back into the console area and click it so that you can work in this area again. You can now proceed with the installation of Windows Server 2008/Server 2008 R2.

23. In the Install Windows window, specify the language to install, such as **English**, in the Language to install drop-down box. In the Time and currency format box, make your selection, such as **English (United States)**. And in the Keyboard or input method box, make your selection, such as **US**. Click **Next**.

24. Click **Install now.** If you see a window prompting for the product key, provide the product key and click **Next.**

If your connection stops before the installation is finished, use the left arrow at the top of the window to go back to the main Status window. Click the virtual machine thumbnail to open a new connection via the Remote Control window. Respond to any security messages, log back in, and respond to any additional security messages. The installation should still be running.

25. Select **Windows Server 2008 Standard (Full Installation)** or **Windows Server 2008 R2 Standard (Full Installation)**—or select a different full installation edition, such as Enterprise Edition if it is available—and click **Next.**

26. Read the license terms, click the box for **I accept the license terms,** and click **Next.**

27. Click **Custom (advanced).**

28. You will see the amount of unallocated disk space highlighted, which is the disk space you specified when you configured the virtual machine. Ensure it is highlighted and click **Next.**

29. The installation program begins installing Windows Server 2008 or Windows Server 2008 R2. You will see progress information about Copying files, Expanding files, Installing features, Installing updates, and Completing installation. This process will take 30 minutes or more.

30. The installation program restarts the operating system.

31. You see the message: *Please wait while Windows sets up your computer.*

32. Next you see the Install Windows window in the Completing installation phase (this step is not in the installation of Windows Server 2008 R2).

33. The system reboots again (this step is not in the installation of Windows Server 2008 R2).

34. You will see the message (a red circle with a white x in it): *The user's password must be changed before logging on the first time.* Click the **OK** button (you may have to click inside the active portion of the console window first to have the mouse function within it).

35. Enter a new password for the Administrator account and then enter the same password again to confirm it. Click the **blue circle** with the white right-pointing arrow inside.

If you enter a password that is not a strong password, you will see the message (with a white x in a red circle): *Unable to update the password.* This means that the value provided for the new password does not meet the length, complexity, or history requirements of the domain. Click **OK** and enter a different password that is over seven characters and uses letters, numbers, and characters such as &.

36. When you see the message *Your password has been changed*, click **OK.**

37. At this point, the Windows desktop is opened and the Initial Configuration Tasks window is displayed. From here you can start configuring Windows Server 2008/Server 2008 R2.

38. You can close the Remote Control window (the Virtual Machine Remote Control Server) or the Status window (the Virtual Server Administration Web site) at any time. The virtual machine continues running in the background. Also, when in the Remote Control Window, you can go back to the Administrator window by clicking the left-pointing arrow at the top of the Remote Control window.

You can shut down a server by first logging on through the Remote Control window. Also, you can use this window and the Status window to turn off a virtual machine (but make sure you shut down the server first).

To access the documentation for Microsoft Virtual Server, click **Start,** point to **All Programs,** click **Microsoft Virtual Server,** and click **Virtual Server Administrator's Guide.**

Installing an OS from an ISO Image

If you have an ISO image file for the guest operating system, you have the option to install it instead of performing a traditional installation through the installation DVD. Here are the general steps for installing an ISO image file in a virtual machine within Microsoft Virtual Server:

1. Follow Steps 1 through 13 in the previous section, "Creating a Virtual Machine and Installing a Guest OS."

2. The bottom portion of the right pane should now show the configuration options for the virtual machine.

3. Click the link for **CD/DVD.**

4. Under Virtual CD/DVD Drive 1, click the option button for **Known image files:.** Next, click the **down arrow** for **Known image files:** and select the image file. If the ISO image file is not listed, then enter the path to the ISO image file in the box for **Fully qualified path to file:.**

5. Click **OK** (the display returns to the Master Status listing).

Configuring Networking and Hardware Options

The Microsoft Virtual Server Administration Web site offers the ability to configure virtual networks. For example, as you learned earlier, a connected network has two default virtual network options: external network and internal network. You can customize settings for both types of networks, such as settings for a virtual DHCP server. You can also create a new virtual network with properties you define.

A virtual network is one used by virtual machines within a network and is independent of other virtual networks. In Microsoft Virtual Server the number of virtual machines connected to a virtual network is unlimited.

The Microsoft Virtual Server Administration Web site also provides options to configure hardware settings, such as adding more memory for use by a virtual server. In the next sections, you learn how to configure virtual networking and to configure hardware for a virtual machine.

Configuring Virtual Networking   In the following steps, you examine how to configure virtual networking:

1. Open the Microsoft Virtual Server Administration Web site tool, if it is not open. (Click **Start,** point to **All Programs,** click **Microsoft Virtual Server,** and click **Virtual Server Administration Website.**)

2. In the left pane under Navigation, click **Virtual Server Manager.** Access each virtual server that is running (if any) and shut it down. To do this, point to the server name (that has a right-pointing arrow) under Status in the right pane, click **Turn Off,** and click **OK.** (You can configure virtual networking while virtual machines are running, but it is advised to turn them off first.)

3. In the left pane under Virtual Networks, point to **Configure** and click **View All.**

4. In the right pane, point to **External Network (***NICname***)** and click **Edit Configuration.**

5. Review the information in the right pane.

6. In the right pane, click the link for **Network Settings.**

7. Review the properties information, including information about the NIC. Click **OK.**

8. In the right pane, click the link for **DHCP server.**

9. You can use the right pane to configure a virtual DHCP server that leases IP addresses through Microsoft Virtual Server (see Figure D-7). To enable the virtual DHCP server, check the **Enabled** box in the right pane. When you enable the virtual DHCP server, you can configure the following:

- *Network address*: Enter the network address for the virtual network
- *Network mask*: Enter the network mask
- *Starting IP address*: Enter the beginning address for the range (scope) of IP addresses that can be leased
- *Ending IP address*: Enter the ending address for the range of IP addresses that can be leased
- *Virtual DHCP server address*: Enter the IP address of the virtual DHCP server
- *Default gateway address*: Enter the IP address of a router that transports packets beyond the virtual network
- *DNS servers*: Enter the IP address of one or more DNS servers already on the network
- *WINS servers*: Enter the IP addresses of any Windows Internet Naming Service (WINS) servers (for converting NetBIOS computer names to IP addresses)
- *IP address lease time*: Enter the amount of time that an IP address can be leased, which can be set in days, hours, minutes, or seconds (typically you would set this for one or more days)

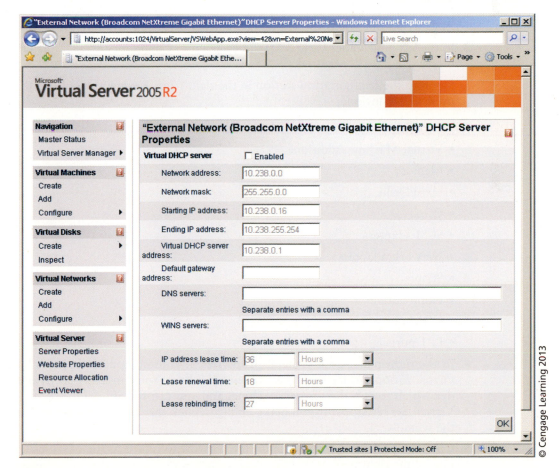

Figure D-7 Virtual DHCP server configuration options

- *Lease renewal time*: Enter the amount of time in which the client can contact the virtual DHCP server to renew a lease (in days, hours, minutes, or seconds, but with a minimum of 30 seconds)

- *Lease rebinding time*: Enter the amount of time it takes to enable the client to contact another server to renew its lease, when the main leasing server cannot be reached (in days, hours, minutes, or seconds, but with a minimum of 45 seconds)

10. In the left pane under Virtual Networks, point to **Configure** and click **Internal Network**.

11. Review the information provided in the right pane for the virtual network properties.

12. Click **Network Settings** in the right pane and review the information provided.

13. Click the **back arrow** at the top of the window.

14. Click **DHCP Server** in the right pane and notice that you can enable a virtual DHCP server and configure it.

15. Leave the window open for the next set of steps.

Configuring Hardware for a Virtual Machine   In addition to configuring a virtual network, you can configure hardware and other options for a virtual machine. In the following steps, you examine the options that can be configured:

 The virtual machine you select in these steps should be turned off before you start.

1. Ensure that the Microsoft Virtual Server Administration Web site tool is opened.

2. In the left pane under Virtual Machines, point to **Configure** and click the name of the virtual server you have configured.

3. Scroll to the configuration section in the right pane. Review the options that can be configured, which include:

- General properties
- Virtual Machine Additions
- Memory
- Hard Disks
- CD/DVD
- SCSI adapters
- Network adapters
- Scripts
- Floppy drive
- COM ports
- LPT ports

4. In the right pane, click **General properties**. If your computer supports hardware-assisted virtualization, notice that you can enable it here. You can also specify a user account under which to run the virtual machine, and you can specify what action to take when the Virtual Server stops. If you make changes, click the **OK** button in the bottom left side of the window.

5. Click the **back arrow** at the top of the window to return to the previous configuration display in the right pane.

6. In the right pane, click **Memory**. Now in the right pane you can change the amount of memory allocated to the virtual machine. If you make changes, ensure that you click the **OK** button.

7. Click the **back arrow** at the top of the window.

8. In the right pane, click the link for **Hard disks**. You see the configuration of the virtual disk used by the virtual machine. Notice the option to *Enable undo disks*. When you select this option, configuration and other changes on the virtual machine are saved so that you can undo those changes, if necessary. Also, notice that you can add a new virtual disk by clicking the Add disk >> button. If you make changes, remember to click the **OK** button so they take effect.

9. Click the **back arrow**.

10. Click **CD/DVD** in the right pane. You can click the Remove box to remove a CD/DVD drive, and you can click the Add CD/DVD Drive >> button to add a new drive. If you make changes, click **OK**.

11. Click the **back arrow**.

12. Click each of the remaining Configuration options in the right pane to view what they cover. In particular, notice that you can add NICs by using the Network adapters option.

13. Close the Microsoft Virtual Server Administration Web site tool when you are finished (or restart your virtual server so it is in use).

Host Key Options

Microsoft Virtual Server designates the right ALT key as the default host key and offers host key options that are similar to those offered by Microsoft Virtual PC. Table D-2 lists important host key combinations you can use while you are accessing a virtual machine.

Table D-2   Host key options for Microsoft Virtual Server

Keyboard Combination	Result
HostKey	Enables you to move the mouse outside of the window area used by the guest OS (move the mouse back into the guest OS display and click when you want to work on the guest OS)
HostKey+DEL	The virtual machine OS responds to this as CTRL+ALT+DEL
HostKey+C	Displays the Connect to server box for connecting to a specific virtual machine (or if you have selected text first, it can be used to copy the text)
HostKey+A	Toggles to the Administrator display window
HostKey+I	Shows the VMRC Connection Properties box with information about the connected virtual machine
HostKey+B	Provides information about the VMRC Client software
HostKey+V	Pastes text and items saved in the clipboard into the active window in the guest OS
HostKey+H	Enables you to configure a different key as the host key

© Cengage Learning 2013

VMware Player

VMware Player enables you to set up virtual machines to run Windows or UNIX/Linux operating systems. At this writing, VMware Player version 4 has the following new features:

- Ability to host newer Windows operating systems such as Windows 7 and Windows Server 2008 R2

- Improved graphics

- Resolution of disk and memory problems

- Support for newer Ubuntu Linux distributions

VMware Player Guest Operating Systems Supported

VMware Player supports the following guest operating systems:

- Windows Server 2008 R2 Standard, Enterprise, Datacenter, and Web Server (x64)
- Windows Server 2008 Standard, Enterprise, Datacenter, and Web Server (x86 or x64)
- Windows Server 2003 Standard, Enterprise, Datacenter, and Web Server with SP1 or SP2 (x86 or x64)
- Windows Server 2003 Standard, Enterprise, Datacenter, and Web Server R2 (x86 or x64)
- Windows Small Business Server 2003 (Standard and Premium Editions)
- Windows 2000 Server and Professional
- Windows XP Professional
- Windows Vista Business and Ultimate (x86 and x64)
- Windows 7 Professional, Ultimate, and Enterprise
- Red Hat Enterprise Linux Server and Desktop versions
- Fedora
- Ubuntu
- SUSE Linux Enterprise Server
- SUSE Linux

VMware Player Host Operating Systems Supported

VMware Player 4 runs inside more different kinds of host operating systems than Microsoft Virtual PC or Server. This is because it can run on several different Linux distributions. It also runs on x86 and x64 computers. The list of VMware host operating systems includes the following:

- Windows Server 2008 Standard, Enterprise, Datacenter, and Web Server (x64)
- Windows Server 2008 Standard, Enterprise, Datacenter, and Web Server (x86 or x64)
- Windows Server 2003 Standard, Enterprise, Datacenter, and Web Server with SP1 or SP2 (x86 or x64)
- Windows Server 2003 Standard, Enterprise, Datacenter, and Web Server R2 (x86 or x64)
- Windows Small Business Server 2003 (Standard and Premium Editions)
- Windows 2000 Server and Professional with SP3 or SP4
- Windows XP Professional and Home through the current service pack
- Windows Vista Business and Ultimate (x86 and x64)
- Windows 7 Home Premium, Professional, Ultimate, and Enterprise
- Red Hat Enterprise Linux Server and Desktop versions
- Fedora
- Ubuntu
- SUSE Linux Enterprise Server
- SUSE Linux

For Windows host operating systems, you must download the VMware Player version for Windows, which is in .exe format. For Linux host operating systems, you must download the VMware Player version for Linux, which is in .tar format.

Windows Server Core is not a supported host at this writing.

Requirements for VMware Player

VMware Player 4 has the following hardware requirements:

- *CPU*: 1.3 GHz or faster and supports x86 and x64 processors as well as multicore processors; also to run a 64-bit guest operating system the host processor must have virtualization capability through AMD-V for an AMD processor or Intel VT for an Intel processor.
- *RAM*: A minimum of 1 GB, but must include enough RAM for at least the minimum requirements of the total number of operating systems you will be running (host and guest).
- *Disk space*: Enough disk storage for the operating systems you plan to run (host and guest).

VMware Player 4 virtual machines can connect to hard, optical, and USB drives, including USB flash/thumb drives. VMware 4 also supports USB version 2 connections.

How to Download VMware Player

VMware Player can be downloaded from VMware's Web site at no cost. To download VMware Player:

1. Log onto your computer.
2. Establish a folder to store the download (such as a temporary folder or a folder under your Program Files folder).
3. Start your Web browser, such as Internet Explorer.
4. Go to the URL **www.vmware.com/products/player**.

Web links and specific instructions change periodically. You may need to search for the most current link at *www.vmware.com* if this link does not work.

5. Click **Download**.
6. Find the latest version of VMware Player (if multiple versions are listed) and click **Download**.
7. If asked to provide registration information, complete the registration form. Or, if you already have a VMware account, provide your account name and password. Click **Continue**.
8. If you see the window containing licensing information, read the licensing information, click the **checkbox** to agree, and click **Register**.
9. Click **Start Download Manager** or **Download** or **Manually Download** for the version of VMware Player that corresponds with the type of host computer you intend to use.
10. Follow the directions to save the program file to the folder in which you want to save it. (For example, you may have to permit Download Manager to install an add-on to your browser, browse to the folder in which to save the download file, and then click **Save**).
11. If you used the Windows download capability, click **Close** in the Download Complete box.
12. Close your Web browser and any open windows.

How to Install VMware Player

The general steps to install VMware Player into the host operating system are (using Windows 7 as an example host):

1. If possible, connect to the Internet so that updates can be installed automatically during the installation process and so that VMware tools can also be downloaded appropriate to specific guest operating systems.

2. Browse to the folder where you saved the install file for VMware Player.

3. Double-click **VMware-player-4.x.x-xxxxxx** (where 4.x.x-xxxxxx is the version of VMware Player). If you see the User Account Control security box for Windows, click **Yes**.

4. You may see a box showing files loading quickly, but you do not need to respond to this box.

5. When the installation wizard for VMware Player starts (see Figure D-8), click **Next**.

Figure D-8   VMware Player installation wizard

6. In the Destination Folder dialog box, click **Next**. (Or, if you want to use a different destination folder location, click the Change button to select a different destination folder location.)

7. In the Software Updates dialog box, ensure that the checkbox is checked for **Check for product updates on startup**, if you have an Internet connection, so that you can automatically check for the most recent updates to VMware Player. Click **Next**.

8. Select whether or not you want to help improve VMware Player and click **Next** in the User Experience Improvement Program dialog box.

9. Select from the shortcut options to place a shortcut on the Desktop or in the Start Menu Program folder and click **Next** (see Figure D-9).

Figure D-9 Choosing shortcut options

10. In the Ready to Perform the Requested Operations dialog box, click **Continue**.

11. Wait for a moment as the files are installed and configured (see Figure D-10).

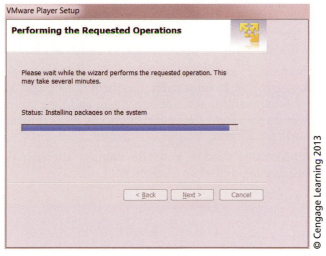

Figure D-10 Installing and configuring files

12. When you see the Setup Wizard Complete dialog box, close all open programs on your computer and click **Restart Now**. Log back into the account you are using on the host machine. Go to the next section to create a virtual machine and install a guest operating system.

Creating a Virtual Machine and Installing a Guest OS

Now that VMware Player is installed, the next step is to create a virtual machine and install the guest operating system. Here are the general steps using the DVD installation method for Windows Server 2008 or Windows Server 2008 R2 (using Windows 7 as an example host):

1. Insert the installation DVD, such as for Windows Server 2008 or Windows Server 2008 R2.

2. Click **Start,** point to **All Programs,** click **VMware,** and click **VMware Player.**

3. In the License Agreement window, select **Yes, I accept the terms in the license agreement** and click **OK.**

4. In the Welcome to VMware Player window, notice that you can use this window to create a new virtual machine or to open a virtual machine that has already been created (see Figure D-11). Select **Create a New Virtual Machine**.

Figure D-11 Options in the Welcome to VMware Player window

5. In the Welcome to the New Virtual Machine Wizard window, ensure that **Installer disc** is selected and specify the disc drive for the installation DVD, such as drive D:. Click **Next**.

6. If requested provide the product key. Also, provide the name of the operating system to install; provide the administrator account name for the guest operating system, such as Administrator; enter the administrator account password; and then confirm the password (this action enables you to bypass Steps 22–24 later that involve setting up the Administrator account and password). Click **Next**.

7. In the Name the Virtual Machine window, enter the name of the virtual machine such as **Windows Server 2008 R2** (see Figure D-12). Click **Next**.

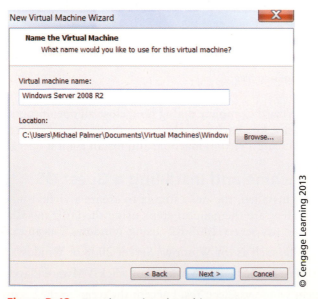

Figure D-12 Entering a virtual machine name

8. In the Specify Disk Capacity window, enter the maximum disk size, such as *40 GB*. Click **Next**.

9. In the Ready to Create Virtual Machine window, review your selections and click **Finish**.

10. Wait for the virtual machine console window to be displayed. Also, if you see the Removable Devices box showing that a removable device can be connected to the virtual machine click **OK**.

11. Perform a normal installation in the console window (or in some cases, the installation process may skip to installing the OS automatically, such as by going to Step 17 below). For example, in the Windows Server 2008/Windows Server 2008 R2 installation, in the Install Windows window, specify the language to install, such as **English**, in the Language to install drop-down box. In the Time and currency format box, make your selection, such as **English (United States)**. In the Keyboard or input method box, make your selection, such as **US**. Click **Next**.

12. Click **Install now**.

13. Select **Windows Server 2008 Standard (Full Installation)** or **Windows Server 2008 R2 Standard (Full Installation)**—or select a different full installation edition, such as Enterprise Edition if it is available—and click **Next**.

14. Read the license terms, click the box for **I accept the license terms**, and click **Next**.

15. Click **Custom (advanced)**.

16. You will see the amount of unallocated disk space highlighted, which is the disk space you specified when you configured the virtual machine. Ensure it is highlighted and click **Next**.

17. The installation program begins installing Windows Server 2008 or Windows Server 2008 R2. You will see progress information about Copying files, Expanding files, Installing features, Installing updates, and Completing installation. This process takes 30 minutes or longer.

18. The installation program restarts the operating system.

19. You see the message: *Please wait while Windows sets up your computer*.

20. Next you see the Install Windows window in the Completing installation phase (this step is not in the installation of Windows Server 2008 R2).

21. The system reboots again (this step is not in the installation of Windows Server 2008 R2).

22. You will see the message (a red circle with a white x in it): *The user's password must be changed before logging on the first time*. Click the **OK** button (you may have to click inside the active portion of the console window first to have the mouse function within it).

23. Enter a new password for the Administrator account and then enter the same password again to confirm it. Click the **blue circle** with the white right-pointing arrow inside.

If you enter a password that is not a strong password, you will see the message (with a white x in a red circle): *Unable to update the password*. This means that the value provided for the new password does not meet the length, complexity, or history requirements of the domain. Click **OK** and enter a different password that is over seven characters and uses letters, numbers, and characters such as &.

24. When you see the message *Your password has been changed*, click **OK**.

25. At this point, the Windows desktop is opened and the Initial Configuration Tasks window is displayed. From here you can start configuring Windows Server 2008/Windows Server 2008 R2 or log out and use the VMware Player console window later to access Windows Server 2008/Windows Server 2008 R2.

26. You can close the VMware console window at any time (the virtual machine keeps running). Also, to go outside of the console window simply move the cursor outside the window. To go back inside the window press Ctrl+G, which directs input to the virtual machine.

27. To shut down a virtual machine, first use the normal key clicks to shut down the operating system. Then click **Virtual Machine** at the top of the console window, click **Power**, and click **Power Off**. Click **Yes**.

 If you see an Install Tools button at the bottom of the console screen, ensure you have an Internet connection and click the button to install VMware tools. These tools can make your use of the guest operating system easier.

Installing an OS from an ISO Image

VMware Player supports installing an operating system via an ISO image file. To install an ISO image file, follow the beginning steps to create a virtual machine. However, instead of specifying Installer disc, select *Installer disc image file (iso)* and specify the location of the file.

Editing Hardware and Network Options

You can edit a virtual machine's hardware and network configuration. The general steps to access the configuration window are as follows:

1. Open VMware Player, such as by clicking **Start**, pointing to **All Programs**, clicking **VMware**, and clicking **VMware Player**.

2. In the left pane, click the name of the virtual machine, such as **Windows Server 2008 R2**. Ensure that the virtual machine is turned off.

3. In the right pane, click **Edit virtual machine settings** (see Figure D-13).

4. Ensure that the hardware tab is selected in the Virtual Machine Settings window (see Figure D-14).

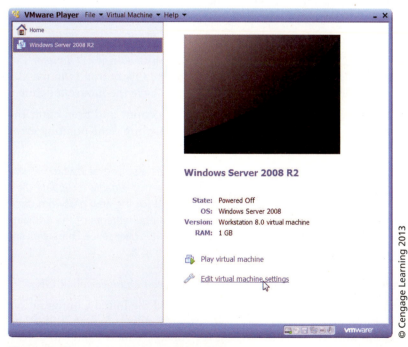

Figure D-13 Selecting *Edit virtual machine settings*

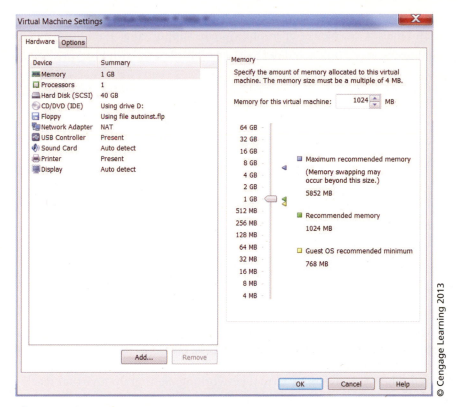

Figure D-14   Virtual Machine Settings window

5. In the Virtual Machines Setting window, you can change a variety of hardware and network settings, such as the amount of memory allocated to the virtual machine or the hard disk size.

6. Click each of the settings under *Device*, starting with **Memory** to see how you can configure them.

7. When you are finished, click **Cancel** (or click **OK** if you have changed the settings) in the Virtual Machine Settings window.

8. In the VMware Player window, click the operating system in the left pane to start it; or if you don't want to start the operating system at this time, close the VMware Player window.

Other Virtual Systems

This appendix has focused on virtualization systems that are free. Other systems are available at a cost and enjoy popular use. On the desktop side, VMware Workstation has grown in use along with desktop virtualization. Another system is Microsoft Hyper-V, which can be included with Windows Server 2008 or Windows Server 2008 R2. The following sections give you a brief overview of these systems, but are not intended to provide instructions about how to use them.

VMware Workstation

VMware workstation is popular among software developers and testers because it provides a safe environment in which to write and test development software before it is released to live production. It is also used by individuals who need to run multiple operating systems on one workstation-class computer, including legacy operating systems. This can be useful to enable a user to run old software without having to convert it for a new operating system. It is also useful for learning a new operating system.

VMware Workstation 8 (and above) supports Windows, Linux, and other operating systems as host and guest OSs. Newer operating systems supported as both hosts and guests include:

- Windows Server 2008/Windows Server 2008 R2 Standard, Enterprise, and Datacenter
- Windows 7
- Windows Vista
- Red Hat Enterprise Linux up to 6.1
- Ubuntu Linux up to 11.x
- SUSE Linux up to 11.x
- openSUSE Linux up to 11.x

VMware Workstation has several of the same new features as VMware Player, which include:

- Handles increased memory (up to 64 GB)
- Can be set up and accessed through cloud computing
- Can be run as a server for testing applications
- Supports HD audio and Bluetooth Devices as well as 3D graphics
- Supports USB 3.0

As with VMware Player, you can configure hardware for the virtual machine including multiple processors, memory, hard disks, USB access, DVD/CD access, and other hardware elements. You can also configure to use Bridged or NAT virtual networks. A virtual DHCP server can be configured when you use NAT virtual networking. Setting up a virtual machine is also accomplished through a step-by-step wizard.

Also, like VMware Player you can install VMware tools that include specialized drivers, such as drivers, for enhanced video and audio functions for the guest operating system. VMware Workstation offers a console display for accessing the guest operating system that resembles the VMware Player console.

You can download a 30-day free evaluation version at *www.vmware.com/products/workstation*.

Microsoft Hyper-V

Microsoft Hyper-V was released just a few months after Windows Server 2008. Unlike the other virtualization systems discussed in this appendix, Microsoft Hyper-V is intended to run only on Windows Server 2008/Server 2008 R2 or later Windows Server systems, including Windows Server 8 (a code name for the new Windows Server version for now). It is loaded through the Server Manager tool like any other server role in Windows Server 2008/Server 2008 R2. In this regard, Windows Server 2008/Server 2008 R2 offer perhaps the smoothest installation process of any of the virtual systems discussed in this appendix. Also, unlike the other systems in this appendix, Hyper-V runs only on x64 computers, which means the host systems include only the following:

- Windows Server 2008 Standard, Enterprise, or Datacenter Editions x64
- Windows Server 2008 R2 Standard, Enterprise, or Datacenter Editions (there are only x64 versions)
- Windows Server 2012 (there are only x64 versions)

Windows Server 2012 comes with Hyper-V version 3.

You can purchase any of Windows Server 2008/Server 2008 R2 Standard, Enterprise, or Datacenter Editions with Hyper-V (for a very small extra cost), or you can purchase Hyper-V separately. The low cost and seamless installation and integration with Windows Server operating systems are designed to make this virtualization system particularly appealing to Windows Server operating system users.

The guest operating systems that can be installed in Hyper-V at this writing include:

- Windows Server 2012
- Windows Server 2008 R2 Standard, Enterprise, Datacenter, and Web Server (x64)
- Windows Server 2008 Standard, Enterprise, Datacenter, and Web Server (x86 or x64)
- Windows Server 2003 Standard, Enterprise, and Datacenter (x86 or x64)
- Windows Server 2003 Web Edition
- Windows 2000 Server and Advanced Server with SP4
- Windows 8
- Windows 7
- Windows Vista
- Windows XP Professional with SP2 or SP3
- SUSE Linux Enterprise Server up through version 11 (x86 or x64)
- Red Hat Enterprise Linux up through version 6 (x86 or x64)

After Hyper-V is installed as a server role, you can open the Hyper-V Manager as a Microsoft Management Console (MMC) snap-in or you can open it from the Administrative Tools menu—all steps familiar to Windows Server 2008/Server 2008 R2 administrators. Use of Hyper-V Manager is relatively intuitive because it is designed in the same format as is used by most Windows Server 2008/Server 2008 R2 administrative tools. For example, to create a new virtual machine, click the New option in the right pane of Hyper-V Manager and follow the steps provided by the New Virtual Machine Wizard.

To configure hardware and management settings for a virtual machine, click Settings under the name of the virtual machine in the right pane of Hyper-V Manager. The Settings window enables you to add hardware, configure hardware, and configure management capabilities.

You can access the Virtual Network Manager from Hyper-V Manager to configure a virtual network. At this writing, there are three types of virtual networks:

- *Private*: Offers communications only between virtual machines on the same virtual server
- *Internal*: Enables communications between virtual machines and the host virtual server
- *External*: Offers communications between virtual machines and the physical network (using a network adapter)

For an external virtual network, you can specify a virtual LAN identification number. This is a unique number used for communications through the network adapter that distinguishes the virtual network from other networks.

The guest operating system appears in a console window that has an Action menu from which to send CTRL+ALT+DEL for logging on, and which can start, turn off, shut down, or pause a virtual machine (as well as other options). You also can expand the console to completely fill the desktop display. The console window can be started by clicking its thumbnail. When the console window opens, it provides a message about how to start the guest operating system.

Windows Server administrators will find that installation and administration is very consistent with how other server roles are installed and administered.

2nd generation (2G) Second generation of mobile telecommunications technology, which is notable because it introduces the use of digital signals instead of analog signals (1G) for mobile radio transmissions and enables the use of codecs for handling many more calls per radio frequency or bandwidth. *See* **codecs.**

3rd generation (3G) Third generation mobile telecommunications technology for cell phones, tablet computers, and other devices that is based on the IMT-2000 standards for mobile communications. The data transfer rate is up to 5.8 Mbps upstream and 14.4 Mbps downstream.

4th generation (4G) Fourth generation mobile telecommunications technology that is faster than 3G and is built on the IMT-Advanced standards. Data transfer rates are based on whether a device is used in a low (100 Mbps) or high (1Gbps) mobility situation.

10 Gigabit Ethernet The IEEE 802.3ae, 802.3ak, 802.3an, 802.3aq, and 802.3ap standards for Ethernet communications at 10 Gbps. *See* **10GBaseX.**

40 Gigabit Ethernet The IEEE 802.3ba and 802.3bg standards (for both 40 and 100 Gigabit) for Ethernet communications at 40 Gbps. *See* **40GBaseX.**

40GBaseX or 40GBaseE The generic reference for 40 Gigabit Ethernet versions, transmitting at 40 Gbps. *See* **40 Gigabit Ethernet.**

10Base2 Used to designate a thin coax or thinnet network transmitting at 10 Mbps.

10Base5 Designates a thick coax or thicknet network transmitting at 10 Mbps.

10BaseT A network transmission approach for 10 Mbps communications using twisted-pair cable.

10GBaseX The generic reference for 10 Gigabit Ethernet versions, transmitting at 10 Gbps. *See* **10 Gigabit Ethernet.**

100BaseVG/100VG-AnyLAN Also called the IEEE 802.12 standard, a network transmission approach that uses demand priority instead of CSMA/CD. *See* **demand priority.**

100BaseX The generic representation for different Fast Ethernet transmission versions, transmitting at 100 Mbps and using the IEEE 802.3u standard. *See* **Fast Ethernet.**

100GBaseX/100GBaseE The generic reference for 100 Gigabit Ethernet versions, transmitting at 100 Gbps. *See* **100 Gigabit Ethernet.**

100 Gigabit Ethernet The IEEE 802.3ba and 802.3bg standards (for both 40 and 100 Gigabit) for Ethernet communications at 100 Gbps. *See* **100GBaseX.**

1000BaseX The generic representation for Gigabit Ethernet versions, transmitting at 1 Gbps. *See* **Gigabit Ethernet.**

802.1X A wireless and wired authentication standard offered by the IEEE that is a port-based form of authentication.

802.11a An IEEE standard for wireless networking at 5 GHz with a top speed of 54 Mbps.

802.11ac An IEEE standard for wireless networking under development at this writing that operates at 2.4 and 5 GHz with a top speed of 1+ Gbps.

802.11ad An IEEE standard for wireless networking under development at this writing that operates at a top speed of about 7 Gbps and is primarily targeted for wireless computer components, phones, TVs, and other short-range wireless devices.

802.11b An IEEE standard for wireless networking at 2.4 GHz, with a top speed of 11 Mbps.

802.11g An IEEE standard for wireless networking at 2.4 GHz, having backward compatibility with 802.11b and a top speed of 54 Mbps.

802.11i A standard for wireless and wired security that builds on the 802.1X standard and implements the Temporal Key Integrity Protocol (TKIP) for creating random encryption keys from one master key. 802.11i also employs Robust Secure Network (RSN) for creating secure communications channels. *See* **Temporal Key Integrity Protocol (TKIP)** and **Robust Secure Network (RSN).**

802.11n An IEEE wireless networking standard at 2.4 and 5 GHz with a top speed of 300+ Mbps.

802.16 Also called WiMAX, an IEEE standard for wireless MANs that can reach up to 48 kilometers (about 30 miles) and transmit up to 75 Mbps. *See* **WiMAX.**

access point A device that attaches to a cabled network and that services wireless communications between WNICs and the cabled network.

access server A unit that connects synchronous and asynchronous devices to a network, providing routing for both types of communications.

Active Directory A directory service used in Windows Server that houses information about all network resources such as servers, printers, user accounts, groups of user accounts, security policies, and other information. As a directory service, Active Directory is responsible for providing a central listing of resources and ways to quickly find and access specific resources and for providing a way to manage network resources.

active hub A network transmission device that connects nodes in a star topology regenerating, retiming, and amplifying the data signal each time it passes through the hub.

adaptive differential pulse code modulation (ADPCM) An audio file creation technique that converts an analog audio signal into an 8-bit digital signal, similar to regular pulse code modulation (PCM), but it transmits voice communications at less than half or one-quarter the speed of regular PCM communications.

Address Resolution Protocol (ARP) A TCP/IP-based protocol that enables a sending station to determine the MAC address of the intended receiving station.

Advanced Encryption Standard (AES) An encryption standard that uses a private-key block-cipher technique in which plain text data is divided into 128-bit blocks. The private key can be either 128, 192, or 256 bits in length. WPA2 uses AES encryption. *See* **Wi-Fi Protected Access (WPA)**.

Airport A wireless networking approach used on Apple computers that includes devices such as WNICs and routers that operate using 802.11b/g/n networking.

American National Standards Institute (ANSI) An organization that works to set standards for all types of products, including network equipment.

American Standard Code for Information Interchange (ASCII) An 8-bit character-coding method consisting of 96 uppercase and lowercase characters and numbers, plus 32 nonprinting characters.

analog A type of transmission that can vary continuously, as in a wave pattern with positive and negative voltage levels.

Android operating system An operating system designed for mobile and wireless devices such as smartphones and tablet PCs. Under the hood, Android is based on the Linux operating system.

antenna A device that sends out (radiates) and picks up radio waves.

anycast Used in IPv6, a packet that goes only to the closest interface and does not attempt to reach other interfaces with the same address.

Anything or Everything as a Service (XaaS) Including a combination of or all of the cloud services options: CaaS, DaaS, IaaS, MaaS, NaaS, PaaS, and SaaS.

AppleTalk A peer-to-peer protocol used on legacy networks for communications between Macintosh computers. AppleTalk is a routable protocol, but is not used on the Internet.

application virtualization Running single applications in their own virtual machine environments.

application-layer attack A malicious attack on any type of application, including an operating system, so that an attacker can control the application or prevent it from working. Application-layer attacks are of particular concern to cloud computing providers.

application-level gateway A proxy that filters application-level protocols and requests between an internal network and an external network. *See* **proxy**.

application-specific integrated circuit (ASIC) A customized integrated circuit on a chip that contains logic for a specific application, such as fast routing logic.

archive attribute A file property that shows whether or not a file or folder has been backed up since it was created or last modified.

Asymmetric Digital Subscriber Line (ADSL) A high-speed DSL technology that can use ordinary telephone lines for downstream data transmission of up to 9 Mbps, and 1 Mbps for upstream transmissions.

asynchronous communications Communications that occur in discrete units, in which the start of a unit is signaled by a start bit at the front, and a stop bit at the back signals the end of the unit.

Asynchronous Transfer Mode (ATM) A transport method that uses cells, multiple channels, and switching to send voice, video, and data transmissions on the same network.

ATM permanent virtual circuit (ATM PVC) A dedicated circuit that has a preassigned path and fixed allocated bandwidth between two designated endpoints.

ATM smart permanent virtual circuit (ATM SPVC) Combines characteristics of PVCs and SVCs. Like a PVC, an SPVC must be manually configured, although only at the end devices; and similar to an SVC, each transmission has its own defined path to the switch or switches through which it must pass.

ATM switched virtual circuit (ATM SVC) A circuit that is set up and used for a discrete communications session and is taken down when that session is finished.

attachment unit interface (AUI) A network interface that connects coax, twisted-pair, or fiber-optic backbone cable to a network node, such as a hub, switch, or workstation. The interface consists of AUI standards for connectors, cable, interface circuits, and electrical characteristics.

attenuation The amount of signal that is lost as it travels through a communications medium from its source (transmitting node) to the receiving node.

authentication The process of verifying that a user is authorized to access a particular computer, server, network, or network resource.

automatic private IP addressing (APIPA) A process in which a computer assigns its own IP address from the range 169.254.0.1 to 169.254.255.254 and assigns the subnet mask 255.255.0.0, when no DHCP server is present on the network.

automatic repeat-request (ARQ) An 802.11 error-handling technique that helps to reduce communication errors created by sources of interference, such as adverse weather conditions.

backbone A high-capacity communications medium that joins networks on the same floor in a building, on different floors, and across long distances.

backbone cabling As defined by the EIA/TIA-568 standard, cable that runs between network equipment rooms, floors, and buildings.

backplane A circuit board with many slots to support plugging in other circuit boards into one unit or chassis.

Typically the chassis provides one or more power supplies (including backup power supplies) and circuits for data signals, and the chassis can even provide one or more forms of network connectivity. For network devices, a backplane can have many slots for circuit boards providing different network technologies.

bandwidth The transmission capacity of a communications medium, which is typically measured in bits per second (for data transmissions) or hertz (for data, voice, and video transmissions) and which is determined by the maximum minus the minimum transmission capacity.

base priority class The initial priority assigned to a program process or thread in the program code.

baseband A type of transmission in which the entire channel capacity of the communications medium (such as cable) is used by one data signal, enabling only one node to transmit at a time.

basic input/output system (BIOS) A program on a nonvolatile random access memory chip that establishes basic communication with components such as the monitor and disk drives. The BIOS also performs memory and hardware tests when a computer is initially turned on. On most computers you can update the BIOS. *See* **nonvolatile random access memory (NVRAM)**.

Basic Rate Interface (BRI) ISDN An ISDN interface that consists of three channels. Two are 64-Kbps channels for data, voice, and video transmissions. A third is a 16-Kbps channel used for communications signaling.

bayonet nut connector (BNC) A connector that is used for thin coax cable and that has a bayonet-like shell. The male BNC connector has two small knobs that attach to circular slots in the female connector. Both connectors are twisted on for a connection. (Different renderings of what BNC stands for are bayonet navy connector, bayonet nut connection, and British naval connector.)

beaconing An error condition on a token ring network that indicates one or more nodes are not functioning.

benchmark A performance assessment of a network under varying loads or circumstances.

bits per second (bps) The number of binary bits (0s or 1s) sent in one second.

blade enclosure A large box with slots for blade servers; the box provides cooling fans, electrical power, connection to a shared monitor and pointing device, and network connectivity.

blade server A modular server unit that looks like a card and that fits into a blade enclosure.

Bluetooth A wireless networking specification for short distances that uses the 2.4 GHz band that is defined through the Bluetooth Special Interest Group.

Bluetooth personal area network (PAN) A network of personal devices used in a small work area, such as around a PC. The devices in the work area may include a keyboard, pointing device, printer, smartphone, camera, tablet PC, another computer, and other devices. Bluetooth is a common and convenient way of connecting such devices to create a wireless PAN. *See* **Bluetooth**.

border gateway A firewall that is configured with security policies to control the traffic that is permitted across a border (in either direction) between a public and private network.

bridge A network transmission device that connects different LANs or LAN segments using the same access method. An example is connecting one Ethernet LAN to another Ethernet LAN. Bridges operate at the Data Link layer.

bridge protocol data unit (BPDU) A specialized frame used by bridges to exchange information with one another.

broadband A type of transmission in which there are several transmission channels on a communications medium, allowing more than one node to transmit at the same time.

broadband ISDN (B-ISDN) A version of ISDN that has not been pursued because of newer WAN technologies.

broadcast One copy of each frame or packet is sent to all points on a network, regardless of whether or not a node has requested it.

broadcast frame A frame sent to all nodes on a network.

broadcast packet A packet sent to all nodes on a network.

broadcast storm Saturation of network bandwidth caused by excessive traffic, as when a large number of computers or devices attempt to transmit simultaneously, or when computers or devices persist in transmitting repeatedly.

buffer A storage area in a device (for example, in a network interface card, a computer system, or a network device such as a switch) that temporarily saves information in memory.

buffer attack An attack in which the attacker tricks the buffer software into attempting to store more information in a buffer than the buffer is able to contain. The extra information can be malicious software.

buffer overflow A situation in which there is more information to store in a buffer than the buffer is sized to hold.

buffering The capability of a device, such as a switch, to temporarily save information in memory.

bus A pathway inside the computer that is used to transfer information to the CPU or to peripherals attached to the computer.

bus topology A network design built by running cable from one PC or file server to the next, like links in a chain.

cable continuity tester A device that enables you to check for opens or breaks in a cable by determining if the signal sent from one end reaches the other end of the cable.

cable modem A digital modem device designed for use with the cable TV system, providing high-speed data transfer.

cable plant The total amount of communications cable that makes up a network.

cable scanner A device used to test the length and other characteristics of a cable.

cableco A cable TV company, such as Comcast or Time Warner.

cache Storage used by a computer system to house frequently used data in quickly accessed storage, such as memory.

campus area network (CAN) Multiple LANs in a specific area or region, such as in buildings on a college campus, that are managed or owned by one organization.

carrier sense The process of checking a communication medium, such as cable, for a voltage level, signal transition, or light, indicating the presence of a data-carrying signal.

Carrier Sense Multiple Access with Collision Avoidance (CSMA/CA) Also called the distributed coordination function, an access method used in 802.11 wireless networking that relies on the calculation of a delay or backoff time to avoid packet collisions.

Carrier Sense Multiple Access with Collision Detection (CSMA/CD) A network transport control method used in Ethernet networks. It regulates transmission by sensing the presence of packet collisions.

cell In wireless LAN networking, the broadcast area around an access point. In cellular phone communications, the broadcast area around a base station. When used in WAN technology, a cell is a fixed-size data unit formatted for high-speed transmission, such as in broadband and ATM.

cell switching A switching method that uses TDM and virtual channels and that places a short indicator or virtual channel identifier at the beginning of each TDMA time slot. *See* Time Division Multiple Access (TDMA).

Certified Cable Modem Project Also called Data Over Cable Service Interface Specification (DOCSIS), a project sponsored by the cable modem industry to provide a set of standards and equipment certification to provide stability to cable modem communications.

Challenge Handshake Authentication Protocol (CHAP) A protocol used to encrypt passwords, such as server account passwords that are transferred over a WAN.

channel service unit (CSU) A device that is a physical interface between a network device, such as a router, and a T-carrier line.

circuit mode On an ISDN network that uses T-carrier communications, this means the communications circuit lasts for the duration of the communications session and is used exclusively by the two connected devices until it is terminated.

circuit switching A network communications technique that uses a dedicated channel to transmit information between two nodes.

circuit-level gateway A proxy that creates a secure virtual circuit through an internal network to a client computer that is communicating with a computer on an external network via the proxy. *See* **proxy**.

Classless Interdomain Routing (CIDR) An IP addressing method that ignores address class designations and that uses a slash at the end of the dotted decimal address to show the total number of available addresses.

client A computer that accesses another computer, such as a workstation that accesses a shared file on another workstation, server, or mainframe. The client may use the accessed computer (host) to process data or may process accessed data using its own CPU.

cloud computing A computing technology that provides a host of scalable Web-based applications and services over the Internet or a private network that are used by clients through Web browsers.

coaxial cable Also called coax, a network cable medium that consists of a copper core, surrounded by insulation. The insulation is surrounded by another conducting material, such as braided wire, which is covered by an outer insulating material.

codec Method of coding and encoding a digital signal to enable loading a specific radio frequency or bandwidth with more individual radio transmissions (calls).

collision A situation in which two or more packets are detected at the same time on an Ethernet network.

collision domain Two network segments connected by one or more repeaters; or the network segments between two or more Layer 2 devices, such as switches or bridges. In a collision domain, two or more computers can transmit at the same time, causing a collision (and slowing network transmissions).

Common Management Interface Protocol (CMIP) A protocol that gathers network performance data and is part of the OSI standards for network management.

Communication as a Service (CaaS) Offering unified communications services through cloud computing. This might include communications services such as VPN, VoIP, or private telephone services.

communications media The cabling or radio waves used to connect one network computer to another or one network to another and transport data between them.

community A group of hosts that share the same SNMP services.

community name In SNMP communications, a rudimentary password (name) used by network agents and the network management station (or software) in the same community so that their communications cannot be easily intercepted by an unauthorized workstation or device.

Compressed Serial Line Internet Protocol (CSLIP) An extension of the SLIP remote communications protocol that provides faster throughput than SLIP. *See* Serial Line Internet Protocol (SLIP).

computer network A system of computers, print devices, network devices, and computer software linked by communications cabling or radio waves.

concentrator A device that can have multiple inputs and outputs all active at the same time.

conditioned power source A device, sometimes combined into a UPS device, that smoothes out small and large fluctuations in the power delivered by the power company, providing a known range of power.

connectionless service Also known as Type 1 operation, services that occur between the LLC sublayer and the Network layer, but that provide no checks to make sure data accurately reaches the receiving node.

connection-oriented service Type 2 operation services that occur between the LLC sublayer and the Network layer, providing several ways to ensure data is successfully received by the destination node.

controlled access unit (CAU) Stackable hubs that count as one MAU and connect nodes on a token ring network.

cookie Information that a Web server stores on a client computer, such as the client's preferences when accessing a particular Web site, or where the client has been on the Web site.

counter Used by Performance Monitor, this is a measurement technique for an object, as when measuring the processor performance by percentage in use.

cut-through switching A switching technique that forwards portions of a frame before the entire frame is received.

cyclic redundancy check (CRC) An error detection method that calculates a value for the total size of the information fields contained in a frame. The value is inserted near the end of a frame by the Data Link layer on the sending node and checked by the Data Link layer on the receiving node to determine if a transmission error has occurred.

data communications equipment (DCE) A device that converts data from a DTE, such as a computer, to be transmitted over a telecommunications line. *See* **data terminal equipment (DTE)**.

Data Encryption Standard (DES) An encryption standard created by the National Institute of Standards and Technology and ANSI. DES uses both a public and a private encryption key.

Data Execution Prevention (DEP) A security feature in Windows Server systems that monitors how programs use memory and stops programs that attempt to use memory allocated for system programs and processes. This is intended to foil viruses, Trojan horses, and worms that attempt to invade system memory.

Data Over Cable Service Interface Specification (DOCSIS) *See* **Certified Cable Modem Project.**

data service unit (DSU) A device used with a channel service unit (CSU) for communications over a WAN connection, such as a T-carrier line. The DSU converts data to be sent over the line and converts data received from the line into a format for the receiving network.

data terminal equipment (DTE) A computer or computing device that prepares data to be transmitted over a telecommunications line to which it attaches by using a DCE, such as a modem. *See* **data communications equipment (DCE)**.

demand priority A data communications technique that transmits a packet directly from the sending node, through a hub, and to the receiving node, without passing through other network nodes.

demilitarized zone (DMZ) A portion of a network that exists between two or more networks that have different security measures in place, such as the "zone" between the private network of a company and the Internet.

denial-of-service (DoS) attack An attack that interferes with normal access to a network host, Web site, or service, for example, by flooding a network with useless information or with frames or packets containing errors that are not identified by a particular network service.

Desktop as a Service (DaaS) Providing the desktop through cloud computing, such as desktop background, icons, or menus provided to start applications, e-mail access, messaging access, and data backup.

device address Also called the physical or MAC address, the hexadecimal number permanently assigned to a network interface and used by the MAC sublayer within the Data Link layer or Layer 2.

diffused infrared Reflecting infrared signals off of a ceiling inside a building. Diffused infrared is used by the 802.11R standard for wireless communications.

digital signal (DS) A transmission method that has distinct signal levels to represent binary zeroes or ones, such as +5 volts and 0 volts.

Digital Subscriber Line (DSL or xDSL) A technology that uses advanced modulation technologies on existing telecommunications networks for high-speed networking between a subscriber and a telco and that has communication speeds of up to 200 Mbps.

Direct Sequence Spread Spectrum (DSSS) An 802.11b/g wireless communication technique that spreads the data across any of up to 14 channels, each 22 MHz in width. The data signal is sequenced over the channels and is amplified to have a high gain to combat interference.

directory service A large database of network resources, such as computers, printers, user accounts, and user groups. The database is replicated to all servers that are responsible for helping to manage network resources, such as authorizing users to log onto the network.

discovery A process used by routers that involves gathering information about how many nodes are on a network and where they are located.

disk quota Allocating a specific amount of disk space to a user or application with the ability to ensure that the user or application cannot use more disk space than is specified in the allocation.

distributed coordination function *See* Carrier Sense Multiple Access with Collision Avoidance (CSMA/CA).

distributed denial-of-service (DDoS) attack A denial-of-service attack in which one computer causes other computers to launch attacks directed at one or more targets. *See* **denial-of-service (DoS) attack**.

DNS dynamic update protocol A TCP/IP-based protocol that enables information in a DNS server to be automatically updated, such as a Windows 7 workstation updating its leased DHCP IPv4 or IPv6 address.

domain A logical grouping of networking resources that centralizes management of elements such as user accounts, computers, printers, and network devices.

Domain Name System (DNS) A TCP/IP application protocol that resolves domain and computer names to IP addresses, and IP addresses to domain and computer names.

dotted decimal notation An addressing technique that uses four octets, such as 10000110.11011110.01100101.000 00101, converted to decimal (for example 134.222.101.005), to designate a network and individual hosts on the network.

driver Software that enables a computer to communicate with devices such as NICs, printers, monitors, and hard disk drives. Also, a NIC driver enables the NIC to communicate with a network. Each driver has a specific purpose, such as handling Ethernet network communications.

driver signing A process in which a digital signature is placed in a driver for a device. The digital signature helps ensure that the driver is tested and is compatible with the operating system and device for which it is written.

Dynamic Host Configuration Protocol (DHCP) A network protocol that provides a way for a server to automatically assign an IP address to a device on its network.

dynamic routing A routing process in which the router constantly checks the network configuration, automatically updates routing tables, and makes its own decisions (often based on guidelines set by the network administrator) about how to route packets.

electromagnetic interference (EMI) Signal interference caused by magnetic force fields generated by electrical devices such as motors.

encapsulate In the context of OSI layers, the process of wrapping the information in one layer inside the information within the next layer. In the context of protocols, the process of placing the information formatted for one protocol inside the information formatted for a different protocol, as is done in TCP/IP communications.

Encapsulating Security Payload (ESP) Used in IPSec communications for encrypting packet-based data,

authenticating data, and generally ensuring the security and confidentiality of Network layer information and data within a packet.

encryption A process that scrambles data so that it cannot be read if intercepted by unauthorized users.

enterprise network A combination of LANs, MANs, CANs, or WANs that provides computer users with an array of computer and network resources to complete different tasks.

Ethernet A transport system that uses the CSMA/CD access method for data transmission on a network. Ethernet typically is implemented in a bus or star-bus hybrid topology.

Ethernet Alliance An international body that works to advance Ethernet standards and consists of users, vendors, educators, and government representatives.

European Telecommunications Standards Institute (ETSI) Develops "globally applicable" radio and broadcast communications standards and Internet standards under the endorsement of the European Union.

Extended Binary Coded Decimal Interchange Code (EBCDIC) A character-coding technique used mainly on IBM mainframe computers and consisting of an 8-bit coding method for a 256-character set of letters, numbers, and special characters.

extended service set (ESS) topology A wireless topology that uses one or more access points to provide a larger service area than an IBSS topology.

external virtual network A virtual network that offers communication between virtual machines and the physical network through a network interface card.

extranet A network that makes an organization's intranet technologies available through a public network, such as the Internet, but usually only for specific users. *See* **intranet**.

Fast Ethernet Ethernet communications at speeds up to 100 Mbps as defined under the IEEE 802.3u standard. *See* **100BaseX**.

fat pipe Fiber-optic cable used on a network backbone for high-speed communications, such as between floors of a building.

fault tolerance Techniques that employ hardware and software to provide assurance against equipment failures, computer service interruptions, and data loss.

Fiber Distributed Data Interface (FDDI) A fiber-optic data transport method capable of a 100-Mbps transfer rate using a dual ring topology; largely supplanted today by faster Ethernet methods.

fiber-optic cable Communications cable that consists of one or more glass or plastic fiber cores inside a protective cladding material, covered by a plastic PVC outer jacket. Signal transmission along the inside fibers typically uses infrared light.

Fibre Channel A type of SAN that enables gigabit high-speed data transfer. *See* **Storage Area Network (SAN)**.

File Transfer Protocol (FTP) A TCP/IP application protocol that transfers files in bulk data streams and that is commonly used on the Internet.

firewall Software or hardware that secures data from being accessed outside a network and that can also prevent data from leaving the network through an inside source.

firmware Software that is stored on a chip in a device, such as in a ROM chip, and that typically composes some type of system software.

flooding When a network device, such as a bridge, retransmits a frame or packet to all of its outgoing ports.

flow control A process that ensures one device does not send information faster than it can be received by another device.

forward lookup zone A DNS zone or table that maps computer names to IP addresses.

frame A unit of data transmitted on a network that contains control and address information corresponding to the OSI Data Link layer, or Layer 2.

frame relay A communications protocol that relies on packet switching and virtual connection technology to transmit data packets and that achieves higher transmission rates by leaving extensive error-checking functions to intermediate nodes.

frame relay assembler/disassembler (FRAD) Also called a frame relay access device, FRAD is specialized equipment often found in the form of a module (card) in a switch or router that converts packets from the local network (LAN) into a format that can be transmitted over a frame relay network, and vice versa.

Frequency Division Multiple Access (FDMA) A switching method that creates separate channels on one communication medium by establishing different frequencies for each channel.

Frequency Hopping Spread Spectrum (FHSS) Used in Bluetooth, a wireless technology in which transmissions hop among 79 frequencies for each packet that is sent. *See* **Bluetooth**.

full duplex The capacity to send and receive signals at the same time on the same medium.

G.lite Asymmetric Digital Subscriber Line (G.lite ADSL) A Plug and Play-compatible version of ADSL that transmits at 500 Kbps upstream and 1.5 Mbps downstream.

gain Ability of an antenna to amplify a radiated signal.

gateway A network device that enables communications between two different types of networked systems, for example, between complex protocols or between different e-mail systems.

geosynchronous satellite Satellite in geosynchronous orbit at 22,300 miles above the Earth. Geosynchronous means that the orbit of such satellites enables them to maintain a position that is stationary with respect to the Earth.

Gigabit Ethernet Refers to the IEEE 802.3z, IEEE 802.3ab, and IEEE 802.3ah standards for Ethernet communications at speeds up to 1 Gbps. *See* **1000BaseX**.

graded-index multimode fiber-optic cable A type of multimode fiber-optic cable in which the light-based signals follow uniform curved routes inside the cable, resulting in signals that all arrive at the same time and with less long-distance distortion than step-index cable.

group identification number (GID) A unique number assigned to a UNIX/Linux group that distinguishes that group from all other groups on the same system.

half duplex The ability to send or receive signals on a medium, but not at the same time.

handle A resource, such as a file, used by a program that has its own identification so the program is able to access it.

hard QoS Providing a minimum level or guaranteed level of bandwidth. *See* **Quality of Service (QoS)**.

hardening Taking specific actions to block or prevent attacks by means of operating system and network security methods.

hardware or **CPU virtualization** Using the CPU to perform virtualization tasks by having virtualization processes work inside a specially designed CPU.

headend On a cable TV WAN, a central receiving point for signals from various sources, including satellite, other major cable sources, and local television sources.

hertz (Hz) The main unit of measurement for a radio frequency; one Hertz represents a radiated alternating current or emission of one cycle per second.

High Bit-Rate Digital Subscriber Line (HDSL) A form of high-speed DSL technology that has fixed upstream and downstream transmission rates of either 1.544 or 2.048 Mbps.

HiperLAN Popular in Europe, a wireless specification compatible with Ethernet and ATM communications and that uses the 5 GHz band.

HiperMAN A European standard for wireless MAN communications and that is compatible with WiMAX while operating between 2 and 11 GHz. *See* **WiMAX**.

home directory In UNIX/Linux, a user work area in which the user stores data on a server or other computer and typically has control over whether to enable other users to access her or his data.

homegroup In Windows 7, a concept intended for home computer networks that enables sharing resources such as files, printers, music, and photos, using Windows 7 libraries.

hop The movement of a frame or packet, point to point, from one network to the next.

horizontal wiring (or **horizontal cabling)** As defined by the EIA/TIA-568 standard, cabling that connects workstations and servers in the work area.

host (1) A computer (mainframe, server, or workstation) that has an operating system enabling multiple computers to access it at the same time for files, data, and services. Programs and information may be processed at the host, or they may be downloaded to the accessing computer (client) for processing. (2) A computer that is connected to a network.

host address (A) resource record A record in a DNS forward lookup zone that consists of a computer or domain name correlated to an IPv4 (or 32-bit) address.

hotspot A public location that provides an access point for Internet and network users, such as a coffee shop or airport. Alternatively, a 3G/4G device that can connect up to 5 client computers through WNICs.

hub A central network device used in the star topology to join networks.

hybrid fiber/coax (HFC) cable A cable that consists of a single cable sheath containing a combination of fibers and copper cables.

Hypertext Transfer Protocol (HTTP) A protocol in the TCP/IP suite that transports information over the Internet for access by Web browsers.

Hypertext Transfer Protocol Secure (HTTPS) A secure form of HTTP that uses Secure Sockets Layer to implement security. *See* **Secure Sockets Layer (SSL)**.

impedance The total amount of opposition to the flow of current.

independent basic service set (IBSS) topology An 802.11 wireless topology that consists of two or more wireless stations that can be in communication; IBSS does not use an access point.

infrared An electromagnetic signal that transmits in the range of 100 gigahertz (GHz) to 1000 terahertz (THz).

Infrastructure as a Service (IaaS) Providing the service equipment in cloud computing, which might include servers, routers, switches, storage arrays or SANs, and firewalls.

instance Used by Performance Monitor, when there are two or more types of elements to monitor, such as two or more NICs/WNICs or disk drives.

Institute of Electrical and Electronics Engineers (IEEE) An international organization of scientists, engineers, technicians, and educators that plays a leading role in developing standards for network cabling and data transmissions.

Integrated Services Digital Network (ISDN) A standard for delivering data services over telephone lines, with a current practical limit of 1.536 Mbps, and a theoretical limit of 1 Gbps.

Integrated Services Digital Network Digital Subscriber Line (IDSL) A DSL version that is compatible with a Digital Loop Carrier device that may be used on some telephone networks. IDSL provides upstream and downstream communications at 144 Kbps. *See* **Digital Subscriber Line (DSL or xDSL)**.

intelligent hub Also called a managed hub, a hub that can be used to perform network management functions using the Simple Network Management Protocol (SNMP).

Interaccess Point Protocol (IAPP) A roaming protocol for wireless networks that enables a mobile station to move from one cell to another without losing connection.

internal virtual network A virtual network that enables communication between virtual machines and the host virtual server.

International Corporation for Assigned Names and Numbers (ICANN) An organization that coordinates domain naming (the Domain Name System) and guidelines for domain registration.

International Mobile Telecommunications-2000 (IMT-2000) 3G standards provided through the ITU that cover voice, mobile telephone, mobile video, mobile TV, Internet, and mobile data communications over mobile communications devices such as smartphones. *See* **3G**.

International Mobile Telecommunications-Advanced (IMT-Advanced) 4G standards provided through the ITU that offer higher data transfer rates, higher quality of services, and better security than IMT-2000. *See* **IMT-2000** and **4G**.

International Organization for Standardization (ISO) An international body that establishes communications and networking standards and that is particularly known for its contributions to network protocol standards.

International Telecommunication Union (ITU) A United Nations agency that develops international communications standards; allocates international radio spectrums; and sets standards for modems, e-mail, mobile wireless communications, and digital telephone systems.

Internet A worldwide network of interconnected LANs, MANs, CANs, and WANs that uses the TCP/IP protocol to enable people to share e-mail messages and computer files and to access a vast array of information.

Internet Assigned Numbers Authority (IANA) An organization that assigns Internet accessible IP addresses.

Internet Connection Sharing (ICS) An option offered on Windows computers that enables one computer connected to the Internet to share its Internet connection with other computers on the same network. This can be a good Internet access solution in a home or small office.

Internet Control Message Protocol (ICMP) A protocol that works behind the scenes to help IP to track error conditions, such as the inability to reach a node or router.

Internet Engineering Task Force (IETF) An arm of the Internet Society (ISOC) that works on Internet-related technical issues. *See* **Request for Comments (RFC)**.

Internet Group Management Protocol (IGMP) A protocol employed by routers to create groups for multicasts, such as for multimedia streaming video.

Internet Protocol (IP) A protocol used in combination with TCP or UDP that enables packets to reach a destination on a local or remote network by using dotted decimal addressing.

Internet Protocol television (IPTV) Broadcasting television services over an IP network, particularly the Internet, in contrast to using cable and satellite communications.

Internet Small Computer System Interface (iSCSI) A high-speed technology used in SANs that employs TCP/IP communications and SCSI disk drives. *See* **storage area network (SAN)**.

Internetwork Packet Exchange (IPX) A legacy protocol developed by Novell for use with its NetWare file server operating system.

intranet An IP-based private network that uses Web technologies for communications internal to an organization.

iOS An operating system developed by Apple for mobile devices such as the iPhone and iPad. Like Apple's Mac OS X for desktop and laptop computers, iOS is based on Darwin UNIX and incorporates concepts from Mac OS X. *Compare to* **Android operating system**.

IP Security (IPSec) A set of IP-based secure communications and encryption standards developed by the Internet Engineering Task Force (IETF) and used to protect network communications through IP.

IP version 4 (IPv4) The current version of IP used on most networks.

IP version 6 (IPv6) The next version of IP after IPv4 that enables more addresses than are available through IPv4. Compared to IPv4, IPv6 also has a longer header coupled with IP extension headers for special communications needs.

IPv6 host address (AAAA) resource record A record in a DNS forward lookup zone that consists of a computer or domain name mapped to an IPv6 (or 128-bit) address.

jamming A flow control technique used by switches to indicate that they are being overrun by too much traffic. In jamming, the switch doubles the carrier signal to simulate a collision.

jumbogram A data payload of 4 GB minus one byte (4,294,967,295 bytes) that is an option provided through IPv6, but is not available in IPv4.

kernel An essential set of programs and computer code built into a computer operating system to control processor, disk, memory, and other functions central to the basic operation of a computer.

latency The time it takes for information to travel from the transmitting device to the receiving device.

Layer Two Tunneling Protocol (L2TP) A protocol used in VPNs that employs authentication techniques and can create special tunnels over a public network, such as the Internet. L2TP uses an additional network communications standard, called Layer Two Forwarding, that enables forwarding on the basis of MAC addressing (which is the physical address of the network interface) in addition to IP addressing. *See* **virtual private network (VPN)**.

library A Windows 7 element that enables a single view of multiple shared folders through a homegroup. *See* **homegroup**.

line-of-sight transmission A type of radio wave signal transmission in which the signal goes from point to point, rather than bouncing off the atmosphere to skip across the country or across continents. Line-of-sight transmissions follow the surface of the Earth.

Link Access Protocol for Frame Mode Bearer Services (LAPF) The frame relay communications layer that corresponds to the OSI Data Link layer.

local area network (LAN) A series of interconnected computers, printing devices, and other computer equipment that share hardware and software resources. The service area usually is limited to a given office area, floor, or building.

local bridge A network device that connects networks in close proximity and that can be used to segment a portion of a network to reduce heavy-traffic problems.

local router A router that joins networks within the same building or between buildings in close proximity such as on the same business campus.

logical link control (LLC) A Data Link sublayer of the OSI model that initiates the communications link between nodes and ensures the link is not unintentionally broken.

loopback address An address used internally by a computer for diagnostics and testing and is usually 127.0.0.1 (or in the range 127.0.0.0 to 127.255.255.255) for IPv4 or is 0:0:0:0:0:0:0:1 for IPv6.

low Earth orbiting (LEO) satellite A satellite that orbits at a distance of between 435 and 1000 miles above the Earth's surface, resulting in faster two-way transmission of signals.

MAC address *See* **device address**.

managed hub *See* **intelligent hub**.

managed switch Has options to configure the switch, manage network traffic, and help monitor the network through SNMP. *Compare to* **unmanaged switch**.

Management Information Base (MIB) A database of network performance information that is stored on a network agent for access by a network management station.

man-in-the-middle attack The interception of a message or data transmission meant for a different computer, by an attacker who is literally operating between two communicating computers.

mapping In Windows-based systems, the process of attaching to a shared resource, such as a shared folder, and using it as though it is a local resource. For example, when a workstation operating system maps to the drive of another workstation, it can assign a drive letter to that drive and access it as though it is a local drive instead of a remote one.

media access control (MAC) A Data Link sublayer that examines addressing information contained in a network frame and controls how devices share communications on the same network.

mesh topology A network design in which every node is connected to every other node, achieving fault tolerance.

message switching A switching method that sends data from point to point, with each intermediate node storing the data, waiting for a free transmission channel, and forwarding the data to the next point until the destination is reached.

metric A value calculated by routers that reflects information about a particular transmission path, such as path length, load at the next hop, available bandwidth, and path reliability.

Metro Ethernet Forum An industry alliance to promote Carrier Ethernet, which is a form of Optical Ethernet. *See* **Optical Ethernet.**

metropolitan area network (MAN) A network that links multiple LANs in a large city or metropolitan region.

Microsoft Hyper-V Microsoft virtual server software that can be included with Windows Server 2008/Server 2008 R2 and above that enables running multiple operating systems on one physical computer.

Microsoft Management Console (MMC) A Windows Server tool that you can customize by adding tool modules to manage different server functions, such as creating accounts or monitoring a server. (The MMC is also available in Windows 7).

mobile hotspot Wireless connectivity through a 3G/4G network, such as through a USB digital modem for a single computer or a mobile wireless hotspot device that can host multiple users.

modem A modulator/demodulator that converts a computer's outgoing digital signal to an analog signal that can be transmitted over a telephone line. It also converts the incoming analog signal to a digital signal that the computer can understand.

Monitoring as a Service (MaaS) The cloud computing process of monitoring software applications to ensure the applications are live and fully performing.

mounted volume A shared drive in UNIX/Linux.

multicast A transmission method in which a server divides users who request certain applications, such as multimedia applications, into groups. Each data stream of frames or packets is a one-time transmission that goes to multiple addresses, instead of sending a separate transmission to each address for each data stream.

multimeter A device that tests voltage and resistance, combining the functions of a voltmeter and an ohm meter.

multimode fiber-optic cable Used for shorter distances than single-mode fiber-optic cable, this type of fiber-optic cable can carry several signals at the same time.

multiple system operator (MSO) A cable TV company that offers WAN or Internet services. *See* **cableco.**

multiple-cell wireless LAN An extended services set (ESS) wireless topology that employs two or more access points.

multiple-input multiple-output (MIMO) A communication technology used in 802.11n/ac/ad and in 4G communications that involves using multiple antennas at the transmitting and receiving devices in wireless communications. It can be coupled with spatial multiplexing. *See* **spatial multiplexing.**

Multiprotocol Label Switching (MPLS) A switching protocol for backbone or label edge routers to optimize IP packet exchange through creating labels that integrate the equivalent of Data Link and Network layer information.

multistation access unit (MAU or MSAU) A central hub that links token ring nodes into a topology that physically resembles a star but in which data signals are transferred in a logical ring pattern.

multistation access unit (MAU) A central hub that links token ring nodes into a topology that physically resembles a star, but in which frames are transmitted in a logical ring pattern.

namespace A logical area on a network that contains a listing of named objects, such as computers, and that has the ability to perform name resolution.

Neighbor Discovery (ND) protocol Uses messages and other means to discover the physical addresses and much more about computers and routers on a network. ND protocol enables a more extensive range of information to be determined beyond the capabilities of Address Resolution Protocol. *See* **Address Resolution Protocol (ARP).**

NetBIOS Extended User Interface (NetBEUI) Developed by IBM and Microsoft in the mid-80s, this legacy protocol incorporates NetBIOS for communications across a network.

Network Address Translation (NAT) A technique used in network communications that translates an IP address from a private network to a different address used on a public network or the Internet, and vice versa. NAT is used to protect the identity of a computer on the private network from attackers, as well as bypass the requirement to employ universally unique IP addresses on the private network.

network agent A managed device that runs agent software that is in contact with the network management station. Most devices connected to modern networks are agents. These include routers, repeaters, hubs, switches, bridges, PCs (via the NIC/WNIC), print servers, access servers, and uninterruptible power sources (UPSs). *See* network management station (NMS).

Network as a Service (NaaS) Offering network services to the cloud and within the cloud for cloud computing, including providing the infrastructure of equipment and communications services.

network discovery A configuration option in Windows operating systems that determines whether computers and devices on a network can be viewed by other computers on the network.

Network Driver Interface Specification (NDIS) A network driver specification and application programming interface (API) for creating and using network interface card drivers that work with many network protocols.

Network File System (NFS) protocol A TCP/IP file transfer protocol that transfers information in record streams instead of in bulk file streams.

network interface card (NIC) An adapter board or USB device designed to connect a workstation, server, or other network device to a network medium.

network management station (NMS) A computer with software that monitors networked devices that are equipped to communicate via SNMP.

Network Monitor A Windows Server network-monitoring tool that can capture and display network performance data.

Network Termination Unit (NTU) On an ISDN network this device provides a U interface for an incoming ISDN line and an S/T interface to connect to ISDN devices, such as computers, ISDN fax machines, and ISDN telephones.

network virtualization Dividing a single network into multiple channels or bandwidths so that the network appears as multiple networks.

node Any device connected to a network, such as a personal computer, tablet PC, mainframe, server, network equipment, or printer. Also called a station.

nonvolatile random access memory (NVRAM) Computer memory that does not lose its contents when the computer is turned off. One way to ensure nonvolatile memory is by connecting the memory to a battery.

open circuit A circuit in which the connection is severed, such as a cable that is inadvertently cut in two.

Open Handset Alliance (OHA) An alliance of vendors such as Google, Motorola, Intel, Dell, and T-Mobile that has provided backing for the Android operating system. *See* Android operating system.

Open Shortest Path First (OSPF) protocol A routing protocol used by a router to communicate to other routers information about its immediate links to other nodes.

open SMTP relay server An e-mail server that not only accepts e-mail, but also resends the e-mail to other servers without restrictions.

open system authentication The default form of authentication in 802.11 in which any two stations can authenticate with each other. There is no elaborate security, only the mutual agreement to authenticate.

Open Systems Interconnection (OSI) reference model Developed by the ISO and ANSI, a model that provides a framework for networked hardware and software communications based on seven layers.

Optical Ethernet High-speed Ethernet, such as Gigabit or 10 Gigabit Ethernet, carried on fiber-optic cable and used for MANs and WANs.

optical time domain reflectometer (OTDR) A device for testing fiber-optic cable distance, bad splices, connector problems, and bending radius problems.

Orthogonal Frequency Division Multiplexing (OFDM) Used in 802.11a/g/n/ac/ad wireless network communications, a multiplexing technique that divides the 5 GHz frequency range into a series of small subcarriers or subchannels and transmits information all at once over all of the subcarriers.

packet A unit of data formatted for transmission over a network that contains control and other information that corresponds to the OSI Network layer, also called Layer 3.

packet analyzer *See* protocol analyzer.

packet filtering Using characteristics of a packet—such as an IP address, network ID, or TCP/UDP port use—to determine whether a packet should be forwarded or blocked in its transport between two networks or across a packet-filtering device (for example, a firewall).

packet mode On an ISDN network that uses T-carrier communications, packet mode means that several circuits can be used during a communications session, and each connected device is assigned an address and sequence number at the start of the session to ensure that data arrives at the correct destination.

packet radio The process of transmitting a data-carrying packet over radio waves through short bursts.

packet switching A data transmission technique that establishes a logical channel between two transmitting nodes, but uses several different paths of transmission to continually find the best routes to the destination.

packet switching exchange (PSE) A switch located at the vendor's site in a frame relay (or X.25) WAN network that connects with a DCE (data communications equipment).

page file Disk space, in the form of a file, for use when memory requirements exceed the available RAM.

partitioning To shut down a cable segment because a portion of the segment is malfunctioning.

passive hub A network transmission device that connects nodes in a star topology, performing no signal amplification as the data signal moves from one node to the next through the hub.

Password Authentication Protocol (PAP) A protocol that is used to authenticate an account password when accessing a server, host computer, or directory service over a WAN.

peer protocol Protocol used to enable an OSI layer on a sending node to communicate with the same layer on the receiving node.

peer-to-peer network A network on which any computer can communicate with other networked computers on an equal (peer) basis without going through an intermediary, such as a server. Peer-to-peer networking enables each computer to offer and access shared resources, such as files and printers.

Performance Monitor The Windows Server utility used to track network, system, or application objects. For each object type there are one or more counters that can be logged for later analysis, or tracked in real time for immediate system monitoring. *See* **counter** and **instance**.

permanent virtual circuit (PVC) Used in frame relay, a continuously available path between two nodes, even when the nodes are not communicating.

personal area network (PAN) A network that typically reaches a few meters, such as up to 10 meters (33 feet; although some PANs can reach farther), and consists of personal devices such as mobile computers, smartphones, and handheld devices. A PAN can be cabled or wireless.

physical address *See* **device address**.

plain old telephone service (POTS) Regular voice-grade telephone service.

Platform as a Service (PaaS) When a cloud provider buys, develops, deploys, and manages software that is available to the end user.

plenum area An enclosed area, such as a false floor or ceiling, in which pressure from air or gas can be greater than the pressure outside the enclosed area, particularly during a fire. Plenum areas in buildings often extend to multiple rooms or extend throughout an entire floor and contain ventilation and heating ducts.

plenum cable Teflon-coated cable that is used in plenum areas because it does not emit a toxic vapor when burned.

point coordination function *See* **priority-based access**.

pointer (PTR) resource record A record in a DNS reverse lookup zone that consists of an IP (version 4 or 6) address correlated to a computer or domain name.

Point-to-Point Protocol (PPP) A widely used remote communications protocol that supports TCP/IP (and other legacy protocols such as NetBEUI and IPX/SPX) communications over WANs.

Point-to-Point Protocol over Ethernet (PPPoE) An addition to PPP that builds in the capability for virtual point-to-point connections (like virtual tunnels between two points) on an Ethernet network consisting of multiple end points. PPPoE is particularly well suited for communications through ISPs on DSL networks.

Point-to-Point Tunneling Protocol (PPTP) A remote communications protocol that enables connections to networks, intranets, extranets, and VPNs through the Internet.

port *See* **socket**.

power budget For fiber-optic cable communications, the difference between the transmitted power and the receiver sensitivity, as measured in decibels. It is the minimum transmitter power and receiver sensitivity needed for a signal to be sent and received fully intact.

preshared key (PSK) An enhancement available for Wi-Fi Protected Access (WPA) intended for home and small office users that employs a password along with frequently changing encryption keys through WPA. *See* **Wi-Fi Protected Access (WPA)**.

primary DNS server A DNS server that is used as the main server from which to administer a zone, such as updating records in a forward lookup zone for a domain. A primary DNS server is also called the authoritative server for that zone.

Primary Rate Interface (PRI) ISDN An ISDN interface that consists of switched communications in multiples of 1.536 Mbps.

primitive A command used to transfer information from one layer in an OSI stack to another layer, such as from the Physical layer to the Data Link layer.

print server A device with software that manages shared printing on a network, such as (1) receiving print jobs, (2) storing the print jobs until it is their turn to print, (3) queuing the print jobs, and (4) sending print jobs to the right printer.

priority-based access Also called the point coordination function, an access method in 802.11 wireless communications in which the access point device also functions as a point coordinator. The point coordinator gives each station that has been polled an opportunity to communicate, one at a time, thus ensuring that only one device communicates at a given moment.

private network A network owned and maintained by an organization, such as a campus network operated by a college.

private virtual network A virtual network that enables communication between virtual machines and the host virtual server.

programmable logic controller attack An attack on a programmable logic controller that interferes with manufacturing or mechanical processes. A programmable logic controller is a computer that is used in industrial manufacturing and other similar environments to control or automate specific manufacturing or mechanical processes.

promiscuous mode Mode in which network devices read frame destination address information before sending a frame on to other connected segments of the network.

protocol Similar to a language, a protocol enables network devices to communicate and exchange information or data. A protocol is an established guideline that specifies how networked data is formatted into a packet or frame, how it is transmitted, and how it is interpreted at the receiving end.

protocol analyzer A network testing device that works in promiscuous mode to capture detailed information about the traffic moving across a network, including protocol and OSI layer information.

protocol data unit (PDU) The information transferred between layers in the same OSI stack.

proxy A computer that is located between a computer on an internal network and a computer on an external network, with which the internal computer is communicating. The proxy acts as a "middleman" to filter application-level communications, perform caching, and create virtual circuits with clients for safer communications.

public network A network that offers services to members of the public, such as network services offered by a telecommunications company or a cable TV company.

public switched telephone network (PSTN) Regular voice-grade telephone service.

pulse code modulation (PCM) An audio file creation technique that converts an analog audio signal into an 8-bit digital signal. PCM is used in frame relay audio communications and on the Internet.

pulse position modulation (PPM) A communications method used in diffused infrared communications in which the binary value of a signal is related to the position of the pulse within a range of possible positions.

Quality of Service (QoS) A measurement of the transmission, quality, throughput, and reliability of a network system.

rack-mounted server A CPU box mounted in a rack that can hold several such CPUs, each with its own power cord and network connection, and that often share one monitor and pointing device.

radio frequencies (RFs) A range of frequencies above 20 kilohertz through which an electromagnetic signal can be radiated through space.

radio frequency interference (RFI) Signal interference caused by electrical devices that emit radio waves at the same frequency used by network signal transmissions.

RADIUS server A server that employs the RADIUS protocol and that is used to configure the protocol in order to manage authentication and access to enterprise networks that use a variety of remote access services including wireless, internal network; virtual private network (VPN); dial-up; Internet; and other forms of remote access. RADIUS servers also keep access statistics. *See* **Remote Authentication Dial-Up User Service (RADIUS)**.

Rate Adaptive Asymmetric Digital Subscriber Line (RADSL) A high-speed data transmission technology that offers upstream speeds of up to 1 Mbps and downstream speeds of up to 7 Mbps. RADSL uses ADSL technology, but enables the transmission rate to vary for different types of communications, such as data, multimedia, and voice. *See* **Asymmetric Digital Subscriber Line (ADSL)**.

redirector A service used via the Application layer to recognize and access other computers.

redundancy Providing extra cable and cabled and wireless equipment to ensure that computers and computer systems can continue to function even when one or more network or computer elements fail.

regional Bell Operating Company (RBOC) A telecommunications company that provides telephone services to a designated region.

remote access server A specialized server that is located on a network for the purpose of enabling remote users to access the resources, such as servers and databases, of the main network.

Remote Authentication Dial-Up User Service (RADIUS) A protocol used by a RADUIS server to enforce rules governing remote access to network services and servers. *See* **RADIUS server**.

remote bridge A network device that joins networks across the same city, between cities, and between states to create one network.

Remote Network Monitoring (RMON) A monitoring standard that uses remote network nodes, such as workstations or network devices, to perform network monitoring, including gathering information for network protocol analysis. Probes can be located on remote sections of the network, such as across bridges or routers.

remote procedure call (RPC) Enables services and software on one computer to use services and software on a different computer.

remote router A router that joins networks in WANs across large geographic areas, such as between cities, states, and countries.

repeater A network transmission device that amplifies and retimes a packet- or cell-carrying signal so that it can be sent along all outgoing cable segments attached to that repeater.

Request for Comments (RFC) A document prepared and distributed by any individual or group as a way to further networking, Internet, and computer communications. RFCs help ensure that network standards and conventions are provided so one network can talk to another. Every RFC is assigned a number to distinguish it from other RFCs and to provide a way to track it. Each RFC is tracked and published by the Internet Engineering Task Force (IETF). *See* **Internet Engineering Task Force (IETF)**.

Reverse Address Resolution Protocol (RARP) A protocol used by a network node or by a software application at a node to determine its own IP address.

reverse lookup zone A DNS server zone or table that contains records, which map IP addresses to computer or domain names.

ring topology A network design consisting of a continuous path for data with no logical beginning or ending point, and thus no terminators.

riser cable Another term for vertical cable; refers to cable that goes between floors in a building.

roaming On a wireless network, moving a laptop computer, tablet, handheld device, or other mobile device from cell to cell.

Robust Secure Network (RSN) A security method used in 802.11i, which is designed to create secure communications channels.

rogue Web site A Web site that performs unlawful activity or that puts the user who accesses it at risk, such as by downloading malicious software to the user's computer, gaining unauthorized access, or stealing account password or other personal information.

root server A DNS server that is on the Internet and is used to find top-level domains (TLDs), such as .com or .net. There are 13 root servers throughout the world that act as final authorities for finding a TLD.

route aggregation A technique for organizing network routes hierarchically. It also enables routes to be summarized resulting in reduced router advertising of routes (equating to less network traffic from routers).

router A network device that connects networks having the same or different access methods and media, such as Ethernet to token ring. It forwards packets to networks by using a decision-making process based on routing table data, discovery of the most efficient routes, and preprogrammed information from the network administrator.

Routing Information Protocol (RIP) A protocol routers use to communicate the entire contents of routing tables to other routers.

Samba Used by UNIX/Linux (and Mac OS X systems), this utility employs the Server Message Block (SMB) protocol, which is also used by Windows systems for sharing folders and printers. Samba enables UNIX/Linux systems to access shared Windows resources.

satellite microwave Microwave transmissions between ground-based units and a satellite.

secondary DNS server A DNS server that is a backup to a primary DNS server and therefore is not authoritative.

Secure Hypertext Transfer Protocol (S-HTTP) A secure form of HTTP that often uses Cryptographic Message Syntax and MIME Object Security Services. S-HTTP is not as commonly used as HTTPS. *See* **Hypertext Transfer Protocol Secure (HTTPS)**.

Secure Shell (SSH) A form of authentication originally developed for UNIX/Linux systems to provide authentication security for TCP/IP applications, such as Telnet and FTP.

Secure Sockets Layer (SSL) A data encryption technique employed between a server and a client, such as between a client's browser and an Internet server.

segment One cable run within the IEEE specifications, such as one run of 10Base2 cable that is 185 meters (610.5 feet) long and that has 30 nodes or fewer (including terminators and network equipment).

Sequenced Packet Exchange (SPX) An older Novell protocol that is used for network transport for application software, such as database information, when there is a particular need for data reliability. SPX is generally paired with IPX.

Serial Line Internet Protocol (SLIP) Designed for UNIX environments for point-to-point communications between computers, servers, and hosts using TCP/IP. *See also* **Compressed Serial Line Internet Protocol (CSLIP)**.

server A computer that provides extensive multiuser access to network resources, such as shared files, shared disks, and shared printers.

server farm A group of servers placed in the same location, as in a computer machine room.

Server Message Block (SMB) protocol A resource-sharing protocol used in Windows-based networking and that is employed by Samba software in UNIX/Linux systems for resource sharing with Windows-based computers.

server virtualization Running multiple server operating systems on a single server computer.

service data unit (SDU) A protocol data unit that has been transferred between OSI layers and then stripped of control information and transfer instructions.

service pack An operating system update that provides fixes for known problems and offers product enhancements.

service resource record (SRV RR) A record in a DNS zone that is created to locate commonly used TCP/IP services. The SRV record is formatted to include information about the service that is provided by a server, the domain that is serviced by the server, and the protocol used by the server.

service set identifier (SSID) Used on wireless devices, an identification value that typically can be up to 32 characters in length, and its purpose is to define a logical network for member devices (each device is configured to have the same SSID).

shadow file With access limited to the root user, a file in UNIX/Linux that contains critical information about user accounts, including the encrypted password for each account.

shared key authentication A wireless 802.11 authentication technique in which two stations use a shared WEP encryption key to encrypt and decrypt a unique challenge text. Authentication is accomplished if the sending and receiving stations properly encrypt and decrypt the challenge text.

shell An interface between the operating system and the user. A shell provides an environment in which to enter commands. The bash shell is popular and usually the default in Linux.

shielded twisted-pair (STP) cable Network cable that contains pairs of insulated wires that are twisted together, surrounded by a shielding material for added EMI and RFI protection, all inside a protective jacket.

short circuit An incomplete or damaged connection, such as when the two conductors in a twisted-pair set come in contact in a poorly built connector.

Signaling System 7 (SS7) A WAN protocol for telecommunications networks that is used to set up the fastest route between two telecommunications carriers.

silence suppression A voice communications method over data communications lines, such as over frame relay, in which voice transmissions are sent during moments of inactivity (silence) on the lines.

Simple Mail Transfer Protocol (SMTP) A protocol in the TCP/IP suite used to transmit e-mail, such as over the Internet.

Simple Network Management Protocol (SNMP) A protocol in the TCP/IP suite that enables computers and network equipment to gather standardized data about network performance.

simplex The capacity for a signal to travel on a medium in only one direction.

single-mode fiber-optic cable A form of fiber-optic cable that supports only one signal transmission at a time and that is used mainly for long-distance communications.

sliding window The agreed-upon number of data bytes transmitted in a packet when two nodes are communicating via TCP. The amount of data can be dynamically varied, hence the sliding window, on the basis of network traffic conditions and available buffer space at each node.

Small Computer System Interface (SCSI) A 32- or 64-bit computer adapter that transports data between one or more attached devices, such as hard disks, and the computer.

smart multistation access unit (SMAU) A multistation access unit with intelligence built in to detect problems at a connected workstation and to isolate that workstation from the rest of the network. *See* **multistation access unit (MAU)**.

sniffer attack When an attacker uses software that can intercept and read packet traffic.

social engineering attack In relation to a computer attack, refers to the use of human interaction to gain access to an individual's personal information or to a computer system to do damage or acquire access or information—for example, through a bogus e-mail or telephone call.

socket A value or means of identifying a service on a network node, such as socket or port 103 for standardized e-mail services in the TCP protocol.

Software as a Service (SaaS) Providing software and software platforms through a cloud provider in which the end-user has little say about the software features. SaaS also entails running the software on the cloud provider's servers, such as through terminal services or a Web browser.

source routing A routing technique in which the sender of a packet specifies the precise path (through hops) that a packet will take to reach its destination.

spam Unrequested commercial e-mail that is sent to hundreds, thousands, or even millions of users in bulk.

spanning tree algorithm Software that ensures that frames are not transmitted in an endless loop and that enables frames to be sent along the most cost-effective network path.

spatial multiplexing Enables a wireless device to transmit and receive two or more data streams over one channel within a frequency. Spatial multiplexing is used with MIMO in 802.11n/ac/ad communications. *See* **multiple-input multiple-output (MIMO)**, **802.11n**, **802.11ac**, and **802.11ad**.

spoofing When the address of the source computer is changed to make a packet appear as though it originated from a different computer.

spread spectrum technology Communications technology that is used by wireless networks for very-high-frequency communications between networks. In spread spectrum, one communication involves using several adjoining frequencies.

spyware Software that is placed on a computer, typically without the user's knowledge, and then reports back information—to an attacker or an advertiser, for example—about that computer user's activities. Some spyware also works by simply capturing information about cookies sent between a Web server and a client.

stand-alone server In Windows Server, this is a server that does not have Active Directory installed. Instead, it manages user accounts and shared access locally through a workgroup.

star topology The oldest type of network design, this topology consists of multiple nodes attached to a central hub or switch.

star-bus hybrid topology Also called the star-wired bus topology, a network design that combines the logical communications of a bus with the physical layout of a star.

star-ring hybrid topology Also called the star-wired ring topology, a network design in which the logical communications are in a ring, but the physical layout of the network is a star.

star-wired bus topology *See* star-bus hybrid topology.

star-wired ring topology *See* star-ring hybrid topology.

start of authority (SOA) resource record The first record in a DNS zone, it indicates if a server is authoritative for the current zone.

stateful autoconfiguration Uses dynamic addressing for an IPv6 host by obtaining the IPv6 address through DHCPv6 and a DHCPv6 server.

stateful packet filtering Tracks information about a communication session, such as which ports are in use, by drawing from the contents of multiple packets.

stateless autoconfiguration When a network host assigns its own IPv6 address without obtaining it from a DHCPv6 server.

stateless packet filtering A packet-filtering technique in which the firewall examines every individual packet and decides whether to pass or block the packet on the basis of information drawn from single packets.

static routing A routing process that involves control of routing decisions by the network administrator through preset routing instructions.

station *See* node.

Statistical Multiple Access A switching method that allocates the communication resources according to what is needed for the task, such as providing more bandwidth for a video file and less for a small spreadsheet file.

step-index multimode fiber-optic cable A type of multimode fiber-optic cable that reflects the light-based signals like a mirror within the cable, resulting in different signals arriving at different times and with an increased likelihood of distortion over longer cable runs.

Storage Area Network (SAN) A grouping of storage devices that forms a subnet. The storage devices are available to any server on the main network and appear to the user as though they are attached to the server they are accessing.

storage virtualization Setting up multiple networked disk storage units to appear as one unit.

store-and-forward switching A switching technique in which a packet is buffered and not sent until it is completely received and there is an open channel on which to send it.

stream cipher encryption An encryption method in which every bit in a stream of data is encrypted.

streaming media Sending audio, video, or a combination of both over an IP network so that the contents of the media files can be played before the entire file is received.

structured network A network that uses a horizontal and vertical wiring design that enables centralizing a network at strategic points, such as placing switches in wiring closets and connecting them via high-speed links into a main chassis switch placed in a machine room or at a main cabling demarcation point in a building.

structured wiring Installing cable that fans out in a horizontal star fashion from one or more centralized switches or routers located in telecommunications rooms or wiring closets.

sub-band adaptive differential pulse code modulation (SB-ADPCM) A variety of ADPCM that is tailored to work over ISDN and frame relay. *See* adaptive differential pulse code modulation (ADPCM).

subnet mask A subnet mask is a designated portion of an IP address that is used to indicate the class of addressing on a network and to divide a network into subnetworks as a way to manage traffic patterns.

swap space Disk space that acts like an extension of memory. *See* virtual memory.

switch A device that links network segments and that forwards and filters frames between segments. Originally, switches operated primarily at OSI Layer 2, forwarding on the basis of physical or device addresses, but newer switches also function at OSI Layer 3 and higher.

switched virtual circuit (SVC) Used in frame relay, a means of connecting for a transmission session by sending a special control signal between two nodes to establish communication. Once the communication is finished, the call control signal issues a command for each node to disconnect. This type of circuit enables the network or T-carrier provider to determine the data throughput rate.

Symmetric Digital Subscriber Line (SDSL) A form of DSL technology that is often used for video conferencing or online learning. It offers a transmission speed of 1.544 or 2.048 Mbps for upstream and downstream communications. *See* Digital Subscriber Line (DSL or xDSL).

Symmetric High Bit-Rate Digital Subscriber Line (SHDSL) Also called G.shdsl, a DSL technology that can be transmitted over one or two wires and that can reach up to about four miles (over two wires). The upstream and downstream rates can vary in the range of 192 Kbps to 2.3 Mbps. *See* Digital Subscriber Line (DSL or xDSL).

synchronous communications Communications of continuous bursts of data controlled by a clock signal that starts each burst.

Synchronous Digital Hierarchy (SDH) A standard that is similar to synchronous optical network (SONET) that is used in Europe.

synchronous optical network (SONET) A fiber-optic communications technology that is capable of high-speed (up to 39.813 Gbps) data transmission. Networks based on SONET can deliver voice, data, and video communications.

T-carrier A dedicated telephone line that can be used for data communications to connect two different locations for continuous point-to-point communications.

TCP port Functioning like a virtual circuit, a TCP port enables communication between individual processes at two communicating nodes or devices. Each communicating process has its own port, and one or more ports can be used simultaneously to handle many communicating processes.

telco A regional telephone company. *See* **Regional Bell Operating Company (RBOC)**.

Telnet A TCP/IP application protocol that provides terminal emulation.

Temporal Key Integrity Protocol (TKIP) Designed for creating random encryption keys from one master key, TKIP creates a unique encryption key for each packet. *See* **802.11i**.

terminal A device that consists of a monitor and keyboard, used to communicate with host computers that run the programs. The terminal does not have a processor to use for running programs locally.

terminal adapter (TA) A device that connects a computer or a fax to an ISDN line. A TA simply converts a digital signal to a protocol that can be sent over a digital telephone line.

terminal emulation Using software to make a computer, such as a PC, behave as though it were a terminal.

terminator A resistor that is connected to the end of a segment on a bus network, so that data-carrying signals are absorbed at the point where the segment stops. Absorbing the signals ensures that they are not reflected back onto the cable after they reach the end—thus preventing communication errors.

terrestrial microwave Microwave transmissions between two directional parabolic antennas located on the Earth's surface.

thread A block of program code executing within a running process. One process may launch one or more threads.

time division duplexing (TDD) A communications method used by Bluetooth in which packets are sent in alternating directions using time slots. A transmission can use up to five different time slots, resulting in packets that can be sent and received at the same time in a process that resembles full-duplex communications.

Time Division Multiple Access (TDMA) A switching method that enables multiple devices to communicate over the same communications medium by creating time slots in which each device transmits.

time domain reflectometer (TDR) A device for cable testing that can monitor line impedance, opens, shorts, RFI/EMI, and cable distances, and detect connector and terminator problems, as well as other problems.

token ring An access method developed by IBM in the 1970s and which is still used on some networks. Variations of the technology are used for WANs. This transport method employs a physical star topology along with the logic of a ring topology. Although each node is connected to a central hub, the frame travels from node to node as though there were no starting or ending point.

topology The physical layout of cable and wireless network devices and the logical path followed by network frames or packets sent on the cable or by wireless transmissions.

transceiver A device that can transmit and receive, such as transmitting and receiving signals on a communications cable.

translational bridge A bridge that converts frames from one access method and media type to another, such as from Ethernet to token ring or vice versa.

Transmission Control Protocol (TCP) This transport protocol, which is part of the TCP/IP suite, establishes communication sessions between networked software application processes and provides for reliable end-to-end delivery of data by controlling data flow.

trap A specific situation or event detected by SNMP that a network administrator may want to be warned about or to track via network management software, for example, when a network device is unexpectedly down or offline.

tree topology Also called the expanded star, it offers features of the basic bus topology combined with features of the star topology. This topology resembles a tree with a trunk and limbs or represents a root node at the base in a hierarchy of nodes built on levels off of the root node.

Trivial File Transfer Protocol (TFTP) A TCP/IP file transfer protocol that is designed for the transfer of files that enable a diskless workstation to boot.

Trojan horse A program that appears useful and harmless, but instead does harm to the user's computer. Often a Trojan horse provides an attacker with access to the computer on which it is running or enables the attacker to control the computer.

trunk line In a cable TV or telecommunications system, a high-capacity communications line that goes between two switches (often over several miles) or it is generally a main line that has multiple channels.

trunking Physically connecting two or more links between two network transmission devices to form an aggregate that is treated as one link that has the total speed of each link added together.

twinaxial or **twinax cable** Coaxial cabling that has two main cores.

twisted-pair cable A flexible communications cable that contains pairs of insulated copper wires that are twisted together for reduction of EMI and RFI and covered with an outer insulating jacket.

unicast One copy of each frame or packet is sent to each destination point.

unicode A character coding standard that enables consistent coding of characters covering 93 scripts for most languages used throughout the world. Unicode enables data to be translated between different systems and languages while retaining the original data integrity.

uninterruptible power supply (UPS) A device built into electrical equipment or a separate device that provides immediate battery power to equipment during a power outage, surge, or brownout.

Universal Serial Bus (USB) A serial bus, such as in a computer, designed to support up to 127 discrete devices with data transfer speeds up to 5 Gbits/s (gigabits per second).

unmanaged hub A simple hub on a network that does not have built-in intelligence for network monitoring and management.

unmanaged switch A switch that has a fixed configuration and that does not support network monitoring through SNMP.

unshielded twisted-pair (UTP) cable Communications cable that has no shielding material between the pairs of insulated wires twisted together and the cable's outside jacket.

user account On a network or in a computer operating system, a vehicle used to give a user access to resources through a user id and password (although it is possible to configure an account without a password). Information about a user is often associated with an account, such as the account password, access permissions, and information about the user.

User Datagram Protocol (UDP) A protocol used with IP, as an alternative to TCP, for low-overhead connectionless communications.

user identification number (UID) A number that is assigned to a UNIX/Linux user account as a way to distinguish that account from all others on the same system.

vertical wiring (or vertical cabling) Cabling and network equipment used between the floors in a building and that often physically links the telecommunications room or rooms on one floor to adjoining floors.

Very High Bit-Rate Digital Subscriber Line (VDSL) A DSL technology that works over coaxial and fiber-optic cables yielding up to 52 Mbps downstream and 2.3 Mbps upstream communications. *See* Digital Subscriber Line (DSL or xDSL).

Very High Bit-Rate Digital Subscriber Line version 2 (VDSL2) An enhancement to VDSL that can offer upstream and downstream speeds of up to 200 Mbps. *See* Very High Bit-Rate Digital Subscriber Line (VDSL).

virtual circuit A logical communication path established by the OSI Network layer for sending and receiving data.

virtual CPU A simulation of a CPU to have the equivalent of more CPUs than are actually in a computer, enabling applications, such as virtual machines to have their own processor.

Virtual Disk Service Software in Windows Server 2008/ Server 2008 R2 that enables management of disk volumes on multiple SANs through one interface at a server. *See* Storage Area Network (SAN).

virtual LAN (VLAN) A logical LAN that links together specific switches on a large LAN or on separate LANs so that the switches act as though they compose one unified logical or virtual LAN.

virtual LAN identification number (VLAN ID) A unique number used for communication through a network adapter that distinguishes the virtual network used by that adapter from other networks.

virtual machine An instance of a discrete operating system running within virtual server software on one computer. Multiple virtual machines can run within the virtual server software on one computer.

virtual memory Disk storage allocated to link with physical RAM to temporarily hold data when there is not enough free RAM. *See* swap space.

virtual network A network on which virtual machines communicate through virtual links.

virtual private network (VPN) A private network that is like a private and secure tunnel through a larger network—such as the Internet, an enterprise network, or both—that is restricted to designated member clients only.

virtual server software Software that enables a computer to house two or more operating systems.

virtualization Ability to disguise the physical or individual hardware elements of computing to enhance or multiply resources. Through virtualization, one resource can be made to appear as many separate resources. For example, one computer can be virtualized to appear to the user as many computers or one storage device can look like multiple storage devices.

virus A program that is borne by a disk or a file and has the ability to replicate throughout a system. Some viruses cause damage to systems, and others replicate without causing permanent damage.

virus hoax An e-mail falsely warning of a virus.

voice compression A method for transmitting voice communications by converting them from an analog format to a digital format, thus creating digital audio files that are played back to the listener.

voice over frame relay (VoFR) Using frame relay to transmit voice signals as a way to replace the need for regular telephone communications.

Voice over IP (VoIP) A network technology that enables telephony communications over an IP network.

voltmeter A device that tests voltage.

well-known ports TCP/UDP network ports 0–1023 that are most commonly used by applications (technically called application end points) that use TCP or UDP for communications. The well-known port designation is included in the TCP or UDP header within a packet or frame. Ports 1024–49151 are registered by IANA (Internet Assigned Numbers Authority) to ensure they remain in the public domain for current or future use. Ports 49152–65535 are ports reserved for private use.

wide area network (WAN) A far-reaching system of networks that usually extends over more than about 48 kilometers (about 30 miles) and often reaches across states and continents.

Wi-Fi Alliance An organization that promotes wireless networking for LANs. The Wi-Fi Alliance also offers a certification program to vendors, which tests wireless devices so that they can be certified to meet IEEE 802.11 standards as well as accepted security practices.

Wi-Fi Protected Access (WPA) A wireless authentication and encryption method that uses encryption keys that are regularly changed to foil attackers. The current version is WPA2. *See* **preshared key (PSK)**.

WiMAX The IEEE 802.16 standard for wireless MANs that can reach up to 48 kilometers (about 30 miles) and transmit up to 75 Mbps. *See* **802.16** and **HiperMAN**.

Windows Firewall A software firewall provided by Microsoft that controls information exchanged between a Microsoft operating system or shared network connection and an external network connection, such as the Internet.

Wired Equivalent Privacy (WEP) A security method that involves using the same encryption key at both stations that are communicating. This method is less secure than WPA/WPA2.

wireless NIC (WNIC) A network interface card that has an antenna and is used for wireless communications with other WNICs or with access points on a wireless network.

workgroup As used in Windows-based networks, a number of users who share drive and printer resources in an independent (and decentralized) peer-to-peer relationship.

workstation A computer that has its own CPU and may be used as a stand-alone computer for word processing, spreadsheet creation, or other software applications. It also may be used to access another computer such as another workstation or server via a network.

workstation or PC virtualization Running multiple workstation operating systems, such as Windows XP, Windows 7, and Linux, on one computer.

worm A program that replicates and replicates on the same computer or sends itself to many other computers on a network, but does not infect existing files.

X.25 An older, very reliable packet-switching protocol for connecting remote networks at speeds up to 2.048 Mbps. The X.25 protocol defines communications between DTEs and DCEs.

X.400 A set of standards for global message handling for e-mail.

zone A partition in a DNS server that contains specific kinds of records in a lookup table, such as a forward lookup zone that contains records in a table for looking up computer and domain names to find their associated IP addresses.

Index